Anton Rubinstein

Anton Rubinstein ca. 1880.

RUSSIAN MUSIC SERIES

Malcolm Hamrick Brown, founding editor

PHILIP S. TAYLOR

Anton Rubinstein

A Life in Music

INDIANA UNIVERSITY PRESS
Bloomington and Indianapolis

Publication is made possible in part with the generous support of Dan and Susan Sterner.

This book is a publication of

Indiana University Press
601 North Morton Street
Bloomington, IN 47404-3797 USA

http://iupress.indiana.edu

Telephone orders   800-842-6796
Fax orders   812-855-7931
Orders by e-mail   iuporder@indiana.edu

Library of Congress Cataloging-in-Publication Data

Taylor, Philip S.
    Anton Rubinstein : a life in music / Philip S. Taylor.
        p. cm. — (Russian music series)
    Includes bibliographical references (p.) and index.
    ISBN-13: 978-0-253-34871-5 (hardcover)
    ISBN-10: 0-253-34871-4 (hardcover)
    1. Rubinstein, Anton, 1829-1894. 2. Composers—Russia—Biography. I. Title.
    ML410.R89T293 2007
    780.92—dc22
    [B]
                                                                    2006032914

1 2 3 4 5   12 11 10 09 08 07

To the memory of my late parents
Thomas and Mary Gwyneth Taylor

Contents

Foreword

The subject of this revelatory book is the Russian composer and pianist Anton Grigoryevich Rubinstein (in no way to be confused with the late Polish master Artur Rubinstein, who was no relation). Born in Balta Podolia (Ukraine) on 28 November 1829 (he died in Peterhof on 20 November 1894), he was Russian of German extraction and Christian by virtue of his progenitors' forced conversion from Judaism. This admixture served his critics well, but it was also the reason for his versatility and solid Western European cultural standards. Anton Rubinstein has suffered the unhappy fate of having his name and fame as composer, pianist, and pedagogue perpetuated while nearly all his enormous catalogue of compositions has disappeared from the general repertoire.

Rubinstein's reputation rests on his having been, by general consensus, the greatest pianist since Liszt, and the many accounts of his performances range from deeply sensitive to electrifying, although, unfortunately, he died just a little too early to leave us any recordings. His repertoire was enormous and all-embracing, and his most famous series of concerts was the cycle of seven Historical Recitals with which he toured Europe in 1885. These programs began with early keyboard music of the English, French, Italian, and German schools, moving through all the important classical and early romantic composers and ending with a selection of Russian piano music. Schumann and Chopin featured in his music above all others. Only early music of Liszt appeared—Rubinstein felt that Liszt's later forays into modern harmony were unacceptable—and Brahms was not featured at all. (Rubinstein's antipathy to Brahms may be easily accounted for: Brahms borrowed a great many ideas from Rubinstein's music without acknowledgment but, aided and abetted by Clara Schumann, then caustically criticized Rubinstein's output, root and branch.) Cutting himself off from both the conservative school of European music as exemplified by Brahms, and the modern school as exemplified by Liszt, left Rubinstein somewhat isolated as a composer, all the more so as he regarded all his Russian forerunners as distinctly amateur, he mistrusted the growing school of nationalism, and he took a very long time to appreciate that a relative cosmopolitan Russian like Tchaikovsky had any worth. He thought all along that real music had died with Schumann and Chopin. Not surprisingly, then, he was a very conservative composer indeed. But this had its virtues: while the Russian school was emerging in something of a hit-or-miss fashion, Rubinstein, with his thorough German background, brought a great deal of order to chaos. He is revered in all books about Russian music for his abiding interest in rich, broad, and highly competent music education, and, of course, he will always be remembered for having founded the St. Petersburg Conservatory. (His brother Nikolay was the director of the Moscow Conservatory and an equally old-fashioned academic, if unfairly remembered for his criticisms of the early works of Tchaikovsky.) Anton Rubinstein believed that all potential Russian composers ought to be given better grounding in the essentials of musical language—up to this point the great classical forms of European music, opera excluded, were almost non-existent in Russia. It was Rubinstein who wrote the first significant body of Russian Sonatas (ten), Concertos (eight), Symphonies (six), and String Quartets (ten), and whose very industry and competence were an inspiration to his compatriot brothers in composition.

What sort of a composer was Rubinstein? The only piece of his music that could be said to have survived, at least in every domestic library, is a pretty but relatively insignificant piano piece written in his seventeenth year. The instant fame of the Melody in F would nearly eclipse the rest of Rubinstein's production in the same way that Paderewski's Minuet in G and Rakhmaninov's C♯ minor Prelude were to do some years later. But in this little piece of Rubinstein's we can sense his interest in Mendelssohn's *Songs without Words*, and he was to produce some hundreds of similar trifles for piano, a good many of which are of more than passing interest. He also composed operas (thirteen of them!) ranging from Russian legends to Jewish and Christian stories—only one of which has survived in the theater, and then only in Eastern Europe: *The Demon*. But it is certainly interesting that Gustav Mahler once turned down Hugo Wolf's opera *Der Corregidor* in order to prepare *The Demon* for the Vienna Opera, and even a cursory glance shows that Tchaikovsky's *Eugene Onegin* is heavily indebted to Rubinstein's work. Among Rubinstein's symphonies, the second (a grand piece which started life with four movements but ended up with seven), the *Ocean Symphony* was for a time very popular and merits a revival, along with the more modestly proportioned but beautifully crafted and delightfully idiosyncratic Fifth Symphony. Although Rubinstein was a cosmopolitan heavily influenced by Mendelssohn and Schumann, every now and then a bit of real Russia breaks through—for example, in songs like "The Asra" or "Gold Rolls Here before Me" (wonderfully recorded by Chaliapin), in the delicate treatment of a folk song in the last movement of the excellent piano quartet, and in the explosive finale of the brilliant first piano sonata.

Just because a composer is rather *derrière-garde* is no reason to dismiss him; after the passage of time it no longer matters so much whether a piece is anachronistic. What counts is that, in its own terms, a work be consistent, interesting, and inventive. There is a great deal of such music by Rubinstein which renders his neglect shameful. Although those hoping for another Tchaikovsky in Rubinstein will be disappointed, it is clear that Tchaikovsky would have been a very different composer without Rubinstein's example. (A case in point: the similarity of the introduction to the cadenza in the first movement of Rubinstein's Fourth Piano Concerto—happily still in the repertoire—and the same moment in Tchaikovsky's First, which appeared the following year, is scarcely likely to have been accidental!)

In recent years there has been an upturn in Rubinstein's fortunes thanks to recordings, and it is now possible to hear the piano music, the symphonies, and the concertos. A few other orchestral works have appeared, and some chamber music and songs, as well as *The Demon,* but there is still a long way to go before the bulk of his work is available. The present writer has had the good fortune to perform in many of Rubinstein's chamber and vocal works, and has played and recorded a good deal of the piano music. To take just one body of work from his vast output, Rubinstein's four piano sonatas make an excellent introduction, even if the performer has quite a bit to do to render the many various elements of some of the movements homogeneous. But this perhaps was the secret of Rubinstein as a pianist—that he could convince the audience of the worth of a piece, and even hold their rapt attention when the work was of lesser importance. It is certain that, as well as being highly respected for his performances of the great piano masterpieces, he had great success with the works of such as Moscheles, Thalberg, and Henselt, composers of the second rank, with the best will in the world! And frankly there is sometimes a touch of the salon in Rubinstein's own music against which one must be on guard to save from itself—as he himself must have done in performance. Sadly much of Rubinstein's music is presently out of print, but some detective work in libraries and on websites will yield results. Clearly his music is a good deal more interesting than its scarcity would suggest, and the present book—filled with information and insight—should prove an ideal impetus for the proper revival of a fine composer.

Leslie Howard
London, 2006

Acknowledgments

The author would like to thank the following for their kind assistance:

Raisa Ourasova of the Foreign Exchange Department at the National Library of Russia, St. Petersburg

Jane Rosen, librarian of the Society for Co-Operation in Russian and Soviet Studies

The Goethe Institute, London

The British Library and the employees of Northamptonshire Public Libraries

D. Holohan, B. Lowe, H. Zajaczkowski, Marius van Paasen, Margaret Fingerhut, and Professor N. Cornwell

Last, but not least, Professor Malcolm Hamrick Brown without whose encouragement this book would probably never have been completed.

Introduction

Wholly devoted to his art, he did not value
the opinion of people and believed but little in the
praises of admirers who were oftentimes partial
towards him; not in transient fashion, but in his
own deep feeling did he try to fathom the
secrets of art.

Vladimir Odoyevsky Sebastian Bach "Russian Nights," 1844

Posterity has not been entirely kind to Anton Rubinstein (1829–1894). Within fifty years of his death his reputation as one of the foremost musical figures in all of Europe had shrunk to a mere nothing. Anyone trying to assess Rubinstein's achievements and the reasons for this paradoxical fall from grace has to keep in mind the three key aspects of his life's work: his career on the concert platform, his educationalist work in founding Russia's first music conservatory, and his achievements as a composer. At the same time one must view these factors from two different standpoints: his reception both inside and outside Russia (after 1872 this also includes America). Rather like Meyerbeer, who began his career in Berlin but went on to write for the Italian and French stages with enormous success, Rubinstein may be considered an internationalist. He remained proud of his Russian nationality, but he also occupied an ideal position to bridge the gap between two separate spheres of musical culture: the newly emerging Russian school and the well-developed musical traditions of Western Europe. This is an important point and largely explains why the "cosmopolitan" Rubinstein fell out of favor in Russia when the Bolsheviks seized power. In fact, political issues consistently played a role in Rubinstein's fate. The Great War of 1914–18 and the October Revolution of 1917 in Russia changed not only the map of Europe but also the tastes and attitudes toward music. Hardened by the horrors of war, death, and deprivation, people no longer found solace in the high romanticism of the late nineteenth century. While tastes and fashions were just as likely to change again, there were always victims. The rise of Nazism in 1933 and the attempts to eradicate all traces of Jewish culture was just the next stage in the effacement of Rubinstein's legacy.

Countless words have been written about Rubinstein the virtuoso. His depth of tone, his skill with the pedal, his perfect phrasing that allowed him to make the instrument sing are but a few of the qualities of his playing most frequently cited. Since his artistry was never captured in actual sounds, however, only his contemporaries' reviews and commentaries can give any impression of it. When he died in the winter of 1894 phonogram recordings were still a novelty, but even had they succeeded in capturing some part of the famous Rubinstein legend, they would probably not have done him justice. He was by the end of his life a bitter and disappointed man and not the Titan who had taken Europe and America by storm in the 1870s. His career as a concert virtuoso lasted for almost fifty years, although even after 1886, when he officially retired from the concert platform, he continued to appear regularly in charity concerts. The fear that people might forget him if he did not maintain his public profile haunted him. In this he was certainly driven by vanity and ambition that sprang not from the transient glory of the concert platform but out of a jealous desire to succeed as a composer. In this he was guided by an instinctive belief in the universality of music as a language, resisting (in his early years, at least) the growing importance of the nationalist schools.

Rubinstein's innate conservatism extended also to his technique of composition at a time when great advances were being made in all aspects of composition, especially harmony and orchestration. He could not, and would not, accept their value and believed that the music of Berlioz, Liszt, and Wagner were aberrations leading composers along a false path in art. In their music he saw nothing more than a "dressing up of ideas," which was "an evil sign of the times, an unhealthy weakness—however strong-willed and well done in itself—as the sign of a lack of solid invention and creative power."[1] In his own music Rubinstein tried to look back to a time before the advent of "musical theories," "programs," and "national styles," and no doubt firmly believed that he was a standard bearer for the lost world of music as it was before the European revolutions of 1848. He did eventually make a few concessions to contemporary trends—the gradual acceptance of program music and the limited use of national folk songs in symphonic music and opera—but generally he refused to bow to any sort of meretricious "fashion." He regarded composition as a craft that must be practiced like any other: sometimes the product might not be very successful, but most important was to keep trying and perhaps one day patience would be rewarded with a masterpiece. By the mid-nineteenth century, that approach was distinctly out of fashion, but, for Rubinstein, composition born of calm reflection and slow maturation was largely alien. The desire for action and impulsiveness were irresistible components of his character.

The era when Rubinstein first began to make an impact on Russian musical life was one of huge social change. Russia was only just beginning to emerge from the oppressive regime of Nicholas I (r. 1825–55) and the paralyzed intellectual life of the country was beginning to revive. Rubinstein's plan to found a music academy in St. Petersburg had been turned down in 1852, but by 1859 the idea had found favor in imperial circles and the Russian Music Society was born. This was followed by the St. Petersburg Conservatory three years later. In the years preceding these events Rubinstein had undertaken a long concert tour of Western Europe and had come under the charismatic influence of Liszt, whose model as an artist he consciously emulated. An inveterate enemy of char-latanism and mediocrity, Rubinstein set very high artistic standards. He had always maintained that only years of patient and selfless devotion could produce an artist of any caliber, and therefore he detested dilettantism of any kind. Even a measure of poverty was beneficial for a budding talent, as it instilled a need to strive and succeed. Rubinstein's contact with Liszt reinforced these values and fueled him once again with reforming zeal. The first fruit was the article "Composers in Russia" which appeared in the Viennese press in 1855 and caused a storm of protest in Russia. Far from assisting Rubinstein in gaining support for musical reform in his own country, the article actually hampered his plans by uniting various disaffected groups (composers, critics, amateur musicians) who, for their own reasons, were radically opposed to his views. This proved to be only the first of several obstacles that he faced. Despite the changes in Russia's political climate, it was not without difficulties that the Conservatory was founded. Rubinstein's endeavors would almost surely have been in vain at that time had it not been for the direct intervention of Grand Duchess Yelena Pavlovna (1806–1873), who used her influence with the Russian Ministry of the Court to put pressure on the government.

Both periods of Rubinstein's directorship of the Conservatory (1862–67; 1887–91) were marked by vigorous attempts to consolidate the authority of the director and limit external interference from the court and various government departments. This brought him into frequent conflict with state bureaucrats, with other members of the teaching staff, and also with certain influential sections of Russian society intent on undermining his authority. He steadfastly refused to be intimidated by any display of animosity toward him and pursued his artistic aims with a tenacity bordering on the tyrannical. In this regard, Rubinstein was almost completely unable to compromise on any matter relating to his artistic principles, and he could be overbearing and inflexible in his dealings with people. Undoubtedly there were some who supported and admired his tough and uncompromising stance, but others saw it only as vanity and an insatiable lust for power. Perhaps his single-mindedness and unswerving determination to achieve his aims were in themselves the source of much hostility, and were interpreted by his opponents as a willful and despotic ambition. In Rubinstein's defense, it would be fair to say that the Russian intelligentsia of that time was replete with "big personalities" who were very vocal in expressing their views, and a man having less moral strength than the Conservatory's first director would never have been able to achieve what he achieved. The antagonism between Rubinstein and his opponents was a specific feature of St. Petersburg's musical development. Acrimonious bickering over the merits and demerits of a conservatory did not play a conspicuous part in shaping the musical life of Moscow. When Anton's younger brother, Nikolay Rubinstein, a man with a more phlegmatic temperament, founded the Moscow branch of the Russian Music Society and the Conservatory a year or two later, he was largely spared personal animosity. Generally speaking Anton simply ignored the polemics, no doubt believing that if the conservatories could prove their worth in the face of rancorous criticism, the argument would be won in his favor simply by default. This turned out to be a vain hope, as the arguments were being constantly juggled by his opponents always with the aim of casting him in an unfavorable light. Most vociferous among them were the critics Serov (until his death in 1871), Stasov, and Cui, all of whom rarely missed an opportunity to attack the work of the Conservatory, and Rubinstein, in any way they could. For them the issue of the Conservatory, whether or not they realized it, had become inextricably entangled with their attitude toward Rubinstein himself.

The source of this antagonism is bound up with the emergence of the New Russian School headed by Balakirev. In Germany Liszt had waged war against philistinism in art with the formation of the Neu-Weimar-Verein and his support for Berlioz and Wagner. Stasov, also guided by an admiration for Liszt, wanted to create a school in Russia that would be both progressive and nationally distinctive. Throughout the 1870s Stasov and the other members of Balakirev's circle maintained contact with Liszt, and the "delegations" headed by Cui in 1876, and Borodin the following year, were intended to seek his protection and patronage. For Liszt there seemed to be absolutely no contradiction in the support that he had once given to the young Rubinstein and the praise that he now lavished on these, his younger compatriots. In Russia, however, things were viewed in a very different light. The St. Petersburg Conservatory and the New Russian School came into being within months of each other, but it was not just open rivalry that divided them. Something went far deeper. Before Rubinstein's departure for Western Europe in 1854, attitudes toward him had not been particularly hostile. When he returned to Russia with his head brimming with ideas about founding a conservatory in 1859, he had already made his mark, not only on the concert platform but as a composer. One of his operas had been performed in Weimar, and his *Ocean Symphony* had been heard at the Gewandhaus subscription concerts in Leipzig. At this time Balakirev and his fellow *kuchkists*[2] had achieved nothing worthy of note, and one can easily see how a reaction set in against the man who was telling them how the musical affairs of Russia were to be organized henceforth. This attitude was at least partially based on envy of Rubinstein's European reputation at a time when even Glinka's works were barely known outside Russia. In publishing his article "Composers in Russia" Rubinstein had unwittingly played into the hands of his critics, providing them with all the ammunition they needed to begin a war of words. With all the skill of trained lawyers, they proved to be quite adept at focusing on the aspects of his writing that could best be turned to their advantage.

In 1855, when "Composers in Russia" appeared, music education in Russia was almost completely unsystematic. The government trained singers and orchestral players for the imperial stage, but in most other respects music was a pastime for members of the aristocratic elite who had studied with resident foreign musicians. Rubinstein's clear intention in the article had been to cultivate a more serious attitude toward the teaching and composition of music in Russia. While stressing the importance of professionalism, he had heaped scorn on the musical dilettantes, and among Russian composers had dismissed everyone except Glinka. In the eyes of his contemporaries, he had made a fateful association between the achievements of the fledgling Russian school and amateurism, and this amounted to nothing less than a slur on national art. Rubinstein made matters worse with his ambiguous attitude toward the undisputed founder of the Russian national school. On the one hand, he had sung the praises of Glinka and declared him a genius, but, on the other, he had also declared that the operas *Zhizn' za Tsarya* [A life for the tsar] and *Ruslan i Lyudmila* [Ruslan and Lyudmila] had failed because the composer had been mistaken in allowing the national style to take precedence over the need to express universal emotions. Rubinstein's critics interpreted this as an attack on the holy grail of the Russian school. Yet, later on, when Rubinstein recanted and tried to write in a pseudo-national style, the same critics despised him even more, as if he were trying to steal the Emperor's clothes.

In his role as principal conductor of the Russian Music Society concerts during the 1860s, Rubinstein was often accused of favoring second-rate German music over works by native composers. Again this was a distortion of the truth, for at that period there were very few works by native composers. That the Russian Music Society struggled to find pieces by Russian composers who are now largely forgotten, for example, Afanasyev and Fitingof-Shel, only proves that the accusation was unfounded. Even more important, it was Rubinstein who conducted some of the very first orchestral works by Cui and Musorgsky as early as the winter season of 1859–60. The programs of the Russian Music Society concerts consistently showed a balanced repertory and frequently included works for which Rubinstein had little personal sympathy, patently demonstrating his impartiality. In an attempt to demolish Rubinstein's standing, his critics trained their sights on the Conservatory and on Rubinstein's compositions. It was an effective stratagem to associate these two targets since the argument could be put like this: listen to this man's music—it is bad, derivative, unoriginal, and the product of dull academic training. This is what a foreign institution like a conservatory will produce when it is transplanted onto Russian soil: all it will turn out is mediocre talents, writing hack works. Then the same critics could effectively contrast this supposed mediocrity with the vibrant works of native composers whose imaginations had not been polluted by alien theories about music, who listen to the songs of the peasants and their own inner voice that has not been stultified by foreign pedantry, and compose works that are meaningful to their fellow Russians.

For Stasov and his cohorts, everything associated with the Conservatory was corrupt and repulsive. Even a talent of Tchaikovsky's stature was suspect, as he was a product of the same Conservatory and was, as they saw it, therefore irrevocably tainted with the same pernicious "defects." Rubinstein's resignation in 1867 cooled the protests, especially as Rimsky-Korsakov was invited to teach at the Conservatory in 1871, but the opposition to Rubinstein as a composer and as a musical educationalist remained. In his speech of the same year, commemorating the ninth anniversary of the Conservatory's founding, Rubinstein paid tribute to the achievements of the New Russian School in an attempt to shore up old differences. Although attitudes between the opposing camps had softened to some extent by the early 1870s, the propaganda war was far from over. In 1880, in Paris, Cui published a 174-page book, *La Musique en Russie,* in an effort to increase awareness of the "kuchkists" in Western Europe. Although it could be said that Rubinstein had done much the same with his article on Russian composers, Cui's work had a far more lasting effect, conditioning Western opinion about the kind of music people should expect to hear from a native Russian composer. It was a masterly coup, for its approachable yet authoritative style made it one of the most important source works on Russian music of the time in a language other than Russian. In a narrower sense, but one of specific importance at the time the book appeared, it also served as a way of counterbalancing the success that Nikolay Rubinstein had recently achieved with his Trocadéro concerts of September 1878 where the spotlight had been trained largely, though not exclusively, on the works of "conservatory composers," namely, Anton Rubinstein and Tchaikovsky. Even three decades later Cui's book had not outlived its usefulness, for when Diaghilev's *Saisons russes* took Paris by storm, it had firmly established the yardstick by which all Russian music was to be judged. The proponents of "real" Russian music had created what Richard Taruskin has called "the mythos of authenticity,"[3] which excluded from its ranks anyone who was not a member of their exclusive club. The same myth was ably and eagerly promulgated by later French and British writers on Russian music and for many decades was responsible for the ambivalent attitude toward Tchaikovsky in Western criticism—that the composer was only as good as the "Russianness" of his works had made him. In the case of Rubinstein, of course, ambivalence was not even an issue, and the critics, one and all, squarely wrote him off because his music was not perceived as Russian at all.

As the old adage goes, "It is the victors who write the history," and therefore it is not entirely surprising that the views of Stasov, Cui, and their Western imitators prevailed for a century and more. Their crusade began as a noble cause but ended as a grotesque caricature. In the campaign to legitimize their own position they had attempted indiscriminately to annihilate that of their opponents. There is a direct comparison here with the polemic that raged around Wagner's operas during the 1870s, for when tempers had cooled, even the implacable Hanslick could write: "I and others who share my views would probably have written more dispassionately about Wagner had our pulses not been agitated by the immoderate, often ludicrous excesses, of our adversaries."[4] For a long time these same excesses distorted the brilliant achievements made by the "kuchka," Tchaikovsky, and the conservatories. The inward-looking and anti-cosmopolitan cultural policies of the Stalinist years only served to strengthen the stereotypical attitudes already established by Stasov, Cui, and others. Balakirev, Musorgsky, and the other "kuchkists" were duly awarded state "canonization," because they were portrayed as radical, "revolutionary," and anti-establishment. Popularity saved Tchaikovsky, despite his having been labeled the morbid poet of a bourgeois, decadent, and dying society, and he, too, received due recognition from the state in 1940, the year of his centenary. In life, as in death, Rubinstein never earned any sort of distinction and remained a perpetual outsider. In a final twist of irony, he even lost out to Rimsky-Korsakov when the St. Petersburg Conservatory was named after him.

Naturally it is Rubinstein's achievements as a musician and public figure that are of the greatest interest to the music historian, but the nature of his upbringing and his relationships with other members of his family clearly cannot be ignored, especially in view of the important role played by his younger brother, Nikolay. The most enduring influence on Anton's life was his Prussian-born mother, Kaleriya Khristoforovna (1807–1891). A stern and highly practical woman, she instilled into her sons a love of order and patient determination in achieving their goals. For all of Anton's adult life she was his personal confidante, and it is largely because she carefully preserved his letters that we are now able to piece together much that would have otherwise remained unknown. Although Anton rarely kept any correspondence addressed to him (the rare exception was Liszt's letters) his letters to Kaleriya Khristoforovna cover a period of more than forty years. In particular, they show that the relations between Anton and his brother, Nikolay, were often far from harmonious. The rivalry between them began quite soon after Anton returned to Russia in 1842, following his first concert tour of Western Europe with his teacher, Villoing. For his elder brother, Yakov, who was a medical student and therefore in no way his professional rival, Anton always showed far more sincere fraternal concern. Yakov died suddenly in 1863 from causes that are not clear from any published material, and the loss must have been a bitter blow to Anton. On the other hand, the coldness shown by Anton at Nikolay Rubinstein's funeral in 1881 was noted by several bystanders, and Tchaikovsky was in little doubt when he concurred with his publisher, Jurgenson, that it was the result of jealousy.

Rubinstein's relations with his youngest sister, Sofiya (1841–1919), do not seem to have been particularly close during the early years of her life in Odessa. She was twelve years his junior and remained close to her mother. In July 1854 Kaleriya Khristoforovna moved to Moscow to take up a post teaching music at a girls' boarding school and remained there until the end of 1859. Judging by Anton's letters, Kaleriya and Sofiya lodged with Yakov in St. Petersburg for a time, and remained in the capital intermittently until 1868. By then Rubinstein was financially secure. He was able to give his mother and sister a yearly allowance of one thousand rubles, and there was even talk of their moving to Germany. In the end, when Anton quitted the Conservatory and departed for Western Europe, his mother and Sofiya returned to Odessa. The Russian musicologist and Rubinstein scholar, Lev Barenboym, took pains to emphasize Sofiya's "revolutionary activities." The true extent of these activities is unclear, but it is quite possible that she was some sort of political activist. In 1879 Vera Figner (1852–1942) had organized a branch of the People's Will group in Odessa, which advocated radical ideas, including the overthrow of the autocracy and the creation of a constituent assembly. Another prominent revolutionary, Andrey Zhelyabov (1850–81), had also studied at the University of Odessa until his expulsion in 1871, and he was later hanged for the part he had played in the assassination of

Alexander II in 1881. When the new emperor, Alexander III, acceded to the throne, vigorous attempts were made to eradicate the activities of the People's Will organizations, and in 1883 Figner was arrested. According to Barenboym, it was Sofiya's association with Figner that resulted in her being placed under police surveillance, and for several years she was prohibited from visiting either St. Petersburg or Moscow. Rubinstein's relations with Sofiya grew much closer after Nikolay's death, and it was with her that he shared his most intimate thoughts about the loss of their brother. The bond between them was strengthened still further after the death of Kaleriya Khristoforovna. By then Rubinstein had separated from his wife, for reasons indicated below, and was living alone in Dresden. His correspondence with Sofiya and with his daughter, Anna, is a particularly useful source of information on his life during this period.

In 1865 Anton married Vera Chekuanova, and between 1866 and 1872 they had three children. The proceeds from the tour in the United States in 1872–73 had enabled him to purchase a villa at Peterhof, a small town not far from St. Petersburg on the Gulf of Finland. Because of his busy schedule of concert engagements, Rubinstein was frequently absent from home for long periods, and the upbringing of the children was left mostly in Vera's hands. Anton's strict upbringing had instilled in him a belief in the need for authoritarianism, but Vera's approach to the children's education was a good deal softer and more liberal. Toward the youngest child, Aleksandr, who was born with asthma and a weak heart, she was especially affectionate. She made a number of costly trips to Italy with the boy to seek out medical help and to allow him time to recuperate. While Anton was able to earn money from his concert appearances, he continued to shoulder the cost without complaint. In January 1886 he told his mother that Vera and the children were spending the winter in St. Petersburg, as they found it more cheerful there than in Peterhof. It was the kind of unnecessary expense that eventually was bound to affect his financial security: "As far as the latter is concerned we have long ago lost all sense of scale. In the final analysis it is a matter of indifference whether more is spent here or abroad. And while everyone here is well, we are spared the torments of moving from one place to another, and that is something you cannot underestimate."[5] After Rubinstein stopped giving concerts in mid-1886, Vera could not tolerate the need to economize. Again he confessed to his mother in January 1889: "Vera is well but unhappy: 1) she loves the South, but she has to live in the North; 2) she loves her husband as all wives do, but she has in me only an artist; 3) she loves a lot of money as all women do, but she has to content herself with little—especially since I stopped giving concerts! All this together makes her nervy, that is, nervously irritable!!"[6] On his reappointment as director of the Conservatory in 1887, Rubinstein rented an apartment in St. Petersburg, which only accelerated the growing rift between husband and wife. He spent the summer of 1890 not at Peterhof as usual but at Badenweiler in Germany. When he returned to St. Petersburg in August of that year, he finally cut his ties with the Conservatory and moved to Dresden. The final illness and death of his youngest son, Aleksandr, in October 1893 brought about a brief reconciliation with Vera, and in June of the following year he returned to Peterhof where he died four months later.

For the most part Rubinstein had forged his way through life with barely a backward glance. "Fais ce que tu dois, advienne ce qui pourra" is the advice he gave his daughter, Anna, when she was about to take her examinations, but it could also have served as his own mantra. "Do what you must and come what may," had served him throughout his life, in all his personal endeavors and had given him the confidence to overcome problems however great they were. This extreme bullishness tends to obscure the fact that this complex and in many ways contradictory man had a vulnerable side. The self-doubts that plagued him in later years became manifest at first in humorous asides, as, for instance, when he remarked wryly in 1880: "This year humanity can breathe easily—it will not be cheered by any new compositions of mine!?" Seven years later he told the German composer, Carl Reinecke, that "my compositions only please because of me, and, in the final analysis, that is not a sufficiently well-founded reason to carry on writing." Enormous industry had eventually led Rubinstein to the belief that he had written himself out, and when his publisher, Barthold Senff, brought out a catalogue of his complete works as part of the 1889 jubilee celebrations, far from being pleased, he felt only utter disenchantment. Yet again in 1892 he declared to his sister, Sofiya, that he planned to give up composing but once more was drawn back to it. A lifetime of perpetual toil had become a habit he found impossible to give up.

* * *

One glance at the extensive bibliographies on Rubinstein provided by Catherine Drinker Bowen and Larry Sitsky reveals an alarming array of source materials for the would-be biographer to assimilate. The majority is contained in late-nineteenth and early-twentieth-century newspapers, periodicals, and other publications that are not always easy for researchers to find and are of variable quality and usefulness. Some are simply too specific for a general biography such as aspects of keyboard interpretation, pedaling, and so on; others make up a large corpus of what could be called memoirist literature. Although some of this material is of value, it is too often anecdotal in character and lacks the benefit of firsthand information. Rubinstein, for example, flatly refused to provide Eugen Zabel, the journalist and editor of the *Nationalzeitung* with any details for his biography, *Ein Künstlerleben,* published by Senff in 1892, and the author was forced to approach Tchaikovsky (in vain, as it happens) in an effort to elicit information about Rubinstein's early years at the Conservatory.[7] In the present work this author has tried to allow Rubinstein to speak for himself, adding commentaries, where necessary, for the sake of narrative structure and clarity. He has also tried to be guided by the published documentary material only, avoiding, as far as possible, anecdotal descriptions. At times this has resulted in rather arid listings of concert itineraries and programs, but since this was the nature of Rubinstein's career as a virtuoso, excluding these details would have somehow robbed him of stature. The concert programs, and particularly those of the

Russian Music Society during the years Rubinstein was the director, are of great historical interest, as they reflect the changing tastes that occurred over the thirty-five-years between 1859 and 1894.

The earliest of Rubinstein's published letters date from 1850, and from that year on it is possible to reconstruct his biography fairly accurately based on those letters. That the letters are available is almost entirely owing to the Russian musicologist Lev Barenboym. Until the late 1940s very little of Rubinstein's correspondence was available to scholars, and the discovery of valuable archival material at times reads like a detective story. Much has been irrevocably lost, however. We know, for example, that around 1909 Rubinstein's daughter, Anna, destroyed a large bundle of his letters to his wife, at Vera's own request. By 1980 Barenboym claimed to have located perhaps a thousand letters, of which approximately half have appeared in print. The first such publication, *A. G. Rubinsteyn: Izbrannïye pis'ma* [A. G. Rubinstein, Selected letters], appeared in 1954 but is quite limited in scope. Three decades later a collection of 510 letters, most of them appearing in print for the first time, was published in the three-volume work *A. G. Rubinshteyn. Literaturnoye naslediye* [A. G. Rubinstein. Literary heritage] (Moscow: Muzïka, 1983–86), along with a number of other key documents listed at the end of Appendix A. Mention must also be made of Barenboym's two-volume biography, *Anton Grigor'yevich Rubinshteyn. Zhizn', artisticheskiy put', tvorchestvo, muzïkal'no-obshchestvennaya deyatel'nost'* [Life, artistic career, creative work, public work in the field of music]. This pioneering and well-documented work contains a wealth of factual information for which any latter-day biographer must be greatly indebted, but it appeared during the Khrushchev "thaw" and was written from a defensive and apologetic position. In order to rehabilitate Rubinstein in the eyes of the Soviet ideologues, Barenboym needed to remind people that Rubinstein had been born a man of the people, that he had high democratic principles and took his civic duties seriously, and, perhaps most important of all, that in his frequent brushes with tsarist officialdom there was a nascent Communist bursting to get out.

The other main source for anyone researching Rubinstein's life is *Avtobiograficheskiye vospominaniya* [Autobiographical reminiscences] that appeared in the newspaper *Russkaya starina* as part of the composer's jubilee celebrations in 1889. Rubinstein himself dictated these memoirs to a journalist in four separate sessions, but given the ad hoc manner in which they were delivered, it is not surprising that there are inaccuracies. Even so, the autobiography remains an important document and is one of the few sources of information on his life up to 1850. Rubinstein's early childhood in Bessarabia (now part of Moldova and Ukraine), and later in Moscow, are shrouded in mystery, as little is known about his parents' origins. To overcome this significant problem, this author has attempted to provide a socio-geographic outline of the milieu from which Rubinstein's descendants originated. This seemed far preferable to the speculative and semi-fictionalized accounts of Anton's childhood that appeared in Catherine Drinker Bowen's earlier biography. Rubinstein's childhood is not the only gray area in need of further elucidation. The publication of new material from Russian archives would greatly enhance our understanding of his life in Russia, and would throw considerable light on his relations with the Russian court and the origins and nature of the opposition toward him from the conservative press. In her recent article, *The Disowning of Anton Rubinstein,* Marina Frolova-Walker has rightly suggested that its causes were complex and anti-Semitism was only one factor.[8] His Jewish origins were undoubtedly an impediment to attaining proper recognition in Russia and certainly account for the anti-Semitic attacks on him, particularly during the reign of Alexander III. But an even greater barrier existed for him, particularly at the start of his career, and that was the problem of class in a country where social standing was infinitely more important than talent or ability. Born the son of a merchant, he did not achieve elevation to the hereditary *dvoryanstvo* [gentry] until 1877. Publicly he appeared to disdain such honors, but privately he coveted them. A fiercely proud man, Rubinstein probably felt that his talent placed him in a class outside the norm. When he was finally awarded the rank of Privy Counselor in 1888, for instance, he declared: "Before I was a king, and for many a god. Now I am a general, so that, properly speaking, means a demotion for me. But in our country a person without a title even to this day is a nothing."[9] An attitude such as this was bound to ruffle imperial feathers, and Rubinstein's irascible temperament and outspoken manner would earn him many enemies.

* * *

The appendixes contain a list of Rubinstein's works, the programs of the Historical Concerts, a genealogical table, and selections from *Gedankenkorb* [A basket of thoughts] (a sort of diary Rubinstein began in the 1880s and continued to write until his death, except during the years when he was preoccupied with other literary works). He gave authorization for it to be published posthumously, and the book eventually appeared in Leipzig in 1897. It consists of 470 entries, or aphorisms, of which a small number are translated in the appendix under rubrics rather than in the random manner of the original. Translating the whole of *A Basket of Thoughts* would take up far too much space, but even the limited selection given here will provide the reader with a vivid insight into Rubinstein's aesthetics and the breadth and scope of his interests in art, morality, religion, history, and politics. The entries may raise a smile of amusement, or a frown of disapprobation, but rarely are they devoid of interest. Whether cynical, paradoxical, true, thought-provoking, prophetic, or false, they make for fascinating and stimulating reading.

Note on Transliteration, Orthography, and the System of Applying Dates

The transliteration of Russian names and words are mostly standard, but note the following:

е = ye, following a vowel or a soft sign. Thus "Taneyev" rather than "Taneev"

ы = ï,	й = y
ь = '	ъ = "
я = ya	ю = yu

I depart from this system where established convention requires it, for example:

Rubinstein, not Rubinshteyn

Tchaikovsky, not Chaykovskiy

Cui, not Kuy

Laroche, not Larosh

The soft sign is omitted in personal names (e.g., Pikkel, Bessel, Sapelnikov, Menshikova, Lvov, Alyabyev, Lyubov, Grigoryevich, Ilich) except in transliterated titles.

The titles of Rubinstein's works are given in accordance with their first publication, when known. Thus *Die Kinder der Haide,* rather than . . . *Heide; Der Thurm zu Babel,* rather than *Der Turm zu Babel; Die Maccabäer,* rather than Die Makkabäer. Since *Néron* was set to a French text, this title is used in preference to *Nero.*

Place names in Poland, Eastern Prussia, the Baltic States, and so on, are given as they were known in Rubinstein's lifetime. Later names are shown in the General Index, for instance, Derpt, later Dorpat, now Tartu (Estonia).

All dates are generally given in their dual form in accordance with the Julian calendar (used in Russia before 1918) and the Gregorian calendar, unless new style (n.s.) or old style (o.s.) is specified. Although cumbersome, this avoids the possibility of confusion when making comparisons between places and dates. In documents that apply only to Western Europe, a single date (the Gregorian calendar) is given. During the period in question, the Julian calendar lagged behind the Gregorian by twelve days.

Abbreviations for Sources

AGR   *Lev Aronovich Barenboym. Anton Grigor'yevich Rubinshteyn: Zhizn', artisticheskiy put', tvorchestvo, muzïkal'no-obshchestvennaya deyatel'nost'* [Life, artistic career, creative work, public work in the field of music]. 2 vols. Leningrad: Gosudarstvennoye muzïkal'noe izdatel'stvo, 1959/1962.

AR   *Avtobiograficheskiye rasskazï* [Autobiographical stories], in *A. G. Rubinsteyn: Literaturnoye naslediye* [A. G. Rubinsteyn: Literary heritage], ed. L. A. Barenboym, 3 vols. (Moscow: Muzïka, 1983–86), 1:65–104.

CBFA *Catherine Drinker Bowen. Free Artist: The story of Anton and Nicholas Rubinstein.* New York: Random House, 1939.

CPSS *P. I. Tchaikovsky. P. I. Chaykovskiy: Polnoye sobraniye sochineniy. Literaturnïye proizvedeniya* [P. I. Tchaikovsky: Complete collected works. Literary works]. 18 vols. Moscow, 1953–81.

FOZD *Nikolay Findeyzen. A. G. Rubinshteyn: Ocherk yego zhizni i muzïkal'noy deyatel'nosti* [A. G. Rubinstein: An outline of his life and musical activities]. Moscow, 1907.

LMBHZ *La Mara (pseudonym of Ida Lipsius). Briefe hervorragender Zeitgenossen an Franz Liszt.* Nach den Handschriften des Weimarer Liszt-Museums mit Unterstützung von dessen Custos Geheimrath Gille herausgegeben von La Mara. Vols 1–2, Leipzig, 1895.

LIS   *G. A. Laroche. Izbrannïye stat'i v 5-i vïpuskakh* [Selected articles in 5 volumes]. Vols. 2–4. Leningrad: Muzïka, 1975–77.

LN   *Lev Aronovich Barenboym, ed. A. G. Rubinshteyn: Literaturnoye naslediye* [A. G. Rubinstein: Literary heritage]. 3 vols. Moscow: Muzïka, 1983–86.

MABS *Alexander M'Arthur [Lillian McArthur]. Anton Rubinstein: A Biographical Sketch.* Edinburgh: Adam and Charles Black, 1889.

NEUS *A. A. Neustroyev. "Aleksandr Villoing i pervoye kontsertnoye puteshestviye po Evropye A. G. Rubinshteyna, 1840–1842"* [Alexander Villoing and A. G. Rubinstein's first European concert tour, 1840–1842). *Russkaya starina* 65, no. 1 (January 1890).

NGR   *Lev Aronovich Barenboym. Nikolay Grigor'yevich Rubinshteyn: Istoriya zhizni i deyatel'nosti* [Nikolay Grigoryevich Rubinstein: The history of his life and work]. Moscow: Muzïka, 1982.

NSCJT *Gerald Norris. Stanford, the Cambridge Jubilee and Tchaikovsky.* Newton Abbot, U. K.: David and Charles, 1980.

RMG   *Russkaya muzïkal'naya gazeta* [Russian music newspaper].

RMM   *Anton Rubinstein. Music and Its Masters: A Conversation.* Translated by Mrs. J. P. Morgan. 2nd ed. London: Augener, [1921?].

Anton Rubinstein

1 Prologue

The Historical Context

The second half of the eighteenth century saw a vast expansion in the territories of the Russian Empire. On the death of Catherine the Great in 1796 the empire extended some 305,794 square miles from the Gulf of Finland to Alaska on the North American continent.[1] These acquisitions were gained chiefly in the West at the expense of Poland in the three partitions of 1772–95 (and later by the annexation of the Duchy of Finland in 1808), and southward in a whole series of largely successful wars against the Ottoman Empire. The new acquisitions Catherine made through her military and diplomatic victories brought with them an increase in population that became increasingly heterogeneous in its ethnic composition. Furthermore, the Russian government frequently adopted an "open-door" policy to attract settlers to the newly won territories. Under Empress Elizabeth (r. 1741–61), for example, several hundred Serbians and Montenegrins had been allowed to settle in an area between the rivers Dnieper and Bug. This autonomous region came to be known as "Little Serbia." Catherine the Great (r. 1762–96) continued this policy when in 1762 she opened the doors of the empire to foreign immigrants, except Jews, in an attempt to colonize the thinly populated tracts of southern Russia. To ensure the economic prosperity of the entire region, Catherine founded many important new cities such as Yekaterinoslav, Kherson, and the great port of Odessa. The first two of these cities became the centers of large provinces (*gubernii*), which in 1764, together with "Little Serbia," formed the basis of the "Government of New Russia" (Novorossiya), later administered by Prince Potyomkin. After the subjugation of the Tatar Khanate in 1783, the new province of Tauris (an area that included the entire Crimean peninsula) was added to New Russia, as was Bessarabia when it became part of the Russian Empire in 1812.

By the last third of the eighteenth century four principal classes (*sosloviya*) formed the bedrock of Russian society: at the top were the nobility (*dvoryanstvo*) and the clergy (*dukhovenstvo*) and beneath them the merchant class (*kupechestvo*) and the peasantry (*krest'yanstvo*).[2] The rigid stratification of society into classes (or estates) was reinforced by a legal structure that defined the obligations toward the state that were incumbent upon each social group. In this well-ordered structure, the policy of the central government toward the Jews was complex and contradictory. Throughout much of the eighteenth century it was marked by hostility tempered by pragmatism. Initially Jews were excluded from New Russia, but then the government had a change of heart. In order to colonize the newly annexed southern territories, Russia needed to expand its urban centers and, to do that, the numbers of merchants and townspeople had to be increased. As John Klier points out, the Jews came to be seen as "the raw material of urban development."[3] In 1769 the Jews finally acquired official permission to reside in New Russia, and the migration of settlers increased greatly after the first partition of Poland in 1772. The acquisition of Belorussia, with its well-developed urban infrastructure and its large Jewish populations, resulted in a steady flow of colonists toward the South. By successive imperial decrees of 1773, 1783, and 1791, the Jews were permitted to reside in Belorussia, Yekaterinoslav, and Tauris, and later the area was extended to encompass the Ukrainian provinces. The success of this policy of colonization initially brought its rewards, and Jews were accorded the same rights and privileges as other subjects of the newly acquired territories. As John Klier remarks, "Jews were at once recognised as Russian subjects and were *not* regarded as foreigners or aliens."[4] This situation continued for more than twenty years, and the Jews were not subjected to discriminatory legislation. However, the confinement of the Jews to designated areas on the fringes of the Russian Empire resulted in the formation of the so-called Jewish Pale of Settlement. By the time that Nicholas I acceded to the throne in 1825 the Pale consisted of the provinces of Grodno, Vilno, Volhynia, Podolia, Minsk, and Yekaterinoslav. Within these areas Jews had right of movement, and first-guild merchants were allowed to visit St. Petersburg, Moscow, and other important commercial centers of the empire.

Paradoxically the Jews paid for the economic transformation of New Russia, for a decree of 1794 forced them to pay taxes at double the rate of Christians living in the Pale. This did not stop the nobility from blaming them for impoverishing their own Orthodox serfs, and as a result the Jewish Statute was passed in 1804. The statute afforded the Jews "the protection of the law on the same basis as other subjects of the Crown" and also confirmed their right to an education, but at the same time it prevented them from residing on the landowners' estates and, more important, prohibited them from leasing agricultural land, from keeping inns, and from distilling or selling intoxicating liquor. The government considered these occupations, in which many Jews were actively engaged, as harmful and, by prohibiting them, attempted to steer the Jews into agriculture and small-scale industry. Despite this, a project for establishing Jewish agricultural colonies, proposed in 1806, never had any real success.

In spite of the discriminatory aspects of the 1804 statute, the situation was still relatively favorable to the Jews. Systematic expulsions from the estates of the nobility were not widespread, and there were still strong incentives attracting Jews from the western provinces to New Russia, and Odessa in particular. The Jewish population of Odessa grew steadily throughout the nineteenth century. In 1815, for example, the Jewish population of the city was less than four thousand, but by 1861 it had more than quadrupled to seventeen thousand. Bessarabia had also traditionally attracted Jewish settlers because of its commercial importance on the trading route between the Black Sea region and Central Europe. Its name derived from the Walachian Basarab dynasty that had ruled it at one time, and, like Moldavia and Walachia, it was once a northern province of the Ottoman Empire. In 1806 Russia contested the region on behalf of its Christian populations, but the fighting had dragged on inconclusively for many years. The war came to an end only in 1811, with the appointment of Field Marshal Kutuzov as supreme commander on the Turkish front. By the Treaty of Bucharest, in 1812, Russia gave up its claim to Moldavia and Walachia but gained Bessarabia, the large region lying between the rivers Dnestr and Prut. The peace was signed hurriedly because of the impending war with France on Russia's western borders. On 24 June 1812 Napoleon crossed the river Nieman, and the invasion of Russia began. After the Napoleonic Wars Bessarabia retained considerable regional autonomy. From 1818 to 1828 it had a Moldavian governor and archbishop, and the Jewish Statute introduced elsewhere in the empire did not apply to Bessarabia. The autonomous status of these newly acquired territories proved beneficial to the Jewish settlers, and, when Bessarabia was absorbed into the Jewish Pale, they crossed the Dnestr and the towns situated along the river gained considerably in economic importance. After 1828 the central government began to reverse the policy of autonomy and the Jewish legislation began to apply equally to Bessarabia.

The period of relative tolerance toward the Jewish settlers had come to an abrupt end with the accession of Nicholas I to the Russian throne. Under the banner of "Orthodoxy, autocracy, and nationality," the state policy championed by Sergey Uvarov, the minister of education, Nicholas strove tirelessly to assert the authority of the Orthodox Church and to russify the diverse peoples of his realm. Although the Jews were by no means the only social group to suffer, they were doubly persecuted because of their faith and also because of their distinct cultural institutions. "The policy of his reign," writes Florinsky, "was to bring about an assimilation of the Jews through the elimination of their 'religious fanaticism and racial exclusiveness.'"[5] The most notorious anti-Jewish legislation of Nicholas's government was the Recruitment Statute of the Jews of 26 August 1827. Under this act Jewish families lost any immunity they might have had from military service, which was set at twenty-five years and was notorious for its harshness. Even minors were not spared, for children as young as twelve were conscripted into Cantonist battalions. The brutality inflicted on the conscripts, on the one hand, and incentives in the form of privileges, tax exemptions, and the offer of land or money, on the other, produced many converts to Christianity. The Jews were forced to "bow down before the Greek cross" through the act of baptism.

Family Background

It was against this complex historical and social background that Anton's paternal grandfather, Roman Ivanovich Rubinstein, had grown up. The year of his birth is unknown, but certain facts point to the late 1770s. This was the period when many families were resettling in New Russia from the western provinces, and we can be certain that he and his immediate forebears had known the hardships faced by Jewish families living on the fringes of the vast

Russian Empire. The Rubinsteins settled in Berdichev, a town then located near the borders of three provinces—Volhynia, Podolia, and Little Russia (Ukraine). For almost three hundred years Berdichev had been a part of the Lithuanian-Polish Commonwealth, and the town's historical ties to Poland were strong. An active Jewish community sprang up around 1721, and, as a major center of Hasidism, Berdichev became known as the "Jerusalem of Volhynia" and the "Jewish capital." From the mid-eighteenth century Berdichev grew steadily in size, especially after 1765 when King Stanisław Augustus issued a decree allowing a fair to be held in the town. Most of the commerce centered on agricultural supplies, but the textile industry also played an important part in Berdichev's economy, and in 1795 Prince Radziwiłł granted seven Jewish cloth merchants the monopoly on the cloth trade in the town. After 1798 trade in the town began to decline, but owing to food shortages and the high cost of bread in Odessa, the merchants of Berdichev grew very wealthy in the period after 1812.

By the early years of the new century Roman Ivanovich had evidently become an influential figure in and around Berdichev. According to Barenboym, "he organized the first settlement of Jewish ploughmen—the village of Romanovka." Beyond these bare facts, little is known about Roman Ivanovich's biography except that he married twice. From the first marriage there were three sons.[6] The two older sons—Abram and Grigory (future father of the composer, who was born in 1807)—followed the family tradition and engaged in farming. As the firstborn, they were spared the rigors of army life, but the third son, Yakov, was conscripted into the army under the terms of the imperial decree of 1827, which stated: "Every Jewish male boy of twelve years, to the proportion of seven in every hundred of population, [is] to be conscripted for the Imperial Army and to proceed immediately to the cantonment school, to remain in the Imperial Army 25 years."[7] Yakov was later appointed to a hussars' regiment and attained the rank of field captain (he died in 1853). Two sons were born in the second marriage: Emmanuil and Konstantin, both later trained as doctors at the medical school of Moscow University.

Abram, his wife's brother, and Grigory hired a plot of land near Dubossarï (now Dubăsari in Moldova) on the river Dnestr, which formed the natural border between Russia and Bessarabia. The land rented by Abram and Grigory belonged to powerful landowners, the Radziwiłłs, who were ancestors of the ancient Polish-Lithuanian family that had played such a prominent role in the history of their country during the fifteenth and sixteenth centuries. Because of the double tax law and various restrictions imposed on Jews living in the Pale, their lives were often precarious. The landowners took full advantage of their privileges, using them to exercise almost unlimited control over their Jewish tenants. Roman Ivanovich suffered much the same fate. As Barenboym tells us: "Persecuted by the Radziwiłłs and local officials, he was finally thrown into the prison at Zhitomir, and only by sacrificing the remnants of his fortune was he able to regain his freedom. The enormous family of Roman Rubinstein, consisting at that time of more than thirty persons, was left with absolutely no means of subsistence."[8] The plight of families like the Rubinsteins was exacerbated by the cholera epidemic of 1830–31. The mortality rate in Podolia and Volhynia was particularly high, and this had direct social consequences for the population. The responsibility for the collection of taxes in the Jewish settlements was left to the *kahals* (Jewish autonomous communities) on the basis of a poll tax set at three rubles, thirty kopecks, per capita times the number of persons recorded in the previous census in 1816. The large numbers of deaths from cholera put an enormous strain on the kahals to maintain the level of payments demanded from them, and government legislation that was intended to ease the tax burden of the badly affected areas was severely hampered by excessive bureaucracy. The desire to escape onerous taxation must have been an important factor in Roman Ivanovich's decision, in July 1831, to accept the Russian Orthodox faith. Deciding to have the entire family baptized was entirely pragmatic, for it would enable them to leave the Pale and reside in Moscow and St. Petersburg. Materially this strategy proved entirely successful, and by the early 1840s (by which time the family was already well established in Moscow), Roman Ivanovich had regained his position in society. Such was his prestige in the Moscow merchants' guild that he had his portrait painted. He is pictured in a short, old-fashioned, velvet jacket, proudly displaying the gold medal from the era of Alexander I that was evidently an award for the charitable work he had performed for the guild. In this portrait Findeyzen saw a likeness to Anton that was even greater than the likeness to his own father: "The broad forehead, the intelligent, penetrating eyes, and the whole cast of the face, except for the large, hooked nose, could have belonged to A. G. Rubinstein had he lived into old age." [9]

Rubinstein's mother, Kaleriya Khristoforovna, came from an impoverished Jewish family originating from Lissa in Prussian Silesia (now Leszno in western Poland). She was born in 1807 (Barenboym claims that other sources give 1811). [10] She moved to Odessa in the early 1820s with her family, and it was there that she met Grigory Romanovich and where they probably married. Nothing is known about their lives in the period after the marriage. Because of the conflict with the Radziwiłłs, it seems likely that Grigory Romanovich soon lost the means of supporting himself by farming. Kaleriya Khristoforovna's family in Odessa and Roman Ivanovich in Berdichev may have helped the couple, but still their lives must have been unsettled by the constant need to find work. It would have been against a background of considerable uncertainty that their first child, Nikolay, was born, but the child did not survive infancy. Two more sons soon followed—Yakov in 1827 and Anton two years later in 1829. Another six years would pass before brother Nikolay was born in 1835.

At Anton's birth, the onset of labor evidently occurred suddenly. That he was not born in any of the larger towns or cities of the region, but at an inn in the village of Vïkhvatinets (sometimes given as Wechwotinez in the German transliteration) suggests that the family was often on the move.

Vïkhvatenets is now part of the urban conurbation of Rîbniţa in the Republic of Moldova and is located on the left bank of the Dnestr River. The river valley route on this stretch of its course is now known as the Transdnistria and extends from Mogilev-Podol'sky (now Mohyliv-Podil'skyi in the Ukrainian Republic) in the north to Odessa where the river flows into the Black Sea. From Mohyliv-Podil'skyi the roads run north to the towns of Vinnitsa (Vynnytsia), Berdichev (Berdichyv) and Zhitomir (Zhytomyr). The inn was no longer standing by the end of the nineteenth century, for Findeyzen says: "The stone ruins of this building have been preserved for posterity on a photograph that is stored at the Rubinstein Museum. On the site of the building, which in 1895 belonged to P. I. Gryaznov, a people's school, named after A. G. Rubinstein, was opened in 1901."[11]

As birth certificates for Jews were not introduced in Russia until 1835, inaccuracies about Anton's date of birth found their way into some early biographical sources. For many years even Anton himself was not clear on this point. The matter was not finally resolved until shortly before the publication of Rubinstein's *Autobiography* in 1889, as testified by the following passage:

> I was born in 1829 on 16 November. Up to the present time I had supposed the year of my birth to have been 1830, and my birthday—18 November, but this has proved incorrect. Only recently did I chance to establish the exact date of my birth: some papers were found which clarified this.[12]

The Rubinsteins Move to Moscow

Rubinstein remembered very little of his life in Southern Russia, as the entire family moved to Moscow when he was only four years old. The Rubinsteins were just one of many converted families that moved north from the Pale to find work in the big cities of the Russian heartland. Rubinstein himself described the journey to Moscow:

> All our relatives (three families) traveled in one enormous wagon. When we crossed some bridge or other over the river Yauza, a large house was rented from Madame Poznyakova. The house was situated by a pond overgrown with trees. Here we managed to set up home relatively well. At first we were comfortably well off. All three families lived and worked together as one household. But this did not last long. Soon we moved to Ordïnka in the Zamoskvorechye. It was here in Ordïnka where father split up with his brother and his brother's wife's brother. His affairs went by turns well, then badly, but this did not especially sadden him.[13]

Grigory Romanovich was still a young man of twenty-five when the family arrived in Moscow, a city then with a population of a mere 350,000 inhabitants.[14] By this time the household had been enlarged by the birth of a daughter, Lyubov, in the early 1830s, and by Nikolay who was born in Moscow on 2/14 June 1835. The Rubinsteins eventually settled in the Zamoskvorechye, an area of Moscow traditionally associated with the manufacture of goods, such as linen and canvas, much of it supplied to the royal court. The occupations of the artisans (*posadskiye lyudi*) who once worked there are preserved in some of the street names, and during the late nineteenth century the Zamoskvorechye became the seat of the Moscow merchant class and enjoyed great prosperity. When Grigory Rubinstein arrived in Moscow the district was considered a quaint corner of old Moscow, full of winding alleyways with small, often single-story buildings, dilapidated and run-down factories, and workshops surrounded by fences of tall planks. It was a world inhabited by merchants, poor factory owners, petty officials, small-time nobility, and factory workers—the very people whom Aleksandr Ostrovsky, himself born in the Zamoskvorechye in 1823, portrayed with such candor and realism in his plays.

It would be some years before Grigory Romanovich obtained the official permission needed to engage in business activities in Moscow. Eventually he obtained a guarantee from one of his acquaintances among the Moscow merchants, and this enabled him to make the transition from "a merchant's son of the Zhitomir first guild into a Golutvin village merchant of the Moscow third guild."[15] His first initiative was to set up a smithy and an enterprise to manufacture wire. Afterward he organized an enterprise to manufacture pins and pencils that at one time employed seventy workers. The workshop was situated on the ground floor of a small stone building, and the family occupied the rooms above. Grigory Romanovich seems to have been industrious and capable but overly trusting in his business affairs, too good-hearted, even sentimental. He was often thought to be a poet and a dreamer, and consequently lacked the qualities needed to make his business thrive. Although his education had been patchy and he had never received any systematic instruction, he was considered an educated man and spoke Russian and German perfectly. In his reminiscences of Nikolay Rubinstein of 1897, Kashkin reported Nikolay as having said: "I am the embodiment of my father: he loved to live it up, love, and play cards."

If Nikolay took after his father, Anton was much closer to his mother. Kaleriya, in all respects, was strong and willful, had stoical courage, and ruled the Rubinstein household with an iron rod. In his reminiscences published in *Russkoye slovo* (Russian word) in 1905, Pyotr Veynberg describes her in these terms: "In all my long years I have hardly ever met a woman with such a lucid mind when it was a matter of everyday life and relationships, with such practical common sense, yet at the same time such strength and a will of iron that sometimes approached real despotism, with such steadfastness in her convictions, and with a purely masculine cast of nature."[16] Many of Kaleriya Khristoforovna's traits later appeared in Anton's character. Like his mother, Anton showed tenacity and patience in attaining his goals and refused to be discouraged by difficulties and setbacks. He also inherited from her a love of order, which became apparent later in his extraordinary organizational and administrative skills. On the other hand, her method of bringing up the children was unquestionably harsh, frequently resorting to beatings and whippings. It was said that Nikolay was his mother's favorite, and for that reason he suffered more than the other children. This is corroborated by a letter from Tchaikovsky to Nadezhda von Meck many years later concerning rumors that Nikolay had physically abused his students:

What you write about R[ubinstein]'s attitude toward the students of the conservatory is entirely correct, unfortunately. There is one thing that justifies it. He tells
me that in their childhood he and Anton went through the most brutal school of
beatings and whippings, and since they both turned out to be bigwigs, he thinks
quite sincerely that an iron hand striking someone's face, which at the same time is
a caring hand, is the symbol of true pedagogy. I have never seen him beat anyone,
although I have heard that it has happened; I confess I didn't believe it.[17]

Findeyzen tells us that Kaleriya Khristoforovna received her first instruction
in music from "a local trumpeter" but had evidently gone on to become a capable pianist and was later to teach in a private music school. She began giving
Anton his first piano lessons when she noticed his special talent for music, but
she made few allowances for his tender years and the lessons were often accompanied by scoldings and beatings. In later years Anton never reproached his
mother for methods that may seem draconian in our more enlightened age. On
the contrary, he wrote: "I am indebted to her in many ways, having found in her
my first and finest mentor."[18]

The Rubinstein children grew up in the very heart of the Zamoskvorechye,
but details of these years are sketchy and even Anton could only half remember
his childhood experiences. Many years later, shortly after the appearance of his
official autobiography in *Russkaya starina*, he attempted to write his memoirs,
asking Kaleriya Khristoforovna: "If you could help me with regard to my early
childhood that would be very nice. When was I Christened, for example? In
which year did we move to Moscow? When did I get lost on the streets of Moscow? I think it was at the Krïmsky brod [Crimea ford] near the Tartars. We lived
for a while at that time on Pyatnitskaya Street before moving to the Ordïnka.
In a word it would be very desirable for me to learn in more detail about that
time."[19] Sadly the proposed (second) autobiography was never completed, and
Kaleriya Khristoforovna's reply to her son's letter is unknown and may well have
been destroyed.

The Zamoskvorechye did not have the reputation of being a particularly intellectual quarter of the city. The authors of *Po Moskvye* [Around Moscow],
writing in 1917, remarked: "Fifty years ago educated people were rarities there.
And where were you to find them? The Zamoskvorechye felt no inclination for
science: only the sixth in number of the Moscow high schools was established
on the right bank of the Moscow River."[20] Nevertheless the Rubinstein household was a small intellectual oasis. The younger half-brothers of Grigory Romanovich, Konstantin and Emmanuil, had also come to Moscow, and, as noted,
both studied medicine at Moscow University. Their presence ensured that a
steady stream of visitors came to the house on the Ordïnka, and informal gatherings were arranged on Sundays, often attended by as many as thirty guests.
The visitors mostly consisted of traders, students, and sometimes even musicians such as the violinist Ivan Iogannis and the cellist Schmidt (subsequently
the teacher of Karl Davïdov). Among the other visitors were young professionals
like Morits Rozenberg, a medical student who later recorded his memoirs of
Anton. Rozenberg would sometimes arrive in the company of his married sister,

Vavara Bogdanovna Grunberg, and her daughter Yuliya, a girl of about ten who was already giving piano concerts in Moscow under the guidance of her teacher, Alexandre Villoing. By this time Kaleriya Khristoforovna was giving piano lessons to Anton which lasted at least two hours a day. In eighteen months he had already made remarkable progress, and his repertory now included works by Moscheles, Kalkbrenner, Czerny, and Clementi. Kaleriya Khristoforovna probably realized that she had taught her son as much as she was able to teach and needed to find a reliable teacher to continue Anton's studies. In view of the progress Yuliya Grunberg had made, and the reputation Villoing enjoyed as a teacher in Moscow, the choice seemed obvious.

Villoing

Villoing's father, Jean, was a French immigrant who had fled France during the Revolution of 1789. He secured himself the position of chef in the household of Count Chernïshyov in Moscow for a salary considered quite colossal at the time. Aleksandr, the fourth of five children, was born on 29 February/ 12 March 1804, and at the age of twelve was apprenticed to a pharmacist at the Golitsïn Hospital in Moscow. His training in pharmacy was short-lived, however, and in 1821 he abandoned it to study music under Franz Xavier Gebel, who had been a pupil of Abbé Vogler and Albrechtsberger in Vienna.[21] Until the 1830s he led a more or less nomadic existence, working at an institute for the daughters of the nobility in Poltava, and as a teacher in the houses of various landowners. In the early 1830s he established himself in Moscow and gave a number of concerts as a virtuoso performer, but eventually he gave up the concert platform in favor of teaching. In 1837 Kaleriya Khristoforovna engaged him to teach Anton, and the next two years was a period of intensive study for the boy.

> He was my sole teacher. I had no other teachers in my life. I studied with him from the ages of eight to thirteen. After that my lessons ceased, and I never studied with anyone again.
> Villoing had a good hand position and a good ear. He paid a great deal of attention to tone. This came from the Field school, of which he was one of the finest pupils.[22]

Anton's studies went so well that by the age of nine Villoing declared him ready for his first public concert. Aleksandr Bashilov, Privy Councilor and Marshal of the Nobility, gave his backing to a charity concert in aid of the poor, and on 11/23 July 1839, in the Petrovsky Park in Moscow, Anton played the Allegro from Hummel's Concerto in A minor, the Fantasy on themes from *Moïse*, an Andante (probably the Andante in D♭, Op. 32) by Thalberg, Liszt's *Grand Galop Chromatique*, and pieces by Field and Henselt. This concert was favorably reviewed by the Moscow journal *Galatea*, which observed: "In this child the soul of an artist and a feeling of elegance is fully revealed; such great musical gifts are concealed within him that, through perfection and the full development of his talent, the young artist may, with time, achieve an honorary place among the musical celebrities of Europe."[23]

The huge success of this concert prompted Villoing to suggest a major European concert tour beginning in the autumn of 1839. Anticipating the possibility of a long separation from his son, Grigory Rubinstein accompanied Anton on an excursion to Mozhaysk during August. There they watched military maneuvers in the presence of Emperor Nicholas I, and they saw the unveiling of a monument on the site of the Battle of Borodino. They found time to attend a performance of a play called *Volshebnaya strela* [The magic arrow] given by a troupe of actors at the local theater, and they also made the acquaintance of a certain I. V. Lokhvitsky, who later published a brief recollection of the Rubinstein family. Lokhvitsky recalled that Anton was "a very lively and extremely sympathetic child."[24]

In the end the proposed tour was vetoed by Kaleriya Khristoforovna, who was strongly opposed to exposing her son to the rigors of the concert platform before he had acquired a comprehensive musical education. As Neustroyev remarked: "Madame Rubinstein told Villoing that she wished to see her son installed at the Paris Conservatory for his subsequent, serious, and all-round education."[25] Villoing appeared to concur wholeheartedly: "She did not meet with any opposition to this plan on his [Villoing's] part but, on the contrary, complete willingness to put it into action."[26] If they were in complete agreement on this point, one wonders why more than a year went by before she was persuaded to let Anton go. Far more likely is that, from the very start, Kaleriya Khristoforovna and Villoing had quite different views on the best way to perfect Anton's musical development. It took Villoing a whole year to convince her that the primary purpose of the tour was not a mercenary one and that the concerts he planned would merely help to defray the costs of the journey and cover living expenses. By the middle of 1840, however, there was another impelling consideration: Grigory Romanovich's business affairs were fast deteriorating, but to what extent Kaleriya Khristoforovna hoped that the tour might ultimately raise sufficient funds to extricate them from serious financial difficulties is hard to say.

First Concert Tour (1840–43)

From the very outset there appeared to be something of a contradiction about the exact purpose of the trip. Was it to further Anton's musical education? Or raise funds? Or was it an opportunity for Villoing to show his pupil to Europe? No one doubted the young pianist's exceptional talent that extended beyond mere virtuosity to a perceptive understanding of the music he was performing. Indeed, this is what distinguished him from the myriad child prodigies touring Europe in the 1830s and 1840s.

Under Louis Philippe's July Monarchy the musical life of France was thriving, and Paris had gained the enviable reputation as the foremost city of Europe for pianists. A measure of the vibrancy of Parisian concert life was evident in the

1835–36 season alone, as more than two hundred piano recitals were given at the two major concert venues: the Salle Erard and the Salle Pleyel. Kalkbrenner, who had returned to Paris from England in 1824, was enjoying the last fading remnants of his distinguished virtuoso career, and if his name slowly disappeared from the Parisian concert bills of the late 1830s, then other equally eminent names took his place. Chopin settled there after the collapse of the Polish Revolt of 1830, and Liszt and Thalberg were frequent visitors to the city. In fact, it was only a few years before Rubinstein's first visit to Paris that the infamous "duel" between Liszt and Thalberg took place at the home of Princess Belgiojoso. Having scored an astonishing coup with this public spectacle, the princess consolidated her achievement by inviting six distinguished composer-pianists (Liszt, Thalberg, Pixis, Herz, Czerny, and Chopin) to collaborate on the set of variations based on *Suoni la trombe* from Bellini's *I Puritani*, which came to be known as the *Hexaméron*.

When the arrival of Anton and Villoing was reported in the *Revue et Gazette Musicale* during the autumn of 1840, these events were still quite fresh, but the 1840–41 season was dominated by yet another contest. This time it was not between giants of the keyboard but between Giulia Grisi, the favorite of the Italian theater, and Pauline Viardot—great sopranos vying for the attention of the Parisian public. The vogue for Italian operas and singers was at its height, and *I Puritani*, *Il Pirata*, and *Norma* were being performed by Tamberlick, Lablache, Grisi, Mario, and Rubini to enormous public acclaim. One of Anton's enduring impressions was of hearing these legendary singers, among whom he was especially impressed by Rubini, whose *bel canto* singing style he tried to reproduce in his own piano playing:

> In Paris I heard Rubini. The famous Italian opera was there, later moving on to Russia. It produced on me, a twelve-year-old boy, a tremendous impression, which has remained with me all my life. He sang magically. I have never heard the likes of it since, but there never has been anything to compare with him. I have always tried to imitate his singing. He was my teacher. But I only became conscious of this later. I met him.[27]

Villoing and Anton remained in Paris for six months, but despite the wealth of new and powerful impressions and a host of new acquaintances, Anton's development as a musician made very little real progress.[28] The most influential voice among the keyboard pedagogues was that of Pierre-Joseph-Guillaume Zimmermann; he had occupied the post of professor of the piano at the Conservatory since 1816 and was the teacher of both César Franck and Alkan. He heard Anton play at one of the musical salons in the spring of 1841 and declared the boy's playing to be "a musical revelation," but Villoing's attempts to secure an official audience with Zimmermann and Cherubini, the aging director of the conservatory, proved unsuccessful, and any notion of studying there was quickly dismissed.

Villoing's own career as a virtuoso had not been particularly successful, and Neustroyev, who knew him in the 1870s, remarked he had "fingers that were so incapable of playing, it seemed to me he could never have had any sort of well-developed technique."[29] Villoing must have realized early on that Anton had a brilliant future before him, and the jealousy with which he guarded him almost certainly stemmed from a vicarious desire to realize his own unfulfilled hopes and dreams.

Anton's first appearances in Paris were given in private salons. On 5 December 1840, for example, he took part in a concert given by the composer Pauline Duchambge, who was celebrated for her drawing-room romances. His first major concert took place at the Salle Pleyel on 23 March 1841, when he performed:

Villoing: Allegro from the Piano Concerto in C minor[30]
Thalberg: Fantasy on Russian themes, Op. 17
Beethoven–Liszt: Adelaida
Liszt: Grand Galop Chromatique

Besides solo playing, Anton also took part in several concerts with other artists. On 25 April he appeared with Jacques Offenbach at a time when the future composer of *Les Contes d'Hofmann* was still striving to become a cello virtuoso, and together they played the second and third movements of Beethoven's Cello Sonata in A. At another concert he accompanied the renowned Belgian violinist Henri Vieuxtemps, the pupil of Charles Bériot; just a few years earlier Vieuxtemps had scored an enormous success in Russia, and his Violin Concerto in E had been rapturously received in Paris in January.

The critics were won over by young Anton's talent. One ecstatic writer observed that in the Thalberg *Fantasy* he had played a two-octave arpeggiated chord with such accuracy and speed that it produced the impression of a single stroke. Villoing had been wise, perhaps, in first presenting his pupil to the Parisian public in advance of Liszt's impending concert in the French capital, for the great Hungarian virtuoso had recently returned from a concert tour of Britain and Ireland and on 27 March 1841 he appeared at the Salle Erard. Anton was stunned by his playing, and perhaps for the first time saw a true model to which he himself might aspire. As Anton later recalled, Liszt's "opinions and directives were sacred and absolute," but they did not quite square with Villoing's way of seeing things. Liszt had long felt a kind of revulsion for infant prodigies performing tricks "as a source of amusement for distinguished society" and, in so doing, cheapening the very art of which they were such dazzling exponents.[31] There developed in him what Robert Wangermée has called the "conscientiousness" and "shamelessness" of the romantic virtuoso, who seduces the public by his brilliant virtuosity but yearns to be recognized as a true artist in the eyes of his enlightened peers.[32]

The moral dilemma which Liszt sought to resolve in his art was of less immediate concern to Chopin, who had become increasingly reclusive as a concert artist. He now only appeared before audiences made up of the aristocracy and his adoring pupils and friends. It was therefore a somewhat extraordinary event when, on 26 April 1841, he was persuaded to make a rare public appearance at the Salle Pleyel. Intimidated by the crowd, Chopin was nevertheless happy to receive guests informally, and Villoing and Anton were able to visit him. Many years later, in his *Lectures on the History of Piano Music*, Rubinstein recalled his first encounter with the great Polish composer-pianist:

> I was eleven years old when, in 1841, I was presented to Chopin. On that occasion he played me his *Impromptu* when it was in manuscript.[33] Although I was still a child, this meeting with Chopin created a strong impression on me, and even now I can remember all the furnishings of his apartment on the rez de chausée, rue Tronchet, 5, near the Madeleine, and the Pleyel piano covered with green baize standing in the middle of the room, and on the piano: "the gift of Louis-Philippe to Frédéric Chopin."[34]

Liszt's advice to Villoing had been to take his pupil to Germany, but first they traveled to The Hague where Anton gave his first concert at the Diligentia Hall on 18 June. On 19 and 24 June 1841 he played for the Dutch court at the palaces of Paauw (Wassenaar) and Soestdyk (Baarn). For ten years the old king William I had struggled to come to terms with the humiliating loss of Belgium, which, through the intervention of France and the other European powers, was established as an independent kingdom in 1830. He eventually abdicated in favor of his son who came to the throne as William II in October 1840. Already in 1816 the new king had married Grand Duchess Anna Pavlovna, the sister of Tsar Alexander I of Russia, whose hand Napoleon had once sought. That summer her grandson, Grand Duke Konstantin Nikolayevich, himself just thirteen years old, visited the Dutch court and heard Anton play. The grand duke was destined to play an important role in the political and cultural life of his country, and this encounter with Rubinstein paved the way for establishing influential contacts with the Russian court. After giving several more concerts in Amsterdam and The Hague, Villoing and his pupil finally arrived in Germany in mid-July. From this point forward all pretense that the tour was intended to further Anton's musical education was clearly abandoned.

The first concert in Germany took place at the theater in Cologne on 19 July, where Villoing accompanied his pupil in a performance of his own Piano Concerto in C minor. Then from July to the end of the year they made further appearances in Ems, Bonn, Baden-Baden, Frankfurt-am-Main, Karlsruhe, Augsburg, and Munich. Villoing was responsible for devising the programs of Anton's concerts, and as the young pianist later remarked: "He [Villoing] observed the greatest discipline with me, and I carried out all his demands."[35] The programs of these early concerts laid great stress on brilliance and were designed to show off the young player's technical accomplishments. In performing such works as Thalberg's fantasies and Liszt's *Grand Galop Chromatique*, (pieces frequently included in Liszt's own programs), the young Rubinstein exhibited eloquent proof of his skill in the mechanical execution of music composed in the grand bravura style.

Early in 1842 the pupil and his teacher arrived in Vienna where Anton gave three concerts. In his first, which took place on 9 January under the auspices of the Gesellschaft für Musikfreunde, Anton played Thalberg: *Fantasy on Russian Themes;* Bach: the fugue from the *Chromatic Fantasy;* Liszt: *Réminiscences de Lucia di Lammermoor;* Schubert-Liszt: *Lob der Thränen;* Liszt: *Grand Galop Chromatique;* Rubinstein: *Zuruf aus der Ferne* (this romance was performed by Henrietta Treffz to the composer's accompaniment).[36] The instrument used on this occasion was a Stein piano with a Viennese action, and as Anton began playing the Bach *Chromatic Fantasy,* the hammers jumped from their resting places and a mechanic had to be called. The critics were unanimous in their praise of the young artist, observing how every note was deeply felt. "Rubinstein hauchte, so zu sagen, die Töne nur an, aber sie gehorchten willig dem belebenden Hauches des Meisters [Rubinstein merely breathed on the notes, so to speak, but they willingly obeyed the invigorating breath of the master]," wrote one critic.[37]

In mid-April Anton and Villoing arrived in London. As usual, before taking any public appearances, Anton gave several private performances, including one for Queen Victoria. He was well received—one reviewer called him a Thalberg "in embryo"—but he seems to have been rather overshadowed by the presence of Mendelssohn who enjoyed enormous popularity with London audiences. Despite this, it was Mendelssohn who led Anton to the seven-octave Collard piano when the latter gave his first major concert at the Hanover Rooms on 20 May. Moscheles remarked in his diary that the boy had "fingers light as feathers, and with them the strength of a man," and William Ayrton, writing for the *Examiner,* observed: "for the force by which, through some unparalleled gift of nature, he is enabled to exert a degree of muscular strength which his general conformation, and especially that of his hands and arms, would have induced us to suppose he could not possibly possess."[38]

From London, Anton returned to Paris and played before a large audience at the newly opened Salle Herz. The concert was a great success and was attended by the musical elite of Paris, including Chopin, Liszt, and Leopold de Meyer. Chopin lavished particular praise on Rubinstein's playing of Henselt, declaring: "Son triomphe est la musique de Henzelt, qui est toute de sentiment."[39] Anton's final appearance in Paris was followed by a month-long series of concerts in Sweden and Norway, but by fall the tour was drawing to a close. In November Anton gave five programs in Berlin. These included his own early composition *Ondine*[40] and Beethoven's Cello Sonata in A in which he performed the piano part with Moritz Ganz, the leading cellist of the royal orchestra in Berlin. Their final destination was to be Breslau. There Anton gave five concerts between 7 and 21 January 1843. It is worthwhile to reproduce the programs here for the light they shed on the kind of repertory Rubinstein played as a young virtuoso:

7 January 1843 in the main hall of the university—Henselt: *L'Orage,* Op. 2, No. 1; *La Fontaine; Poème d'Amour; The Little Bird;* Beethoven: Sonata *Pathétique;* Liszt: *Réminiscences de Lucie di Lammermoor;* Rubinstein: *Ondine;* Mendelssohn: *Lied ohne Worte,* No.1; Thalberg: Thème original et étude in A minor, Op. 45; Handel:

Adagio and fugue; Schubert–Liszt: *Ave Maria;* Liszt: *Grand galop chromatique.*
14 January in the main hall of the university—Kittl: Impromptu; Chopin: Mazurka; Goldschmidt: Study; Mozart: Gigue in G; Mendelssohn: Scherzo in F♯ minor; Thalberg: *Fantasy on Don Giovanni,* Op. 14; Schubert–Liszt: *Ständchen; Der
Erlkönig;* Bach: Chromatic fantasy and fugue; Herz: Ballade; Liszt: *Heroischer
Marsch im ungarischen Styl.*
17 January:—Henselt: Romance; Rhapsodie; Handel: Gigue; Thalberg: Andante in
D♭, Op. 32; *Fantasy on Russian Themes,* Op. 17; Kalkbrenner: Study; Taubert: *Cam-
panella;* Henselt: *Poème d'Amour;* Schubert–Liszt: *Ave Maria;* Thalberg: Fantasy on
themes from *Moïse.*
19 January—Villoing: Piano Concerto in C minor (Allegro)
21 January, the theater in Breslau—Villoing: Piano Concerto in C minor (movements 2 and 3); Schubert–Liszt: *Ständchen; Der Erlkönig;* Thalberg: Fantasy on
themes from *Moïse;* Herz: Ballade; Liszt: *Heroischer Marsch im ungarischen Styl;
Grand galop chromatique.*

Finally Anton and Villoing arrived in St. Petersburg on 28 February/12 March
1843. Anton remained in the Russian capital for a month and, with the assistance of Grand Duke Konstantin Nikolayevich, an audience with the court was
arranged. Before Anton could make his appearance at the Winter Palace, however, his seven-year-old brother, Nikolay, had arrived from Moscow. In the intervening years Nikolay had received piano lessons from Franz Xaver Gebel, Villoing's own teacher and a much-respected figure in the musical life of Moscow
during the 1830s.[41]

The brothers played for the court, and Tsar Nicholas I himself greeted Anton
sardonically with the words: "Ah, your Excellency." "I was a child," Rubinstein
recalled, "and I was told that the word 'royal' was law. They told me what I ought
to say to him, and I would become 'an excellency.'"[42] Within the next few weeks
Liszt was expected in St. Petersburg on his second visit to Russia, and Anton's
mimicking of the Hungarian virtuoso's style of playing quite delighted his royal
masters. The audience was a great success, and legend has it that the tsarina
ordered the young Anton to be stood on a table so that he could receive his sovereign's embraces. When the brothers returned home from the Winter Palace at
about 10 o'clock in the evening both were hungry. It seems that Villoing had
gone away, leaving his young protégés with only twenty kopecks in their pockets. As Barenboym tells it: "The elder brother (considering it undignified for
him, a celebrated artiste, to run through the streets) sent his younger brother
to the nearest greengrocer to buy twenty kopecks' worth of black bread and
salted cucumbers."[43] In later years Nikolay expressed his indignation at the way
he had been treated, considering that Anton had wounded his pride.

Shortly after his appearance at the Winter Palace, Anton played the solo part
in Villoing's Piano Concerto at a Philharmonic Society concert on 20 March/1
April. Over the next few weeks he appeared in three more concerts at the Engelhardt Hall playing some of the works he had performed earlier in Breslau and
elsewhere. With the arrival of Rubini and Liszt in St. Petersburg, however, Anton
retired to Moscow, where he repeated his earlier successes in a concert of 18/30

April that included works by Thalberg, Wielhorski, Handel, Liszt, and Mendelssohn.

The successes of the Rubinstein brothers seemed to be in an inverse ratio to the success of their father's business affairs. During his concert tour Anton had been unable to provide his parents with any material support, as "the money had been used to cover my and Villoing's living expenses."[44] He did return with several valuable gifts, however, including a clock with precious gems: "I once brought father a number of valuable articles, but they were unable to raise the material position of our family. They were pawned but were never redeemed." Despite the family's considerable financial hardship, it was decided that Kaleriya Khristoforovna would travel to Berlin with Anton, Nikolay, and Lyuba, leaving two-year-old Sofiya in the care of her father. Kaleriya Khristoforovna had concluded that the aristocratic patrons of the arts in Russia would only acknowledge the musical gifts of her sons if they had studied under respected foreign maestros. Her resolve was strengthened after Liszt's visit to Moscow in the spring of 1843, when the Hungarian virtuoso was favorably impressed by Nikolay's playing of one of Moscheles's fantasies and repeated his earlier advice: the need for a solid grounding in the theory of music.

With the death of Gebel, Villoing took charge of Nikolay's piano lessons until the latter's departure for Berlin. Anton's musical development was already more advanced, but neither brother had yet received any formal training in all the aspects of music theory, form, and harmony. Kaleriya Khristoforovna believed that merely giving concerts could not advance their general musical education. Since Villoing could no longer provide the advice she needed in these matters, she now sought the opinion of more celebrated musicians in Western Europe. Kaleriya Khristoforovna turned to her father-in-law, Roman Ivanovich, to help finance the trip, but the amount was insufficient and the rest of the money had to be raised through concerts given by the two brothers. The concerts were arranged at the Engelhardt Hall in St. Petersburg during the winter season of 1843–44, and one of them was attended by the tsar himself. In two concerts of 16/28 March and 30 March/11 April 1844 Anton and Nikolay appeared together playing various works by Field, Chopin, Liszt, Henselt, and Thalberg, as well as Anton's own paraphrase from Meyerbeer's *Les Huguenots* for four hands and the transcription of Liszt's *Heroischer Marsh im ungarischen Styl* which had been completed earlier that year. Unfortunately the returns from these concerts proved much less than were hoped for because of the Schumanns' arrival in Russia. Between mid-March and early May 1844 Clara gave several concerts in St. Petersburg and Moscow.

As a precocious fourteen year old, Anton had not been able to resist the compulsive urge to compose. Besides the four-handed paraphrase on *Les Huguenots* and the transcription of Liszt's *Heroischer Marsh im ungarischen Styl*, noted above, the romance *Zuruf aus der Ferne* had already been performed in Vienna during the concert tour with Villoing and *Ondine*, the little study in Db, had been published by Schlesinger in Berlin. To this small group of compositions

Anton added four polkas and the four songs, Op. 3–6, in the original numbering. These new works were published in Moscow by Julius Gresser.

Berlin and Vienna, 1844–48

In the late spring of 1844 the Rubinsteins left St. Petersburg. Their route took them through the Baltic cities, where they gave several concerts, and then on to Warsaw. In Paris Kaleriya Khristoforovna approached Chopin for an appraisal of the musical abilities of her children, but their final destination was to be Berlin, and they arrived there toward the end of 1844. Although hardly anything is known about Kaleriya Khristoforovna's family, there is good reason to suppose that she had relatives in the Prussian capital. Moreover, during the late eighteenth century Berlin had been the home of the *Haskala*, or the Jewish enlightenment movement in Germany. The major figure in this movement had been the philosopher Moses Mendelssohn (the composer's grandfather), who, while defending Judaism, advocated the assimilation of Jews into the mainstream of Western European culture. Even in the mid-nineteenth century his writings still absorbed Jewish intellectuals, for his collected works (seven volumes) were published in Berlin in 1843–45. The atmosphere of religious tolerance and the support of Mendelssohn and Meyerbeer (two of the foremost composers of the day and themselves converts to Christianity) must have been key factors in Kaleriya Khristoforovna's decision to settle in Berlin.

Mendelssohn would clearly have remembered Anton's appearance in London three years earlier, but Kaleriya could count on his direct support only for a brief period. Although Mendelssohn had been director of the Berlin opera during the 1843–44 season, his visits were rare in later years owing to his conducting commitments with the Gewandhaus orchestra and the new music conservatory he had founded in Leipzig. Kaleriya Khristoforovna's own family had been distant acquaintances of the Mendelssohns, and this association, together with the letters of recommendation provided by Prince Odoyevsky and the Wielhorski brothers, gained her entry to the musical gatherings arranged by the composer. On one of these visits the Rubinstein brothers heard Mendelssohn play Chopin's Three Mazurkas, Op. 59, still in manuscript at that time. They also called on Meyerbeer whose success in Germany had been assured after the first Berlin performance of *Les Huguenots* in May 1842. Within a month he was appointed court composer and general music director of the Königliche Schauspiele, a post he held for six years until a quarrel with the theater director, Küstner, led to his dismissal. The following year a fire destroyed the theater and the new opera house only reopened in December 1844, shortly after Kaleriya Khristoforovna had arrived in Berlin with her children. Meyerbeer's new Singspiel *Ein Feldlager in Schlesien,* later remodeled for the Paris Opera as *L'Etoile du Nord,* inaugurated the theater. The opera began its run on 7 December 1844 with Leopoldine Tuczek in the role of Vielka, but after only a few performances her place was taken by Jenny Lind making her Berlin début in this role. The Rubinsteins must have attended one of these performances, and the young Anton's *Homage à Jenny Lind* (Op. 7 in the original numbering) was probably inspired by seeing her in this opera. The support of Meyerbeer, one of the most popular opera composers of the day with contacts throughout Europe, was of great benefit to Rubinstein.

Meyerbeer and Mendelssohn both had the same opinion concerning the musical education of the Rubinstein brothers. They concluded that Anton, now nearly sixteen, had reached the stage where he alone could perfect his art as a performer; as for Nikolay, they recommended lessons with Theodor Kullak, perhaps the finest piano teacher in Berlin, and music teacher to members of the Prussian royal family and the aristocracy. Kullak himself had been a pupil of Siegfried Dehn, the celebrated theorist from whom Glinka had received lessons in the 1830s. In 1842 Dehn had been appointed librarian of the royal music collections on Meyerbeer's recommendation. From 1824 he had edited the scholarly journal *Cäcilia, eine Zeitschrift für die musikalische Welt* and was noted for his editorial work on the German masters. Meyerbeer concluded that the Rubinstein brothers would benefit greatly by making a thorough study of the broad musical disciplines under Dehn. The brothers took two lessons a week from February 1845 to March 1846. Working with Dehn's book on harmony and thorough bass, th……………………………re harmony course, simple, two-, three- and f……………………………on and elementary fugue, the practical applica-…………ces, and the analysis of free forms with special emphasis on the piano sonata.[45] Both excelled in these lessons, ten-year-old Nikolay in particular, and they earned the approbation of Meyerbeer, whose laudatory remarks were carefully translated into Russian for the newspaper *Moskovskiye vedomosti*.

Besides paying Dehn for his lessons, Kaleriya Khristoforovna also had to pay for lessons in the Russian language and scripture from a Russian priest (Father Dormidont Sokolov) and also lessons in French and German for both brothers. Their German teacher was Rudolph Levenstein.[46] The money that had been raised by giving concerts in St. Petersburg, Revel, and Köningsberg had almost run out, but Kaleriya Khristoforovna had decided that her sons would give no public concerts in Berlin (although they did appear at private societies and clubs). She was determined that nothing would interfere with their education. The Russian government provided no assistance, but when the empress Aleksandra Fyodorovna arrived in Berlin for a state visit in 1845, Anton and Nikolay played for her and received valuable gifts. The gifts were quickly sold to help raise money for their lessons.

The lessons with Dehn halted abruptly in the spring of 1846, however, because news arrived from Russia that Grigory Romanovich, threatened with imminent bankruptcy, was seriously ill. Kaleriya Khristoforovna hurried back to Russia with Nikolay and Lyuba, but Anton remained in Berlin. The next four years were probably the most difficult in Rubinstein's life. In her memoirs of her husband, Vera Rubinstein later wrote: "As a child he did not live with children, as a youth he had no comrades. Alone and abroad . . . he struggled with need, early on he learned the dark side of life, developed his own convictions, character, and ideals."[47] Rubinstein himself spoke about his lack of a childhood: "Well, I never did look young, that is why I have grown old so quickly. I began to live too early."[48] The experience of having to fend entirely for himself at the ripe age of sixteen surely left an indelible mark on his character. He did not remain in Berlin but traveled to Vienna, where he intended to give music lessons. Before leaving, however, he renewed an old acquaintance. Five years earlier in Paris he had played in a concert with Vieuxtemps, and now their paths crossed again in the Prussian capital. A musical autograph was found at the Gesellschaft für Musikfreunde in Vienna, showing the first bars of the Rondo finale (*Allegretto*) of Vieuxtemps's Concerto in E with the inscription: "H. Vieuxtemps, Berlin, 15 mars 1846. A son ancienne connaissance, l'intéressant A. Rubinstein." This autograph is reproduced in L. Ginsburg's work on Vieuxtemps.[49]

In Vienna Rubinstein had counted on the support of Liszt, but, to his dismay, the Hungarian virtuoso told him: "A man must achieve everything by himself, that my talent would support me, and that no other support was necessary."[50] After this, Liszt departed on a long concert tour, initially to Prague but then to Hungary, Ukraine, and Turkey. If Liszt had not given him any practical assistance, at least Rubinstein had had the good sense to arm himself with fifteen or so letters of recommendation from Baron Meyendorff, the Russian ambassador in Berlin. When these letters failed to achieve the desired objective, however, he opened one of them and read: "We are obliged to offer protection and assistance to our fellow countryman. This young man has so requested, and therefore I recommend him . . . " His country, he felt, had let him down, and he was amazed at the ambassador's behavior. His situation was becoming increasingly desperate. The lessons he gave brought in very little money, but that he would not compromise his artistic principles and integrity was entirely characteristic. He could have earned a comfortable living by playing in the fashionable Viennese cafés or by dazzling undiscriminating audiences with brilliant fantasies and potpourris, but this ran counter to his noble concept of art. So he took a small room in the garret of a large house, sometimes going without food for two or three days. Instead, he found spiritual nourishment in composing vast quantities of music: "I wrote a frightful amount. The whole room was strewn with oratorios, symphonies, operas; the devil knows what I didn't write at that time! I even composed a newspaper for myself. What can I say? I lived in my room and wrote, wrote, wrote, and my life in the material sense was simply very bad."[51]

Rubinstein acknowledged that his situation became so desperate that "I stopped visiting even Liszt." In reality, he had very few occasions when he could have seen him. Liszt's busy concert schedule, and his acceptance of an invitation to spend much of the summer as the guest of Prince Lichnowsky in Graz, allowed him only fleeting visits to Vienna, each lasting little more than a few days. Nevertheless Liszt evidently became sufficiently concerned about Rubinstein's disappearance from public life that on one of these visits he appeared unannounced at Rubinstein's lodgings, accompanied by the thronging entourage that it was his custom to take with him. Rubinstein tells us that Liszt was visibly shaken by his living conditions and promptly took him dinner. "Since then," the Russian virtuoso declared, "I have remained on warm and friendly terms with Liszt. Envy, you say? But what envy could there have been on his part, there never was the slightest trace of envy."[52]

Given the impoverished conditions in which Rubinstein lived in Vienna, it is quite remarkable that he was the only pianist in the Austrian capital who responded to an appeal launched by the *Wiener Allgemeine Musikzeitung* to raise funds for the employees of a theater in Pest that had burned down. In a characteristically charitable gesture, Anton appeared in two concerts on 19 and 20 February 1847 in aid of the fire victims and was rewarded by being made an honorary member of the local music society. One of Rubinstein's new acquaintances in Vienna was a flautist named Heindl with whom he made a concert tour of Hungary. At the end of the concert season the two young men, in the company of their new acquaintance, Baron Fühl, decided to try their luck in the United States. They traveled to Berlin with the intention of making the crossing to America from the ports at Bremen or Hamburg. Rubinstein felt obliged to call on his old teacher, Dehn, who was able to dissuade him from embarking on such a reckless plan without having first established his name in Europe. Nor did Heindl make the journey to America; it seems he died rather tragically a few years later when he accidentally stumbled into a shooting range and was killed. Rubinstein remained in Berlin, and, thanks to the support of Mendelssohn and Meyerbeer, soon found some wealthy clients to whom he gave music lessons. Sadly he was soon to lose the support of Mendelssohn who died in Leipzig on 4 November 1847.

One of the distinguishing features of the Berlin intellectual milieu was the musical and literary salon whose patrons were often wealthy Jewish families. During the 1820s and 1830s the salon of Karl August Varnhagen von Ense and his wife, Rahel Levin, had been the focus of lively political debates and had seen the emergence of a Goethe cult. Abram Mendelssohn and Jacob Herz Beer (Meyerbeer's father) also hosted regular meetings where guests discussed politics and exchanged ideas, and where music was constantly playing. Through the circles in which Rubinstein moved, he clearly became increasingly drawn into the stimulating world of the salons. That summer Rubinstein's German teacher introduced him to a literary club that had been founded in 1827 with the assistance of Moritz Saphir, one of the editors of the newspaper *Berliner Schnellpost* and a contributor to a theater almanac. Originally known as *Tyll Eulenspiegel*, the club was revived in 1844 by Theodor Fontane as *Tunnel über der Spree*. Another prominent member of the club was Count Moritz Strachwitz, who had been born in Silesia and was considered one of the most promising German lyric poets of his generation. He died tragically in Vienna a few years later at the age of twenty-five, shortly after returning from a tour of Italy. He and Fontane were particularly noted for their ballads, and Fontane later became the drama critic for the newspaper *Vossische Zeitung*.

The main point about this society was that anyone accepted as a member was not called by his real name; he was given a pseudonym associated with the sphere of his work. A poet, for instance, might be called Goethe, Heine, or Moore, a doctor—Hufeland,[53] a writer by the name of some eminent *littérateur*. And what people there were in this circle! But they all addressed one another in the familiar *du*. I was there when Geibel read his ballads and was made a member of the Society.[54] The circle gathered every Sunday for about two hours. The aim of the meetings was to read one's works and listen to criticism, but not personal criticism (there were no personalities, only Goethe, Schiller, and so on), only that which flowed from the very essence of the artistic composition.[55]

The experience of attending the meetings of the *Tunnel über der Spree* undoubtedly made a lasting impression on young Rubinstein, and it developed in him a strong tendency to intellectualize art and crown it with the aura of a sacred duty. It also made him feel that he belonged to a set apart, which probably accounts for the rather elitist views he later espoused on the nature, role, and duty of the creative artist. For the time being, however, the somewhat cool picture of intellectual aloofness was rudely shattered by political events. The fall of Louis-Philippe's July Monarchy and the rise of the new radical and socialist ideas expounded by Saint-Simon, Fourier, and Louis Blanc resonated throughout Europe. Even Rubinstein sensed that the storm would soon overtake the Prussian capital. He witnessed the dramatic events unfold on the barricades of the Bernstraße in March 1848, when the insurgents clashed with the royal troops and decided that music had little place amid such political turmoil. There was little Rubinstein could do but return home to Russia.

2 Return to Russia and First Opera, 1848–53

At the end of 1848, after the outbreak of the revolutions that swept through France, Germany, and Austria, Rubinstein, nearing nineteen years of age, returned from Berlin to St. Petersburg. The turbulent political events that had overtaken Europe were certainly one factor in his decision to return to Russia. Fueled by a growing nationalism, the *Risorgimento* movement in Italy and the National Liberation movement in Hungary were shaking the foundations of European stability established at the end of the Napoleonic Wars. In an atmosphere so highly charged, nationalism also began to play an increasingly important role in music, sweeping aside the sentimentality and mechanical virtuosity that had prevailed for a decade or more. Rubinstein must have been acutely aware of this shift away from the cherished values of "absolute" music toward music with a more overtly social or political purpose. "After 1848, everything changed. Before 1848 they demanded brilliance, virtuosity, whereas after 1848 they began to demand the very substance of art to the point of satiation, to the point of Wagner!" he declared.[1] But there were other reasons, too. He had left Russia as a fourteen-year-old child prodigy—now he was returning home as a mature artist with a practical knowledge of his craft. The musical life of Russia was flourishing. Some of the greatest pianists of the day had been greeted with rapturous acclaim in the Russian capital—Henselt[2] in 1838, Thalberg in 1839, Dreyschock in 1840–41, Liszt in 1842, and Clara and Robert Schumann in 1844. Even Berlioz had given concerts in St. Petersburg in March 1847. Rubinstein must have felt that the time was right for the appearance of a new "star." Almost immediately he was drawn into the musical life of the capital. In keeping with the fashion of the time he was invited to play in the houses of wealthy patrons of the arts, but he also gave public concerts in St. Petersburg in November and December 1848. A number were given in collaboration with Vieuxtemps. On 21 November/3 December, for example, the two musicians appeared together, performing a jointly composed "Grand duo" for violin and piano on motifs from Meyerbeer's *Le Prophète*. At a later concert, on 28 February/12 March 1849, Rubinstein played his early Piano Concerto in C major at the Mikhaylovsky Theater with Vieuxtemps conducting.[3] These appearances continued regularly from the beginning of 1849 until the end of the concert season. One of the last included a performance of the early Piano Concerto in D minor (later reworked as the *Octet*, Op. 9) which Rubinstein played at a Philharmonic Society concert conducted by Karl Albrecht on 14/26 March. It was probably not before April 1849 that Rubinstein left St. Petersburg to join his mother in Moscow.

There were pressing reasons that prevented him from leaving earlier, namely, his lack of a passport and the recovery of the trunk with his musical manuscripts that he had brought with him from Berlin. There is no reason to doubt the veracity of Rubinstein's account of these events in his *Autobiography*, even though he mistakenly attributes them to 1849. When he left Russia in 1844 he had been registered on his mother's passport, but she had returned to Moscow with Lyuba and Nikolay two years later. Fearing that the trunk full of musical manuscripts that Rubinstein had brought with him from Berlin contained ciphers intended to spread revolutionary ideas to Russia, the customs officials at the frontier immediately confiscated it. If this were not misfortune enough, upon arriving in St. Petersburg he found it impossible to register at a hotel as this required a passport. He located one of the few acquaintances he had in the city, Carl Lewy, a musician whom he had known since childhood. Lewy provided him with lodgings, and together the two friends decided on a course of action. Rubinstein went to see the chief of police in St. Petersburg, Aleksandr Galakhov, but despite his protestations that he was well known to several prominent aristocratic families, Galakhov was implacable and gave the young man two weeks to obtain an official passport. Undeterred, Rubinstein referred the matter to the governor-general of St. Petersburg, Dmitry Shulgin, but he was received in a rude and uncivil manner. Rubinstein wrote to his mother, and she in her turn wrote to the town council in Berdichev in an attempt to get a passport issued. At the end of two weeks Rubinstein was required to appear before Galakhov again and was made to stand for two or three hours in the official's waiting room. The purpose of this visit was to prove to Galakhov that he really was the same Rubinstein who had once given concerts in the city. Subjected to this humiliating ordeal, one can well imagine how the young virtuoso contemptuously hammered the instrument that he was given to play. Nevertheless the audience with Galakhov provided him the reprieve he needed, and within the next three weeks the passport finally arrived.

The Petrashevsky Incident

The reactionary government of Nicholas I had an obsessive fear that the revolutionary movement which had engulfed Western Europe would spread into the heart of Russia itself. His fears were not unfounded, for the old order was being seriously challenged by dangerous ideas of social reform and national sovereignty. Nicholas's response was to tighten his grip on the press and to root out all elements in society that were suspected of subversive views or seditious activities. An oppressive censorship attempted to muzzle all free expression of public opinion from wherever it came: the radicals, the liberals, even the Right. The seven-year period from 1848 to 1855 has been called "the era of censorship terror" and "one of the darkest periods in the history of Russian thought."[4] The political situation in Russia was aggravated by a serious cholera epidemic that was fanning the flames of public unrest, and Russian citizens returning home in 1848 were subjected to close scrutiny from the secret police. If Rubinstein's brush with Russian officialdom over the lack of a passport were not a serious enough matter, his brief association with the Petrashevsky circle could have had even more serious implications for him. The activities of Mikhail Butashevich-Petrashevsky and the members of his radical circle had been under surveillance from the secret police since 1844, but in the wake of the revolutions in Europe the membership of the circle had increased and so, too, had the surveillance. The circle, in fact, consisted of two closely associated groups: the main parent body, committed to the socialist ideas of Fourier, and a splinter group known as the Palm-Durov group. This latter group (founded by Aleksandr Palm, a lieutenant in the guards, and Sergey Durov) was far more interested in art, music, and literature than in politics and its members refused to subscribe to Petrashevsky's notion that art was only useful for promoting socialist ideals. The Palm-Durov group met on Saturdays, and music played an important role at these gathering: "Music was regularly performed because the group included a pianist, two violoncellists, and a singer; part of the subscription paid by each guest (three silver rubles a month) was even used to rent a piano."[5] Rubinstein was evidently persuaded to attend one of these meetings by a university student, who was, mostly likely, an *agent provocateur* in the service of the government, and there he came into contact with Petrashevsky himself. Using a secret agent, Pyotr Antonelli, the Ministry of the Interior had succeeded in infiltrating the meetings of the Petrashevsky circle and during March and April 1849 reported on all that was discussed there.[6] Antonelli's report included details of a dinner given on 7 April to commemorate the birthday of Fourier at which the guests spoke enthusiastically about Fourier's ideas of achieving greater social equality through a system of *phalanstères*. As a result of the report, on 29 April 1849, 123 people were arrested, including the writer Fyodor Dostoevsky. Twenty-one of them were sentenced to death, although at the very last moment the sentence was commuted to one of hard labor in Siberia. Rubinstein was not seriously implicated in the Petrashevsky affair, and there was probably never any real likelihood of his being arrested, but it was a fitting moment to quit St. Petersburg and he wisely decided to remain in Moscow until the dust settled.

The situation of Kaleriya Khristoforovna and her children was still precarious. She had returned to Moscow with Nikolay and Lyuba in 1846 after receiving the news that Grigory Romanovich had suffered a stroke. Grigory died on 9/21 January the following year, leaving behind huge debts. There were grave fears that the family would be turned into the street. The situation was indeed so alarming that it prompted one of the family's Moscow acquaintances to write to Grigory's father: "It is difficult to describe here in words the lamentable position in which he [Grigory Romanovich] has left his family: one would have to be here and know in detail all the circumstances in order to have the slightest notion of the disastrous and unfortunate position in which the destitute family now finds itself after your late son passed away."[7] It was only Kaleriya Khristoforovna's strength of character and resourcefulness that averted the catastrophe. She succeeded in rescuing the small pencil factory that her husband had left her and sold it three years later. Having settled her husband's debts, she eventually took up a post as a music teacher at Madame Knol's boarding school for girls. It was there that her youngest daughter Sofiya was educated. Nikolay and Yakov were living together in furnished rooms: the former being coached by Villoing, and the latter attending the medical school at Moscow University. The period between April 1849 and the fall of 1850 was the only time when the adult Anton lived in close proximity to the rest of his family, and Findeyzen reproduces a rare daguerreotype of the three brothers—Anton, Nikolay, and Yakov—that dates from this time.[8] This also must have been the time when the relations between Anton and Nikolay Rubinstein were formed. They had both been trained by the same teacher, but their lives were quite different. Nikolay had been born in Moscow in 1835, and even in 1849 when Nikolay was only fourteen, it must have become apparent to Anton that his younger brother's future life would be associated with that city. He was already playing in public and was even composing his own salon trifles: for example, on 15/29 April 1849 he appeared at the Hall of the Nobility in Moscow playing his own *Etude charactéristique* and *Bolero*. Anton probably realized that if he remained in Moscow, eventually he and his brother would become rivals, and, besides, ancient Moscow with its quaint, patriarchal ways did not appeal to him. He was drawn far more toward Europeanized St. Petersburg.

In Moscow, however, there were fewer distractions, and when Anton was not giving lessons for a ruble each, he was composing. With an eye to the new concert season he was already thinking about two new works that would be his most important up to then: his First Symphony in F major, Op. 40, completed by the end of 1849, and his Piano Concerto No. 1 in E minor, Op. 25, completed early in 1850. Although clearly derivative, neither work is entirely lacking in interest. The symphony may be a somewhat pallid imitation of Mendelssohn, but its classical proportions, freshness, and unself-conscious spontaneity give it a certain modest appeal. The concerto was Rubinstein's fourth attempt at the genre and he dedicated it to Villoing.[9] Partly influenced by the languid style of Field and the brilliance of Hummel, its heroic gestures are also a tribute to Beethoven. As the musicologist Jeremy Norris has pointed out, the dialogue between the piano and orchestra in the *Andante con moto* of Beethoven's Fourth Concerto served as the model for the corresponding movement of Rubinstein's concerto.[10] Neither the symphony nor the concerto was published until 1858, but it is significant that Rubinstein abandoned the first system of opus numbers he had adopted in Berlin and began all over again as if he wished to show that his composing career was now associated with Russia. His growing conviction that success could be achieved in his homeland must have stemmed from the major changes taking place in the cultural life of Russia. Throughout the 1840s the stream of international artists and virtuosos visiting St. Petersburg and Moscow had grown steadily, and this had had a positive effect on public taste. Interest had been stimulated at virtually every level of educated society and had led to the first serious critical reviews in the press. To better understand the artistic milieu to which Rubinstein had returned after his long absence abroad, it is worth summarizing briefly some of the main features of musical life in Russia, specifically St. Petersburg and Moscow, at the start of the 1850s.

It was without doubt the operatic stage that attracted the broadest sections of Russian society, and for that reason it is hardly surprising that the first major successes achieved by native composers were in this field: specifically the operas of Glinka and Dargomïzhsky. For more than twenty years, however, the Italian troupe had consistently enjoyed the favors of the court, which, in effect, chose the repertory of the imperial theaters. During the years from 1828, when the emperor recalled the Italian opera from Moscow to St. Petersburg, the troupe had staged several of Rossini's operas, Mozart's *Don Giovanni,* and many of Verdi's early operas: for example, *Ernani* in 1846, *I Due Foscari* in 1847, and *Giovanna d'Arco* in 1849. While great Italian singers such as Rubini, Lablache, Tamberlick, Giovanni Mario, his wife Giulia Grisi, and Pauline Viardot were lavishly feted, Russian artists struggled to gain recognition. One of the few exceptions was the great bass Osip Petrov who had made his début as Sarastro in Mozart's *Die Zauberflöte* in October 1830, and four years later went on to sing Figaro in *Il Barbiere di Seviglia* and Bertram in *Robert le Diable* with brilliant success. His greatest achievement came in 1836 when he created the role of Ivan Susanin in the premiere of Glinka's *Zhizn' za Tsarya* [A life for the tsar]. The prevailing taste for Italian opera at this time did not entirely suppress the works of native composers. Apart from Glinka, whose two operatic masterpieces eventually eclipsed all other Russian operas of the 1830s and 1840s, there were a number of other industrious composers working alongside the creator of *A Life for the Tsar.* Among the most important were Cavos (Italian by birth, but resident for most of his life in Russia), Dmitry Struysky, Verstovsky, and Dargomïzhsky whose *Esmeralda* had been first heard in Moscow in 1847. Such was the indifference to Russian opera, however, that when *Esmeralda* was later revived at the Aleksandrinsky Theater in St. Petersburg on 29 November/11 December 1851, it was so badly staged that it closed after only three performances.

While opera enjoyed great privilege and was patronized by the crown, the performance of orchestral music was rather less frequent. Consequently, in 1842, Aleksandr Fitsum von Eckstedt, the inspector of St. Petersburg University, organized a series of public concerts and invited Carl Schuberth to direct them. These concerts were known at first as "Musical Exercises for Students of the Imperial University" and later as "University Concerts."[11] The orchestra, made up of fifty to sixty players, gave ten concerts during the winter season on Sunday mornings. The programs consisted mainly of the classical repertory, including all the symphonies of Beethoven, as well as those of Haydn, Mozart, Mendelssohn, and Schubert, but also a good deal of new music including works by several Russian composers. Although Schuberth was an able musician, the concerts did not adhere to a high standard and this was aggravated by the lack of rehearsals. Rubinstein appeared several times as soloist and occasionally even deputized for Schuberth as conductor. With the formation of the orchestra of the Russian Music Society, these University Concerts gradually ceased.

In addition to the University Concerts, a few concerts were also given in the hall of the Imperial Cappella each year. During the period when Aleksey Fyodorovich Lvov was the principal conductor, the repertory was fairly conservative and included standard works by Beethoven, Mozart, and Mendelssohn, and also choral works including Lvov's own *Stabat Mater*. From 1856 the orchestral concerts were also organized under the direction of Ludwig Wilhelm Maurer. Tickets to these concerts were costly, and the orchestra was partially made up of aristocratic amateurs whom Rubinstein later criticized severely.

Dmitry Donskoy

Like Glinka before him, Rubinstein had returned to Russia with the idea of composing an opera on a national theme. During the winter of 1848 Rubinstein was introduced to the writer Count Vladimir Sollogub, who had provided the libretto for Aleksey Lvov's opera *Undina*, which premiered at the St. Petersburg Bolshoy Theater in September of that year. Fourteen years earlier, in 1834, Sollogub had also had a hand in writing the patchwork libretto for Glinka's *A Life for the Tsar*, and he now agreed to adapt Dmitry Ozerov's tragedy, *Dmitry Donskoy*, as an operatic libretto for Rubinstein. Sollogub worked quickly, for when Rubinstein arrived in Moscow from St. Petersburg in April 1849 the libretto of *Dmitry Donskoy* was already finished. Much of the opera was most likely composed during the summer months, as Rubinstein was eager to present the overture during the new concert season.

Early in 1850 he returned to St. Petersburg and on 8/20 January made his début as a conductor, presenting his own First Symphony in F major and the overture to *Dmitry Donskoy* at a University Concert. Rubinstein had decided that Sollogub's libretto for the new opera was too short and, accordingly, asked Vladimir Zotov to provide a Tartar scene, which became act 2 of the opera. Just a few years later Zotov was to become editor of the revamped weekly journal *Illyustratsiya*, but he was already the author of many plays and novels. Rubinstein was evidently pressuring Zotov, for he wrote to him twice in February 1850, excusing himself for his persistence but also justifying it, pointing out his "impatience to continue with the work in which so much has been done already; only your assistance is needed to finish it."[12] The concert season was by then in full swing, and Rubinstein did not miss the opportunity to appear before the St. Petersburg public with his latest compositions. Prince Vladimir Odoyevsky had organized two charity concerts which proved to be one of the highlights of the season. The concerts consisted exclusively of works by Russian composers, and in the first of them, on 15/27 March, Karl Albrecht conducted the first performances of Glinka's *Kamarinskaya* and the two Spanish overtures, the first performance of the overture to Dargomïzhsky's opera-ballet *Torzhestvo Vakhka* [The triumph of Bacchus], excerpts from Mikhail Wielhorski's opera *Tsïganye* [The gypsies] and the overture to Rubinstein's *Dmitry Donskoy*.[13] A few days later, on 21 March/2 April, Rubinstein played the first movement of his new Piano Concerto in E minor, his *Fantaziya na dve russkiye narodnïye pesni* [Fantasy on two Russian folk songs] and the Symphony No. 1 at the St. Petersburg

Bolshoy Theater. On 9/21 April he conducted the second of Prince Odoyevsky's "Russian Concerts," which included works by Wielhorski, Glinka, Alyabyev, and Verstovsky, as well as another performance of his own overture to *Dmitry Donskoy*. Toward the end of April he returned to Moscow, and on 9/21 May played his Piano Concerto in E minor in its entirety at the Hall of the Nobility. A few days later he wrote to his publisher, Bernhard: "In the financial respect my concert was a failure, but the public was happy."[14] Rubinstein needed a more regular source of income, and he tried to secure a position that would give him a better living, but, as he reported to Bernhard, the general (i.e., Aleksandr Mikhaylovich Gedeonov, who headed the Directorate of Imperial Theaters from 1834 to 1858) had categorically refused him two recently announced posts, claiming they had already been filled.

In mid-June Rubinstein set off on a concert tour of Kharkov and Odessa but returned to Moscow at the beginning of July to begin setting the Tartar scene of *Dmitry Donskoy*, completing it in October. The opera concerns the liberation of Russia from the "Tartar yoke," as the period of Russia's domination by the Golden Horde is generally known. Grand Duke Dmitry, advancing his army toward the Don (hence the later appellation "Donskoy"), met the Tartar Khan Mamay on Kulikovo field on 8 September 1380 and routed him. This was the first significant defeat that the Russians inflicted on their oppressors, and the battle is considered a milestone in Russian history. In reality the victory, if not entirely hollow, failed to secure complete emancipation from the Tartars, which took about another hundred years to achieve. In the hands of Glinka or Borodin, a heroic subject such as this might have produced a work of great national significance, but Rubinstein was content merely to use it as a pretext for introducing a clichéd and trivial love story. Dmitry and the boyar Tverskoy are rivals for the hand of Kseniya. When Dmitry is betrayed by his erstwhile allies, he is forced to face Mamay alone. His victory over the Tartars, of course, secures for him the prize of Kseniya's hand.

With the score of the opera completed, Rubinstein rented an apartment on the Bolshaya Konyushennaya in St. Petersburg for twenty rubles in silver a month and began looking for pupils. He also brought with him two works that he had begun the previous year: the set of *Six Studies* for piano, later published as Op. 23, and the *Six Fables of Krïlov*.[15] Given Rubinstein's implicit belief in the need for musical professionalism, he must have taken particular delight in "Quartet," the fourth song of the cycle. Here a monkey, a donkey, a goat, and a bear sit down to play a string quartet, but they cannot decide how to arrange themselves in order "to captivate the world with their art." Whichever position they choose, the music still comes out badly, so they ask a passing nightingale to resolve their dilemma. The nightingale replies: "In order to be a musician you need skill and ears a little more sensitive than yours. However you sit, my friends, you will still be no good as musicians."

Rubinstein had received vague assurances from the Directorate of Imperial Theaters that *Dmitry Donskoy* would be staged "after Easter," but his doubts about this were well founded. As a young and largely unknown composer, he needed the patronage of some influential person, and therefore he sought to renew his acquaintance with the grand duke Konstantin Nikolayevich. The grand duke was the second son of the reigning emperor Nicholas I and from birth had been destined for a career in the imperial navy. He had received a broad European education, spoke several foreign languages, held liberal views, and was a keen amateur musician; it was therefore not without a certain satisfaction that Rubinstein reported to his mother, on 1/13 November: "The day before yesterday I put my name in the visitors' book of the grand duke." He had also established good relations with Aleksandr Gedeonov and hoped that this would augur well for the future of *Dmitry Donskoy*. For the time being, however, there was little he could do to advance the fortunes of his opera, so he settled back to enjoy the forthcoming concert season. Among the musicians who had arrived in St. Petersburg that winter were the singers Anna Hassel-Barth and Henrietta Nissen-Saloman,[16] the renowned Norwegian violinist Ole Bull, and the Danish cellist Kellerman.

Toward the end of December 1850 the censor returned the libretto of *Dmitry Donskoy* to Rubinstein with the terse comment: "Prince Dmitry Donskoy must not sing." According to Russian law, it was forbidden to represent any personage of the imperial dynasty on the stage. With the emperor's permission, the law was occasionally relaxed in the case of drama, but in opera it was considered undignified for royal personages to sing: either they had to appear mute or were banned altogether. Sollogub suggested changing the names or making some other revisions in the libretto. This prevarication likely made Rubinstein realize the serious difficulties he faced in staging a Russian opera in St. Petersburg. As noted above, from 1834 to 1858 the Directorate of Imperial Theaters was headed by Aleksandr Mikhaylovich Gedeonov, whose tastes inclined increasingly toward ballet and French drama. His treatment of artists was autocratic, and he regarded them with little more respect than serfs: "Gedeonov was rude to the artists. He invariably addressed everyone, including me, in the familiar personal pronoun," Rubinstein recalled.[17] During the premiere of *Dmitry Donskoy*, Gedeonov humiliated Pavel Bulakhov, the young tenor who sang the role of the Dervish, reprimanding him rudely for removing his hat as he concluded his aria. "In the first place a Dervish must not remove his hat," Gedeonov had roared at him, "and in the second place, the hat was new and I might crush it!"[18]

At the end of 1850 Rubinstein was still trying to obtain an official passport that would allow him to travel abroad again. He had decided that if his new opera succeeded in reaching the stage and it pleased the public, he would remain in Russia for two or three years; if not, he planned to seek his fortune in the broader European arena. Two major obstacles were barring his progress in Russia, he told his mother somewhat immodestly, namely, his youth and his talent in a Russia that could only tolerate veneration for old age and mediocrity. He had also reached an important decision about his future development as an artist:

My idea is not to appear as a pianist, playing opera fantasies, but as a composer performing his symphonies, concertos, operas, trios, etc. . . . We are on the threshold of the New Year. I do not know what it will bring me. I am beginning it with the composition of a new concerto, a symphony and a number of small-scale works, specifically, Russian romances, small salon pieces for piano, etc.[19]

These new works included the Second Piano Concerto in F major, Op. 35 (published in 1858), and Symphony No. 2 in C major, Op. 42, "Ocean" (in its four-movement version published in 1857).

The start of 1851 heralded important events both for the Rubinstein family in general and for Anton in particular. First, Lyubov (often referred to as Amaliya or Lyuba in correspondence) had become engaged to the lawyer Yakov Veynberg of Odessa and was soon to marry him. Second Kaleriya Khristoforovna finally succeeded in selling the pencil factory which she had inherited from her husband to the merchant Sbroevsky. The young Nikolay Rubinstein was making rapid progress in his musical studies and had composed some piano works and a duet with his friend, the violinist Yuly Gerber. Anton's long-awaited passport finally arrived from the Ministry of the Interior soon after the holiday, and a few weeks later, at the request of the grand duchess Yelena Pavlovna, he presented himself at the Mikhaylovsky Palace: "The day before yesterday I played for the grand duchess Yelena; true, this does not mean anything yet, but since she said to me that she had it in mind to hear me this winter, I can count on taking part in the wedding festivities[20] and this will give me something."[21]

The operas being presented by the Italian opera troupe at the St. Petersburg Bolshoy Theater during January 1851 included Donizetti's *Alina, regina di Golconda* and Giuseppe Persiani's *Il Fantasma*. A few weeks later Persiani's wife, the celebrated soprano Fanny Tacchinardi-Persiani, appeared in Moscow with the troupe, and Rubinstein advised his mother: "Do not miss the chance to hear Mario. Persiani still has something left [of her voice]; she is already old, but I still think she is one of the very greatest of artists!"[22] Meanwhile, the fate of Rubenstein's opera remained undecided. "What you write about me is full of kindness, but not quite true," he wrote to Kaleriya Khristoforovna.

As far as the opera is concerned, you are wrong in assuming that everything has disappeared into oblivion: in the first place, it will be presented to the tsar for his approval; he will decline it—I shall only have to change the names, make certain changes in the text and it will be accepted; second, if it is not staged even then, this is not such a big calamity because such things are never a waste of time![23]

Within a few weeks his misgivings became a reality. The censor's office demanded that the title be changed to *The Battle of Kulikovo* and that the main protagonist become a different character entirely. "This is not so dreadful," Rubinstein reported to his mother. "The public will gradually find out what the real names are. If William Tell can be called Charles the Bold,[24] then Dmitry Donskoy can be called Mikhayla Volïnsky."[25]

Some of the frustration he had experienced over the opera was alleviated by the new concert season and the arrival in St. Petersburg of some of the most renowned musicians of the day. Among them were the sisters Amalie Nerudová, the pianist, and Wilma Nerudová, the violinist, who, since their first appearance together in Prague in 1847, had made a triumphant tour of Germany with their father, Josef Neruda, visiting Leipzig, Berlin, Breslau, and Hamburg. Then there were the brothers Henryk and Josef Wieniawski and the singer Augusta Miller: "Augusta Miller is here from Berlin, but she suffered a terrible fiasco. The Neruda sisters and Schulhoff are creating a furor," Rubinstein told his mother.[26] He was especially impressed by the Czech pianist and composer Julius Schulhoff, whose popularity with the St. Petersburg public, however, still failed to overshadow Rubinstein's own concert. The season was indeed particularly brilliant and concerts were being given all over the city: at the St. Petersburg Passage, the Aleksandrov Theater, the Bernardaki Concert Hall, the Hall of the Nobility, the Mikhaylovsky Theater, and the St. Petersburg Bolshoy Theater. Rubinstein's only appearance that season was at the Bernardaki Hall when he presented his Piano Concerto in E minor, Op. 25, and the Piano Trio in F major, Op. 15, No. 1, on 12/24 March 1851. The hall, intended for three hundred people, was filled to capacity, although a hundred tickets had been distributed free of charge. Still, he was satisfied with the financial gain from this concert, as he still had 128 rubles in silver in hand even after covering his costs. In spite of this, he decided against a second concert because of the "inundation of concerts" in the capital.

Meanwhile, the score of the *Dmitry Donskoy* had been with the censor for more than a month and no decision had yet been made about its fate. Rubinstein had grown almost indifferent to it. Only on 14/26 March was he finally able to report to his mother:

> The censor has passed it; the score is with the Directorate, which must first of all look through it and decide how much the staging will cost, what must be acquired, to whom the roles should be entrusted. After that, I will be given a definite answer whether it will be accepted—and that will take two weeks.[27]

The preparation of the sets and copying of the orchestral parts proceeded, even though another month was to pass before Rubinstein was officially notified that the opera was to be staged. Finally on 16/28 April he informed his mother:

> The opera will be copied and the parts distributed for learning, so that in September she will be out of dry dock. However good this news may sound, it only half gives me any joy, as now it will be essential to stay here for the summer. Rehearsals begin in August, so learning the parts has to be completed by then. Since various things can crop up in these circumstances—that is, one place has to be changed, another taken out entirely, and something new composed—I shall have to take charge of all this myself.[28]

Rubinstein was fortunate in the choice of artists, for some of the foremost Russian singers of the day were engaged to perform in the opera. The cast list has survived and has been recorded by Findeyzen:

Dmitry Mikhaylovich Volïnsky [Donskoy]	Osip Petrov
Boyar Tverskoy	Mr. Leonov
Boyar Belozersky	Mr. Gumbin
Boyar Torussky	Mr. Zhivov
Kseniya	Mariya Stepanova
Svetlana	Mlle Kalkovskaya
Mamay	Semyon [Gulak]-Artemovsky
Uzbek (Mamay's emissary)	Mr. Zarussky
Gusli player	Mr. Strelsky
Dervish	Pavel Bulakhov
Sets	Andrey Roller[29]

With the fate of the opera secure, it is very likely that Rubinstein considered applying for the post of opera director at the Moscow Bolshoy Theater to replace the outgoing Iogannis. The matter had evidently been discussed with Gedeonov of the Directorate of Imperial Theaters, for Rubinstein wrote to his mother:

> On the subject of the position in Moscow, the general said to me that it is out of the question. In the first place he will not risk appointing such a young man over so many older ones. In the second place I have no experience as a conductor. In the third place the post is already filled. . . . The name of the person who is to replace Iogannis is Elkamb; he is a very serious musician.[30]

By early August Rubinstein learned that the staging of his opera was to be rescheduled for after Easter 1852, even though all the preparations had been rushed through for its premiere in September. The Directorate excused itself by telling Rubinstein that the Italian opera was due to present Meyerbeer's *Le Prophète* at the beginning of the season, but he suspected that this was merely a convenient pretext. He was beginning to despair at the demands and constant questions to which the Directorate continued to subject him. The result was an outburst of extreme frustration that was not at all typical of Rubinstein:

> This is enough to bring a nervy person to the point of despair. But for me this is far worse; the pain it causes me is beyond all measure, and if in the near future God does not send me some successful ideas for a large-scale work, I don't know what is going to happen to me, I am so overwrought.[31]

Aggravating the situation further was that the attention of the authorities was firmly focused on the impending celebrations to commemorate the twenty-fifth anniversary of Nicholas I's accession to the throne. "Soon the entire court will be arriving in Moscow, and then there will really be something to look at," Rubinstein wrote Kaleriya Khristoforovna sardonically. "I am so sated with all this, that only one desire remains for me—to see my opera! I have no desire to see anything else. Yes, and something else, too—not to see myself here any longer!?"[32] Having vented his frustration, however, Rubinstein quickly regained his capacity for viewing matters in a completely detached and positive way: "As for giving lessons—I have one pupil, and compositions—I haven't sold a single one. But what hasn't come to pass may come to pass, definitely will come to pass, I am not bothered about this. I am just lacking in patience, but with each day I acquire more of it."[33]

During the fall of 1851 Count Dmitry Sheremetyev asked Rubinstein to compose a Russian Liturgical Concerto for his celebrated choir. This choir, which consisted of up to eighty singers, was formed to celebrate the Orthodox liturgy in the count's private church, but the choir also gave annual concerts of liturgical and secular music. Like the Imperial Cappella, its repertory included a lot of music from the classical and pre-classical era: Palestrina, Nanini, Carissimi, Lotti, Durante, and Bach, and was greatly admired by visiting artists such as Liszt, Berlioz, Viardot, and Rubini. Rubinstein indeed composed a work for Sheremetyev's choir, although there is no known material relating to its performance and the score may have been lost. Two years later Sheremetyev came to Rubinstein again, requesting him to set some psalms. It is possible that he made a selection for Sheremetyev to approve, for he wrote to Kaleriya Khristoforovna on 6/18 May 1853: "I am again filled with hope regarding Sheremetyev to whom I have handed the psalms for his cappella. If he wishes it, something good will come of this." Despite his optimism, Rubinstein apparently did not work on any psalm settings. He was rather more fortunate, however, in his settings of duets to words by Russian poets which probably date from this period. The set of twelve duets, eventually published as Op. 48 in 1852, demonstrate the composer's lyrical gifts to their best advantage.

In December Rubinstein moved into a new apartment on Malaya Morskaya Street in St. Petersburg. The Italian opera was enjoying enormous success with performances of Verdi's *Nabucco* and Mozart's *Le Nozze di Figaro* at the St. Petersburg Bolshoy Theater, and an indignant Rubinstein raged against Vieuxtemps for his lack of principle (as Rubinstein saw it) in capitalizing on it. "Yesterday," he wrote Kaleriya Khristoforovna, "Vieuxtemps's concert took place, earning him five thousand rubles in silver, all because the entire Italian troupe took part in it. I find this completely unworthy of an artist like Vieuxtemps, but God gave him a wife who would agree to his taking part in a concert of tightrope dancers if she could make a profit out of it."[34]

The start of 1852 saw Rubinstein anticipating two events: the staging of *Dmitry Donskoy* and a concert to be given at the Lichtenthal Hall, which would feature his latest compositions. It was the most brilliant period of the traditional winter season, and at a reception given by the Wielhorski brothers he met Mario and Grisi. At almost midnight he, the Belgian cellist Adrien François Servais, and Vieuxtemps played the Beethoven Trio in B♭, Op. 97, to the inexpressible delight of the assembled guests. It was not without a certain irony that Rubinstein remarked on the effect that this performance had on the listeners, who were all representatives of the cream of Russian society: "It was impossible to imagine anything comparable. You would have least expected it, since this Trio is not intended for crowned personages, nor for ladies dressed to kill, nor for gentlemen wearing stars."[35]

The concert at Lichtenthal Hall took place on 23 February/6 March 1852. The program included an overture by Mendelssohn, conducted by Vieuxtemps; the premiere of Rubinstein's *Ocean Symphony,* conducted by Rubinstein; Rubinstein's Second Piano Concerto in F major, with Rubinstein as soloist and Vieuxtemps as conductor; the Two Melodies, Op. 3; the Mazurka in E major, Op. 5, No. 3; the Barcarolle No. 1 in F minor, Op. 30, No. 1; and the Krakowiak in E♭ major, Op. 5, No. 2.

By early spring Rubinstein was deeply absorbed in the final preparations for the staging of *Dmitry Donskoy:*

> On Friday 18 [April], here at the Bolshoy Theater, my opera was first performed. The success was brilliant; I was summoned two or three times after each act and they let me go to the thunder of applause; many numbers were encored. In brief, people can scarcely remember such a success for a first night. You must not forget that the performance was very unsatisfactory because of the lack of good artists and the miserliness of the Directorate which did not want to risk anything for the sake of the first work by a young composer. Besides, it was staged very late, when the public is not as receptive to music as at the start of the season. None of this got in the way, however, and the theater was filled to capacity. The success was enthusiastic![36]

There were four performances of *Dmitry Donskoy* between 18 and 27 April, but it did not enjoy the success that Rubinstein had supposed. The production of this new Russian opera was more of a historic landmark than a great artistic event. Prince Odoyevsky greeted it joyfully with the words, "Our numbers have increased," and although the press was generally sympathetic, Serov did not miss the opportunity to snipe at Rubinstein from the pages of the journal *Panteon.* He did so by appearing to moderate the enthusiasm of those he called Rubinstein's "panegyrists," among whom was a certain Mr. Z. writing in the *Sankt-Peterburgskiye vedomosti.* The approach was subtle but still one designed to inflict maximum damage. Serov prefaced the discussion of *Dmitry Donskoy* with a long preamble about the sterility of technique if it contains no poetry. The "ouvrier en intervalles" shouldn't be confused with the creative musician in the same way as the bricklayer should not be confused with the architect or the paint grinder with the artist. German obsession with technique had caused the purveyors of such art to drown in a sea of notes: "The creator of an opera must be as much a dramatic poet as a musician. A musical gift alone is not sufficient here."[37] In the choice of a subject for an opera, Serov judged that "the most disadvantageous subjects are grand historical events involving historical heroes," and he blamed young composers for their immaturity in believing that they could express in music any situation they chose. Having set the scene, so to speak, he eventually began his discussion of *Dmitry Donskoy.*

His first task was to cast doubts on Rubinstein's competence to write a Russian opera: "Having received assurance that Mr. Rubinstein is a Russian and that he has had the opportunity to accustom himself with the spirit of our Russian national themes . . . " This had done him little good, according to Serov, for it had been merely arrogant on Rubinstein's part to think that he could compete with Glinka, whose style, in any case, he had simply plagiarized. "He himself knows very well how much he strove to capture the national spirit of Russian music with his imitations of Glinka's style (for instance, Kseniya's first aria has merely been copied from Antonida's aria in the first act, and copied in a servile manner, even down to the orchestral figuration, and traces of this imitation can be seen in many other places, particularly the choruses)." Serov saved much of his scorn for the mixture of styles in the opera: "French in the tenor solo in the duet with Kseniya in the second act, Italian in many places, German, especially à la Mendelssohn, in the choruses—for instance, in the prayer before the battle—and in many features of the orchestration."[38] He accorded a measure of success in the Andante of the duet between Dmitry and Tverskoy (act 1), and in the Dervish's narration, considering them the best moments in the opera. As a whole, however, he roundly dismissed the work for its weak orchestration, and blamed Rubinstein for having written it for the piano and at the piano. Serov's claim that some conservatory or other might award the opera a silver medal, or even a gold one, was, in his view, clear proof of its dull academicism. It was perhaps solipsism on Serov's part, but essentially his article set the tone for much of the criticism directed at Rubinstein in the coming years. The threefold attack had been carefully planned: (1) bring into question Rubinstein's credentials to be considered a Russian composer; (2) suggest that he was a plagiarist and that his music was derivative, whether of Glinka or Mendelssohn was of little importance; and (3) point out that his work was dull and academic, and therefore not merely uninteresting but even damaging to the creative instincts of inspired artists. Serov's article had the effect of splitting public opinion in a very distinctive manner. According to Findeyzen, the same factions that defended or reviled *Dmitry Donskoy* would be the very same that would later support or reject the future conservatory.

Although the tsar and the empress had not attended a performance of *Dmitry Donskoy*, most of the imperial family had been present at the premiere. Rubinstein received compliments from Prince Pyotr Oldenburg and, more important, from the grand duchess Yelena Pavlovna, who invited him to spend the summer at her palace, "Kamennïy Ostrov" [Rocky Island]. Moreover, for the first three performances of *Dmitry Donskoy* he received 150 rubles in silver from the Directorate. Rubinstein had hoped that his usual publisher, Bernhard, would bring out the vocal score of the opera, but Bernhard had spent all his available funds to pay for his daughter's dowry, as she recently married. This delay probably is why the unpublished manuscript full score and vocal score were lost. Only the overture to the opera was ever published, although, according to Barenboym, the Central Music Library in St. Petersburg still has "the vocal line and a sketch of the orchestral accompaniment for one of the male roles of the opera."[39]

Despite the excitement over the premiere of the opera, Rubinstein continued to appear regularly at Lichtenthal Hall as a soloist and an ensemble player in chamber concerts. Later that year a new virtuoso appeared in the Russian capital. Twenty-two-year-old Theodor Leschetizky had come to St. Petersburg to take up a teaching appointment at the home of Baron Alexander Stieglitz, the court banker and president of the St. Petersburg Stock Exchange Committee. Leschetizky played for the Russian court and gained entry to the highest echelons of the aristocracy. According to Aniela Potocka, one of Leschetizky's new acquaintances was Princess Ustinova (née Trubetskaya)[40] who maintained a salon frequented by musicians and prominent figures in public life. We may safely assume that Rubinstein played at her soirées and that both he and Leschetizky came into contact with the Russian foreign minister Count Nesselrode and his niece, the pianist Countess Kalergis; General Todleben, who would mastermind the defense of Sevastopol during the Crimean War a few years later; Yekaterina Mikhaylovna, Comtesse de Ribeaupierre (née Potyomkina), whose husband, Aleksandr Ivanovich, was the grand master of ceremonies at the Summer Palace in Peterhof; Countess Yelizaveta Vorontsova, who had once been Pushkin's mistress; and the tragic actress Élisa Rachel, who excelled in her reading of La Fontaine's *Les Deux Pigeons.*

The "Musical Stoker"

Within a month of the first performance of *Dmitry Donskoy,* Rubinstein was already thinking about another opera. This time the subject was to be Stepan Razin, the seventeenth-century leader of a mutinous uprising, with a libretto by Mikhail Voskresensky. The idea was eventually shelved as such a politically dangerous subject would almost certainly have been rejected by the censor. Also by mid-June Rubinstein had taken up residence at Kamennïy Ostrov, the out-of-town palace belonging to the grand duchess Yelena Pavlovna located outside St. Petersburg: "Today I am traveling out of town to the Grand Duchess, where it will cost me nothing for my board and lodging."[41] Yelena Pavlovna was the daughter of Prince Paul of Wurttemberg and most of her childhood had been spent in Stuttgart and Paris until her marriage, in 1824, to Grand Duke Mikhail Pavlovich, the brother of Nicholas I. Mikhail died suddenly of a stroke in September 1849, and in the years that followed she was guided in large measure by her devoted secretary, Baroness Edith von Raden, a woman of extraordinary intellect and refinement.[42] The patronage of such a highly placed figure, who had the ear of the tsar, proved a crucial factor for the development of music in Russia. Rubinstein was engaged as her musician-in-residence, and one of his chief functions was to accompany the singers she maintained as part of her entourage. They included Mariya Stepanova, a singer whom Sollogub once characterized as having "not a voice but a draught," and Osip Petrov, the great bass, who created major roles in the operas of Glinka, Dargomïzhky, and Musorgsky. Both singers had taken the leading roles in *Dmitry Donskoy.*

Rubinstein's relations with Yelena Pavlovna were often extremely irritable, especially in the years after the founding of the Russian Music Society. In his *Autobiography* he calls her "capricious, willful, in a word a tyrant," but he never ceased to feel sincere respect for her:

Her position was quite unique because in the upper ranks of the court Aleksandra Fyodorovna [the empress] loved toilette, balls, glitter: artists never played for her, not even sometimes. The major artistic soirées were held by Yelena Pavlovna. It was at her residence that Nikolay Pavlovich [Tsar Nicolas I] and Hamilton held the conversation that led to the Crimean War.[43]

As we know from Rubinstein's own memoirs, the period he spent as *podogrevatel', istopnik muzïki* [musical heater, stoker] to the grand duchess did not carry a regular salary, but his accommodation and upkeep were paid for. In August the grand duchess and her entourage went to Oranienbaum, an imperial palace on the Gulf of Finland, where, as Rubinstein himself acknowledged, they led "a life of paradise." During this visit Rubinstein played for the Crown Prince of Saxony and the son of the Crown Prince of Prussia and began the huge cycle of piano pieces *Kamennïy Ostrov*—twenty-four musical portraits inspired by the ladies whom he had met during his stay. The dedicatees of these pieces in their Gallicized form are shown in the index of Rubinstein's works in Appendix A. The first nine bear only the initials of the dedicatees in large Gothic letters (except for No. 5, *Romance,* which has no dedicatee). A few of the named persons (Edith von Raden, Yelizaveta Eiler, and Anne de Friedebourg) later played a significant role in Rubinstein's biography, but most were just representatives of aristocratic Russian and German families. A few are worth mentioning: Yekakerina Apraksina (née Golitïsina) (dedicatee of No. 10) was known in her time as the "whiskered countess" and was thought to be the prototype for the countess in Pushkin's novella, *The Queen of Spades,* and Countess Antonina Dmitryevna Bludova (the dedicatee of No. 19) acquired a certain public recognition. She was the daughter of Count Dmitry Bludov, who was a friend of the historian Karamzin and the poet Zhukovsky, and, toward the end of his life, the president of the St. Petersburg Academy of Sciences. Her memoirs [*Zapiski*] later appeared in the Russian press.

During the visit to Oranienbaum the grand duchess commissioned from Rubinstein a one-act opera based on Lermontov's narrative poem *Hadji Abrek,* a grisly tale of vengeance set against the exotic backdrop of the Caucasus. In the poem an old man tells how he was once forced to flee into the hills with his youngest daughter, Leila. The girl is abducted by Prince Bey-Bulat, and the heartbroken old man begs the young tribesman Hadji Abrek to seek her out and bring her back to him. Hadji Abrek's search leads him to a distant village where he finds the girl. She seems indifferent when she learns of her father's grief, but then in a dramatized middle section Hadji reveals his true purpose. He wants vengeance for his own brother, himself once the innocent victim of Bey-Bulat's cruelty. But killing Bey-Bulat is too merciful: "Is that vengeance?" he asks. "What is death!? Will one moment pay me for so many years of sorrow, grief, and torment?" No, it is the object of Bey-Bulat's love that he wishes to kill, and with a blow of his saber he cuts off Leila's head. He then brings the head back to the old man who dies from grief. A year later nomads discover two foul and bloodstained corpses still bearing the curse of hatred on their foreheads. One corpse they recognize as Bey-Bulat, but no one recognizes the other corpse.

Plan for a Music Academy

The opera had to be ready by the winter of 1852, and Rubinstein began working on it immediately. When he returned to the capital from Oranienbaum in mid-October, however, he brought with him not only sketches for the opera but also a plan for a music academy:

> The plan is ready and today I shall give it to the grand duchess who will hand it to the tsar. This may have great consequences for the future of music in Russia and also for me. But one must know how to be patient and this is the difficult task. I wrote the plan in French and everyone who has heard it says that it is very good. We'll see!?[44]

The plan has only been published in the Russian translation by Dmitry Stasov which first appeared in the *Russkaya muzïkal'naya gazeta* in 1909. It was later republished in the monograph by Boris Asafyev, *Anton Grigor'yevich Rubinshteyn* (1929), and most recently in Barenboym's three-volume *A. G. Rubinshteyn: Literaturnoye naslediye.*[45] In this important document, dated 15/27 October 1852, Rubinstein suggested setting up a music section within the framework of the Imperial Academy of Arts on the lines of the Academy of Arts in Berlin, which had been reorganized in 1840 to include a music section. Catherine the Great had founded the Russian Academy of Arts in the mid-eighteenth century, but even by the mid-nineteenth century a person's standing in Russian society was still defined exclusively by his position within the fourteen grades of the civil service established by Peter the Great 130 years earlier. Painters, sculptors, and architects who had studied at the academy and received diplomas could take their rightful place in Russian society as a "Free Artist," but the profession of musician in Russia was not formally recognized. Rubinstein argued that anyone who wished to devote his or her life to music in Russia and earn a living by it could not do so. He pointed out that only a lifelong dedication to this art could produce accomplished musicians. Therefore those who felt drawn to it as a vocation ought to be spared the necessity of earning their living by other means (the army, trading, etc.), for this only robbed them of the time needed to perfect their skills and their knowledge. As servants of the state, artists employed by the imperial theaters were in a different position, but the theater needed only performers and technicians (singers, orchestral players, set designers, etc.) and the Imperial Theater School already existed to train them. Rubinstein was thinking primarily about the future of composition and the performing arts. In rudimentary form he set down the minimum requirements for the teaching of composition. For this, teachers in the following disciplines would be needed: thorough bass, counterpoint and fugue, orchestration, practical composition, and musical literature. For the performing arts, teachers were required for each of the individual instruments. Under the strict authoritarian rule of Nicholas I the time had not yet come for this ambitious project to be implemented, but essentially it laid the foundations for the future conservatory, which came into being just ten years later.

At the start of 1853 St. Petersburg was gripped with excitement. After an interval of seven years, Pauline Viardot had returned to Russia and was to appear as Rosina in *Il Barbiere di Seviglia*. Everyone in St. Petersburg was talking about it, but this did not discourage Rubinstein from giving a public concert at Lichtenthal Hall. On 10/22 January he appeared with the violinist Ludwig Maurer and the cellist Carl Schuberth in a program that included his own Cello Sonata, Op. 18, the Violin Sonata, Op.19, and the Piano Trio, Op. 15.[46] Two days later he reported to his mother: "Only now am I writing to you, as I wanted to wait for my concert so as to tell you the results. On this occasion, even more than usual, there were more honors than money since the success was brilliant but the takings were poor."[47]

Meanwhile, Rubinstein had continued working on the operas which the grand duchess had commissioned from him: *Sibirskiye okhotniki* [The Siberian hunters] had been completed, *Mest'* [Vengeance] (the opera based on *Hadji Abrek)* was finished except for the overture. A third opera had already been envisaged and was to be completed in time for Lent. These three operas were to be in different styles: *The Siberian Hunters* was to be a romantic opera; *Vengeance,* a tragic opera; and *Fomka Durachok* [Fomka the fool], a comic opera. The grand duchess intended the operas to reflect the various nationalities of the Russian Empire—Siberia, Georgia, and Great Russia—and they were to be performed together in a single evening.

On 3/15 February Rubinstein wrote to Kaleriya Khristoforovna to say that the plan to perform *Vengeance* at the grand duchess's Mikhaylovsky Palace had proved disastrous, and his idea of a music academy had not been received favorably: it was "sleeping the sleep of the righteous."[48] In his personal life things were also going badly, for he had become enamored of the singer Anna Karlovna Fridberg (more often her name is given as Mlle Anne de Friedebourg), a pupil of Pauline Viardot who had appeared with him during soirées at the Mikhaylovsky Palace. It was to her Rubinstein dedicated the twenty-second piece of the cycle *Kamennïy Ostrov,* which subsequently came to be known as "Rêve angélique." Their liaison, however, was not destined to blossom, for, as Rubinstein declared to Kaleriya Khristoforovna, "I cannot have that which I ought to have."[49] Some time later he actually proposed to her, but three years later, on 16 February 1856, she married Theodor Leschetizky. Anne is characterized by Aniela Potocka in her biography of Leschetizky as: "Always graceful, but always cold, she was not made to create happiness around her. She was one of those natures that by mere force of passivity inflict suffering they apparently cannot understand."[50] Fridebourg served as one of Yelena Pavlovna's ladies-in-waiting and the active interest the latter took in the social attachments formed by the members of her entourage may have played an important part in Rubinstein's rebuff. "It is true, God created the world from nothing, but he did not leave to people the secret how to do it. This is the cause of my eternal disfigurement: from much comes nothing," Rubinstein remarked in the same letter to his mother.[51] Here was one of those strange paradoxes which he liked so much and with which he often masked a feeling of bitter disappointment.

Despite his difficulties, an air of defiant independence is evident in the reply to his mother's letter from Odessa a few weeks later:

> I told you that I love to write when I have something pleasant to tell you, but since that happens very rarely I write rarely. But you want me without fail to write about everything. When I do this you are upset. When I write that my affairs are bad you become agitated and put yourself out of pocket to send me something. I can always muddle through alone, but you need the money far more. Of course, if I knew that you would not be angry I would send the 25 rubles back to you, but I am not doing this because I hope that this will be for the last time.[52]

Perhaps he realized that the tone of this letter had been too insensitive, for on 6/18 April he made a noticeable effort to mollify Kaleriya Khristoforovna by holding out the prospect of a visit to Odessa where she and his sister, Lyuba, were living. He had not been offended by the money she had sent him, he told her, only that he was sorry to have deprived her of it. "Besides the cholera, we are suffering from another epidemic," he continued, "it is a concert season the likes of which there has never been: 3–4 concerts every day, each worse than the other and all of them to empty houses."[53] Meanwhile he had been up to his ears with the rehearsals of "my three operas, which have to come out of dry dock on 5 March." A month later he was already trying to excuse himself from the proposed trip to Odessa, saying that the grand duchess had invited him to spend the summer with her again: "There is nothing unpleasant for me in this, as it will not cost me anything and I shall be able to work calmly."[54]

In his *Autobiography* Rubinstein claimed that *Fomka the Fool* was first given in 1854. In fact it was premiered on 30 April/12 May 1853 at the Aleksandrinsky Theater in St. Petersburg, and the other two one-act operas were to have been staged shortly afterward. Things did not go so smoothly, however, for, as Rubinstein himself recalled: "The first opera was performed in such a way that I gathered everything up and do not intend to give any more of my works to the Russian stage here."[55] He would have to write a whole book, he told his mother, if he wanted to describe everything that took place before, during, and after the production of the opera. Essentially he had been advised against presenting his work; he had enemies, he was told, and even if they could not actually prevent the performance from going ahead, they would do everything in their power to ensure that it was a fiasco. Rubinstein was skeptical and thought it was too late to cancel the production, as it had already been announced and the work was in rehearsal. "But you cannot imagine anything more pitiful. They missed out whole bars, came in early, forgot their parts, in a word, what happened was quite unheard of. I was ready to stop the performance, but the opera went on to the end and I was so happy when it finished that I ran straight out of the theater.

The audience summoned me for half an hour. Twice someone had to come out and tell the audience that I was not in the theater."[56]

It has been suggested that Rubinstein chose to blame the artists for the failure of *Fomka the Fool* rather than accept that the fault was his. The cast included able and reputable singers as the surviving cast list shows:

Miron (village elder)	Mr. Zhivov
Annyushka (his daughter)	Emiliya Lileyeva [Schefferdecker]
Fyodor (her betrothed)	Pavel Bulakhov
Panteley	Semyon [Gulak]-Artemovsky
Stepanovna (a matchmaker)	Darya Leonova

Given this cast, it is hard to imagine quite the fiasco Rubinstein describes. Even allowing for an element of exaggeration, the incident highlights two important factors. First, despite all attempts to sabotage the work, Rubinstein's character and professionalism required him to see the performance through to the end. Second, it caused him to abandon the Russian stage for many years: "Now I am resolved to carry out the decision which I ought to have carried out long ago: not to produce anything further on the Russian stage."[57] The day after the disastrous performance he went to the offices of the Theater Directorate and demanded that the score be returned to him. The incident is vividly highlighted by the composer in his reminiscences:

I appeared at the theater office and vehemently demanded that the score of the opera be returned to me. A certain Semyonov, who worked for Gedeonov (he alone in the theater office was slightly interested in Russian opera), tried to reason with me. But I was distraught and would hear nothing of his consoling words. "I do not wish to know anything. Give me back my score immediately."[58]

The bitter failure of *Fomka the Fool* was a key factor in Rubinstein's decision to quit Russia and make his name as a serious international composer. Pauline Viardot's successful performance of Zulima's aria from *Vengeance* at a concert of the Patriotic Society on 22 April/4 May 1853 provided him some small measure of solace (this is the only number from the opera that has survived).[59] Viardot also told him that she had heard his brother, Nikolay, in Moscow and, like many other artists who had heard him play, was enraptured. "He is generally the favorite of the Moscow public, he plays with great success in all his concerts, he gives lessons, and he has passed his examination; now he is in the third class [his third year at Moscow University]."

In the spring of 1853 Rubinstein returned the libretto of *Stepan Razin* to its author, Mikhail Voskresensky:

Mr. Bernhard has repeated his request for me to return the libretto belonging to Mr. Vokresensky, which I am doing without delay. I am sorry that, under the impression I would not have to return it, I have made some penciled notes on it. I hope that Mr. Voskresensky will not take this to be some wicked intent on my part. Nor [object to] my retaining the subject and of handling it with the assistance of some other writer. It should be borne in mind that this subject has been my property for some time.[60]

Some time later he evidently asked Mikhail Mikhaylov, who had furnished him with the libretto of *Fomka the Fool,* to prepare a text for *Stepan Razin*. During the 1850s Mikhaylov had acquired a reputation as a genre writer. He had graduated from the University of St. Petersburg in 1848 and then accepted a government post in Nizhny Novgorod, where he translated Goethe's *Faust* into Russian. One of his own best-known works, the tale *Adam Adamïch,* was published in 1851, and the following year he retired from government service and returned to St. Petersburg, where he evidently became acquainted with Rubinstein. Rubinstein was probably well aware of Mikhaylov's radical sympathies and most likely thought him a good candidate for a subject like Stepan Razin. Mikhaylov prevaricated, however, and on 18/30 June an irate Rubinstein wrote to him, demanding to know whether he intended to honor his word and write the libretto. Perhaps Mikhaylov's growing involvement in the radical movement, as well as the politically sensitive subject of Stepan Razin, prevented any further collaboration with the writer, and even if the libretto was completed, it was never used.

By the early 1850s the circle of Rubinstein's acquaintances in St. Petersburg had become extensive, and he was a frequent visitor at various high-society salons. Despite the extreme censorship affecting Russian society as a whole, the salons provided a venue for intellectuals and prominent public figures to exchange views on a wide range of political, philosophical, and artistic matters. One of the most important of these salons was organized by Grand Duchess Yelena Pavlovna at the Mikhaylovsky Palace, and it came to play a crucial role in attracting young energetic men who would later implement the great reforms of Alexander II's reign. Not surprisingly, the role played by the aristocratic salons and their patrons in shaping the cultural and political development of Russia received scant attention in Soviet scholarship, but Prince Odoyevsky was perhaps a rare exception. His salon has been described as "the visible center of the literary-musical life of St. Petersburg in the 1830s," and the prince himself was dubbed "the founder of scholarly musical studies in Russia" and "the first outstanding Russian musicologist."[61] In his youth Odoyevsky and the poet Dmitry Venevitinov had founded the Obshchestvo lyubomudriya [Society for the Lovers of Wisdom] in Moscow. After moving to St. Petersburg, and after his marriage to Princess Olga Lanskaya in 1826, Odoyevsky established a salon that was frequented by the greatest literary and musical luminaries of the age: Pushkin, Zhukovsky, and Glinka, and in later years Turgenev, Tolstoy, and the young Dostoevsky.[62] Odoyevsky was a unique phenomenon in Russian culture and his interests were vast: philosophy, literature, music, astrology, magic, alchemy, animal magnetism, and hypnotism. In the 1840s he published the unique series of stories known as *Russkiye nochi* [Russian nights], and he was also active as a serious music critic. Liszt was invited to play at his home during the former's concert tour of Russia in 1842, Glinka had turned to him for advice during the composition of *A Life for the Tsar,* and after the formation of the Conservatory,

Odoyevsky was elected a member of the committee set up to examine works submitted to the Russian Music Society by aspiring composers. As a music critic, Odoyevsky had been very supportive of Glinka and Dargomïzhsky, and in 1853 he suggested to Dargomïzhsky that he give a charity concert consisting of arias from his recently performed opera *Esmeralda*, based on Victor Hugo's *Notre Dame de Paris*, and some romances and piano pieces. Little is known about the relations between Rubinstein and Dargomïzhsky in the years before the founding of the Conservatory, but it is evident that Rubinstein had been asked to lend his support in this concert and had been given a four-handed version of Dargomïzhsky's recently completed *Fantaziya na motïvï iz operï "Ivan Susanin"* [Fantasy on themes from Glinka's opera *Ivan Susanin*], which he was to perform. The concert was arranged for 9/21 April, and the artists who took part included the pianists Mikhail Santis and Mariya Kalergis; Dargomïzhsky's younger sister, Erminiya (a harpist); and the singers M. V.Shilovskaya, A. A. Latïsheva, Pauline Viardot, Osip Petrov, and Pavel Bulakhov.

For reasons still unclear, Rubinstein wrote to Dargomïzhsky, refusing to take part in the concert:

> I have only just discovered that Mme Kalergis will be playing in your concert next Sunday. I assume, therefore, that you no longer have any need of me and I advise you that in the contrary case you must not rely on me, since not for anything in the world will I play in a concert in which Mme Kalergis plays or intends to play. I am returning to you with a thousand thanks your beautiful *Fantasy* with which I was delighted to acquaint myself and I beg you to regard me always your completely devoted Ant. Rubinstein.[63]

Mariya Kalergis was the niece of Count Nesselrode, foreign minister to Nicholas I. In 1839 she had married the Greek diplomat Johann Kalergis, but she soon separated from him. Some years later she married Count Sergey Mukhanov, who was appointed intendant of the imperial theaters in Warsaw in 1868 and chairman of the Directorate of Warsaw Theaters two years later. Neil Cornwell writes of Countess Kalergis-Mukhanova: "Sometimes referred to as a gifted pianist, sometimes as a courtesan—a kind of aristocratic nineteenth-century groupie—or even a spy, she is reputed to have been a pupil of Chopin, the some-time mistress of Liszt, Alfred de Musset, Gautier (who wrote *Symphonie en blanc majeur* to her), and Heine."[64] Whatever Rubinstein's misunderstanding was at that time regarding Mariya Kalergis, two years later he dedicated his Piano Sonata No. 3 in F, Op. 41, to her.

Rubinstein planned to leave St. Petersburg for Western Europe in the spring of 1854, but first he needed to find a new Russian publisher. He had quarreled with Bernhard and had a mass of unpublished romances on his hands (these must have included the six Russian songs eventually published as Op. 8 and at least some of the Koltsov settings from Op. 27). He also needed to arrive in Berlin with a newly completed opera believing that the ones he had written so far would not be to the taste of German audiences. He was considering Pushkin's narrative poem, *Poltava*, as the subject for an opera, but, disillusioned with the librettists in St. Petersburg, he set his sights on collaborating with Dmitry Lensky (pseudonym of Vorobyov) or Countess Rostopchina in Moscow. In the end, nothing came of the idea.

That winter Rubinstein was busily preoccupied with preparations for his forthcoming trip abroad: renewing his passport, completing the works he wished to take with him, and copying the orchestral parts of the compositions that he wanted to perform. Nevertheless, he still found time to attend the Italian opera and found it disappointing, with the exception of the troupe's prima donna, Madame de Lagrange. He also saw the tragic actress Élisa Rachel and declared: "she is making good and bad weather here this year, but she is truly inexpressibly great." [65] He also found, to his delight, that he was on the best of terms with these artists since he was visiting them at the behest of the grand duchess Yelena, and therefore "they receive me wonderfully." [66] In November he also renewed an old acquaintance, for the family of the priest who had given him Russian lessons in Berlin during the 1840s had arrived in St. Petersburg. Old Father Sokolov had died, but his eldest daughter, Aleksandra Dormidontovna, Anton confessed to Kaleriya Khristoforovna, "is very beautiful and sings superbly." [67] In view of the dire financial position of her family, Aleksandra needed to give lessons to support her family. To do so, she needed to pay for lessons herself and Rubinstein planned to speak to the grand duchess about assisting her. In later life she became the famous soprano and teacher Aleksandra Aleksandrova-Kochetova.

During the fall and winter of 1853 Rubinstein completed a Symphony in B♭. It was performed in St. Petersburg the following March and then in Berlin a year later, but the composer evidently became disillusioned with it. The score was eventually discarded, and the material was reused in other works. The first movement was subsequently published as the Concert Overture in B♭ (1861), and the second and third movements were added to the *Ocean Symphony* (in the six-movement revision of 1863). He also continued work on the cycle *Kamennïy Ostrov*, but his most significant work at this time was the Piano Concerto No. 3, completed early in 1854. Many years latter, in *Gedankenkorb*, Rubinstein wrote of this concerto:

> I once had a strange dream. I saw a temple in which the various instruments of the orchestra had come together. A piano approaches this temple with a defiant air and demands to be accepted as one of the devotees. The orchestral instruments subject him to an examination and suggest that he should reproduce their various timbres and melodies; in the end, however, they find this insufficient. As a result the piano is overcome with despair and grief, but then rousing itself, declares itself in a haughty manner to be an independent orchestra and makes fun of the other instruments. They resentfully show it the ways in which it cannot imitate their playing, and they throw it out of the temple. I tried to convey this dream in sounds (Piano Concerto No. 3); I even wanted to append a program to it but abandoned the idea, convinced that in a prescribed program one person will hear one thing and another something quite different. [68]

In his résumé of 1853 Rubinstein declared that year to have been "a mixture of good and bad, of the pleasant and the unpleasant." [69] True success seemed to elude him, at least partly because of his inferior social status. Despite the acclaim of audiences, music critics, and the patronage of the court, his standing in Russian society remained unchanged. No level of artistic achievement could alter the fact that he was "the son of a merchant." He had already ruled out working in a musical establishment in Russia, as that would have limited his ability to travel abroad. He could not apply for a post in a ministry, as he had not attended any of the official schools nor passed the appropriate examinations. Without having first gained a solid European reputation, the opportunities for advancing his career in Russia were restricted. In these circumstances he judged that the impending foreign trip would be "decisive for the fate of my life, and therefore, in greeting it, my look is serious and my soul agitated."[70]

3   Foreign Tour, 1854–59

Before leaving Russia, Rubinstein was engaged to appear a number of times at various concert venues in St. Petersburg. In an all-Rubinstein concert at the Lichtenthal Hall on 2/14 March he performed the solo part in his Piano Concerto No. 3 under the baton of Carl Schuberth and then conducted the premiere of his Symphony in B♭. On 14/26 March he performed his Piano Trio in F, Op.15, No. 1, with Pikkel and Schuberth at Myatlev Hall. Two weeks later the Philharmonic Society gave a charity concert under the direction of Schuberth, performing works by Dargomïzhsky, Rubinstein, Mikhail Wielhorski, Glinka, Lvov, and Maurer.[1] On 31 March/12 April he appeared with Ludwig Maurer at the Mikhaylovsky Theater, and on 15/27 April he played some of his own works at a concert given by the Italian clarinetist Ernesto Cavallini at the Lichtenthal Hall. This was the last concert in which Rubinstein appeared in Russia before embarking on his long concert tour.

As the European winter season was almost over, he realized that it was not the most propitious time to begin a concert tour, but when the necessary permission to travel arrived, he resolved to go: "The die is cast: it will be one thing or the other," he wrote to Kaleriya Khristoforovna in Odessa. "I still hope to achieve the goal I have set for myself. The most important thing is to familiarize people with my works, to get them printed, to listen to good music more often, and to work myself."[2]

Rubinstein set out from St. Petersburg on 30 April/12 May 1854 and his first stop was Warsaw, where the company of a certain Laura Sveykovskaya caused him to dally for four days longer than he had intended. "When you see Fredro," Rubinstein told his brother Yakov, "tell him that in the near future I shall write to him much about her. Tell him that she has asked me to pass on her respects. I gave her his letter."[3] Maksimilian Fredro was the son of the celebrated Polish playwright Count Alexander Fredro, known in his time as "the Polish Molière." Born in 1820, Maksimilian was an amateur artist and a music lover, and held the post of an official in St. Petersburg. Rubinstein kept his promise, for he eventually wrote to Fredro:

> Laura [Sveykovskaya] is more beautiful than ever, and although suffering, even ill, she completely captivates all the young people; she feels a real affection for you; she favored me like an out and out coquette; besides, I find that for a beautiful woman she is very natural and good, which is rare in this milieu. Constanze, her sister, is becoming the observer of the weaknesses of human nature; in my opinion—a bad omen. Sobansky, Branitssky, etc., the one has tabes dorsalis, the other consumption,

in short, it is curious to observe, but since I considered it essential to look after my health, I stayed but a few days.[4]

From the context it is evident that Laura Sveykovskaya was ill (probably suffering from tuberculosis), but one can only conjecture what her relations with Rubinstein, his brother Yakov, and Fredro were. A few years later, Rubinstein dedicated to Sveykovskaya his *Acrostic*, Op. 37, which appeared in 1856. Finally, Rubinstein arrived in Berlin on 16/28 May and from there traveled to Weimar.

Liszt and Weimar

Rubinstein arrived in Weimar around 1 June, as confirmed by Liszt's letter to Hans von Bülow of 7 June 1854: "Rubinstein has been installed at the Altenburg for a week now, and although he expresses consistent prejudice against *Zukunftmusik*, I esteem him as a talent and as a person."[5] The genial and enlightened atmosphere of the court at Weimar must have seemed to Rubinstein like a blessing after three years of servitude to Yelena Pavlovna.

Weimar was the capital of the small Duchy of Saxe-Weimar-Eisenach, and during the great classical age of the 1770s and 1780s Goethe and Schiller had worked there under the protection of Grand Duke Carl August (1757–1828). The poet and novelist Wieland had been appointed tutor to the children of the grand duke, and Herder received the post of court chaplain and superintendent. In 1804 Carl August's son, Grand Duke Carl Friedrich (1783–1853), had married the grand duchess Mariya Pavlovna (1786–1859) of Russia. She was the sister of Tsar Nicholas I, and her presence at the Weimar court ensured that close ties with Russia were maintained. The special relationship that existed between the two courts, which endured almost up to the time of the First World War, led to the establishment of a Russian diplomatic mission. During the mid-nineteenth century it was actively supported by the chargé d'affaires, Apollon von Maltitz, the Russian provost, and his daughter, Martha von Sabinina. The grand duchess herself had been a pupil of Hummel and was keenly interested in music. Even before her husband's death in 1853, she and her son, Carl Alexander (1818–1901), were largely responsible for Liszt's appointment as Kapellmeister in außerordentlichem Dienst [Grand Ducal Director of Music Extraordinary] in 1842. Although the post required him to spend at least three months of the year in Weimar, it was not until 1848 that Liszt finally took up permanent residence at the Altenburg just outside the city.

From 1848 on, Liszt succeeded in surrounding himself with a host of highly talented musicians and men of letters, the majority of whom were devoted to his advocacy of the New German School and the "music of the future." Prominent among them were Hans von Bülow, who was Liszt's pupil from 1851 to 1853, and the composer, writer, and translator Peter Cornelius. Cornelius had studied with Siegfried Dehn (the composition teacher of both Glinka and Rubinstein) in Berlin from 1844 to 1852, and immediately afterward he joined

Liszt in Weimar. His own first opera, *Der Barbier von Bagdad,* was staged at Weimar under Liszt's direction in 1858. Its failure was due to the intrigues of the intendant general of the Weimar Theater, Franz von Dingelstedt, whose real purpose was to remove Liszt. Hired *claqueurs* were engaged to stir up fierce opposition to the opera and Liszt took their action to be directed against him. The incident eventually caused Liszt to resign his post at Weimar and prompted Cornelius to remark dryly: "Liszt wants—Art; Dingelstedt—himself."

Besides composition (in the mid-1850s Cornelius was principally noted for his song settings), Cornelius was highly valued in the Weimar circle as an able translator. It was he who provided the German translation for a performance of Berlioz's *Benvenuto Cellini* at Weimar in February 1855 and of Rubinstein's opera *Die Sibirischen Jäger* (the revised German version of *Sibirskiye okhotniki*) when it was produced in November 1854. Rubinstein evidently also furnished Cornelius's sister with letters of recommendation for a planned trip to St. Petersburg where she intended to launch a stage career in the chorus of the Italian opera. Rubinstein commented to Liszt in his letter of 5 August: "Herein are enclosed letters for Mme Cornelius: she is heading for a country where it is not enough to have just means in order to hit your target in musical art; that is why I would advise her to see Carl Schuberth first of all and ask him to speak to Cavos, and also to other influential people; that is what I am earnestly advising her to do in my letter."[6]

Another recent arrival in Weimar was August Heinrich Hoffmann von Fallersleben. He had been appointed professor of German poetry at Breslau University in 1836 but was exiled in 1849 for his revolutionary verses. He arrived in Weimar in the spring of 1854 and played a leading role in the activities of the Altenburg circle. Rubinstein set two of his poems in his Six German Songs, Op. 33. Another frequent visitor to the Altenburg was Karl Brendel, a staunch supporter of Liszt, Wagner, and the New German School, and the influential editor of the *Neue Zeitschrift für Musik.* Besides residents and regular visitors, Weimar's reputation as an intellectual center attracted many other visitors who remained for a few months at a time. Rubinstein's arrival in June, for example, was followed in the fall by the appearance of the novelist George Eliot and G. H. Lewes, who had come to research his book, *The Life and Works of Goethe.*

During the few weeks that Rubinstein spent at the Altenburg, he was invited to compose a Solemn Overture on the theme of *Heil dir im Siegerkranz* to mark the thirty-sixth birthday of Carl Alexander. He had only six days to complete it, he informed Fredro, but "it has turned out to be not the worst of my compositions."[7] The overture was conducted by Liszt on 24 June in the theater at Weimar as a curtain raiser to a performance of Schubert's opera, *Alfonso und Estrella.* According to Rubinstein, the overture scored a success: "In general my works are finding people who appreciate them."[8]

Toward the end of June, Rubinstein and Liszt traveled to Hamburg where their routes took them separate ways—Liszt to Mainz and Rubinstein to Berlin. There was just time to pen a few lines to Kaleriya Khristoforovna and apologize for not having written to her, for, as he explained, he had spent most of his time "in stagecoaches, trains, and so on."[9] Rubinstein rejoined Liszt at Cologne, as testified by Liszt's letter to Carolyne von Sayn-Wittgenstein of 11 July:

> At Cologne the evening before last, Rubinstein came aboard the *Agrippine* [a Dutch steamer boat]. He was coming back from Berlin, where he had spent a few hours with Fraülein Emilie Genast."[10] The two musicians then arrived in Rotterdam for a three-day music festival organized by the Dutch composer and conductor Johannes Verhulst to mark the twenty-fifth anniversary of the Maatschappij ter Bevordering der Toonkunst [Association for the Advancement of Music]. It was held between 13 and 15 July and was attended by some of the foremost musicians of the day, including Berlioz, Hiller, Sterndale-Bennet, Reinecke, and others. Liszt took no active part in it, but wished to be there in what he described as "a supernumerary capacity."

The performances of Handel's *Israel in Egypt* and Haydn's *Die Schöpfung* that were given during the festival must have delighted Rubinstein and inspired in him the idea of writing a grand oratorio of his own—this resulted in *Das Verlorene Paradies* a few years later.

Rubinstein was finding that his trip had generally been productive. "The change in climate, the exchange of ideas, the new faces and other impressions," he told Kaleriya Khristoforovna, "all this is extremely important for a person, and especially for an artist. At the moment I am drowning in this, and I hope that it will bear fruit."[11] Since the summer was not a lucrative time to arrange a tour, he used the time to renew old acquaintances. Among them was François-Joseph Fétis, the eminent director of the Brussels Conservatory, to whom he provided biographical information for the celebrated *Biographie Universelle des Musiciens*.[12] On 21 July, in the company of Liszt, he also attended the second of two soirées given by Hubert-Ferdinand Kufferath. This distinguished teacher and composer had played host to the violinists Wieniawski and Charles de Bériot and also to Clara Schumann (Kufferath had been instrumental in popularizing Robert Schumann's music in Belgium). The highlight of the evening was a performance of Beethoven's Ninth Symphony played by Liszt and Rubinstein in Liszt's own transcription for piano four hands.

The successful performance of his overture in Weimar had been reported in the Leipzig newspapers, but the prospect of the Weimar staging of *Fomka the Fool* in November delighted him even more. These triumphs had owed more than a little to the generous support of the Wielhorski brothers. This is made explicit by Rubinstein's letter to Fredro of 15/27 July: "But if you see them [the Wielhorski brothers], do not forget to pass on my earnest respects and express all the gratitude that I feel toward them. In essence, this makes it impossible for me to write to them, but I shall do it, and do it when I am able to tell them that their goodness toward me has brought forth fruit and that the musical world is thanking them as well as me."[13]

Rubinstein's assertion that he lived in Weimar for "five or six months"[14] was not strictly true, for by 27 July he had already taken up residence at the summer water spa of Biebrich near Mainz, enjoying the company of a lady to whom Liszt and Rubinstein refer in their correspondence as Madame S. From Biebrich and elsewhere Rubinstein penned letters to Liszt which are not only an important source of information about his activities up to the middle of 1855 but are remarkable on another account. The style is quite unlike anything we find in Rubinstein's letters to other correspondents. In the refined language of the letters, so full of metaphor, keen observation, and linguistic dexterity, we can see his evident attempt to emulate Liszt's distinctive epistolary manner.[15] Rubinstein spent almost the entire summer in Biebrich, but a few days before his departure he appeared before the grand duchess Mariya Pavlovna: "She is an excellent pianist, a pupil of Hummel and Liszt," Rubinstein told his mother, "and besides, she has fifty years of experience. It was difficult but it came off well."[16] The dowager duchess Mariya Pavlovna had arrived in Weimar in 1804, and, principally to please her, Liszt marked the occasion by staging an opera by a Russian compatriot.

There can be little doubt that Rubinstein found the company of Liszt and his entourage immensely stimulating, but it was something he could tolerate only in small doses. By moving to Biebrich he was able to distance himself from the heady intellectualism of the Weimar circle. "I have been in Biebrich now for some time, but I am not very happy with myself as regards work: it is barely making any progress because of the proximity of Wiesbaden, Mainz, and other attractive towns. All I am gaining by this is that I shall no longer be a composer of quantity," he remarked to Liszt, taking to heart the accusation that he had not been sufficiently self-critical in his writing.[17] He found the company of Carolyne von Sayn-Wittgenstein especially taxing:

> She was a Pole, the most fervent Catholic there ever was. She was not only a blue stocking but also a stocking of I do not know what hue. She was educated in the extreme, to the point of nausea. Conversation with her was a trial, but she was also a very intelligent woman. She was not beautiful, but she had an enormous influence on Liszt. It was she who discouraged him from virtuosity so that he could make himself known in another sphere: with his musical compositions and his protection of others. He thought up Wagner. The "Wagner question" and "the music of the future"—all this came about from the Weimar period, from Liszt and Madame Wittgenstein.[18]

Rubinstein's relations with Liszt himself were highly ambiguous. In the early days of his concert tours, he had delighted audiences by mimicking Liszt's style of playing, moving his body about and sweeping back his hair. There is no doubt that he was hugely influenced by Liszt, above all by his immense artistry, his rejection of everything banal, and the high opinion he had of his art and of himself. From the first moment he had heard Liszt play in Paris in 1841, he had consciously followed his example in his own career as a performer. In 1839 Liszt had given concerts in aid of flood victims in Hungary and lent his support to the formation of a professional conservatory in Pest. These acts of charity and public generosity rekindled Rubinstein's own sense of civic responsibility after his plan for a Music Academy failed. The first result of this influence came a year later with the publication in the Viennese press of the article "Russische Komponisten."

However, while Liszt's irresistible charisma as an artist dazzled Rubinstein and he admired the musician and the personality without reserve, he simply could not abide the composer. He had an innate dislike of contrived or preconceived artifice and a mistrust of theories, and he fiercely opposed what he saw as the "false prophets" who threatened to divert art from its well-defined path. Rubinstein's marked ambivalence toward Liszt is clearly evident in his letter to Fredro of 15/27 July 1854:

> Liszt is a person about whom I should write a book if I wanted to analyze him. I can only tell you that this is a person who is, in all respects, such that you rarely find—and that is as an artist, as a person, and as a writer. He behaves perfectly toward me and predicts that I will have absolute success in my plans, although we completely disagree on the principal points of his views on music, which consist in the fact that he sees in Wagner the prophet of the future in opera, and in Berlioz—the prophet of the future in the domain of the symphony. I confess that I have learned a great deal from him and that many things would have passed me by quite unnoticed had I not known him and had we not exchanged views."[19]

Rubinstein's antipathy toward Liszt's music extended to Liszt's support of Wagner and Berlioz, as he made clear in this letter. Of Rubinstein's hostility toward the music of Berlioz we shall have eloquent proof in the coming pages. His attempts to familiarize himself with Wagner's music led to his very tactful remark, "I heard and saw *Der Fliegende Holländer* and *Tannhäuser* in Wiesbaden, but I cannot say anything since I find that it is necessary to hear such works many times in order to be in a position to judge them."[20]

Liszt's opinion of Rubinstein as a composer was initially one of genuine sympathy but ultimately it gave way to growing disappointment. This is not surprising. By the mid-1850s the views of Liszt and his musical adherents had crystallized around the Neu-Weimar-Verein, founded to obtain a "centralization of common endeavors" in the struggle against musical philistinism in Germany. The purpose of the association was to build on the aims of the Society of Murls, which had been formed at the end of 1853 with Liszt as its president (the Padischah). A *Murl* is a contraction of two German words *Mohr* (Moor) and *Kerl* (a fellow) and, just as in the expression "Einen Mohren kann man nicht weisswaschen" [A Moor cannot be whitewashed], so a *Murl* "was one whom the Philistines could never whitewash to their colorless ways."[21] This led Liszt to later remark of Rubinstein: "Murlship alone is wanting in him still."[22] Despite his conviction that Rubinstein's development as a composer was stagnating, the sincerity of his support for the man whom he jocularly addressed as "Van II" (owing to Rubinstein's alleged physical resemblance to Beethoven) was never in question. Nevertheless he was often vexed by Rubinstein's peevish pranks, which he labeled "*murrendo*"—a word sometimes thought to derive from *morrendo* but perhaps more fittingly associated with the Spanish *murrio*, meaning sulky.

As noted, the opera *Fomka the Fool* had been proposed for the celebration to commemorate the fiftieth anniversary of the arrival of Grand Duchess Mariya Pavlovna in Weimar. Consequently Rubinstein pressed Fredro to send him drawings of the costumes of Russian peasants and peasant girls, and also a drawing of a village square with a drinking house. His doubts about the poor reception that a Russian subject (*Fomka the Fool*) might receive in Germany were entirely consistent with his views about national themes in a "universal" medium like opera. He expressed these doubts in a letter to his mother: "I am curious to know what is going to happen with the staging of my opera due for production in November. Besides curiosity, fear also steals in: not everything that is good in music for Russia will be evaluated the same way in Germany. I still hope for a good outcome."[23] Rubinstein toiled over the scenario, which it was Cornelius's task to turn into a workable German libretto, and also the final version of the score, which Liszt had requested should be delivered to his copyist in Weimar between 15 and 20 September. "You will receive in the next post," Rubinstein informed Liszt, "a prosaic and very bad translation of my opera, but nevertheless it will give you a more accurate idea of the piece than just the scenario; that is why I have decided to do it. If a decision is taken to stage it—about which I graciously ask you to inform me—I shall come to Weimar in the first few days of September to work with Cornelius."[24]

Die Sibirischen Jäger at Weimar

A few days later, on 9 August, Rubinstein sent Liszt rough German translations of *Fomka the Fool* as well as *Die Sibirischen Jäger* and *Vengeance*: "I am sending you herewith the subject of the opera which was under discussion and also the two others, so as to leave you a free choice; I have translated them quickly into bad German, but in such a form as to give you an idea about the unfolding of the dramatic action."[25] In the end *Die Sibirischen Jäger* was substituted for *Fomka the Fool*.

Apart from the opera, one of Rubinstein's principal concerns during the summer of 1854 was attempting to find German publishers for some of his recently completed piano works. The stay in Biebrich had given him the much-needed time to complete the work on his first two piano sonatas, begun as far back as 1848, and also the massive cycle of twenty-four musical portraits *Kamenniy Ostrov*. In addition, he composed the fantasy *Le Bal*, and a number of shorter salon pieces. He duly informed Liszt:

> I have been successful with Schott as regards my solo piano pieces—he is taking all of them, and is beginning with the twenty-four portraits.[26] The strangest thing is that on the same day that Schott fell into the trap, Charles Voss was in Mainz—poor Schott is becoming decidedly old.
>
> Schloss in Cologne also wanted a few pages of my manuscripts, but when he came into my room and saw that he would be inundated with them, he made good use of the swimming lessons he once used to take, and hastily swam to safety.
>
> André from Frankfurt, it seemed, was also ready to swallow the bait, but I know

the deadly power [*faculté funeste*] of my head—the head of the Medusa for the publisher who would look at me—and I shall allow him a little more time to breathe freely amid the springs of Blumenthal, the lakes of Goria, and generally amid the limpid waters of Voss and the likes of him; however, I shall lie in wait for him."[27]

In the end, as Rubinstein himself tells it, the music dealer and piano maker Carl August André in Frankfurt did escape "the nets, which I set for him with my compositions."[28] This metaphor of "angling" and "setting traps" seems to have amused both composers, for it reappears a number of times in their correspondence, and also in Liszt's celebrated remark to Brendel about Rubinstein fishing in Mendelssohnian waters: "He is a clever fellow, possessed of talent and character in an exceptional degree, and therefore no one can be more just to him than I have been for years. Still, I do not wish to preach to him—he may sow his wild oats and fish deeper in Mendelssohn waters, and even swim away again if he likes. But sooner or later I am certain he will give up the apparent and formalistic for the organically Real, if he does not want to stand still."[29]

The Biebrich summer of 1854 proved to be highly productive, and in addition to the composition of instrumental pieces, Rubinstein planned two large-scale works. In the months before his departure for Western Europe, he, Dargomïzhsky, and Prince Odoyevsky had been appointed honorary members of the St. Petersburg Philharmonic Society, and, as a mark of gratitude, Rubinstein felt obliged to provide a new symphony. This eventually resulted in Symphony No. 3 in A major; it was only completed the following year, however, as its composition was temporarily interrupted by another symphonic work. Finding himself under Liszt's irresistible spell, Rubinstein broke with one of his own cardinal rules. At this time Liszt was putting the finishing touches to his *Faust Symphony*—program music of the kind that was usually abhorrent to Rubinstein. His sudden attraction to the same subject was reputedly inspired by having seen Ary Scheffer's picture, *Faust*, in Brussels and in July he informed his mother: "The first movement will be called 'Faust', the second movement—'Gretchen', the third movement—'Mephistopheles', the fourth—'The Poet.' The subject is excellent but difficult. We shall see what comes of it."[30] The final decision to write the *Faust Symphony* was made during Rubinstein's visit to Leipzig. He worked on the symphony in the fall and winter of 1854, but in the end abandoned it, as he eventually abandoned the Symphony in B♭ of a year earlier, and most of this *Faust Symphony* was destroyed. Only the first movement survived and was published separately, in 1864, as his *Faust Overture*, Op. 68. Another pressing task that occupied Rubinstein in the summer of 1854 was to prepare the *Ocean Symphony* for performance. This work had been first heard in St. Petersburg in 1852, and with it he planned to mark his début in Leipzig as a composer.

Toward the end of August Rubinstein learned from Liszt about the decision to stage *Die Sibirischen Jäger* rather than *Fomka the Fool*. He replied to Liszt on 28 August: "I consider the choice of libretto for 9 November to be successful for a number of reasons: to put across expressions of love is easier than satire because feelings of love are universal, whereas satire is typical of only a few nations." Rubinstein's own perception of love appears to be somewhat cynical, for in the same letter to Liszt he continued: "I am very much looking forward to our meeting, and, believe me, a certain Madame S. will not be able to detain me when it is a question of visiting you; I never had a clearly expressed taste for paradise, if paradise there is in a woman or near her [si Paradis il y a dans une femme ou auprès d'elle]; I always felt a great respect for Satan, whom I personify in the form of Prometheus, whom I personify in *you*."[31]

On the eve of his departure for Weimar, Rubinstein wrote to his brother, Yakov, who had taken up a post as a military doctor and was shortly to leave for Warsaw with his regiment. He was keen to ensure that the Russian press was kept fully apprised of his successes and asked Yakov to call on Messrs Mann and Andrey Kraevsky and notify them that the romantic opera *Die Sibirischen Jäger* and not *Fomka the Fool* was to be performed in Weimar in November.[32] He also told his brother about the recent composition of three instrumental pieces for violin, Op. 11, which were eventually dedicated to Joseph Joachim, leader of the orchestra at Weimar from 1849 to 1853. Rubinstein wrote to Yakov: "Give my cordial regards to Kologrivov, and tell Pikkel that I have written for Joachim three violin pieces which he will enjoy playing."[33] This dedication to Joachim was somewhat premature, however, since Rubinstein had not yet even made his acquaintance.

Rubinstein arrived in Weimar on 3 September, and during the month he remained there the final alterations were made to the libretto and score of *Die Sibirischen Jäger*. At the beginning of October, however, Rubinstein traveled to Leipzig in the hope of getting his *Ocean Symphony* accepted for performance by the Gewandhaus orchestra, but he received a cold reception. The Gewandhaus was fiercely proud of its traditions—Mendelssohn had conducted it from 1835 until his death in 1847, and Ferdinand David was still its highly respected Konzertmeister. After Mendelssohn's death, Julius Rietz took over directorship of the Gewandhaus orchestra and of the Leipzig opera, but the two posts proved too much for him and he was obliged to give up the Gewandhaus concerts (in his absence they were conducted by Gade and David). Finally, in 1854, Rietz gave up the directorship of the opera and returned to the Gewandhaus, remaining there until his appointment as Kapellmeister at the Dresden court in 1860. Not surprisingly, Rietz was a staunch supporter of Mendelssohn and was hostile to new music, regarding Liszt's symphonic poems as "sins against art." At this time Rubinstein's symphonic music was still unknown in Leipzig, and as an "outsider" he was treated with considerable aloofness. Writing to Liszt on 6 October, he observed: "If I have not sent you news about my sojourn here, it is because I am in a mood of '*murrendo assai*' to the highest degree. I do not like anything here; the people seem to be the haughtiest, and matters seem to be unpardonably vile. Your letter to David has elicited the immortal phrase: '*Seien sie versichert, dass alles, was ich für Sie thun kann* [Be assured I will do everything I can (Germ.)],' etc."[34] He made obligatory calls on the resident bigwigs, whom Liszt derisively called "the little Leipzigers": Julius Rietz, Moritz Haupt-mann (the formidable theorist from the Leipzig Conservatory and founder of the Bach Gesellschaft), and Ferdinand David. His visit to Julius Rietz and Schleinitz, however, produced only "searching and mistrustful looks [des re-gards scrutinateurs et méfiants]."[35] Nevertheless, he managed to have the *Ocean Symphony* submitted to the Gewandhaus commission for possible performance in November: "They want to measure *The Ocean* with the yardstick of criticism and much good may it do them [à l'aune de la critique, grand bien leur en fasse]."[36]

The indifference to his music that Rubinstein encountered in Leipzig sorely wounded his artistic pride. The only people who had actually returned his visits were Brendel, Moscheles, and Langer. He had shown Langer his quartets for male voice choir, and Rubinstein commented dryly: "I imagine he did not like them, since he said that he found them 'très beaux.'" None of this prevented him from haranguing the Leipzig publishers: "Senff, after I had seen him off, left behind the smell of sulfur; he is a devil, and I am in despair of coaxing him if he is not a good devil. Härtel and his cohort maintain a defensive posi-tion with regard to me. I try to maneuver so as to keep them under constant pressure; I am counting on waging a battle with them only when a favorable wind blows from *The Ocean*."[37] He also went to see the music seller and pub-lisher Klemm and took delight in the fact that the latter had also taken Agnès Street-Klindworth for a man,[38] yet neither he nor Klemm had realized that Agnès was deliberately disguised. Her father, Georg Klindworth, was a secret agent working for the Hapsburg court and for the Russian government during the time of the Crimean War. It is known that his daughter assisted him in gath-ering information, and her appearance in Weimar during the fall of 1853 was not coincidental. As Alan Walker observes: "The house of Sachsen-Weimar had treaties with Prussia, Hanover, and St. Petersburg . . . In brief, she was what she had never ceased to be: a part of her father's intelligence-gathering network."[39]

The Gewandhaus committee finally approved the *Ocean Symphony* and a performance was set for 16 November. According to the rules of the committee, however, Rubinstein was prevented from playing in the same concert in which his symphony was being performed, so it was agreed that he would give a solo concert a few weeks later. Liszt had instructed Rubinstein to return to Weimar by 4 November, as the rehearsals of *Die Sibirischen Jäger* were due to begin in the last week of October. The premiere actually took place on 9 November 1854 at the Weimar Theater. It is a one-act opera in nine scenes with an astonishingly naïve plot: Tanya (soprano) is grieving about her betrothed, Ivan (tenor), who has disappeared. Her father, Semyon (bass), is consoling her in a duet, "Es singt der Sturm, ein Jäger wild." Some huntsmen, headed by Udaloy (baritone), re-turn from the bear hunt without Ivan. Everyone decides to go off and look for him. Scene 2 opens in a forest thicket, where snow maidens evoke a snowstorm. Ivan appears and sings a recitative "Froh lebt der Jäger und frei" followed by an aria "O Tania! Nun kehret dein Jäger." The lovers are reunited and Ivan shows them the bear he has killed. One of the huntsmen, Fyodor (tenor), who also aspires to Tanya's hand, accuses him of witchcraft. Everyone except Tanya recoils from Ivan, and Fyodor challenges him to a duel. At this point magical forces come into play, and the snow maidens return and dance around. The leader of the snow maidens announces to Fyodor that his final hour has come, and then the maidens submerge him in snowdrifts. A love duet and an ensemble conclude the opera.

Rubinstein informed his mother that the performance of the opera had been so successful that Dingelstedt had asked him for another which could be performed during the spring. He was already thinking about the Caucasian opera *Vengeance*, but, before this, he had a second trip to Leipzig ahead of him and the Gewandhaus premiere of his *Ocean Symphony*. As on his earlier trip, the welcome he received was rather cool, and he expressed his unhappiness at the paralysis of social life in a letter to Fredro. If he had not previously steeled himself against such setbacks, he told Fredro, there would have been no alternative but to return to accompanying nightingales and delight in the society of nymphs—an allusion to his musical duties as musician to Yelena Pavlovna. But instead he concludes, "be patient and the cossack will become an ataman."

The *Ocean Symphony* at the Leipzig Gewandhaus

Julius Rietz, during his term as director, had attempted to turn the Gewandhaus into a "bulwark against tastelessness,"[40] a position that was keenly perpetuated by his successor, Carl Reinecke. Yet, despite the extreme conservatism of Leipzig audiences during the 1850s, the Gewandhaus had maintained a tradition of "special concerts" in which contemporary composers were allowed to appear with their own compositions. It was under the banner of this tradition that the long-awaited performance of the *Ocean Symphony* took place on 16 November 1854. On the very same day Rubinstein wrote to Liszt:

> I have just returned from the Gewandhaus where my symphony was performed. I suggested that Rietz, who has become very friendly toward me of late, conduct it. He and David are the principal artists of the orchestra, and even certain local composers who were at the rehearsals predicted a great success for me. This evening, before the concert, the greater part of these gentlemen congratulated me beforehand, and said that I would be called out to take a bow. I replied to everything with the kind of smile that is distinctive of any composer when the performance of one of his works is about to take place. This smile says: do you want to make fun of me? Or must I make fun of you? At last they start—the first movement is played well and people applaud; the second movement is played superbly and the applause is louder; the third movement is a miracle of execution and the applause is much less; the last movement—the orchestra is delirious [*bat la campagne*] and there is no applause at all. So, I do not know whether this is a failure, or whether the Leipzig audience is doing me the honor of failing to understand me—it is all the same. I am just curious about one thing: before the concert Gurkhaus met me in the concert hall and said that he would come to see me tomorrow on business; if he does not come the first of my suppositions about the symphony is correct, if he does come then it is the second. I hope that this will not stand in the way of my

intention of playing at one of these concerts; so far, nothing has been decided in this respect. Anyway, it will not be on the 30th, as I had previously supposed, for Mr. Jaëll is playing that evening. My appearance will be in the first or second week of December: I shall know in a few days. None of this, however, has prevented me from composing preludes: I have just finished the fifth and I am beginning the sixth; I shall be very happy when I have finished them because they are starting to bore me. When I was listening to my symphony today many thoughts were conflicting in my head, one more amusing than the next. Here are a few examples:

> A conversation between the Audience and the Symphony!
> Audience: "Ocean, du Ungeheuer! Wie wässerig bist du!"
> Symphony: "Publikum, du musikalische Einkommensteuer, wie ledern bist du!"
> Audience: "Symphonie, que me veux-tu?"
> Symphony: "Te prouver que ton Leipzig est un faux nid."
> Audience: "Hon y soit qui mal y pense!"
> Symphony: "Béni soit qui vertement te tance!"
> Italian: "Che porcheria musicale!"
> Composer (aside): "Se non è vero, è ben trovato."
> Symphony (to the audience): "To be or not to be?"
> The audience puts off the question.
> Symphony: "Eppur si muove!!!" etc. etc. etc."

> [A: "Ocean, you monster, how watery you are!" (Germ.)
> S: "Public, you payer of musical income tax, how leathery you are!" (Germ.)
> A: "Symphony, what do you want of me?" (Fr.)
> S: "To prove that your Leipzig is a false nest." (Fr.)
> A: "Evil to him who thinks evil!" (Fr.)
> S: "Blessed be he who gives you a sharp reprimand!" (Fr.)
> I: "What a musical obscenity!" (It.)
> C (aside): "If it is not true, it is well-founded." (It.)
> S (to the audience): "To be or not to be?" (Eng.)
> The audience puts off the question. (Eng.)
> S: "And yet it moves!!! etc. etc. etc." (It.)][41]

The Leipzig reviews about the performance of the *Ocean Symphony* were mixed. For some the music was simply too "watery," but Rubinstein himself believed that the audience had failed to understand the symphony: "It is a very serious work," he wrote to his mother, "and therefore the success could not be unanimous. Nonetheless, it was applauded and the experts have given a high opinion of it."[42] Some of these experts visited Rubinstein the day after the concert, for he was able to tell Liszt in a bemused tone: "The day after the concert in which it [the symphony] was performed, all these gentlemen came to congratulate me, and the journals have expressed themselves in a favourable fashion. 'Du hast die schönsten Augen, mein Liebchen, was willst du noch mehr?'" [You have the most beautiful eyes, my dear, what more do you want? (Germ.)].[43] The *Ocean Symphony* could scarcely be considered ahead of its time, even by the standards of the mid-nineteenth century, but the work decidedly gave Moscheles much cause for alarm: "The clarity of the first movement, for me, was soothing as a mirror-calm sea. Then came the modern capers and roars and it became incomprehensible and stormy, and my thoughts could no longer find anchorage in those daring harmonic shallows. Nevertheless I do not recognize in him an excellent composing talent."[44] The symphony had not yet grown into the colossal work that it was later to become by the addition of three more movements in the revisions of 1863 and 1880. In its original form, as published by Senff in 1857, the symphony bore a dedication to Liszt and consisted of the following four movements:

I Allegro maestoso, (3/2) C major
II Adagio ma non tanto, (4/4) E minor
III Allegro, (2/4) G major
IV Adagio (4/4) C minor—Allegro con fuoco (2/2) C major

If the critics were unsure about Rubinstein's talent as a composer, the publishers were a good deal more generous. Gurkhaus from the publishing firm Kistner did indeed come to see Rubinstein the day after the performance of the symphony, as he had promised, and they came to an agreement about publishing the cycle of *Persian Songs*, which Rubinstein wished to dedicate to Grand Duchess Sophie at Weimar.[45] According to Barenboym, the songs were originally intended for voice and orchestra (he bases this assumption on newspaper reports of the 1850s), but Liszt advised that it would be difficult to find a publisher willing to take them in such a form. The songs were eventually published by Kistner in 1855 in a version for voice and piano. Stanford University now possesses Rubinstein's manuscript score of the songs which are listed in the library catalogue.[46] The first performer was the mezzo-soprano Emilie Genast whom Rubinstein had visited in Berlin in July.

Rubinstein had also brought with him to Leipzig the *Octet* that he had reworked from the early D minor Piano Concerto (last played in Moscow in 1849), and he sold it to Peters. "The publication of my works is going ahead very slowly, but probably by the spring most of them will have already been published," he told Kaleriya Khristoforovna.[47] More important than his dealings with Kistner and Peters were Rubinstein's relations with Barthold Senff, for in the years to come this Leipzig music firm would become Rubinstein's most important publisher outside Russia. If the impression of Senff that he had formed during his first visit to Leipzig had been accompanied by the "smell of sulfur," now the publisher had become "a good devil." Rubinstein did not miss the opportunity to attend as many of the Gewandhaus concerts as he could, and he looked forward to the opportunity of seeing Clara Schumann and Joachim: "Mme Schumann and Joachim are proposing to come here and give a concert on the 19 [December]; I am delighted because this will give me the opportunity of becoming acquainted with Joachim."[48] In fact, Clara Schumann's concert with Joachim at the Gewandhaus took place on 21 December.[49] Rubinstein was then writing his Six Preludes, Op. 24, which were eventually dedicated to Clara, and it was probably then that he approached Joachim about the dedication of the three violin pieces from his Op. 11 set.

His own solo concert at the Gewandhaus had taken place on 14 December.

Again the press reviews were mixed but were largely favorable. Rubinstein hastened to advise Liszt once more about his success: "This time I can inform you about a great success. Yesterday I played at the Gewandhaus, first the Fantasy for piano and orchestra in F [Second Piano Concerto, Op. 35], then a Nocturne, the first Prelude, and a Study—I scored a great success and the audience made amends to me in an honorable way. I must thank you for your kind advice in using a trumpet in the *Adagio;* this is an indisputable effect, and it drew the attention of all the musicians."[50] The success he had achieved in Leipzig had exceeded his expectations despite some harsh newspaper reviews. "But who can stop them," he complained to Kaleriya Khristoforovna, "especially I who will not take a step to acquire the good favor of people for myself."[51] On 25 December Rubinstein's Octet for piano, violin, viola, cello, double bass, flute, and horn was performed at a Gewandhaus chamber concert, and a few days later, on 28 December, the composer took the piano part in a performance of his Trio in F with Ferdinand David.

For some time Rubinstein had been thinking seriously about composing a grand oratorio. Liszt had recommended the German writer Arnold Schloenbach as a possible librettist, and during his visit to Leipzig Rubinstein commissioned him to prepare a text on the subject of Milton's *Paradise Lost.* The oratorio would occupy Rubinstein's thoughts a great deal during the coming months, but there was also another work, which was giving him serious cause for concern. In mid-December he received a letter from St. Petersburg concerning the symphony that he had promised to the Philharmonic Society. His work on the Third Symphony was progressing slowly, and although he was pinning his hopes on an early performance in April, he doubted that he would finish it in time.

After a short visit to Weimar at the start of the New Year Rubinstein arrived in Berlin, and wrote at length to Liszt about his reception there: "True to his custom of keeping you informed about "childe Rubinstein's pilgrimage through the musical world," I hasten to advise you that last week I gave my first concert and paid 160 thalers from my own pocket, but scored a great success, even though the journals tear me to pieces [*me déchirent à belles dents*]. 'Formlosigkeit et harmonisch wirr [Formlessness and harmonically incoherent (Germ.)]'—these are the accusations they throw at me."[52] At this concert Rubinstein played his Concerto in F under the baton of Leopold Ganz, and then the composer took the rostrum for a performance of the *Ocean Symphony*. After the concert he called on several important figures from the musical world of Berlin. His old teacher Dehn, who liked his concerto very much but found that the symphony was "music which it is unusual to listen to, and so is bad"; the great musical theoretician Adolf Marx, who was not at home when Rubinstein called, even though he had been present at his concert; Heinrich Dorn, the eminent conductor of the Berlin opera and coeditor of the *Berliner Allgemeine Musikzeitung,* whose operatic saga *Die Nibelungen* Rubinstein heard and "found to be a worthy composition"; the composer and court Kapellmeister Wilhelm Taubert, who "smiled slyly at my expense and took me to hear one of his symphonies (a work which, despite everything, was good)"; Julius Stern, who treated him with particular affection; and the critic Ludwig Rellstab, who, as Rubinstein himself declared, "was totally in raptures so long as I do not go any further, for then he would feel sorry for me."[53] Rellstab's review, entitled "Ocean, du Ungeheurer" appeared in *Vossische Zeitung* on 27 January 1855 under the nom de plume "K.M.Weber." The critic was enthusiastic about Rubinstein's playing but was more reserved about his music. Other critics were far less magnanimous and were especially critical of the fact that Rubinstein had mostly played his own compositions. Ernest Kossak was particularly scathing and reviled Rubinstein's playing as "coarse, noisy, and crude [*rohes Spiel*]" and entirely lacking in charm. "Die anderen Hunde bellen mich an [The other hounds bark at me (Germ.)],"[54] he told Liszt, "in particular Kossak, who reviles me so shockingly that people are advising me to give him a box around the ears the first time we encounter one another; but I intend to leave that concern to my future if God will grant me as much." His reply to such critics would be "Du gleichst dem Geist, den du begreifst, aber nicht mir [You resemble the spirit that you understand, but it does not resemble me (Germ.)]," and he would silence them with his musical portrayal of *Faust*. "For at least another fifty years Berlin will remain in the eighteenth century in its relations to music, and here there is only a small circle of people who say "eppur si muove" [And yet it moves (It.)]."[55] In a second concert on 5 February Leopold Ganz conducted the orchestra in a performance of Rubinstein's Third Piano Concerto in G, and then the composer conducted his own Symphony in B♭. This symphony had been heard in St. Petersburg in March 1854 and was originally destined to have been his third numbered symphony, but Rubinstein had become disillusioned with it, and after the publication of his Symphony No. 3 in A major, he destroyed it. Some of the music was salvaged, however, for the first movement was eventually published in 1861 as a concert overture, and the second and third movements were absorbed into the enlarged six-movement version of the *Ocean Symphony* in 1863.

A Berlioz week at Weimar

By mid-February 1855 Rubinstein was back in Weimar. This was the occasion of the second week of Berlioz concerts given between 16 and 25 February. The birthday of Mariya Pavlovna fell on 16 February and, out of regard for her admiration of Berlioz's music, a performance of *Benvenuto Cellini* inaugurated the festivities. The following day Liszt gave the first performance of his own First Piano Concerto in E♭ under Berlioz's direction, and a few days later, on 20 February, the French composer was made a member of the Neu-Weimar-Verein and a grand dinner was given in his honor. The climax of the festivities was to be a performance of the three parts of *L'Enfance du Christ* and the *Symphonie Fantastique*. On the eve of this concert Rubinstein fled Weimar without telling anyone. An astonished Liszt wrote to Rubinstein the same day: "Your flight (fugue) this morning, my dear Rubinstein, was not entirely to my taste, and to this 'fugue' I incomparably prefer the 'Preludes' composed by you in the same room, which, to my great astonishment, I found to be empty, as I called in on you in order for us to set off together to the Berlioz recital."[56] Rubinstein considered Berlioz to be an entirely unmusical phenomenon in art. He questioned the value of the innovations that he had introduced into the symphony orchestra and declared that melodic invention, beauty of form, and richness of harmony were lacking in him.

Rubinstein's sudden flight from Weimar did not sour his relations with Liszt, for he continued to send news about his activities. Arriving in Vienna, he wrote on 24 March:

> First of all I must thank you for the mark of benevolence shown toward me in your letters to your friends here—benevolence which has ensured me a favorable reception. On the 22nd I gave my first concert; I played the Concerto in F, a few salon pieces, and had my Symphony in B♭ performed. The paying public was small: quite the reverse, the non-paying members of the public being numerous; in general it is impossible to see an empty auditorium here, as critics and artists of the first rank are represented in such a large number that they occupy half the hall. Then, each artist has several families of his acquaintance who have known him for many years, have borne him in their arms and feel a true concern for him—but not paying; this makes up three quarters of the auditorium. One quarter remains for the charitable souls who attend the concert out of idleness; but the present times are so serious and occupy people to such an extent that this last part of the auditorium was represented very poorly, with the result that I had to pay from my own pocket 260 florins for this concert. The success was most satisfactory, but, as usual, I was not to the critics' taste; there is only one person who, from a strange accident of fate, had to be favorable to me, even if he did not want to be, simply because he is marrying a girl from a family of my close acquaintance, and this is precisely the Bogeyman of the pack."[57]

The bogeyman was Leopold Zellner, who, in fact, had defended Rubinstein against his harsh critics in the pages of the *Blätter für Musik, Theater und Kunst*. Rubinstein must have been immensely grateful to Zellner and rewarded him by dedicating to him his recently completed Symphony No. 3 in A major.[58] "Mr. Zellner, however, is a good musician, a composer himself, and he can be numbered among those rare critics who write for the sake of art and not against artists," he told Liszt.[59] Some of the hostility toward Rubinstein in the Viennese press may have been prompted by the anti-Russian stance of Austria at the end of the Crimean War. This, however, had very little direct influence on his relations with musicians, and he probably sought the acquaintance of many of the leading figures in Viennese musical life: Carl Eckert, who had been appointed the first permanent conductor of the court opera the previous year; Joseph Hellmesberger, the artistic director of the Gesellschaft für Musikfreunde; and Johann Herbeck, the then choirmaster of the Piaristenkirche. As far as the publishers were concerned, Rubinstein found that the ground was "infertile." "Haslinger does not want to take anything large, and since I have dried up as far as salon pieces are concerned, we agreed that he would take the fantasy *A Ball in 1750*,[60] to match the *Le Bal* for Bock,[61] with gigues, sarabandes, etc.—as soon as I finish it. Spina seems to be prepared to take the Concerto in F, but nothing is yet resolved; the others do not count, as they only want to take little pieces and I am tired of turning them out."[62] His *Persian Songs*, on the other hand, were soon to be published by Kistner in Leipzig, and he had given instructions to Gurkhaus to send a copy to Liszt as soon as they were ready.

A few weeks later Rubinstein wrote to Carl Schuberth about his enthusiastic reception in the Austrian capital, which had been marred only by the hostility of the critics who had abused him more than the cholera epidemic. Gustav Lewy (the owner of the music shop in Vienna) had produced a lithograph portrait of him and he asked Schuberth to recommend it to Bernhard, along with a subscription to Zellner's journal *Blätter für Musik, Theater und Kunst*. Although he had finished his A major Symphony two months earlier, Rubinstein had decided against sending it to Schuberth, as he had assumed that there would be no concerts of the Philharmonic Society because of the death of Nicholas I (on 18 February/2 March 1855). For similar reasons he had also withheld his recently composed *Ouverture Triomphale* in C for the accession of the new emperor. With the Crimean War still dominating European politics, Rubinstein's plans for the coming months were uncertain. Until the war was over, it would be unseemly for him, a Russian patriot, to travel to Paris or London. His other options were to return to Russia in November or remain in Germany for another year. Some time in late April or May he returned to Biebrich, where he received a letter from his mother that quite dumbfounded him.

Marriage of Nikolay Rubinstein

In his reply on 10/22 May 1855 he wrote to Kaleriya Khristoforovna: "Your letter received today astounded me extraordinarily. So Nikolay is getting married! I did not take him to be such an idiot: to get married at twenty is unheard of. Apply all your efforts to ensure that he completes his university studies at least and does not become unhappy for the rest of his life for the sake of this marriage. Perhaps he thinks that he will find a good position because of this; but could he not have just restricted himself to courting the girl? I hope that nothing more will result from this because that would be extremely sad."[63] The woman whom Nikolay was to marry was Yelizaveta Dmitriyevna Khrushchova, his senior by around ten years, and the daughter of a prominent Moscow official. The marriage was not only impulsive but also unequal, and it was to last little more than three years. Nikolay's later recollections of the event were apparently vague, and he attributed his actions to "the stubbornness of youth."[64] From the start the marriage was opposed by Kaleriya Khristoforovna and her daughters. They were particularly outraged by one of the principal conditions laid down by the Khrushchovs: Nikolay had to abandon his career entirely as a public performer, as it was thought unseemly for their daughter to be associated with someone who entertained people for money. Yelizaveta's father, Dmitry Mikhaylovich Khrushchov, had served in the Preobrazhensky Regiment life-guards and was later made a chamberlain and an actual state councillor. Catherine Drinker Bowen also intimates that the Khrushchovs opposed the marriage on anti-Semitic grounds but were persuaded to acquiesce because of Nikolay's high-society connections.[65] After his marriage Nikolay gave music lessons for about a year and a half, and eventually, at the beginning of February 1857, secured himself a permanent position at the Nikolayevsky Institute for Orphans in Moscow. Anton's reaction to the sudden news of Nikolay's imminent marriage highlights a degree of ambiguity on his part. Outwardly he shows complete brotherly concern and expresses his indignation that both Villoing and Yakov Veynberg should have approved the match. He protests to his mother: "If I knew that my words would have any significance for him, I would write and try to dissuade him while there is still time."[66] At the same time the old feeling of rivalry, which is never apparent in his relations with his elder brother, Yakov, bubbled to the surface. His own attempts at "social climbing" through a liaison with Anne de Friedebourg had failed miserably, and he may have felt some envy at the possibility that Nikolay was marrying into such an influential family: "Please write to me which Khrushchova Nikolay is marrying . . . Is it the family of the knight marshal of the Grand Duchess Yekaterina?" he asked his mother. Most important, at a time when Anton was himself contemplating a return to Russia, he was anxious to know whether "Nikolay intends establishing himself in Moscow or St. Petersburg and does he have any expectations of a post, and what sort of post he could lay claim to."[67]

Meanwhile, Anton remained in Biebrich until the beginning of October, still wondering whether to go back to Russia. There were compelling reasons for him to stay, for, as he informed Kaleriya Khristoforovna: "I am getting closer and closer to my aim—to make my name as a composer. Already artists are playing my compositions in their concerts . . . in short, everything is going well."[68] Some of his compositions were already being published, including certain songs and the cycle *Kamennïy Ostrov*, which Schott brought out toward the end of 1855. Liszt continued to send him words of warm encouragement from Weimar, where Berhard Cossmann and Edmund Singer had taken part in a performance of the Piano Trio in G minor and where the Duchess Sophie had been delighted with the *Persian Songs* dedicated to her. There were cautionary words, too, for a recently completed fugue (possibly one from Rubinstein's Op. 53 set) had not pleased Liszt. He likened it to the turgid counterpoint in an oratorio by Friedrich Karl Kühmstedt who had conducted his work in Weimar at the beginning of April, and which Liszt characterized as being like an unsalted and unpeppered sausage. None of this discouraged Rubinstein from intensive composition. The few months spent in Biebrich had enabled him to complete his work on the ten-movement suite of old dances, but, despite previous assurances to the contrary, he complained: "that monster Haslinger does not want to take it."[69] He had also written some shorter salon pieces that he had promised to Gustav Lewy in Vienna, as well as his Third Piano Sonata dedicated to the Countess Kalergis, the Viola Sonata in F minor, and he had also made a start on his String Quintet in F. The most important work that absorbed him, however, was the setting of *Das Verlorene Paradies*, which, as he told Liszt: "I have begun, but very much fear has proved lost to me in view of the difficulty of the task . . .

I shall send you the first part and the vocal score when I finish it. Please be so kind as to return it with your comments because I feel that this work can only be completed in consultation with those people who are closest of all to these rarefied spheres."[70]

Composers in Russia

Another of the tasks occupying Rubinstein during the summer months was an article about composers in Russia. At the beginning of April Liszt had written to him: "for the few artists who have sense, intelligence, and a serious honest will, it is really their duty to take up the pen in defense of our Art and our conviction."[71] Rubinstein took up this challenge with a highly contentious article called "Russische Komponisten," declaring to his mother somewhat naïvely (or condescendingly, depending on one's viewpoint): "I have to do something for my countrymen!"[72] The article appeared in the Viennese journal *Blätter für Musik, Theater und Kunst* and was greeted with howls of derision by many Russian composers and musicians. In one of the key points of the article Rubinstein questioned whether national art could have any significance within the broader context of European culture. His perception of the Russian folk song, in particular, was bound to bring him into bitter conflict with Glinka, Dargomïzhsky, Stasov, and Serov. While acknowledging the great beauty of the Russian folk song, he continues: "they are characterized by a melancholy and plaintive coloring, and a certain monotony, and since this gloomy character is maintained for the most part even in cheerful or dance melodies, it is understandable that an entire opera (in this spirit) would hardly be understood abroad, where there is no nationalist interest in it."[73] Although Rubinstein had praised Glinka, describing him as the Russian composer of the greatest genius, he reproached him for the bold and unhappy (unglücklichen) idea of writing a national opera. *A Life for the Tsar* and Glinka's later opera *Ruslan and Lyudmila*, in his opinion, both suffered from the same deficiency: monotony. He argued that national music could only exist as folk songs and dances, and therefore "national opera, strictly speaking, does not exist." For Rubinstein, the range of human feelings—love, jealousy, vengeance, happiness, and sorrow—were common to all peoples, and therefore their expression in an opera should not have a national coloring but a universal character:

> In Vienna I happened to write about the position of music in Russia for a German newspaper. I praised Glinka to the heavens, since I had always respected him: I compared him to Beethoven. Toward other Russian composers I was very disparaging. They were so embittered that they wanted to have the matter taken up through the courts or the police. I believe Yelena Pavlovna helped me out. Writing this article was an act of rank stupidity on my part, although I do not regret it, since it is not my habit, in general, to regret the foolish things I may have happened to do.[74]

But the damage was done and Rubinstein's critics in Russia would never forgive him. Even Glinka, whom Rubinstein had genuinely praised in his article, was incensed for he wrote to his friend Vasily Engelgardt: "Rubinstein has taken it upon himself to familiarize Germany with our music and has written an article in which he has played dirty tricks on us all and has even offended my old girl *A Life for the Tsar* in a rather impertinent way. On this matter, a few days ago the *St.-Petersbourger Zeitung*, no. 3, published a feuilleton in defence of my old girl, and heaping scorn on the impudent . . . "[75] Henceforward, in the eyes of many of his countrymen, Rubinstein would never be able to avoid derision for having equated nationalism with dilettantism. A rift had opened up between him and the nationalists that only widened as the years went by. Every action, every proposal he put forward, came to be treated with the utmost suspicion and was often opposed simply on principle.

Rubinstein was still considering a trip to London, but he abandoned the idea out of "patriotic feelings." The idea of returning to St. Petersburg still haunted him, for, as he confided to Kaleriya Khristoforovna, "all the time I have the urge to return to Russia. But who knows what will face me there. I am becoming more serious in my art, and that will be little to the taste of our dilettantes in music. I would also solicit a post now, but if I am refused again, that would be decisive for my future work. However, I am speaking about those things which are in the unknown future."[76] In mid-July 1854 Kaleriya Khristoforovna had moved from Odessa to Moscow and had already been engaged as a teacher at Madame Knol's boarding school on Kislovka for more than a year. The work was evidently a strain, but Rubinstein advised her not to allow her teaching duties to tax her: "Things will go best if you can reach that stage in teaching where the teacher conducts his lesson with absolute coolness and does not ruin his life for the sake of a pupil. That is the way all great teachers do it."[77]

By early October 1855 Rubinstein had already arrived in Leipzig, where on 7 October he played the solo part in his Piano Concerto No. 3 at one of the Gewandhaus subscription concerts. Writing to Kaleriya Khristoforovna two days later, he told her that he was still thinking about returning to Russia, as he felt physically tired and dissatisfied with his role as a "commercial traveler" with his works. Within a month, however, he had already decided to delay his return to Russia for a year, explaining that he wanted to finish *Das Verlorene Paradies,* a work that could not be given in Russia, only in Germany. "If the oratorio is a success," he wrote, "I shall consolidate my name, and in that case I can rest calmly in Russia for a prolonged period of time."[78] During these fall months he was already composing part 2 of the oratorio and planned to spend the summer of 1856 orchestrating it, with a view to a performance the following fall. He also found time to work on the group of three string quartets that make up his Op. 47, and on 10 November he wrote to Liszt enclosing one of them, asking him to oversee the preparation of the work if he found it worthy of a public performance.

On 8 November Rubinstein attended the first performance of Wagner's *Faust*

Overture at the Gewandhaus and accorded it a rare accolade: "In my opinion, as an instrumental work this piece is the most important of those I know [by Wagner], and in some places this is a first-rate work in terms of its design."[79] At the same concert he played some of his own salon pieces, including the "Valse" from his fantasy *Le Bal.* Before he began playing, he turned to Rietz who was seated near the piano, and proclaimed "Res severa est verum gaudium" [A serious work is a true joy], reiterating the words inscribed in large letters over the auditorium. According to Rubinstein, this remark quite delighted the audience. The next day he walked to Halle with David in order to attend the first concert of the Masonic lodge where David played in the orchestra. "I paid court to Mlle Wunderlich, who, if not exactly a prima donna, is at least a bella donna,"[80] Rubinstein joked cynically with Liszt. The composer Robert Franz had shown him several new pieces, which had impressed him by their elegance, but Rubinstein was less enthusiastic about Franz's treatment of folk songs. He had been hard on the Russian nationalist composers for their inappropriate (as he saw it) use of folk songs, but, in Rubinstein's view, Franz, too, had been unable to escape "their monotony." The end of the year was drawing near, but Rubinstein declined Carolyne von Sayn-Wittgenstein's invitation to spend Christmas at the Altenburg. He had decided to remain in Leipzig.

The start of the New Year found Rubinstein in Hamburg, where he again performed his Piano Concerto No. 3 and some smaller piano pieces on 6 January 1856. A few days later he was obliged to pen a rather tactful letter to Edith von Raden, the secretary of Grand Duchess Yelena Pavlovna, concerning his former relations with Anne de Friedebourg. Before departing from St. Petersburg, Rubinstein had clearly proposed to de Friedebourg. She in her turn had agreed to await his return before accepting his offer. "I set myself a fundamental aim—to try to secure a more brilliant position than I could have offered to Fridebourg previously," Rubinstein told Raden. Because of his long absence from Russia and his failure to achieve the kind of material success he had dreamed of, Friedebourg had broken (or had been persuaded to break) her promise and had agreed to marry Theodor Leschetizky. Rubinstein does not appear to have been particularly upset by this development: "This is, of course, the best thing she could have done. I congratulate her with all my heart and I am grateful that she has thereby lightened my load, since henceforth I shall have to work for myself, which is easier than working for two." It is apparent, however, that Raden had been against the match from the beginning, and perhaps she had even encouraged Friedebourg to change suitors, for Rubinstein concludes, "and I hope that the actions which have been taken and the circumstances, annulling in this way your reproaches to me before my departure, will convince you to accord me fairness, while preserving a happy memory of me and allowing me the gift of your respect, which you once thought necessary to deprive me of, and toward which all my thoughts are directed."[81]

After Hamburg Rubinstein gave concerts in Bremen and Hanover, informing Senff in a letter of 6 February that he was pleased about the corrections of his *Six Songs,* Op. 8, that were dedicated to Aleksandra Sokolova. Senff published them later that year in the German translations by Wilhelm Osterwald. In Hanover Rubinstein met Brahms and Grimm, and renewed his acquaintance with Joachim. "Of the three of them," Rubinstein told Liszt, "it was he [Joachim] who interested me most; he produced the impression of a lay brother in a monastery who knows that he still has the choice between the monastery and the secular world, and has not yet resolved which it is to be. As far as Brahms is concerned, I cannot define precisely the impression he produced on me; for the salon he is not sufficiently gracious, for the concert hall he is not sufficiently fiery, for the fields he is not simple enough, and for the town he is insufficiently versatile. I have little faith in such natures. Grimm appeared to me like an unfinished sketch of Schumann."[82]

From Hanover, Rubinstein traveled first to Brunswick and then to Cologne, where he visited Ferdinand Hiller, Kapellmeister of the city, and the pianist and music editor Hans Bischoff. "Hiller is very courteous to me," he informed Liszt, "although he does not yet know what opinion he should have about me as a composer. Bischoff and his cohorts are exact copies of what you will find in any town where there are musicians—that is, so to speak, an urban, musical Cerberus: you risk being devoured as you enter, and you can rest assured that you will not be spared as you leave, even if you have managed to flatter Satan (the audience) and the other evil spirits (the musicians)."[83] From Cologne Rubinstein proceeded to Bonn, Coblenz, Mainz, and then Stuttgart, where he remained for almost three months.

Das Verlorene Paradies

Rubinstein's chief purpose in resting in Stuttgart was to complete the orchestration of *Das Verlorene Paradies,* and on 19 July he was able to inform Senff with a certain self-satisfied conviction: "I have created, in as far as my strength has allowed, something good." On 8 August he left for Weimar, taking with him his *berüchtige* [notorious] trunk full of manuscripts, but the Hungarian composer was not at home. As a consequence he headed straight for Berlin in an effort to get his oratorio performed there. His endeavors, however, were beset with difficulties. He offered it to Julius Stern, the eminent conductor of the celebrated Sternscher Gesangverein, but Stern turned it down, saying that the king had requested an oratorio by Karl Reinthaler and that he was already engaged in preparing Beethoven's *Mass* in D, Handel's *Israel in Egypt,* and Mendelssohn's *Paulus* for other concerts. The Singakademie, then directed by Eduard Grell, also rejected it on the grounds that "it proposes to be involved only with works by famous composers and those who died long ago." There were hopes that Julius Benedict might perform it at the Norwich Festival in England the following year, but Rubinstein doubted his sincerity, for "a promise which has to be fulfilled in a year's time is easily given."[84] The only other option was to have the oratorio performed at his personal expense, but that was completely impossible, especially since the annual salary he received from the grand duchess Yelena had ceased after his departure from Russia in 1854.

On his return to Weimar, Liszt learned of Rubinstein's visit and promptly dispatched to him some of his own scores that Breitkopf and Härtel had recently published (the symphonic poems *Tasso, Prometheus, Les Préludes, Orphée, Mazeppa, and Festklänge*). Despite Rubinstein's intense dislike of Liszt's music, he responded affably, congratulating Liszt on the success of his *Messe à Gran* written for the inauguration of the basilica at Esztergom. It was not without a note of envy, however, that he added: "You are a lucky man, having the opportunity to hear and have so much of what you compose performed."[85] Rubinstein must have seen that there were distinct advantages in securing an appointment to one of the city orchestras. On 21 August Peter Lindpainter, the Kapellmeister of the court orchestra in Stuttgart had died. Mendelssohn had once declared him to be the "best conductor in Germany," and Rubinstein briefly considered applying for his job, for this would have given him an excellent opportunity to have his own works performed regularly. In the end this idea came to nothing.

Having completed his oratorio, Rubinstein was already thinking about a new opera libretto. Carolyne von Wittgenstein came up with the idea of an opera based on the Hussite revolt, but Rubinstein rejected it, claiming that Meyerbeer had already exhausted all the possibilities for expressing religious strife in music with *Les Huguenots*. He had high hopes that the writer Max Ring would find him a suitable operatic subject, but so far nothing had materialized. During his stay in Berlin Rubinstein often met Joachim at the home of Bettina von Arnim. He also went to see Meyerbeer, who recorded in his diary on 30 October: "Rubinstein played me the second part of his oratorio *Das verlorene Paradies*."[86] When Rubinstein called on Glinka, however, the latter was still mortified by the article on Russian composers published in *Blätter für Musik, Theater und Kunst* and received him coldly. "Rubinstein is here," he wrote to Dmitry Stasov on 11/23 August 1856, "he is spending the winter here with the intention of presenting his *Le paradis perdu* after Milton."[87] In his *Autobiography* Rubinstein described his meeting with Glinka:

> The attitude of Mikhail Ivanovich Glinka toward me was very strange. In past years, here in St. Petersburg, he was affable, as all people are affable to one another. In the 1850s, when I had already become a composer, he did not treat me in an affable manner. In Berlin in 1855, after the appearance of the above-mentioned article, I visited him. He received me very badly and began to read me a lecture to the effect: "I do not understand . . . " Had he been referring to others! But he ought not to have been speaking of himself in such a fashion! I had, after all, compared him to Beethoven. We parted politely enough. But by then he was ill and irritable.[88]

Glinka died in Berlin on 3 February 1857. Many years later, on 20 May/2 June 1885, a monument to him, sculpted by Aleksandr Bok, was unveiled at his birthplace—Smolensk. The funds for this monument had been collected on the initiative of Glinka's sister, Lyudmila Shestakova, and Balakirev conducted concerts of the composer's works for the unveiling. The event was attended by all the most prominent Russian musicians of the day, including Rubinstein, who would later recall with irony:

I gave a concert in aid of erecting a monument to Glinka. I can almost say that without me this monument would not have been erected so soon. At the inauguration ceremony they invited everyone except me. I was invited by public notice as ordinary members of the public are. This is rather strange. Everyone thinks that I am piled high with laurels and honors, but I have never had anything but insults.[89]

In the fall of 1856 the grand duchess Yelena Pavlovna recalled Rubinstein to Moscow to take part in the coronation celebrations for Alexander II. He also received a one-time payment of one thousand rubles to accompany her on a visit to Nice, where she and the dowager empress Aleksandra Fyodorovna took up residence at the Villa Abigore and the Villa Bermine. Rubinstein's nominal position as the grand duchess's secretary suited him, for it gave him an official rank which assisted in eliminating some of the problems he was having with his passport.

The Crimean War had ended at the beginning of 1856, and the peace was concluded with the Treaty of Paris in February. While Russian public opinion was extremely hostile toward Great Britain and Austria, the attitude of Russian official circles to France was somewhat different. Despite French participation in the war against Russia, the years 1856–59 saw "an ostentatious display of Franco-Russian friendship," motivated principally by the political interests of the two governments.[90] On the Russian side, this rapprochement was fostered by the new foreign minister Prince Aleksandr Gorchakov and involved visits by high-ranking officials and members of the immediate imperial family. The visit of the dowager empress Aleksandra Fyodorovna and Grand Duchess Yelena Pavlovna to Nice in January 1857, for example, was one such diplomatic move devised by Gorchakov. Rubinstein joined Yelena Pavlovna's suite early in 1857, and, amid the diplomatic moves intended to repair the damage done by the Crimean campaign, the idea of the Russian Music Society was born:

After the coronation, Aleksandra Fyodorovna and Yelena Pavlovna went to Nice. I received an invitation to spend a little time there. Yelena Pavlovna summoned me to go there as her "stoker." This was something akin to a position, true, but it was not an official position and the salary was not monthly but now and again. The ageing Aleksandra Fyodorovna was very ill (she had lost her husband and the Crimean War) . . . Victor Emanuel, the King of Sardinia, came here more than once. He arranged balls and soirées, was very charming with the ladies, tried to brighten them up and, in so doing, to smooth away the bad memories of his involvement in the Crimean campaign.[91] It was then that I chanced to see Cavour. The court spent its time in Nice very pleasantly. Aleksandra Fyodorovna did not spare the money. A frigate was standing in the bay. People came from Russia. Yelena Pavlovna bought a villa. It was here that the idea of founding the Russian Musical Society and a Conservatory was born. There were discussions with Matvey Wielhorski (the other brother was already dead) about the necessity of doing something, since the position of music in Russia was lamentable in all respects. Yelena Pavlovna became interested in this. To undertake what and how: we could not yet envisage.[92]

While Rubinstein was in the employ of the grand duchess he was prevented from appearing in any public concerts, and he complained that he was living the life of an idler: "I am doing nothing and I regard this winter as lost time for me."[93] Only toward the end of February was he free to travel to Paris, bearing the lavish gifts he had received from the royal visitors to the Villa Abigore. From Paris he wrote to Kaleriya Khristoforovna on 3/15 April: "It is already three weeks since I left Nice, showered with gifts and compliments from the court. Still, I am sincerely glad that I have finished with it, for as a thinking person this cannot be pleasant for a long time."[94] On 14 April he gave his first concert in the French capital at the Salle Erard. On this occasion his String Quartet in C minor was performed by Jacquard, Lalo, Kazimir Ney, and Lepré, and Vieuxtemps joined him in a performance of his A minor Violin Sonata.[95] He described the success as being "more in honor than in gold,"[96] for the concert was given for publicity purposes and without a paying audience. A second concert followed eight days later at the Salle Herz on 23 April, when Rubinstein accompanied Pauline Viardot and Julius Stockhausen in some of his songs (including the *Persian Songs*) and he performed some smaller piano pieces.[97] A final concert followed toward the end of April when Rubinstein performed his Piano Concerto No. 3 and took the baton for his Symphony in B♭ major.

Rubinstein arrived in London in mid-May. He had received a letter of recommendation to Prince Albert from the grand duchess and had forwarded it to the court via the Russian Embassy. Some days later he was accompanied to the palace by Colonel Phipps, one of Prince Albert's adjutants, and found "to his astonishment the entire royal family—cousins, aunts and uncles—wearing full decorations and orders, standing in a semi-circle to receive him."[98] Rubinstein was perplexed by the stiffness and silence with which they greeted him and later learned that his "letter having come through the Russian Embassy, while several secret diplomatic missions connected with the late war were going on at the same time, he had been mistaken for a secret agent of the Russian court coming to London in the disguise of a musician."[99] This misapprehension was apparently soon remedied by Rubinstein's brilliant playing. At his first public appearance in London on 18 May Rubinstein performed his Piano Concerto No. 3 at a Philharmonic Society concert conducted by William Sterndale Bennett at the Hanover Square Rooms. Few people, except the conductor, liked the work, and Gerald Norris quotes from a letter of Arthur Sullivan who heard Rubinstein play the concerto. While according Rubinstein great technical skill, he deplored the concerto, considering it "a disgrace to the Philharmonic. I never heard such wretched, nonsensical rubbish."[100]

On Friday 5 June the music critic Henry Chorley took the Russian novelist Ivan Turgenev to a musical soirée at the Beethoven Rooms in Harley Street, and there they heard Rubinstein play.[101] Turgenev was apparently unimpressed, but Chorley wrote an enthusiastic review for the *Atheneum*. Rubinstein also appeared in several of John Ella's Musical Union concerts, which at that time were held at the Willis's Rooms on King Street. Ella, himself a violinist, had founded the Musical Union in 1845 to encourage the performance of chamber music, and as a result the Beethoven Quartet Society was founded. The program for Tuesday, 9 June, was as follows:

Onslow: Quartet in B♭, Op. 21
Goss: Glee: "Ossian's Hymn to the Sun"
Rubinstein: Trio in B♭, Op. 52
Mozart: Recitative and aria "Mi tradi" from *Don Giovanni* with Mme Stubbe
Beethoven: Quartet in A from Op. 18
Rubinstein: Romance and Impromptu, Op.26; Courante in A minor from the Suite, Op. 38; and Etude No.2 in C from the *Six Etudes,* Op. 23
Rubinstein: Two songs: *Die Lerche,* Op. 33, No. 2, and *Lied,* Op. 32, No.5

The quartet had its regular players: Herr Goffrie (second violin), Richard Blagrove (viola), and Alfredo Piatti (cellist), but it was the custom to invite foremost violinists of the day to lead the quartet: on this occasion it was the eminent Italian violinist Camillo Sivori. Despite the distraction of the races at Ascot, "the concert was fully attended by the musical aristocracy," wrote the music critic for the *Globe*. However, the same critic was at pains to warn his readers: "To those who prefer the passive inanimate style of running quietly over the notes, as a satirist once observed, without disturbing the dust on the keys, Rubinstein's powers of execution will give them cause for alarm." The trio, however, "was rapturously received" and the *presto* movement was encored.[102] Goffrie gave a special entertainment in honor of Rubinstein at rooms on Harley Street, where Rubinstein performed his own Cello Sonata, Op. 18, with Guillaume Paque, and Herr von der Osten sang some of his *Persian Songs*. Rubinstein's last appearance in London that season was in another of John Ella's Musical Union concerts on 23 June. This time the French violinist Prosper Sainton led the quartet in works by Mendelssohn and Beethoven, and Rubinstein took the piano part in a performance of his own Cello Sonata.

Toward the end of June Rubinstein returned to Paris for a few weeks, but he was soon summoned to Baden-Baden by Yelena Pavlovna who held court there during July and August. Rubinstein wrote to Senff that he wanted to write a violin concerto—and if that is successful, then a cello concerto as well. For the time being only the Violin Concerto in G, Op. 46, was completed, and it was published by C. F. Peters in Leipzig in 1859. During the late fall and winter season Rubinstein played in Leipzig and Vienna. In Leipzig he was joined by Ferdinand David in a performance of the Trio in B♭, Op. 52, at a Gewandhaus chamber concert, and on 12 November the Gewandhaus orchestra performed his Symphony in F major, Op. 40.

In Vienna Rubinstein gave five concerts and Hanslick devoted a separate article to Rubinstein (subsequently reprinted in the book *Aus dem Concert-Saal* in 1897). "In the artistic sense I was extraordinarily happy in Vienna," Rubinstein told his mother in a letter of 29 December 1857/10 January 1858. "There were many honors, and on this occasion even a little money."[103] He also informed her that before leaving Vienna he expected to receive an opera libretto: "That is, to see my cherished dream fulfilled, for at the present time, only with an opera can one achieve real success; we may assume that it will be successful—my passionate desire is a guarantee of this."[104] There was good news about *Das Verlorene Paradies,* too, for after Rubinstein's unsuccessful efforts to secure a performance in Berlin, Liszt had agreed to perform it at Weimar in the spring.

Rubinstein knew that the coming season would be a taxing one, and he even considered abandoning his career as a concert virtuoso when the season was over. His busy schedule took him first to Pest in Hungary, where he gave six concerts between 28 December 1857 and 27 January 1858. In these concerts he repeated the Vienna programs but also included his *Fantaisie sur les mélodies hongroises* which had hastily been completed that winter. His next destination was to be Dresden via Prague, where he gave two more concerts. Yakov's duties in Poland were due to end in December, and Anton had tried to persuade his brother to accompany him on his winter-season tour of Europe. Yakov would be able to help him arrange his concerts, and the trip would also give him a good opportunity to familiarize himself with the latest medical practices in other countries. The brothers had arranged to meet in Dresden at the end of January, and now Rubinstein was eagerly awaiting news. "If he doesn't come now," he told his mother, "it will hardly be worth it, for only five months [of the season] remain, and in Germany, where, as a doctor, it will be most interesting for him to be, the chance will have been lost entirely."[105]

Relations between Nikolay and his wife were reaching a crisis, and Anton felt that the situation would now soon be resolved: "I am sincerely pleased that Nikolay has chosen the correct path, that he is not making coup d'états at home, and that he does not need to have recourse to the protection of his mother-in-law. All this and time will yet bring him happiness and, perhaps, free him from the regret of the reckless step he took in his youth."[106] No doubt he was also gratified to hear from Kaleriya Khristoforovna that Nikolay had played the piano part in a performance of his brother's Trio in B♭ in Moscow. Banned from giving public performances under the marriage conditions imposed by the Khrushchovs, Nikolay still appeared in semi-public performances of chamber music with the violinists Yuly Gerber and Karl Klamrot and the cellist Schmidt. It was no great surprise to Rubinstein to learn from his mother shortly afterward that Nikolay and Yelizaveta Krushchova had separated (although they were never actually divorced).

From Prague Rubinstein traveled to Weimar for the premiere of *Das Verlorene Paradies* on 1 March 1858, and on the next day reported to Senff that it was a brilliant performance—"or Liszt is a wizard."[107] Everyone had claimed to like the music, especially the second part, and he had been complimented by the grand duke. The oratorio was conceived on a grand scale. It is divided into three parts and requires eight soloists. There is much in the general design of part 1 of the oratorio that anticipates the first act of the opera *The Demon*: the use of opposing choruses of "good" and "wicked" angels, for example, and the set aria for Satan. As in Rubinstein's portrayal of the Demon, we are not meant to see in Lucifer merely the incarnation of evil. He is Prometheus stealing fire from the Gods; he is the tragic Byronic hero who suffers because of noble pride and love of freedom. Against such restless and vital passions the forces of heaven can seem almost dull: "Lucifer, of light the Angel, seeks a monarch now to be.

And the lovely flower wreath of duty and humility rashly snatches from his head. Therefore, Prince of Heaven's armies, Raphael, Michael, Gabriel, commence the fight! Chase hence the Fiend to the brink of Heaven. Then hurl him downward into Hell's depths, 'mid flaming chaos,"[108] exclaims the voice in No.4. Satan rises to the challenge (No.5): "Come all to me, who are ready to combat for freedom!" and in the ensuing chorus Rubinstein provides quite vigorous and rousing music for: "On, on, on, on, attack the Tyrant's throne," where the basses, tenors, altos, and sopranos enter in canonic imitation (D minor). At the beginning of part 2 the Voice (narrator) calls for an end to the chaos. The culmination of the act of Creation is a magnificent choral fugue in C major: "Praise ye the Mighty one." In the final part Adam and Eve are banished from Paradise, while in another grand fugue the Rebel Angels rejoice over the undoing of "Creation's masterwork." The two rival choruses continue to battle it out with increasing fury. The archangels express the hope that mankind may yet regain paradise, but the oratorio ends with the closing of the gates of Paradise.

After Weimar, Rubinstein traveled first to Paris and then to London. His endeavors to obtain a satisfactory opera libretto had been unsuccessful: the one commissioned in Vienna from Hebbel had proved useless, but under the terms of the contract he was still obliged to pay eight hundred guelders. It was a matter of great regret, he lamented, that Scribe would not write for young composers. In Paris Rubinstein gave four concerts in March and April, and also accompanied Wieniawski in a program that included the *Kreutzer Sonata*. In the first concert on 18 March Richard Hammer directed the orchestra in a performance that the composer gave of his Piano Concerto No. 2. The second concert followed on 11 April, when Rubinstein performed both his piano concertos No. 2 and No. 3 at the Salle Herz. A year earlier, when Rubinstein had made appearances in Paris, the young Camille Saint-Saëns had failed to make the personal acquaintance of the Russian pianist. In the spring of 1858, encouraged most likely by Pauline Viardot and Turgenev, he was more successful. Saint-Saëns vividly recalled Rubinstein's appearances the previous season: "As for the gods of the piano, the race of them seemed to be forever extinct, when one fine day a little full-length notice appeared on the walls of Paris, bearing this name: Antoine Rubinstein, of whom no one had yet heard anything; for this great artist had the foolhardy coyness to disdain the assistance of the press, and no publicity, none, you understand me, had announced his appearance."[109] When Rubinstein conducted a performance of the *Ocean Symphony* at his third Paris concert in mid-April 1858, the young Frenchman astounded him by sight-reading complex passages from the score at the piano. Subsequently they often played duets together, and this seemed to seal their friendship. Saint-Saëns was genuinely impressed by Rubinstein's artistic integrity: "I was so happy to have met an artist who was truly an artist, devoid of the paltriness that sometimes so sadly attends the greatest talents."[110]

In London, Grisi, Mario, Rossi, and Tamberlick were appearing to full houses at the Crystal Palace and at the Royal Italian Opera, Covent Garden, where Meyerbeer's *Les Huguenots* was being performed. On Friday 11 June 1858 the

Times announced that the Musical Union had engaged Rubinstein for the remaining Tuesdays of the month (i.e., 15, 22, 29 June) for their subscription concerts that were now held at the St James's Hall. The same day (11 June) Rubinstein appeared in a concert with Joachim given by the Royal Society of Female Musicians under the direction of William Sterndale Bennett.[111] His first Musical Union concert was on 15 June, as indicated above, and the program included Spohr's Double Quartet in E minor; Rubinstein's Piano Trio No. 2 in G minor, Op. 15, No. 2 (wrongly billed as "the first time"), and Mozart's Quartet in D. The artists were listed as Sainton, [Henry] Blagrove, Goffrie, Piatti, [Louis] Ries, [Richard] Blagrove, Webb, and [Guillaume] Paque. Piano—Rubinstein. During this same London season Rubinstein played Weber's *Concertstück* at a concert of the Philharmonic Society (7 June) and solo piano works by Mozart, Beethoven, Field, and Mendelssohn. It was also on this visit to London that Rubinstein made the personal acquaintance of Julius Rodenberg, who ten years later would furnish him with the text for the oratorio *Der Thurm zu Babel*. For the moment Rodenberg beguiled Rubinstein with his literary refashioning of Solomon's *Song of Songs*, but it was not until 1882 that his texts eventually found their ultimate incarnation in the opera *Sulamith*.

At the beginning of July Rubinstein returned to Paris for eight days, where he performed with Wieniawski, and then traveled to Leipzig via Weimar.[112] Finally, he returned to Russia, arriving in Petersburg around 4/16 September. He went to see Yakov, whom he found in good health, but few people, including the grand duchess, had yet returned to St. Petersburg for the start of the winter season. A few weeks later Rubinstein went to Moscow, but Kaleriya Khristoforovna had rented a dacha in the nearby village of Bogorodskoye, and it was there that a notable event took place—after many years of separation, the entire Rubinstein family assembled (Kaleriya Khristoforovna, Anton, Nikolay, and Yakov, Sofiya and Lyuba). By this time Nikolay's separation from Yelizaveta Khrushchova was already a fait accompli, and Kashkin tells us that, "the couple separated without any quarrel or anger, but also without regret."[113] Anton was pleased at Nikolay's separation from Yelizaveta Khrushchova and enthusiastically supported his intention to resume his career as a concert artist. He even suggested that Nikolay should go abroad with him for a six-month period to find a lucrative post somewhere. The plan did not materialize, as, in the words of Barenboym, Nikolay "did not want to live on the money of his elder brother."[114] What did materialize during those late summer months, however, was a coming together of minds; the entire family took part in discussions about reforming musical education in Russia, and many of their cherished ideas began to take on a more positive shape. In his writings on the founding of the Moscow Conservatory, Kashkin suggests that the broad ideas about the formation of a Russian music society belonged to the elder Rubinstein and the practical details to the younger one.

By mid-October Anton and Yakov were already speeding their way toward St. Petersburg, where the former rented an apartment. Anton was awaiting the return of Yelena Pavlovna, who once again engaged him as her "musical stoker" (in the intervening years Leschetizky had fulfilled this function). Rubinstein described himself to Kaleriya Khristoforovna as a "court jester," spending his time now in the palace of the old empress, now at the palace of the new empress, and, of course, at Grand Duchess Yelena Pavlovna's Mikhaylovsky Palace. Even in court circles the hapless position in which Rubinstein found himself was noted. In her reminiscences, Anna Tyutcheva, the daughter of the celebrated poet and a lady-in-waiting to the empress Mariya Aleksandrovna, recalled the following incident. On 11/23 October 1858 she recorded in her diary that she had attended a concert at the Arsenal where Rubinstein and the singer Mlle Stubbe were performing. The dowager empress wanted the youngsters to play race-and-catch at the other end of the Arsenal while the concert was taking place. Their game caused a terrible noise, and Rubinstein did not attempt to disguise his annoyance. Acclaimed throughout Europe as one of the foremost pianists of his generation, he was forced to play for "two Russian empresses to the shouts and noise of the reveling youngsters."[115] Tyutcheva also noted that Rubinstein was obliged to play at court soirées, where he accompanied charades and played parodies of operatic scenes for which any ballroom pianist would have been suited. It was a form of humiliation that Rubinstein found hard to bear. At this critical moment he needed to find a new direction for his life in Russia: he had ruled out taking a post in the imperial theaters because he feared that the terms of his employment would be too restrictive. Although people were talking seriously about conservatories, no one was actually doing anything, and he doubted that anything positive would happen for at least another five years. His greatest hope was to obtain the permanent official position of court pianist, but it was not offered to him and, in the end, Rubinstein received a salary of one thousand rubles for his work in assisting at court functions and continued to receive this payment for a number of years.

Having been deprived of a permanent court position, Rubinstein looked for other ways to channel his energies. He set about trying to goad his fellow musicians into action by organizing Saturday soirées at the Bernardaki Hall. There he joined Pikkel, Veykman, Drobish, Schuberth, Leschetizky, Lewy, Santis, Kross, and other musicians in playing the classical repertory and also some of the latest pieces available from the music shops of Bernard and Bitner. "I have driven the local musicians mad," he told Kaleriya Khristoforovna, "that is to say I have made them rouse themselves and given them a taste for music; I think that this is quite incredible for anyone who knows what life here is like."[116] He also took advantage of Yelena Pavlovna's offer of a room at the Mikhaylovsky Palace to found a "singing academy," where he assumed the unpaid role of artistic director of a mixed choir. "The singing academy is to open this week," he told his mother. "It is opening without any prior claims, but I hope that sooner or later something significant will emerge from it."[117] The existence of choral academies in Russia was not a new phenomenon. At the beginning of Nicholas I's reign, during the second half of the 1820s, two rather short-lived associations had been founded: the Academy of Singing formed by Count Mikhail Wielhorski and the Music Academy (1828) founded by Aleksey Lvov. Throughout the first half of the nineteenth century Lvov had also been the leading representative of the Russian violin school, and two years after his appointment as director of the Imperial Court Cappella in 1837 he introduced instrumental classes. The academies that he and Wielhorski had founded were eventually disbanded, but their example clearly suggested to Rubinstein a way in which institutionalized reform could be introduced in Russia. Although it is not clear whether he resurrected the former institution for his "singing academy," he would certainly have known about it from Mikhail Wielhorski's brother, Matvey.

In October 1858 Nikolay Rubinstein had fallen ill with nervous stress after the breakdown of his marriage to Yelizaveta Khrushchova. He had rented an apartment on Sadovaya Street (the Volotsky house near the Church of St. Ermolay) in Moscow, and early in the New Year he visited Anton in St. Petersburg to discuss their plans to form a music society. Anton informed Kaleriya Khristoforovna on 19/31 January: "I was very pleased at Nikolay's visit. He ought to have spent at least a month here to recuperate from his illness and from the cares of life. But he has become so accustomed to taxing work that even during the days he spent here he was worried that he might have forgotten to do something important at home. I dissuaded him as best I could from giving too many lessons. I hope that he has understood the rightness of this and that from now on he will pay more attention to public duties."[118] By public duties Anton evidently meant a resumption of Nikolay's career as a concert artist, and also playing his part in the long-term plan to found a Moscow branch of the Russian Music Society. This would come into being little more than a year later.

Meanwhile, the news from Vienna was good and Anton was delighted to hear that Josef Hellmesberger had played his recently published String Quintet in F at one of his chamber concerts. At this time Hellmesberger was the artistic director of the Gesellschaft für Musikfreunde. He was shortly to take up a new appointment as professor of the violin at the Vienna Conservatory, but before quitting his old post, he planned to perform the oratorio *Das Verlorene Paradies*. An ecstatic Rubinstein eagerly set about organizing the dispatch of the parts and the vocal score. "This is a large and complex work," he told Hellmesberger, "The choruses, which are its foundation, need to be learned very carefully and require large forces. Things are simpler with the orchestra."[119] He was evidently anxious about the Viennese public's reception of the oratorio, and he warned Hellmesberger about the occasional "harmonic harshness" in the work. Most of all he feared a comparison with Haydn's *Die Schöpfung*, especially in part 2, which also dealt with the Creation. Such factors might seriously affect the financial viability of the performance, and he even told Hellmesberger that he was prepared to defray a few of the costs of performing the oratorio. Two months later, on 6 April 1859, the work was indeed performed. Rubinstein was unable to attend, but he received a telegram from Hellmesberger, informing him that the performance had been a success.

Several important engagements in St. Petersburg prevented Rubinstein from attending the Vienna performance of *Das Verlorene Paradies*. On 28 January/ 9 February he appeared at the Bernardaki Hall together with Pikkel, Veykman, and Schuberth in a concert of chamber music and solo piano music. This was followed by a concert on 4/16 February at which he introduced his Viola Sonata in F minor. A month laterm on 11/23 March, a concert mostly consisting of Rubinstein's works was given at the Bolshoy Theater in St. Petersburg. The program included Rubinstein: Piano Concerto No. 2 in F; Barcarolle No. 2 in A minor; Scherzo; Romance in F, Op. 26, No. 1; a study from Op. 23; Field: Nocturne; Mendelssohn: Lied ohne Worte; Chopin: Nocturne; Study; Berceuse in D♭ major, Op. 57; Beethoven-Rubinstein: March from *The Ruins of Athens;* and Rubinstein: Symphony No. 2.[120] Judging from Turgenev's correspondence, it seems highly likely that the great novelist attended this concert.

Serov and the Anti-Rubinstein Campaign

Serov's review of one of Rubinstein's February concerts was highly critical and marked the beginning of a new phase in the campaign to discredit Rubinstein. The American musicologist Richard Taruskin has given some interesting sidelights on this theme. Serov, for example, praised the appearance of Balakirev's collection of Russian songs published in 1859 but warned him against the difficulty of being a Russian composer in Russia. Serov continues (Taruskin's translation): "A Russian musician must remember at all times that fame, esteem, and money are not for him. For all these things to materialize as in a dream, one needs, besides talent (which hardly matters), first of all not to be Russian, even if born in Russia."[121] Taruskin sees in this remark an "anti-Semitic envy of Rubinstein," which became even more pronounced in the same critic's review of Balakirev's *Overture on Russian Themes*, where he "commiserates with the composer because his name is not Balakirstein."[122] Reference to the anti-Rubinstein campaign (with no references to anti-Semitism) is also made in Marina Cherkashina's book on Serov:

> The criteria that he had worked out for himself as a result of assimilating the lessons of Glinka had an effect on Serov's evaluation of Anton Rubinstein. At that time the cosmopolitan circles of aristocratic melomanes and of German musicians making a career for themselves in the Russian press began actively to extol the musical works of Rubinstein as models of the *new* word in art. The St. Petersburg public's favorite, the "second Beethoven," as his particularly zealous devotees called him, was surrounded with an aura, as a result of which an involuntary shadow was cast over the work of the foremost national talents—Glinka and Dargomïzhsky. The values had been displaced because the same people who praised Rubinstein to the skies reacted casually, superficially, and to some extent with evident disdain toward the creator of *Ruslan* and the composer of *Rusalka*.[123]

One of the zealous devotees of whom Cherkashina speaks was Berthold Damcke, who had first written about Rubinstein in the journal *Biblioteka dlya chteniya* in the early 1850s. Now this German music critic and composer declared in the leading newspaper *Sankt Peterburgskiye vedomosti* (1857, no. 114): "I can say boldly that I was the first in Russia to recognize the noble virtue of his talent; I was the first to speak about him."[124] Such people needed to be taught a lesson, and "Serov set about systematically contesting the musical superiority that Rubinstein's unquestioning admirers attributed to him."[125] In his article "Kontsertï v Peterburgye" [The concerts in St. Petersburg] published in the journal *Sovremennik* in 1851, Serov had ridiculed Damcke, whom he portrayed as "a critic, who knows all the musical wisdom contained in the numerous volumes of the German musical lexicons and histories of music."[126] Serov lampooned Damcke's review of a concert given by Rubinstein: "He [Damcke] has decided, forthrightly and without mincing his words, that Rubinstein is a true genius, that he stands higher than all the musicians that Russia has produced, and that sooner or later the name of this Russian composer will rank among the most prominent celebrities of our age."

As Cherkashina correctly points out, Serov had declared war against those who had taken up what he regarded to be a false position with respect to Russian art. The entire purpose of his campaign was to shape public attitudes toward Rubinstein, a process that was subsequently perpetuated by Stasov and Cui. He was seen as a feeble imitator of Mendelssohn, and the *Ocean Symphony* was the constant target of their mockery. Serov's growing hatred for Rubinstein was fueled still further when Serov was not invited to become a member of the Russian Music Society when it was formed in 1859. To his credit, Rubinstein kept aloof from the insults that were aimed at him, although Serov's attacks cannot have failed to annoy him:

> I had bad relations with Serov all the time. There never was an occasion when we became friendly or conversed. We saw each other in society but I do not think we acknowledged each other. I do not know what art he favored in his youth, but it is true that he unquestionably wanted to make it to the top, and he was vain. He could have gone a long way in opera because he had a flair for the stage, but there was much in him that was coarse and unrefined. His writings—and he wrote volumes—I did not read; they did not interest me. He was a remarkable man, but there was something stupid, frankly mad, about him. And his lectures against music schools, against God knows what! He did not know what to do, where to apply his talents.[127]

The taunts about his music were probably a good deal easier for Rubinstein to bear than the alienation he must have felt at having his Russian nationality constantly brought into question. Many years later, in a discussion on Händel, he made a telling reference to the way in which his compatriots had ostracized him as a "foreigner": "The English also call Händel an English composer, because he wrote his oratorios in the English language. I cannot say that this kind of patriotism displeases me. There is at least more pride in that than in disowning one born and bred in a country and avowing its religion, because his name is a foreign one."[128]

Rubinstein had made an arrangement with John Ella of the Musical Union to give five concerts in London for a fee of around one thousand rubles, a concert in Dublin, and concerts in a number of British provincial towns. He arrived in a chilly London in early May: this was at the time of the Indian Mutiny and the War in China, and Rubinstein commented that the British were entirely absorbed in the political events of the day:

> I shall be glad when I can finally leave. I do not know of another country which inspires such revulsion with regard to music as this one. Nowhere is music played as much as here, and nowhere do people treat it so badly and so affectedly as here."[129]

Rubinstein's dissatisfaction with musical life in London was softened to some extent by the presence of Wieniawski and other visiting musicians. He had the opportunity of renewing his acquaintance with Clara Schumann, Joachim, and Meyerbeer, who was in London for the rehearsals of his opera *Le Pardon de Ploërmel*.[130] Unfortunately Rubinstein succeeded in upsetting Joachim during a performance of Beethoven's *Kreutzer Sonata*. Wilhelm Ganz, who was second violinist in Henry Wylde's New Philharmonic Society, and subsequently associate conductor, later recalled that Joachim was "very angry with Rubinstein for taking the last movement at such a terrific rate, and said he would never play it again with him. I was present at the time, and I think Joachim was quite right. Rubinstein was of such an exuberant disposition that he really could not help himself and was carried away by his own enthusiasm."[131] During his stay in London Rubinstein often met Vladimir Sollogub and his family, as well as Dmitry Stasov, who was making a grand tour of Western Europe in the summer of 1859. Dmitry Stasov told his brother, Vladimir, that he had read in an English newspaper that "Rubinstein is the greatest pianist who has visited England after Thalberg and Liszt." The critic went on to observe that Russia, "with each day, is acquiring greater and greater significance in music," and to speak of Balakirev as "another pianist of very high esteem and an almost European reputation."[132]

Rubinstein made several London public appearances in May and June. These were interspersed with numerous private engagements, and his circle of acquaintances in the British capital continued to grow with each successive visit. Among the new acquaintances that Rubinstein and Wieniawski made were the Hamptons. Mrs Hampton was the sister of the pianist and composer George Osborne, and her daughter, Isabel, became Wieniawski's wife in August 1860. The most important event of Rubinstein's London season was the concert of 11 June at the Hanover Square Rooms. The program of this concert was as follows:

Beethoven: Coriolanus Overture
An aria from *Freyschütz* [*sic*]
Rubinstein: Piano Concerto No. 2
Boïeldieu: An aria from the opera *La fête du village* (soloist: Julius Stockhausen)
Field: A nocturne
Mendelssohn: *Lied ohne Worter*
Chopin: A nocturne } Rubinstein
Liszt: *Valse caprice d'après* Schubert
Rossini: an aria from *Il Barbiere di Seviglia* (soloist: Désirée Artôt)
Rubinstein: Romance; Scherzo; Etude

Rubinstein: Symphony No. 1 in F major
Rubinstein: Ballads and songs accompanied by Karl Klindworth

At the end of the year Anton learned that the title "Member of the Philharmonic Society in London" had been bestowed on him. It was, as he remarked dryly to his mother, "a mark of distinction which is as flattering as it is rare."[133]

Rubinstein spent the remaining part of the summer in Baden-Baden. Before leaving for Germany, however, he played for the king of Belgium and the grand duchess Yelena Pavlovna at Ostend during the celebrated bathing season. He was among a galaxy of artists that included Wieniawski, the violinist Vasily Bezekirsky, who for more than forty years had played in the orchestra of the Bolshoy Theater, and the eminent cellist Alfredo Piatti. The grand duchess presented Wieniawski with a brooch and diamond earrings for his wife-to-be. This mark of distinction must have appeared to Wieniawski a good omen, for he was to spend the next twelve years in St. Petersburg as the "soloist of His Majesty the Tsar."

On 15/27 September Rubinstein returned to St. Petersburg and learned from his mother that Nikolay and Kologrivov had performed his Trio in B♭ in Odessa. On returning to Moscow, however, Nikolay had tendered his resignation from the Nikolayevsky Institute for Orphans, and his place had been taken by Anton Door. Finding himself with no prospects, Nikolay even intimated that he was considering leaving Moscow for good. Anton seemed actively to encourage the idea, suggesting that Nikolay could find a good position in either Paris or London, for "in both cities, after he has given public appearances, he will find sufficient means for existence through giving lessons."[134] Anton's suggestions did not sit well with Nikolay, for in his next letter to his mother on 12/24 October the elder son found himself having to justify his motives:

Did I not always advise that in no circumstances should he give up working in Moscow, that he should come to an agreement with his wife and concern himself with material profit, since he does not believe in achieving an ideal happiness? Only if it were completely impossible to reach harmony in his family affairs would I have advised him to go abroad."[135]

Now Anton urged Nikolay to remain in Moscow and build on his achievements there: "A person with his talent at his age would not miss out anywhere. But to acquire once more the position that he is leaving behind in Moscow would be difficult, even quite impossible."[136] He strongly advised against Nikolay making concert tours as, in his own experience, the rewards were not commensurate with the energy expended on them:

Earn money through concerts—let him get that out of his head. You feel content if you can get away in one piece, i.e., not have to pay out yourself—especially with his character and principles. Then he might as well go to Australia or China, because giving concerts in Germany, France, and England is becoming more difficult by the year. If he wants to earn his bread through lessons, he can do so very well. But also—only after remaining in one place for a while, and with sufficient funds to wait patiently. Besides, I have told him this verbally many times, but he has probably forgotten about it. And since he has never followed anyone's advice, nor heeded it, let him do as he wants but not blame anyone. I think he is mad to have given up his position. Did he ask anyone? No! So there is nothing to be said. Let him do as he sees fit.[137]

The barely concealed antagonism between the brothers also manifested itself in Nikolay's reaction to Anton's offer to help him find clients in St. Petersburg. The younger brother declined any help, saying that he would feel "subservient." As usual, it was with a sense of relief that Anton turned his attention to Yakov. At this time Yakov was awaiting a reply from the Senate concerning the outcome of a long-standing lawsuit. Barenboym observes: "Judging from unpublished letters from A[nton] Rubinstein to his mother, after the death of his grandfather, Roman Ivanovich, the heirs of the latter (including K. Kh. Rubinstein) fought unsuccessfully in the Senate for ten years a law case against the powerful magnates, the Radziwiłł princes, who, in their time, had ruined R. I. Rubinstein."[138]

4 The Founding of the Russian Music Society and Russia's First Conservatory, 1859–67

For many Russian liberals and the intelligentsia the death of Nicholas I in 1855 and the accession of his son as Tsar Alexander II held out the hope of great social change in Russia. Alexander's reign (r. 1855–81) is known in Russian history as the "era of great reforms," and the first evidence of a change in direction came with the abolition of serfdom in Russia in 1861. In reality, the new "tsar-liberator" continued to cling to the autocratic and bureaucratic policies of his father, but Russia's defeat in the Crimean War had forced the autocracy reluctantly to acknowledge that changes were inevitable. "It is better to begin to abolish bondage from above than to wait for the time when it will begin to abolish itself spontaneously from below," the tsar told the Moscow nobility in March 1856.[1] The following year Alexander appointed Grand Duke Konstantin Nikolayevich, a supporter of emancipation, as chairman of a committee to report on the entire issue of serfdom. Another of the prominent members of the imperial family who was in favor of emancipating the serfs was Grand Duchess Yelena Pavlovna, and it is known that she brought considerable pressure to bear on her nephew, the tsar. By 1859 the legislative framework had been drawn up by an editorial committee under the chairmanship of General Rostovtsev, and the government was heavily preoccupied in implementing the enactments. Alongside these matters of momentous national importance, the petition to form a Russian Music Society (RMS) must have been largely unnoticed. Yet, such was the immense suspicion toward societies of any kind in bureaucratic government circles that the founders of the RMS found it easier to resurrect an old institution than create an entirely new one.

> It was not in the spirit of the era of Nicholas to set up societies! To organize a Russian Music Society as a *new* society was impossible. We had to resort to a dodge, and this is how we did it. Kologrivov remembered that there existed at the Imperial Cappella a circle for musical amateurs which had been approved by the government, and that concerts had been given by them. For some years this circle had not been active at all, but its charter had not been destroyed. So we took advantage of this and asked for it to be continued. Naturally the request *to continue* was granted. This is how it all began. So, on the basis of the old regulations, and in the guise of resurrecting a circle of amateur orchestral players, a completely new Russian Music Society was born.[2]

The circle to which Rubinstein refers in the above passage was the defunct Symphonic Society which Count Matvey Wielhorski had helped to found in 1841.[3] From 1826 the Wielhorski brothers had been active in the musical life of St. Petersburg. Mikhail, who died in 1856, was the composer of the opera *Tsïganye* [The gypsies], and Matvey, an accomplished cellist, had played with Vieuxtemps and Liszt. Such was the renown of the brothers that Mendelssohn had dedicated to Matvey his Cello Sonata No. 2 in D major, Op. 58 (1843), and Liszt, Berlioz, and Schumann had all made appearances in the Wielhorskis' salon during their visits to Russia. On 27 January/8 February 1859 the former members of the Symphonic Society gathered at the home of Matvey Wielhorski on Mikhaylovsky Square and passed a resolution to continue their work. Wielhorski, Vasily Kologrivov, Anton Rubinstein, Dmitry Kanshin, Dmitry Stasov, Aleksandr Shustov, and V. I. Lavonius were elected directors. Their functions were as follows:

Rubinstein: responsible for administering the musical aspects
Kanshin: responsible for the accounts
Kologrivov: responsible for managing the concert hall and any dealings with the administration
Dmitry Stasov: responsible for the secretarial work, including maintaining the *Journal of the Committee of Directors*
Shustov: Stasov's assistant
Lavonius: responsible for organizing the choirs

On 1 May 1859 the Charter of the Russian Music Society was approved on the basis of the obsolete Symphonic Society. It declared its primary aim to be "the development of musical education and musical taste in Russia and the encouragement of native talents." To achieve this aim, the Music Society would "(a) perform to the highest possible degree of perfection the finest instrumental and vocal works, that is symphonies, overtures, quartets, trios, oratorios, masses, cantatas, etc.; and (b) give native composers the opportunity to hear their own works performed."[4] The next task facing the RMS was to acquire imperial patronage. The grand duchess Yelena Pavlovna was the obvious choice, and she made a room in the Mikhaylovsky Palace available for rehearsals. It was decided that the RMS would be mostly funded by private subscription. The annual subscription for full members was set at one hundred rubles, visiting members at fifteen rubles, and performers and members of the chorus at five rubles. During its first season the Music Society had five hundred members, although the exact composition is unknown. The first meeting did not take place until 11/23 October, leaving very little time before the start of the winter concert season. The Sunday "University Concerts" were already being arranged, as were the concerts of the St. Petersburg Philharmonic Society (founded in 1802) and Lvov's "Concert Society" (founded in 1850). News that the RMS had been formed had already been reported in the press, and Rubinstein feared that any delay might lead to a loss in public interest. "We will be stranded in the shallows," he told

Wielhorski.[5] As most of the newly appointed directors were absent from St. Petersburg that fall, Rubinstein asked the missing directors to appoint proxies; thus, for instance, Vladimir Stasov would represent his brother Dmitry, Carl Schuberth would stand in for Kologrivov, and so on.

During the period when the RMS was being organized one of Rubinstein's staunchest allies was Vasily Kologrivov, who had long been active in the musical circles of St. Petersburg and was a close friend of Dmitry Stasov. Concerts of chamber music were frequently arranged at his home, and Rubinstein, Karl Albrecht, Ieronim Veykman, Aleksandr Drobish, Carl Schuberth, Ivan Zeyfert, Carl Lewy, and Gustav Kross all lent their enthusiastic support. Kologrivov's contribution in helping to found the RMS was evidently never given the recognition it deserved, and in his *Autobiography* Rubinstein was at pains to set the record straight by giving a glowing account of his selfless zeal and dedication.

One of the chief issues the new music society wished to address was the question of musical education. At that time, opportunities to train professionally in Russia were limited. The Theater School had initiated music classes in 1833, and when Aleksey Lvov took over the directorship of the Imperial Cappella he began instrumental classes in 1839. The Women's Institutes also offered systematic instruction to some degree, and standards were greatly raised after Henselt was appointed as inspector in 1863;[6] but all these were governmental institutions intended to meet the needs of the bodies to which they were attached. Anyone not in government service who wished to study music turned to resident foreign musicians like the Czech-born theorist Josef Gunke, who had settled in St. Petersburg in 1834.[7] All the leading Russian composers of the time had studied with foreign maestros: Glinka under Charles Mayer, himself a pupil of John Field; Dargomïzhsky with Franz Schoberlechner, a pupil of Hummel; and Verstovsky with Ludwig Maurer. When the first meeting of RMS directors convened, the committee passed a resolution that music classes would be opened under the aegis of the RMS. These classes were to begin in the fall of 1860, and Rubinstein set about attracting suitable teachers. On 5/17 November he wrote to Siegfried Saloman, suggesting that Saloman and his wife come to St. Petersburg. He enticed them with the prospect of earning good money with singing lessons, and assured them of the support and favor of the grand duchess Yelena Pavlovna. The couple eventually accepted the offer, and a room in the Mikhaylovsky Palace was made available to them.

One of the first actions of the newly formed RMS was to send out invitations to Russian composers who wished to have their compositions performed at its concerts. Dargomïzhsky, Lomakin, Prince Odoyevsky, and Carl Schuberth were called upon to form a committee to examine the scores submitted. There were to be ten concerts in the season, each with two rehearsals, and the RMS aimed to achieve balanced programs that would reflect the best of the European and Russian tradition, as well as the music of the new and old schools. It is to Rubinstein's credit that he did not allow his own strongly expressed preferences and prejudices to interfere with this aim. Despite his intolerance toward the music of Liszt and Wagner, he wrote to Liszt on 12/24 November: "I do not know whether you are sufficiently interested in the musical events of Russia, and whether you know that we have founded a music society here, which, among other things, has set itself the aim of performing the works of all composers, all schools and all times. The first concert is set for the 23rd of this month; in the second Nelisov[8] is to play your Concerto in E♭, and for future concerts I am preparing *Les Préludes* and *Orphée*. Besides these, I would like to play something by Wagner, other than the *Faust Overture* already included in our program. I am thinking about the introduction to the second act of *Der Fliegende Holländer* with a choir of eighty amateur ladies, but I do not know how to procure the score. Has it been printed? Do you have it? And could you lend it to me?"[9]

Alongside his work rehearsing and directing a French opera for the grand duchess, Rubinstein was also thinking about a new opera of his own. He had earlier complained to Siegfried Saloman: "I have absolutely no luck with opera texts. I have wasted a lot of money and everything has been unusable. Besides, I have such a passionate desire to write an opera that I am unable with the required inclination to involve myself in any other kind of work. I am hoping that with my present attempt, I shall have more luck and then the world will have something novel in store for it!"[10] The new four-act opera by which Rubinstein was setting such store was to be *Die Kinder der Haide* based on the novel in verse *Janko, der Ungarische Rosshirt* by the Hungarian poet Carl Beck. The libretto had been prepared by the German playwright Solomon Mosenthal, who had once provided Nicolai with the libretto of *Die Lustigen Weiber von Windsor*. With his usual confidence that the opera could be written quickly, Rubinstein expressed the hope that it might be completed by the end of the winter and set his sights on Vienna, for, as he informed Liszt: "I would like to stage it in this city, which has, in my opinion, the best opera house in Germany as regards resources."[11]

Meanwhile, the first concert of the new RMS took place on 23 November/ 5 December 1859. Rubinstein conducted the overture to *Ruslan and Lyudmila*, Beethoven's Eighth Symphony, the unfinished fragment of Mendelssohn's *Loreley*, and the finale of Handel's oratorio, *Jephtha;* Carl Schuberth took the baton for a performance of Rubinstein's Piano Concerto No. 3 in G, with the composer as soloist. Five more concerts were given through November and December that included a balanced mixture of classical and contemporary music, both Russian and European. A few weeks after the first concert of the RMS Rubinstein learned from Kaleriya Khristoforovna that Yelizaveta (Nikolay's estranged wife) had left Moscow. He hoped that this would be the end of the matter but foresaw difficulties in the future, and remarked: "If she takes it into her head to return sometime, then, with her eccentricity, all the tears, repentance, entreaties, anger, vengeance, etc. etc. etc. will begin. Then he will be lucky if he can get by without recourse to litigation."[12]

The RMS season of concerts continued throughout January. It is interesting that, in spite of the bitter hostility displayed toward Rubinstein by the nationalists and their sympathizers, it is a stroke of irony that it was Rubinstein who gave the first public performances of orchestral works by Musorgsky and Cui. The fourth concert of the season given on 14/26 December 1859 had included the premiere of Cui's Scherzo in F major, and the seventh concert given on 11/23 January 1860 included the first performance of Musorgsky's Scherzo in B♭ major.[13] From Musorgsky's correspondence, it is evident that the RMS Directorate had considered giving a chorus from his incidental music to *King Oedipus* later in the 1860/61 season. Musorgsky wrote to Balakirev on 9/21 November 1860 about his meeting with Dmitry Stasov: "Today I was with D. Stasov to get the tickets for the Shilovskys. He said of my chorus that the commission had decided:—if, at the rehearsal, I find that it could be performed before the public, then it will be performed. Out of an intense feeling of self-preservation, I said to Stasov that this chorus is short and marked *agitato*, and that to make this *agitato* come out effectively it must be preceded by the *Andante*, even though it is short. Therefore I asked him to return it to me. I suppose this disorderly mob wanted to teach me something. The chorus was returned, and I am heartily glad that I avoided colliding with Rubinstein."[14] The date given on the orchestral score of Musorgsky's chorus is 1/13 March 1860, so the work was probably being considered for inclusion in one of the concerts of December 1860 or January 1861. In the end, the chorus was performed in a concert given by Konstantin Lyadov at the Mariinsky Theater on 6/18 April 1861. Despite their animosity toward Rubinstein, the *kuchkists* could not remain entirely indifferent to the influential position that he held, nor to the fact that his music was being regularly performed in Russia and Europe. Even Balakirev found himself compelled to study it. From Nizhny-Novgorod he wrote to Vladimir Stasov on 14/26 July 1861: "I would very much like to look at Grubinstein's second concerto dedicated to Lewy.[15] I absolutely cannot remember what form the *Andante* takes, and I need this very much for my own that is shaping itself so strangely that I cannot place it under any of the forms that I know."[16] Stasov duly obtained a copy from Johansen's music shop in St. Petersburg and sent it to Balakirev with the remark that, according to Johansen himself, the theme from the *Andante* had been taken directly from the religious march that occurs in the introduction to Meyerbeer's *Le Pardon de Ploërmel*.

At the end of the St. Petersburg concert season Rubinstein gave two concerts in Moscow to help raise money for the Moscow branch of the RMS which was due to begin functioning in October. The programs of these concerts included his *Ocean Symphony* and Piano Concerto No. 2. Then in mid-March he set out for Riga[17] and Königsberg, and eventually arrived in Vienna, where he installed himself at the Hôtel Elisabeth. At this stage very little of the opera *Die Kinder der Haide* had been written, and most of the work was completed in the small town of Dornbach near Vienna where there was no postal service and Rubinstein could be assured of the rest he needed. In fact, the only major commitment he had that summer was to attend a jubilee concert in Vienna for the fiftieth anniversary of Schumann's birth, when he played the piano part in the Piano Quintet in E♭ on 8 June.

A Report to the Minister of Education

Rubinstein returned from Austria with the draft of a report destined for Yevgraf Kovalevsky, the Minister of Education. The French original was translated into Russian by Dmitry Stasov and was first published in the *Russkaya muzïkal'naya gazeta* in 1909. Rubinstein did not date the report, and Stasov assumed it was written in 1859. Barenboym questions this, however, and remarks: "From the contents of the letter it would appear that it was written after the RMS had already opened its first classes and the Society had been convinced by the flood of students wishing to study music—consequently no earlier than March 1860."[18] In fact, the classes did not begin until the fall of 1860, so it would seem more logical to date it to the end of 1860, especially as Rubinstein had rested the entire summer in Dornbach and would have had the time needed to draft it. Like his earlier plan for a music academy written in the fall of 1852, this new plan is typically thorough. It begins as follows: "The Russian Music Society, whose chief aim is to facilitate opportunities for the people to receive a musical education, while providing them with training from the best teachers in all branches of this art for the most modest payment or even free of charge if necessary, is unable conscientiously to fulfill this task owing to the large number of people wishing to study. This is in view of the lamentable fact that the government has hitherto shown no concern about giving any civil rights to those who wish to devote themselves exclusively to music, and in view of the limited financial resources at the disposal of the Society."[19] From his appraisal of the educational responsibilities of the RMS, it becomes immediately clear that Rubinstein was concerned about civil rights (*droits civils*). Graduates from the Academy of Arts received the award "Free Artist," which carried with it certain rights and privileges in the civil hierarchy, and Rubinstein wished to obtain similar rights for vocational students of music. This point should be borne in mind in the light of later criticism that the Conservatory would foster only a "mercenary desire" (Vladimir Stasov) in aspiring to diplomas, certificates, and awards. The other key issue raised in the report (if only obliquely) concerned the graduates' social status. Only the government had the right to change or confer the rights of estate and that is why the RMS Music School, from which the Conservatory would eventually emerge, needed to be a government institution.

In the remainder of his report Rubinstein set out the prerequisites to achieve his goal. He called for a music school to be opened for a trial period of seven years under the aegis of the RMS, and asked for it to be called the "Imperial Music School" with rights and privileges analogous to the Academy of Arts. The students of the school would have to be spared levies and conscription, and at the end of their studies they would be examined by persons appointed by the government. He recommended appointing an inspector as the intermediary between the government and the directors of the school. The latter were to be accountable to the government and would be required to give annual reports about their work and financial accountability. On the matter of financing, Rubinstein suggested a number of options: an annual subsidy to the school of fifteen thousand rubles; a building to house the school and a subsidy of ten thousand rubles; provision of a building and permission to arrange a national subscription throughout the country; a percentage of the takings from every concert given in Russia; levying a tax on every musical work published in the country; and a tax on every music teaching post in the government institutions. He provided a fourteen-point charter for the school and a detailed analysis of the teachers required for it (more than twenty-one assistants, approximately) and their salaries. He proposed that the school should have five directors, one of whom (the inspector) would preside over the board and inspect the classes. This inspector was to be elected annually. One of the most important points in Rubinstein's plan was to make the school independent from the RMS: "In no way must the School be dependent on the members of the aforementioned Society, and they have no rights in regard to it other than electing its directors."[20] Moreover, the annual report submitted to the government by the school was to have nothing to do with the report of the Society to its members. At the end of the seven-year period the government would decide on the future of the school.

In September 1860 the RMS opened its first classes, which continued to function until 1863, by which time the Conservatory proper had come into existence. The teachers were Nikolay Ivanovich Zaremba (theory and composition),[21] Gavriil Yakimovich Lomakin (singing and choral class), Theodor Leschetizky and Fyodor Begrov (piano),[22] Henryk Wieniawski (violin), and Carl Schuberth (cello). At the same time Otto Deutsch began a free class of choral singing under the aegis of the RMS. Assistance was clearly given by other teachers, including Nissen-Saloman, Pyotr Lodi, and Luigi Piccioli. Concerts were also given regularly to raise funds, and for these the artists gave their time and effort for a modest fee.

Rubinstein was still thinking about the setting of the *Song of Songs* (Sulamith and Solomon), which Rodenberg had given him in London. Catherine Drinker Bowen has claimed with justification that Rubinstein's particular fascination with biblical opera was a reaction against Wagnerism and anti-Semitism. Wagner's article, *Das Judenthum in der Musik,* was first published under a pseudonym in two issues of Brendel's *Neue Zeitschrift für Musik* in September 1850 and may have had some impact on nationalist thinking in Russia—at least in the sense that national art like the national roots on which it fed needed to be kept free of foreign or alien "impurities." Rubinstein probably did not see the article until the revised edition appeared in 1869. His obsession with spiritual opera began to appear at almost the same time and increased rapidly after 1876, when *Das Ring des Nibelungen* was first staged in Bayreuth. It should be remembered, paradoxically, that Rubinstein's interest in the genre was not the result of religious zeal. In *Gedankenkorb* he shows himself to be atheist in outlook and declared art to be "pantheistic" (see Appendix E, Religion [6]). In 1860 there can be little doubt that it was, above all, the poetic imagery of the *Song of Songs* that most appealed to him.

In November 1860 the concert season began again. In his reminiscences, Dmitry Stasov recalled that the artistic committee established a tradition (possibly even supported by a resolution) that each concert would include at least one work by a Russian composer,[23] which posed a problem. At that time the Balakirev circle was only just beginning to show that it was a significant force in Russian music, and, besides the music of Glinka and Dargomïzhsky, there were few established names. The Society tried to encourage native talent and works by Baron Fitinghof-Shel and Nikolay Afanasyev, composers now almost completely forgotten, briefly found their way onto RMS programs.[24] Despite such efforts, the critics of the concerts accused them of being too Teutonic and of failing to encourage Russian music.

The Opposition Redoubles

By late 1860 the general opposition to Rubinstein and the attacks on him were gaining momentum. With his irascible and obdurate character, he constantly made matters worse by his complete refusal to compromise. "He was a born dictator," Ippolitov-Ivanov declared. "He could not tolerate objections, he could not get on with people, nor did he want to."[25] In a rehearsal of Beethoven's Eighth Symphony he harried the horn players to such an extent in the *Allegretto* that they walked out. Then, in December 1860, an incident occurred which was clearly intended to undermine his authority. In March 1861 he was to conduct an RMS concert that included a performance of Mendelssohn's *Die Erste Walpurgisnacht.* Prince Odoyevsky recorded the following in a diary entry dated 14 December 1860:

This is what Rubinstein told me about what happened at the Singing Academy (at the Mikhaylovsky Palace). They were rehearsing Mendelssohn's *Walpurgisnacht;* the sopranos sang wrong notes; he made the first sopranos sing—they sang wrong notes; he made the first row sing—again wrong notes; just the second row—no wrong notes; that means that only the first row were singing wrong notes; he went through them in groups of three, and discovered that one group of three was responsible for the wrong notes [of the choir]. He invited these ladies to sing on their own, but they would not agree. With his usual curtness, Rubinstein said: "Ces dames sont priées de ne plus revenir [These ladies are requested not to return]." Then a scandal occurred . . . Rubinstein would not give in to the demands and left the hall. The next day he sent notification to the directors that he was giving up teaching in the Academy, giving up his directorship and his conducting duties. Tomorrow he is writing his apologies to the three ladies and is announcing to them his intention of standing down. Rubinstein was not right in the form . . . but in reality he was right; he was the one responsible for the wrong notes of the choir . . . With Rubinstein's resignation the Society will fall apart; it can be held together only by a general letter or a request from all members of the Society, or at least of all those who are members of the Singing Academy.[26]

When the directors of the RMS received the letter of resignation, the majority of the chorus members submitted a petition, threatening to disband the choir if Rubinstein were not re-instated. Everything was settled, and on 27 December/7 January 1861 Rubinstein again took up his post at the Singing Academy. The incident merely reinforced Odoyevsky's conviction that the Society had been absurdly organized. Even when the RMS Charter had appeared in May 1859, he had warned Rubinstein that his position as director would be a difficult one, declaring: "Vous n'avez personne à invoquer . . . car la Société n'a donné de mandat à personne [You have no one to appeal to . . . for the Society has not given a mandate to anyone], but only in its own name."[27]

If matters were not going entirely right for Rubinstein in Russia, at least he had the consolation of knowing that his opera, *Die Kinder der Haide,* was shortly to be produced at the Kärntnetor Theater in Vienna. The plot of this work (see Appendix B) contains echoes of Dargomïzhsky's *Rusalka,* although in this version the male protagonist who is torn between two women is not a highborn prince but the simple horse herdsman (Rosshirt) Wania. Spina included the original 1861 cast when he brought out the vocal score:

Count Waldemar, an officer (tenor)	Herr Walter
Conrad, a German tavern owner on the Count's estate (baritone)	Herr Hrabanek
Maria, daughter of the above (soprano)	Frl. Krauss
Wania, a horse herdsman (tenor)	Herr A. Ander
Isbrana, a Gypsy girl (mezzo-soprano)	Frau Csillag
Grigori (bass) ⎫	Herr Mayerhofe
Bogdan (baritone) ⎬ Gypsies	Herr Lay
Pawel (bass) ⎭	Herr Koch
A Gypsy girl (mezzo-soprano)	
Tavern owner's servant	
A Gypsy	

The list includes at least a few distinguished names. Nine years later Gustav Walter sang Walter von Stolzing in the first production of *Die Meistersinger* in Vienna, Gabrielle Krauss had been one of Mathilde Marchesi's most promising pupils at the Viennese Academy, and the Czech tenor Aloys Ander had also had a notable career on the opera stage.

Rubinstein's relations with the court circles were taking a decided turn for the worse. In a letter to Edith von Raden of Tuesday 14/26 February 1861, he spoke of the successful staging of his *Die Kinder der Haide* in Vienna the previous Thursday: "What a strange coincidence. Precisely on Thursday—the day on which I play the most lamentable role in St. Petersburg—proved to be the day on which I played the greatest role in Germany?! Is this not a system of compensation?!"[28] Rubinstein's allusion to Thursday in St. Petersburg was the day he played as the accompanist during the musical soirées given by Yelena Pavlovna at the Mikhaylovsky Palace. His disaffection was primarily caused by an awareness of his own artistic self-esteem and the autocratic demands of the grand duchess. At the same time the issue was broader—her perpetual interference in matters which he considered the musician's exclusive concern. As secretary to the grand duchess, it was Edith von Raden with whom Rubinstein was most directly involved, and his relations with her were far from harmonious. In a letter of 2/14 March 1861 he declared to her: "I shall never understand why you always interpose your person in things which relate to me. I assure you that, although your letter of today is curt, it is not sufficiently curt to cause me to be mistaken in my feelings toward you—this is out of malice toward the grand duchess. I shall not come, whatever you may think. I am used to being unrecognized."[29] This letter was followed by a further one dated Tuesday 21 March/2 April in which he asked to be relieved of his duties as musical accompanist at the Thursday soirées of the grand duchess, finding them "incompatible with the dignity of the art which I hold like a religious fanatic."[30] As the grand duchess continued to send him invitations to appear at her soirées, he told Raden that he considered it necessary to resign from a position which "until today was so flattering and so honorable." He asked Raden to take steps to stop paying his salary, "no longer considering myself in the service of her Imperial Highness."[31] It is clear from subsequent letters to Raden that this did not lead to a complete rupture with the grand duchess. He continued to carry out his musical duties at the Mikhaylovsky Palace until his departure for Vienna a few months later, but his anger bubbled away for a whole year and then finally erupted in a conversation with Raden which took place in early March (n.s.) 1862.

Music in Russia

Early in 1861 Pyotr Isaeyevich Veynberg (the brother of Rubinstein's brother-in-law, Yakov, who had married his sister Lyuba) asked Rubinstein to provide an article for his weekly journal *Vek* [The age]. Veynberg had been educated at the Odessa Gymnasium and the University of Kharkov from which he graduated in 1854, and was a poet, translator, and literary historian. In the mid-1850s he wrote the poem *Titulyarnïy sovetnik* [The Titular Councilor] that Dargomïzhsky had famously set to music in 1859. The poem was written while Veynberg was in the service of the governor of Tambov (while there, he earned the nickname "The Heine from Tambov") and it is thought to be a reflection of Veynberg's unrequited love for the governor's daughter. He moved to St. Petersburg in 1858 and was appointed editor of *Vek* a few years later. In an attempt to reverse the fortunes of the journal which was failing to attract readers, Veynberg wrote a scandalous feuilleton about a woman, who, seemingly breaking all the laws of morality, reads Pushkin's *Yegipetskiye nochi* [Egyptian nights] at a literary soirée in Perm, and presents herself toward her audience as Cleopatra. Perhaps Veynberg had correctly judged the impact Rubinstein's article might have on public opinion and saw in it a way to draw attention to the journal. If so, his instincts did not fail him. The first issue of *Vek* for 1861 carried Rubinstein's article, *O muzïkye v Rossii* [On music in Russia] and it was a bombshell.[32]

This article ferociously attacked what Rubinstein saw as dilettantism in Russian music. He scorned the amateurs who studied music solely for their own pleasure and compared them with the true artist who, in the words of Goethe, has "moistened his bread with tears."

Musical art, as any other, demands that the person who is involved with it should sacrifice to it all his thoughts, all his feelings, all his time, his entire being; only on that person, who in this way devotes all of himself to art, will art sometimes smile, and allow him to discover its secrets. Only then can the elect gain the right to call himself an artist and the privilege to proclaim to the world his art—that awesome fate which imposes on the artist the obligation for providing endless pleasure for his neighbor, and rewarding him only with the palm branch of a martyr.[33]

The conclusions Rubinstein reached in his article were deeply rooted in his own personal experiences, and he attempted to set out the preconditions that, in his view, needed to exist in order for a musician to achieve success in his chosen art:

An artist who demands admiration for his work, who has made art a means for earning his living, will surrender himself to worldwide criticism by that very fact— without this, he will never produce anything great. Disillusionment, fine dreams scattering before sorrowful reality, the struggle of pride and fate, artistic fanaticism, unacknowledged and ridiculed by the indifferent and uncomprehending masses, but respected and valued by a small number of people, strict but fair criticism—these are the conditions without which the artist cannot develop.[34]

In coming to the defense of the vocational artist, Rubinstein stressed that only professional training (a conservatory) could overcome mediocrity and establish the correct attitude (as Rubinstein saw it) of the artist to his art in Russia. His criticism of the amateurs for the "exclusivity" of their views, in particular, was seen by many contemporaries as a veiled attack on Dargomïzhsky, Serov, and the Balakirev circle. As relatively wealthy landowners, Glinka and Dargomïzhsky had never had to earn their living through music. Balakirev was mostly self-taught and his most famous pupils were not musicians by vocation: Musorgsky was a retired guards officer; Rimsky-Korsakov, a naval cadet; Cui, a military engineer; and Borodin (who became a member of the circle in 1862), a doctor and research chemist. Musorgsky read Rubinstein's article and dismissed it with the words: "What are Rubinstein's prerogatives for such strictures —it is glory and money, quantity and not quality. O Ocean! O puddle!"[35] The mere suggestion of criticism sent the implacable Stasov into paroxysms of rage, and he swiftly retaliated in an article entitled *Konservatorii v Rossii* [Conservatories in Russia] published in the newspaper *Severnaya pchela* [The northern bee], 24 February/8 March 1861.[36] In the first half of this article Stasov set out to defend dilettantism, seeing no reason to hinder the amateurs "in an occupation that is pleasant for them and harmless for others." Far more pernicious, he argues, are "the bad works of musicians who are not dilettantes, especially when they belong to people who are celebrated for some reason or other." He then turns his attention to Rubinstein's "remedy" against the allegedly harmful effects of dilettantism but completely rejects the idea of a conservatory and asks why Russia should in a servile manner copy an institution, which even in Europe (according to Stasov) had already been discredited. He regarded the awarding of titles as fruitless and "merely the source of a mercenary desire." For

Stasov, the European conservatories and academies were just "bastions of mediocrity," which had helped "to confirm harmful ideas and tastes in art." They "have created not artists, but only people who crave attaining this or that rank, or this or that privilege." What he found most distasteful about a conservatory, however, was that it:

> interferes in the most harmful way in the *creativity* of the artist being trained, extends its despotic power (from which nothing can protect him) onto the mold and the form of his works, tries to give to them its own direction, to drive them toward a quantified academic yardstick, to instill in them its own recognized habits, and, finally, worst of all, to put its claws into the very understanding of the young artist, to foist on him opinions about artistic works and their composers from which it is impossible, or extremely difficult, for a person who has devoted himself to art to disassociate himself.[37]

Stasov's language is highly emotive, and by personalizing his arguments he was being deliberately provocative. Rubinstein had criticized the "amateurs" and declared: "In Russia there are almost no artist musicians in the usual sense of this word," but nowhere had he referred to any Russian musician by name. Yet, within just a few sentences of beginning his article, Stasov had accused Rubinstein of being a foreigner, "who has nothing in common with our national roots and our art." By disowning Rubinstein, and depriving him of the right to an opinion on any matter concerning national art, he was able to reject his ideas on musical education in Russia. Stasov loathed the notion of a conservatory on principal because he saw it as a foreign institution foisted onto Russian soil: "Each of us knows how many foreign products have been grafted onto us, and how few of them have grown. It seems that it is time to stop these graftings, which have no meaning, and to think about what is really useful and suitable for our soil and for our national roots."[38] There is much that is negative and unconstructive in Stasov's arguments, and his frankly obscurantist convictions are simply indicative of a hell-bent determination to fight a corner and to defend at all costs the values of the New Russian School, which he supported with an all-consuming passion bordering on religious fanaticism. The thought that the "foreigner" Rubinstein and his equally foreign patroness might steal a march on the "real" Russian school filled him with horror, and he wrote to Balakirev:

> Or perhaps you think that I wrote it [the article] to prove critically that "Anton" is ridiculous and doesn't know how to write articles. . . . No, the fact is that out of his zeal for Russia and his stupidity, Anton has started up something whose repercussions, to my mind, must do dreadful harm. If there is just the slightest chance, I want to prevent this, or at least to make those people, who, like industrious little ants bustling about and trying to drag the log that the brilliant maestro has pointed out to them, should stop and think. I want the entire stupid Rubinstein camp of Odoyevskys and Yelena Pavlovnas, etc., at least to know what this is about.[39]

The issue of the conservatory was becoming dangerously confused with xenophobic sentiments surrounding Rubinstein. Balakirev's hatred went even further for, as he replied to Stasov: "If Grubinstein were intelligent he would despise Russia more than he does so now, and he would be entitled to. It is only we who can love her by force of that law which says that sheep love rams and not bears."[40] By some strange quirk of fate, they had demonstrated that they detested Rubinstein far more for being Russian than for being a foreigner.

It was not only Stasov who was stirring up trouble. The indefatigable Serov joined the fray with two articles—*O muzïkye v Peterburgye* [On music in St. Petersburg] and particularly *Zalogi istinnogo muzïkal'nogo obrazovaniya v S.-Peterburgye* [The pledges of the true musical education in St. Petersburg] (*Severnaya pchela*, 9/21 May 1862)—which derided Rubinstein in barely concealed anti-Semitic terms and declared that the conservatory would be "a breeding-ground for untalented musical bureaucrats." Part of this tirade is included by Yury Kremlyov in *Russkaya mïsl' o muzïkye*:

> Let everyone in Russia who sincerely loves art understand that expensive government apartments for the housekeepers and intendants of the patented music school are completely useless for the proper advancement of our cause, that we have no need of musical bureaucrats to swell the ranks of the ungifted and the mediocre (that is death for art!); we have no need of patented judges to issue prizes and diplomas for the encouragement of useless exercises, because no true talent will ever want to subject itself to being assessed by privileged pedants, ignoramuses, and the envious.[41]

In later years Rubinstein himself came to realize that the article had not achieved the goal for which he was striving. The effect on certain very vocal elements in Russian society had been absolutely negative, just as it had been when his earlier article on Russian composers had become known in Russia. Nevertheless, it had played its appointed part in the propaganda war aimed solely at trying to win public support for the future Conservatory. That Rubinstein's endeavors had merely served to strengthen the resolve of the opposition was of little consequence. Quite undeterred, he forged ahead with the drafting of a charter and of a report, *The Necessity of Opening a Music School in St. Petersburg,* which was signed by all the directors of the RMS and submitted to Yelena Pavlovna.

By the late spring of 1861 Rubinstein was already in Vienna. He stayed only a few weeks, however, because on 1 June he left for Interlaken in Switzerland, where he spent most of the summer. Before his departure he penned a few lines to Julius Rodenberg, who had hoped to complete the libretto for the *Song of Songs* by the end of May. Rubinstein had now become fired by an entirely new idea—the oriental legend *Lallah Rookh,* about which he had earlier spoken to Rodenberg. This operatic subject (later called *Feramors* to distinguish it from an opera by David) was based on a part of Thomas Moore's grand epic of 1817. The libretto eventually turned out to be something of a cross between *Die Entführung aus dem Serail* and *Il Barbiere di Seviglia.* From the former, the librettist drew on the exotic setting and also on certain character types—a heroine who proves her constancy in the face of adversity, the buffo Fadladin with his Mozartean counterpart Osmin, and the secondary pair of lovers Hafisa and Chosru. At the same time the king's desire to test the fidelity of his future bride by appearing to her in the guise of a poor singer also allies it with Rossini's opera.

> Lallah Rookh, in love with the singer Feramors, has been betrothed to the unknown King of Kashmir by her father. She spends the last night before her betrothal in the valley before entering Kashmir. In act 2 Lallah Rookh and Feramors declare their love for one another, but Feramors is caught by the grand vizier Fadladin in the princess's tent and demands that he be put to death. The king's envoy Chosru has Feramors taken captive and sentences him to death at dawn. Act 3 is set in the royal harem where Lallah Rookh, deeply distressed by Feramor's fate, is being attired for the marriage ceremony. When she is brought before the king, he turns out to be none other than Feramors himself. Her friend Hafisa is betrothed to Chosru, and the plans of the vengeful Fadladin are foiled.

In his enthusiasm, Rubinstein had already begun making sketches for the new opera and asked Rodenberg to set aside his work on the *Song of Songs* and concentrate instead on the new libretto. "I have a passionate desire to take up this subject," he declared. Resting at Interlaken, Rubinstein learned from English newspapers that his brother, Nikolay, was in London. He had been invited there by the brothers Thomas and Samuel Arthur Chappell, who organized the Monday and Saturday Popular Concerts at the St. James Hall. The newspapers reported that Nikolay was ill, and this prompted Anton to write to Kaleriya Khristoforovna: "Let us hope that everything is well with his health and that the news of his illness is probably only rumors. . . . After all," he commented wryly, "last year they buried me," referring to the canard published in the English newspapers that he [Anton] had died in the spring of 1860.[42] At the same time he must have taken great comfort from the fact that a few weeks earlier Karl Klindworth had conducted the English premiere of his *Ocean Symphony* at a Musical Art Concert. During his visit to London Nikolay had met Aleksandr Herzen, editor of the radical Russian Free Press. His association with Herzen was reported to Vasily Dolgorukov, the head of the notorious Third Section (the tsarist secret police) in St. Petersburg, and when Nikolay returned home to Russia in the fall he was searched thoroughly by customs officials. According to Barenboym, this cost him the post of conductor of the Bolshoy Theater when he was later considered as a replacement for Ivan Shramek. A few years later Anton himself was introduced to this "dangerous acquaintance," but he made no secret of it and even reported to Edith Raden that he had met "the wandering Bell," a reference to *Kolokol* [The bell], Herzen's radical journal published in London during the 1850s.

While Rubinstein was resting in Switzerland, the Conservatory was never far from his thoughts. His own future plans were to be decided by the success or the failure of the enterprise, and he asked Yakov to try and find out from Lavonius, Dmitry Stasov, or Shustov how the affairs of the RMS stood and whether any decision had been reached about opening a conservatory. Using as a pretext the fact that he had found a new singer for the grand duchess's suite, he also dispatched Yakov to the palace at Kamennïy Ostrov in order to glean some information out of Raden or Eiler. Finally, he could not endure these "backdoor" attempts any longer and instead wrote directly to Edith Raden from Interlaken on 2/14 July 1861. In a letter that barely conceals his indignation, he complained: "I still have no information about this matter which is so important for Russia and for me."[43] In fact, behind the scenes Yelena Pavlovna was using her considerable influence with Count Adlerberg, the Minister of the Court. Although her efforts were eventually successful, she had had to compromise and the original report received from the RMS was suppressed and replaced by another version in which Rubinstein had no part. The significance of the changes became apparent when the Charter of the Conservatory was published that fall.

Rubinstein had been unable to attend the Vienna premiere of his opera, *Die Kinder der Haide,* in February, but now there were plans to stage it again in the fall. He traveled to the Austrian capital at the beginning of September, but once more his hopes were dashed because the principal tenor had fallen ill and the performance was postponed. The score of the opera was about to be published by Spina, and it was not without a measure of irony that he reported to Raden that his publisher's request to have the opera dedicated to Tsar Alexander II had been accepted.

With the fate of the Conservatory still in the balance, Anton's future plans seemed very uncertain. Once again he asked for Yakov to be dispatched to the Mikhaylovsky Palace in an attempt to elicit information but to no avail. In September 1861 he met up with Nikolay, and the brothers concluded that the proposal to set up the Conservatory had been rejected. Anton recommended that Nikolay remain in St. Petersburg and take his place as resident musician with the grand duchess; this was prompted by rumors that the Moscow branch of the RMS was on the point of financial collapse. On 19 September Anton left for Berlin, where he planned to stay for four or five weeks to discuss the libretto of *Feramors* with Rodenberg. He called on Meyerbeer and Liszt; the latter, having relinquished his old post in Weimar, was in the Prussian capital for a few weeks en route to Rome. Within a few days, however, Anton received news from Nikolay and Shustov that the Conservatory was to be founded after all. He wrote immediately to Kaleriya Khristoforovna (24 September) to advise her that his return to Russia would be delayed by a month, asking her to find him an apartment in St. Petersburg, and a valet.

Charter for a Conservatory

The appointment of Aleksandr Golovnin as the new Minister of Education at the beginning of 1862 ushered in a period of reforms that directly concerned the schools and the higher educational establishments. Golovnin was well known for his liberal views, and talk of charters was in the air. The official committee set up in 1858 to revise the charter of the University of St. Petersburg had finally published its report, and Konstantin Kavelin had been hastily sent abroad to find out how universities in France, Germany, and Switzerland were organized.[44] At about this time the charter of the new Conservatory was published in an appendix to *Senatskiye vedomosti,* dated 17 October 1861, no. 95.[45] The opening paragraph reads: "Under the aegis of the Russian Music Society, a music school is to be founded for instruction in the art of music in all its disciplines. The school, on a par with the Society, is under the direct patronage of Her Imperial Highness the grand duchess Yelena Pavlovna." Despite Rubinstein's wish for the new institution to be known as a conservatory, the government had objected to the foreign sounding word and insisted on it being called a "school." The title of "Conservatory" was not formally adopted until 1873.

It was claimed that the charter would be published in *Senatskiye vedomosti* "without any change," but Rubinstein had already noticed that a deception had been carried out, and he wrote to Vasily Kologrivov in Tula:

> But I do not know how it happened that the report we submitted with the charter, in which we requested a site or other form of assistance from the government, was not submitted, but some other drawn up at the Mikhaylovsky Palace was sent, which says that the Society undertakes to support the school through its own resources. Where are they? . . . We are thinking of opening the school in September and from that time the first year will be counted. With what funds? God knows. I have no idea.[46]

The most pressing question facing Rubinstein was to finance the new institution. Because of prevarication on the part of the government, and its refusal to lend any direct financial assistance, he needed to raise a considerable sum in a very short time. Yelena Pavlovna was generous, donating one thousand rubles a year from her own purse. She had also succeeded in persuading the Ministry of the Court to provide a subsidy of five thousand rubles annually for the music school, but the remaining funds had to be raised by private means:

> So we started the enterprise, for which, in the first year, we should have had about twenty thousand rubles. What did we start with? We praised Christ and went to see the wealthy: Yusupov, Bernardaki, and the wood merchant Vasily Fedulovich Gromov. Some gave three hundred, some five hundred rubles and all this came to about three thousand rubles. Sofiya Yakovlyevna Verigo (the wife of the member of the State Council), driving around St. Petersburg, collected three thousand rubles on a subscription sheet. . . . Yelizaveta Wittgenstein (née Eiler) collected money, literally a ruble at a time. That is how it was.[47]

Rubinstein was no less energetic in trying to attract good musicians to the Conservatory, among them, the eminent cellist Karl Davïdov, and Nissen-Saloman.[48] Henrietta Nissen-Saloman was considered one of the finest singing teachers, but she had more or less rejected the terms of her engagement by the RMS. Rubinstein cajoled her with persuasive arguments, and eventually she accepted the engagement offered to her, although it was not without some external pressure and Rubinstein was not entirely happy with the terms that she demanded. As director, he would tolerate no challenge to his authority, and this applied no less to the illustrious patroness of the new institution than to its teachers. What he wrote to Edith von Raden on 23 February/7 March 1862 is remarkably bold and demonstrates quite clearly that Rubinstein had no intention of kowtowing to the whims of the grand duchess or of acquiescing in the face of her constant desire to meddle in matters that he regarded as his exclusive prerogative:

You did me the honor in very frankly setting out your point of view on the question which we discussed verbally yesterday at your residence, and which I considered resolved in my favor. As this is not the case, allow me, for my part, to express my view also very frankly. I cannot do battle with you, who possess eloquence and beauty of style, sufficient sincerity, nobility, and refinement of feeling. Unfortunately I notice, true, rather late, that we shall never understand each other, since your actions and words derive from humility, and mine from a sense of worth. The one and the other are falsely interpreted by society here, which sees in the first servility, and in the second only haughtiness.

I consider it beneath me to reply to the hidden reproaches of ingratitude contained in your letter, and I only wish to prove how wrong you are in mixing up two things which have nothing in common between them: art and personal relations. I do not reproach the mighty of this world for the fact that they do not understand or love art; their education, unfortunately, has such a pernicious character that they will never be able to attain that which is noble, divine, life-giving, and ennobling in art. I shall even go as far as to say that I respect those who are frankly conscious of this. But what I cannot tolerate is the bigotry of important personages who make themselves out to be a Maecenas. To become involved as a patron of the arts and to trample it underfoot wherever the opportunity arises— that is what causes my indignation. I always say: you do not love art, you do not understand it—leave it in peace: "König, bleib bei diener Krone." Well, let them concern themselves with it from time to time in order to make their peoples believe in it, or to have a clear conscience from the consciousness of having fulfilled, so to speak, their obligations as important people—but that is all. Do not pretend to the world that you are encouraging it, and at home do not force it to earn its living in the anteroom and to endure what lackeys endure. I have already said to you, Maecenae—patronage obliges you.

But now, as far as my position with regard to her is concerned, then here in very few words is my point of view: as her "leader of the orchestra," I am responsible for the position occupied by music there, I am responsible for the music they perform there; I am responsible for the way artists are treated—I am responsible, not before her, but before myself, before the artistic world. The acts fulfilled there, fall not on her but on me. And then, what could be more natural than to suggest that which you consider to be right? And if people do not heed you for some reason—to go away. I shall never forget the moral support with which she honored me during my precarious youth, and, of course, she will always have in me a loyal and devoted servant, but I shall never be a despised artist, who allows his art to be treated badly under the pretext that the patron has the right to demand everything from him. Once more I detach the personality from the artist.[49] Let her demand my hand when people attack her, my purse when she needs it, my help if she deems it necessary, but not that I should serve toward the humiliation of my art. That is once and for all my point of view. Render unto art that which is due to art. You see that

I do not take seriously what is insulting in your letter regarding me personally—I am only defending César.[50]

Immediately clear from this letter is a sharp contrast in the views of Raden and Rubinstein. Raden, as the grand duchess's secretary, saw her role as entirely subservient: her "actions and words derive from humility." Rubinstein, on the other hand, acts out of a "sense of worth," which society interprets as "haughtiness." It is surely not too fanciful to see in this clash of wills the acrimonious encounter between the Demon and the Angel in the prologue to the opera *The Demon*, where the "humility" of the Angel is pitted against the "pride" of the Demon. If this is the case, then was not Rubinstein secretly depicting Raden/Yelena Pavlovna in the role of the meddling Angel? Much of his anger stemmed from a feeling of intense resentment at the peremptoriness with which he was being treated within the walls of the Mikhaylovsky Palace. He complained bitterly to Raden that he did not know who he was to accept the grand duchesses's instructions from concerning music and the Thursday soirées: through her (Raden) or through Runtsler or Chekalov (palace officials). Exasperated, he told Raden: "You say that Davïdov, Becker and Mme Leschetizky need to be invited.[51] Along comes Runtsler and says that they want Mendelssohn's Octet and Mme Kochetova. Chekalov tells me that it will be upstairs, but Runtsler assures me that it will be downstairs on the stage of the Small Theater. In a word, everyone has something to say—and best of all—everyone has something different to say."[52] He demanded to know once and for all who he was to take the grand duchess's orders from, and told Raden that until the matter was clarified he intended to heed no one. This is just one of several incidents that caused Rubinstein to feel that he was being treated no better than a lackey.

At the end of March Rubinstein was due to leave for Weimar, but before setting out he had a few public engagements in St. Petersburg, including an RMS concert intended to raise money for the Conservatory.[53] Just a few days before, a similar concert had taken place at the Hall of the Nobility to raise money for another new institution—the Free Music School, founded jointly by Balakirev and Gavriil Lomakin. The official opening of the school took place on 18/30 March 1862, thereby preempting the opening of the Conservatory by six months. Possibly on the recommendation of the grand duchess, Kologrivov tried conciliation and evidently approached Balakirev in an attempt to smooth relations and strive for cooperation rather than open rivalry. A reflection of this is to be found in Musorgsky's letter to Balakirev of 31 March/12 April when he writes: "What about the notorious matchmaker? Is Dubinstein still keeping him on tenterhooks; does he dare, or has he stopped caring about getting you engaged?"[54] The gap between the aims of the two institutions was far too wide and Kologrivov's overtures fell on deaf ears. A month later Musorgsky wrote to Balakirev in a disdainful tone:

Two schools, wholly contrasting in character, have been formed in St. Petersburg at a negligible distance from each other. The one is a "professoria," the other a free association of people who have a kinship with art. In one, Zaremba and Tupinstein, in their professorial, anti-musical togas, stuff the heads of their pupils with all manner of abominations and infect them beforehand. The poor students see before them not people but two motionless pillars covered with some sort of idiotic scribbling in the form of musical exercises. But Tupinstein is dense—therefore he conscientiously fulfills his duty and is horridly dense. Now Zarema is different: he's a valiant little chap! He cuts out just the right yardstick for art. Raised to the position of a doctor of music, he's a cobbler in a college cap, and not such a child as to base his views and advice on aesthetics and musical logic, oh no! He's been taught the rules and inoculates everyone who hopes to master the art with this smallpox vaccine against free learning. On your knees in the dust before Mendel! That's Zaremba's motto, and Mendel is Zaremba's god, just as Zaremba is his prophet.[55]

While Kologrivov was trying to win over Balakirev, Rubinstein was far away in Weimar attending the final rehearsals of his opera *Die Kinder der Haide*, which was finally presented on 8 April. Liszt had quit his old post six months earlier, and Rubinstein did not count on a great success, for the theater was small and the musical forces were, in his opinion, only middling. Eagerly awaiting news from Kologrivov about the preparations for the opening of the Conservatory in September, Rubinstein left Weimar for Berlin, where he purchased some new clothes and reported to his mother "I look like a prince."[56] From Berlin, Rubinstein traveled to Copenhagen at the invitation of Princess Anna of Prussia and spent about seven weeks there. Although he gave no solo concerts, he agreed to play in a concert of the Danish Music Society and made the acquaintance of Niels Gade, whose works later appeared in RMS programs.[57] Julius Rodenberg joined him for part of the time in order to work on the libretto of *Feramors*, in which Rubinstein had discovered serious dramatic flaws, and together they set about reworking it.

Despite his intensive work on *Feramors*, Rubinstein remained constantly in touch with Kologrivov by post. He advised him that he had received confirmation from the Czech pianist Alexander Dreyschock that the latter would join the staff of the Conservatory. Villoing, too, was to be appointed one of the piano teachers, and Rubinstein himself agreed to teach (free of charge) but not more than one hour a day. Konstantin Lyadov had been approached and Rubinstein asked Kologrivov to make it clear to him that his duties as a teacher would mean teaching music theory: "He is a gifted person and a Russian, and this latter fact we must bear in mind above anything else," Rubinstein told him.[58] He had also written to Mañuel Garcia, Giovanni Mario, Tamberlick, Calzolari, and Francesco Chiaramonte, inviting them to St. Petersburg as singing teachers. He also wrote to the Italian clarinettist Ernesto Cavallini with whom Rubinstein had performed in St. Petersburg in the 1850s. Cavallini would eventually accept a teaching post at the Conservatory and remain in St. Petersburg from 1862 until his return to Milan in 1870.

The Conservatory opened its doors on 8/20 September 1862. In his inaugural address Rubinstein paid dutiful tribute to the government and to Grand Duchess Yelena Pavlovna. The debt of gratitude, he added, needed to be justified by actions and by results, and, addressing the assembled pupils of the Conservatory, he demanded that they not be content with mediocrity but "strive for the greatest perfection."

> Seeing before us so great a number wishing to devote themselves to art, I cannot but depend on the successful advancement of our undertaking; many people of both sexes, of all ages, of all social strata, from every corner of our vast empire have turned toward our school. This striving cannot be false, it even serves as a guarantee that our Conservatory may in the not too distant future stand alongside the greatest establishments of this kind.[59]

The first teachers at the new Conservatory included:

Piano: Anton Rubinstein; Alexander Dreyschock; and Anton Gerke, with assistance provided by a few advanced students including Frants Czerny, Pavel Petersen, and Karl Karlovich Fan Ark.
Music theory: Nikolay Zaremba; Otto Deutsch (died in 1863); and Konstantin Lyadov
Violin: Henryk Wieniawski
Cello: Carl Schuberth
Double-bass: Ivan Ferrero
Flute: Cesare Ciardi
Oboe: Johann Heinrich Luft
Clarinet: Ernesto Cavallini
Bassoon: Krankenhagen
Horn and trumpet: Hermann Metzdorf
Harp: Albert Heinrich Zabel
Organ: Heinrich Stiehl
Singing: Henrietta Nissen-Saloman; Gamieri; Catalano; and Piccioli
Other teachers were Karl Davïdov and Theodor Leschetizky.

There were 179 students in the first intake that fall, including Tchaikovsky and Laroche.[60] Laroche, in fact, has left us a vivid picture of the students who were drawn to the fledgling Conservatory: "Flocking to the new institution from the most varied strata of society and, in part, from the most far-flung corners of Russia, we were a motley crowd. There was Kross, a retired official from the customs department; Rïbasov, the son of a singer from the court cappella; Rubets, a former coroner's assistant from the Chernigov criminal department; Tchaikovsky, a senior *stolonachal'nik*[61] from the Ministry of Justice; Tiron, a student from Derpt; the Georgian Savanelli; Miretsky, a military engineer; Baranetsky, a lawyer; von Zur-Muhlen, a lieutenant of the Life Guards in the Semyonovsky regiment; Ludger, an Englishman from Newcastle who was a clerk with a steamboat company in St. Petersburg;[62] and the son of the junior French teacher at the Third St. Petersburg High school, Laroche."[63]

The first classes were held on the corner of Demidov pereulok [lane] and the Moyka Embankment at 64/1 (the so-called Demidov House). The classes continued to be given there until 1866, when new premises were found on Zagorodnïy Prospekt. From the outset, the Conservatory aimed to provide an all-round education for its students, and classes in Russian, German, and Italian, history, geography, and mathematics were organized. The full course was set at six years, and students who successfully completed it, and passed a public examination, would receive the title "Free Artist." Students from classes other than the *dvoryanstvo* received exemption from military service during their period of study (a provision that later prompted accusations that the Conservatory was fostering unpatriotic sentiments). Rubinstein threw himself into the organization of the classes with characteristic gusto. As he told Leopold Zellner, the editor of the Viennese journal *Blätter für Musik, Theater und bildene Kunst,* "I have to forget completely that I am a pianist and a composer. I am busy and now only live by the allocation of time and the organization of classes, etc., etc."[64]

Rubinstein's teaching and administrative duties at the Conservatory, as well as the taxing schedule of rehearsals for the RMS concerts between October and March, occupied almost all his time. Between 1860 and the end of 1863 he composed hardly anything except the German part songs that comprise his Opuses 61 and 62, and the setting of Lermontov's *Rusalka* for soloist, female choir, and orchestra (all three works were completed in 1861). He was still hoping to get *Feramors* staged, but Berlin had turned it down because the subject was the same as Spontini's opera *Nurmahal.*[65]

A highlight of the winter concert season was the premiere of Wieniawski's recently completed Violin Concerto in D minor, with the composer playing the solo part under Rubinstein's direction.[66] The remainder of the concert schedule for 1863 was a particularly busy one, including guest appearances by Richard Wagner who had been invited to Russia by the Philharmonic Society. In February/March 1863 he conducted several concerts in St. Petersburg and Moscow, and his appearances made a strong impression on many Russian musicians who praised his novel methods of conducting. Even Cui, who refused to pander to the general chorus of adulation, found something good to say: "Wagner has come at last and proved to us . . . that our orchestra is superb in the fullest sense of the word and you need only to know how to direct it; the only things difficult for our orchestra are those that are difficult for the conductor himself; that since the conductor is conducting not the audience but the orchestra, it is fitting for him to face the orchestra and not the audience."[67] Rubinstein attended these concerts, as he did a dinner given by Matvey Wielhorski in honor of the German composer. No record remains of Rubinstein's reaction to the concerts. His own opinion of Wagner was expressed at length in *Music and Its Masters,* and even if it shows that he failed to appreciate the nature of Wagner's genius, it does show that he was well aware of its impact on the development of European music:

> Had Wagner composed, brought out, and published his operas without expressing his own opinions about them in his writings, they would have been praised, blamed, loved, or not, as in the case of other composers; but to declare himself as the only source of happiness awakened opposition and protest. Some of his works are indeed worthy of respect (*Lohengrin, Meistersinger,* and the *Faust* overture I like best of his works), but the principles and pretensions in his musical creations

disgust me with most of them. The lack of naturalness, simplicity, makes them unsympathetic to me.[68]

Free Artist

Early in February 1863 Rubinstein and Villoing wrote to the Directorate of the St. Petersburg RMS, announcing that they wished to take the examination entitling them to the award "Free Artist." With this request Rubinstein enclosed copies of all his compositions. In her memoirs of Theodor Leschetizky, Countess Potocka noted: "Now Rubinstein, having no diploma from any conservatory, was simply put down as A. Rubinstein, son of a merchant. Strange as it may seem, this insignificant circumstance had been a serious annoyance to the great artist. One day he said to some of his friends, professors at the Conservatory: 'Please look at this abominable thing, my passport! Could anything look worse? Gentlemen, give me an artist's certificate.' Dreyschock and Leschetizky signed Rubinstein's document."[69] On 23 February 1863 (o.s.) an official record was made in the register of the Conservatory: "Mess. Professors, having examined the works of Mr. Rubinstein and Villoing, and taking into account the universal artistic recognition of Mr. Rubinstein and the services shown by Mr. Villoing in piano teaching[70] . . . have unanimously acknowledged that Mess. Rubinstein and Villoing are entirely worthy of the title Free Artist."[71] The description in his passport, "son of a merchant," was a constant reminder to Rubinstein that his social standing in Russia was a lowly one, and it was clearly the source of immense irritation.

Feramors in Dresden

Meanwhile, Rubinstein had received a telegram from Rodenberg telling him that *Feramors* had been successfully staged at the Hoftheater in Dresden on 24 February 1863. Karl August Krebs had taken up the post of music director of the theater from Wagner in 1850, but it was the arrival of Rubinstein's old friend, Julius Rietz, in 1860 to take charge of the opera and the orchestra that probably assisted in getting *Feramors* accepted for production. The original cast is shown in the full score of the opera published by Senff, and it indicates that Krebs's wife sang the role of Hafisa and Ludwig Schnorr von Carolsfeld, the famous Wagnerian tenor and creator of the role of Tristan, sang the role of Feramors:

Lallah Rookh, Princess of Hindostan	Frau Jauner-Krall (soprano)
Hafisa, her friend	Frau Krebs-Michalesi (alto)
Feramors, a singer	Herr Schnorr von Carolsfeld (tenor)
Fadladin, high vizier of Hindostan	Herr Frenz (bass)
Chosru, envoy of the King of Bothara	Herr Degele (baritone)
A muezzin	Herr Schloss (tenor)
A messenger	Herr Hollmann (tenor)

Although Rubinstein had been unable to attend the premiere, he was particularly pleased to hear that Hülsen, administrator of the Berlin theaters, had been present, for this might ultimately lead to a performance in the Prussian capital.[72] That same year Félicien David's opera *Lallah Rookh* on the same subject as *Feramors* was being accepted by opera houses all over Germany, but because of his teaching responsibilities, Rubinstein had been unable to promote his own opera. He complained about his situation: "I no longer belong to myself, nor to my art, but I am forced in the broadest sense to give myself over to teaching. My present post is neither honorable nor interesting in many respects, and I do not think that I shall be able to bear it for a long time. Sooner or later I shall give up this entire story and return to my muse, that charming coquettish bride, and I shall live only for her, even if I have to sacrifice my post."[73] Rubinstein was annoyed by the setbacks over the staging of *Feramors* and asked Rodenberg to supply another libretto; only this time he wanted it to be not a lyrical subject, but a highly dramatic one. He was still hoping that the libretto for the *Song of Songs* would be ready soon.

In May Rubinstein was at last able to go abroad. He headed first for Köningsberg, where he conducted *Das Verlorene Paradies* on 29 May, and then for Dresden via Baden-Baden, where he could not resist the gaming tables. Having missed the premiere of *Feramors*, he finally heard the opera in Dresden on 22 July. His verdict to Rodenberg was: "In the music there are shortcomings, in the text—*longeurs*—but this work will not bring shame on us, and we can boldly put it out into the world, and the world will be unjust if it turns it down."[74] He was pleasantly surprised by the staging, which he thought brilliant, and the sets exceeded his expectations. All this inspired in him the desire to compose yet another opera: "Only no more oriental settings—one work of this type is enough for the moment; now something European with a general and intriguing interest!"[75] For the time being, however, no new libretto, nor even the almost forgotten *Song of Songs*, materialized. In reality, there was little time to think about composing an opera, and Rubinstein's only achievement that summer was to revise the *Ocean Symphony*, adding to it the two discarded movements from the Symphony in B♭. The score, in this enlarged form, was published by Senff in 1871.

When Rubinstein returned to St. Petersburg, he brought with him the draft of a new charter for the RMS and the Conservatory, and lost no time in submitting them for approval. The main purpose of the new charter for the Conservatory was to strengthen the authority of the director and reduce external interference, but many months would pass before he received a response. Meanwhile, the RMS season began as usual in October, and on 7 and 21 November, and 5 and 19 December (o.s.), he conducted concerts in the Hall of the Nobility. Among the works heard were Brahms's *Serenade* for orchestra, choruses by Handel and Schubert, a romance by Gurilyov, and works by Beethoven, Schumann, Gounod, David, Litolff, Liszt, Chopin, and Glinka. Rubinstein also played on evenings devoted to chamber music at the Bernardaki Hall: the repertory was exclusively classical from Haydn to Schumann.

In the New Year Rubinstein conducted more RMS concerts on 9 and 29 January, and 5 February (o.s.). The programs consisted primarily of the German classical and romantic repertory (Michael Haydn, Mozart, Beethoven, Schubert, and Weber) prompted most likely by the arrival in St. Petersburg of Clara Schumann. She took part in chamber music evenings at the Bernardaki Hall in January and February and also played the solo part in her husband's Piano Concerto in a concert of 29 February/12 March. Laroche recalled that during this visit Clara Schumann heard a performance of a flute quartet by Kuhlau played by the young Tchaikovsky in the company of three other students (Pugni [the son of the ballet composer], Gorshkov, and Pomerantsev). Rubinstein had been striving for more than a year to form an orchestra of conservatory students. "Apart from a respectable contingent of violinists attracted by the name of Wieniawski," Laroche recalled, "there was in the first year, as far as I remember, not a single student who could even tolerably play any orchestral instrument. Rubinstein, who at that time received a very meager income, forfeited fifteen hundred rubles each year to provide free training on the missing instruments needed to make up a complete orchestra."[76] Laroche himself played the timpani, Vasily Bessel—the viola, and Ludwig Homelius—the cello, but the orchestra was mostly lacking in woodwind players, and it was on Rubinstein's initiative that Tchaikovsky studied the flute under Cesare Ciardi, and then occupied the position of second flute in the Conservatory orchestra from 1863 to 1864.

Some months earlier, the Directorate of Imperial Theaters had intimated to Rubinstein that his opera *Die Kinder der Haide* would be staged in St. Petersburg. In February he wrote to Count Aleksandr Borkh, director of the Imperial Theaters, explaining that Pavel Fyodorov, the head of the repertory section, had given him permission to distribute the roles in the opera himself. He wanted the eminent soprano Kseniya Prokhorova to take the role of Maria and had already promised it to her, but now the Directorate had given it to the much less notable singer Mikhaylovskaya. He also wanted the role of the Count to be entrusted to Komissarzhevsky, Nikolsky, or Bulakhov (all prominent tenors of the day), but this request was also ignored by the Directorate. Rubinstein felt that he had been treated abominably, and on 1/13 February he wrote directly to Andrey Krayevsky, editor of the influential paper *Golos,* asking him to publish an open letter in which he insisted that the opera was not being staged because of the Directorate's blatant disregard for the composer's wishes. Opposition to the opera came not only from official circles and the press. Balakirev, too, was stirring up hostility toward it. After the publication of the vocal score, he wrote to Rimsky-Korsakov on 11/23 January 1863: "he [Rubinstein] has done a lot of imitating, and do you know of whom? Gurilyov, Alyabyev, and the other Gypsy composers, turning out their wares in the center of that servile, obscene, and anti-artistic place—Moscow."

In March Rubinstein dismissed Konstantin Lyadov for failing to show up for classes, although this did not prevent him from taking part in a concert given by Lyadov on 9 April.[77] His relations with Raden were also giving him much cause for concern. In the period since she last entered our narrative, his relations with her had become more intimate—at least that is the way Rubinstein saw it. But she was avoiding him, and one wonders whether the attention he had been paying to her had become just a little too personal. With his customary habit of confronting matters head on, he finally he wrote to her, asking her to clarify how he must behave toward her: "If it is to be as a lady-in-waiting of the court, then I have grounds for terminating our acquaintance decisively and for good; if it is as Mlle Edith von Raden, then I shall always value the honor and feel proud of my friendship with you. And I assure you (although I suppose I do not need to): whatever happens, from the depths of my soul, I wholly belong to you even if circumstances force you to avoid my company. Ah! For how long have I wanted to kiss your sweet hand ardently. How fine it would be if you wanted to accept me such as I am. But God be with you, do as you wish."[78]

St. Petersburg was enjoying a rare festival of symphonic concerts, for Balakirev was now conducting the concerts of the Free Music School at the Hall of the Nobility. On 9/21 March Lomakin conducted choruses by Bach, Marcello, Handel, Dargomïzhsky, Weber, and Schumann, and Balakirev conducted orchestral works by Glinka, Dargomïzhsky, Cui, and Liszt. Nor did Rubinstein ignore the contemporary repertory, for, despite hostile claims in the press that the RMS concerts in the hands of Rubinstein had become a bastion for second-rate German music, on 12/24 March at the Hall of the Nobility, he conducted, alongside choruses from the operas of Lully, Rameau, and Mozart, the overture to Cui's opera *Sïn Mandarina* [The son of the Mandarin], and orchestral works by Wagner and Schumann. A notable appearance during the concert season was that made by Hans von Bülow at an RMS concert of 26 March/7 April. On this occasion the German pianist played the Liszt Concerto in E♭ under Rubinstein's direction. A week later Rubinstein gave a concert of his own works (as well as works by Chopin, Mendelssohn, and Liszt) at the City Duma in St. Petersburg, and on 3/15 May he and Konstantin Lyadov shared the rostrum in the popular concert organized annually by Lomakin and Kologrivov at the St. Petersburg Mikhaylovsky Manège; this concert included Balakirev's *Second Overture on Russian Themes* (revised a few years later as *1000 Years* and finally as *Rus'*) and works by Handel, Wagner, and Glinka.

Some time in May Rubinstein left for Berlin, where Dreyschock visited him and told him about a long conversation he had had with Count Aleksandr Borkh, the director of the Imperial Theaters in St. Petersburg, concerning the idea of closing the government-supported Theater School and transferring its subsidy to the Conservatory.[79] Rubinstein informed Kologrivov: "The report concerning the Theater School will be signed by the minister in the next few days on the following basis: the Conservatory is obliged to accept all the pupils from the Theater School without compensation; the minister is to adopt this measure as an economy and the music section at the Theater School is to be done away with; a specialist school is to be established at the Theater School for all the branches of music for the benefit of those who have successfully graduated from the Conservatory for the purpose of higher education and entering the service of the Directorate. What nonsense," Rubinstein complained to

Kologrivov. "Have they understood you? And have you understood their reasoning? I hasten to inform you about this so that you can clarify this important question in time (if this is still possible)."[80] Rubinstein had still received no response to his proposal for a new charter for the Conservatory, and he had decided that a sine qua non of his remaining director was that the charter had to be accepted.

In Leipzig Rubinstein met the eminent German violinist and teacher Ferdinand David. The latter joined Dreyschock and Rubinstein in a performance of the Piano Quartet in C, Op. 66, and David even intimated that he would not object to moving to St. Petersburg if a good position could be found for him. Rubinstein reveled in the thought of the prestige this would bring to the Conservatory: "It's better than Laub, Becker, and even Vieuxtemps," he told Kologrivov gleefully, asking him to bring the subject up with Borkh and of letting Wielhorski and the grand duchess know about the idea.[81] In the end David turned the proposal down and did not go to Russia.

At the end of 1863 Pauline Viardot and her husband, Louis, had settled permanently in Baden-Baden. They were attracted to it by the delightful surroundings and the active musical life. Deeply in love with Pauline, Turgenev followed shortly afterward, renting an apartment on the Schillerstraße. Rubinstein's professional association with Pauline inevitably brought him into contact with Turgenev, and earlier in the year he had worked with the great novelist on preparing an edition of Russian songs that Pauline had composed. Arriving in Baden-Baden in June, Rubinstein gave Sunday matinees attended by a host of especially invited guests, and lost heavily at the casino. Balakirev remarked derisively to César Cui: "He constantly plays roulette and has squandered everything, even some of his clothes, so that the next day he had to put on an old frockcoat and, for the temptation of the locals, went gloveless."[82] Almost every day he visited Pauline Viardot, whom he called "a remarkable woman." Before long, Clara Schumann had also arrived in Lichtenthal, just outside Baden-Baden. Here, in the house which she regularly occupied during the summer months, Rubinstein visited her in July, and together they played Brahms's Sonata in F minor for two pianos. Rubinstein probably felt little sympathy for this work, but it can hardly be a coincidence that he composed his own Fantasy in F minor for two pianos, Op. 73, over the next few months. As one might expect, the two works are completely unlike. Brahms's concentration on organic development, his predilection for complex textures (a factor that eventually led the composer to recast the work as the Piano Quintet, Op. 34), as well as his avoidance of ostentatious virtuosity, were largely alien to Rubinstein's musical nature. In his Fantasy, Rubinstein was aiming, above all, to create a rich sonority, and in this, the first of his extended piano works (except for the sonatas) he achieved his goal with a tempestuous first movement (*Lento. Allegro con fuoco*), and the imaginative set of variations with which the work concludes.

Before leaving Russia, Rubinstein had had discussions with the writer Vsevolod Krestovsky about adapting Mey's play *Pskovityanka* [The maid of Pskov] as an opera libretto. Krestovsky had evidently asked too high a fee, and

Rubinstein never set *The Maid of Pskov* (it was Rimsky-Korsakov who would set the subject of Mey's drama some eight years later). He had also hoped to write an opera called *Figlia del Tintoretto,* but the libretto had turned out to be so vile that it was completely unusable. He turned to writing piano pieces, a task for which he felt no particular enthusiasm, while continuing his search for a libretto. He told Kaleriya Khristoforovna that Turgenev had made a start on turning his own novel *Rudin* into an opera libretto for him, but the task proved too great, and on 28 June 1864 Turgenev wrote to Moritz Hartmann, encouraging him to provide Rubinstein with a libretto.[83] The Austrian writer and journalist Hartmann had translated several of Turgenev's works into German and had known many of the radical Russian exiles (Herzen, Bakunin, and others). Four years later, in 1868, he became chief editor of the Viennese newspaper *Neue Freie Presse.* The result of the collaboration between Hartmann and Rubinstein was *Rosvita,* an opera in three acts for which the composer paid three thousand francs. Rubinstein began work but demanded changes; Hartmann refused, and Rubinstein abandoned the opera altogether. In his search to find an appropriate subject for an opera Rubinstein had even discussed his plans with Edith von Raden,[84] for she had suggested the novella *Veronica Cybo* by Francesco Guerrazzi. Her choice of Guerrazzi seems strange, as his historical novels, although very popular in their time, were considered extremely radical, republican, even revolutionary. The relentless search for a suitable operatic subject that summer suggests that Rubinstein was brimming with new creative ideas, but none of the proposals put forward seems to have sufficiently captured his imagination. If he had been denied an opera, he said, he would compose a symphony, but this plan did not materialize either; his Symphony No. 4 in D minor was not written until 1874. Instead, he wrote two concertos that may be counted among the most successful of his works: the Cello Concerto No. 1 in A minor, Op. 65, and the Piano Concerto No. 4 in D minor, Op. 70.

The idea of writing a cello concerto had been in Rubinstein's mind since 1857 when he completed his Violin Concerto in G. The influences on the earlier work were clearly Beethoven (the concerto and violin romances), Mendelssohn, Vieuxtemps, and especially Wieniawski, but the concerto is quite faceless, and not even the considerable demands made on the soloist in terms of technique and delicacy of shading can redeem the work from mediocrity. The Cello Concerto, on the other hand, is in all respects a much finer piece. In the first place, the thematic material is altogether richer and more varied, the overall structure is tauter, and the very tonal qualities of the cello seemed to draw from the composer a power of expression that is wholly lacking in the Violin Concerto. This becomes immediately apparent from the soloist's first entry in the *Moderato con moto* and the second subject group, where subtle touches of humor provide an effective contrast to the more dramatic moments. Rubinstein was quite adept at writing slow movements full of dreamy sentimentality, and the *Adagio* of this concerto is one of his finest. Many of the same good qualities are to be found in the Piano Concerto No. 4, the only one of Rubinstein's five published piano concertos to have retained a tenuous hold on the repertory. This is understandable: the musical ideas in this concerto are fresher and more imaginative than in Rubinstein's earlier works in the same genre, and the overall design is more satisfactory. "Only in this concerto," as Jeremy Norris has pointed out, "did Rubinstein achieve "a well-balanced distribution of the material between soloist and orchestra."[85] Cui found the finale to be "original" but "strange and antiartistic," yet, despite his criticism, the concerto served as one of the most important models for several later Russian piano concertos, notably Tchaikovsky's Bb minor concerto of 1874.

Rubinstein was eagerly awaiting news from Kologrivov. The most pressing matter was the charter. The grand duchess had made changes, but Kologrivov had not sent him the amended copy so he did not know what they were. If he knew, he told Kologrivov, he would go to Carlsbad and try to sort it all out with her and Matvey Wielhorski. "She will play dirty tricks on us, and that is all on account of me, isn't she a minx? Who is right? Well, the main thing is to try and become 'imperial' and to be attached to the Ministry of the Court or the Ministry of Education."[86] On 3/15 August Rubinstein reported to Kologrivov that he had been to see the grand duchess in Switzerland about the affairs of the RMS and the Conservatory (specifically the charters of both), and more suitable premises for the Conservatory. He planned to be back in St. Petersburg by 1/13 September, followed by the grand duchess a little later in mid-October. By the time of her arrival the committee would have to be in a position to give a reply to all her proposals and enquiries point by point.

On 19 September/1 October 1864 Rubinstein wrote to Niels Gade in Copenhagen, recalling their acquaintance in the summer of 1862 and offering him the dedication of his *Faust Overture*, Op. 68 (one of the surviving movements of the abandoned *Faust Symphony* of 1854).[87] Meanwhile, the new concert season was about to start, and, given Rubinstein's deeply rooted dislike of Berlioz's music, it is remarkable that he conducted a performance of *La Fuite en Egypte* at the Hall of the Nobility on 22 October/3 November. Just a week later, on 29 October/10 November, he played the solo part in the first performance of his Piano Concerto No. 4. Further RMS concerts under Rubinstein's direction followed on 19 and 26 November, and 3, 10 and 17 December (o.s.) (these concerts included Liszt's *Mazeppa*, Schumann's *Das Paradies und die Peri*, and Wagner's *Ride of the Valkyries*).

Tchaikovsky

The relations between Rubinstein and his most famous pupil were extremely complex and require careful examination. Tchaikovsky had first heard Rubinstein's name in 1858 when he was still an eighteen-year-old student at the School of Jurisprudence. At that time he was taking private piano lessons from Rudolf Kündinger, and it was the latter who had told him that the great virtuoso had returned to Russia. That same year Tchaikovsky had the opportunity to hear Rubinstein play and to see him conduct concerts. He attended one of these concerts in the company of his twin brothers, Modest and Anatoly. As Modest later recalled in the biography of his brother:

> At the house of Prince Beloselsky there was a charity concert for amateurs. Pyotr Ilich and we, the twins, were among the audience. There, too, was Anton Grigoryevich Rubinstein in the prime of his unique, "monstrous"—if you can put it like that—beauty, as a man of genius and then at the height of his artistic fame. Pyotr Ilich pointed him out to me for the first time, and now, forty years later, I can vividly remember the agitation, the delight, and the reverence with which the future pupil gazed at his future teacher. He no longer looked at the stage, but, like a love-crazed youth, nervously followed the unapproachable maiden at a distance— he did not tear his eyes away from his "divinity," and, during the intervals, he walked behind him unnoticed, trying to catch his voice, and envying the people who were fortunate enough to shake his hand. . . . Indeed, Anton Grigoryevich was the first one who gave the budding composer the model of an artist boundlessly devoted to the interests of his art and honest to the smallest detail in his strivings and in his methods for attaining his goal. In this sense, incomparably more than because of the lessons in composition and orchestration, Pyotr Ilich was his pupil. With Pyotr Ilich's inherent talent and the thirst for study which gripped him, any other teacher could have given him essentially that which Anton Grigoryevich gave him, without impressing in any way his influence on the compositions of Pyotr Ilich. As an energetic, irreproachably pure figure, as an artist of genius, as a person incapable of any compromise with his conscience, the indefatigable enemy of char- latanism, majestically disdaining inflated banality, and allowing no concessions to it, and as an unceasing toiler—he was unquestionably a teacher who left a pro- found impression on the artistic career of Pyotr Ilich.[88]

When the Conservatory opened in 1862 Tchaikovsky was still working as a clerk at the Ministry of Justice, living the carefree life of a socialite and taking his first tentative steps toward a career in music. He finally resigned his post at the ministry in the spring of 1863 but began receiving composition lessons from Rubinstein only in the fall of that year; previously (1861–62) he had worked through Marx's course in harmony with Zaremba, and then, during the conser- vatory's first year, strict counterpoint and church modes from the book by Bel- lermann.[89] Thus, in the fall of 1863, he was attending Zaremba's class in form and simultaneously Anton Rubinstein's recently opened class in orchestration. Laroche has left us a lucid portrait of Rubinstein at this period: "The mighty personality of the director of the Conservatory inspired in us students endless love mixed with not a small dose of fear. In reality, there was not a head more indulgent and good-natured, but his gloomy look, quick temper, and turbulent character, combined with the charm of a name famed throughout Europe, nevertheless acted on people in an unusually imposing manner." It was the cher- ished desire of all piano students to get into his large classes, Laroche tells us, which consisted of three male students and a veritable flock of female ones. One of the tasks he set for students was to play Czerny's *Tägliche Studien* in all twelve keys and with the same fingering. As a lecturer, Laroche compares him to Zaremba. The latter, despite his Polish origins, spoke Russian perfectly with no trace of an accent and, moreover, with "brilliant eloquence," whereas, in Laroche's view, Rubinstein was quite inarticulate, and although he knew many languages he spoke none of them perfectly—not even German. "In a private conversation he could express himself in Russian very fluently, sometimes finding felicitous and well-aimed expressions, but the grammar left much to be desired, and in the coherent presentation of a theoretical subject the defects showed themselves even more forcefully." What Rubinstein did bring to his pupils was "massive practical knowledge, a vast mental outlook, and incredible experience of composition for a man of thirty." Such qualities "gave to his words an authority that we could not help but feel. The very paradoxes which he rained down on us, now teasing us, now mocking us, bore the stamp of a person of genius and of a thinking artist."[90]

In his orchestration class Rubinstein acknowledged only the orchestra of the classic composers, that is, the orchestra of Beethoven with the addition of three trombones and the substitution of chromatic trumpets and horns for natural ones. He forbade his pupils to use the full orchestra in their exercises: "before allowing them [the pupils] to work with a full orchestra, I would straightjacket them into exercises, using the various individual orchestral groups. It is astonishing how much beauty Beethoven could express in his five string trios," Rubinstein declared in *Gedankenkorb*. Rubinstein once asked Tchaikovsky to orchestrate Beethoven's D minor Piano Sonata, using four different methods: "One of these methods came out in a refined and complicated manner, with a *cor anglais* and other such rarities, for which Tchaikovsky immediately received a dressing down," recalled Laroche.[91] He [Rubinstein] was not putting himself to the trouble of teaching the art of composition to create idiots [*pour former des imbéciles*]. Rubinstein's disapproval of his pupil's methods is best illustrated by the incident over Tchaikovsky's first major orchestral composition, the *Storm Overture,* based on Ostrovsky's play *Groza.* Here were all the ingredients which were anathema to Rubinstein: the use of the afore-mentioned *cor anglais* in an orchestral work (not to mention the harp), a Russian folk melody, a complex use of harmony and colorful effects. Tchaikovsky was wise in not presenting the score to Rubinstein himself; when safely out of harm's way, he posted it to Laroche, asking him to deliver it to the formidable director. Laroche recalled:

In the summer of 1864 Pyotr Ilich had to write a large overture, and he himself chose as a program Ostrovsky's *The Storm.* He picked the most heretical orchestra that ever was with bass tuba, *cor anglais,* harp, *tremolo* in the divided strings, bass drum, and cymbals. Probably with his characteristic optimism, he hoped that under the flag of a program, these departures from the regime prescribed for him would pass unpunished.[92] As always, he finished his work on time, even a little earlier. I do not remember why, instead of presenting it personally, he sent the score to me by post, charging me with the task of taking it to Anton Grigoryevich. Rubinstein instructed me to see him in a few days to hear his response. Never in my life have I received such a wigging for my own actions as I had to endure (I remember it was a fine Sunday morning) for someone else's as on that occasion. With an instinctive humor Rubinstein put the question thus: 'If you had dared to bring me such a thing of your own composition . . . ,' and then proceeded to fulminate against me. Having completely exhausted the store of his anger, the hot-tempered director of the Conservatory had kept nothing in reserve for the real culprit, so when Pyotr Ilich arrived a few days later and went, in his turn, to hear the verdict, he was greeted extremely affectionately and received only a few brief complaints.[93]

Tchaikovsky erred on the side of caution when he came to write his graduation piece the following year—the cantata *K Radosti* [Ode to joy] set to the words of Schiller. The work is a good deal more conventional, but it still failed to gain the approbation of the Conservatory's director. According to Laroche, Tchaikovsky asked whether Rubinstein would include the cantata and his Overture in C minor in RMS concerts, but Rubinstein steadfastly refused, or at least agreed to conduct the cantata only if Tchaikovsky made substantial changes. Despite Rubinstein's apparent mistrust of Tchaikovsky's judgment in composition, he nevertheless set his pupil the task of translating into Russian Gevaert's *Manual of Orchestration.*[94] The work was completed by 1 September, and Jurgenson published it in 1866.

During January, February, and March 1865 Rubinstein appeared as conductor in RMS concerts and as a soloist, although less frequently than in earlier years. On 7/19 January, for example, he conducted Schumann's overture *Die Braut von Messina* and excerpts from Moniuszko's cantata *Nijola.* There were also concerts of chamber music at the Bernardaki Hall, where Rubinstein appeared with the pianists Mikhail Santis and Mariya Harder in works by Mozart, Beethoven, Mendelssohn, Schumann, Schubert, and Volkmann. The musical life of Russia had been much enlivened by the concerts of the Free Music School given by Balakirev and Lomakin in St. Petersburg and also by the RMS concerts in Moscow, conducted by Nikolay Rubinstein. By this time, the programs of the Moscow concerts had become as enterprising and varied as their St. Petersburg counterparts, and appearances by artists such as Clara Schumann helped to establish Moscow as a center of musical excellence. The works of many contemporary European composers, such as Gade and Volkmann, were already being heard in RMS concerts, and other composers were approaching Rubinstein with their work. That winter, for example, Rubinstein received the score of the program symphony *Columbus* by the Czech-German composer Jan Abert who headed the court orchestra in Stuttgart.[95] Abert's Symphony was performed in Moscow by Nikolay Rubinstein in an RMS concert at the Hall of the Nobility on 16 December 1865, together with extracts from Anton's *Die Kinder der Haide.*

Rubinstein's delicate negotiations with the government and the court concerning the provision of new charters for the RMS and the Conservatory had become bogged down in bureaucracy. Matters had been made worse by the decision to restructure the organization of the Russian Music Society which, by 1865, had branches in Moscow (1860), Kiev (1863), and Kazan (1864). With the prospect of further branches of the RMS being opened in other Russian cities, the government decided to create a Chief Directorate to which the directorates of all the branches would be subservient. This meant that, even though Yelena Pavlovna remained its president and Prince Dmitry Obolensky its vice president, control would pass into the hands of people over whom Rubinstein had little influence. In a last-ditch attempt to force the issue, he wrote directly to the grand duchess on 28 May/9 June, enclosing copies of the revised charters together with his report *The Obligations and Rights of the Director of the Conservatory*. Rubinstein's report has never been published in its entirety, but Barenboym quotes a part of it:

> The director is to choose the professors, appoint the subjects to be taught and the classes and the periods of study; he is to keep watch over the method and manner of teaching and the success achieved by the students . . . and he is to arrange everything that he finds necessary for the successful progress of art at the Conservatory. In all the aforesaid points he is to be guided by a Council of Professors over which he presides and in which all questions are to be resolved through a majority of votes. . . . For his entire tenure he is the chief person in charge of the Conservatory; no one has the right to make any arrangement without his knowledge. . . . At his discretion he may reply or not to public accusations, but in any case he is obliged to accept full responsibility.[96]

Rubinstein pointed out to Yelena Pavlovna that the term he had set himself as director to establish the two institutions (the RMS and the Conservatory) had almost expired: "Now I can say boldly that they have sufficient material funds and they can blossom and attain their noble aims." He told her that all this had deflected him from his career as a composer, but he was prepared to make the sacrifice "if Your Imperial Highness finds that my labors are not without use even now, but on no other terms than those expressed by me in the charters."[97] If these conditions could not be satisfied, he told her, he would consider himself relieved of his duties at the Conservatory and the RMS as of 1 January 1866. To issue an ultimatum such as this was indeed a high-risk strategy. He may have felt that his position as the head of an institution which had achieved so much in just three years was virtually unassailable, but his demands for greater autonomy ran contrary to the policy of centralization and bureaucratization that was the hallmark of the tsarist government. The Conservatory's dependence on arbitrary decisions taken by the Ministry of Education and the Ministry of the Court was a constant source of irritation to Rubinstein.[98]

Marriage to Vera Chekuanova

Shortly after sending his letter to the grand duchess, Rubinstein set out for Leipzig via Berlin. He stopped in Leipzig just long enough to pen a few lines to Rodenberg, telling his librettist that he did not want to return to Russia without the libretto of the *Song of Songs* in his suitcase.[99] He had promised the opera to a music festival in Köningsberg and must have it *"coûte que coûte* [whatever the cost]."[100] There is nothing in the published documents to prepare us for what happened next. Rubinstein's next communication is addressed to Kaleriya Khristoforovna and informs her of his marriage to Vera Chekuanova the previous day: "Yesterday on the day of my marriage I telegraphed you in Helingsfors. I hope that you received it."[101] On 12 July Rubinstein had married Vera Chekuanova in Baden-Baden. Of his immediate family only Nikolay was present, and there were no more than sixteen persons in the church to witness the ceremony. His sponsors (i.e., those standing in for his parents) were Mme Chernïsheva and Mr. Myuller, and his best man was Mr. Volkov. Those for Vera were her mother, and Mr. Stolïpin (a certain Mr. Bruner gave her away). "As you see," he remarked to his mother, "unfamiliar people, or very distant acquaintances. But since the marriage was held abroad, it could not be any other way."[102] After the ceremony, the couple went directly to Stuttgart. They planned a trip to Paris, then to take a short holiday in Switzerland. After this they intended returning to St. Petersburg via Baden-Baden.

Barenboym tells us that Vera was the youngest of several daughters in an impoverished family of landowners with a small estate in the Province of Novgorod called Glubokoye.[103] The family spent the winter months in St. Petersburg, and, according to Vera herself, she met her future husband at a costumed ball at the Academy of Arts in 1859. He was dressed as a pilgrim and she, as an Italian girl, and, as they were both fond of dancing, they soon found themselves partnered in a Strauss waltz. Vera's father was a retired officer and was arrogant and conceited. He opposed the match from the start and considered it degrading for his daughter to marry an artist with no material standing, who had originated from the Jewish merchants' estate. Fortunately for Rubinstein, Vera became a pupil of Pauline Viardot in Russia, and most of the courtship took place at her convivial home in Baden-Baden.[104] In all probability the engagement was announced in the summer of 1864 when both Anton and Vera were visiting Pauline.

Rubinstein returned to St. Petersburg with his bride on 28 August/9 September 1865. Yakov Becker met them at the railway station, and they drove straight to Vera's father, where they spent an hour. When they arrived at their new home, they found Kologrivov, Aleksandr Shustov, Vera Ivasheva,[105] and two lady friends of his wife waiting for them. Evidently Kaleriya Khristoforovna had taken great care to arrange the apartment for the homecoming of the newlyweds, for Rubinstein thanked her effusively for all the care she had taken and for "all your love and kindness." On 26 October/7 November 1865 he wrote to her that he and Vera were settling in well and that they had instituted Sunday evening receptions attended by many people who came to chat and play cards. "As a rare exception there is a little music, that is, singing with piano accompaniment, with Wieniawski, etc."[106]

One of the eagerly awaited events that fall in St. Petersburg was the premiere of Serov's new opera, *Rogneda*, which was presented at the Mariiinsky Theater on 27 October/ 8 November 1865. The opera scored a huge success with the public because of its colorful historical setting and vivid folk scenes. Serov had become "intoxicated with his success," Rubinstein remarked, and the public is intoxicated by his music, but "that is not surprising," he added sarcastically, "for so much drinking is done in the opera."[107] With his own compositions Rubinstein was not making much headway, for he had only completed the first movement of a piano sonata since returning to Russia, and even that had not yet been written down. In fact, Rubinstein completed no further piano sonatas until his Fourth Sonata in A minor, Op. 100, in 1877, so the movement was either abandoned or incorporated into some other work (in 1866 he completed his Fantasy in E minor, Op. 77). In any case, the time for examinations was fast approaching, and this would mean there would be little time for composing. He had received another opera libretto, which he had found suitable: this was *The Oprichnik* adapted by Pyotr Kalashnikov from the play by Ivan Lazhechnikov.[108]

The latter part of 1865 had seen the first public performance of works by Tchaikovsky. Johann Strauss had conducted his *Characteristic Dances* at the pleasure gardens in Pavlovsk on 30 August/11 September, and the first performance of the Quartet Movement in B♭ (probably first heard privately at the Conservatory in August) had its official premiere on 30 October/11 November. Tchaikovsky made his first appearance as a conductor with the original version of his Overture in F major for a small orchestra on 14/26 November at the Mikhaylovsky Palace. Finally, on 29 December/10 January 1866 his cantata *Ode to Joy* was performed as part of the first public examination of the St. Petersburg Conservatory. Among the audience were the directors of the RMS and an examination committee consisting of government delegates appointed by the Ministry of the Imperial Court (the director of the Court Cappella Bakhmetyev and the conductors of the Imperial Theaters Viktor Kaźiński, Konstantin Lyadov, and Ricci). The program of the graduation concert is published in *Dni i godï P. I. Chaykovskogo.*[109] The program shows that seven examinees that had completed the full course were eligible to receive the diploma and the award "Free Artist" (some of these "students" were already junior teachers at the Conservatory):

Tchaikovsky (Professor Zaremba's class) for theory;
Messrs. Homilius and Kross[110] (Professor Rubinstein's class), for piano
Mr. Reykhardt (Professor Dreyschock's class), for piano
Mr. Rïbasov (Professor Gerke's class), for piano
Mr. Bessel (Professor Veykman's class), for viola
Mr. [Ludwig] Albrecht (Professor Davïdov's class) for cello

There were an additional five graduates who had completed the course for instrumentalists:

Mme Malozyomova (Professor Leshchetizky's class), piano
Mess. Ivanov, Pushilov, and Salin (Professor Wieniawski's class), violin
Mr. Makarov (Professor Ferrero's class), double-bass

The examination began at 12.30 PM and commenced with "the handing out of theoretical assignments." The program of the examination concert itself included nine items by Mendelssohn, Ferrero, Chopin, Viotti, and Ernst, but

Tchaikovsky's name as the author of the *Cantata* was not flushed to the right under the names of the "established composers." Rubinstein conducted the orchestra. A further examination took place at the same time on 31 December/ 12 January. It commenced with an examination of the theoretical assignments presented to the students two days earlier and an analysis of the musical compositions. The graduates who had completed the entire conservatory course had to perform a work that they had prepared: the first movement of a Beethoven piano concerto (Reykhardt), the *Romance* and *Finale* of a viola concerto by Friedrich Dotzauer (Bessel), a *Prelude* and *Fugue* by Mendelssohn (Homilius), a cello concerto by Davïdov (Albrecht), Liszt's *Réminiscences de Don Juan* (Rïbasov). They were then examined in the history of music, score reading, piano, sight-reading, and transposition. At the end of the examination a magnificent banquet was organized by the grand duchess at the Mikhaylovsky Palace in honor of the new graduates.

By mid-December 1865 Rubinstein had still not received any positive news from the grand duchess about the new charter, and on 14/26 December he informed his mother: "I am quite firmly decided that as of 1 January I shall have nothing more to do with the Conservatory unless matters have been resolved to my satisfaction."[111] He was gradually accustoming himself to the idea that he would have to leave the Conservatory in the spring.

The successes achieved by the Conservatory during its first three years were striking, and Rubinstein could later claim, not without a certain pride, that the St. Petersburg Conservatory (and after 1866 the Moscow Conservatory as well) had produced "a whole new division of Russian citizens bearing the title "Free Artist" (in the domain of music). What was done more than a hundred years ago for painters and others, and even earlier, at the instance and on the initiative of Sumarokov, for Russian actors and actresses, was done in these years for Russian artist-musicians of both sexes."[112]

Despite the new charter not having been approved, Rubinstein remained for another year as director of the Conservatory. He justified his decision, in part, by the fact that the examinations had not gone quite the way he had wanted. He was delighted with the results, and told Kaleriya Khristoforovna that "six students received diplomas and four received certificates."[113] This apparent oversight was caused by Rubinstein refusing to sign the diplomas of students who had failed to appear at the examination ceremony. He actually withheld Tchaikovsky's diploma, because the latter had absented himself from the graduation concert, fearing public examination.[114] Tchaikovsky's failure to appear on 29 December, however, was not mentioned in any of the official documents.

Work on the opera *The Oprichnik* was progressing slowly, and in two months Rubinstein had managed to complete only the introduction and the first chorus of act 1. He had grown disillusioned with the opera and turned to Sollogub for advice about the quality of Kalashnikov's libretto, asking for suggestions about the way it could be changed. Sollogub concluded his reply with the solemn pronouncement: "I close with the wish never to collaborate with Mr. Kalashnikov.

He will be a heavy encumbrance upon your genius."[115] This put an end to Rubinstein's work on *The Oprichnik*. As the concert season in St. Petersburg was about to resume, Rubinstein was unable to attend the first performance of *Die Kinder der Haide* at the Bolshoy Theater in Moscow on 10/22 February. The opera received four performances but was not heard again in Russia until 1903, when it was revived by Savva Mamontov's private opera company at the Hermitage Theater. Reviewing this later production, the critic Yury Engel acknowledged perceptively: "There is a lot of the old-fashioned in it, especially in the role of Wania . . . and as if conforming to this, the composer interpreted it, from the musical point of view, in an outdated Alyabyev-Varlamov style." Engel also observed that the opera contains real Gypsy themes, one of which was used for Isbrana's song at Wania's wedding: "The tragic end of this song, with its unexpected melodic turn, can serve as an example of those flashes of talent that are not uncommon in Rubinstein . . . and by its freshness and strength so often adorns the vapidity of the music surrounding it."[116]

During the Lent season Rubinstein conducted performances of Raff's First Symphony and a symphony by Gade. He was also engaged to take part in the popular concert given by Kologrivov each spring at the Manège. On 1/13 May Lomakin, Konstantin Lyadov, and Rubinstein conducted a program that included works by Glinka, Dargomïzhsky, Balakirev, Serov, Lomakin, Tchaikovsky, and the first performance of Rubinstein's cantata *Utro* [Morning], to a text by Yakov Polonsky.[117] Rubinstein had agreed to conduct Tchaikovsky's Overture in F major[118] but when the latter submitted his First Symphony to his old teachers in the fall, both Rubinstein and Zaremba were highly critical. After Tchaikovsky had revised it, Nikolay Rubinstein conducted the *Scherzo* from the symphony at an RMS concert on 10/22 December 1866, and Anton conducted the *Andante* and *Scherzo* in St. Petersburg at an RMS concert on 11/23 February 1867. Anton's refusal to conduct the entire symphony infuriated Tchaikovsky, for he wrote to his brother Anatoly: "The attitude of those villains [Rubinstein and Zaremba] toward me is too cavalier; I should spit on them and let them see that I have my self-respect."[119]

Rubinstein's relations with conservative elements in the RMS had by this time taken a decided turn for the worse, and in May 1866 it became clear that his departure from the Conservatory could not be long delayed. He had written in a defiant mood to Senator Andrey Markovich: "Yesterday I was in Pavlovsk and found out that you have asked the grand duchess, through General Kepen, not to sign the confirmation for the inspector I have appointed for the Conservatory. I acknowledge the formalities of confirming my orders concerning the Conservatory, but I do not acknowledge the formalities of non-confirmation. I suggest the following way out of the situation—either I leave, or you go, or the inspector I have appointed will take his place before 1 June."[120] This ultimatum was the last straw for the grand duchess and her acolytes in the RMS.

In June the Conservatory moved from Demidov pereulok to Zagorodnïy Prospekt and Rubinstein was involved in transferring to the new premises the music library and the collection of instruments which Count Matvey Wielhorski had bequeathed to the Conservatory after his death on 26 February/5 March 1866.

In October the concert season began again and performances of Gade's "symphony" [sic] *In Scotland*,[121] a concert overture by Azanchevsky, the overture to Spohr's opera *Der Berggeist*, Berlioz's overture *Le Carnival Romain*, and excerpts from a mass by Liszt were given under Rubinstein's direction. His position was looking increasingly more isolated. Having provoked the fury of Yelena Pavlovna and the court circles, he now alienated himself from the teaching staff of the Conservatory. At a meeting of the Council of Professors on 21 October/2 November he came into conflict with the majority over their right to choose the works which their pupils could perform at Conservatory soirées and in examinations. The same day he wrote to the council:

> I cannot agree with the opinion of the majority because I consider that the aim of the Conservatory is to shape the musical tastes of the students, to acquaint them with the model works of the classical composers, to open up for them the lofty horizon of musical art, etc. To achieve this aim I consider it impossible to permit any teacher to give a student works which do not have artistic merit and are based only on more or less elegant passages and melodies, that is, so-called fashionable music. Or, at least, to permit a choice of this sort I consider possible only in the classroom in the form of exercises for the complete development of the mechanism, in the rarest circumstances, as an exception, but not at Conservatory soirées where the programs must bear witness to the direction and spirit of our institution.[122]

A further disagreement arose two months later on the matter of awarding diplomas, when Rubinstein disagreed with Wieniawski. Once again Rubinstein wrote a letter of protest to the Council of Professors:

> I cannot agree with the opinion of the majority because I consider that the diploma is too great an award for people who are not absolutely mature in musical art; it is desirable to avoid the accumulation of mediocrity in art and not to encourage it. It is possible to award certificates of various sorts to people who have more or less satisfactorily completed the institution's program, but a diploma must be awarded only to a student who stands out from the mundane. In the first year of graduation blunders of that kind were made, in the second year they ought to be avoided, and the same blunders not committed because of poorly thought-out resolutions. Therefore I protest against awarding the diploma to Mr. Altani, Mlles Altani, Tarnovskaya, Smiryagina, Terminskaya, Shchetinina, Dobzhanskaya, Khvostova, Klemm, and Loginova, and I find it necessary for all these people to remain at the Conservatory and continue their studies for at least another year.[123]

These two disagreements ultimately led to Rubinstein's resignation.

Resignation as Director of the Conservatory

Toward the end of February 1867 matters had reached a head and Rubinstein wrote to Dmitry Obolensky, vice president of the Chief Directorate of the RMS, stating the conditions he insisted upon if he were to remain director of the Conservatory. The original of this letter is no longer extant, but the record of meetings convened by the Directorate of the RMS indicates that Obolensky included a report in which these conditions were set out. They were as follows:

1. Diplomas and certificates in variable form are to be produced quickly and presented to the persons due to receive them before the start of the vacation.
2. Diplomas with the names of those I have not approved, I will not sign.
3. The examinations for 1865 and 1866 are to be considered valid only for those persons who have received their diploma or certificate with my approval. The graduation of anyone in the obligatory subjects with a mark of 3 or 4 I consider invalid, and I demand their reexamination, for up to the present time the guide rules for conducting examinations were not fully understood by anyone and the marks were awarded by everyone without appreciating their proper value.
4. Henceforth, examinations must be conducted in accordance with my instructions and my program, and the final awarding of the diploma or certificate, with due regard for the opinion of the council of professors, depends on me and is approved by the grand duchess.
5. Contracts are to be concluded with all the professors.
6. The Council of Professors is to assemble each month for consultations with me about various matters concerning the Conservatory. The opinions of the majority are to be recorded in a journal (as a document), but if I disagree with them I act according to my own conviction.
7. The journals and the resolutions of the professors up to the present time are considered invalid and everything is subject to reexamination.
8. The students are wholly subject to my instructions and they cannot make reference to any lack of agreement between their professors, that is, in the event of an ad hoc test which I may deem it necessary to subject someone to at any time, my demand for someone to take part in a Conservatory soirée or a concert of the Russian Musical Society, my assigning them to this or that class among the classes I have devised.
9. I retain the right to transfer a student from one professor to another within the same specialization.
10. All documents and papers issuing from the Conservatory, and also invitations for examinations, etc., are written in my name and not in the name of the Russian Music Society, as it has been done up to now.
11. I receive a monthly salary of thirty-six hundred rubles without accommodation, or three thousand rubles with accommodation, inseparably from the Russian Music Society, and on a nine-monthly basis.[124]

Barenboym tells us that points 1, 2, 3, 4, 6, and 7 were declined by the RMS Directorate and he includes a fragment of a letter from Yelena Pavlovna in which she states her reasons: "I find, however, that the proposed letter of Mr.

Rubinstein cannot in any way serve as the basis for discussions with him. . . . It even seems improbable that the government would agree to concentrate in the hands of one person the authority to confer a title which is associated with the rights of estate."[125] Rubinstein was left with no other alternative, and on 10/22 April Andrey Klimchenko, one of the directors of the RMS, reported to the board that Rubinstein was resigning. The official resignation made by Rubinstein himself came a few months later in a letter of July 1867, addressed to Prince Obolensky.

News of Rubinstein's imminent departure from the Conservatory was greeted gleefully by the nationalists. In a wave of pan-Slavic sentiment, Balakirev had been recently dispatched to Prague to conduct Glinka's operas *A Life for the Tsar* and *Ruslan and Lyudmila* at the national opera. He had suffered considerable opposition from the conservatives headed by Smetana and even more hostility from the Poles living in the city. The crushing of the uprising in Poland in 1863, the attempted assassination of Alexander II by pro-Polish revolutionaries, and the depiction of the Poles as the villains in Glinka's *A Life for the Tsar* had the effect of turning these opera productions into a sensational political event, aggravated by rumors that the costs of staging the operas had been financed by the Russian government to the tune of fifty thousand rubles. The operas scored a resounding triumph with the public, but the political turmoil they caused proved too much for the Czech authorities, and after only one performance of *A Life for the Tsar* on 10/22 February 1867 Balakirev was politely asked to return home to Russia.[126]

A clear reflection of xenophobic, anti-Polish, anti-Jesuitical, and anti-Semitic sentiments can be readily found in the correspondence between Balakirev and Musorgsky from this period. In one particularly malicious letter dated 23 January/ 2 February 1867, Musorgsky replied to a letter Balakirev had written to him from Prague on 11/23 January. Musorgsky addressed his mentor as "My dear Mily-Czech, pane professore," and then goes on to tell him:

> On 16 January you honored me with a pleasant awakening—I received your dear letter and roared with laughter about the conservatory alumni-capons in Bohemia, and about General Capon Tupinstein,[127] this most esteemed of capons, whose immaculateness you suspect. Such a brilliant idea leaves an important gap in the most Catholic fantasies of the indefatigable Pius IX—pontifex maximus! You know what, Mily? I dare to think that if by misfortune (the Lord spare us from this!) you happened to have a chat with the Most August and the Most Stinking Pius IX on the subject of the secret illusions of the *quasi* Orthodox intelligentsia, then you, as a Russian, would not be slow in advising the Glorious (read, Freakish) Pius, in raising Pater Druklin (in the monkish trade corporation) to the rank of a saint, to excite a treatise on his immaculateness; there is no need that Druklin grammatically speaking belongs to a person of the male gender, for Catholics, acknowledging the infallibility of the Pope with his stink, must be, in all probability, genderless.
>
> Three facts have occurred during your absence: the St. Petersburg Conservatory is in disarray; General of Music Tupinstein has quarreled with the conservatory

clique and plans to resign; [and] the poor professors are crestfallen, and now you can see them in the streets wearing sackcloth, with cheap penitential cigars (instead of candles) between their teeth (hands) out of penitence, and their heads are sprinkled with ash (from these cigars)—your heart is heavy when you meet them.[128]

One of Rubinstein's last duties as director of the Conservatory was to stage Gluck's *Orphée*. This was the first opera staged entirely through the efforts of the Conservatory students, and the cast included two of Nissen-Saloman's best pupils, Yelizaveta Lavrovskaya and Natalya Iretskaya. The performance took place at the theater of the Mikhaylovsky Palace on 18/30 May and 21 May/ 2 June 1867.[129]

On 25 May/6 June Rubinstein left Russia, asking Andrey Markovich to take his place on the board of directors of the RMS. He headed for London, where he received from Rodenberg the libretto of the oratorio *Der Thurm zu Babel*. Between 18 June and 4 July he gave three concerts, joining Vieuxtemps in a performance of his own Violin Sonata, Op. 19, and Léon Jacquard in Chopin's Cello Sonata in G minor. He also gave a performance of Beethoven's Piano Concerto No. 5, and on 1 July played the solo part in his own Piano Concerto No. 4 at a Philharmonic concert conducted by William Cusins. During his stay he met Karl Klindworth, asking him (at the behest of Nikolay) to join the staff of the Moscow Conservatory, but Klindworth's debts would not allow him to leave London for at least one year. On 5 July 1867 Rubinstein left for Paris, where he remained for about a week. The Universal Exhibition, which had opened in April, was still drawing enormous crowds of visitors to the Champs-de-Mars. It was an event intended to show off the finest achievements of the Second Empire and to stimulate trade. Almost all the crowned heads of Europe had visited the French capital, including Wilhelm Friedrich of Prussia, his consort, Queen Augusta, and their chancellor, Otto von Bismarck. That summer American piano manufacturers came away with two out of the four medals awarded for their category. It was widely considered that the system of construction they had patented and the technical innovations they had introduced placed their pianos in the forefront of piano technology. The Steinway Company was particularly successful in combining technical excellence with effective strategies to market their products. Engaging Rubinstein for a tour of the United States would be a prestigious achievement for the company, and it seems more than probable that Rubinstein entered into tentative negotiations with the Steinway agent during his stay in Paris. For the time being, however, he made no outright commitment.

From Paris Rubinstein headed for Baden-Baden. He had decided against returning to St. Petersburg and planned a concert tour of Europe, and "even a trip to America. Any boot shine has more standing than I in St. Petersburg," he complained bitterly to Kaleriya Khristoforovna.[130] He was only waiting for all the directors, teachers, and pupils to return to the Conservatory, and then he would announce his formal resignation.

Finally, on 16/28 July 1867, Rubinstein wrote to Prince Obolensky from Baden-Baden:

Your Excellency,

I have the honor of informing you and of begging you to inform whomever it is necessary that I have finally decided to leave the Conservatory and the Russian Music Society, and also St. Petersburg from 1 September.

When I promised to remain for another year at the end of April it was only with the purpose of (1) being able to show that in the moral sense the Conservatory is standing on a firm foundation and on sturdy legs, and (2) because of my promise to hold on to the professors and students of the Conservatory who wanted to abandon the Conservatory if I had left it.

As far as the first point is concerned, the staging of Gluck's *Orphée* has shown fully that I kept my word and achieved my aim. My second point has also succeeded, and if you do not make public my intention of leaving the Conservatory before September, when the professors and students again return, the whole matter will sort itself out without the slightest difficulty.

Since my opinion was never heeded by anyone and it was always overturned by the majority of votes and by the practical views of the committees which are so numerous in our affairs, then I must desist from offering it now, although, out of love for my offspring, I would like to give so very much advice for the future.

The constant concerns of the grand duchess, and also the felicitous choice of president and other new directors on the Committee of the St. Petersburg Society are a guarantee that the undertaking may proceed successfully and without my assistance. With this assurance it only remains for me to beg you to accept the assurance of my absolute respect with which I have the honor of remaining the humble servant of your Excellency.

A. G. Rubinstein.[131]

5 Europe and America Concert Tour, 1867–73

Rubinstein's departure from the Conservatory was accompanied by a great deal of speculation. The immediate cause was his disagreement with other members of the teaching staff about some fundamental points of principle. He wished to defend music as a pure and noble form of art; many of the other professors wished to bow to public pressure in admitting more "fashionable music" as models for the students to study and play. "I have therefore decided," Rubinstein told his mother, "to let these good folks chat and write everything about me they want, but I am out of it."[1] Not surprisingly, critics like Stasov ascribed Rubinstein's departure to the inevitable consequences of his despotism: "Under the influence of that adulation which his supporters and admirers heaped on him, he began in the end to demand for himself such dictatorial and unlimited rights as were inappropriate for anyone, and which even his most fervent admirers could not arrange for him."[2] There were, in fact, many loyal supporters at the Conservatory who were genuinely sorry to see him go. He received, for example, a tearful three-page letter from Henrietta Nissen-Saloman bewailing his departure, and there were also letters from several female students, including Terminskaya, Sokolovskaya and Iretskaya. His chief concern was that the RMS might suppose that their protestations had been prompted by him, and he asked his sister Sofiya, through Kaleriya Khristoforovna, to try and calm any dissenting voices.

Nikolay Rubinstein had been forthright in his criticism of his brother. The pragmatically minded director of the Moscow Conservatory thought that his brother should have compromised with his opponents. To the unyielding Anton this seemed like treachery, and, as usual, it was left to Kaleriya Khristoforovna to try to reconcile her sons' opposing views. Anton would have none of it:

What you write concerning what Nikolay has to say about your attitude toward the Russian [Music] Society exactly confirms my opinion that he views this whole affair from the point of view of a man with a great civic duty who puts to one side the insults caused to me, while my endeavors were able to further the cause of Russia! This is all very fine in a book called "A Description of Great Characters," but I do not like it, since this points to coldness and even to farce. However, it is superficial to speak of this, such is his wont, and "si cela peut faire son bonheur, soit le! [If that makes him happy, then so be it!]." As far as letters are concerned, he owes me one, not vice versa. I once dragged him out of a stupid and idle life in Moscow, paved the way for his new work, and pointed this out to him; without this he would have sunk further into the quagmire of his good-for-nothing way of life at that time. Thank God I was able to do so, and I wish him well-being in the future; in me he will always find a loving brother and a loyal friend, I do not care about the rest.[3]

On 28 August/9 September Rubinstein sent Senff his newly composed Fantasy in E minor, Op. 77, with the remark "I am satisfied with this work, and I hope it will not shame either of us." Shortly afterward Rubinstein set out for Leipzig, and from there he wrote to Rodenberg that he had received the revised text of *Der Thurm zu Babel* and was delighted with it.[4] His enthusiasm for the *Song of Songs*, however, had not diminished and he confided to Rodenberg: "I am attached to it more than ever." Ahead of him, however, was a grueling concert tour that would last five years and take him all over Europe and to America, with only brief visits to Russia. A notable feature of Rubinstein's concerts of this period is that, if until then he had performed mostly his own compositions, his program now began increasingly to include the works of other composers.

His travels began in Leipzig, where he appeared at a Gewandhaus concert on 17 October 1867. Two days later he boarded a train for Dresden, where he played his Piano Concerto No.4 (conducted by Julius Rietz) and works by Beethoven (Sonata No. 32), Schumann (*Kreisleriana*), Chopin, and Mendelssohn. Almost immediately he had to return to Leipzig for a second concert on 21 October in which he performed his own Piano Quartet in C major, Op. 66, with Ferdinand David as the principal violinist, one of his preludes and fugues from the Op. 53 set, a barcarolle and a study, and other solo piano works that he had previously performed at the Dresden concert. Then it was back to Dresden on 22 October for another concert that same evening. He had just enough time to pen a few lines to Kaleriya Khristoforovna, confiding to her that he felt a certain dread: "Such things should be undertaken when one is between twenty and thirty years old, and not, like me, nearly forty. Shall I reap my reward in the financial sense? Heaven only knows! I had to do it, and now I am only waiting to see what comes of it."[5]

Thoughts about the Conservatory still dogged him, and he had asked some acquaintances in Vienna to arrange for him to receive the program of the RMS concerts "as this interests me incredibly."[6] He foresaw the many problems facing those who continued to teach at the Conservatory: "I can vividly imagine what relations between people must be like—they must be rather jolly," he remarked ironically to his mother.[7] His sister, Sofiya, had suggested sending an open letter to the St. Petersburg newspapers, but Rubinstein rejected the idea: "I think it is better to ignore all this, because if I write I shall quarrel with the whole of society for good. What frightens me most is the thought that you cannot restrict yourself to one letter, and you cannot keep things within limits, since it will entail objections which you must follow up with other objections, etc., ad infinitem; I cannot get embroiled in this."[8] On 31 October Rubinstein returned to Vienna for a second concert, where he played his Piano Quartet in C major with Hellmesberger and other Viennese musicians. More concerts followed on 3 and 7 November 1867 at which Hellmesberger joined him in a performance of the Piano Trio in G minor, Op. 15, No. 2. In mid-November he gave more concerts in Pest, Trieste, and Prague. At the beginning of December he returned to Vienna, gave a fourth concert, and then traveled to Salzburg, Munich, Augsburg, and Würzberg. On 18 December he gave a fifth concert in Vienna, performing Beethoven's Piano Concerto No.4 and some of his own solo piano works.

With the Christmas holidays fast approaching, Rubinstein arrived in Baden-Baden on 20 December to join his wife, Vera, and their son, Yakov (Yasha). From there he wrote to Kaleriya Khristoforovna that his concert tour would continue without a break until June. Despite the enormous strain of these concerts, he now had no regrets about leaving the Conservatory and felt optimistic about his future plans. "By comparison with what I would have lost in St. Petersburg had I stayed there, this is still preferable."[9] He had decided that, provided he could earn a little money, he would be able to live where and how he wanted, "independent of noble favors and the instructions of various Comités."[10]

Rubinstein had planned to leave Baden-Baden on 1 January 1868, but his departure was delayed because on New Year's Eve he had a fainting attack, fell unconscious onto the floor, and injured his knee. As a result he was forced to spend several weeks convalescing in bed. The boredom was alleviated by news from Edith Raden, to which he responded in a long letter dated 1/13 January 1868. The most interesting part of the letter concerns the Conservatory:

I do not share your view about the Conservatory. This institution did not need perfecting in order for it to transform itself finally into a national institution, since through its very inception it was that already (you do not belong, I hope, to that party which gives preference to national art). In order to become good—more than that—better than many others (even famous institutions), this institution needed money and individuality, which would have led it to its aim, to its ideal. But since it grew up in a country where art is still not understood even in its elementary prerequisites, and, moreover, where it is not encouraged, then all resolutions by a majority of votes, all committees (since their character is not simply consultative) only hold back and damage the cause. Independent of this, there is one more circumstance: scarcely was the Conservatory founded and brought to life than nearby another institution was founded with the same prerogatives and of the same size[11]—this is in all respects a mistake and will not result in anything good. The second basic mistake consists in the fact that this institution is private. In America, where everything is set up and supported by private associations, establishing a government institution would be an unnecessary matter, whereas in Russia, where the government sets up everything, it would be odd to leave an artistic institution in private hands.

When I organized the Conservatory with the help of the Russian Music Society it was done—as I have explained many times and in detail to the grand duchess—to show, as a counterbalance to the government which was and continues to be extremely indifferent to questions of art, the initiative and, having achieved the kind of brilliant results that we have had in the past few years, to force it, the government, in the end to take control of the Conservatory. Such has been my opinion for many years, as proved by the report (it would be a pity were it lost) which I submitted in 1852 to the grand duchess concerning the organization of a Conserva-tory, and in which I also said that the musical institution ought to be affiliated with the Academy of Arts. Matters stand differently with the Russian Music So-ciety which ought to remain in private hands since its aim consists only in dissemi-nating music and broadening the taste for this art by means of concerts, competi-tions, incentives, etc. For this, it needs principally money, a number of passionate music-lovers and enthusiasts, and a central directorate. Besides this, it needs a high-ranking patron who would surround the undertaking with an aura—in a country where aura depends on noble origin.

As regards me, this institution became quite alien to me from that moment when basic principles other than mine were adopted.

I repudiate the assertion that this institution needed perfecting, and I claim that, if from the very beginning the necessary financial resources had been made available, and the undertaking had not depended on such a vast number of people, the institution would have been from the very beginning that which it ought to be for all time.

My program—artistic as well as administrative—was of the broadest kind and met all the requirements. Because of constant discussions, shortages of money, pre-mature (as far as Russia is concerned), immature, philanthropic, and charitable views expounded by many colleagues of the most varied types, this program was distorted, as being too despotic, unnecessary, etc. Only the fulfillment of these pro-posals could improve this institution and nothing else.

What could be improved over a period of years? The introduction of new theo-ries for thorough bass? Or a new method for placing the fingers on the keyboard? Or to sing, not with the throat, but with something else?

Rules of discipline, contact with the teachers, the allocation of the classes and subjects, years of training and much else—all this was put in order many years ago; and all these things taken together were not put into practice because of the charitable considerations of the committees. Thus it was not the institution that needed time to perfect itself but the people who study in it, the public in its rela-tions to the institution, the people who play such a major part in its life, and those who "hear the ringing of the bells, but do not know from which parish it is coming."

There is imprinted on my mind something that I wanted to accomplish differ-ently from the way it has been done until now everywhere; I started out with the idea about the need to perfect not only this institution but all artistic institutions. But I was defeated out of people's fear of doing something new and because of their stupidity. Here is my idea: during the graduation examination to make a decision based not on the marks awarded out of the hunger and boredom of the examiners but to assess the true value of a student by means of seriously testing his knowledge. This is one of the main reasons why I left the Conservatory and will never again take upon myself the administration of it unless my require-ments are placed as its basis: even if, in people's opinion, the institution becomes a model specimen with the assistance of Mess. Gromov, Vargunin, Dargomïzhsky, Kologrivov et tutti quanti.[12]

Toward the end of January 1868 Rubinstein had sufficiently recovered from his knee injury to resume his concert tour. As a farewell, Pauline Viardot orga-nized a morning concert at which Rubinstein played his own arrangement of

Beethoven's *Egmont Overture* and Schumann's *Carnaval*. Then he set off, his route taking him through Basel, Coblentz, Frankfurt-am-Main, Düsseldorf, Barmen, Krefelt, Elberfelt, Cologne, The Hague, and Rotterdam. From there he again wrote to Edith Raden to thank her for her "kind letter," which he had received a few days earlier in Cologne.[13] The demands placed on him by eager concert organizers had led him to make a number of appearances in small German towns, such as Barmen and Krefelt, where he was astonished to hear local townspeople saying, for example, "Yesterday we performed Handel's *Messiah*," or "at the next concert we are giving Beethoven's Ninth Symphony with a big chorus of two hundred singers." "Will we ever live to hear people in Tula, Tambov, or Orenburg talking about performing Glinka's *A Life for the Tsar*?" he lamented to Raden. "Try to ensure that the Russian Music Society sees in this its main task or else it will lose its purpose and *à la langue* will be worthy of ridicule."

Paris and London

From 19 March to 29 April 1868 Rubinstein gave eight concerts in Paris. His first Paris concert took place at the Salle Herz:

Rubinstein:	Piano Concerto No. 4
Prelude and fugue	
Sarabande, Passepied, Courante	
and Gavotte from Op. 38	
Nocturne	
Caprice	
Barcarolle	
Etude in C "On false notes"	
Mozart:	Rondo in A minor
Mendelssohn:	Scherzo a capriccio in F♯ minor
Beethoven-Rubinstein:	March from *The Ruins of Athens*

In his third Paris concert at the Salle Herz on 3 April he performed his Piano Concerto No. 3 under the baton of Camille Saint-Saëns. It had been ten years since the two men had first met, and the young Frenchman was beginning to score his first successes as a composer. He greatly admired Rubinstein's playing and found it in no way inferior to Liszt's, even though the two pianists were quite different. If Liszt was an eagle, then Rubinstein was a lion, and Saint-Saëns vividly recalled the way the latter stroked the keyboard with his huge sheathed claw.[14] "And when he joined forces with the orchestra itself what an amazing role the instrument played under his fingers through this sea of sonority! Only lightning passing through a storm cloud can give any idea of it. . . . And how he could make the piano sing. By what sorcery did these velvety sounds have a lingering duration, which they do not have and could not have under the fingers of others."[15] A token of the high esteem in which Rubinstein held Saint-Saëns can be seen in the rather flattering request for a new concerto with which the former could make his debut in Paris as a conductor. "I haven't yet conducted in Paris; so give me a concerto so I can take up the baton," Rubinstein declared to him.[16] Fortunately, for Saint-Saëns, this somewhat impossible demand proved feasible only because the composer had been carrying about with him the idea of a concerto for several months, and it took him just seventeen days to set it down on paper. The result was the Piano Concerto No. 2 in G minor, which Saint-Saëns performed on 13 May at the Salle Pleyel under Rubinstein's direction.

On 12 April Vera Rubinstein arrived in Paris with their son, Yakov. She told him about the concert in Moscow given by Nikolay Rubinstein and Ferdinand Laub on 27 February/10 March, during which Nikolay had given the first performance of Tchaikovsky's Scherzo in F, Op. 2, No. 2. The concert had been a failure in the financial sense, and Anton put this down to the fact that it was a mistake for the head of the Conservatory to give concerts unless the proceeds were donated to some charitable cause. He had understood the importance of this and had abstained from giving solo piano concerts while he had been director of the St. Petersburg Conservatory. He was also amused to hear that back in Russia he was now being called "our Russian composer and artiste." "Just for that alone I was right in going away; thanks to this, even in Russia they will finally consider me Russian," he told Kaleriya Khristoforovna with a note of bitter irony.[17]

A few days earlier he had met Alexander Herzen at the Café de l'Opéra. Herzen recalled that Rubinstein ordered a bottle of *Roederer frappé* and fearlessly raised a toast to "this happy meeting." As the café was full of people and there was every possibility that their conversation might be overheard by police informants, Herzen suggested that the meeting might not prove such a happy one for him, but Rubinstein played the hero and said loudly: "I don't care a straw."[18] During his many years of exile in London and Geneva, Herzen had campaigned tirelessly against serfdom and the iniquities of the tsarist government and autocracy, but Rubinstein boldly reported this encounter with the "wandering Bell" to Edith Raden in an extended letter of 10–14 April. Well aware that this was not a matter that could be freely discussed in writing, he reserved the details for a time that he could communicate them to her verbally. He told her about the "brilliant success" he had had at the Paris Conservatory when he had played his Piano Concerto No. 2 (1/13 April), but he had refused to play in Pasdeloup's "Concerts populaires," even though the public was clamoring for him. Something inside had forced him to despise popular art: "je suis pour les concerts impopulaires [I am for the unpopular concerts]," he told her. He felt that art in France was in serious decline and expressed his horror at the idea that "To be or not to be" could be set to music and garnished with musical roulades. The premiere of Ambroise Thomas's *Hamlet* took place at the Opéra on 9 March 1868, but Rubinstein regarded the opera as nothing short of hackwork. By comparison, Meyerbeer seemed like a giant and even the weakest of his operas seemed like a masterpiece. Generally, he regarded opera as a form of popular art at a time when the symphony was considered unpopular. The symphony "stands far above the former from the aesthetic point of view," he told Raden, and even declared himself ready to write a dissertation on the subject. With his usual feeling for the nobility of art, he defended what he saw as the true values: "There is no democracy in the arts, for painting will then become only a photograph, music—only Liedertafel or choral societies, architecture—only an exhibition bazaar, sculpture—little busts of great people, mime (that is, theater) will become a parody, and dancing will become the cancan."[19]

Despite this avowed preference for symphonic music over opera, Rubinstein had nevertheless entered into detailed discussions with Émile Perrin, the director of the Paris Opéra, and the dramatist Jules Vernoy de Saint-Georges concerning the commissioning of an opera for the French stage. Saint-Georges had provided librettos for Auber, Adam, and Halévy, and had been the coauthor of the libretto for Bizet's *La Jolie Fille de Perth*, premiered at the Théâtre Lyrique in December the previous year. News of the proposed commission was reported in *Signale für die musikalische Welt* and in *Neue Zeitschrift für Musik*, but negotiations dragged on for more than a year and in the end the project was shelved. Rubinstein had also approached François Hainl, the conductor of the Paris Opéra and of the Société des Concerts du Conservatoire, about the possibility of conducting the concerts of the Paris Conservatory. Like the commission for the opera, however, this attempt proved equally unsuccessful, and ultimately Rubinstein was obliged to acknowledge: "In general, I hear so much about so many things from all quarters that clearly nothing will be realized."[20]

Rubinstein's final concert at the Salle Herz on 29 April included his *Ocean Symphony* and Beethoven's Piano Concerto No. 4. His appearances in Paris, as well as the concerts that he gave in Lille, Brussels, and Mons during April, were very successful and he had every reason to feel pleased with the reception he had received: "You have probably found out about my successes here from the newspapers: they are truly grandiose and afford me very much pleasure," he told Kaleriya Khristoforovna.[21]

After Paris, Rubinstein moved on to London for a series of concerts in May and June. On Monday 8 June he gave a concert with the Philharmonic Society that included Handel's *Air and Variations* from the Suite in D minor, but he generally found British audiences unsympathetic: "I like England less and less," he reported to Edith von Raden. "I imagine her like a woman full of qualities worthy of respect, but ugly. In general, I could represent, quite to the point, the various countries of Europe in the shape of women. If we should meet some time I shall clarify this, and it will make you laugh."[22] At the end of June Rubinstein, Vera, and Yakov left London and returned to Paris where they stayed for a few days before heading for Munich. There Rubinstein planned to hear Wagner's new opera, *Die Meistersinger von Nürnberg*, which had received its premiere at the Königliches Hof- und Nationaltheater on 21 June under the direction of Hans von Bülow. The vocal score was already in print and Rubinstein had evidently examined it thoroughly, for he confided to Raden: "In the music there is something good, but as a whole it affords little pleasure, it seems to me. However, I consider the text a masterpiece—not as an opera text but, in general, as a literary work; perhaps this is the best thing that recent literature has produced. It is not malice which causes me to consider the music bad and the text good—this really is my conviction." He concluded this discussion of Wagner with one of his favorite paradoxes: "It is well said of Wagner, 'He is greater than Beethoven and Goethe, since Goethe could never have written such music, and Beethoven—such verses as Wagner.'"[23]

Der Thurm zu Babel, Ivan the Terrible, and Don Quixote

Rubinstein spent most of the summer in Odessa. It had been ten years since he had last seen his sister, Lyubov, and the visit was no doubt intended to give her and her husband the opportunity to meet Vera and see their two-year-old nephew, Yakov. Rubinstein spent much of his time working on the composition of the musical characteristic picture *Ivan the Terrible* and the oratorio *Der Thurm zu Babel*, but between 24 August/5 September and 6/18 October he also undertook a short concert tour of Odessa, Yelizavetgrad, Kharkov, and Kursk. He now had no doubts that his decision to leave the Conservatory and return to the concert platform had been the right one. Zaremba had replaced him as director of the Conservatory, with Balakirev as the music director of the Free School concerts and the RMS concerts. The old rivalries persisted, and Rubinstein felt happy not be associated with them. He wrote to Siegfried Saloman: "People there understand that I would now only accept an invitation on entirely different terms, and those terms would not be acceptable to anyone. People are wisely leaving me in peace, and they are right to do so because I have finally settled into that métier which I ought never to have left. Despite my expectations, I am having success, and it only remains for me to regret that I did not go down this road nine years ago."[24]

After his troubled departure from the Conservatory, Rubinstein was clearly unsure about the reception he might expect in the Russian capital. He decided to accept an invitation from Nikolay to give some concerts in Moscow. During RMS quartet evenings on 9/21 and 11/23 October he performed Schumann's *Carnaval* and other solo piano works, as well as taking part in a performance of Beethoven's Piano Trio in Bb, Op. 97, with Ferdinand Laub and the German cellist Bernard Cossmann. Tchaikovsky wrote to his brother, Anatoly, on 21 October: "Rubinstein was here: he played twice like a God, and created an indescribable furor. He has not changed at all and was just as charming as before."[25] Hearing of Tchaikovsky's infatuation with the soprano Desirée Artôt and the rumors of his proposal of marriage to her, Rubinstein forced the bashful composer to renew his acquaintance with the famous singer. As subsequent events later proved, the liaison was short-lived, and within a few months she had married the Spanish baritone Mariano Padilla y Ramos. During his visit to Moscow, Rubinstein went to see Jurgenson about the publication of his set of *National Dances*, Op. 82. He had intended dedicating the first number (the *Russian Dance* and *Trepak*) to Balakirev, but he later had a change of heart and told Nikolay: "I am afraid that Balakirev might refuse this honor, since he and his party give me no credit whatsoever for anything; let this item be dedicated to A. I. Dubuque instead of him—he is an old servant of the art of piano playing and, moreover, a pupil of Field, that is, almost a comrade-in-arms to me."[26]

Rubinstein decided against making any public appearances in St. Petersburg that fall, but he appeared at a private gathering of musicians on 17/29 October and promised to return to the Russian capital in December. He arrived in Berlin on 20 October/1 November and on the same day wrote to Nikolay, thanking him for the cordial welcome he had received in Moscow: "Be assured that I know how to appreciate your selflessness in this affair and everything, and the manner in which you arranged it all. . . . My reception in St. Petersburg touched me, and convinced me that what I did, even though it came up against ill-will and even baseness, has also left deep roots with many people from whom I would have never expected it; and to such a degree that it has almost reconciled me to the idea that the nine years which I devoted to this cause were not wasted."[27] A few months later, on 21 December/2 January 1869, Nikolay gave an all-Anton program at the Hall of the Nobility during which the musical picture *Ivan the Terrible* was first performed. The following year Bessel commissioned Tchaikovsky to make an arrangement of the work for piano duet, and it was published in October 1869.

Anton arrived in Berlin in time for his first concert on 3 November 1868 and the start of the concert season. His taxing schedule took him from Berlin to Breslau, Schwerin, Ketten, Hamburg, Bremen, back to Berlin, and then on to Danzig, Gumbinnen, Elbing, and Köningsberg (22 October/3 November—8/20 December). He returned to St. Petersburg around 11/23 December. Amid a constant stream of guests and visitors, and endless invitations to dinners and soirées, Rubinstein gave the two concerts promised during his visit in October. These concerts were arranged by Yakov Beker, who had founded his St. Petersburg piano company in 1841.

According to Rubinstein's own account, his first concert (15/27 December) "went off superbly in all respects" and his net profit (excluding 600 rubles in costs) amounted to 3,125 rubles in silver. He expected to earn at least another 2,000 from his second concert the following Sunday. With this sum added to the income he had already accumulated from his concerts in Western Europe, he would have a total of 25,000 rubles. "Beker is quite content with the results," he told Kaleriya Khristoforovna. "But, of course, there is no man happier than I. I hope that this year will see the end of my concert tours and I shall not have to go to America which would be terrible for me."[28]

With the start of the New Year, the concert season began again. From 14 January to 11 April Rubinstein gave a huge number of concerts throughout Germany: Breslau, Posen, Neisse, Kattowitz, Brieg, Dresden, Hamburg, Kassel, Danzig, Bremen, Magdeburg, Halle, Hanover, Bremen, Brunswick, Weimar, Brussels, Cologne, Elberfeld, Darmstadt, Stuttgart, Frankfurt-am-Main, Zürich, Basel, Geneva, and Hamburg. On his way through Weimar Rubinstein called on Liszt, who had recently accepted the invitation of Grand Duke Carl Alexander to take up residence at the Villa of Hofgärtnerei. Rubinstein shared his impressions of

Liszt with Edith von Raden: "What an incomparable man he is! Despite all his weaknesses (and he has far more of them than many others), he still compels me to be captivated by him. Je trouve qu'il pose devant Dieu even in his mystical works, and even, perhaps, when praying to God. But other people, especially musicians, are only pathetic worms by comparison with him. He is one of those rare individuals whom only God has the right to judge, and not any of his peers."[29] During his stay in Weimar Rubinstein discussed his ideas on spiritual opera with Liszt and Grand Duke Carl Alexander. Liszt evidently considered Rubinstein's plans impractical, for he informed Carolyne von Sayne-Wittgenstein:

> He [Rubinstein] is tormented by an ideal that is not only inadequate but even a little incoherent! His great project now is to set the Bible to music, in the form of dramatic oratorios for which would be needed—as with Wagner's *Nibelungen*—a separate theater, a Prince or a company of shareholders who would see to the costs, and an impresario—whose choice would present no difficulty, for Rubinstein would himself be this impresario. Wagner's theatre will be built—but Rubinstein's will be postponed to the Greek calends!"[30]

Rubinstein, however, was inclined to believe that the grand duke supported his idea, for he informed Edith von Raden: "The Grossherzog von Goethesgnade wants to keep me back at all costs and it is not out of the question that I'll go along with it. It would be particularly attractive for me if he wished to assist my plan to organize a theater of spiritual opera; I think he is disposed to do this."[31] In the end the heavy schedule of concerts drew Rubinstein back into the maelstrom of concert appearances.

At the end of March he made a six-week tour of Denmark and Sweden, visiting Copenhagen, Stockholm, Gothenburg, and Upsala, and in May he returned to London in time to take part in the concert marking the twenty-fifth anniversary of John Ella's Musical Union. The concert took place on 27 May, and the program was as follows:

Rubinstein:	Violin Sonata (with Wilma Neruda)
Schumann:	Dichterliebe (with A. Goetze)
C.P.E.Bach:	Rondo in B minor
Handel:	Gigue from the Suite in A
Mendelssohn:	Lieder ohne Worte
Rossini-Liszt:	La gita in gondola
Schubert-Liszt:	Der Erlkönig

Songs by Rubinstein, Schumann, Julius Benedict and K. Bank (Goetze and Rubinstein)

On his return to Russia, Rubinstein received the news that he had been awarded the Order of St. Vladimir, class 4. The months of June and July were spent resting at Glubokoye, the estate in the Province of Novgorod belonging to Vera's family. Vera was already pregnant with their daughter, Anna, and Anton took the opportunity of working quietly on *Der Thurm zu Babel* and the Fantasy in C for piano and orchestra, Op. 84. Then, at the beginning of August, he left Vera and Yasha behind and traveled to Berlin en route to Arnstadt in Thuringia, where J. S. Bach had once been organist. "I am leaving here on Friday by the 8 AM train for Halle,"[32] he told Rodenberg, who had invited him to Arnstadt for discussions concerning the final changes in the draft of *Der Thurm zu Babel* and the progress being made on the libretto of the *Song of Songs*. The composer and librettist also spoke about two more possible subjects for operas: the biblical *Joab* and *Don Quixote*, in which they saw "two human comedies of the noblest kind." Before returning to Russia, Rubinstein found time to visit Paris for further discussions about the composition of an opera for the Paris stage: "I have received the flattering proposal to write an opera for the Paris Grand Opera," he told Kaleriya Khrisoforovna. "The libretto is being prepared now, and I shall start work on it next summer."[33] It had now been decided that the libretto would be written, not by Saint-Georges but by another respected writer, Thomas Sauvage, who had earlier collaborated with Meyerbeer in the period following the success of his opera *Il Crociato in Egitto* on the Parisian stage. "My future is beginning to shape itself fairly clearly. From next summer I shall settle in Paris and remain there until the opera has been staged. If the opera is a success, I shall remain there for good; if not, then I shall probably move here [Vienna], where I have been offered entirely acceptable proposals." He was already thinking about giving up his career as a concert pianist after one more year.

On Saturday, 28 August 1869, Rubinstein began his homeward journey to Russia. He stopped over in Munich to attend the unveiling of a statue to commemorate the birth of Goethe. Liszt, Henselt, Saint-Saëns, and Pasdeloup were also present, and Rubinstein had the opportunity to attend one of the dress rehearsals of Wagner's *Das Rheingold* at the Königliches Hof- und Nationaltheater (the premiere followed on 22 September). It is unlikely that the performance pleased him, not least because earlier that year Wagner's pamphlet *Das Judenthum in der Musik* had been issued again in a revised version. Rubinstein was filled with repugnance and wrote to Edith von Raden: "Have you read Wagner's brochure on Jewishness in music which he dedicated to Mme Mukhanova[34] (the poor woman—what a backhanded compliment)? I think that he will soon be ripe for the madhouse. And now, when all the theater directorates are making the greatest efforts to stage his operas, and when almost everywhere the public and artists are showing him the keenest favor and interest, at a time like this, to come forward with a litany about persecutions—one can hardly believe it. It turns out that the Jews want to crucify him, the Messiah of art, in order to remain faithful to their traditions! It would be laughable were it not so sad."[35]

Rubinstein finally arrived back in St. Petersburg early in September and very quickly completed his work on *Der Thurm zu Babel*. It was possibly at this time that he sat for the portrait by the artist, Vasily Perov, completed in 1870. For some time he had been considering a concert tour of Poland and the western provinces, and had even approached Semyon Veynberg (his brother-in-law's brother) to arrange it for him. As there were no concert engagements planned for St. Petersburg or Moscow until December, he began his tour on 7/19 October with concert appearances in Riga, Wilno, Kovno, Warsaw, Vitebsk, Ryazan, Kharkov, and Kiev. In Warsaw Rubinstein received a particularly warm welcome from Apollinary Kątski (Kontsky), the director of the Conservatory, who expressed his deep appreciation of Rubinstein's endeavors to obtain official recognition of Chopin in his homeland. A year earlier Rubinstein had attempted to persuade the Russian government in Warsaw to erect a monument or bust to Chopin. He had induced Prince Orlov, the Russian envoy in Vienna, to write to the hard-line viceroy of Poland, Count Fyodor Berg, and even when the latter turned down the proposal Rubinstein did not give up. He wrote to Edith von Raden in the hope that she would be able to exercise her influence at the Russian court. The monument would "meet general approval and would produce a good impression abroad," he had remarked, sensitive to the objections raised by many European governments to the harsh subjugation of nationalist feeling in Poland.[36] Rubinstein even had a sculptor in mind (the Pole, Cyprien Godebski, the son-in-law of the cellist Servais).

Rubinstein's tour ended on 2/14 December 1869 just in time for his first concert in Moscow on 5/17 December, when he played the solo part in Beethoven's Piano Concerto No. 4. This concert had been organized by Nikolay Rubinstein to mark the centenary of the great composer's birth. Two days later, on Sunday 7/19 December, Anton gave another concert at which he played his own Piano Concerto No. 4 and the Fantasy in C for piano and orchestra, Op. 84 (as yet unpublished). Laroche reviewed the second concert for *Sovremennaya letopis'*. Parrying the blows of Rubinstein's opponents, he praised "this great artist, this national figure, this Russian, of whom we, his compatriots, are proud before all Europe . . . The concert of 7 December is once again eloquent proof of the extraordinary popularity which Anton Rubinstein enjoys in Moscow and throughout Russia. This proof has great and joyful significance. Where a rigorous and untainted artist, a stranger to the attractions of fashion and its unworthy allure, is rewarded by the instinctive understanding of the masses, by their unfeigned and universal rapture, that is where art has a future, that is the basis on which it can rely for a broad and rich development."[37] Nor had St. Petersburg forgotten Rubinstein. On 1/13 November Nápravník had conducted an RMS concert which had included a performance of the *Faust Overture,* and the following day even the hostile Balakirev had consented to give the first St. Petersburg performance of the musical picture *Ivan the Terrible* at a Free Music School concert. In later years, this musical picture was one of the very few works by Rubinstein of which the "Mighty Handful" approved. Tchaikovsky's arrangement of the work for piano four hands was published by Bessel in October, and in the course of the next year the same publisher commissioned him to work on Russian translations of Rubinstein's songs Ops. 32, 33, 72, 76, and 83. Tchaikovsky's first task, however, was to translate the German texts of Rubinstein's *Persian Songs* into Russian. Jurgenson published them in 1870.

In December Rubinstein gave two concerts in St. Petersburg. The first (14/26 December) included *Ivan the Terrible* and the Fantasy in C for piano and orchestra, and Lavrovskaya performed *Sulamith's Song* from the as yet unfinished opera. Shortly after his second concert (21 December/2 January 1870) Rubinstein set out for Dresden and Breslau en route to Berlin. Julius Stern, the conductor of the Berlin Choral Society, had agreed to perform the ballet music and choruses from *Feramors*, but in the full score held by Bote und Bock it was discovered that some pages were missing. Clearly the purpose of Rubinstein's detour to Dresden was to obtain the missing numbers of the ballet from the court theater where the opera had first been staged in 1863. More important, however, Rubinstein was also counting on Stern's support in arranging a performance of *Der Thurm zu Babel* in Berlin.

Despite his high hopes, Stern had proved unwilling to perform *Der Thurm zu Babel* at such short notice and the premiere of the oratorio actually took place in Köningsberg on 9 February 1870. A second performance followed in Vienna on 20 February, and Rubinstein wrote to Edith von Raden the following day to inform her that the work had been "brilliantly performed and very cordially received by the public." His standing in the Austrian capital was now so high that when Johann Herbeck, the director of the concerts of the Gesellschaft für Musikfreunde, resigned his post at the end of April, Rubinstein was invited to succeed him. Brahms may have felt slighted, for he secretly coveted the post himself (he was finally offered it in the fall of 1872). Brahms evidently attended the Vienna performance of *Der Thurm zu Babel*, for in a letter to the conductor Karl Reinthaler he remarked: "Sunday we had Bruch's symphony, today the first rehearsal of Rubinstein's 'Tower of Babel', tomorrow 'Meistersinger', then [Schumann's] 'Paradise and the Peri.'"[38]

Rubinstein continued his concert tour to Pest, Munich, Mannheim, Stuttgart, and Stettin, and arrived in Paris toward the end of March. He gave six concerts in the French capital—the first on 1 April when he played the solo part in his Fantasy in C, Weber's Sonata in A♭, and some shorter pieces by Chopin. It had become customary with Rubinstein to intersperse his major appearances in capital cities with short visits to the provinces. This strategy was clearly designed to give him the maximum exposure to audiences and also to allow time for public interest in his most important concerts to develop. As a result, Rubinstein gave concerts in Bordeaux, Toulouse, and Marseilles. On his return to Paris he gave an additional four concerts. In his final appearance on 11 May, he conducted the revised six-movement version of the *Ocean Symphony* and played Schumann's Piano Concerto under the direction of Saint-Saëns. By this time it had become clear that the commission to provide an opera for the Paris stage was not going to materialize. Vera and the children had planned to join Anton in Paris in early May, but since the opera project had been finally abandoned, they decided to spend the summer in the small spa town of Bad Liebenstein, not far from Eisenach in Thüringia. Before this, however, Rubinstein had one more commitment—attending a festival to commemorate the centenary of Beethoven's birth which the Tonkünstler-Versammlung in Weimar organized between 25 and 29 May.

A few days later Rubinstein was already in Bad Liebenstein. From there, he wrote to his brother Nikolay, asking him to join him on a trip to see the

Oberammergau Mystery Plays: "It is a most interesting thing which it would not harm you to see."[39] His own thoughts about a spiritual opera were still haunting him, and as a reaction against Wagner's *Das Judenthum in der Musik,* perhaps, he became fired with the idea of writing a brochure on the subject (this eventually led to the article *Die Geistliche Oper,* although it was not published until 1882). The idea of spiritual opera was in the air, so to speak, and Rubinstein noted with interest the growing trend toward enlivening the static character of the oratorio: "So mysteries will be staged at the theater in Seville, the artists of Düsseldorf recently staged Mendelssohn's *Paulus, Judith* is being prepared for productions in Vienna and Paris," he wrote to Edith von Raden. "It is always so: when something great is being prepared for humanity, the essence of it hovers over people (is this not the Holy Spirit in the final analysis?!). Atoms of this are picked up by various people and refashioned. One person (and let us hope that on this occasion it is I) picks it up in its entirety and refashions it. And lo and behold, it exists!"[40] Alongside these rather metaphysical deliberations, he continued to harangue Rodenberg with requests for the libretto of the *Song of Songs,* and was also awaiting the arrival of a new libretto based on Byron's *Cain* that was being prepared for him by Karl-August Heugel.

During the first few weeks of his stay at Bad Liebenstein Rubinstein was able to work quite intensively until the whirl of society life became too distracting. He complained about the time lost in visits, court functions, luncheons, and balls, but, even so, he managed to complete his Piano Trio No. 4 in A minor, Op. 85, the *Romance and Capriccio* for violin and orchestra, Op. 86, and the *Waltz-Caprice* in E flat, destined to become a bravura encore piece not just of Rubinstein himself but of generations of later pianists. His original intention of writing an opera based on *Don Quixote* with the assistance of Rodenberg had now transformed itself into the idea of a musical and characteristic picture for orchestra and he had begun to sketch out the new work. His planned trip to Oberammergau in mid-August was becoming less of a certainty with the prospect of war between Prussia and France looking more and more likely every day. When the Franco-Prussian War eventually broke out, Nikolay Rubinstein was in Wiesbaden and much closer to the scene of possible military action, which eventually centered on Alsace and Lorraine. This did not deter Nikolay in the slightest. Since February he had been locked in a bitter legal wrangle with the state councilor and historian Pyotr Shchebalsky, whose daughter, Vera, Nikolay had expelled from the Moscow Conservatory for her insolent behavior. The incident had been the talk of all Moscow, and Nikolay, still under the depressing effects of this lawsuit, found the casino at Wiesbaden even more of a temptation than usual. Throughout August he gambled at the roulette tables and returned to Moscow with hardly a kopeck in his pocket.

By fall the two brothers were back in Russia, and Anton took a train to Moscow for two concerts Nikolay had arranged for him during October. In the first of them, on 23 October/4 November, Anton played the solo part in Schumann's Piano Concerto, with his brother conducting. Two days later, at an RMS chamber concert, Anton gave the first performance of his Piano Trio in A minor when he was joined by Ferdinand Laub and Wilhelm Fitzenhagen. Anton had also brought with him the newly finished score of *Don Quixote*. It was not publicly performed, although it was tried out at rehearsals so that some fine-tuning could be made to the scoring before being presented by Nikolay later in the season. Tchaikovsky, who was present at all of Rubinstein's concerts, also mentions that Anton had brought with him from St. Petersburg his Violin Concerto, although there is no suggestion that it was played publicly.[41]

After his appearances in Moscow, Anton embarked on a whirlwind tour, starting in southern Russia and ending in the Baltic provinces: Odessa, Kishinyov, Kherson, Nikolayev, Kharkov, Tambov, Oryol, Riga, and Revel. From Odessa he wrote to Nikolay, enclosing the manuscript score of *Don Quixote*, and telling him to get the score and parts copied quickly, as the original had to be sent to Senff for engraving. Tchaikovsky had already undertaken to make the arrangement for piano four hands, and Nikolay lost no time in scheduling the new work on a program of the RMS concerts during the coming winter season. The premiere of *Don Quixote* took place at the seventh RMS concert on 8/20 January 1871. Laroche reviewed the work for *Sovremennaya Letopis'*, where he observed: "Having sided with the Weimar school with regard to a program and absolute freedom of form, Mr. Rubinstein has managed to retain his complete independence in terms of the musical texture: here he has remained quite true to himself, and we can recognize in his music that energetic individuality which he brought to composition in his earliest essays."[42] As in the earlier musical picture *Ivan the Terrible*, Rubinstein had finally shown that he had overcome his abhorrence of program music, and although Rimsky-Korsakov later claimed that Rubinstein had written the piece as "a parody of Liszt," the concession was duly noted and even appreciated to some extent by the nationalist composers. For once, even the sharp-tongued Cui had words of praise: "It is full of interest, it has talent and humor," he wrote in the *Sankt-Peterburgskiye vedomosti*.[43]

Composition of the Opera *The Demon*

Anton's Russian tour ended in Revel on 15/27 December 1870, and he returned to St. Petersburg. There was only a short respite, however, for a large number of concerts were scheduled for the coming season. On 21 February/ 5 March he conducted the St. Petersburg premiere of his *Don Quixote*, and Leopold Auer played his *Romance and Caprice* for violin and orchestra. In another concert of 28 February/12 March Auer, Pikkel, Veykman, and Davïdov performed Rubinstein's String Quartet in C, Op. 90, No.1, Anton and Nikolay played the Fantasy for two pianos in F minor, Op. 73, and the Sonata for four hands in D, Op. 89, and Auer and Davïdov joined Rubinstein in a performance of the Piano Trio in A minor. According to Rubinstein's own account, the earlier concert was a financial success and, after a deduction of 1,250 rubles for expenses, he had made a net profit of 2,400 rubles. Unfortunately the second concert was poorly attended, and the net profit had amounted only to 1,300 rubles. Anton ascribed this disappointing turnout to the "very serious program," and to the fact that only his own works had been performed. Nevertheless, after more than three years of almost continuous absence from Russia, he was doubtlessly gratified to realize that he had not been forgotten. Despite the relentless hostility that still dogged him in certain quarters, his undisputed contribution toward music in Russia had finally been acknowledged. The conservatories, in spite of all the opposition, had survived, and the realization of this fact was not wasted on Rubinstein. In September he delivered a speech to commemorate the ninth anniversary of the St. Petersburg Conservatory (the text was published in the *Journal de St Pétersbourg* in the French translation by Feofil Tolstoy). With a tactfulness that does him great credit, Rubinstein paid homage to Glinka, Dargomïzhsky, and even the hurtful Serov who had died in February of that year. His attempts to heal old wounds extended also to the new generation, and he looked to Tchaikovsky, Laroche, and the members of the "Mighty Handful" (naming each of the five individually), calling them "our glory and our musical future." This was indeed apposite, for Azanchevsky, the new director of the Conservatory, invited Rimsky-Korsakov to join the teaching staff during the summer of 1871.

The Conservatory could no longer afford to ignore the growing importance of the Free Russian School and Balakirev who had been its co-founder, but at the same time the director did not wish to abandon everything that Rubinstein had achieved during his tenure there. On 21 February/3 March Andrey Klimchenko, rear-Admiral Vladimir Opochinin, and Baron Fitingof-Shel addressed a letter to Rubinstein: "The St. Petersburg Conservatory retains a vivid memory of your useful work in developing musical art in Russia. Knowing of your constant endeavor to ensure access to this Conservatory of young people gifted with an aptitude for music but lacking the material means to receive a musical education, people who sympathize with your endeavor have offered capital funds so as to set up at the St. Petersburg Conservatory a permanent stipend in your name, and they ask you to accept this stipend as a sign of their sincere respect for you, and also to inform the Conservatory of the rules under which you would like your stipend to be awarded." On 5/17 April Rubinstein wrote to the outgoing director, Nikolay Zaremba, requesting two rules to be taken into account in awarding the stipend: "(1) that it should be without fail a male person; and (2) the subject of study should be without fail composition and piano."

There was something of a newfound optimism in Rubinstein's attitude toward his native Russia. His commendation for the Order of St Vladimir seemed to signal imperial approval of him, but the reality was never that simple. During the spring of 1871 St. Petersburg was buzzing with rumors that he was to be offered some important and lucrative post attached to the court. Had such a post been forthcoming, there is every probability that he would have declined the directorship of the Gesellschaft für Musikfreunde concerts in Vienna and would have remained in St. Petersburg. He had even gone so far as to give a guarantee "to persons interested in my remaining here" that he would not confirm any foreign commitments until at least the end of May. In the end, his optimism proved ill-founded, although a beneficial offshoot resulted from his extended stay in the capital—the prospect of writing something for the Russian stage once again. In the winter of 1870–71 the poet Yakov Polonsky had suggested Lermontov's narrative poem *The Demon* to Rubinstein as the possible subject for an opera. Many years earlier Rubinstein had set Lermontov's *Hadji Abrek* as the opera *Vengeance,* and once again it was the power of Lermontov's verses that captured the composer's imagination. There are several reasons why *The Demon* must have seemed an ideal choice. First, Rubinstein had been toying with Karl-August Heugel's libretto based on Byron's mystery *Cain,* and Lermontov's own incarnation of the Demon owed a considerable debt to Byronic prototypes: proud and solitary outcasts disowned and misunderstood by the common herd. Second, the intrinsic musicality of Lermontov's verses lent itself to a musical setting—indeed, the Demon's success in seducing Tamara is through the power of his songs. Third, the great choral prologue to the opera and the epilogue gave Rubinstein the opportunity to put into practice his ideas on sacred drama where the stage is divided into three levels representing heaven, earth, and hell. Finally, the wealth of local color in the poem would give him every opportunity to introduce exotic Georgian themes for the scene with Tamara on the banks of the river Aragva, the scene for Prince Sinodal in the mountains, and in the dances from act 2.

Rubinstein was counting on Polonsky to provide him with a libretto, but the poet demurred and recommended Apollon Maykov. Using a scenario devised by Rubinstein himself, Maykov made a start at piecing together a libretto, but then for some reason declined further cooperation. In the end, the task fell to Pavel Viskovatov, who had studied at the University of St. Petersburg and in Germany. At the University of Leipzig Viskovatov had received a doctorate for his research on the humanist and theologian Jakob Wimpfeling, and he would later be appointed a professor of Russian literature at the University of Derpt. In 1867–71 Viskovatov was in the service of Prince Aleksandr Baryatinsky, the governor-general of the Caucasus, but it was for his pioneering work on Lermontov that he was, and still remains, best known. By late February Rubinstein was cajoling him for the text: "I cannot sleep at night! Fragments of notes and musical phrases are flying all around me (schwirren um mich herum). Can you not send me something? An aria, a scrap of text? The dances are almost ready! I have made a sketch of the skirmish between the betrothed prince and the Pharisees, and his death."[44]

On 4/16 March 1871 Rubinstein conducted his *Ocean Symphony* in a concert of the St. Petersburg Philharmonic Society, and on the same day he attended a meeting at the Demut Hotel to promote a new Literary and Artistic Circle he wished to found:

> In St. Petersburg there was an artists' club in Troitsky pereulok, but the direction of this club was not at all what ought to have been expected from an artistic association: it did not fulfill its obligations and aims. In Berlin and Brussels these *cercles artistiques* play a huge role. Something similar should be created here in Russia. How could musicians, actors, writers, and painters be introduced and brought

together? How could they be gathered together in order to create a truly artistic circle? This is what I was thinking about at that time.[45]

Rubinstein's idea was not really so new. The Society for Assisting Needy Writers and Scholars [Obshchestvo dlya posobiya nuzhdayushchimsya literatoram i uchyonïm] (popularly known as the "Literary Fund") had been founded in St. Petersburg in 1859 on the initiative of Aleksandr Druzhinin, and it held regular gatherings and public readings. In Moscow an Artistic Circle [Artisticheskiy kruzhok] had been formed by Nikolay Rubinstein and the playwright Aleksandr Ostrovsky in 1864. Although Nikolay's direct involvement in this circle had ended when the Moscow Conservatory was founded, it is possible that Anton had something similar in mind for his own project. Unfortunately, when the first meeting convened in September, none of the organizers had foreseen the possibility of police intervention; as Rubinstein comments wryly: "The times were such that they looked in a very strange way at socializing of that kind." Undeterred, he went to see Fyodor Trepov, the chief of police, who just a few years later, as the governor of St. Petersburg, was to become the target of a failed assassination attack by the famous revolutionary Vera Zasulich. Trepov received him coldly, and it became clear that no further meetings of the circle would be permitted. "So, our enterprise went to the wall," a disappointed Rubinstein complained. "It was so very interesting and our two evenings were very successful. Of politics there had not been a mention; the times were dreadful."[46]

During his visit to Moscow the previous October Rubinstein had come to an arrangement with Jurgenson about giving a concert during Lent. Nikolay Rubinstein was due to appear in a Vienna Philharmonic concert in mid-March. Under the terms of Nikolay's contract, the Viennese organizers had paid only his traveling expenses, but Anton considered that his brother had been right in accepting, if only to avoid overtaxing himself by having to appear in numerous concerts in Moscow over Lent. During his absence, Anton gave a concert of his own at the Bolshoy Theater on 8/20 March. Nikolay returned to Russia a week later on 15/27 March in time for his benefit concert in Moscow three days later. Anton had earlier confided to Jurgenson that he had misgivings about the timing of his own Moscow concert: "I keep thinking that I ought not to come, that people have heard me enough, and that Patti has scarcely left the public with enough money to buy a ticket for my brother's concert."[47] These misgivings were not without foundation, for Nikolay's benefit concert was actually very poorly attended and Anton discretely asked Jurgenson to let him know what the state of his brother's finances were. If necessary, he suggested returning the proceeds of his own concert to help him out, but asked Jurgenson to arrange matters without Nikolay's knowledge: "but only in a way that this money can be set against the sum he owes me, and so that, if God grants that his affairs should be straightened out, he can return it to me."[48]

Anton's own future seemed quite secure, for, as he told Kaleriya Khristoforovna: "Now, without thinking about my gains and without even touching the interest from my capital, I am secure in the financial sense for the entire year."[49]

However, as the weeks passed by with no news about the rumored government post, he began to fear that he would fall between two stools if he delayed any longer in accepting the offer of conducting the concerts of the Gesellschaft für Musikfreunde in Vienna. In April Herbeck stepped down after eleven years in the post, and Rubinstein knew it was imperative that he come to an urgent decision. He opted for Vienna. The post involved conducting eight major concerts in the 1871–72 season and managing the choral society, and although Rubinstein did not consider the salary of three thousand rubles to be adequate, he counted on other opportunities presenting themselves.

It was not altogether with regret that Rubinstein had decided to leave St. Petersburg, which was then in the throes of a cholera and smallpox epidemic. Before quitting the capital, however, he had told Dmitry Stasov that he wished "to have a precise understanding about the state of music in Russia at the present time,"[50] and eagerly accepted Stasov's suggestion of attending a private run-through of Dargomïzhsky's opera The Stone Guest which Cui had completed and Rimsky-Korsakov had orchestrated after Dargomïzhsky death.[51] Almost another year was to pass before the opera was first heard on the stage of the Mariinsky Theater, but the vocal score had already appeared. In the end, Rubinstein's departure from St. Petersburg was delayed until the end of May. He had been particularly alarmed by news of disturbances (a pogrom) in Odessa during Lent, which had resulted in a three-day rampage through the Jewish quarter of the city and several fatalities. "We are following the events in Odessa with revulsion," he wrote to Kaleriya Khristoforovna. "Now everything is behind us, but the impression must have been painful and indelible. . . . I can only hope that you have now grown completely calm again and you have returned to the 'status quo ante bellum.'"[52] Finally, on 29 May/10 June, he set out for Traunkirchen on the shores of Lake Gmunden in Austria, taking with him the libretto of the first two acts of The Demon.

Besides his work on the composition of The Demon, Rubinstein was already thinking about the concerts that he was to give in Vienna during the winter. In July he wrote to Liszt, asking the Hungarian composer for his newly completed oratorio Christus: "Will you not entrust it to me? I should like to give it in a concert on the Tuesday of Holy Week. If by chance you wish to conduct it yourself, I would be very happy; I put myself at your disposal entirely for the preliminary rehearsals with both chorus and orchestra."[53]

Three days later Liszt replied to Rubinstein from Wilhelmsthal: "Thank you for having thought of the Christus oratorio. It is not a light work; may it not seem too heavy to the public! My intention was to bring out, in the first place, only its opening section, Christmas Oratorio, around Christmas this year. The score is now being engraved at Leipzig, and I shall send it to you in September."[54] Rubinstein had also spoken with much regret about Tausig, who had died of typhoid fever in Leipzig on 17 July at the age of twenty-nine. Only a year earlier Rubinstein had heard him perform the Emperor Concerto during the Beethoven celebrations at Weimar, and he told Liszt: "He, together with my brother and Bülow, was [among] the last of the great piano virtuosi. Instrumental music will only lose by the disappearance of virtuosity; after all, is it not 'gute Musiker' who move art forward!!? It was well said: a 'guter Musiker' can be the representative of the right, the center, the left, but art demands a dictator, a 'commander'; composition is the law and the virtuoso is the executant."[55] To this Liszt responded: "You characterize the good musician very justly and wittily. Indeed, he is only the lining of the material needed—which is supplied by the masters. However, we must appreciate and even extol this lining, provided it is of good quality."[56]

Throughout the summer Rubinstein worked hard on *The Demon* to complete the opera in time for his return to St. Petersburg in the second half of September. He had decided that if the Imperial Directorate turned it down, he would commission a German translation and offer it to one of the German opera houses. The main problem was that Viskovatov was dragging his feet with the last act, and Rubinstein implored him to come to Traunkirchen: "I am in a feverish state," Rubinstein told him. "I have thrown out the Pharisees." He did not wait for Viskovatov to respond but pressed ahead with the last act, setting the music directly to Lermontov's verses. In the dramatic sense this was entirely feasible, as the last act of the opera is essentially one extended duet between Tamara and the Demon, but Rubinstein's impetuosity resulted in a serious conflict with Viskovatov when the vocal score was published. By the beginning of September 1871 the entire score was ready.

Nikolay Rubinstein had spent most of the summer in Baden-Baden, where he performed in concerts with Ferdinand Laub and the cellist Bernhard Cossman. On his way home to Russia, he went to see his brother in Traunkirchen. The financial affairs of the Moscow Conservatory were in a serious state, and there were grave fears that it would be forced to close. The Shchebalsky affair had sparked off a newspaper campaign against Nikolay that had caused him much anguish. Several times he had been on the verge of resigning from the Conservatory and the Russian Music Society, and the failure of his benefit concert only added to his conviction that public opinion had turned against him. He contemplated leaving Moscow, and Anton had evidently approached the grand duchess Yelena Pavlovna about appointing his brother as director of the St. Petersburg Conservatory. As later events showed, Nikolay was able to resolve the difficulties he faced, and from 1872 the Conservatory was awarded an annual government subsidy that greatly eased the financial strain.

Anton returned to St. Petersburg around 10/22 September 1871. On the same day the first meeting of the artistic circle that he had proposed during the spring took place. In an attempt to stimulate public interest, he had approached the actor Vasily Samoylov and Turgenev, but the latter had not been impressed at all by Rubinstein's initiative: "He must always be organizing something . . . He's a devil of a man and as obstinate as a mule," the great writer wrote to Pauline Viardot.[57] In the end, some thirty to forty people (including Suvorin, one of the future owners of the journal *Novoye vremya*) turned up. Barenboym quotes part of a letter from the writer Nikolay Leskov, who was also present at the meeting, to the historian and journalist Pyotr Shchebalsky: "There was a quartet, there were speeches, Rubinstein played and people talked about the union of churches."[58] There were even proposals to set up a commission of Russian musicians with Rubinstein and Balakirev as members. With the composition of his new opera for the Russian stage, Rubinstein clearly hoped to build bridges with his old rivals. As Musorgsky informed Vladimir Stasov: "(1) Yesterday I beheld the charming Rubin—he thirsts for a meeting just as passionately as we do; (2) He is setting next Wednesday for this purpose; (3) He will come on Wednesday with his new opera and will show it to us, in other words, to General Bach [V. V. Stasov], Dimitry [D. V. Stasov], Sir Vasilich [Vasily Bessel?], the Admiralty [Rimsky-Korsakov?], Kvey [Cui?], and to me (great sinner that I am); (4) He will sing his opera, and for that reason he has begged that no one should be present except us. . . . Rubin was enthusiastic to the point of charm—a lively and excellent artist."[59] A few days later, on 15/27 September, Anton and Nikolay Rubinstein played through the newly completed opera at Dmitry Stasov's apartment. Present were Vladimir Stasov, Musorgsky, Rimsky-Korsakov, Cui, Laroche, and Azanchevsky.[60] On 6/18 September he sent the score of the opera to the Imperial Directorate with the following letter: "In presenting herewith the opera *The Demon* composed by me, and the libretto and score, I most humbly implore you to examine it and to stage it in the coming season on the basis of the existing regulations."[61] It seems quite clear that he expected the new opera to be accepted for production very quickly, but he had not counted on the objections that would be raised by the religious censor.

Conductor of the Gesellschaft für Musikfreunde

Within a few weeks Rubinstein had set out for Vienna where the concerts of the Gesellschaft für Musikfreunde were due to begin in November. He wrote to Rodenberg concerning the libretto of the *Song of Songs*: "Unfortunately I cannot immediately undertake a new work, nor continue with the old one. Therefore I relieve you, unfortunately, very willingly from your promise."[62] In reality the composition of this opera was still many years away, and Rubinstein joked with Rodenberg that he did not want to compose an opera about love when he was an old man, for then the desire would remain but the ability would be gone. By a strange quirk of fate, at almost the same time the conductor Herman Levi had proposed *Schulamith* as an opera libretto to Brahms, but the German composer had replied: "He could not make a symphony out of a duet for two flutes, and he could not see how to make a modern drama out of a biblical love song."[63]

The first concert of the Gesellschaft für Musikfreunde took place on 5 November when Rubinstein conducted two of Handel's Coronation Anthems (Kröhnungshymnen) for double choir (*Zadok the Priest* and *Let Thy Hand be Strengthened*), Beethoven's Symphony No. 3, and Mendelssohn's Psalm 114 for double choir and orchestra. Another concert followed on 26 November when he conducted Bach's *Ein feste Burg ist unser Gott*, Schubert's *Symphony* in C major, Calvisius's *Weihnachtslied* for six-part a cappella choir, Haydn's *Non no-*

bis Domine for four-part unaccompanied choir and Schumann's overture to *Genoveva*.

The successful start of the Vienna concert season was marred only by disappointing news from Russia. In a tone of bitter regret, tinged with unconcealed irony, Rubinstein wrote to Edith von Raden about the decision of the censorship committee to reject the opera *The Demon*:

> My *cara patria* has again shown herself to be on brilliant form in her relations toward me. I wrote an opera for St. Petersburg. I myself brought the completed score to the Directorate. My work was subjected to an ordeal in a commission made up of vaudevilles conductors!? When the latter brought forth their verdict, I received a reply that the opera cannot be staged this year, since the repertory has already been decided on. And, since I objected, saying that such a reason was unfounded, I have now been told that the libretto has been forbidden by the theater censor! Nothing better could have happened to me! This is only an excuse, since the censor usually crosses out the places which he thinks dangerous, and suggests replacing them with something else. But here they say simply "forbidden." So, nothing has come of it! And a year's work wasted, and the idea of devoting my abilities to my country has turned into a mockery. This is really too stupid. All my work in Russia would be highly comical were it not so sad. And then people say that there should not be any expatriation! I have an absolute right to this, more than anyone. Nevertheless, I will not do this. More than anything I like it when the entire Russian people weeps bitter tears as I set off for the railway station to go abroad.[64]

The rejection of his new opera by the Imperial Directorate strengthened Rubinstein's conviction that he needed to achieve complete financial independence. It was just one more factor in his final decision to undertake the American tour that he had long been contemplating. "That which I have always opposed has to happen to me," he told Edith von Raden. "I have accepted a concert engagement in America next season. That means from next September until June I shall have to appear publicly six times a week! I must become a sort of operating engine which brings a few pence to him who needs them, and who wants to liberate himself from all protection, courtly posts, directorates, and similar levels of authority."[65] The *Revue et Gazzette Musicale* announced that the impresarios Maurice Grau and Charles A. Chizzola had been in Paris to conclude contracts with artists for a concert tour of the United States, Havana, and Canada. Contracts were successfully concluded with Rubinstein, Wieniawski, Mlle Liebhart (from Vienna), the contralto Mlle Ormény and her accompanist, Rembielinski. Four years later Maurice Grau[66] organized a concert tour of the United States for Jacques Offenbach, and later he became closely associated with the New York Metropolitan Opera when it was founded in 1883. The financing of this massive tour, however, was sponsored by the American piano manufacturer Steinway & Sons. Rubinstein himself refers to the terms of the contract in his *Autobiography*:

> An engagement was concluded with me. I took advice with Jacques, a lawyer in Vienna. Of the 200,000 francs (60,000 rubles) offered to me, a part of the money was deposited by the entrepreneur in a bank beforehand; the rest was to come later.

I was not given anything in cash. I might have spent it. For his concert voyage to the New World, Wieniawski was to receive 100,000 francs.[67]

Wieniawski, in fact, had had a serious quarrel with the governor-general of Poland, Count Berg, and consequently resigned his post in St. Petersburg. According to Wladyslaw Duleba: "He could not stay any longer among people who demanded little less than servility, on the one hand, and, on the other, did not know how to protect the artist against disrespect and arrogance."[68] Therefore the American tour was not only a lucrative inducement for Wieniawski but also made it possible for him to escape the constraints of the tsarist bureaucracy. In fact, when the contract ended, he remained in the United States for more than a year.

Far away in Moscow on 26 November/8 December 1871 at the second RMS concert of that season, Nikolay Rubinstein conducted extracts from *Der Thurm zu Babel*. Reviewing the concert for *Sovremennaya letopis'* on 6/18 December, Tchaikovsky, who had only made his debut as a music critic a few years earlier, wrote: "Extracts from A. Rubinstein's oratorio *Der Thurm zu Babel* (one of his recent compositions that scored a great success in Vienna last year) were wonderfully performed by the choir of the Russian Music Society and greatly pleased the public. The chorus of Semites is particularly good, being wholly imbued with the melancholy, tender mood characteristic of the melodies of this race. The touching, almost plaintive, melody of this chorus, depicting with amazing accuracy the sadness of the new arrivals from the distant and fair homeland, makes a deep impression on the listener."[69] Laroche later wrote a long analytical essay on the same work, noting perceptibly that the composer had clearly envisioned *Der Thurm zu Babel* as a piece requiring stage representation. At the same time he observed that the libretto was "devoid of any dramatic interest" and that "the musical interest is immeasurably greater than its scenic interest." The two principal character roles in the oratorio are Abraham and Nimrod, who personify good and evil, respectively, and Laroche judged that "Mr. Rubinstein is rather happier in his depiction of vice than virtue: his Nimrod came out very successfully."[70]

On 12 December Rubinstein took part in a concert of the Hellmesberger Quartet, playing the piano part in the Beethoven Trio in Bb, Op. 97, and also performing Handel's Variations in E. Then, on New Year's Eve, he conducted the "Christmas Oratorio" from Liszt's *Christus* in the composer's presence (the organist was Anton Bruckner). The following day, New Year's Day 1872, Liszt wrote to Carolyne von Sayn-Wittgenstein: "Rubinstein conducted with great care."[71]

Rubinstein continued to give a few solo recitals, including one on 3 January that introduced his recently completed Variations in G, Op. 88, one of the strongest of his works for solo piano. Later that month he partnered Liszt in some works for piano four hands at the home of Dr. Joseph Standhartner, the physician and amateur musician who was a friend of Wagner and Cornelius. Shortly afterward Liszt left for Hungary, where he witnessed the triumph of

Hans von Bülow in Poszony. In a letter to Carolyne von Sayn-Wittgenstein of 21 January he remarked:

> By his three Beethoven soirées—the programs of which consisted exclusively of works by the master—Bülow very intelligently avoided entering into too provocative a rivalry with Rubinstein. The latter can from now on make no better decision than that of applauding with conviction such a colleague. He will, I hope, do it with good grace—notwithstanding his rather autocratic artistic temperament. On this point he resembles Berlioz. Two of his best lady friends and admirers, Mmes Schleinitz and Dönhoff, told me in confidence that he was reproaching them bitterly for their enthusiasm for Wagner, "after he himself had declined to understand him" early enough in Weimar. He even indicated that they showed me too partial an affection. Without always being of his opinion, I very sincerely esteem and admire Rubinstein. He is a noble, ardent, richly gifted, prodigiously hard-working personality—and far superior to the greater part of celebrated and distinguished artistes that one encounters.[72]

Liszt's generous opinion was not shared by everyone. On 21 January Rubinstein conducted the fourth concert of the Gesellschaft für Musikfreunde in a program that included:

Gade: Concert Overture *Hamlet*
Brahms: *Schicksalslied* for chorus and orchestra
Meyerbeer: Incidental music to *Struensee*
Goldmark: *Regenlied* for unaccompanied choir
Rimsky-Korsakov: *Sadko*

Brahms was clearly present at one of the rehearsals of this concert, for he wrote to Hermann Levi, then Hofkapellmeister in Karlruhe: "My *Schicksalslied* came off badly here on Sunday. Rubinstein is simply a mediocre conductor, and did not offer to let me conduct. Consequently I let the thing run its course."[73] Brahms's dissatisfaction with Rubinstein's conducting was aggravated by the fact that Rubinstein was due to conduct the German composer's *Triumphlied* at the forty-ninth Niederrheinishe Musikfest, which that year was to take place in Düsseldorf. Styra Avins tells us that the incident over the *Triumphlied* led to a complete rupture in Rubinstein's relations with Brahms, who actually withdrew the *Triumphlied* from the festival, informing the organizers, when the work was still in manuscript, it could not be conducted by anyone but himself.

Rubinstein continued to keep in touch with Liszt by post, but declined an invitation to join the Hungarian composer in Pest. Rubinstein replied from Vienna: "I am unable to express how touched I was by your benevolent regard for me, and I am flattered by the sympathy which you express on all manner of occasions. But it is absolutely impossible for me to get away from here, even for a day—even to earn some money (of which, unfortunately, I am in dire need); rehearsals, concerts, the opera, etc., etc., and, finally, all kinds of matters are piled up one on top of the other, so that I cannot manage even to finish those few compositions which touch me to the quick, and which I was imprudent enough to promise to Mr. Senff in the immediate future."[74] The works to which

Rubinstein was referring were clearly *Hecuba,* the concert aria for contralto, set to a text by Ludwig Goldhann; the dramatic scene *Hagar in the Desert* [*Hagar in der Wüste*] for soprano, tenor, and contralto, set to a text by the Austrian writer and dramatist Ferdinand von Saar; and the Goethe setting *Verses and Requiem for Mignon,* Op.91.

While working on these compositions, Rubinstein continued to fulfill his numerous concert engagements with the Gesellschaft für Musikfreunde. On 2 February he conducted a performance of Mozart's *Requiem* in commemoration of the eminent Austrian playwright and author of Beethoven's funeral oration, Franz Grillparzer, who had died on 21 January. In an extraordinary concert on 1 March he conducted the Overture to Glinka's *Prince Kholmsky,* the surviving fragment of the first movement of Beethoven's unfinished Violin Concerto in C (completed and performed by Hellmesberger), two excerpts from Schumann's opera *Genoveva,* Beethoven's Piano Concerto No. 4 (in which he was the soloist), and Mozart's Symphony No. 41.[75] On 16 March he played the piano part in his Wind Quintet in F, Op. 55, and the Piano Trio No. 4 in A minor, Op. 85 (with Hellmesberger and David Popper). In a second extraordinary concert on 24 March he presented his oratorio *Das Verlorene Paradies.* Several more concerts followed throughout April, including the first performance of excerpts from his *Verses and Requiem for Mignon,* Op. 91.

While Anton was in Vienna, Nikolay Rubinstein was performing his brother's works in Moscow. On 19/31 December a performance of the *Ocean Symphony* with the additional two movements added in the 1863 revision was reviewed by Tchaikovsky for *Russkiye vedomosti:*

Rubinstein's *Ocean Symphony,* written about fifteen years ago, is the work of an ebullient and youthful though wholly defined talent. This work is almost the high point of our famous compatriot's activities as a composer whose shortcoming, as we know, consists in his excessive productivity. This naturally entails a failure to develop the details to a sufficient degree, and a certain carelessness in selecting his themes that arises from his inability to treat his musical sketches with a critical and objective eye. What is to be valued above everything in the work of Mr. Rubinstein is that in our times, which suffers from a lack of distinctive creative talents, he is almost the only, and at the same time highly sympathetic, musical individuality who stands wholly aloof from the morbidly impotent strivings for originality found in many contemporary composers, and who is able to express in sounds "his own" deeply felt word. *The Ocean* originally consisted of four movements, among which, in terms of inspiration, beauty, and the breadth of his masterly brushstroke, the first stands out in particular. Afterward, Mr. Rubinstein added two more movements to his symphony. True, they are very charming, but, on the other hand, they break the artistic equilibrium of the classical sonata form and make his fine work excessively spun out. The exhausted listener is barely able to maintain throughout the entire piece the required mood that so irresistibly wafts over him at the start of the work. When a person is sated, feed him with ambrosia alone and he loses the sensitivity of his taste buds and he will turn away with revulsion from the delicate aromas of the viands being offered to him. One cannot with due attention and receptiveness walk around five different art galleries in one day, so in exactly the same way it is impossible in a comprehensive way to evaluate the delights of a symphony when it is played after several large compositions and, moreover, when it consists of six lengthy movements. Thus I conclude my review of Mr. Rubinstein's fine symphony with an expression of deep regret that his lack of feeling for measure has resulted in a lamentable prolixity in the form of the work, and perhaps, in so doing, has paralyzed the elements of public success that are undoubtedly contained in *The Ocean*.[76]

If the revised version of the symphony had failed overly to impress Tchaikovsky, he was a good deal more enthusiastic about a performance of the String Quartet No. 8 in G minor: "A. Rubinstein's quartet was written two years ago in St. Petersburg for the Russian Quartet of four young local virtuosi[77] that was being formed at that time under his influence and initiative. It is perhaps for that reason so much of the Russian melancholy element goes through the entire work with great success. Particularly successful is the *Allegretto* composed in a highly piquant and original five-beat rhythm and delightfully scored. A broad melody in the Russian style makes its appearance in the finale. and it is brilliantly and richly developed."[78]

Fermamors in Vienna

The high point of Rubinstein's appearances in Vienna in the 1871–72 season should have been a new production of his opera *Feramors*, revised after its Dresden premiere and not heard in its entirety since 1863. In this form it was staged at the Staatsoper on 24 April 1872. Unfortunately the opera was heckled by the members of the Wagnerverein, and the performance turned into a near fiasco. As Rubinstein informed Rodenburg:

My dear *Feramors* has NOT been fortunate here, and the Directorate must have much *vis artistica* to keep the opera in the repertory—I am even ready to admit that they will not stage it anymore. I have to admit that I must accept the major part of the blame for this, as, in the first place, I refused to conduct the opera, which led to many errors in the tempi and the learning of the work, and, in the second place, I insisted on a distribution of roles that proved to be entirely at fault. Thus Fadladin was a disaster, Feramors was not satisfactory enough, Hafisa could be considered sacrificed already since there was no choice for this role; there was only one artiste who could perform it, but she is by nature stupid, helpless, ponderous, and, although the sets are delightful, the orchestra and choruses faultless, Lallah Rookh and Chosru good, the thing as a whole has not succeeded. It is very painful, because, despite everything, I like this opera very much.

Besides, other significant factors played a role in this affair. Thus the Wagner society, with the aim of mounting a demonstration, sent the opposition to the opera, then the critics, with whom I have strained relations always and everywhere, made use of a convenient incident to make me feel the full weight of their right hand; moreover, all these pamphlets about opera and drama, about principles and new methods, about the future, and the constant jangling of these phrases, have so deluded the public that a sincere, purely lyrical, scenically musical work, and, moreover, one by a Russian-Jewish composer, must have left these people entirely cold, or, in any case, must have made them antagonistic toward me. The times are devilish—but I live in the conviction that whether it will be for a long time or a short time, it is only transitory, and then my *Feramors* will acquire its rights—unless people stop finding joy in a simple, well-executed melody. Then, of course, woe to music, woe to the musician, and for me more woe than for anyone.[79]

In fact, the Vienna premiere of *Feramors* came only a matter of weeks before the first stone of the theater at Bayreuth was laid on Wagner's birthday (22 May), an event that Rubinstein pointedly shunned. Only a few days earlier, he had been the guest conductor at the traditional Whitsuntide Niederrheinishe Musikfest, and a performance of his oratorio *Der Thurm zu Babel* was given in Düsseldorf on 20 May with a choir of 673 and an orchestra of 132 players. During the festival Rubinstein had the opportunity to see Julius Rodenberg, and they were able to discuss various operatic projects. The failure of *Feramors* was a bitter disappointment to the composer, and he began to see in the scenario of the *Song of Songs* too many similarities that would have to be avoided: "Almost without exception it is a total repetition of *Feramors,*" he told Rodenburg, "with one difference: that Sulamith is a grape-picker and Lallah Rookh a princess. Even the jester at the wedding is none other than Fadladin, and the stage effects are the same, as, for instance, the presentation of the gifts, the march, as well as other things. What can be done? Yes, the coloring is oriental again, as it is too difficult to make the Hebrew come out in music in any other way than as Persian or Arabic. I feel bluntly unhappy about this."[80]

After Düsseldorf, Rubinstein traveled to Weimar where he ran into the Countess von Schlenitz and Frau Dönhoff on their way back from the Bayreuth festivities. He seemed more irritated than even by their pro-Wagner sympathies, and even Liszt observed to Carolyne von Sayn-Wittgenstein that he had become "more anti-Bayreuth than ever after the exaggerated failure of his opera *Feramors.*"[81] Liszt tried unsuccessfully to persuade Rubinstein to take part in the Kassel music festival, which the new German emperor had subsidized to the tune of a thousand thalers, and had offered the use of the city theater. Rubinstein's resolute refusal may have had something to do with his antipathy toward the rising tide of German militarism in the wake of the Franco-Prussian War and the declaration of the German Empire. A reflection of these sentiments is to be found in his *Autobiography* and in some of his letters to Edith von Raden. As far back as 1868 he had written to her with an uncanny presentiment of future events: "Happy Germany. For fifty years she was so funny in the political sense but stood so high in the moral sense. Who knows, perhaps in the next half century there will be an attempt to make it in the political sense worthy of respect and united (that is, under the supervision of some clown)."[82] For him, the era of Bismarck had represented a "reexamination of all former traditions about patriotism and the unity of Germany." Now, according to Rubinstein, people had been seized by "militaristic, political, and religious fervor: imperialism and patriotism to the last degree, and together with that, a sort of pietism, even mysticism."[83] For Rubinstein, these notions had become inseparably bound up with his perception of Wagnerism. It must have seemed to him that the pure, classical traditions that he so revered had been betrayed. Now he saw only falseness and a reversal of artistic truth in which allegory had become the very essence of stagecraft.

Rubinstein spent most of the summer months in the small town of Ischl near Salzburg. Vera joined him with a new addition to the Rubinstein household: a son, Aleksandr (Sasha). On 12 June Rubinstein wrote to Senff from Salzburg that circumstances had made it difficult for him to finish the two works for voice and orchestra, namely, *Hecuba*, dedicated to the Austro-Hungarian contralto Karoline Gomperz-Bettelheim, and *Hagar in the Desert*, but by the first week in August both were ready. With them he enclosed a corrected copy of the *Verses and Requiem for Mignon* as well as the song *Die Heimath meiner Lieder* on a text by Boddien which, Rubinstein told Senff in a jocular vein, "you can publish after my death, along with the other songs"—this was the last of the six German songs published without an opus number in 1875.[84] The score of *The Demon* had also been deposited with Senff, and Rubinstein told him to save it for him until his return from the "other world."

Concert Tour of America

Having arranged matters with his publisher, Rubinstein and Wieniawski set out for Liverpool and from there made the long crossing to the United States on board the steamship *Cuba*. The ship departed on 1 September 1872, and the journey took about twelve days. By 14 September Rubinstein was able to report to Kaleriya Khristoforovna from his room at the Clarendon Hotel in New York: "I am completely well and passionately await the time when this whole story will be over and I shall be in Europe again. I have been promised a very great success. The first concert will be on the 23rd of this month, and then they will continue without respite. These ten days of rest are very pleasant for me, and I am thinking of using them for composition. Everything still seems to me like a dream in this entirely different world which, though extremely interesting, appears to me not very sympathetic, so I feel rather lonely."[85] The two newly arrived artists were to inaugurate their tour of the United States with a concert performed at New York's Steinway Hall. Not since the time of Jenny Lind and Thalberg, who had visited America almost twenty years earlier, had European artists enjoyed such acclaim. If they suffered competition in vying for the favors of the public, then it came only from Pauline Lucca. Earlier that year the celebrated Austrian soprano had broken her contract with the Berlin opera, risking a fine of eight thousand thalers, and her incomparable appearances as Sélika in Meyerbeer's *L'Africaine* at the Music Academy won her immense popularity with American audiences. Lucca, Rubinstein, and Wieniawski, declared the *Revue et Gazette Musicale* on 8 December 1872, were considered to be the "idols of the day," and Rubinstein can have been left in little doubt about the high esteem in which he was held.[86]

During the concert at the Steinway Hall on 23 September Theodore Thomas's orchestra accompanied Rubinstein in his Piano Concerto No. 4. Then Rubinstein played the Turkish March from Beethoven's *Ruins of Athens*, Schumann's Symphonic Studies, some variations by Handel, and Mozart's A minor Rondo, and Wieniawski played Mendelssohn's Violin Concerto in E minor and his own *Légende*. During the tour that followed, Rubinstein and Wieniawski gave an average of six concerts per week over an uninterrupted period of thirty-five weeks. This was at a time when musical taste outside large cities such as New York, Philadelphia, and Boston was not considered particularly sophisticated. The tour, in fact, consisted of a series of extended loops radiating outward from New York. They began on the eastern seaboard and returned to New York a number of times during October, but from mid-November the loops became larger and more ambitious. From the beginning of 1873 they began the most taxing part of the tour which took in Albany, Philadelphia, Indianapolis, St Louis, south to New Orleans, and then north again to Chicago. Chicago then became the starting point for several smaller loops through Indiana, Ohio, and Michigan. The final part of the tour was centered on New York state and Canada. With the purpose of calculating the sum of money that would be due him, Rubinstein kept a precise itinerary of his appearances in the New World:[87]

Week 1 (23–29 September)   4
   New York (4 concerts)
Week 2 (30 September–6 October)
   Brooklyn (1 concert); New York (4 concerts)   9
Week 3 (7–13 October)
   Brooklyn (1 concert); Newark (1 concert); New York (4 concerts)   15
Week 4 (14–20 October)
   Providence (1 concert); Boston (5 concerts)   21
Week 5 (21–27 October)
   Springfield, Massachusetts (1 concert), Hartford (1 concert),
   New Haven (1 concert), New York (3 concerts)   27
Week 6 (28 October–3 November)
   Philadelphia (3 concerts), Baltimore (3 concerts)   33
Week 7 (4–10 November)
   Washington (2 concerts), Wilmington (1 concert), Philadelphia (3 concerts)   39
Week 8 (11–17 November)
   New York (6 concerts) plus an additional concert in Brooklyn with the
   Philharmonic Society of New York—rehearsal and public concert—for
   which he received an additional 500 dollars   46
Week 9 (18–24 November)
   Albany (1 concert), Troy (1 concert); Utica (1 concert),
   Syracuse (1 concert), Elmira (1 concert), Rochester (1 concert)   52
Week 10 (25 November–1 December)
   Buffalo (1 concert), Cleveland (2 concerts), Columbus (1 concert),
   Dayton (1 concert)   57
Week 11 (2–8 December)

Week 29 (7–13 April)
   New Haven (1 concert), Farmington (1 concert), Hartford (1 concert),
   Worcester (1 concert), Boston (3 concerts)   171
Week 30 (14–20 April)
   Washington (3 concerts), Baltimore (1 concert), Newark (1 concert),
   New York (1 concert)   177
Week 31 (21–27 April)
   Montreal (1 concert), Burlington (1 concert), Troy (1 concert),
   New York (2 concerts)   182
Week 32 (28 April–4 May)
   Albany (1 concert), Buffalo (1 concert), Cleveland (1 concert),
   Dayton (1 concert), Akron (1 concert), Erie (1 concert)   188
Week 33 (5–11 May)
   Toronto (1 concert), Hamilton (1 concert), Springfield (1 concert),
   Portland (1 concert), Boston (1 concert)   193
Week 34 (12–18 May)
   New York (4 concerts), Brooklyn (1 concert), Boston (1 concert)   199
Week 35 (19–23 May)
   New York (3 concerts), Boston (1 concert)   203

Given the distances covered and the huge number of concerts, the strain was bound to show. The intense pressure under which Rubinstein worked eventually caused him to feel certain distaste for the mercenary, and in some respects anti-artistic, tenor of the tour:

> We traveled with that gentleman who had brought us. We donned our ballroom attire and . . . we played wherever we were taken and wherever we were required. We began with New York. In the course of eight months we did the rounds of the United States as far as New Orleans but no further. The route was determined precisely by the agreement, and the entrepreneur did not have the right to take us into the southern states, nor South America, nor to Havana. During this period I appeared 215 times on the concert platform in various towns, and not once did I exhaust my strength. . . .
>
> God grant that I should never be driven into such servitude again! There is no place for art in this: this is sheer factory work. The artist loses his worth—he earns money and nothing more. The audiences were always numerous, but, I repeat, what a terrible thing this journey was! I felt constantly dissatisfied with myself, and I ended up hating art, myself, and humanity. How many times after that was I offered half a million marks to go to America. Not for anything would I go there! You would have to be devoid of all human worth to become some sort of screw which someone else drives in![88]

In addition to his dissatisfaction with the general terms of the tour, Rubinstein's relations with Wieniawski proved to be far from harmonious. The violinist was constantly rankled by the fact that the fee he was to receive for each of his performances was half that of Rubinstein's, and also that his name was always printed in a smaller typeface on the billposters. Catherine Drinker Bowen suggests that for much of the tour the two men hardly spoke to each other and only met for the actual concerts. After Wieniawski's death in 1880, it cannot be denied that Rubinstein showed himself to be less than generous to his fellow musician:

> Man is a loathsome creature: for money he will do whatever you please. This is what prompted my thought about human weakness: Wieniawski was a very ill man. He often failed to appear for work in the orchestra of the Bolshoy Theater in St. Petersburg because of failing health. If he came once, he would miss ten other times. Now along comes a contract in America. If you failed to appear you lose a thousand francs. So, believe it or not, in eight months he wasn't ill once.[89]

When Rubinstein wrote to Kaleriya Khristoforovna from New York on 3/15 November, he had already given forty-two concerts in six weeks. "Concerts, forever concerts, I see nothing and no one except hotels, railways and concert halls." Nevertheless, he had had the opportunity to make many observations about this "new land," but he wished to communicate them verbally, because "for letters they are too vast" and he would need a literary talent, he told her, that he did not possess to describe everything he had seen.[90]

Having spent Christmas and the New Year of 1873 in New York, Rubinstein set out again on the next leg of his tour that eventually took him south to New Orleans and Memphis. From Detroit, Rubinstein told Kaleriya Khristoforovna that he was surprised at his own good state of health: "It is as well that amid all these ordeals and this bestial work I remain in good health, since each day of illness would cost me, in accordance with the contract, one thousand francs. So, there remains another two and a half months of work, and if everything goes as well as it has until now, I hope to be at home in three months. It really will be no joke to have six months of such an engagement behind me! Up till now they have paid me meticulously up to the minute, and there are no grounds for thinking that this will not continue to the end."[91] He was clearly starting to feel very homesick, and thoughts of Europe were tormenting him. On 9/21 January the Grand Duchess Yelena Pavlovna had died in St. Petersburg, and Rubinstein received the news with genuine regret. He felt as if twenty years from his past were flashing before him, as his entire career had begun from the moment he first went to see her. "For all her enormous defects," he wrote to Kaleriya Khristoforovna, "this is still a great loss for music in Russia, and I do not believe that any other members of the family will devote themselves to this cause with the same devotion and, most important, will spend so much money on it."[92] At the back of his mind he felt constantly concerned that his wife, Vera, was hiding bad news from him, and he longed for the time when he could spend the summer at Glubokoye, the family estate of his wife's parents. His nostalgic thoughts had even brought back memories of his childhood on the Ordïnka and Polyanka, the Moscow streets where he had grown up, and he suggested arranging a reunion of the entire family in Moscow. It would be what he called, a "souvenir d'enfance." He planned to leave America on 24 May and told Kaleriya Khristoforovna: "I shall have two days in London, two to three days in Paris, two days in Leipzig, and only then shall I know, most likely, what we shall be doing during the summer. All that, of course, is provided I am still alive by then, since I have ahead of me another four weeks of the most intensive work here, and then at least ten days journey by sea. It makes you think, perhaps, about the frailty of everything earthly. But we hope for the best!"[93]

Before leaving America, Rubinstein gave a cycle of seven "farewell concerts" at the Steinway Hall in New York on 12, 14, 16, 17, 19, 20, and 21 May.[94] Essentially they anticipated the "Historical Concerts" that crowned his public career more than a decade later. Each of these concerts was devoted to a specific musical period or a composer, beginning with J. S. Bach, C. P. E. Bach, Handel, Haydn, Scarlatti, and Mozart (concert 1), and continuing with Beethoven, (concert 2), Schubert, Weber and Mendelssohn (concert 3), Schumann (concert 4), Chopin (concert 5), Field, Henselt, Thalberg, and Liszt (concert 6), and Rubinstein (concert 7). The final concert included his Variations in G, Op. 88, and numerous salon pieces, and concluded with the *Variations on Yankee Doodle,* later published as Op. 93, No. 8, with a dedication to the American pupil of Liszt, William Mason.

6   A Villa at Peterhof and Operatic Successes, 1873–85

The period from the end of Rubinstein's American tour until his reappointment as director of the St. Petersburg Conservatory in 1887 can be regarded as a period of consolidation. It saw the end of his forty-seven-year career as a concert artist and established his name as a composer with a European reputation. While continuing to give regular solo concerts, his endless peregrinations around Europe in the 1870s and 1880s stemmed as much from the need to supervise and conduct his operas and symphonies as from appearing on the concert platform. He strove tirelessly to promote his works, and for several decades his operas were regularly performed in Russia, Germany, and elsewhere. Although ultimately his reputation as a successful composer proved illusory, undoubtedly some of his music genuinely struck a chord with audiences of the day. His repudiation of Wagnerism, his nostalgic harking back to the era of sentimental romanticism, and his innate conservatism must have seemed to many a sobering antidote to contemporary excesses. In later years he made some small concessions to "modernist" trends, especially in his works with a Russian element, but this was never enough to satisfy his critics. At the same time he realized that, despite all the accolades he had received as a first-rank concert artist, his fame would not outlive him. For that very reason Rubinstein wished passionately to succeed as a composer.

By early June 1873 Rubinstein was back in Europe. He stopped briefly in London, Paris, and Leipzig for discussions about the publication of his works. "Here I am again safely arrived in Europe," he wrote to Kaleriya Khristoforovna. "I am hurrying to St. Petersburg and hope to arrive there on 12 [June]."[1] After the exhausting schedule of his American concerts he was delighted to hear that an apartment was being made ready for him outside the city in Peterhof. The large sum of money raised by his concert tours now enabled him seriously to consider an ambition he had long cherished: acquiring a large villa that could accommodate his own growing family, as well as his mother and younger sister Sofiya.

Before leaving for America, Rubinstein had signed a contract with the publisher Ricordi, indicating the terms under which his works would be published in Italy, and a performance of *Feramors* was to be scheduled for production at La Scala Milan. Details had been announced in *Signale für die musikalische Welt* and the same journal later reported that the libretto of the opera had been translated into Italian. By the end of October Rubinstein was resting on the shores of Lake Como, anticipating the start of his concert tour just four weeks later. Never having had the opportunity to visit Italy before, he used the time for sightseeing and for making a start on a new opera that he had discussed with Salomon Mosenthal. This was to be a reworking of the dramatic canvas by Otto Ludwig called *Die Maccabäer*. The action of Mosenthal's libretto is based on books 1 and 2 of the *Books of Maccabees*, describing historical events during the Seleucid period of Greek rule over Judea by Syrian kings. In 167 BC King Antiochus Epiphanes IV began a campaign against the Jews, forcing them to abandon their customs and adopt Hellenistic practices. In the same year he invaded Jerusalem and erected a statue to Zeus in the temple. This sparked off a revolt by the priest Mattathias whose son, Judas Maccabeus, led a force to evict the Seleucids from the city.

Italian Tour

Rubinstein's Italian tour began at the end of November. In Milan he was introduced to the Russian soprano Aleksandra Santagano-Gorchakova, who was later the teacher of the celebrated tenor Leonid Sobinov. During the 1870s and 1880s her opera troupe actively promoted Russian music in Italy, and she not only appeared as Antonida and Lyudmila in Glinka's operas but also translated the texts of both operas into Italian. It was on her initiative that *A Life for the Tsar* was first produced in Milan in the spring of 1874. Quite clearly Rubinstein had no prior knowledge of this, and on 4 December he wrote impatiently to Bessel from Florence, asking him to find out the details from Dmitry Stasov: "Mme Gorchakova is making a fuss. Everyone is asking me questions, how, what, where, when . . . I don't know anything. It seems to me that these matters are not being dealt with as they ought. Perhaps I could be useful to some extent in this affair: I would do so with the greatest pleasure but earnestly ask you to give me an urgent and precise reply." Glinka's opera was eventually staged on 20 May 1874 at the Teatro Del Verme. It is not certain whether Rubinstein took any active part in facilitating the production, but the newspaper *Russkiye vedomosti* despatched Tchaikovsky to Milan to review it.

The Italian tour came to an end in late January 1874, having taken in several major cities: Bologna, Turin and Venice, Naples, Florence, Genoa, and Rome. In Genoa Verdi heard Rubinstein play and wrote to his Parisian publisher Escudier full of sincere enthusiasm. In Naples he met the composer and pianist Giuseppe Martucci, who had studied under Beniamino Cesi at the Naples Conservatory (Martucci's work later appeared in an RMS program conducted by Rubinstein). Rubinstein had planned to return to Odessa with Vera to collect the children, but he was suddenly called away to Paris and Vera returned to Odessa alone. Rubinstein's journey to Paris was almost certainly prompted by the need to see Jules Barbier about the libretto of a new opera (*Néron*) being planned for the French stage, and a performance of *Der Thurm zu Babel* which was being considered for the spring of 1875.

Rubinstein returned to Russia on 11/23 February 1874. Two concerts were scheduled for St. Petersburg and two for Moscow during Lent. In these concerts he performed his Variations in G, Op. 88, and some of the pieces from the recently published *Miscellanées*, Op. 93 (Près du ruisseau, Menuet, Sérénade, Valse in F, Nouvelle mélodie, Impromtu, and the Fifth Barcarolle). In Moscow Rubinstein attended a private performance of Tchaikovsky's newly completed String Quartet in F, Op. 22 (possibly a day or two before its official premiere at an RMS concert on 10/22 March). The quartet was performed by Ivan Gržimali (who headed the RMS String Quartet in Moscow from 1874 to 1900), Ferdinand Laub, Wilhelm Fitzenhagen, and Yuly Gerber. In his reminiscences Kashkin noted: "All the time, as the music progressed, Anton Grigoryevich listened with a gloomy and disapproving look and, at the end, with the merciless candor characteristic of him, said that this was not at all the style of chamber music, and that he could not understand it at all, etc. All the other listeners, as well as the performers, on the other hand, were in raptures."[2]

If Rubinstein's verdict on Tchaikovsky's quartet was less than flattering, Tchaikovsky's review of Rubinstein's first Moscow concert on 5/17 March contained only words of praise: "This virtuoso of genius came to us after his triumphs in St. Petersburg, where in two concerts he made unheard of earnings of fourteen thousand rubles in silver. Half this sum was given partly to the Chief Directorate of the Russian Music Society and partly to assist the poor." The main work in the program was the Variations in G, Op. 88, which Tchaikovsky characterized as being "extremely pretty, although somewhat long, requiring constant attention and considerable musical knowledge to keep track of the long sequence of rich transformations that are seasoned with all the luxury of his fantasy and technical mastery."[3] In addition to the variations, Rubinstein played his own Barcarolle No.5, the Serenade in D minor, Beethoven's Sonata in C♯ minor "Quasi una fantasia" (Moonlight), some preludes by Chopin, and Schumann's *Studien für den Pedal-Flügel*, Op. 56. Tchaikovsky observed that the "studies by Schumann are unusual in that they are written for a piano arranged not unlike a church organ with a pedal keyboard that performs the main lowest voice, the bass. Mr. Rubinstein found it possible to play these charming but difficult pieces using an ordinary manual keyboard. This is one of those virtuoso feats that only artists of the first caliber can manage, and the effect produced by this technical contrivance is amazing."

A few days later, on 8/20 March, Rubinstein conducted his own *Ocean Symphony* in the six-movement version. Once again, Tchaikovsky covered the concert for *Russkiye vedomosti*. As in his review of a year earlier, he was not entirely convinced that Rubinstein had been wise in adding the two new movements which he characterized as follows: "The *Andante* with its tender, amorous atmosphere has no points of contact with our notion of the ocean or life on the ocean, while the second [movement], although charming because of its original, sharply accented rhythms, harmonic details, and the fiery and ardent exposition of the main idea, is much less distinctive than the original scherzo, which in an unusually plastic way reproduces the coarse merriment and dancing of sailors." In Rubinstein's compositions as a whole Tchaikovsky found that he was "an artist who matured early. Already in his earliest compositions we can see the cohesion of an organically established form, which usually comes at the cost of many years' steadfast work. On the other hand, justice demands it be said that in this composer's work there is no progression, no perfecting, and no development. Mr. Rubinstein's best compositions undoubtedly belong to his early period."[4]

In March Rubinstein learned that the proposed staging of *Feramors* in Italy had been postponed. His disappointment was softened to some extent by the decision to make Peterhof his new permanent place of residence. He had found a house on Znamenskaya Street in Old Peterhof that was far away from the noisy park. Although the building required some alteration, he planned to have the work done in the fall when it would be cheaper and there would be more workmen available. His new opera, *Die Maccabäer,* was finished, and he promptly set off for Berlin to sound out the possibility of having it staged there. Returning to Peterhof in May, he reported to Kaleriya Khristoforovna that his trip had been successful. *Die Maccabäer* had been accepted for production during "the coming winter" and he had sold the rights to Bote and Bock "for a significant sum."[5] In fact, for the rights of publication and the performances in Germany and Austria he received forty-five hundred guldens, from which Mosenthal was to receive one-third.[6] Rubinstein was also heartened by the prospect of a performance of *Die Kinder der Haide* in Prague, and he set about re-orchestrating the opera. During May he was in correspondence with Smetana, and preparations for the production went ahead, only to be abandoned a few months later. But perhaps the greatest disappointment of all was that he had still received no firm date for the premiere of *The Demon* in St. Petersburg. The young soprano Wilhelmina Raab, a pupil of Henrietta Nissen-Saloman, had been cast as Tamara, and Rubinstein himself went through the role with her during the winter of 1874.

With the score of *Die Maccabäer* finished, Rubinstein began work on several new major compositions. It had been twenty years since he had completed his Third Symphony, but in the summer of 1874 he set to work on his Symphony No. 4 in D minor and the Piano Concerto No. 5 in E♭, reporting to Senff that these works were causing him a lot a trouble.[7] He also completed a *Konzertstück* for cello and piano, and offered it somewhat sheepishly to Senff in November. He had wanted to call it a concerto, but was conscious that his earlier work in the same genre (the Cello Concerto No. 1 in A minor, published by Senff in 1864) had not sold well. This does not appear to have discouraged the publisher, who boldly put it out as Rubinstein's Cello Concerto No. 2 the following year.[8]

The Premieres of *The Demon* and *Die Maccabäer*

Only toward the end of December did Rubinstein finally receive news from the Imperial Directorate that rehearsals of *The Demon* had begun at the Mariinsky Theater and that the opera would be given between 10 and 15 January 1875. In the meantime he conducted the first performance of his Symphony No. 4 in D minor "The Dramatic" at an RMS concert on 11/23 January.

Then two days later he finally attended the premiere of *The Demon* at the Mariinsky Theater.[9] The opera was given for the benefit of the baritone Ivan

Melnikov, who sang the title role, and Eduard Nápravník conducted. Bessel had brought out the libretto and the vocal score at the end of 1874, but this event sparked off a newspaper polemic with the librettist. Viskovatov had asked the composer to acknowledge in the printed libretto that he (the composer) had made changes to the text. When Rubinstein failed to do this, Viskovatov wrote to the editor of the newspaper *Golos* and published an article (8/20 February 1875) in which he refused to accept the libretto as his own work. Under instructions from Rubinstein himself, Bessel counterattacked, attempting to justify why the textual changes were not properly acknowledged (*Golos*, 9/21 May 1875). Proofs had been sent to Viskovatov in Derpt, but for some reason he had not received them. With the premiere of the opera imminent, Bessel had decided to publish the text as it stood, without waiting for further communication from Viskovatov. This did not satisfy Viskovatov, although Rubinstein was spared any personal wrangling with his librettist, as he had left for Berlin shortly after the staging of *The Demon.*

Rubinstein had assumed that *Die Maccabäer* would be staged in February, but when he arrived in Berlin he discovered that it had been postponed until April. The Directorate of the theater wanted some ballet music to end the second act. Rubinstein was attracted by the idea of depicting the entrance of the Greek gods into the Temple of Jerusalem, but no such ballet music appears in the published vocal score. He found himself with two months on his hands and quickly organized a series of concerts throughout Germany and Austria. He began in Berlin on 12 February with the world premiere of his Piano Concerto No. 5 and the Berlin premiere of his Fourth Symphony, repeating the same program in Leipzig five days later. He spent most of March in Vienna, making trips to Dresden, Prague, and Pest. He was pleased with his concert appearances and wrote to Kaleriya Khristoforovna that his travels had brought him "both financial and artistic success."[10] In Vienna he found German translators for *The Demon,* but, as he reported to Senff, he thought the fee of two hundred thalers too high, despite what he acknowledged to be a very difficult task.[11]

At the beginning of April Rubinstein returned to Berlin. Vera joined him for the premiere of *Die Maccabäer* which took place on 17 April 1875 under the composer's baton. The leading roles of Leah and Judah were taken by Marianne Brandt and Franz Betz. Almost immediately afterward Rubinstein set out for Paris, but Vera stayed behind for the second performance of the opera and sent a telegram to her husband that it had gone off even more successfully than on the opening night. "This really makes me happy," Rubinstein wrote to his mother. "If the opera can hold its own for a few more successful performances, it can be considered a repertory piece, and that's the most important thing for an opera."[12]

In Paris Rubinstein gave six highly successful concerts between 1 and 17 May. The French premiere of *Der Thurm zu Babel* was given on 4 May under the baton of Jules Danbé. Rubinstein considered that the performance of the oratorio had been a failure, and he put it down to "the excessive economy" of the publisher who had organized the performance. During his visit to the French capital Rubinstein had spoken to Jules Barbier about the libretto of *Néron,* and, under the impression that the work would be given in the 1876–77 season, he anticipated several months of intensive work ahead of him.

During Rubinstein's absence from Russia, Nikolay had performed his brother's new Fourth Symphony at an RMS concert in Moscow (ninth RMS concert of 14/26 March 1875). Tchaikovsky reviewed the performance for *Russkiye vedomosti,* saying of the work that it was "one of the most interesting that I have had occasion to hear in recent times." He defended Rubinstein against accusations of overproductivity and "the stereotypical phrase about composers' critical attitude toward themselves." In so doing, he could not resist a jibe at an old arch-enemy: "In the voice of critics, especially the critic of the *Sankt-Peterburgskiye vedomosti,* Mr. Cui, an opinion has become rather firmly entrenched that to write much is, as it were, to write badly. However, the biographies of all great musicians serve as the best means of repudiating this entirely false premise." If Tchaikovsky could find fault with the symphony, it was because of "the excess of principal ideas, among which many appear only episodically, not being developed." He found that the opening *Allegro* suffered from "incoherence of form" and that the *Scherzo (Presto)* was "marred by a lack of organic cohesion." On the other hand, he thought the finale of the symphony was its most successful movement: "Here, both primary themes stand out for their unusual charm, inspiration and fire."[13] Reviewing the same work some years later, Laroche found that while Rubinstein's manner of writing had little in common with that of Beethoven, this symphony stood alone among the composer's orchestral compositions, being an attempt to imitate the style of Beethoven's "third period": "and it has to be admitted," wrote the critic, "that in certain places (especially in the first *Allegro* and in the *Adagio*) the forgery is a remarkably good one."[14]

Rubinstein returned to Peterhof on 13/25 May. The renovation of the dacha was now completed and he had no plans to go anywhere for at least six months. He forged ahead with the work on *Néron.*

Néron

The new opera had turned into a sprawling four-act work (eight scenes) in the grand Meyerbeerian manner with contrived dramatic confrontations, mass scenes, elaborate stage devices, processions, and the obligatory ballet. The opera had a large cast, including several supporting and mute roles, and concerns the rebellion raised against Nero by Gaius Iulius Vindex. The main singing roles are:

Nero Roman emperor	tenor
Vindex, the governor of Gallia Lugdunensis	baritone
Gaius Ofonius Tigellinus, praetorian prefect	baritone
Balbillus of Ephesus, an astrologer	bass

Saccus, a poet		tenor
Sevirus, high priest of the temple of Evanders		bass
Terpnos, a zither player and a freeman serving Agrippina		tenor
Poppaea Sabina, the wife of Otton		soprano
Epicaris, a courtesan		alto
Chrysis, her daughter		soprano
Agrippina, widow of Emperor Claudius		alto
Lupus, a Roman boy		soprano
Calpurnius Piso		bass
Faenius Rufus	conspirators	baritone
Sporus		tenor
Valerius Messala		tenor

In Moscow, on 26 October/7 November, Rubinstein's Piano Trio No. 4 in A minor was performed in an RMS chamber music program that also included Beethoven's Trio in B♭ and Volkman's Trio No.2 in B♭. In *Russkiye vedomosti* Tchaikovsky reviewed the concert, noting, "Rubinstein's Trio is distinguished for its impetuous drive, brilliance, the power of its thought, and the sincere fervor that is inherent generally in the finest works of this composer. It is well known that Mr. Rubinstein, amazing the musical world by his fabulous productivity, is distinguished more for the richness of his melodic invention and the general beauty of harmony and form than for his subtlety in the finishing of the details. All these qualities have been reflected in this fine Trio. The *Scherzo*, swift, energetic, full of delightful rhythmic combinations, unexpected harmonic turns, and piquant groupings of the three instruments, is especially effective. It was performed with extraordinary mastery by N. G. Rubinstein."[15]

A notable event that winter was the arrival in Russia of Camille Saint-Saëns, who gave successful concerts in St. Petersburg and Moscow. He was warmly received and not only renewed his old friendship with Rubinstein but also met Tchaikovsky for the first time. On 15/27 November the French composer played his Piano Concerto No. 3 at an RMS concert conducted by Nápravník, and then took the baton for a performance of the *Danse Macabre*. A few weeks later, on 23 November/5 December, Anton took the second piano part in Saint-Saëns's recently published *Variations sur un thème de Beethoven*. A more painful duty for Rubinstein was to perform in a concert to raise money for Aleksandra Platonovna, the widow of Vasily Kologrivov, who had steadfastly supported him throughout the difficult early years of the Russian Music Society and the Conservatory. In the last few years of his life Kologrivov had been active in helping to set up the Kievan branch of the Society. Toward the middle of December Rubinstein went to Moscow where he played his Fantasy in F minor for two pianos with his brother Nikolay. The concert took place on 19/31 December 1875 and made a net profit of twenty-five hundred rubles. The brothers, content with their success, traveled together to Peterhof for the New Year celebrations.

Early in January 1876 Rubinstein gave two concerts in St. Petersburg. On

4/16 he performed his Fifth Piano Concerto (with Nikolay conducting) and on 11/23 January a solo concert. The following day Anton went abroad, missing a performance of his rarely heard Piano Concerto No.1 given by Sergey Taneyev.

In early February Rubinstein gave three concerts in Leipzig, including a performance of *Das Verlorene Paradies* at the Gewandhaus (3 February), and from there traveled to Hamburg where he conducted the first performance there of *Die Maccabäer* at the Stadttheater on 9 February. In Paris he had discussions about the proposed production of *Néron* (it was eventually dropped, and even at this early stage the Opéra must have begun to express reservations about the production). On 28 February Rubinstein attended a soirée given by Vieuxtemps. Among the guests were Ferdinand Hiller, the critic and composer Ernest Reyer, and the seventeen-year-old Belgian violinist Eugène Ysaÿe. After Paris, Rubinstein had a three-month concert tour ahead of him, beginning on 4 March in Strasbourg and concluding at the end of May in London. With the prospect of so many concerts and conducting engagements, he began to feel his age (he was forty-seven). In his *Autobiography* he says that his memory was beginning to falter, but he dismissed these feelings, determined to continue working while he still had the strength.

Rubinstein arrived in London on 1 May and remained there for the entire month. British audiences may have had the reputation of being excessively cold and reserved but on this occasion Rubinstein scored a resounding success, and the *Musical Times* boldly declared: "No such excitement has been produced within our recollection by the performances of any artist."[16] His first major engagement was at a Philharmonic Society concert when he performed his own Piano Concerto No. 5 under the baton of William Cusins, who had succeeded William Sterndale Bennett as principal conductor in 1867. He also gave solo recitals and appeared with Wieniawski on 2 May in a concert that included Beethoven's *Kreutzer Sonata*. In a vivid description of Rubinstein's concert of 3 May, which included Beethoven's *Appassionata Sonata* and Schumann's *Kreisleriana*, Alexander Ewing wrote of the unreserved enthusiasm that greeted the artist: "The people fairly shouted at him in a way I have never heard an audience shout in England." These sentiments were echoed by the *Times* (6 May) in a review of Rubinstein's first St. James's Hall recital. The writer noted, in particular, that although the recital continued for a full two hours with only two short intervals, the program was so well balanced that it produced no sense of monotony. The two characteristic traits of Rubinstein's playing that the writer noted were his capacity both for "repose" and "uncontrollable impetuosity." These two contradictory features were perfectly displayed in Chopin's B minor Sonata where the finale was characterized as "a prodigious feat of mechanical daring." On 27 May Rubinstein performed his Piano Concerto No. 4 at a concert of the New Philharmonic Society (founded in opposition to the Philharmonic Society by Henry Wylde in 1852). Two days later William Cusins conducted the first performance in England of the Symphony No. 4 at a Philharmonic Society concert. Rubinstein had good reason to be pleased with his successes in the British capital, reporting to Kaleriya Khristoforovna that it had exceeded his expectations. The Philharmonic Society conferred on him their gold medal, ahead of Brahms who only received the same award a year later. After a private performance for Queen Victoria he received "some fine cuff links" but attached little importance to this token of royal esteem. Cultivating the company of influential artists and intellectuals was another matter. At the home of John Ella he met the poet Robert Browning and renewed his old acquaintance with George Eliot and George Lewes. Although it had been more than twenty years since their paths had last crossed in Weimar, Rubinstein had evidently created a powerful impression on the writer, for in her novel, *Daniel Deronda,* she had modeled the character of the musician Julius Klesmer on the great Russian pianist.[17]

Rubinstein returned to Peterhof from London on 31 May (n.s.) and spent the summer months working on three major chamber works which he planned to present when his foreign travels resumed the following spring. These were the String Sextet in D, Op. 97, the Violin Sonata No. 3 in B minor, Op. 98, and the Piano Quintet in G minor, Op. 99. Another pressing matter was to copy out the score of *The Demon* with a new German translation by Alfred Offermann. The original one commissioned in Vienna had turned out to be "lamentably bad,"[18] and Rubinstein had complained bitterly to Senff that the accents had been placed in a completely unmusical way. The translator needed to be a poet who was also a musician and therefore the task of re-translating the libretto had been entrusted to Offermann whose work Rubinstein found to be satisfactory. By September the copying of the score with the new text was still progressing slowly. Rubinstein predicted a number of problems with the changes, but Senff's belief in the future of Rubinstein's music was such that he published the vocal score and full score of the opera by the end of 1876.

Rubinstein had also promised his latest opera to Senff. The last act of *Néron* was probably completed in London, but the task of orchestrating the work had yet to be started. Rubinstein still believed that it would be staged in Paris during the 1877–78 season, although the focus of his interest had now shifted from the Opéra to the Opéra-National-Lyrique, which in the 1876–77 season was based at the Théâtre de la Gaîté under the administration of Albert Vinzentini. But now Rubinstein was inveigled by a further offer from the Intendant of the Hamburg Opera Pollini (Bernhard Pohl) to stage the opera the following January "in the finest manner." In fact, this offer of an early production was later withdrawn, and the opera was not heard there until 1 November 1879.

It was also widely rumored that *Die Maccabäer* was to be presented on the Russian stage during the coming winter. The celebrated baritone Bogomir Korsov had approached Nikolay Lukashevich, a member of the Directorate and later head of the repertory department of the Imperial Theaters, on Rubinstein's behalf. The opera was eventually accepted for production, but the minister imposed a restriction: "It can be staged, but without any expenses on sets and costumes."[19] Rumors about the staging of *Die Maccabäer* also reached the ears of Tchaikovsky, who was anxiously anticipating the premiere of his new opera *Kuznets Vakula* [Vakula the Smith] at the Mariinsky Theater. Rubinstein had been a member of the RMS committee, which in 1875 had awarded Tchaikovsky first prize in the competition to set Polonsky's libretto. After two long years the opera was finally premiered at the Mariinsky Theater on 12/24 November with Wilhelmina Raab in the role of Oksana, but the idea that his own work might be postponed or dropped altogether because of Rubinstein's opera maddened Tchaikovsky to the point of despair. He wrote in an angry and belligerent tone to his brother, Anatoly, on 20 September/2 October:

> If you can, then tell Anton Rubinstein: "My brother has instructed me to tell you that you are a son of a bitch, and you can [go to hell]." Heavens above, how profoundly I have come to detest that man of late! He has never, never treated me with anything other than condescending nonchalance. No one has wounded my feeling of self-esteem, my sense of justified pride (forgive my self-adulation, Tolya) or my own abilities so much as this Peterhof house owner. And now he comes creeping with his mangy operas to get under my feet again! Is not the glory he has achieved abroad enough for this most stupid and most puffed up of mortals? Is Berlin, Hamburg, Vienna, and so on, not enough for him? If it were not for the penal code and volume XV, I would go to Peterhof and happily burn his wretched villa to the ground.[20]

It was not only the opera that irritated Tchaikovsky. Rubinstein's total indifference toward him, which, so it seemed to him, bordered on outright antagonism, was like a constant running sore. In 1873 Bessel had published Tchaikovsky's Six Pieces on a Single Theme, Op.21, with a dedication to Rubinstein, but the great pianist had pointedly declined to play them, despite Tchaikovsky's evident attempt to please his old teacher with the "scholastic" Prelude and four-part Fugue which opens the set.[21] Anton and Nikolay Rubinstein attended the premiere of *Vakula the Smith*, but the former left for Munich immediately afterward to conduct his own *Die Maccabäer* on 26 November. He returned to Russia in time to conduct the first complete performance in the capital of *Das Verlorene Paradies*, which the St. Petersburg Philharmonic Society gave in a charity concert on 5/17 December.[22]

Nikolay Rubinstein had remained in St. Petersburg during his brother's absence, and when Anton returned from Munich he found his brother looking nervous and prone to feverish states. Anton ascribed this to Nikolay's constant anxiety about the RMS concerts and the affairs of the Conservatory. Nikolay had been persuaded to see the eminent physician Dr. Botkin, who found his patient's constitution to be generally poor. He urged Nikolay to take particular care of his health, and Anton invited him to spend the New Year in Peterhof.

The major event that was dominating Rubinstein's thoughts at the start of 1877 was the St. Petersburg premiere of *Die Maccabäer*. He had wanted Lavrovskaya in the role of Leah but in the end had to content himself with Anna Bichurina. This renowned contralto excelled in character roles and had delighted Tchaikovsky a month earlier as Solokha, the playful witch in his own *Vakula the Smith*. Rubinstein himself conducted the final rehearsals but found the orchestral playing unacceptable. The argument that ensued almost resulted in the opera being withdrawn, but a compromise was reached and the premiere took place on 22 January/3 February under the composer's direction. The following day Rubinstein wrote to his mother in Odessa that, against all his expectations, the performance of the opera had been excellent in all respects. The principal members of the cast were:

Leah—Anna Bichurina
Judah—Bogomir Korsov
Naomi—Wilhelmina Raab
Cleopatra—Aleksandra Menshikova
Antiochus—Josef Paleček
Simeon—Osip Petrov

The performance was extensively reviewed: Famintsïn (*St. Petersburger Zeitung*), Ivanov (*Pchela*), Cui (*Sankt-Peterburgskiye vedomosti*), and others. Not surprisingly, Cui characterized it as "nothing but triteness dragged out into three huge acts."[23] Laroche was more enthusiastic and he had earlier written a very detailed article on the opera published in four issues of *Muzïkal'nïy listok*, 1875–76. He found that the subject had strong dramatic force: "I have in mind the criminal passion of the young Jew for Cleopatra who has forced him to abandon his country and the faith of his fathers. This love appears almost episodically—but the main content of the poem is the struggle for a faith and for a homeland, and this gives it a unique style, free from the obligatory repetition of amorous effusions in a routine libretto."[24] At the same time Laroche admonished the composer for his excessive use of the diminished seventh chord, calling it "the Achilles heel of *Die Maccabäer*."

Rubinstein headed for Leipzig, where his new chamber works were all performed: String Sextet in D, Op. 97; the Violin Sonata No. 3 in B minor, Op. 98; and the Piano Quintet in G minor, Op. 99. These works were clearly still in manuscript at this stage, although Senff was later urged to hurry with the engraving of the sonata which was needed for performances in London. Rubinstein arrived there in early March and gave concerts throughout the British Isles. In five weeks he gave sixty concerts in Liverpool, Manchester, Birmingham, Bradford, Brighton, Dublin, Edinburgh, Glasgow, Leeds, and Cheltenham, as well as a private performance for Queen Victoria at Windsor. According to John Ella's *Musical Sketches*, the 1877 trip earned him some twelve thousand pounds: "No such amount was ever obtained by a vocalist or actor in England in the same space of time."[25] In Edinburgh Rubinstein met the eminent Scottish conductor and composer Alexander Mackenzie, who was somewhat taken aback by the poorness of Rubinstein's eyesight. As they walked arm in arm up a rainy Princes Street, Mackenzie recalled, Rubinstein "heedlessly and deliberately stepped into every puddle that lay in his way."[26] The two men met again in London at the Hotel Dieudonné, where Rubinstein hosted elaborate soirées and received a great many visitors, including Frederic Cowen, Sir Charles Hallé, Robert Browning, Oscar Wilde, and the pre-Raphaelite painter Sir John Millais.

Despite the fact that Wagner, Joachim, and Clara Schumann were all in London during this lengthy visit of 1877, Rubinstein succeeded in capturing the attention of British audiences.[27] His first London concert took place at the Crystal Palace on 21 April and was a major all-Rubinstein concert: "A compliment we cannot recall to have been paid to any living composer," declared the *Monthly Musical Record*. The concert included the *Ocean Symphony*, the Piano Concerto No. 2 conducted by Augustus Manns, the Overture to *Dmitry Donskoy*, piano solos, and songs. This was followed by six recitals between 30 April and 4 June, including one in which Sofie Menter took part. The reviews on this occasion were mixed. In a review on 8 June of a St. James's Hall concert the *Times* columnist complained that the pianist had allowed too many personal mannerisms to creep into his performances of works by other composers: "Herr Rubinstein is by no means the most retiring of virtuosos; on the contrary, he is the most demonstrative and, we may say it with deference, the most egotistical of our time. Instead of being absorbed in the work he is interpreting, the work would rather seem to be absorbed in him." Beethoven, for instance, had not "written up to his standard of virtuosity" and, consequently, the final *presto* of the *Appassionata Sonata* had come out "little better than confusion." The same reviewer was also critical of a second all-Rubinstein concert at the Crystal Palace on 4 June. On this occasion Rubinstein played his own cadenzas (first and last movements) in a performance of Beethoven's Fourth Piano Concerto, and the critic found that such "preponderating self-assertion among our executants . . . is becoming intolerable." The concert also included a duet from *Die Maccabäer* performed by Helen Lemmens-Sherington and Isidor Henschel, the ballet music from *Feramors*, and Rubinstein's Fourth Symphony, of which the *Times* critic remarked: "so long a work, and one so comparatively destitute of interest, is almost without parallel."

During Rubinstein's stay in Britain a new crisis broke out in the Balkans, where unrest had been fomenting for more than two years. The revolt against Turkish suzerainty that began in Bosnia and Herzegovina had engulfed Serbia and Montenegro. The small Serbian army was no match for the might of the Ottoman Empire, and Russia felt that she was fulfilling her historical destiny in coming to the aid of fellow Slavs and fellow Orthodox Christians. On 14/26 April Russia declared war on Turkey, and on the same day Rubinstein wrote to Kaleriya Khristoforovna from Cheltenham: "This war is something rather special—either it will end in nothing, or else it will explode into a global fire the likes of which we have never known! (And then farewell for a long time, of course, to art and music.) But let us hope that the whole world will take fright and not allow this to happen. However, in civilized Europe everything is possible." So wrote Rubinstein prophetically of the Balkan Question that would haunt European politics right up to the First World War and beyond (see Appendix E, nos. 1–3, in this volume).

Rubinstein spent the summer in Peterhof. It was there he learned that the Russian government had finally acknowledged his contribution to Russian art by raising his social status. After almost forty years as "the son of a merchant of the second guild," he had finally been elevated to the ranks of the "hereditary nobility." He had had little opportunity to compose on his travels, and the condition of his right eye was quickly deteriorating. The Piano Quintet in G minor had already been sent to Senff for engraving, and from June to mid-October he worked on the corrections and the orchestration of *Néron*. There were some new compositions, too: his Fourth Piano Sonata in A minor, Op. 100; a *Konzertstück* for piano and orchestra;[28] the twelve Aleksey Tolstoy song settings;[29] and the ten arrangements of Serbian songs inspired by the war. He was also continuing to think about his opera *Sulamith* and to contemplate a new one. The new opera was to be *Kupets Kalashnikov* [The merchant Kalashnikov], and, like *The Demon* before it, it was to be based on a work by Lermontov.

When the concert season began again in the fall of 1877, Rubinstein appeared in an RMS charity concert on 15/27 October, conducting his *Ocean Symphony* and performing Liszt's Concerto in E♭ and a Hungarian Rhapsody, as well as some shorter works of Chopin and his own. Shortly afterward he set out for Vienna, Leipzig, Paris, and Berlin. In Vienna he had the opportunity to see his sister, Lyuba, and on November 11 he performed his Piano Quintet in Leipzig with the eminent violinist Heinrich Schradieck, who was the leader of the Gewandhaus concerts from 1874 to 1882. In Paris he conducted his *Ocean Symphony* at a Pasdeloup concert on 25 November, and a few weeks later he appeared at the Bote and Bock Concert Hall in Berlin where he played his Piano Quintet, Violin Sonata No. 3, and the Piano Sonata No. 4. He also accompanied the Austrian mezzo-soprano Marianne Brandt in a performance of *Hecuba*.

Rubinstein returned to Peterhof for the New Year of 1878 and for a guest appearance at an RMS concert in Petersburg on 28 January/9 February, when he conducted Beethoven's Leonora No. 3 overture and Dargomïzhsky's *Kazachok*. Then he set out for Vienna, where he conducted two performances of *Die Maccabäer* and gave several concerts in the city. From mid-March to mid-April he made appearances throughout the Netherlands. In a major all-Rubinstein concert in Brussels on 24 April, he conducted the Overture to *Dmitry Donskoy*, the Piano Concerto No. 5, the Symphony No. 4, the dances from *Feramors*, and choruses from *Der Thurm zu Babel* and *Die Maccabäer*. He returned to Peterhof in May to continue his work on *The Merchant Kalashnikov* and to begin a new composition, the *Caprice Russe* in C minor for piano and orchestra.

Far away in Paris, Nikolay Rubinstein was preparing concerts for the Paris World Exhibition. Three scheduled concerts (plus an additional charity concert) were given at the Trocadéro Palace on 9, 14, 21, and 27 September. Nikolay conducted a Russian program that included the oriental dances from *The Demon* (9 September). The second concert (14 September) included the musical picture *Ivan the Terrible*, and Nikolay performed his brother's *Valse-Caprice*. These concerts were extensively reviewed by Vladimir Stasov in a series of articles called *Pis'ma iz chuzhikh krayov* [Letters from foreign parts], which were published in *Novoye vremya*. Stasov's primary objective in these articles was to bewail the fact that the work of "conservatory hacks" (Anton Rubinstein and Tchaikovsky) had been offered to French audiences as the voice of Russian music rather than the "real Russians" represented by Balakirev, Rimsky-Korsakov, and the other members of the "Mighty Handful." "He [Nikolay Rubinstein] played the absolutely dreadful *Valse-Caprice* of his brother, Anton Rubinstein, which concludes with a celebrated concerto-style brilliance of leaps, passage work, rapid bass notes, and thunderous chords but completely lacking in music (which, for a mixed audience, was most pleasant of all), and before that he performed a *Romance sans Paroles* by Tchaikovsky—a thin, scroufulous imitation of Chopin."[30] "No matter," Stasov remarked sarcastically, "they were still conservatory works, and not works by those damned self-taught and rebellious new Russian musicians; the former need to be well promoted and the latter need to be pushed down!"[31] Nevertheless the concerts were enormously successful, and even Stasov had to acknowledge that fact amid all his frantic ranting and raving about the lack of works by composers from the New Russian School.

Anton remained at Peterhof until the end of October. On 12/24 October he sent the newly composed *Caprice Russe* to Senff. The work was dedicated to Anna Yesipova and Rubinstein remarked to his publisher that he considered it effective. Yesipova should be able to show it off well, he added, provided that she is not put off by the coldness and indifference of audiences and critics to every element of Russianness in art and science (this was prompted by a certain anti-Russian feeling in Europe as a result of the Russo-Turkish War). At the beginning of November Rubinstein was to begin a tour of Eastern Prussia, but before his departure he gave an RMS program in St. Petersburg on 14/26. In this concert he conducted Schumann's Symphony No. 4, and performed his own Fantasy for piano and orchestra, Op. 84 (Nápravník conducted), and Nikolay Ende performed his *Krïlov Fables* to the composer's accompaniment. The tour of Eastern Prussia began in Danzig and continued through Elbing, Bartenstein, Tilsit, Insterburg, and Lyck. The highlight of this tour was a performance of *Feramors,* which Rubinstein conducted in Köningsberg on 2/14 November.

The major event Rubinstein was anticipating at the start of 1879 was a new production of *Feramors* in Berlin. He had been invited to rehearse the work and conduct the first few performances. Before setting out for the German capital, however, he played the solo part in his own Piano Concerto No. 2 at an RMS concert under the direction of Nápravník on 11/23 January. That same day Karl Reinecke had conducted a performance of Rubinstein's Symphony No. 4 at a subscription concert of the Gewandhaus Orchestra in Leipzig. The success of this concert greatly pleased the composer, all the more so since he had not attended it personally. As he told Senff, if one of his works enjoyed success when he was present at the performance, he was inclined to think that it was his piano playing that the audience was cheering rather than the actual composition. This thought had always robbed him of half the pleasure of any success. That his compositions seemed to be holding their own ground delighted him, and he must have been equally pleased to hear about a performance of his *Ocean Symphony* in London a few months later when William Cusins conducted it with the Philharmonic Society on 11 June.

All through February Rubinstein rehearsed *Feramors* on the stage of the Royal Opera. He also gave two concerts in Berlin, including the premiere of his *Caprice Russe* in the second of them (26 February). The opening night of

Feramors was set for 4 March 1879, but a full dress rehearsal was given to a packed audience on 3 March. Mathilde Mallinger, the Croatian soprano who took the title role, had refused to sing certain *fioritura* passages in the first act, and the theater director Botho von Hülsen had supported her in this. Rubinstein, however, flatly refused to sanction any cuts, and when Mallinger stopped her performance in the disputed passages, Rubinstein roared: "Why are you not singing, Mme Mallinger?" The theater director roared back from the audience: "I have exempted her!" After several more heated exchanges between the two men, Rubinstein snapped his baton and marched out of the theater. He refused to have anything more to do with the production, and when the opera opened the following evening it was conducted by Carl Eckert. A few weeks later Tchaikovsky was in Berlin and tried to obtain a ticket for the opera. He wrote to Nadezhda von Meck on 4/16 March: "Today at the opera *Feramors* is being given. This opera by Rubinstein dates from the time when his best pieces were written, that is, twenty years ago. I like it quite seriously, and wanted to get a seat for the performance today, but it turned out that there was not a single ticket to be had. Rubinstein himself was here for two months and only went back to St. Petersburg yesterday."[32]

Shortly after his return to Russia, Rubinstein attended the premiere of Tchaikovsky's new opera *Yevgeny Onegin* at the Malïy Theater in Moscow staged through the endeavors of the Conservatory students. The performance took place on Saturday, 17/29 March 1879, and was attended by the entire Moscow Conservatory headed by Nikolay Rubinstein. Aleksandra Panayeva (better known by her married name, Panayeva-Kartsova) later wrote her reminiscences of Tchaikovsky and relates that, arriving in Moscow at short notice, she found it difficult to obtain a ticket for the performance. Anton Rubinstein, who had traveled to Moscow with her in the same train compartment, offered her a place in his box. A rather disheveled Tchaikovsky appeared to take a bow, and Panayeva observed that this was the first time she had ever seen her "favorite composer." In her reminiscences she recalled her conversation with Rubinstein:

> "You don't know him? You, his admirer and the advocate of his music," Rubinstein mocked. Then I told Anton Grigoryevich about all my fruitless attempts to become acquainted with my favorite composer and his evident unwillingness to give in to these attempts. "Well wait, I shall get on to it," said Anton Grigoryevich, smiling slyly, and he went out of the box. My father had left even earlier, and I was left alone. Suddenly the door of the box opened and I saw Tchaikovsky, and Rubinstein laughing behind him. On seeing me, Pyotr Ilich was on the point of backing out, but Rubinstein shoved him in the back, and, stumbling against the doorstep, he fell into the box. Rubinstein roared with laughter, repeating the phrase, "that's your place, at her feet. Beg her forgiveness." Pyotr Ilich stood up, embarrassed, redder than ever, and sat on the edge of a chair. To all my efforts to strike up a conversation with him he was stubbornly silent, looking around at the exit with a suffering expression, and, finally, having bid Rubinstein farewell, he flew headlong from the box."[33]

These events took place in the aftermath of Tchaikovsky's disastrous marriage to Antonina Milyukova in July 1877, and public appearances were a torment for him. Nevertheless, a sumptuous dinner was organized for Tchaikovsky at the Hermitage Restaurant attended by both Rubinstein brothers. Anton had never forgiven Tchaikovsky for failing to attend the public examination which formed part of the graduation formalities in December 1865, and he seemed to dislike Tchaikovsky's excessive shyness: "I really do not know whether he liked or disliked *Onegin*. At least, he did not say a word to me about it," Tchaikovsky wrote to Nadezhda von Meck two days later on 19/31 March.[34]

The Merchant Kalashnikov

When Rubinstein returned to Peterhof he set about completing *The Merchant Kalashnikov* in the hope that it would be staged in St. Petersburg during the following season. He seemed to take particular pride in this work which was based on a narrative poem by Lermontov called *Pesn' pro tsarya Ivana Vasil'yevicha, molodogo oprichnika i udalogo kuptsa Kalashnikova* [The song about Tsar Ivan Vasilyevich, the young *oprichnik* and the bold merchant Kalashnikov]. The work is set in the sixteenth century at the time of Ivan the Terrible. The cast is as follows:

Tsar Ivan the Terrible	bass
Malyuta Skuratov (his henchman)	baritone
Kiribeyevich	tenor
Vyazemsky	tenor
Basmanov ⟩ oprichniks	tenor
Gryazny	baritone
Kolïchov	bass
Stepan Paramonovich Kalashnikov (a merchant)	baritone
Alyona Dmitriyevna (his wife)	soprano
Efim (Kalashnikov's brother)	tenor
Sergey (Kalashnikov's brother)	bass
Timofey Biryuk (Kalashnikov's farm-hand)	bass
Nikitka (Timofey's nephew, and the Tsar's jester)	tenor
Solomonida (trader)	alto
Simeon Kolchin (a rich tradesman, a gray-haired old man)	bass
Filat (a butcher)	baritone
Chelubey (a Tartar strongman)	tenor
Chief police officer	baritone
1st and 2nd heralds	tenors
1st, 2nd, 3rd, and 4th oprichniks	2 tenor/2 basses
Prince Mikhail Temgryukovich Cherkassky	(mute role)

The Merchant Kalashnikov is unique among Rubinstein's operas, as it is the only one with a Russian historical theme (leaving aside the lost score of *Dmitry*

Donskoy and the later *Goryusha* which is essentially a domestic drama). It was written at a time when Rubinstein was beginning to accept the use of national elements, even in his own music. His striving for historical authenticity led him to write to Vladimir Stasov, bombarding the critic with questions about the Russian melody, "*Slava Bogu na nebye, slava* [Glory to God in heaven, glory]," used in the processional chorus when Ivan attends the contest on the Moscow River. On what occasions did the people sing this melody in olden times? Rubinstein enquired. "Which text is better: the one by Prach or the one by Sakharov?[35] Could it be used as an anthem for those times? . . . Also on the matter of martial music, or more correctly, instrumental music, during processions or festivals—was such music in use? Or was it only percussion instruments (drums, bells, and so on?) and trumpets?"[36] One can well imagine that Stasov roundly dismissed Rubinstein's attempts at authenticity, and probably guessed that his advances were prompted simply by the need to gain a sympathetic ear in the hostile nationalist camp.

A month later *The Merchant Kalashnikov* was completed, and on 12/24 June 1879 Rubinstein wrote to Nápravník, requesting that the opera be staged the following season. "Would you like to hear it? I am ready to play (sing!?) it for you," he wrote to the conductor. Nápravník's son, Vladimir, detected in the composer's brashness a wholly characteristic trait, noting that the repertory for each season was approved before the end of the previous one:

> My father would take the scores of the operas that were due to be staged and study them at his dacha during the summer, so that when he returned to town in the fall, he already knew these new operas by heart and from the first rehearsals he could give everyone involved general instructions as well as correct the slightest inaccuracies in the performance. But of what concern to Rubinstein were such tiny details? Wasn't it just a matter of indifference to him that the people from theater administration [the Directorate of Imperial Theaters] had gone away on leave, that there wasn't anyone to approve his opera, that Nápravník was fanatical in his conscientious regard for his duty, that he was bogged down with work for the winter period, and during the summer he had enough to do in studying just the operas that had been approved for production.

Not surprisingly, when Nápravník sent Rubinstein his reply, it "brought forth something of an awesome growl from the angry lion."[37] The conductor was evasive, complaining about the "moral humiliation" caused by the theater administration on the matter of renewing the contracts and approving the repertory for the coming season. He reminded Rubinstein that the administration chose the repertory and not him: "In the new order of things my voice would be a voice wailing in the wilderness." If Nápravník had not given him the unqualified support that he had wanted, then at least Rubinstein was encouraged by the news that the official censor had not raised any objection to the libretto of *The Merchant Kalashnikov*. Only one formality needed to be observed, he was told: the libretto had to be sent to the Main Committee of Printing. In the long and tortuous history of *The Merchant Kalashnikov* the first round had gone to Rubinstein, but an opera in which the tsar seems to flout the sanctity of marriage and defend his cronies against the rightful justice of his people was not going to have an easy passage with those in authority.

In the fall Rubinstein went abroad, missing the first production of *The Demon* at the Bolshoy Theater in Moscow. The opera was heard on 22 October/ 3 November for the benefit of the Italian conductor Enrico Bevignani, and Bogomir Korsov took the title role. In his review of the production for *Moskovskiye vedomosti,* Laroche made an interesting observation: "The whole of Wagner, the whole of the new (post-Meyerbeerian) French School, even the whole of *Ruslan* have passed before him, leaving no trace. As a result, neither in the instrumentation, nor in the harmony, nor in the declamation will you find the material with which our modern operas and cantatas are filled but, rather, the music of the 1840s and 1850s with the addition of Rubinstein of the 1870s."[38] The opera was old-fashioned even at the time of its composition, yet its old-fashioned romance idiom had (and still has) enormous appeal for Russian audiences. Melodies written in the manner of the *bïtovoy romans* (the domestic, urban romance), greatly popularized by Varlamov in the 1840s, were the backbone of this opera, as they were of a much greater one—Tchaikovsky's *Yevgeny Onegin.* Indeed, it would be difficult to imagine *Yevgeny Onegin* as we know it today had it not been for the model of Rubinstein's opera. "Slïkhali l' vï?" [Did you not hear?], the opening duet for Tatyana and Olga, is set to the same text as Rubinstein's *The Singer,* Op. 36 No. 7, and is a skillful stylization of that song. But the influence goes far beyond stylization. In the final scene of both operas, the male protagonist (a baritone in each instance) is pleading for a love to which he has forfeited the right. His entreaties almost succeed, but at the very last moment they fail because the heroine realizes her devotion to heaven (Tamara), to duty (Tatyana). Tchaikovsky may have seen this parallel on an abstract artistic level, and for this reason there are distinct similarities in the dramatic structure of the two scenes. The most interesting similarity, however, can be found in Tamara's short phrase, "Kto b ni tï bïl, moy drug pechal'nïy" [Whoever you are, my sorrowful friend]. One wonders whether Tchaikovsky had not remembered this melodic fragment, which encompasses the interval of a sixth, when he created one of the principal themes associated with Tatyana in *Yevgeny Onegin.*

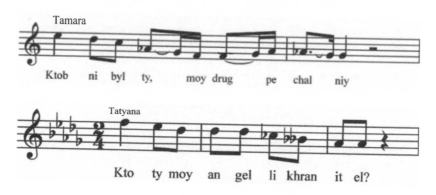

Tamara's E minor Romance, "Noch' tepla, noch' tikha" [The night is warm, the night is calm], also prefigures a situation in another of Tchaikovsky's operas. Act I, scene 2, of *The Queen of Spades* shows Liza alone at night illuminated by candlelight. Tchaikovsky's heroine, like Tamara, cannot sleep because she is dreaming of a stranger whose fateful appearance is about to change her life. Betrothed to a handsome, wealthy prince, Liza is perplexed by her own feeling of profound sadness. Her melancholy, expressed in the lyrical line "Otkuda eti slyozï, zachem onye?" [What reason for these tears, why?], as in Tamara's romance, is supported by rhythmically incessant sixteenth notes. Tamara's startled question, "Kto b on bïl?" [Who might he be?], over a sustained chord also has its counterpart in Liza's "Vï izme*nili mnye!*" [You have betrayed me!], where the final bar of the phrase (italicized above) is fretfully echoed by the woodwind (falling G♭ to F). The resemblance here is less dependent on any direct thematic relationships, but the similar mood and atmosphere of the two scenes is striking.

In Hamburg Rubinstein conducted the long awaited premiere of *Néron* on 1 November. He was well pleased with the "remarkable production." The opera scored a resounding success, and Hans von Bülow wrote a glowing article titled *Ein Nero Brief* for the *Neue Hannovershche Landreitung*. The successful productions of *Néron* and *The Demon* in Moscow were overshadowed by the illness of Rubinstein's youngest son, Sasha, who had been suffering from asthma and a weak heart. Despite this, he would not yield to Vera's demand to leave Hamburg and join them on a trip to Italy, where, it was hoped, the climate would have a beneficial effect on the boy's health. It would be stupidity on his part, he reasoned, to throw away all the material and moral gains he had achieved with the present trip to watch over a thirteen-year-old boy. He remained in Hamburg and conducted another four performances of *Néron,* and also gave several concerts in the city. His subsequent itinerary took him to Stuttgart, Munich, Leipzig, Breslau (where he conducted *Die Maccabäer*), Dresden, Köln, Prague, and Berlin, where he made appearances throughout November and December. Rubinstein spent Christmas in Berlin where he met the young English composer Ethel Smyth, then studying privately with Heinrich von Herzogenberg. In her reminiscences Ethel Smyth recalled that a young woman, who wanted a career in music, had approached Rubinstein for advice about her playing:

> A totally talentless maiden, relying I suppose on her great beauty—for his weaknesses were notorious—had insisted on playing to him with a view to being advised as to whether she should make music her career. When she had done he remarked quite simply: "How should *you* ever become an artist?" and then, taking up her hand, he pointed in succession to her fingers, her forehead, and her heart, slowly saying "hier nix, hier nix, und *hier* nix!"—a terrible sequence of nothingness that needs no translation.[39]

When Rubinstein returned to St. Petersburg the vocal score of *The Merchant Kalashnikov* had been published by Jurgenson, and the composer learned that the Imperial Directorate had yielded to his request for the opera to be included in the 1879–80 opera season at the Mariinsky Theater. Nápravník had declined to rehearse it, and Karel Kučera (the deputy conductor at the Mariinsky Theater) had been suggested as a replacement. "I do not know Kučera," Rubinstein wrote in a letter to Pavel Petersen, the piano manufacturer who in recent years had been acting as his agent and business manager. "If Nápravník has disassociated himself entirely from this affair, then it goes without saying that rehearsing *Kalashnikov* will have to be entrusted to another person; but I do not want testing the reliability of a new person to be at my expense."[40]

On 11 January 1880 Rubinstein conducted *Feramors* in Danzig and returned to St. Petersburg in mid-February to conduct the premiere of *The Merchant Kalashnikov*. This took place at the Mariinsky Theater on 22 February/5 March 1880. A second performance followed three days later, but then the imperial censor banned the opera. According to Barenboym, people of the time saw a close parallel between the execution of Kalashnikov in the last act of the opera and the execution of the populist Ippolit Mlodetsky who had attempted to assassinate Mikhail Loris-Melnikov, the chairman of the Supreme Administrative Committee on 20 February (o.s.). Nevertheless, a review appeared in *Novoye vremya* on 23 February (o.s.) entitled *O prem'erye operï A. G. Rubinshteyna "Kupets Kalashnikov"* [On the premiere of Rubinstein's opera *The Merchant Kalashnikov*]. Seeing little probability of the ban on the opera being lifted in the immediate future, Rubinstein agreed to Senff's request that the libretto be translated into German. The vocal score with a German text by Hermann Wolff appeared in 1881 and the full score in 1883.

From mid-March to the end of April Rubinstein undertook a concert tour of Russia, beginning with two concerts in Moscow, and then taking in Kharkov and Kiev. The programs of these concerts show Rubinstein's tendency to consolidate his core repertory in the 1880s, much of it forming the basis of the later Historical Concerts.

During the summer break he began to think seriously about a new symphony in which he had decided to employ folk-song material. In July he wrote to the Finnish musicologist Friedrich Faltin, asking him whether he could find him "a few Finnish folk melodies of different types, that is, cheerful, sad, and in dance rhythms. I need them urgently."[41] He also wrote to his mother, who was spending the summer in Yalta, asking whether Sofiya could find him a few authentic Tartar folk songs or dances: "They are urgently needed for one work which I am writing at the moment, but quickly—just two or three items, but they must be authentic."[42] The work for which these themes were needed was to be his Symphony No. 5 in G minor, Op. 107, *The Russian*. Barenboym has suggested that the first movement is constructed from two contrasting Russian themes, while the second movement (Scherzo) employs motifs from the folk music of other nationalities of the empire. The symphony, in fact, develops the compositional style that Rubinstein had adopted a year earlier with *The Merchant Kalashnikov*, and although the composer does not abandon the techniques well established by earlier symphonic works, his use of folk melodies was a patent concession to *kuchkism*. Indeed, the melodic contour of the opening theme is strikingly similar to the motif that begins Musorgsky's *Boris Godunov*. For Stasov and the nationalist composers, however, Rubinstein's use of folk songs amounted to little more than exotic decoration lacking true organic kinship with the traditions established by Glinka and his successors. Laroche observed: "Rubinstein has remained, and probably will always remain, a representative of the universal element in music, an element needed in an art that is not mature and is subject to all the enthusiasms of youth." He clearly saw Rubinstein as a moderating influence against the excesses which, he believed, had infiltrated Russian music since the time of Glinka: "The more passionately the author of these lines has throughout his career defended the Russian trend and the cult of Glinka, the more he recognizes the need for a sensible counterbalance to the extremes into which any trend can fall. . . . Mr. Rubinstein is a composer who follows a predominantly cosmopolitan direction, but, I add, his G minor Symphony has again shown how easily and brilliantly he can adopt the techniques of the opposing camp when he wants to."[43]

While working on the new symphony, Rubinstein was also composing the two string quartets of Op. 106 and an additional seventh movement (*Lento assai*) for the *Ocean Symphony*. This new movement was so lengthy, he wrote to Senff, that it constituted "an entirely new symphony." In the definitive version, the new A minor movement was to be placed second in the order of movements, and Rubinstein tried to integrate it musically by beginning with a descending chromatic phrase in quarter notes (C–B–B♭–A) to match the opening of the *Adagio* in D with the same phrase in half notes. In this massive movement Rubinstein seemed to be attempting to dispel the myth that his musical horizons had ended with Mendelssohn and to prove that he was a modern master with a rich and varied orchestral palette. Rubinstein's final word on the *Ocean Symphony* was suitably grand in conception. Most remarkable is that the whole movement is an extended exercise in tone painting. The wind howls, the lightning flashes, the waves heave and groan, the thunder roars. And this is not just as a colorful episode in a classically proportioned movement but is present from beginning to end. In its final seven-movement form the symphony consists of the following:

1. Allegro maestoso, 3/2 C
2. Lento assai, 4/4, a
3. Adagio 3/4, D
4. Allegro 2/4, G
5. Adagio 8/8, e
6. Scherzo, 3/4, F (Presto with a brief trio: Moderato assai in B flat)
7. Adagio—Allegro con fuoco, 8/8 c > C

On 20 September/2 October 1880 Rubinstein appeared in a concert of the Chamber Music Society, when Karl Davïdov joined him for a performance of the Cello Sonata in D, Op. 18; the first performance of the String Quartet in F minor, Op. 106, No. 2, was also given. Twelve days later, on 2/14 October, Rubinstein took part in an all-Rubinstein concert. He conducted the premiere of his Symphony No. 5, Aleksandr Verzhbilovich was the soloist in his Cello Concerto No. 2, Iretskaya and Lavrovskaya sang some of his vocal duets, and he performed his own *Caprice Russe* (Nápravník conducted).

On 3 November Rubinstein conducted *The Demon* in Hamburg, where almost exactly a year earlier the premiere of *Néron* had been given under the composer's direction. The directorate of the opera was very attentive and had sought Rubinstein's advice on the stage directions, the costumes, and the distribution of roles. For once Rubinstein was delighted, and he wrote to Kaleriya Khristoforovna: "My opera *The Demon* has been staged here with brilliant success and better than in St. Petersburg and Moscow."[44] This success was followed by several more productions of Rubinstein's operas in Germany, most of them conducted by the composer:

Die Maccabäer (Hanover, 19 November)[45]
Feramors (Mannheim, 17 December)
Néron (Berlin, 3 December)
Die Maccabäer (Königsberg, 19 January 1881)[46]

After the fiasco with *Feramors* in Berlin, Rubinstein refused to conduct *Néron*. Even worse, the performance at the Royal Opera House failed to please him; he became embroiled in a bitter argument with the theater administration and boycotted the premiere altogether.

The first German performance of the Symphony No. 5 took place in Berlin on 12 January 1881. It was with a certain relief that Rubinstein reported to Karl Davïdov in St. Petersburg: "Now I am calm on its account; I think that it can please even abroad—something I doubted, as you know, because of its exclusively Russian character."[47] In this same concert Rubinstein performed his *Le Bal Costumé* for two pianos, Op. 103, with Anna Yesipova. A week later he conducted *Die Maccabäer* in Köningsberg, and on 23 January gave another performance of *Le Bal Costumé* in Hamburg, this time with his former pupil Monika Terminskaya.

Immediately afterward he headed for Madrid and the start of a tour of the Iberian Peninsula in the company of Hermann Wolff, who had earlier provided Senff with the German translation of *The Merchant Kalashnikov*. Highly literate and intelligent, Wolff had been a former editor of the *Neue Berliner Musikzeitung*, but he had recently set up a concert agency in Berlin. Among his first commissions was that of organizing Rubinstein's Iberian tour, which began with six concerts in Madrid between 31 January and 28 February and then took in other towns throughout Spain and Portugal.

Death of Nikolay Rubinstein

On 23 March 1881, three months short of his forty-sixth birthday, Nikolay Rubinstein died in Paris at the Grand Hôtel on the Boulevard des Cappucins. His health, which had never been good, took a decided turn for the worse in November. In spite of this, Nikolay had continued to fulfill his concert engagements in St. Petersburg and Moscow punctiliously, and few people in his circle had appreciated the seriousness of his condition. According to the medical reports of his doctors in St. Petersburg (including the eminent physicians Lev Bertenson and Sergey Botkin), the cause of Nikolay's illness was chronic hepatitis that resulted in cirrhosis of the liver. It was hoped that a period of rest in Nice would restore his health, but the patient only succeeded in traveling as far as Paris, arriving there on 17 March. Only then did it become clear that the situation was grave and there was little hope of recovery. It seems unlikely that Anton was aware of the critical state of his brother's health. The telegrams that his sister Sofiya sent to Sintra in Portugal and then Paris took him completely by surprise, and when Anton eventually arrived in the French capital Nikolay had already been dead for several hours. He sent a hastily written note to Sofiya:

> I received your telegrams there and here. At least mamma and all of us are well. Much water has flowed since I left St. Petersburg. If only you could go to Moscow, do not disturb mamma.[48]
>
> I juggled my way around Spain with Wolff. This time not without something pleasant—something new! It has become easier to contemplate life. About Nicholas I thought—why did he not travel? Nikolay played better than me, and I always asked myself why great success fell to my lot. Of all of us, only he inherited from our father that *légèreté de l'esprit,* but in life (in his youth) and not in his art. Why was that? Surely it is not just because ponderous thoughts did not make him languish? . . . We had not seen each other for a long time, but I felt his hand as a brother, and perhaps he—mine. Now he is no more. What we have, we do not keep, but having lost it we weep. All around it is quite deserted. I cannot even weep! Maybe I shall soon come and see you, and then I shall have to start up my English barrel organ. And there—has not the time come for rest, shouldn't I abandon this charming world? Soon the Knochenmann will come for me, too. I must hasten to take stock of things.[49]

On 28 March Anton accompanied the lead coffin with the body of Nikolay Rubinstein on its long journey back to Russia. Contemporaries speak of Anton's cold reserve during the elaborate funeral rites in Moscow: "He did not weep," wrote one eyewitness, "but effused a sense of horror. It was as if death had looked him in the eyes."[50] Tchaikovsky went much further: "Not only is he not crushed by his brother's death but is *apparently* very pleased about it. Jurgenson, with whom I spoke about this, explains this incomprehensible fact by Anton's *jealousy* of Nikolay. For what? Why? I don't understand. But if this is so, what could be more offensive than such jealousy?"[51]

After observing a period of mourning, Rubinstein arrived in London on 15 May 1881 for a five-and-a-half-week stay. His numerous commitments in the British capital included solo recitals and conducting the London premiere of his Symphony No. 5 which was heard on 21 May. On 11 June Rubinstein appeared in a mammoth concert at the Crystal Palace concert hall. In the first part he played the solo part in Schumann's Piano Concerto under the direction of Augustus Manns, and Auer was the soloist in his Violin Concerto in G. The second part of the concert was wholly taken up with *Der Thurm zu Babel.* The

Musical Times devoted a long article to the oratorio, but the writer reproached the composer for his declamatory style, which "should be (and is, for example, in Wagner) always supported by an undercurrent of musical inspiration." On the other hand, he found the destruction of the tower by lightning to be "rendered by the orchestra in a truly masterly manner"[52]—a view, coincidentally, wholly endorsed by the *Times* columnist (14 June). For Rubinstein, however, the major event of his London visit was a performance of *The Demon* at Covent Garden (this is usually credited as being the first Russian opera ever heard in Britain). He conducted the opera, which was sung in Italian, on 21 June, and the distinguished cast included the French contralto Zélia Trebelli and the Canadian soprano Emma Albani.

The Demon: Jean Lasalle
Tamara: Emma Albani
Sinodal: Signor Marini
Angel: Zélia Trebelli
Gudal: Edouard de Reszke

The opera was well received by the public, and one reviewer commented that Rubinstein was given an ovation such as the theater had not heard since the days of Weber. Unfortunately *The Demon* fared less well with the critics who were perplexed by the fantastical subject "lacking unity and dramatic grasp."[53] Even though the opera achieved only a *succès d'estime*, it was heard again in London seven years later when the touring company, *The Russian National Opera Company*, gave it in Russian at a theater in Great Queen Street (probably the Novelty Theater, then known as the Jodrell Theater).

After two appearances in Paris, Rubinstein returned to Peterhof in late June. On 8 July the *Sankt-Peterburgskiye vedomosti* again reported the news of Rubinstein's failing eyesight. Stasov wrote to Balakirev on the same day: "But have you heard that Anton Rubinstein has almost lost his eyesight, plans to give up playing, and finally to give himself up to composing!!" And, as if to underscore Stasov's indignation at the thought of yet more works flowing from Rubinstein's pen, the composer was indeed hard at work that summer on a new ballet, *Die Rebe* [The grapevine]. This work was being composed to a scenario by Paolo Taglioni, the director of ballet at the Wiener Staatsoper, in collaboration with the French writer Charles-Jean Grandmougin and the Belgian ballet master Josef Hansen, who worked at the Moscow Bolshoy Theater from 1879 to 1883. Rubinstein also continued his work on the opera *Sulamith* and the orchestral piece *Russia* (intended for the opening of the Moscow Exhibition of Industry and Art in the spring of 1882).

In November he was engaged to conduct the first three concerts of the new RMS season in memory of his brother. Before setting out for Moscow, however, he wrote to Senff, enclosing the *Lento assai* movement of the *Ocean Symphony:* "I do not think that I am doing you or the public any service," he told his publisher. "But it is necessary; only now do I consider this symphony complete. It always seemed to me that something was lacking in it—now it is the way I want it."[54] The first RMS concert in Moscow took place on 31 October/ 12 November and, in accordance with Nikolay Rubinstein's own wishes, Anton conducted Schumann's *Requiem* and concluded the concert with Beethoven's Symphony No. 3, a work for which Nikolay is reputed to have had a particular fondness. The following day he conducted *The Demon* at the Bolshoy Theater, and then he took up the baton for the final two RMS concerts on 7/19 and 14/ 26 November. These concerts, the first without Nikolay as their principal conductor, struck contemporaries by their poignancy. On his return to St. Petersburg, he conducted the first performance of the *Ocean Symphony* in its seven-movement revision (28 November/10 December). Two weeks later he joined Leopold Auer in a charity concert organized by the Polish soprano Marcellina Sembrich, having earlier given his consent to appear in her concert only if a piano from the firm Becker were provided for his use.

Immediately following the New Year celebrations Rubinstein headed for Leipzig where he conducted his Symphony No. 5 to great acclaim on 12 January 1882. From 28 January to 23 February he gave a series of solo concerts at the Salle Erard and the Conservatory in Paris, and also conducted several of his own works. On 14 February he gave the French premiere of his Symphony No. 5 and *Don Quixote* at the Conservatory, and five days later conducted a *concert populaire* at the Cirque d'Hiver, the traditional home of the Pasdeloup concerts. The program included works by Glinka, Dargomïzhsky (*Kazachok*), Tchaikovsky (*Romeo and Juliet*), and Rimsky-Korsakov (*Sadko*), and Aleksandr Verzhbilovich performed one of Davïdov's cello concertos. Among his own works Rubinstein conducted a performance of the cantata *Rusalka* and the dances from *Feramors,* which had to be repeated. On 20 February, at a concert arranged for the pupils of the celebrated singing teacher Mathilde Marchesi, Gounod conducted the introduction to his opera *Mireille,* and Rubinstein took the baton for *Rusalka* in which Mme A.M. Rïndina sang the contralto solo.

These concerts were extensively reviewed by Hermann Laroche for *Moskovskiye vedomosti,* and the critic devoted considerable space to Rubinstein as a performer. His description of the effect that Schumann's Fantasy in C had on listeners is particularly illuminating. Laroche considered the work difficult: "It is completely devoid of melody in the popular sense of the word; on an uneducated listener it must produce the impression of military exercises, of limbering up for the fingers . . . For all of this, under the fingers of Rubinstein this difficult work, so bristling with complexities, acquires a fantastical charm which rivets a huge mass of listeners in some incomprehensible fashion."[55]

From Paris, Rubinstein traveled to Cologne, where he conducted the first performance there of his opera *The Demon* on 1 March. There is no doubt that his endeavors to popularize his works were paying handsomely. His successful London season in the spring of 1881 had resulted in two more British premieres of his works without the composer's direct intervention. On 9 March 1882 the Philharmonic Society chorus and orchestra gave the first British performance of *Rusalka* with Janet Patey, considered the leading British contralto of the day. Three months later, on 9 June, London first heard *Das Verlorene Paradies* at a

Philharmonic Society concert. The oratorio, in an English translation by Henry Hersee, was given by the Philharmonic chorus and orchestra conducted by William Cusins, and the performers were all leading artists of their day: Rosa Hersee, Marian Fenna, Eleanor Farnol, Sophie Hudson, Barton McGuckin, and Signor Foli.[56] Thomas Pettit was the organist.

In early May 1882 Rubinstein undertook a concert tour of Scandinavia with the Belgian violin virtuoso Eugène Ysaÿe. In 1879 Ysaÿe had been engaged by the impresario Benjamin Bilse as a violinist (and soloist) for his so-called *Brasserie-Konzert* in Berlin—open-air concerts of serious music where beer and other refreshments were served.[57] Rubinstein remembered his meeting with Ysaÿe at Vieuxtemps's soirée in Paris six years earlier and was outraged that such a fine musician should be playing in an orchestra instead of establishing a career as a soloist. Although Ysaÿe was bound to Bilse under the terms of a contract, Rubinstein managed to convince the impresario that a successful concert tour would increase the artist's prestige and ultimately boost the takings of his own concerts. The stratagem appeared to work, for the pianist and violinist immediately set out for Denmark.

On returning to Peterhof, Rubinstein set to work on scoring his ballet *The Grapevine*, reporting to Senff, on 7/19 May, that the work would be completed during the summer. However, this task was interrupted by the necessity of conducting three RMS concerts connected with the opening of the Exhibition of Industry and Art in Moscow. Nikolay Rubinstein had pledged to conduct the concerts as far back as 1880 and Anton agreed to stand in for his late brother. The concerts included his Symphony No. 5 and the first performance of the orchestral work *Russia*. In the opening concert on 18/30 May Rubinstein conducted the first performance in Russia of Tchaikovsky's Piano Concerto No. 2 in G with Sergey Taneyev as the soloist, and twelve days later, on 30 May/11 June, he also conducted Tchaikovsky's Serenade in C for string orchestra. Jurgenson wrote to Tchaikovsky the following day: "Your Serenade scored a huge success. Jupiter [nickname for Anton Rubinstein] at the first rehearsal said to me: 'I think that this is Tchaikovsky's best piece.' He praised the work to other people no less unconditionally and at the final rehearsal said: 'You can congratulate yourself on the publication of this opus.'"[58] This uncharacteristic gesture of approval was symptomatic of a general change in Rubinstein's outlook which had become more noticeable since the death of his brother Nikolay. He had never had much sympathy for Tchaikovsky or the "Mighty Handful," yet the popular concert he had given in Paris in February seemed almost an attempt to emulate the kind of program his brother had devised for the Russian concerts at the Paris World Exhibition in 1878. Hitherto he had done virtually nothing to assist Tchaikovsky, whereas Nikolay had been a steadfast champion of his music for more than fifteen years, despite the occasional disagreements that marred their relationship. Yet here was Anton conducting two new compositions by Tchaikovsky, and even singing the praises of the Serenade. His attitude to the Nationalists was even more ambiguous. Despite the rancor that had been poured out in the press, Rubinstein maintained cordial relations with Stasov, and they still met socially and at public events. Perhaps Stasov had been mollified to some extent by Rubinstein's confession to Bessel of the error of his ways in not having recognized the significance of the New Russian School. As Stasov told Balakirev on 5 July 1882: "Now he sees that there is no little talent and merit among these musicians, and he intends to give them a fairly extensive place in his concerts."[59]

In June Rubinstein returned to Peterhof. His wife Vera was still nursing their ailing son Sasha in Italy and the only residents of the house were his son Yasha, his father-in-law Aleksandr Chekuyanov, and the English governess. Still working on the orchestration of *The Grapevine*, Rubinstein wrote to Marius Petipa on 30 June/12 July, inviting him to Peterhof for discussions concerning the scenario and choreography: "You may spend the night here since my family is abroad taking the waters, and I am here alone in a fairly large house. It makes absolutely no difference which day and time you come, as I do not go out anywhere."[60] It is not known whether Petipa accepted the invitation but, with or without his intervention, the ballet proved to have a difficult stage history. The completed score remained with the Imperial Directorate of Theaters for some weeks before it was eventually refused. Jurgenson agreed to publish the piano score, but despite Rubinstein's endeavors to secure a performance of the work in St. Petersburg, he was unsuccessful. Odd numbers were played at concerts in Moscow in 1886 and in St. Petersburg in 1889, but the entire ballet was only produced in Berlin on 24 April 1893.

Die Geistliche Oper

During the summer Rubinstein was also preparing an article for publication on spiritual opera, which he had probably been thinking about since the late 1860s. The article, *Die Geistliche Oper*, took the form of a letter to Josef Lewinsky, the actor and editor of a work on the theater called *Vor den Coulissen*.[61] The article was reprinted in Senff's journal *Signale für die musikalische Welt* and was considered highly contentious at the time, as it attacked the fundamental idea of sacred oratorio. For Rubinstein there was something incongruous at the sight of gentlemen in dress coats and ladies in extravagant toilettes singing the parts of imposing figures from the New and Old Testaments. He felt that it was more fitting to represent these religious subjects as sacred operas, citing the Mystery Plays of the Middle Ages as adequate proof that the form had historical legitimacy. He saw no trace of profanity in this; after all, paintings of scenes from the Holy Scriptures were not considered profane, so it followed that musical representation of these scenes should be viewed in the same way. He claimed to have held views on the desirability of transferring the action of oratorios to the stage for more than twenty-five years. His own *Das Verlorene Paradies* and *Der Thurm zu Babel* had been wholly conceived as sacred operas, but, in view of the impracticability of seeing them produced in that way, he had refashioned them as oratorios. In the past he had tried to win support for his ideas from influential patrons: the Grand Duke of Weimar, for example, had told him that such a plan could only be carried out in the larger towns; and von Mühler, the Prussian Minister of Religion, had referred him to the Minister of Culture and intimated that the idea would be approved only for the Old and not the New Testament. He had approached Dean Stanley of Westminster in London, but the latter had replied that the plan could only be realized in popular venues such as fairs and markets. He had approached the Jewish community in Paris, which was prepared to support him financially but did not want people to suppose that the initiative had come from the Jewish community. Then he had thought of America, but the shortage of suitable artists caused him to abandon the idea. It was his conviction that the realization of this goal could be achieved only through the construction of special theaters designed solely for the purpose of presenting sacred opera, and that, practically speaking, they would become "churches of art." One of the specific features of the genre was the frequent need to divide the set into representations of heaven, earth, and hell, which necessitated alterations in the construction of the auditorium and stage. Just six years after Bayreuth had first staged Wagner's *Der Ring des Niebelungen*, Rubinstein was advocating something similar for the art form that he fondly believed he had created. Perhaps these reflections on sacred opera had galvanized his own creative urges, for when he set out on his next journey to Western Europe in October, his interest in the *Song of Songs* was already rekindled and he was eagerly anticipating a meeting with Rodenberg.

Meanwhile, Artur Nikisch was busy rehearsing *Die Maccabäer* in Leipzig, although it was the composer himself who conducted the first performance there on 4 November. Rubinstein did not miss the opportunity to send Rodenberg a telegram asking his librettist to join him for discussions about *Sulamith*. After this, he returned to St. Petersburg and wrote to Kaleriya Khristoforovna on 6/18 November: "Now I am here again busy with preparations for the winter which promises to be rather tiring. I am getting old, and I feel this particularly at public appearances: rehearsals, concerts, stage productions, everything that I used to overcome with a joke, I now manage with difficulty, and it soon tires and bores me!"[62] In September he had sent his son, Yasha, to the lycée, but the boy had played pranks and had been expelled until Christmas. "It is not a tragedy, but it is unpleasant. Still, youth must be allowed to get mischievousness out of its system," Rubinstein wrote to his mother. And on a rather more reflective note, he added: "I was never mischievous—probably I was never young?!"

In November and December Rubinstein conducted a series of RMS concerts, largely consisting of classic works from the Western European repertory; the programs included a rare performance of Henselt's Piano Concerto in F minor on 4/16 December. During the season there were ten concerts in all, but in four of them Rubinstein handed the baton over to younger composers for a reading of their own work. For 4/16 December concert it was Nikolay Solovyov with his *Fantaziya na temu "Ey ukhnem"* [Fantasy on the "Song of the Volga Boatmen"]. In the concert of 18/30 December Taneyev conducted his Overture in C on Russian themes, a work written for the Exhibition of Art and Industry in Moscow, where it had first been introduced in June.

On 22 January 1883 Rubinstein conducted the fifth RMS concert which included the first performance of Glazunov's *Uvertyura na grecheskiye temï* [Overture on Greek themes], Op. 3. Two weeks later, at the sixth RMS concert, he conducted a concert of music by Haydn, Gluck, Beethoven, and Schumann, and Ippolitov-Ivanov took the baton for the premiere of his overture *Khmel'-Yar*. It was after this performance that Rubinstein, supported by Karl Davïdov, recommended the young composer for the work of establishing a branch of the RMS in Tiflis.

At the beginning of the year Rubinstein received the piano score of his ballet, *The Grapevine*, from Jurgenson, and he informed his publisher: "There are many mistakes in it, but this is not a disaster. I cannot obtain the full score from the Directorate, that is, from the music office; it simply makes me sick having to deal with them. As soon as I receive it, I shall send it on to you. It seems that the ballet will not be staged this season!? Why? Only God knows; that is the way they do things—they are a pack of fools and that is all!"[63] The delay in recovering the manuscript from the Directorate, and consequently the delay in having the score and parts engraved by Jurgenson in Moscow and Senff in Leipzig, meant that it would be difficult to get the ballet staged anywhere. A week later he sent his sister, Sofiya, a copy of the piano score, advising his mother: "On the subject of Sofyia, tell her from me that she must now be more cautious than ever with respect to all she is doing and to what she says to each and every person she meets." According to Barenboym, this cautionary note was prompted by Sofiya's association with Vera Figner, the Russian revolutionary of the People's Will movement, who was arrested on 10/22 February.

On 19 February/3 March Rubinstein was scheduled to perform Beethoven's Ninth Symphony in an RMS concert, but some of the orchestral players (specifically the principal horn, the principal clarinet, and the principal bassoon) had refused to play under the pretext that "the program is too long (?!) and too arduous."

The full program that Rubinstein was to conduct was the following:

Wagner: Faust Overture
Popper: Suite for cello and orchestra (played by David Popper)
Musorgsky: Intermezzo in modo classico
Shcherbachyov: Interlude
Arensky: Scherzo from Symphony No. 1 in B minor
Beethoven: Symphony No. 9

Four days before the concert was to take place Rubinstein wrote to Yevgeny Albrecht, the Inspector of Music for the Imperial Theaters in St. Petersburg from 1877 until his death in 1894, to say that if the conflict could not be resolved to his satisfaction he would not conduct the concert, even hinting that he would also renege on all the remaining RMS concerts that season. "I do not wish to become odious to the orchestra, which I respect and love," he told Albrecht, "but in the final analysis I would have to. The director of the theater is also a director of the Society, and Messieurs MM. orchestral players should not forget this.

Moreover, all these gentlemen, without exception, gave a written commitment at the start of the season to take part in ten Society concerts." Rubinstein asked Albrecht to make his position in this matter clear, and concluded his ultimatum with the words: "I hope that the rehearsal for 9:00 AM tomorrow will go ahead without any hitches."[64] Barenboym notes that Rubinstein brought in new measures during the preparations for these concerts: instead of the usual rehearsals for each concert, Rubinstein demanded two or three preparatory rehearsals and then a final rehearsal. It seems that this (and other measures) is what the players really objected to. Rubinstein evidently got his way, as the concert went ahead as scheduled.

At the same time another conflict was rocking the very foundations of the Moscow Conservatory. In this conflict the main protagonists were Nikolay Hubert, its director, and Max Erdmannsdörfer, professor of orchestration and conductor of the Moscow RMS concerts. The problem centered on the fact that the Artistic Council of the Conservatory had been provoked by the presence of a teacher whose independence threatened to undermine the director's authority. As one of the members of the Artistic Council, Taneyev, explained in a long letter to Tchaikovsky of 2/14 March 1883:

> This question consists of the following: is it possible to admit into the Conservatory and into the Artistic Council a person who holds in his hands the concerts of the Musical Society, and whose refusal to direct the concerts might lead to losses for the Musical Society and, consequently, undermine the existence of the Conservatory, which depends financially on the Musical Society? Such a person, even though he occupies the secondary post of a teacher, will be something like a second director, but a director who bears no responsibility for his actions. The presence in the Conservatory of such a person, who is there in completely abnormal circumstances, is harmful for the Conservatory.[65]

Hubert demanded the removal of Erdmannsdörfer from his post at the Conservatory, and while the majority of the Artistic Council supported him, the Directorate of the Moscow RMS sided with Erdmannsdörfer, fearing that he would refuse to conduct the concerts on which it and the Conservatory depended for their financial support. At this point an appeal was made to Rubinstein, but the situation was suddenly resolved when Hubert resigned, and the acting director Konstantin Albrecht was elected to replace him. Erdmannsdörfer also resigned his teaching post at the Conservatory but was persuaded to continue conducting the RMS concerts.

When Rubinstein arrived in Moscow a few weeks later, the purpose of his visit was primarily to conduct the first performance of *Die Maccabäer* (23 February/7 March), which, as he wrote to his mother on his return to St. Petersburg, had "a brilliant success."[66] During his visit to Moscow, Rubinstein was approached by the commission responsible for organizing the coronation celebrations for Alexander III. However, he turned down the request to compose a march and a cantata for the coronation in May because of his other commitments and proposed Tchaikovsky for the job. Despite some initial reluctance, because of the six-week deadline for both commissions, Tchaikovsky completed the march and the cantata on time. Unfortunately this led to rumors in the Parisian press, and also in Russia, that Rubinstein had turned down the commission out of personal animosity toward the Russian court and the new emperor in particular. Tchaikovsky informed Nadezhda von Meck on 12/24 May: "As Anton Rubinstein's children are being brought up in Russia, and it could be harmful to him in general, since calumny however unfounded always leaves its mark, on the day of my departure I sent the newspaper *Gaulois* a brief repudiation of this fact."[67] A similar repudiation had also been published by *Novoye vremya* in St. Petersburg six days earlier.

When Rubinstein returned to the capital, he finally recovered the manuscript of his ballet, *The Grapevine*, from the Imperial Directorate and lost no time in sending it to Senff. At the same time he inquired with a note of hopeful optimism: "Is it true that Vienna is thinking about putting it on?" Unfortunately for Rubinstein, Vienna was not thinking about it, and nor was Berlin after his heated disagreements with the theater administration over *Feramors* and *Néron*. "If it is not staged in both places," he told Senff, "I am sorry for you. For then you will be left only with concert halls and bandstands."[68] A week after dispatching *The Grapevine* to his publisher, Rubinstein addressed a curious open letter to Senff, dated 7/19 March. This letter was republished shortly afterward in *Signale für die musikalische Welt* as *Über die Edition der Klassiker* (a Russian translation appeared in the journal *Nuvellist* later that year). It begins: "I must with gratitude decline your flattering proposal to edit a new edition of our classics." Whether Senff actually made any such proposal is open to question, for Rubinstein frequently resorted to dialogues or interviews (sometimes with entirely fictitious persons) for the purpose of putting over his views on issues that he wished to draw to public attention. The letter was intended to throw down the gauntlet to other musicians in an attempt to resolve various contentious matters about performing practice in the Baroque and Classical repertory. The letter contains Rubinstein's own ideas about markings, embellishments, and playing the music in the spirit of the time at which it was written. "Good musicians cannot agree about these things," he says, so the idea of producing a standard edition of the classics is "beyond the power of a single publisher or a single performer." He calls for a collective approach so that an edition could be produced "detailed to the utmost degree, explaining everything, an edition that would be supportive to the public, the standard for performers (teachers), and authoritative enough to be the starting point and guideline for the village teacher and for the professor of the conservatory."[69]

It is tempting to speculate whether Rubinstein wrote *On Editing the Classics* under the influence of Reinecke, who was in Russia that spring and played his Piano Concerto No. 1 in F♯ minor under Rubinstein's direction at an RMS concert on 12/24 March. The two men must have found much in common. Both were musically conservative, both believed in the necessity of the highest teaching standards at the conservatories, and both believed that students should receive the most rigorous and solid training. Like Rubinstein, Reinecke regarded himself as a guardian of tradition and was very much concerned with preserving the classical heritage stretching back to Bach and earlier. The article also reflected Rubinstein's then current preoccupations, such as the choice of edition when performing Handel's oratorios. This was clearly prompted by the actual performance of *Israel in Egypt* that Rubinstein conducted at an RMS concert on 6/18 April.

Besides works from the Western European classical repertory, Rubinstein began to include more works by native composers in the RMS concerts. Concert programs that included works by Glazunov, Ippolitov-Ivanov, Musorgsky, Shcherbachyov, and Arensky—predominantly young, contemporary composers—were noted earlier. In addition, Rubinstein conducted Tchaikovsky's Festival Overture "1812" in an RMS concert of 26 March/7 April and Blaremberg's overture *Umirayushchiy gladiator* [The dying gladiator], and handed the baton to Rimsky-Korsakov for a performance of the overture and entr'actes from the opera *Pskovityanka* [The maid of Pskov] in a concert of 5/17 February. He even began to include a few Russian works, other than his own, in his solo recitals: Tchaikovsky, Lyadov, and Nikolay Rubinstein in a concert of 3/15 April. These significant concessions were noted by contemporaries, and the day after his solo recital he wrote to Kaleriya Khristoforovna: "my concert was brilliant in all respects." [70] On 12 April Rubinstein left for Odessa, but his last concert before leaving St. Petersburg was another charity concert to raise funds for the Glinka monument. The program is interesting in that it foreshadows the later Historical Concerts, being a miniature survey of piano music from Handel to Liszt.

Sulamith, Unter Räubern, and *Der Papagei*

During his stay in Odessa, Rubinstein had discussions about organizing a local branch of the Russian Musical Society. The branch was founded the following year on the basis of the former Odessa Music Society. When he returned to Peterhof in mid-May, he composed a new piano trio, continued his work on *Sulamith*, and began a new one-act opera *Unter Räubern* [Among the brigands] based on Théophile Gautier's *Voyage en Espagne* with a libretto by Ernst Wiechert. Set in Spain during the early nineteenth century, this work concerns a group of travelers who fall victim to two rival bands of robbers. Pedro Torez complains to Prince Edgar, who is traveling incognito, about the hardships of a brigand's life since those in authority are no longer willing to pay for hostages. The prince helps the robbers give up their life of crime and, in the process, resolves various love intrigues. [71]

Prince Edgar		baritone
Nelke, his manservant		tenor
Pedro Torez, head of a band of robbers		baritone
Antonio	⎫	tenor
Perez	⎬ robbers	tenor
Rodrigo	⎭	bass
Rullo, head of another band of robbers		bass

Mados, a traveling merchant	bass
Donna Urica	alto
Laura, her daughter	soprano
Eufemia, a singer	soprano

* * *

By 7/19 August Rubinstein was able to inform his mother that *Sulamith* was finished, but not without a great deal of discussion with his librettist, Julius Rodenberg, whom he had visited in Germany. "You have to do it if you do not have Wagner's ability to write your own text!"[72] he told her. The opera had been many years in the making, and in its final form the action was spread over five scenes:

Solomon, King of Israel	baritone
Sulamith, a grape picker from Lebanon	soprano
A young shepherd also from Lebanon	tenor
Captain of the Jerusalem city watch	bass

Scene 1. Women's quarters. Harem in the king's palace in Jerusalem. Solomon has abducted Sulamith and has a passionate desire for her, but she rejects the king because she loves a simple shepherd.
Scene 2. Landscape in Lebanon. The spring festival. The shepherd is grieving for Sulamith and discovers that she has been abducted by Solomon.
Scene 3. The harem in the king's palace. Night. The shepherd has found Sulamith, and they flee together.
Scene 4. An open space in Jerusalem. The captain of the city watch captures the fugitive lovers.
Scene 5. Throne room in Jerusalem. The king is preparing for his marriage to Sulamith, unaware that she is languishing in chains. When Solomon discovers the events that have taken place during the night he forgives the couple and sets Sulamith free.[73]

Rubinstein's other one-act opera, *Unter Räubern*, was completed shortly afterward, as it was due to be presented in a double bill with *Sulamith* in the fall. In addition to the prospect of hearing his new operas, he had received several other attractive proposals, including one to stage *The Merchant Kalashnikov* in Moscow. He eventually left Peterhof for Germany on 8 October 1883, just finding time to write to his mother another anxious word about Sofiya whose belongings had been searched by the authorities: "You must be very cautious! and even with close acquaintances speak (and particularly write) only about the weather, the theater, and the like; do not keep anything in the house—books, compositions, letters that might in some distant degree arouse suspicion. You must be ready for everything, especially in the provinces."[74]

In the summer of 1880 Rubinstein had made an arrangement with Jurgenson to publish the vocal scores of his opera in Russia at intervals of roughly a year apart. As he had informed his publisher: "It seems to me that we should start with *Néron*, and perhaps, as this will be more desirable for the provincial stages, with Feramors."[75] *Néron*, with the text in French and a Russian translation by Yelena Andreyevna Tretyakova, appeared in the fall of 1883 in time for the St. Petersburg production the following February. The opera, however, never held the Russian stage, and a few years later Tchaikovsky played through the score and wrote in his diary:

> I still cannot find sufficient words of amazement for the composer's impudent lack of ceremony. You buffoon! Heavens above, it infuriates me looking at this score. But the reason I play this loathsome thing is the consciousness of my own superiority, at least in the sense of conscientiousness—and that keeps up my strength. You think that you are writing abominably, but then you look at this drivel which people have performed in all seriousness, and your soul feels lighter. I feel ashamed to treat an event like this with such malice, but to whom am I pretending in a diary?[76]

Several important productions of Rubinstein's operas were scheduled for the 1883–84 winter season. The first performance of *The Demon* in Tiflis, with Varvara Zarudnaya (the future wife of Ippolitov-Ivanov) in the role of Tamara, took place on 2/14 October, and Rubinstein himself conducted the first performance of *Die Maccabäer* in Frankfurt-am-Main on 15/27 October. The most important event for Rubinstein, however, was the joint production of *Sulamith* and *Unter Räubern* that he conducted at the Dammtor Theater in Hamburg on 8 November. He had also received news from Jurgenson about the proposed production of *The Merchant Kalashnikov* in Moscow. When the publisher suggested making cuts in the libretto to get the opera past the censor, Rubinstein replied curtly: "No cuts in Kalashnikov are envisaged! I myself would very much like to see this opera staged in Moscow." His intransigence in this matter scuttled any hope of the opera being staged in Russia in the foreseeable future. In addition to his operas, Rubinstein also conducted a performance of his oratorio *Das Verlorene Paradies* in Kassel on 1 November. In Berlin he conducted his own Symphony No. 4 and played the solo part in Beethoven's Piano Concerto No. 5 at a concert on 12 November 1883.

Rubinstein traveled on to Leipzig, Dresden, Prague, Berlin, and Köningsberg, returning to St. Petersburg around the beginning of December. His opera *Néron* was to be given by the Italian Opera in St. Petersburg, but he found the affairs of the theater to be in "great disarray,"[77] and he had grave doubts that the opera would be staged. He saw Hubert, who was seeking a post at the St. Petersburg Conservatory after his resignation as director of the Moscow Conservatory. He also saw Anna Yesipova and Sofie Menter, who had both recently returned from Odessa. He rated them both as the greatest of female pianists: "If you could blend them into one, a goddess of pianism would come out, although I willingly accept each of them separately," he confessed to his mother.[78]

During his travels the previous fall Rubinstein had made a commitment to Alexis Holländer, the conductor of the Cäcilien-Verein in Berlin, that he would conduct a performance of *Das Verlorene Paradies* early in the New Year. However, because of the delay in rehearsing the production of *Néron*, Rubinstein was obliged to excuse himself and wrote to Holländer on 14 January 1884: "An operatic composer proposes, but (unfortunately) the Theater Directorate disposes."[79] In the end the proposed performance of *Das Verlorene Paradies* at the Cäcilien-Verein did not take place until 17 November 1884.

The performance of *Néron* was finally given by the Italian opera troupe on 29 January/10 February 1884, and the following day the composer wrote to Kaleriya Khristoforovna: "A grandiose success, everything was magnificent in all respects."[80] During the rehearsals of the opera Rubinstein had made significant revisions in the score. The day after the performance he set out for Vienna and Pest and from there wrote to Senff: "My misfortune (and in particular the misfortune of my publishers) is that I only get a proper idea of one of my works when I see it engraved before me. Only then do I see what needs to be done in another way, and what would be better. I agree that this is a terrible trait in my character, but that is how it is."[81] With this he enclosed the amended score and the vocal score of *Néron*, warning Senff about the extent of the correcting.

For the next two and a half months Rubinstein was continuously on the move. Between 14 and 27 February he gave five concerts in Vienna which were extensively reviewed by Hanslick. Despite colossal takings from his concerts and the royalties on the performance of his works, Rubinstein seemed more preoccupied than ever about his financial status. To some extent this was prompted by his wife's notorious extravagance and by the need to finance the frequent trips that the doctors prescribed for his youngest son, Sasha, who had always been sickly. From Copenhagen he wrote to Kaleriya Khristoforovna: "Exactly a year has passed since we last saw each other. In the musical sense it has been one of the most brilliant for me, but in other respects this is not the case: sickness in the family, unpleasantness for you, constant ignorance about the near future, what we shall do, where we shall live (it is quite possible that Vera will remain abroad for the next year with the two little children)." Although his concerts had been highly successful and financially rewarding, he confessed to his mother: "I cannot wait for the day when they end. I am too old for this. They do not afford me the slightest pleasure. Even earning money bores me, and is, in fact, pointless anyway as I give half of it away, so that I can never achieve my goal. . . . A limit must be set to all this. How many times have I said this! Even I find it funny!"[82] He had thought about retiring from the concert platform before, but this time there was an air of seriousness about it.

At the end of his tour Rubinstein went to join his family in Marienbad. By this time he had completed yet another one-act comic opera for Hamburg to a libretto by Hugo Wittmann. As Cornelius had done earlier in *Der Barbier von Baghdad*, Rubinstein turned to an oriental subject—this one based on a Persian fairy tale called *Der Spruch des Papageis* [The parrot's slogan]. The main singing roles included:

Almanzier, a merchant	baritone
Feth-Ali, the son of a poet	tenor
Suleika, Almanzier's daughter	soprano

Fathme, Suleika's companion	alto
The Kadi	bass
A Dervish	tenor

Feth-Ali arrives in Isfahan with a mirror, the sole heirloom of his deceased father, a once-famous poet. He sees the reflection of the beautiful Suleika in the mirror and kisses it. Suleika's companion, Fathme, has him tried for this outrage, but the Kadi is somewhat confused by the verdict. The parrot belonging to a Dervish has spoken truthfully "Maß gegen Maß. Da Feth-Ali das Spiegelbild geküßt hat, werde sein Schatten gepeitscht [Measure for measure. Since Feth-Ali has kissed the image in the mirror, his shadow will be whipped]." Feth-Ali kisses his beloved Suleika, and her father recognizes him as the son of the famous poet who had once been banished. The parrot has pronounced that, as "Schatte(n)" (shadow) rhymes with "Gatte" (husband), Feth-Ali will become Suleika's husband.[83]

When Rubinstein dispatched the manuscript, both full score and vocal score, to Senff on 22 July, he suggested *Der Papagei* as a good name for the new opera, as "the title does not mean anything to the listener—only in the course of the action does the significance of the parrot become evident."[84] Pollini had given a promise to stage it in Hamburg by 1 November, and therefore the vocal score needed to be ready as quickly as possible. Rubinstein rarely had reason to reproach Senff with dilatoriness in publishing his works, and, as if to prove it, the revised edition of *Néron* was already in the composer's hands by August. As a mark of gratitude, Rubinstein presented Senff with a cycle of piano pieces for which he had not yet devised a name. Senff eventually suggested *Soirées musicales,* which Rubinstein approved, but the unpretentious title somewhat belies their ferocious difficulty. It was not for nothing that Rubinstein referred to them as works for *gens pianistica* and inscribed each of them to leading pianists of the day. For the time being, he sent only seven of the pieces, the remaining two numbers being completed in Odessa where Rubinstein spent part of the summer. Sending them to Senff, he told him that the dedication of the final Étude in E flat was to Eugen d'Albert. It was a fitting tribute to a young pianist for whom Rubinstein had predicted a glorious future. The whole opus was published by both Senff and Jurgenson toward the end of the year.

Shortly after returning to Peterhof at the beginning of September, Rubinstein was delighted to find the vocal score of *Der Papagei,* which Senff had published "in a superb manner . . . That the inner value might match the external one!?"[85] Rubinstein declared to his publisher. Ivan Vsevolozhsky had also written to Rubinstein, inviting him to mark the hundredth performance of *The Demon* on the Russian stage by conducting the performance. The composer replied that he would willingly conduct the opera provided no cuts were made, but the Directorate, well aware of Rubinstein's irascible temperament, gave instructions for the staging to be organized without the composer's direct involvement. He was told the dates of the rehearsals and of the performance, and was politely informed that the rest did not concern him. The new production, which Rubinstein conducted at the Mariinsky Theater on 1/13 October, did not please him, and he recorded his outrage in his *Autobiography* and also in a fictional dialogue with newspaper reporters called "Po povodu sotogo predstavleniya operï *Demon*" [Concerning the hundredth performance of the opera *The Demon*].[86] What angered him principally was that in the new production the action had been transferred from the Caucasus to a setting that was "quasi-Persian, quasi-Indian, quasi-Byzantine." It was not the Caucasus depicted in Lermontov's narrative poem but some sort of travesty, and Rubinstein was infuriated that the Directorate had made this radical change without having first discussed it with him. Despite his harsh criticism of the mise-en-scène, nine days later he reported to his mother that the opera had gone off "brilliantly."

Over the next two months Rubinstein had several important engagements in Germany and Belgium to fulfill, but before setting out he conducted the opening RMS concert of the season (6/18 October), which included his new *Eroica Fantasy*, Op. 110. The new work was dedicated to the memory of the Russian general Mikhail Skobelyev, who had distinguished himself in the Russo-Turkish War of 1877–78. The sudden death of the general in June 1882 had sparked a wave of pan-Slavic jingoism, and his heroic status was later enshrined in an imposing monument erected in the center of Moscow.[87] Rubinstein gauged the strength of patriotic feeling well, for the *Eroica Fantasy* scored a considerable success and was later published by Jurgenson. Four days later Rubinstein set out for Germany. In Hamburg he wrote to Senff, thanking him for the sumptuous edition of the *Soirées Musicales*, remarking: "Si le ramage était aussi beau que le plumage! [If the warbling were as fine as the plumage!]."[88] On 11 November he conducted the first performance of *Der Papagei* and came away with the impression that it had been "a charming production in all respects."[89] From Hamburg he traveled to Berlin to conduct the postponed performance of *Das Verlorene Paradies* at the Cäcilien-Verein on 17 November. Then it was on to Schwerin to conduct *The Demon* on 30 November, and to Antwerp for *Néron* at the Royal Theater the following month. "All this drags on endlessly to the point of repugnance," he told his mother.[90] He had received worrying news from Peterhof. Sasha had been ill again and had been confined to bed for three weeks, but by the time Rubinstein arrived home in Peterhof for Christmas the boy's health had much improved.

At the beginning of January 1885 Rubinstein approached Aleksandr Polovtsov, a court official and state secretary, petitioning him for premises in which the RMS could give its concerts, but the request was received coolly. Rubinstein was also engaged to give three concerts in Moscow and to conduct two RMS concerts in St. Petersburg. His Moscow appearances took place on 8/20 and 11/23 January (solo concerts) and 12/24 January (Fantasy for piano and orchestra, Op. 84, and *Eroica Fantasy*, Op. 110). Because of his absence from St. Petersburg (perhaps intentional), Rubinstein succeeded in avoiding any odious comparison with his old rival, Hans von Bülow, who was in the capital to conduct the premiere of Tchaikovsky's Suite No. 3 in G. His Moscow appearances earned him a net profit of twelve thousand rubles: "Not bad, don't you think?" he wrote to

Kaleriya Khristoforovna. "But I was much in need of it, as this winter is costing such a devilish lot of money. Yesterday my Anenka was sixteen (so she can marry!)"[91]

The energy with which Rubinstein continued to fulfill his engagements was truly amazing, but even he had begun to tire of them. The strain was beginning to show: "It is one and the same story which has bored me to the last degree. But, like all musicians, one has to submit to it."[92] Vienna was preparing for its premiere of *Néron* in March and Rubinstein had been invited to conduct it. Before this he was in Leipzig to conduct *Der Thurm zu Babel* (26 February) and in Frankfurt-am-Main for a performance of *Das Verlorene Paradies* and his Symphony No. 4 (26 March). He then discovered that the Vienna premiere of *Néron* had been postponed a whole month, and he used the time for a whirlwind concert tour of Holland, giving around ten concerts between 12 and 30 March. He returned to Vienna in time to conduct *Néron* at the Court Theater on 20 April and then began the journey homeward to Peterhof via Warsaw and Wilno. After four exhausting months, he had already decided that his career as a solo artist was nearing its end. On 13–14 April he had appeared at a charity concert in Pressburg that was intended to raise money for a monument to Hummel. This event was the occasion for a final reunion with Liszt, who had little more than a year to live. Pressburg sparked many memories for Rubinstein. "I remembered my youth," he wrote to Kaleriya Khristoforovna, "I remembered the concerts I gave (I think it was in 1847?). If it had not been for these appearances in Pressburg, the whole further course of my life would have probably been quite different and I would not have been dissuaded from moving to America. Consequently everything has been for the best!"[93] With that memorable appearance in Pressburg he had somehow come full circle, but the man who had become a living legend throughout the New and Old Worlds was not going to quit the concert platform without some suitably grand gesture:

In the 1885–86 season I realized an idea which I had long cherished. As the finale to my virtuoso career, I wanted to present in a series of concerts in the main centers of Europe a review of the gradual development of piano music. I had once begun this in America. There had been lectures on the history of music before, but historical concerts, at least on the scale that I undertook them, had never been tried. Fifty years, a whole lifetime, were needed to prepare for these concerts.[94]

7 The Historical Concerts and Second Term as Director of the St. Petersburg Conservatory, 1885–91

Rubinstein spent the greater part of the summer of 1885 working on the programs of the Historical Concerts. There were to be seven in all covering the entire history of European piano music from the English virginalists to contemporary Russian composers (see Appendix C for programs). Rubinstein began his triumphant tour of Europe in Berlin during the autumn of 1885, ending it in London the following May. Moreover, all the concerts given in St. Petersburg, Moscow, Vienna, Berlin, London, Paris, and Leipzig were to be given twice: once for the general public and a second performance on a different day for students. He also gave historical concerts in Prague, Dresden, Brussels, Utrecht, Liverpool, and Manchester, making a total of 107 concerts. During the American tour of 1872–73 Rubinstein gave almost twice that number in a similar eight-month period, but it was the scope of the Historical Concerts that astounded his contemporaries. As Tchaikovsky remarked, the concerts were "unprecedented for the vastness of their program and the difficulty of their execution."[1] Rubinstein's enormous programs often led to heated arguments with his agent, Hermann Wolff, about their length and complexity. Nevertheless the artist was resolute in his undertaking and would not be persuaded to shorten them.

Rubinstein arrived in Odessa around 24 September, having first given a charity concert in Grodno for the victims of a fire. He stayed for about a week with the aim of trying out the programs of the Historical Concerts and of testing his memory and staying power. During the last days of September a number of close friends and acquaintances gathered at the Witzmann Hall, and for seven consecutive days he played the entire program.[2] A month later Rubinstein began the tour in earnest with concerts in Berlin on 20, 23, 27, 31 October and 4, 8, 11 November. When all these concerts were over, he wrote to Kaleriya Khristoforovna from Vienna on 7/19 November: "I have finished with Berlin in a brilliant fashion. Yesterday I began here."[3] In the Austrian capital he saw his wife Vera and son Sasha, who were en route to Italy again for the sake of the boy's health. He instructed his banker, Zak, to provide Vera with as much money as she needed for the trip, but the drain on his resources was clearly giving him much cause for concern. "I work like an ox," he told Petersen, "and I am not achieving my aim to increase my capital and must be content if I can manage to keep it topped up. But that is what I married for. There will have to be a radical reform in our life—selling the house in Peterhof, etc. I can get out of scrapes as long as I go on playing. But I am no longer in a condition to play. Therefore I will have to take stringent measures. For now, the main thing is to concern myself with the health of the family and to send them abroad."[4] The Historical Concerts in Vienna followed in November and early December, and in Prague he gave the three programs devoted to Beethoven, Schumann, and Chopin. All these concerts were received with rapturous acclaim, but Rubinstein was hoping for his greatest successes in Russia. His hopes were fully justified, for on the same day as notices of his St. Petersburg concerts were posted in the city, the ticket sales amounted to twenty thousand rubles. "That is colossal!!" he remarked to his mother.[5] At the end of December he returned to Peterhof for the New Year's celebrations. There, most likely, he would have heard about the death of Edith von Raden on 9 October (o.s.).

With the resumption of his concerts in January 1886, Rubinstein appeared in St. Petersburg on 4/16, 11/23, 18/30 January, 25 January/6 February, and 1/13, 8/20, 15/27 February, interspersing them with concerts in Moscow on 7/19, 14/26, 21 January/2 February, 28 January/9 February, and 4/16, 11/23, 18 February/2 March. "Now I am the personification of a train trundling between St. Petersburg and Moscow: three days there, four days here, and it will be like that every week until 20 February," he told Kaleriya Khristoforovna.[6] In fact, Moscow treated Rubinstein with particular affection. The lavish banquet that Hubert arranged on 27 January/8 February was one of several that were given to mark Rubinstein's triumphs in Russia's second capital, and two weeks later the city administration organized a special tribute to him at the Bolshoy Theater. Taneyev did not miss the opportunity to present Moscow's best talents. One of his own piano students, sixteen-year-old Arseny Koreshchenko, was asked to improvise on the theme of one of Bach's fugues for solo violin. Although Rubinstein himself had a formidable reputation as an improviser, the young artist fulfilled the assignment brilliantly and even earned the praises of the great maestro. Nikolay Zverev was also eager to show off his pupils. One of the most promising was Sergey Rachmaninov, who had begun his studies with Zverev only a few months earlier. His performance of Bach's English Suite in A minor clearly pleased his teacher, for he was given the task of conducting Rubinstein to his place of honor at the supper table (this was considered necessary because of the guest's failing eyesight). Zverev ensured that his pupils attended all of Rubinstein's Historical Concerts in Moscow, including the programs repeated at the German Club for the benefit of students.

Between 24 and 30 January Tchaikovsky was also in Moscow. He wrote to his brother, Modest: "I was at Rubinstein's Schumann concert. He has never pleased me more than on this occasion. As I noticed he was touched that I had finally honored his fourth concert with my presence, and as he was somehow so particularly affectionate toward me, I now consider myself, as it were, obliged to attend all his remaining concerts, the celebration in his honor which is set for the 10th, and various other dinners and binges that are being arranged for him.

Life will be busy."[7] Tchaikovsky returned to Moscow in time for Rubinstein's fifth recital: "There is little artistic merit in all this," he remarked to Nadezhda von Meck, "but the performance was truly amazing."[8] On 10/22 February Rubinstein was fêted with a gala celebration at the Bolshoy Theater in which he was honored by the whole of artistic Moscow. Actors as well as the opera and ballet troupes of the Imperial Theaters, the Directorate of the RMS, and the Moscow Conservatory took part in it. No fewer than three conductors lent their support: Ulrich Avranek, principal choirmaster of the Bolshoy Theater; Pyotr Zolotarenko, conductor of the Bolshoy Theater ballet orchestra; and Max Erdmannsdörfer, chief conductor of the RMS concerts. The sets for the tableaux vivants, too, were produced by the leading stage designers and painters of the time: Karl Valts, Vladimir Makovsky, and Vasily Polenov. Some of the tickets in the stalls and the first two tiers were sold, but the rest were distributed without charge to students. The celebration began with the appearance of Rubinstein on the stage surrounded by the musicians and representatives from the drama troupe: Glikeriya Fedotova of the Moscow Malïy Theater and the soprano Mariya Korovina, who had graduated from the Moscow Conservatory in 1883 from Giacomo Galvani's class. The program consisted of the following:

Part 1:

1. "A Word of Welcome," verses by the actor Nikolay Vilde (read by the author)
2. A tableau vivant representing the Chorus of Angels from the oratorio *Das Verlorene Paradies*, with tenor solo (Anton Bartsal)
3. Adagio from the String Quartet in G minor played by a string orchestra
4. A scene from *Die Maccabäer* with the baritone Bogomir Korsov and chorus

Part 2:

5. Two *tableaux vivants* for the symphonic poem *Don Quixote*
6. Romances: *Song of Love*, performed by the soprano Mariya Klimentova-Muromtseva; *Hebrew Melody*, performed by the contralto Aleksandra Svyatlovskaya; *Pandero*, performed by the mezzo-soprano Aleksandra Krutikova; *Thu' nicht so spröde schönes Kind* from the *Persian Songs* and *Räthsel*, performed by the tenor Dmitry Usatov; *The Winds Blow*, performed by the baritone Pavel Khokhlov; and *The Prisoner*, performed by the bass Ivan Butenko.
7. Dances from *Le Bal Costumé* staged by the dancer, producer, and ballet master of the Bolshoy Theater Aleksey Bogdanov (music orchestrated by Max Erdmannsdörfer)
   (a) *Tarantella (Pêcheur napolitain et Napolitaine)*
       Performed by Mmes Lidiya Nelidova (Barto) and Kalmïkova; Mess. Nikolay Domashov and Nikolay Tatarinov; Mme Nadezhda Andrianova, Yermilova, Karpakova, Yevgeniya Konstantinova, Yevdokiya Pukireva, Anna Andrianova, Mariya Nikitina, and

Yelizaveta Cherepova; Mess. Viktor Belov, Aleksandr Vinogradov, Zhivokini, Vasily Tarasov, Nikolay Svetinsky, Ivan Rïzhov, Ivan Yezhov, and Viktor Lobov

(b) Spanish Dance (*Toréador et Andalouse*)
Performed by Mme Lidiya Geyten, Ivan Khlyustin, Yevgeniya Markovskaya, Glafira Samoylova, Anna Polyakova, Mariya Mikhaylova, Sofiya Cherepova, Lyudmila Vinogradova, and Sofiya Dmitriyeva

8. March from the opera *Néron*—Apotheosis (*tableau vivant*)

"The celebrations given by Moscow to honor Rubinstein have been very successful," Tchaikovsky reported to Nadezhda von Meck. "He was clearly very touched by the love which Moscow so energetically and passionately showed him. It is necessary to tell the truth, Rubinstein is worthy of the honors accorded him. Besides being an exceptionally gifted artist, he is indisputably honest and magnanimous, and he stands, and has always stood, above all those horrid petty squabbles which fill the life of all possible musical circles."[9] Tchaikovsky was much less enthusiastic about the endless public functions into which he was inevitably drawn by the celebrations. "How intolerable these Rubinstein concerts are!" he complained to his brother. "That is, of their own accord they give me enormous pleasure (I think he has never pleased me more as a pianist), but these dinners! These formal dinners! The indispensable prerequisite of going off to them every time for at least three days that is what makes it so gloomy . . . Laroche is playing a rather comical role just now in sulking before Anton, and attributing significance to his every action or lack of action in relation to him. He imagines that Rubinstein notices all this, whereas in fact he doesn't care a straw."[10]

That winter Rubinstein put into action a plan for organizing an international competition for composers and pianists. His idea was that the competition would take place in August every five years, starting in St. Petersburg in 1890, followed by Berlin in 1895, Vienna in 1900, and Paris in 1905. After this the venue would continue on a rotating basis. The organization of the competition was to be in the hands of the St. Petersburg Conservatory, and Rubinstein himself drew up the General Provisions, putting up the capital of twenty-five thousand rubles to initiate the project. "The competition is open to persons of the male sex of twenty to twenty-six years of age of all nations, religions, and estates, and regardless of where they studied the art of music," he instructed Andrey Markovich,[11] and the top prize for each winner was set at five thousand francs. According to the rules of the competition, the prize for composition could be awarded for a concerto, chamber music, or other compositions for solo piano. Prizes for the best performers were to be awarded for works in the same musical categories.

By early March Rubinstein was in Leipzig where he gave all seven programs of the Historical Concerts at the Gewandhaus on 12, 14, 21, 23, 27, 29, and 31 March, and three more in Dresden on 15, 17, and 22 March. Joking with

Wolff about his *Elfenbeinkragen* (ivory collar), he proceeded to Paris, and continued with the next cycle of programs on 5, 8, 12, 15, 19, 22, and 27 April. During his concert of 19 April Rubinstein suffered a fainting fit and all the Parisian newspapers reported the incident. After two days of recuperation he gave his next concert on schedule but felt the need to write reassuringly to his mother: "In Paris, where it was unusually warm (moreover, I do not suffer from the cold when I am playing), I fell into a faint. This event immediately found its way into all the newspapers and was described as a tragic event. But this does not have any significance: a day later I was playing again."[12] He also gave a charity concert for an association intended to help Russian artists in Paris and attended a concert organized by Mathilda Marchesi de Castrone, who had established a famous singing school in the French capital. At the concert Rubinstein heard some of her Russian pupils but refused to accept the flowers they presented to him, and called on them to be patriots by completing their musical education in Russia. He was particularly vexed that singers being trained for the Russian stage were not being taught to sing in their native tongue, and he recommended to Marchesi a "maestro au piano"[13] familiar with the Russian repertory. Rubinstein's last appearance in Paris was on 10 May; the crowds were so numerous that the accesses to the Eden Theater were blocked with carriages until midnight.

On 30 April and 2 and 4 May 1886 Rubinstein gave Historical Concerts in Brussels, and on 8 May he conducted a performance of *Das Verlorene Paradies* in Utrecht. In mid-May he arrived in London, where the June issue of the *Monthly Musical Record* devoted a verbose panegyric to him, noting that his appearance in the British capital had been "unheralded by the flourish of bombastic newspaper paragraphs." Indeed, he had had no need of them for his reputation alone was enough to excite intense public interest. After each of his concerts, as Wilhelm Ganz tells us in his reminiscences, he would invite his friends to a reception at the Hôtel Dieudonné in Ryder Street. He clearly felt at home there and had a large circle of acquaintants and well-wishers. Apparently on one occasion, when some young girl was taken to see him, he asked her to sing something for him. She sang his romance, *Du bist wie eine Blume*. Her plummy tones evidently amused him, for when she had finished singing, his verdict was, "Too much Belgrave Square!"[14] Rubinstein's last visit to London had also encouraged the public performance of his compositions. On 31 May the American contralto Antoinette Sterling sang the solo part in his *Rusalka* at the St. James's Hall.

Rubinstein returned to Peterhof on 5/17 June 1886. "It is as if I had been born again," he wrote to Kaleriya Khristoforovna the following day. "So, my career as a pianist with the public has ended for good. Another, new life (whether it will be better I do not know) is beginning for me."[15] He remained almost completely indifferent to the news that he had been awarded the highest degree of the *Légion d'Honneur*, but when he learned that Liszt had died in Bayreuth on 31 July he was genuinely saddened. "Liszt has died!" he wrote to Kaleriya Khristoforovna on 3/15 August:

This is a sorrowful event. Not to speak of his musical magnitude, he was an entirely unusual phenomenon as a man and as a personality. But in our times, a time of terrible leveling off, of the absence of major individualities, both in terms of character and external appearance, a time of absolute egoism—he (in opposition to all this) appeared amid us as a man belonging to a former age, and with his end we lose even the notion of this. The piano loses together with him its magnitude and its element of the fantastic and the poetical; musical art loses a bold and progressive man, and musical youth loses a champion and a patron. This is a great and irrevocable loss! Besides, the advent of old age was a sorrowful phenomenon for him (there are people whom we wish to see among us only at the height of their powers).[16]

As ever, Rubinstein was full of praise for the man and the musician but could never square this with his opinion of Liszt as a composer:

I remember only too well that he was pretentious and very pompous. I was very aware of all this, but I also respected him as one of the most highly gifted people, but as a performer and not as a composer. Being a musician does not mean that you are a composer. He understood everything and knew everything, but in his compositions there is falseness—it was all affectation.[17]

* * *

That summer Rubinstein completed his Symphony No. 6 in A minor. On 8/20 September he posted the manuscript to Senff: "I am sending you herewith the Symphony No. 6, score and parts. It would be very nice if the orchestral parts were printed in time for the performance in Leipzig."[18] The symphony proved to be an effective work that contained some of the best, and sadly some of the worse, features of Rubinstein's mature symphonic style. He continued to adhere to the universal language he had always advocated, although it must be said that the balance between the movements in this work is particularly successful. The first movement, *Moderato con moto*, contains strong thematic material and is cogently presented; the romantic second movement harkens back to Schumann and is shot through with a deep vein of poetic lyricism; the scherzo is truly delightful for its spontaneity and piquant combination of humor and melodic invention. In the finale Rubinstein again employed Russian motifs, as he had done in the Symphony No. 5, but, sadly, this is the weakest movement of the symphony. The two folk themes heard at the start are wonderfully contrasted, one a melancholy lament and the other a spirited dance song. As self-contained melodies Rubinstein treats them in a highly effective way, but the problem is that he does not know what to do with them afterward. The development section begins with an imperious Beethovenian gesture but is not strongly enough associated with the themes that gave rise to it and the music ends up sounding merely rhetorical. Even the lack of cohesion might be overlooked were it not for the completely lopsided conclusion. Having worked through his development section, Rubinstein seemed to lose interest. Briefly he brings back the slow folk melody as though it was an onerous task, and then winds up the symphony with almost indecent haste. This is a great pity, as the work, despite its defects, contains many delightful pages.

Two weeks after sending the manuscript of the symphony to his publisher, Rubinstein conducted the 101st performance of *The Demon* at the Bolshoy Theater in Moscow for the benefit of Karl Valts who was celebrating twenty-five years of service in the Imperial Theaters. The fine cast was as follows:

The Demon	Pavel Khokhlov
The Good Genius	Aleksandra Svyatlovskaya
Prince Gudal	Otto Fyurer
Tamara	Mariya Klimentova-Muromtseva
Old Retainer	Ivan Matchinsky
Nanny	Anna Ivanova
Prince Sinodal	Anton Bartsal
Messenger	Pyotr Grigoryev

The young Rachmaninov was in the audience and recalled an incident that illustrates the composer's "autocratic attitude in front of an audience numbering two thousand people." When the curtain rose on the third scene of the opera, depicting the advance of Prince Sinodal's caravan, Rubinstein halted the orchestra with a few impatient taps of his baton:

> Through the sudden stillness that hung over the whole theater one heard Rubinstein's disagreeably grating voice: "I have already asked for better stage lighting at the rehearsal!" There was some hurried movement behind the scenes, and suddenly the stage was flooded with brightness almost as strong as daylight. Rubinstein calmly picked up his baton, which he had placed on the score, and began conducting the scene all over again.[19]

The Moscow production prompted Tchaikovsky to compare the opera favorably with another based on the same subject. Baron Fitinghof-Shel's opera *Tamara*, composed sporadically between 1860 and 1871, had finally reached the stage of the Mariinsky Theater on 22 April 1886 under the direction of Karl Kučera (the vocal score was published by Bernard the same year). "My God," Tchaikovsky exclaimed, "what a feeble thing this is! He has a little more talent than Solovyov, but the latter still has something akin to compositional technique; but the dilettantism of Fitinghof is terrible. He is like a little child and not a mature musician. By God, it is shameful that such operas are given on the imperial stage. What a service the Directorate did to Rubinstein. Now his *Demon* seems to me like a masterpiece when compared with Shel."[20]

After the performance of *The Demon* in Moscow Rubinstein set out for Leipzig, where he conducted the first performance of his Symphony No. 6 at a subscription concert of the Gewandhaus on 28 October.[21] A couple of days later he wrote to Kaleriya Khristoforovna: "My symphony had a great success here and was superbly performed."[22] Twelve days later he conducted his opera *Die Kinder der Haide* at the Königliches Schauspielhaus in Kassel, while far away in New York the National Opera Company, under its musical director, Theodore Thomas, was preparing a production of *Néron*, in English. When the opera was finally heard on 14 March 1887, it would be the first of Rubinstein's operas to be heard in the New World.

Rubinstein returned to St. Petersburg on 23 November/5 December in time to begin the rehearsals of ten Historical Concerts of the RMS intended to chart the course of symphonic music from the eighteenth century to contemporary Russian composers.[23]

Second Term as Director of the St. Petersburg Conservatory, 1887–91

At the very beginning of the year the St. Petersburg Conservatory was faced with internal difficulties. Since 1876 the directorship had been in the hands of Karl Davïdov, but his tenure had been soured by a long-running feud with the conductor Eduard Nápravník, who had left the RMS in 1881 as a result of it. The directors of the RMS were divided in their support for Davïdov, and he was persuaded to step down owing to ill health at the end of 1886. In all probability certain influential figures in the Directorate had been waiting for this opportunity for some time. Andrey Markovich and Vyacheslav Tenishev lost no time in approaching Rubinstein, and on 12/24 January he once again took up his old post as head of the institution he had founded. Two days later he wrote to Kaleriya Khristoforovna: "You probably know that because of illness Davïdov has gone away, and I am again the director of the Conservatory—twenty years on. I have taken on a difficult task, as it will scarcely be any easier to change (improve) what is old than to start from scratch. I shall do everything I can, but what will come of this—let us leave that to time and fate."[24] Among Rubinstein's first tasks as the new director of the Conservatory was to write to the grand duchess Aleksandra Iosifovna, the wife of Grand Duke Konstantin Nikolayevich, and also to the Directorate of the RMS. In his report to the grand duchess dated 11/23 May[25] Rubinstein maintained that the prestige of the conservatories was being undermined by the Shostakovsky Music School in Moscow. This school had been founded in 1883 by Pyotr Shostakovsky, who became its first director, and was upgraded into a School for Drama and Music under the aegis of the Moscow Philharmonic Society in January 1886. What vexed Rubinstein was that this measure had resulted in the school being granted the same privileges as the conservatories. His most surprising recommendation, however, was the closure of the Moscow Conservatory and the transfer of the entire staff to the southern cities. His argument was based on the premise that the South, with its warmer climate, would become a center of excellence for the development of vocal music, and that the North, based in St. Petersburg, would become Russia's great bastion of orchestral and instrumental music. For all this, one cannot help wondering at Rubinstein's apparent willingness to sacrifice the legacy of his brother's contribution to Russian music in the interests of this grand plan. Rubinstein's final request was viewed with more sympathy by the government. The Conservatory was then situated in cramped and unsuitable premises on Theater Square. Rather than spending money on celebrating the Conservatory's twenty-fifth anniversary, he suggested that the government provide the institution with new premises in the form of classrooms and halls for concerts and opera. This was the only part of Rubinstein's report that was successful, and he was promised the Bolshoy Theater in St. Petersburg which had formerly been home to the Italian opera troupe. The renovation of the building, which is now the St. Petersburg Conservatory, began in 1890–91 and took more than seven years to complete. It was said that the cost of the work amounted to a colossal two million rubles.

A few days after writing his report to the grand duchess, Rubinstein also presented to the Artistic Council of the Conservatory his *Provisions for the St. Petersburg Conservatory*.[26] The provisions, which reinforced the director's administrative authority, were accepted by the Artistic Council and ratified by the St. Petersburg division of the RMS. While the authoritarian character of Rubinstein's leadership perturbed many, his *Report to the Directorate of the St. Petersburg Division of the Russian Music Society*[27] was warmly received, as it advocated the organization of an opera theater and concerts specifically for the works of native composers under the auspices of the Russian Music Society. Operas were to be performed only in Russian, and tickets were to be kept at moderate prices. Rubinstein also saw the undertaking as a way to provide employment to the growing corpus of qualified musicians and singers who were not able to find positions in the Imperial Theaters. The St. Petersburg Mariinsky Theater and the Bolshoy Theater in Moscow were the only places in the capital cities where graduates of the conservatories and music schools could hope to find gainful employment. In an interview published in *Novoye vremya* (28 March/9 April 1887), Rubinstein says: "The idea of setting up such an opera house in St. Petersburg occurred to me, as it would offer a free outlet for our Russian musical art and would provide work for all our free and unemployed musical talents, to singers who have not been engaged, to musicians and conductors, etc. In particular, I should like to bind the Conservatory more closely to the new opera house. After all, such a link is perfectly natural."[28] In an attempt to enlist Tchaikovsky's support, Rubinstein wrote to him on the same day: "We would like to lure the public with the new works of its favorite composers —give us an opera! If you have not given *Charodeyka* [The enchantress] to the Directorate of Imperial Theaters, give it to us, and if you have given it, then write us a new one by 1 September."[29] It seems unlikely that Rubinstein was ignorant of the fact that *The Enchantress* was already being rehearsed at the Mariinsky Theater, but the request to write another opera in six months was politely refused. In any case, Rubinstein had decided to write one of his own for the new enterprise. This was to be *Goryusha* [The doleful one] with a libretto by Dmitry Averkiyev (after the librettist's historical novella, *Khmelevaya noch'* [A night of intoxication]). In fact, Tchaikovsky, too, had once considered this same subject in 1881 for an opera called *Vanka-klyuchnik* [Vanka the steward].[30] In Rubinstein's opera the main singing roles include:

Prince, aged 50	baritone
Princess, his second wife, aged 18	soprano
Dashutka, an orphan brought up in the prince's house	mezzo-soprano
Ivan, a poor nobleman, the prince's steward	tenor
The Boyar Poltev	bass
Shelog Skomoroch	tenor

The orphan Dashutka loves the poor nobleman Ivan and believes that her love is returned. The prince, who plans to see the two married, leaves on a journey. Dashutka pleads in vain for Ivan's love. She discovers the young princess and Ivan in a secret rendezvous. Ivan wants to kill the eavesdropper, but the princess asks for the girl to be spared. Dashutka reflects on her revenge. Thunderstorm.

The boyar Poltev is entertaining his guests, including the prince, with a troop of German players. The long-winded allegorical play is enlivened by the prince's jester, who interrupts the play with insinuations about the alleged adultery of the princess and Ivan. The prince has Dashutka arrested. The fool warns Ivan of the prince's fury, but Ivan, who protests his innocence, does not flee and is to be executed. Dashutka repents, defends Ivan from his accusers, and then takes her own life. All are shaken. The prince releases Ivan and sends the princess into a convent.[31]

* * *

At the same time that Averkiyev was preparing the libretto of *Goryusha*, Rubinstein had begun work on the sacred opera *Moses* to a libretto by Mosenthal. Tableaux 1–3 were probably already completed, for on 26 February/10 March Rubinstein informed his publisher: "I hope that shortly you will receive Tableaux 5 and 6, on which I am working at the moment. Whether I can manage to send off Tableaux 7 and 8 in September, as I would like, is still questionable. Since taking on the Conservatory, I have so little free time, and the millstones spinning about in my brain can be little applied to creating musical thoughts."[32]

During the ten years Davïdov had headed the Conservatory he had allowed the number of students to grow steadily and even planned to introduce preparatory classes for minors. In Rubinstein's view, this "relaxed policy" had only served to encourage mediocrity and was entirely at odds with his uncompromising insistence on the very highest standards. He was especially determined that the title "Free Artist" should be conferred on none but the most gifted pupils. But his decision to reorganize the teaching staff and replace a number of Russian professors with foreign ones proved to be the most unpopular measure that he introduced. Sofie Menter resigned in protest, and the appointment of Beniamino Cesi from the Conservatory of Naples and Eduard Goldstein was seen in some quarters as an attempt by Rubinstein to surround himself with dutiful acolytes. Balakirev was outraged, seeing in Rubinstein's actions a desire to replace talented people with mediocrity in order to enhance his own glory. Those who condoned his actions were deemed "Unitarians" [members of the Greek Orthodox Church who acknowledge the supremacy of the Pope—P.T]. "Whatever Rubinstein is," Balakirev wrote to Stasov, "he is still cleverer than they are and far more practical. It is not for nothing he has Jewish blood. Surely it cannot be that Auer's appointment did not make them see reason, and they still will not understand that their Pope is the most ferocious enemy of everything that rises above the mediocre, as being something that detracts from his own grandeur and his own self-esteem without limits. Try to ram this into their stupid brains. Let them ponder over the fact that Mme Menter has been replaced by the talentless Cesi. And, lastly, why doesn't he like Tchaikovsky, his own prodigy? . . . I can find no reason other than that he cannot abide anything that rises above the commonplace."[33]

Henselt was one of the few teachers who supported Rubinstein in his measures to reorganize the staff, and Bettina Walker remarked:

> Is he not brave and strong and resolute? For when the professors in the Conservatorium objected to the new order of things which Rubinstein wished to introduce there, and he would not yield a jolt to them, the majority turned out in a body, without giving him time to fill their vacant places. But Rubinstein faced them, saying, "You think that you can frighten me, gentlemen, but I feel in myself the strength of an ox, and both will and shall be able to give all the lessons myself."[34]

Rubinstein's doggedness won the day, but earned him few friends. Stasov was in an apoplectic rage brought on by the thought that Rimsky-Korsakov and Lyadov would have to kowtow to "the great Ruler." "I wrote a letter to Rimlyanin the day after Whit Monday," he told Balakirev "in which I said that all this makes me sick, that their relations with the Conservatory and Rubinstein is Unitarianism (and on the part of Cui, unadulterated apostasy), that the Russian School must remain independent, not join the farmhands and the apprentices of Rubinstein working for his 'glory' and for his 'good,' but conduct its affairs in its own name."[35]

At this time Rimsky-Korsakov was heavily embroiled in completing Borodin's opera *Prince Igor*, after the composer's sudden demise in February 1887, and it was Rimsky-Korsakov's wife, Nadezhda, who answered Stasov's letter on 29 May/9 June:

> All your leonine fulminations are inappropriate and even comical. . . . You ought to study the facts before you write about them. What right do you have in suspecting my husband of base acts, apostasy, and the devil only knows what else! To that person who has been telling you slanderous things about him, you write and tell him off. And I hope that Nikolay Andreyevich does not need anyone's advice in order to act in all circumstances of life in a noble and honorable fashion; for this he has sufficient nobility and intellect of his own."[36]

Rimsky-Korsakov himself saw Balakirev at the beginning of June, and the latter wrote to Stasov that he could see no reason for Rimsky-Korsakov and Lyadov to leave the Conservatory, which gave them their bread, simply because Rubinstein ruled it autocratically: "I think that Rubinstein will never drive them out but, on the contrary, will try to make them into scaffolding up to his throne." But Stasov was implacable, hardly knowing where to vent his anger: against Rubinstein for his "despotism" or against Rimsky-Korsakov for his timid acquiescence. The tirade continued all through the summer of 1887 in his correspondence with Balakirev and even with Kruglikov in Moscow:

> We keep on having abominations here: Rubinstein has demanded despotic power for himself from the Council of Professors, and they, like the grovelers they are, have invested him with the knout in a servile manner . . . But what is more shameful than anything, Rimsky-Korsakov and Lyadov out of the goodness of their hearts, and, I suppose, because they have their hands tied to some extent, without understanding the crux of the matter, have taken part in these abominations, put their necks under R's foot, and have voted for all these obscenities!!!![37]

Because of his duties at the Conservatory, Rubinstein had rented an apartment in St. Petersburg, and he moved from the smaller premises at 27 Troitskaya ulitsa (now ulitsa Rubinshteyna) to No. 38. There, baton in hand, he posed for a new portrait that Repin had made of him. At the end of May, however, he was already installed in Peterhof for the summer vacation. He quickly got down to work on *Moses,* and on 31 May/12 June he sent the corrections of Tableau 4 to Senff. The following three months were entirely devoted to the secular opera *Goryusha,* and throughout the summer Rubinstein remained in regular correspondence with his librettist Dmitry Averkiyev. Unfortunately the latter could scarcely keep up with the pace at which Rubinstein composed the opera: "Much respected Dmitry Vasilyevich," the composer wrote to Averkiyev on 8/20 July, "have you completely forgotten about me? Where is the promised continuation of acts 2, 3, and 4? I have finished what you sent me, and I am waiting, waiting. Only five weeks of time free for work remain to me—once the Conservatory vacation has ended there can be no thought about composition."[38] Despite his hectic productivity, Rubinstein began for the first time seriously to question whether he was written out as a composer. In April he had written to Reinecke to thank him for the dedication of the German composer's recently completed *Zenobia* Overture, and confessed to him: "I propose to stop writing music. I have written a very great deal, and, to tell the truth, my compositions only please because of me, and in the final analysis that is an insufficiently well-founded reason to continue writing."[39] As the years passed this theme increasingly dominated his thoughts.

In addition to composition, part of the summer was devoted to preparing a series of fifty-eight lectures on the history of piano music up to the death of Chopin. The lectures were intended principally for the students of the Conservatory, but they proved so popular that they were repeated in an abridged form comprising thirty-two lectures during the 1888–89 season for a much wider audience.[40] Although Rubinstein never published the texts of his lectures, they were recorded by, among others, Cui, Sofiya Cavos-Dekhteryova, and Adelaida Gippius, and their accounts later appeared in the Russian press. Taking the programs of the Historical Concerts as his starting point, Rubinstein greatly expanded the repertory to include some 1,302 separate works, prefacing his performances with comments on the context and style. As one would expect, important figures like J. S. Bach, Beethoven, Schubert, Mendelssohn, Schumann, and Chopin were considered in great detail, but he also made interesting excursions into the less familiar byways of the repertory for the purpose of illustration. Not all the pieces he chose were intended to represent the very best in keyboard literature. In his lectures on the French harpsichordists, for example, he played a minuet and an *Allegro molto* by Johann Schobert to illustrate how the style had declined after Rameau. When the lecture course was finally completed in April 1889, he was able to report: "I could not do everything owing to a lack of time. However, I demonstrated much and saw, to my great satisfaction, that this was useful. The gratitude of the listeners was warm and sincere, so I can feel contented."[41]

After the death of Liszt in 1886, Stasov had asked Rubinstein for permission to make copies of his correspondence with the Hungarian composer. Rubinstein agreed, and on 29 July/10 August Vladimir Stasov personally traveled to Peterhof in order to return the letters to their owner.[42] As he waited for Rubinstein to come down for this uneasy meeting, Stasov surveyed the music room at the Peterhof villa where two large grand pianos stood side by side. His attention was caught by a bookcase and a mass of bound scores. "Russian music and the Russian School given high esteem," he told Balakirev, and there, to Stasov's surprise, he found, among other scores, *The Stone Guest, The Maid of Pskov, William Ratcliff, Angelo, A Life for the Tsar,* and *Ruslan and Lyudmila.* When the conversation began, however, Rubinstein pointedly refused to be drawn into any discussion about Russian composers with the New Russian School's most vociferous champion. "Clearly," Stasov informed Balakirev, "Rubinstein talks about new Russian musicians and the concerts only with Cui and Rimsky-Korsakov, knowing beforehand how favorable they are."[43]

The New Year of 1888 began with examinations at the Conservatory, and Rubinstein rejoiced that for two precious weeks he would not have to listen to students' exercises. He had also received the news that he had been awarded the title of Privy Counsellor—fourth civil rank, which was equivalent to the military rank of major-general. "I am a general!!!" he wrote to Kaleriya Khristoforovna. "What appellation is this? And what for? No one knows the answer to this. Personally I did not consider myself less than that before I was given this appellation. Before I was a king, and for many a god. Now I am a general, so that, properly speaking, means demotion for me. But in our country a person without a title, even to this day, is a nothing. In this sense the appellation has a certain value and I console myself with this."[44] The elevation in Rubinstein's official status brought with it certain privileges and, most important, the favor of the court. "Alexander III had a high regard for another musician at that time—A. G. Rubinstein," wrote Vladimir Nápravník, the son of the conductor. "The latter's opera, *The Merchant Kalashnikov,* had been banned for eight years . . . it was staged on 22 February 1880, and after the second performance it was taken out of the repertory at the insistence of the attorney-general of the Holy Synod Pobedonostsev. Now, Alexander III wanted this opera to be revived."[45] By the early spring the matter had been entirely resolved, and Nápravník senior had approached Rubinstein about the distribution of the roles in the opera, which was to be staged during the coming season. One of the company's finest basses, Fyodor Stravinsky (the father of the composer Igor Stravinsky), was cast in the role of Ivan.

Rubinstein's duties at the Conservatory, and his intensive work on the lecture course devoted to the history of piano music, absorbed much of his time during the spring term. He had relinquished his conductorship of the RMS concerts to Leopold Auer, and, as soon as the summer vacation arrived, he retreated to Peterhof to continue his work on *Goryusha*. "Wie der Hirsch schreit nach Wasser, so sehnt sich mein Herz nach Ihnen [As the stag cries for water, so my heart longs for you (Germ.)]," he rather poetically began a letter to Averkiyev of 2/14 July. "I have already put three acts of our opera in order, and now I have started on the fourth. It is necessary to think seriously and talk about this; little free time is left for me—by 20 August my Conservatory duties begin and I will need to bid farewell to this work again until next summer."[46]

That summer saw the start of a veiled anti-Semitic campaign launched in the pages of *Grazhdanin*, whose editor was the reactionary Prince Meshchersky. Meshchersky's newspaper attacked the design of a new statue to Alexander II, which had been put forward by Mark Antokolsky, a respected sculptor of the realist school. Antokolsky had graduated from the St. Petersburg Imperial Academy of Arts in 1871 (one of the first Jews to do so) and in the same year completed an imposing study of Ivan the Terrible in marble. The writer of the article suggested that the design for the statue to the late tsar had been commissioned unfairly without the usual declaration of a competition, and scornfully referred to the sculptor as a "zhid" [comp. "yid"]. While Stasov respected Antokolsky's talent and defended it, Balakirev was unable to hold back his xenophobic prejudices: "In what way is he a representative of the Russian School when he is a Jew through and through, even an un-baptized one, who lives permanently in Paris and even speaks Russian badly?—Surely not just because he has Russian nationality? Then you would have to acknowledge even Rubinstein as a Russian musician."[47] A year later this same campaign was renewed, and this time Rubinstein himself would be the target.

On 25 November 1888 celebrations were held to mark the twenty-fifth anniversary of Eduard Nápravník's association with the Russian opera. Throughout the day deputations of visitors, musicians, and friends came to visit the conductor at his apartment on the Kryukov canal where he lived from 1877 until his death in 1916. Among them was Rubinstein who read an address from the St. Petersburg Conservatory and the St. Petersburg branch of the RMS. Vladimir Nápravník recalls that, after giving this address, Rubinstein kissed his father and said very loudly: "Now the official side is done with. Now we can have a smoke."[48] With that, he lit up a cigarette, went into Nápravník's adjoining study, and sat down. Nápravník was to conduct the revival of *The Merchant of*

Kalashnikov planned for January 1889, and on 3/15 December Rubinstein wrote to the conductor, asking him to replace the brief introduction to the opera (just two pages in the published vocal score) with the musical picture *Ivan the Terrible*.[49] According to Vladimir Nápravník, this request was fulfilled.

Toward the end of 1888 a scheduled performance of Rubinstein's *Ocean Symphony* in Berlin under the direction of Hans von Bülow was removed from the program at the last moment. The conductor apparently remarked that the symphony was "antiquierte Scheußlichkeit [antiquated monstrousness (Germ.)]" written by a pianist with long hair. In December Rubinstein sent an open letter to the editor of the *Berliner Signale:*

> If the aforementioned conductor, the same Herr Hans von Bülow, whom I have known for more than thirty years, and who, after the first performance of *Néron*, kissed my hands at the Hotel Schreit, and more than once showered me with praises in the newspapers, then I make public that I remain entirely indifferent to his evaluation of my compositions, and even cherish the hope that that which he has denigrated today will be declared by him tomorrow to be grandiose and majestic, just as he has done with regard to the works of Mendelssohn, Brahms, and Reinecke. What surprises me is that amid all the vast number of his preoccupations he could have found spare time to measure the length of my hair. I never even thought of measuring his ears, but perhaps I should have done so. Be that as it may, I hope that his opinion has no effect on musicians or the public, who, to the present time, have shown my compositions much indulgence and sympathy[50]

Another Berlin orchestra, apparently to avenge itself on von Bülow, performed the symphony, displaying Rubinstein's bust on the concert platform, and the composer thanked the orchestra for the "rehabilitation" of the symphony.

The dress rehearsal of *The Merchant Kalashnikov* took place on 10/22 January 1889. Grand Duke Konstantin Konstantinovich, who was present at this performance, recorded in his diary:

> I saw this opera long ago. I think it was in '79 on the one occasion that it was presented. Since that time it has been forbidden. A few years ago it was rehearsed again, and again it was forbidden. Now it has been rehearsed once again, but, before the performance, doubts were expressed as to whether it should be performed. It was curious to see the opera in an almost empty theater. The only people admitted to see it were the artists of the Imperial Theaters and certain members of the aristocracy, so a few of the boxes were occupied. The emperor himself and all our family occupied seats in the stalls . . . The music was beautiful. But the impression it produced was slightly alarming, even painful. These villains—as they are shown in the opera—start by praying, then dance and get drunk. . . . My opinion is that it would be best not to allow the opera. It would not be right for the government to entertain our audiences with this sort of spectacle at times like these when there are aspirations to overturn everything that over the centuries has been raised onto a pedestal. It is painful for our past when you see a villainous tsar on the stage, and all the more so when, in my opinion, the brutality of Ioann Vasilyevich IV [Ivan the Terrible] has been exaggerated in this country. But the opera has been allowed, and it will be presented on Tuesday.[51]

This second performance took place on 13/25 January, and then, as in 1880, it was banned by the religious censor and taken out of the repertory. Barenboym quotes from the diary of a court official, Count Vladimir Lamsdorf: "The emperor says that the dress rehearsal [of *The Merchant Kalashnikov*] did not make a particularly strong impression on him, but when he went to hear this opera for a second time, it agitated him greatly and he found it impossible to allow it to be given to the public. His Highness regrets that Rubinstein chooses only such subjects."[52]

With his request for better premises in which to house the St. Petersburg Conservatory, Rubinstein was more successful. The petition addressed to the grand duchess Aleksandra Iosifovna had produced the desired effect, and in January the tsar made the building that housed the Bolshoy Theater available. In Rubinstein's opinion even this was insufficient, and another court official, Aleksandr Polovtsov, remarked in his diary on 29 December (o.s.) 1889: "Rubinstein explained to me that the Bolshoy Theater presented to the Conservatory is too small because Rubinstein considers that the Conservatory building ought to have one auditorium seating two thousand people, one—eight hundred people, and one—three hundred people, fifty-two classrooms, not to mention accommodation for the staff—this in true Russian fashion is beyond the pale."[53] The other problem was that the government had not provided the money to reconstruct the building, and Rubinstein set up a special fund, later contributing thirty thousand rubles toward it from the money raised during his jubilee celebrations in the fall.

Meanwhile, Rubinstein's life at the Conservatory was following its usual monotonous routine: "Music from morning until night, meetings, rehearsals, student performances (so successful that they could be teacher performances), and teacher performances (so bad that they could be student performances)."[54] In February Karl Davïdov, the professor of cello at the Conservatory, had died, and Rubinstein invited Franz Neruda, the cellist from the Neruda Quartet in Copenhagen, to take his place. A few weeks later, on 3/25 April, he attended a concert at the Marble Palace when Grand Duke Konstantin Konstantinovich made his début as the soloist in Mozart's D minor Piano Concerto, K. 466, before two hundred guests, including the empress and tsarevich, the future Nicholas II. News about this concert was even reported in the French newspapers, for Tchaikovsky, who was passing through Marseilles, had read that Konstantin's mother, the grand duchess Aleksandra Iosifovna, had played the cello in the orchestra. According to Konstantin Konstantinovich, the performance went off without mishaps, despite his first-night nerves. In his diary he records Rubinstein's wry comment to him at the end of the concert: "Grand dukes can become artists, but the latter can never become a grand duke."[55]

The whole of May was taken up with examinations, but when they were finally over Rubinstein was able to think once again about Peterhof and composition. His duties at the Conservatory had absorbed a great deal of valuable time, and it was not without a certain irony that he remarked: "Mankind was glad of this because it was spared my compositions, but in this respect I am no philanthropist, and I am unspeakably jubilant when I can offer a symphony, an opera, or some other thing. 'Gorge yourself, little bird, or die.' Now I shall have to take up my *Moses* again."[56] In addition to *Moses,* Rubinstein was also working on the three-movement *Konzertstück* in A♭, Op. 113.

Rumors had been circulating in the press that grandiose jubilee celebrations were being secretly planned in Rubinstein's honor during November, but he found them distasteful: "The so-called jubilee celebrations I find in the highest degree unpleasant. I would have forbidden them entirely had I not seen in them the means to achieve my social aims for music."[57] His social aim was to raise cash for the reconstruction of the Bolshoy Theater and to establish a permanent home for the Conservatory. Rubinstein understood very well that he had influential enemies, and he worried that the jubilee celebrations would simply provide the pretext for attacks on him. There was little affection for Rubinstein, for example, on the part Ivan Vsevolozhsky, director of the Imperial Theaters, who wrote to Nápravník on 23 May 1889:

> There's another piece of trouble—that is the Rubinstein jubilee on 18 November. The minister has spoken with the emperor, and we have been commanded to make it a celebration. I proposed an act from *The Demon,* an act from *Kalashnikov,* perhaps an act from *Feramors,* and a divertissement from *Phylloxera.*[58] It has pleased the emperor to cross out *Kalashnikov* and command an act from *Néron.* But then along flies Georgy Georgiyevich of Mecklenburg, who is protesting about a performance that has been cobbled together, demands a new production, and intends speaking to the emperor about it. He confirms that Rubinstein's *new opera is completely ready.* I objected to this, saying that there is no time to learn the opera and paint scenery, and if the order comes, then it will be necessary to *recall* the periods of leave due to the artists and to give us an additional credit to order the scenery from abroad."[59]

Once again, however, the real assault on Rubinstein came from the conservative press, which was bent on sabotaging the jubilee celebrations by whipping up public hostility toward the Conservatory. A short article in *Grazhdanin* suggested that the conservatories, while receiving generous government subsidies, had produced very meager fruit in their undertaking to train Russian musicians. Another newspaper, *Novoye vremya,* fanned the flames with an article entitled *Nashi konservatorii* [Our conservatories], suggesting that the conservatories would gain a good deal if they were run by military men and not by musicians. Rubinstein's achievements were repudiated. There was criticism of his idea of a general musical education, which, in the view of the writer, would "only lead to the increase in Russia of the number of nervy people with a psychopathic temperament." There were also anti-Semitic attacks on the director.

Rubinstein rarely responded to a bruising in the press, but on this occasion he saw that the attack was directed not only at him personally; more important, it was an act of defamation against the Conservatory he had helped to found. On 8/19 July he sent an open letter entitled *Yeshchyo o konservatoriyakh* [More about conservatories] to the editor of the newspaper *Novoye vremya.*[60] The article begins: "Having read in your newspaper the article entitled 'Our

Conservatories,' I, as one of the principal champions of these institutions, consider it my duty to say a few words in justification of them." Then Rubinstein repudiated the matters raised by the author of the article point by point. Among the most important of them, he rejected the notion that the conservatories had produced "absolutely insignificant results," citing a long list of composers (headed by Tchaikovsky) and performers like Sapelnikov, Taneyev, Siloti, Yesipova, Brandukov, and so on. The allegation that the Russian conservatories were a copy of their French counterparts was also rejected: "You find that in our conservatories *we give* a superficial musical education? This I deny in the most categorical fashion." The program offered by the Russian conservatories, Rubinstein insisted, was far more serious and demanding.

Not being qualified to speak about nerves and psychopathic disorders, he continued, he had decided to leave that matter aside. Nor did he accept that students were dodging their obligations to complete their military service by attending the conservatories, and he regarded such an insinuation as "slander." The presence of Jews in the capital had nothing to do with the Conservatory, he retorted. Only Jews who had obtained official permission to reside in St. Petersburg were being accepted. During his travels abroad he had discovered that many Russian Jewish musicians had been obliged to enroll at foreign conservatories because they had been barred from attending their own. "Abroad they are naïve enough to take any Russian for a Russian subject," he added, hinting that in Russia native Jews were not considered to be Russians at all.

On the subject of the national character of the music taught in the conservatories, he replied:

> The purpose of the conservatory is to give a correct musical education, that is, to teach the theory of music (nationalism has nothing to do with this), to introduce the students to the forms and spiritual content of the classics (again nationalism has nothing to do with this), and, as for introducing students to our native works, the conservatory does everything that is necessary: the students are provided with boxes for the opera, free entry at rehearsals and concerts, and in classes they are required to perform vocal and instrumental works by the most remarkable native composers.

He acknowledged that "a school helps geniuses, but does not create them," and, using Glinka as an example, he suggested that the author of *Ruslan and Lyudmila* would not have considered his studies with Dehn in Berlin a waste of time. In his final paragraph Rubinstein declared: "In conclusion, I cannot help but express my total astonishment at the tone of ill-will, or at least irony, that the entire press assumes whenever the subject of the conservatories or the Imperial Russian Music Society is brought up. Here the truth of the saying *Nul n'est prophète en son pays* is wholly justified."

The polemic did not end there, for *Novoye vremya* and *Grazhdanin* both took up a stance against Rubinstein's reply, and in the autumn of 1889 Prince Meshchersky (the proprietor of *Grazhdanin*) even entered the fray. This prompted Tchaikovsky to write to his brother, Modest, saying that it would be a good thing if Laroche came to Rubinstein's defense in *Moskovskiye vedomosti:* "It would be a marvelous opportunity for Laroche, with his inherent wit, to flip that son of a bitch Meshchersky on the nose in a little article! . . . And it would not hurt to teach Suvorin a little lesson either."[61] Tchaikovsky's advice seems to have produced the desired effect, for on 5/17 November an article entitled *Slovo o Knyazye Meshcherskom i Antonye Rubinshtyenye* [A word about Prince Meshchersky and Anton Rubinstein], signed "Bich" [The scourge], appeared in *Moskovskiye vedomosti,* satirizing, in the words of Barenboym, the "high society publisher"[62] of the newspaper *Grazhdanin.*

On 23 August/4 September Rubinstein sent Tableaux 5 and 6 of *Moses* to Senff, and he joked with his publisher that he hoped it would not take him the forty years it took Moses to get the tribes of Israel out of Egypt to finish the opera. Rubinstein's faith in his work was again beginning to falter. In September Senff had marked the fiftieth anniversary of the composer's musical career with the publication of a complete catalogue of his musical works, *Katalog der im Druck erschienenen Kompositionen von Anton Rubinstein.* The composer's response on 11/23 September shows not the energetic, self-confident man of former times but one oppressed by deep contradictions:

> My heartfelt thanks for your most cordial letter in which you have kindly presented to me my entire artistic career, and which nevertheless, or perhaps as a direct result of it, has put me in a sorrowful frame of mind. Yes, I acknowledge to you frankly and honestly the most utter disenchantment—here is the summary result of all my artistic work! And I sing together with King Solomon: vanity of vanities is all human expectation and undertakings, everything is vanity of vanities!
>
> That which I supposed to be the most important thing in my life, on which I directed all my knowledge and my hopes—my musical composing—has met with failure; people do not want to acknowledge me as a composer, neither artists (on whom I always counted above all others) nor the public (I would rather forgive them for this)—yet so much human frailty has remained with me that I imagined both were wrong. I am to blame for the failures, because I always readily told people what I like and what I do not like in music, and particularly because I so little foisted myself on people as a composer. Believe me, however paradoxical the last claim may sound, this is the honest truth. It is necessary to tell people that you are a god; they will crucify you for this, but in the end they will still come to believe in it. Mohammed had to tell people that he was a prophet, Wagner that he was the savior of art, etc. A philosophical or ironical vein, which was always my nature, kept me back from any such thing, but it was not for the best as I see. Only, the devil take it, if the mountain does not come to me, I shall not go to it. My whole existence is worthy of ridicule—let God forgive my parents, I cannot forgive it because what is ridiculous here is profoundly tragic as well. Judge for yourself— the Jews consider me a Christian, the Christians a Jew; the Russians—a German, the Germans—a Russian; the pedants consider me an innovator, the innovators—a pedant, etc. Do you know another personality as funny as mine? I do not know one.
>
> My present work is also a sheer absurdity, as I am of the firm conviction that musical art has finally died, that not eight bars will be written whose value would

be worth a cent. I am convinced, above all, that the art of performing, both in to-day's vocal and instrumental music (whatever it is), would not reach even the boot-strap of playing in earlier periods. And I devote all my time to teaching the young generation composition and playing, knowing full well that all this is a fruitless labor of love.

After everything I have said, you can easily imagine how much irony I shall need for the fast approaching, so-called jubilee celebration.

So, I await the end of my life with impatience, since I am forced to see myself as the personification of a lie (I say this out loud—but, to myself, I think I am the living truth that stands against the universal lie), and the one and the other are equally superfluous.

I wish you well Herr Senff. Tear up this letter and think kindly as before of your not mad, unfortunately, but no longer performing nor composing Anton Rubinstein.[63]

As part of the jubilee celebrations, Mikhail Semyonovsky, the editor in chief of *Russkaya starina*, wrote to Rubinstein to say that he wished to include the composer's portrait in one of the issues of the journal. Rubinstein replied that the best portraits, in his opinion, were those produced by the St. Petersburg photographers Shapiro and Yasvoin. The November issue carried the portrait by Yasvoin as well as Rubinstein's *Avtobiograficheskiye vospominaniya* [Auto-biographical reminiscences]. The composer himself dictated these reminis-cences, which were recorded in four separate shorthand reports during October–November 1889. The text, as it was published in the November issue of *Russkaya starina*, became the basis for translations into several other European languages —the English translation by Aline Delano, for instance, appeared in Boston in 1890. The original shorthand reports were lost for many years and were redis-covered only in 1948 by N. G. Rozenblyum, who worked for the USSR Academy of Science's Institute of Russian Literature. When these reports were compared to the version in *Russkaya starina*, it was found that there were significant dif-ferences. Barenboym, who later published the original text, claimed that Semyo-novsky had subjected the reports to "a free literary reworking,"[64] which had often distorted the sense intended by Rubinstein himself or colored his words. In particular, Barenboym found it difficult to square the "servile character" of the autobiography "in respect to persons of the imperial dynasty," with the fact that Rubinstein's relations with the Russian establishment were often belliger-ent. At the same time he accepted that there were other views, namely, that Ru-binstein "sympathized with the reworking of his memoirs in the reactionary spirit in which it was done."[65] That Rubinstein raised no serious objection about their accuracy when the memoirs were published for a second time by *Russkaya starina*, seems to have given them the author's seal of approval. The only amend-ment he made to this second edition was a rejoinder: "All this leads me to the resolve—myself to take up the pen, which I shall do at the first available mo-ment I have, and I shall write about what I have seen and experienced in my life."[66]

Jubilee Celebrations

The publication of the reminiscences in *Russkaya starina* seems to have prompted Rubinstein to reassess his entire life. The mood of profound dejection that had filled his letter to Senff had not passed. On 15/27 October 1889 he wrote to Kaleriya Khristoforovna: "As always, in art I aspire but do not attain, in life, I attain but do not aspire. The jubilee is nonsense, and, as always, your friends do more harm than your enemies. The jubilee is taking on such proportions that it must call forth objections from everyone . . . 'Trop de fleurs'—they are dying from the perfume of the flowers!"

The celebrations to commemorate the fiftieth anniversary of Rubinstein's first public appearance in Moscow on 11/23 July 1839 were timed to coincide with his sixtieth birthday. A committee was set up under the presidency of Duke Georg Alexander of Mecklenburg-Strelitz, the grandson of Grand Duchess Yelena Pavlovna, to organize the celebrations which were to take place in St. Petersburg over a six-day period from 17/29 November to 22 November/ 4 December. The duke wrote to Tchaikovsky on 20 September, asking him to attend the committee meeting in which the program of the celebrations was to be decided. As Rubinstein's most famous pupil, Tchaikovsky was to conduct two concerts in his honor. In addition, as part of the celebrations, Rubinstein was to be awarded an annual lifetime pension from the tsar of three thousand rubles. Peterhof granted him honorary citizenship, and the University of St. Petersburg gave him an honorary membership. Besides these acts of public recognition, personal tributes came from number of leading composers. Tchaikovsky composed the chorus *Privet A. G. Rubinshteynu* [A greeting to A. G. Rubinstein] and the Impromptu in A♭ (not a virtuoso work but a gentle, heartfelt piece), and Lyadov dedicated his *Pro starinu* [Of times of yore], Op. 21, and Bagatelle in D♭, Op. 30, to Rubinstein, and orchestrated five of the so-called *Miscellanées* Op. 93 piano pieces.

The first of the two concerts conducted by Tchaikovsky took place on 19 November/1 December with a program that included the Symphony No. 5 in G minor, Op. 107, the newly composed *Konzertstück* in A♭, Op. 113, in which Rubinstein played the solo part, and the orchestral work *Russia*. The second concert took place the following day and included the Overture to *Dmitry Donskoy*, *Rusalka* for contralto and female choir, Op. 63 (with Yelizaveta Lavrovskaya), the dances from *Feramors*, romances performed by Yelizaveta Lavrovskaya and Aleksandra Panayeva-Kartsova, and the first performance in St. Petersburg of the oratorio *Der Thurm zu Babel* with a chorus of seven hundred drawn from the Churches of St. Peter and Paul, St. Anna, St. Catherine, and the Cappella Academy. All the proceeds from these concerts were donated to the fund for reconstructing the new building for the Conservatory. The day after the second concert, the premiere of *Goryusha* was given on the stage of the Mariinsky Theater (21 November/3 December), but the opera was not a success and disappeared from the repertory after a very short run. Findeysen, who attended the fourth performance, ascribed the failure primarily to Antonina Fride, who "literally wailed through [*pronïvshaya*] her entire role (Dashutka)." The opera was revived just once in 1902 by Savva Mamontov's private opera company. Only the finale of the second act drew sympathetic words from the critics. Yury Engel, for instance, wrote: "Dashutka has overseen the rendezvous between Ivan and the princess but swears that she will not disclose the secret, and she remains alone with her grief, half out of her mind, in a thunderstorm. The music here adheres to the action; it does not attract our attention of its own accord, but in sharp brushstrokes underlines the drama of the situation; the result is something garish but unquestionably vivid and powerful. This is Rubinstein at his best."[67] Perhaps the effectiveness of the scene gave Tchaikovsky the idea for the masterly finale of the first scene of *The Queen of Spades* where, amid a howling storm, Hermann swears to make Liza his own. Also, as Marina Frolova-Walker has pointed out in her article *The Disowning of Anton Rubinstein,* the "mouse-trap pantomime" about Diana and Apollo that occurs in Rubinstein's *Goryusha* may have given Tchaikovsky the idea of including the episodes of eighteenth-century pastiche in the second act of his opera.[68]

* * *

Tchaikovsky had avoided the banquet at the Demut Restaurant that followed the concert on 1 December: "Almost everyone expressed their regret that Pyotr Ilich could not be present at the banquet where everyone was in such high spirits," wrote Aleksandra Panayeva-Kartsova, "whereas he, the poor thing, was working himself to exhaustion with sweat on his brow. I remember a short speech given by Cheremisinov and [Avgust] Gerke to this effect, and, to my surprise, I noticed, as it were, a sort of irritation on Rubinstein's part."[69] In fact, rehearsals for the concert on the following day, which included the massive oratorio *Der Thurm zu Babel,* went on through much of the night. Lavrovskaya, who had attended the banquet, dashed off at 11:00 in the evening to rehearse one of her numbers. In her reminiscences, Aleksandra Panayeva-Kartsova recalled:

> The following day, when I arrived for the concert, I saw an expanded stage and a decorated box arranged for Anton Grigoryevich on the left-hand side behind the columns. Until my number I did not see Pyotr Ilich, who was conducting the dances from *Feramors* and I don't remember which other works. I sang a few *Serbian songs* with cello (I don't remember who was playing), and *Night,* one of Anton Grigoryevich's favorite songs, in which he also added a high C for the voice. Having sung my number, I went into the artists' room feeling calmer (my number ended the first part of the program), and I saw Pyotr Ilich sitting on a little sofa, his head lowered onto both arms which were stretched out on a table. Agitated, I approached him: "What is the matter?" I asked. He lifted his head impulsively, waved his arms, and in a desperate voice suddenly started sobbing: "Ah, all of you, leave me alone!" With that he attracted everyone's attention. I rushed to call his brothers, and they conducted him, sobbing, into another room. I returned to my husband in the hall in a distressed state and told him what had happened. The

entr'acte was extended. My husband went to find out about Pyotr Ilich. "My uncle is feeling better," he said to me, "the attack of hysteria has passed. He was just over-tired, working day and night with unprepared choruses and orchestra, without getting any proper sleep and enough to eat." My husband tried to calm me, but I saw that he himself was anxious. Finally, the choruses assembled, and we awaited our dear maestro with baited breath. He appeared to a thunder of applause from the entire hall, the orchestra, and choruses. News of Pyotr Ilich's illness had already spread among the latter, and by their ovation they wanted, as it were, to encourage everyone's favorite. In the three days of concerted work, everyone involved in the performance of *Der Thurm zu Babel* had grown to love it. . . . The oratorio came to an end as a triumph for Pyotr Ilich. The public, the orchestra, and choruses—everyone seemed to forget about the man celebrating his jubilee, and they were noisily doing honor to the conductor.[70]

Tchaikovsky's triumph in conducting the oratorio cannot have failed to irritate Rubinstein profoundly. At the supper that followed the concert, Aleksandra Panayeva-Kartsova was seated between the composer and the conductor. She recalled the following scene:

Of course, the usual banal toasts came along. Finally, Pyotr Ilich stood up with a glass in his hand. It is annoying that I can only put across the substance of his words: he was happy that he was able to take an active part in the celebrations, and by this, even in a small way, to prove his love and his delight for the colossal artist, and that he was proud to have been his pupil. . . . Suddenly Anton Grigoryevich, leaning across me toward Pyotr Ilich, interrupted him with laughter: "Well, Pyotr Ilich, let us suppose that you do not love me but you do love my brother, and for that, thank you." Pyotr Ilich began to protest in embarrassment, but Rubinstein repeated: "You only love my brother, and for that, thank you."[71]

This was a public humiliation for Tchaikovsky, and he sank to his chair in abject misery. The event underscored yet again Rubinstein's dislike of his former pupil, who had had every reason to feel gratitude to Nikolay Rubinstein for his staunch support during the 1870s. That Anton found Tchaikovsky's music disagreeable can be explained quite rationally, given his strongly expressed views on art, but his frequent personal antipathy toward Tchaikovsky must have been rooted, at least in part, in that old feeling of rivalry with his sibling brother that Anton could never shake off, even eight years after Nikolay's death.

Whatever Anton's innermost feelings were about his brother, he always made a public display of loyalty toward him. The New Year started with a visit to Moscow where he played his *Konzertstück* at a concert on 6/18 January 1890, with Tchaikovsky conducting. On this occasion the composer was out of sorts and played badly. Matvey Presman recalled: "Almost at the very start of the concert, a bass string in the piano broke while Rubinstein was playing. Even though there was a second piano right there on the stage (which, by the way, was always the case during his concerts), Rubinstein continued to play the piano with the broken string, the constant jangling creating a hideous impression. Rubinstein played without any sense of atmosphere, in a pallid and limp manner and without technical accuracy. It was clear he didn't want to play."[72] The next day he gave a solo concert to raise money for the construction of a hall in memory of Nikolay (this was the origin of the new building of the Moscow Conservatory). Safonov, who had been appointed director of the Conservatory in 1889, worked hard to gather the funds needed, but the actual construction did not begin until a year after Rubinstein's death. The teaching block and small auditorium were completed in 1899, and the large auditorium in the spring of 1901.

On 8/20 January Rubinstein planned to return to St. Petersburg with his daughter, Anna, and her husband. There he had intended to conclude his artistic career with two final concerts: one of these included a performance of the oratorio *Der Thurm zu Babel* under the composer's own direction in aid of the Patriotic Society.[73] At the same time he had begun to write his own autobiography, as he had declared that he would do in the second edition of his reminiscences for *Russkaya starina*. In late February he visited his mother in Odessa to gather information about his childhood. On returning to St. Petersburg in March, he played his Fourth Piano Concerto at an RMS concert for the benefit of the orchestra, and a week later he appeared in his last official public concert—a popular concert of the RMS at the Chinizelli Circus. There he played his Piano Concerto No. 2 under the direction of Lyadov. "Today I finished with my public appearances at the piano," Rubinstein wrote to Kaleriya Khristoforovna, "I am pleased. I hope that the public is not, as that would not be very flattering."[74] That spring Rubinstein's opera *Unter Räubern* (known in Russian as *Sredi razboynikov* [Among brigands]) was performed for the first time in Russia by the students of the St. Petersburg Conservatory (25 March/6 April, 1890) under the direction of the Russian bass Stanislav Gabel.[75]

In May an argument flared up with Senator Andrey Markovich, one of the members of the Chief Directorate of the RMS. Rubinstein had approved the appointment of a new inspector for the Conservatory, but Markovich had asked General Kopen to advise the grand duchess Aleksandra Iosifovna, the patroness and president of the Chief Directorate, not to approve Rubinstein's choice. Incensed by this interference, Rubinstein wrote to Markovich: "Either I go, or you go, or the inspector I have appointed will be approved in his post with your petitioning before 1 June this year."[76] Such ultimatums only exacerbated Rubinstein's relations with the Directorate, and from this point on his involvement with the Conservatory became increasingly statutory rather than executive. He spent more and more of the last years of his life abroad. Relations with his wife, Vera, were becoming increasingly strained, and there were even plans to sell the villa at Peterhof. Rubinstein's Silver Anniversary fell on 12 July, but he did not celebrate it. As he told his mother: "I did not celebrate my Silver Wedding because what is there to celebrate, patience or a lie? I am amazed that there are people who understand each other and can call twenty-five years of living together silver. Iron—that would be the proper name for it."[77]

On 3/15 June Rubinstein set off for Germany, and the summer of 1890 was spent at Badenweiler, a small resort in the Black Forest set back from the Rhine about midway between Freiberg and Basel. A visit to Oberammergau for the Mystery Plays especially attracted him, and he described the spectacle as "exceedingly interesting, and producing on everyone, including me, a huge impression."[78] For a few days his Leipzig publisher, Barthold Senff, joined him, and Rubinstein told his daughter: "He is forcing me to work for him, and I sit writing all day long. Other people go walking. The place is charming, the air wonderful, and I try to forget everyone and everything, but I can't. I feel like a 'person living independently from his family'—all alone, and I wait, wait impatiently for the end."[79] With Senff breathing down his neck, Rubinstein managed to complete a few more pieces, and he dutifully sent the first batch on 16 July: nine songs, Op. 115 (an additional song, No. 8 of the set, making ten in all, was dispatched the following day), and two substantial vocal works, the ballad *Das begrabene Lied* for tenor and piano to words by Rudolf Baumbach and the duet for soprano and tenor *Glück* to words by Faust Pachler. "Here things are starting to become rather anxious for me," he told Senff, "letters, requests, visits, even concerts! Besides, there are too many rising geniuses whose laurels I have to foretell. There is always enough eternal monotony for the earthly existence of a tired musician. Besides, only four weeks of the holiday have passed, and I am already quivering and shaking when I think what awaits me in the so near future."[80] Despite the interruptions, Rubinstein continued to compose new pieces throughout the summer. Among them were the five pieces "Acrostic No. 2," dedicated to his pupil, Sofia Poznańska (they were published by Senff as Op. 114). The major new work of this period, however, was for orchestra: "Now I am writing an overture for orchestra to Shakespeare's tragedy *Anthony and Cleopatra*," he told Anna on 13/25 July. "I would very much like this work to be a success—it is a good subject."[81]

The prospect of resuming his duties at the Conservatory filled him with dread. Nevertheless, by early August 1890 he was already back in St. Petersburg in time to attend the "First Anton Rubinstein International Competition" which was held at the Conservatory between 15–17 August (o.s.). The official rules of this competition had been approved on 15/27 June 1889 as part of the jubilee celebrations. In his capacity as director of the St. Petersburg Conservatory, Rubinstein was the president of the jury, but Nápravník had declined the invitation to serve with him. Worse, the star on whom Rubinstein was pinning his hopes in the piano section, Vasily Sapelnikov, did not even take part in the competition, and there had been a dearth of young Russian composers sending in their compositions. As a result, the prize for composition was awarded to Feruccio Busoni and for piano to Nikolay Dubasov. The competition had not been the glowing success that Rubinstein would have liked, and he was becoming ever more disillusioned with his life at the Conservatory. The new autobiography he had started earlier in the year had not made appreciable progress, mainly because he felt prevented from writing about those things and people that most interested him; two years later he destroyed the manuscript. Instead, he put his energies into a new book that he wrote in German—*Eine Unterredung über Musik*. "I will probably gain myself a lot of enemies, but I think that it will not be without interest," he told his mother on 15/27 September.

The new book, dedicated to Duke Georg Alexander of Mecklenburg-Strelitz, was subsequently translated into several languages and has become known in English as *Music and Its Masters: A Conversation*. Rubinstein's aim, as he later admitted to Pyotr Veynberg, was to steer young musicians from what he saw as "a false road in art" and to encourage them to seek out ideals for the present in the greatest works of the past. The work takes the form of a dialogue with a certain Madam von xxxx[82] and begins with a discussion of the merits of certain composers and musical forms. The author divided the development of European music into eras: the first he calls "the organ and vocal epoch," which reached its pinnacle with the works of Bach and Handel. The second he calls the "instrumental epoch," that is, the development of the piano and orchestra, which begins with C. P. E. Bach and concludes with Haydn, Mozart, and Beethoven. The third era is the "lyric-romantic epoch," characterized by the works of Schubert, Weber, Mendelssohn, Schumann, and Chopin. The fourth epoch Rubinstein calls "the new era" and is prefaced by an assessment of Glinka's position in the period from the 1820s to the 1850s. According to the writer, this era could be understood only by examining the nature of virtuosity: "Virtuosity exercises an immediate influence on composition in general, widens the range of expression, and multiplies the means for composition."[83] He offers as an example the *più Adagio* section of Beethoven's Piano Sonata, Op. 110 (1821) where the note A is struck twenty-eight times, thus becoming a challenge to instrument makers to lengthen the tone produced by the piano. The standard bearers of the fourth epoch were Berlioz, Wagner, and Liszt, but Rubinstein rejected the value of their innovations as composers, and his much-quoted assertion, "I think that with the death of Schumann and Chopin—'*finis musicae*,'" has tended to place its author firmly among the ranks of inveterate reactionaries.[84]

After his clash with Markovich, Rubinstein did not disguise the fact that he had decided to leave the Conservatory. In a conversation with the music critic Vladimir Baskin he declared:

> There is nothing for me to do there. Anyone can sign papers . . . I have done everything that I could, and that I thought necessary and useful for it, but this is still not everything that I would have liked. You come up against serious obstacles, and chiefly against indifference from those persons who could have come to your assistance, and against enmity from a well-known section of our press toward everything I do. . . . You have to agree, when musical matters are placed in such a position, it is very difficult to undertake anything: here enmity, there indifference, here people who cause harm, there people who suppress [your initiatives].[85]

8 Dresden, 1891–94

The minutes of the Artistic Council of the Conservatory for 18 January 1891 show that Rubinstein intended to relinquish his post at the Conservatory at the end of the academic year. He clearly wished Nápravník to take his place (Barenboym refers to the journal of meetings of the Directorate of the St. Petersburg division of the RMS dated 28 March 1891). Nápravník wrote to Tchaikovsky on 5/17 April:

> A few days ago the epilogue to the puppet tragicomedy regarding my appointment to the post of director of the St. Petersburg Conservatory took place. Despite my declaration that I cannot take on so responsible a position with the way things stand at present, the Directorate of the Russian Music Society, at A. G. Rubinstein's insistence and advice, passed a resolution to charge the latter to make an official proposal to me that I become his successor. Rubinstein accepted this commission in the full certainty of success. The two-hour, heated conversation and row, full of various insults directed against me and against the Directorate of the Theaters, did not lead to any result. As an example of his tactlessness, let me refer, by the way, to the phrase he used before he said good-bye: "Remember my words," he said. "You will soon regret your refusal, if not today then tomorrow you will be hounded out of the theater!" The Directorate of the Russian Music Society wanted my refusal in writing, and so I succinctly, but without indicating my motives, scribbled my answer on a piece of paper and sent it off. Auer personally assured me that he would never accept this post; that means Safonov is left, and he seems to be the most likely candidate. The reconstruction of the Bolshoy Theater started on 1 April. Rubinstein is beside himself with malice that about a million will be wasted on this reconstruction. The money is needed for the cause and not for the construction of a palace. "You can get results more surely in stables than in palaces." These were his words. When I assured him that it was for his sake that the grand duchess had requested this building, he replied angrily that this was false, that he had been slandered, that people were telling lies, and so on. How do you like that? What contradictions! What a character! I suppose, and I hope, that they will leave me in peace now, even if they do hound me (his words) out of the Russian Opera.[1]

In the end the post was offered to Yuliy Iogansen, but the Council of Professors wanted to retain the procedures that Rubinstein had put in place and asked him not to quit the institution completely but to take extended leave. To this end, Rubinstein wrote to Nikolay Ivanovich Stoyanovsky, the vice president of the Chief Directorate of the Russian Music Society on 27 May/8 June 1891: "The Council of Professors, fearing that with my departure the rules which have become established and the instructions which I have introduced might be altered, have asked me not to leave the Conservatory, and to this I have consented.

But because of my completely shattered health, I beg you to grant me leave for an extended period so that I can live both in Russia and abroad."[2] After protracted correspondence with the Ministry of Internal Affairs, Alexander III finally agreed to allow Rubinstein to go abroad for eleven months. Thus, from the summer of 1891 Rubinstein effectively left the post of director but remained attached to the Conservatory and was merely on "extended leave."

Rubinstein had been incensed about the reconstruction of the dilapidated Bolshoy Theater, as he considered the premises too small. Furthermore, the work had to be financed by public subscription and on 6/18 April he gave a concert to raise funds. This concert included a symphony by Haydn, Beethoven's Ninth Symphony, and Rubinstein's own Third Piano Concerto, with the composer as soloist. Meanwhile, far away in London, Frederic Cowen had conducted the British premiere of Rubinstein's overture *Anthony and Cleopatra* at a Philharmonic Society concert on 5 March.

When the summer vacation arrived, Rubinstein left for Kodzhory, a mountain resort some eighteen kilometers from the Georgian capital Tiflis. Isaiah Pitoyev, the president of the Tiflis branch of the RMS, and the founder and president of the Artists' Society in Tiflis, had invited Rubinstein to spend two months at his dacha. At Kodzhory Rubinstein's twenty-five-year-old son, Yasha, visited him. Yasha was expecting to receive a posting with General Mikhail Annenkov, who at the time was in charge of constructing the Trans-Caspian railroad, but because of a serious crop failure the government had temporarily appointed him to direct the relief work for the people affected by it. Rubinstein traveled some time in August from Kodzhory to Odessa where he saw his mother, who was by then very frail and ailing. From there he sent Jurgenson his own Russian translation of *Eine Unterredung über Musik*. It was agreed that the Russian publisher would bring out the book on the same day as it was published in Germany by Senff. It seems, however, that the German publisher had forged ahead with typesetting the work even before Jurgenson had managed to have it translated. As the terms of their agreement stipulated that the work had to be published simultaneously in both Russia and Germany, Rubinstein himself had hastily translated it. With his letter to Jurgenson of 22 August/3 September 1891, Rubinstein enclosed the translation, but in a number of respects the two versions differ from each other. Even the title of the book was confused: Rubinstein called it *Eine Unterredung über Musik*, which he translated as *Razgovor o muzïke* [A conversation about music], but Senff published it as *Musik und ihre Meister*. As Rubinstein had heard that America was offering one thousand dollars for the book, his daughter Anna had translated it into English, but he asked Jurgenson to have it revised. In the end the book was published in four languages—the German, Russian, and British editions at the end of 1891, and the French and American editions in 1892.

With his letter to Jurgenson, Rubinstein enclosed several new compositions, asking his publisher to bring them out urgently: six romances dedicated to Natalya Iretskaya in a single volume. These songs are without opus—No. 1

"Spring" (Nadson); No. 2 "Lithuanian Song" (Władysław Syrokomla); No. 3 "Golden Spring Shines" (Pavel Kozlov); No. 4 "With You, My Sorrow" (Merezhkovsky); No. 5 "Southern Night" (Merezhkovsky); and No. 6 "Do Not Say to Me 'He Has Died'" (Nadson). Another five songs were dedicated to various persons, and he told Jurgenson that he could publish them either singly or as a set, as his publisher saw fit. These songs were for Russia only, he told Jurgenson, and he did not intend to offer them abroad. All the songs appeared that same year without opus numbers. The batch of five songs clearly included "Autumn" (Eristov); "The Looking Glass" (Eristov); "Serenade" (Minsky); and "O Child, Dear Heart" (Merezhkovsky). The fifth song could either have been the ballad "He Stood before the Voyevoda" or, more likely, "The Heavy Clouds Reach across the Sky," as both appeared in 1891. In addition to the songs, he also sent a Waltz in A♭ for piano which Jurgenson and Senff published in the same year. For all twelve works Rubinstein requested a fee of three hundred rubles, asking his publisher to send the money to Yevgeny Ganeyzer in Saratov as payment for the libretto of *The Gypsies* (after Pushkin), which the composer had commissioned from him. This libretto was never used.

Dresden

Rubinstein spent the second half of August in Odessa. After the final break with his wife, he made Dresden his permanent home. At the beginning of September, he took up residence at 6 Lüttichaustraße, remaining there until the following spring. Soon after arriving in Dresden, he learned about the death of his mother on 17/29 September, and in an undated letter to his daughter, Anna, he wrote: "The death of mamma, the fate of Sonyia, Sasha's illness—all this has agitated me in the extreme. Leaving Odessa, I knew that all was over with mamma and that it was only a question of a few days. However, the catastrophe has dealt me a blow. Well nothing could have been done, but what about Sonyia? She does not want to live with Lyuba because of her husband—and that is quite understandable. But what will she do? I have already suggested that she move in with me here, but she is her own mistress, and she does not want good deeds from anyone. O women!—especially when they have theories about nobility, independence, etc.—then they are even more intolerable!"[3]

That autumn Rubinstein received the order *Pour le Mérite* (the highest Prussian order for a commoner) from Kaiser Wilhelm. He was, by then, used to receiving decorations and was generally indifferent toward them. Perhaps, for once, this award pleased him, since he had always felt that his music had been better received in Germany than elsewhere. During the autumn months, Rubinstein was putting into order the penultimate (seventh) and longest tableau of *Moses*, and the epilogue (Tableau 8). He despatched Tableau 7 to Senff on 24 October and Tableau 8 on 19 November, declaring *Moses* to be "the most significant of my works." However, Rubinstein's "*pia desiderata*" of seeing the entire biblical opera staged in Dresden was never fulfilled. The cast of this grandiose work is as follows:

Asmath, Pharaoh's daughter	soprano
Johebet, an Israelite woman	alto
Miriam, her daughter	soprano
Asmath's slave girl	alto
Moses	baritone
Warrior captain	tenor
An overseer	bass
Job, an Israeli elder	tenor
The voice of God	tenor
Jethro, a Midianite priest	bass
Zipporah, his daughter	alto
Pharaoh of Egypt	tenor
A messenger	tenor
Aaron	bass
Korah	tenor
Kur	baritone
Joshua	tenor
Balak, king of Moab	bass
Bileam, a prophet	tenor
Four priests, Levites	2 tenors and 2 basses

The eight tableaux follow the traditional biblical events as related in the Old Testament:

Tableau 1. The banks of the Nile in Egypt. As an infant, Moses is brought up by Pharaoh's daughter Asmath.

Tableau 2. Before the colossus of Rameses. The Egyptians force the Israelites to perform socage. The subjugated people are indignant. Moses declares his lineage to his people and slays an oppressive overseer.

Tableau 3. An oasis in the desert. Zipporah is threatened by the Edomites and is rescued by Moses. Zipporah wishes her rescuer good fortune. However, Moses decides to follow the word of God and to lead his people from Egypt.

Tableau 4. A hall in Pharaoh's palace. God sends harvest failure, a solar eclipse, and storms to force Pharaoh to release the Israelites.

Tableau 5. On the shores of the Reed Sea. Moses leads his people through the Red Sea. Pharaoh's warriors, who are pursuing them, drown.

Tableau 6. The opposite bank. The Israelites thank God for their deliverance.

Tableau 7. At the foot of Mount Sinai. Desert. Moses goes into the mountains to receive the commandments. Indignant with Moses, Korah and his sons dance around the golden calf. Moses announces a forty-year journey as their punishment. He drives Korah's people to hell.

Tableau 8. Hill in Jordan. A place set with vines; a laughing landscape.

A chorus of night spirits and celestials interprets the events.[4]

* * *

Toward the end of November Rubinstein made a short visit to Paris in connection with the French edition of *Eine Unterredung über Musik* that the publisher Heugel planned to bring out the following year. This was followed by a four-day visit to Milan, where he visited Verdi's villa at Sant'Agata and recalled with Boito his concert tour of seventeen years earlier. The visit had its practical side, too, for Rubinstein had evidently entered into negotiations with Ricordi with regard to the Italian translation rights of his book.

Around 21 December/2 January 1892 Rubinstein returned to St. Petersburg. There he took part in two concerts on 27 December/8 January and 4/16 January 1892; in the latter the piano soloist was his pupil, Sofiya Yakimovskaya). The nineteen thousand rubles raised by these concerts were donated to the victims of the great famine that ravaged the Russian countryside in 1891–92, affecting around thirty million people. In Moscow, on 8/20 January, Safonov conducted, and Lavrovskaya sang some of his songs. It seems likely that this was the occasion when Safonov chose to introduce Rubinstein to his star pupil, the young Aleksandr Scriabin, who had been studying the piano with him since 1888. According to the reminiscences of Scriabin's aunt, Lyubov Aleksandrovna, Rubinstein had first heard the future composer of *Poema ekstaza/Le poème de l'extase* play when he was only seven and had been much impressed with his talent. Furthermore, as a young woman, Scriabin's mother, Lyubov Petrovna Shchetinina, had been one of Leschetizky's most gifted pupils at the St. Petersburg Conservatory during the 1860s and had been well known to Rubinstein. During a concert Rubinstein heard Scriabin play some of his recently completed mazurkas; in his reminiscences the young Aleksandr Goldenweiser recalled: "When he had finished . . . Rubinstein agreed to play something. Stepping out onto the platform, he played a rather long and very successful improvisation on one of Scriabin's mazurkas, an improvisation that was a modulation to the key that he had planned to play."[5] Jurgenson had also proposed another concert to raise money for the new Conservatory building in Moscow in memory of Nikolay Rubinstein (like the one given in January the previous year), but this time Anton politely turned the idea down, saying that he had done enough for the Russian Music Society and that if he served this cause as well, it would be to the detriment of "the other," presumably referring to the reconstruction of the St. Petersburg Conservatory.

In view of the strained relations with his wife and the death of his mother, Rubinstein began to rely more and more on Anna for news about his family. It was from her that he learned that his son, Yasha, had at last found himself a position: "But what rank?" he inquired, "What is he doing now? What salary does he receive? I am extremely interested to know about this."[6] Rubinstein's own financial position was much reduced, as he had handed over all his property to his family and allowed himself an annuity of three thousand rubles a year to live on, plus any additional revenue that came from the performance of his works. Despite this, he refused to undertake another American tour. "Happiness is not to be found in money," he told Anna. "I am becoming old, so that inclination, enterprise, and energy, all of it has disappeared. I hope that I shall not have long to wait, but until then I shall be content with what there is."[7] Some of this deep pessimism is captured in the Heine song setting "Wo wird einst des Wandermüden" in which a weary traveler wonders where he will find his resting place. After Anna's marriage to Sergey Rebezov, Rubinstein had entrusted the task of collecting his royalties to his son-in-law, who had become a kind of personal confidant. However, neither he nor Anna had been able to patch up the differences between Rubinstein and his wife, which had several root causes. Rubinstein's letter to his son-in-law from the Hôtel de l'Europe in Dresden on 16 April clarifies a great deal in their relations:

I am very grateful for your letter. It proves the concern that you take in our family. But I do not consider myself in any way to blame. A hundred times I have remonstrated, and by all means have tried to convince each and all of the falseness of people's notions about upbringing and about the wrong direction Vera Aleksandrovna has taken. I tried to direct Yasha and Sasha toward a serious and true outlook on life and their position, and, finally, when I became convinced that it was all in vain, I separated from my family and decided to leave it to its fate, and to allow myself to live in seclusion in my own way.

The reduction in our revenue is the fault of the Ministry of Finances and the extravagances of Vera Aleksandrovna, and I am not in a position to help; to live in Peterhof, where, as it has been proved to me, nothing belongs to me, I refuse to do. To rent an apartment in St. Petersburg is too expensive for me, and to live in three households would be too idiotic. What do you expect me to do? I cannot reeducate Yasha. Everything he has understood is what I have repeated to him a hundred times. Sasha has been sent to the lycée, that is, they have set him on the path toward silly willfulness. I was always in favor of the gymnasium [high school] and the university (but his illness has remained exactly the same even in the lycée). But where the whole thing is about glitter, you cannot do anything with the arguments.

The squandering of one-third of our capital is also making itself felt, but I could not have known anything about this, and the news has fallen on me like a thunderbolt. Now I am struck by the fact, and convinced that however much I had earned, it would all have gone and would have proved to be too little.

So those blaming me for the way I am treating my family are only those who do not know the heart of the matter.

Now I am alone. I cannot help anyone or make things other than they are; the children have almost all come of age; all that is mine will in time be theirs (if they have not managed to squander the remainder beforehand). Vera Aleksandrovna always acted without asking me or else did not listen to me. So who needs me? Leave me in my lair. I hope that it will not be too long that I shall have to go on living—and *après moi le déluge.*"[8]

One of the chief causes of Rubinstein's break with his wife was about the way the children had been reared. For much of their childhood Rubinstein had been almost constantly on concert tours and was not able to influence their education. Vera wanted Sasha to attend the privileged Aleksandrovsky Lycée near St. Petersburg, where young men from the nobility were prepared for high posts in the ministries. Clearly she had used the excuse of Sasha's illness as one of her chief reasons for choosing the lycée, but it was far more likely that she was attracted by the social status attached to being educated at such an elite establishment. Rubinstein, on the other hand, favored the "no nonsense" gymnasium and university over the airs and graces of the lycée.

In March Rubinstein gave charity concerts in Leipzig and Prague, and during his stay in the Czech capital he saw Angelo Neumann, the director of the New German Theater. His opera company had already learned the biblical opera *Moses* and Neumann told Rubinstein that he intended touring Europe with it. Two months later the composer attended a private dress rehearsal of the opera on 25 and 27 June, but it was never given publicly because of the company's financial difficulties.[9] If *Moses* did not ultimately fare well in Prague, then at least Rubinstein had the opportunity to hear his *Die Kinder der Haide* staged on 3 April: "I have not heard [it] for thirty years," he wrote to his sister, Sofiya.[10] The following day he returned to Dresden and began looking over some of his old compositions. On 15 April he wrote to Senff, enclosing a complete revision of his String Quartet in E minor, Op. 90, No. 2, originally composed and published in 1871. Senff agreed to Rubinstein's request to issue the work in its revised version, and the score appeared later that year.

On 12 May Rubinstein conducted the opening night of *Die Maccabäer* at the Krol Theater in Berlin. When he returned to Dresden on 16 May he found that the Hôtel de l'Europe had been colonized by visitors from Russia: "The Davïdovs, Narbut, and Yakimovskaya are here, and they say that Shura, Zherebtsova, and others are coming. All this is very nice and very kind, but 'trop de fleurs,'" he told Anna.[11] In May the eleven-month extended leave that Rubinstein had been granted by the Conservatory ran out, and he was forced to write to the senator, Count Aleksey Bobrinsky, who was the chairman of the St. Petersburg division of the RMS from 1891 to 1894. Rubinstein wrote to him from Dresden on 28 May, telling him that he was officially on extended leave from the Conservatory, a measure designed "to ease the position" of the teaching staff. "I really do not know what is going on. I do not intend to return to the Conservatory and am taking up residence in St. Petersburg. I shall do so only when the musical affairs of Russia (the Charters of the music societies and conservatories, as well as the Imperial Theaters, the Cappella, and the institutes) are all set down on the soil of good sense; you must agree, why then must I ask for a lifetime of leave!?"[12]

Moses in Prague

The following week Rubinstein set out for Prague and Vienna. Having attended the dress rehearsals of *Moses* at the New German Theater, he returned to Dresden and rented summer quarters in Klein Schachwitz, a location just outside the town, until 1 September. The Russian contingent had also followed him: "I live here calmly and pleasantly; the Russian colony, i.e., the Yakimovskys, the Davïdovs, Malozyomova, Zherebtsova, and Shura, are also here, and they spoil me terribly. Yesterday they thought up some sort of jubilee (fifty-three years since my first appearance on the concert platform), and they organized festivities with illuminations and fireworks which roused the entire neighborhood," he wrote to Anna on 23 July 1892.[13] These festivities were to mark Rubinstein's first concert given in Moscow, and the Russian families engaged the services of a local choral society which gave an open-air performance of Mendelssohn's *Lobegesang* ("Heil dir, du großer Mann").

In Rubinstein's twilight years, private teaching played an important part in his life. For some time he had been coaching two piano students, Sofia Poznańska and Sofiya Yakimovskaya, as well as the young singer Anna Zherebtsova-Andreyeva. That summer, however, Rubinstein took on Josef Hofmann as his sole pupil. The young pianist was already considered a child prodigy, having given his début at a philharmonic concert in Berlin at the age of nine, followed by a triumphant appearance at the New York Metropolitan Opera in 1887. At the tender age of eleven, however, he was considered far too young to begin a career on the concert platform, and his father sent him to Germany for further study. After five unsuccessful lessons with Moszkowski, Hofmann was finally sent to see Rubinstein, who put the young artist through his paces with a thorough examination of the keyboard works of Bach and Beethoven. During this short period of study, Rubinstein came to exercise a huge influence over the development of his young protégé. As Abram Chasins, himself a pupil of Hofmann's, recalled:

> Rubinstein's playing and tutelage made a monumental impression on Hofmann. Once, when I tried to express to Hofmann the overpowering drama and vastness of his playing of Beethoven's opus 111, he looked at me pityingly and said: "I'm very sorry for you that you never heard my master. Why . . . I'm a child—all of us put together are infants—compared to his titanic force."[14]

Rubinstein came to see in Hofmann an artist of the highest genius, who combined technical brilliance with intuition, understanding, and spontaneity.

As Hofmann was just beginning his career, so Anton Rubinstein was coming to the end of his. There is a sense of resignation and finality about the last two years of his life, tinged with a feeling of disappointment, even bitterness. He was like a man who knows that he has only a limited time to remain among the living and wishes to take stock of his life. Perhaps this accounts, in part, for his desire to take up the incomplete autobiography again. As he told his sister, Sofiya, on 23 July: "I have started writing my biography in German; what will come of this I do not know because it will require me to recall a great deal, and I'm afraid that I will not be able to remember."[15] He categorically refused to assist Eugen Zabel in correcting the new biography *Ein Künstlerleben* which Senff brought out later in the year, and in May the author had approached Tchaikovsky, asking for details of Rubinstein's life during the early years of the St. Petersburg Conservatory. As Zabel explained to Tchaikovsky, he did not want his work to be "a dry, scholarly book for specialists, but a fresh and graphic description for every layer of society."[16] In the end, Tchaikovsky was unable to provide much information, as he had only seen Rubinstein fulfilling his duties as a teacher and as the director of the Conservatory, and never knew anything of his personal life.

Another recurrent thread in Rubinstein's life at this period was the decision to abandon composing. "I do not intend to compose anymore," he told Sofiya.

"I have composed too much—for those wishing to get to know my works that will be enough. Only if I receive [a libretto for] *Christus* will I set to work again. This is my long-standing dream!"[17] The revision of his String Quartet in E minor had produced in Rubinstein an earnest desire to reexamine all his old manuscripts. He confided to Senff on 3 September: "I have no manuscripts and I shall have no more. I have worn myself out with suffering (written myself out); is it that philosophy with its awesome word 'why' has taken possession of me?" Most of his works, he told Senff, had been written on his travels and he often had little opportunity to hear them played. Therefore they had been published without a "calm and critical eye." The new editions would give him the opportunity to make all the changes he regarded necessary: "Believe me," he continued, "my works are good, or at least they are more worthy of attention than my colleagues think. While looking at them I always console myself with the Cardinal's dictum *Quand je me juge je suis sévère, et quand je compare je deviens indulgent.*"[18]

The Biblical Opera *Christus*

In fact, Rubinstein had not given up composition entirely, for in Heinrich Bulthaupt he had found a librettist for the sacred drama that he would have wished to be the crowning glory of his composing career. It is difficult to see what drew Rubinstein to the work of Bulthaupt, who was the municipal librarian for the town of Bremen and was later to make his mark with two monographs, *Dramaturgie der Oper* and *Dramaturgie des Schauspiels*. In 1885 he had collaborated with Max Bruch on the oratorio *Achilleus* and later furnished Eugen d'Albert with the libretto of his one-act opera *Kain*. Although this could be taken as an adequate endorsement of his skills as a librettist, Bulthaupt also appears to have been a Wagnerite and, for that reason, may not have wholeheartedly shared Rubinstein's exclusive views on sacred drama. The composer of *Christus* clung steadfastly to the notion that sacred drama could thrive as a counterbalance to Wagnerism, and that, in their own way, *Der Thurm zu Babel*, *Moses*, and ultimately *Christus* would take their rightful place alongside *Der Ring des Nibelungen*. In his article on Rubinstein's sacred operas, Henry Edward Krehbiel suggested: "I am compelled to see in his project chiefly a jealous ambition to rival the great and triumphant accomplishment of Richard Wagner." Rubinstein's ideas about spiritual opera had been set out earlier in the pamphlet *Die Geistliche Oper*, and *Christus* was to be their final embodiment. Not for nothing had he been drawn to the Oberammergau Mystery Plays, but in *Moses* and *Christus* the composer sought to raise those unpretentious and naïve rituals to the level of colossal music dramas. The hopelessly overambitious concept would have pushed the art of stagecraft to its very limits, and it is hard to imagine what exactly Rubinstein envisaged in his attempts to re-create the grandiose dramas of the Old Testament at a time when Hollywood was not even dreamt of. Krehbiel was surely correct when he said: "That Rubinstein dared to compose a Christ drama must be looked on as proof of the profound sincerity of his belief in the art form which he fondly hoped he had created; also, perhaps, as evidence of his artistic ingenuousness. Only a brave or a naïve mind could have calmly contemplated a labor from which great dramatists, men as great as Hebbel, shrank back in alarm."[19]

The completed opera consists of a prologue, seven scenes, and an epilogue. The roles are:

The Angel of the Annunciation	soprano
Three kings	2 baritones, bass
Shepherd	tenor
Jesus Christ	tenor
Satan	bass
John the Baptist	baritone
Simon Petrus	bass
John	tenor
Jacob	baritone
Judas	baritone
Mary, mother of Jesus	alto
Maria Magdalene	soprano
Kaiphas, high priest	bass
Pontius Pilate	baritone
Pilate's wife	soprano
Temple guardian	tenor
Watchman	baritone
A Pharisee	bass
Paul	baritone

Prologue. Open field. The angels announce the birth of Christ to the shepherds. The three kings come to pay homage to the new sovereign.

Tableau 1. Desert. Sand and rock. Dawn. Christ is tempted by Satan but rejects him.

Tableau 2. A plain crossed by the river Jordan. John the Baptist recognizes Christ, pays homage, and baptizes him. Young disciples follow Jesus.

Tableau 3. Open landscape near Jerusalem. Jesus preaches, feeds the starving, supports Mary Magdalene, and resurrects someone from the dead. The people praise him.

Tableau 4. Jerusalem. Temple forecourt. Jesus reprimands the dealers offering their wares for sale in the forecourt. The dealers side with the high priest against Jesus. Judas would have liked God to prove his omnipotence and offers himself to the high priest as their henchman.

Tableau 5. A room in which the table is prepared for communion. Jesus's mother is tormented by a presentiment. Mary Magdalene washes and anoints Jesus's feet. Jesus holds communion with his disciples.

Tableau 6. Open space in Jerusalem before the palace of Pilate. Christ's followers plead in vain for his release. The mob, goaded by the priests, demands his death. Pilate bows to the mob.

Tableau 7. A broken bank of clouds. In the distance three crosses are to be seen. In the heavens—angels, and in the depths—Satan and the demons. The angels and demons fight.

Epilogue. A distant, sun-lit landscape in the middle of which on a hill, illuminated in splendor, a cross rises up. Paul gives news of the transubstantiation. All praise Christ.[20]

* * *

On 21 September Rubinstein informed his sister, Sofiya, that his family in St. Petersburg was well: "The cholera has not yet harmed any of us. I hope that it will continue to leave us in peace."[21] To his delight, the proceeds from the sale of *Eine Unterredung über Musik* were more than he had expected, and he promised the surplus (twelve hundred rubles) to his sisters, Sofyia and Lyuba, "for the Christmas tree," as he put it. That autumn he had given himself four tasks: to continue with his autobiography, to make a start on the biblical opera *Christus*, to give lessons, and to try to prevent his fingers from getting stiff at the piano. "It seems to me that I am not making a success of any of them," he told Sofiya, "but at least I can say that I am stopping myself from getting a vacant look."[22] A month later Anna arrived in Dresden and spent three weeks with her father before departing for Italy with her husband.

During the second half of October and the first half of November 1892 Rubinstein traveled around Germany, partly to promote the careers of his protégées and partly to popularize his own works. In Berlin he took part in the inauguration of the Bechstein Hall, accompanying Anna Zherebtsova in some of his songs. On 9 November he conducted some of his own works in Breslau with Sofiya Yakimovskaya as the soloist. Back in Dresden, he wrote again to Sofiya on 19 November: "I have returned here again, and for a few days I am free from my musical worries."[23] Progress on his opera *Christus* was advancing slowly because of the constant round of concert engagements, but he felt unable to refuse them "as they are undertaken for the benefit of my composing career."[24] After the debacle over *Néron*, Paris had never staged any of Rubinstein's operas, but when he read in the newspapers that the French contralto Marie Delna was about to make her début at the Opéra Comique, he seized the opportunity to write to Philippe Maquet, the co-owner of the music publisher Joubert, asking whether the singer could be shown the part of Leah from *Die Maccabäer*:

Perhaps the role will interest her, and she will consider it possible to urge the director to stage this work in the theater and to perform the role in Paris. I guarantee the success of the opera in a good performance. I would so like to hear one of my works in Paris, especially *Die Maccabäer*. And really, is there no possibility of seeing this work staged before a Parisian audience? I truly cannot find an explanation for the boycott to which I am subjected as a composer when all my endeavors are directed toward this city. I repeat, this concerns *Die Maccabäer* above all. . . . So, let us gather our patience, perhaps after my death all this will change.[25]

Rubinstein's endeavors were all in vain, but the young singer went on to create the role of Charlotte in Massenet's *Werther* in January the following year.

The year ended with a benefit performance of *Die Kinder der Haide* conducted by the composer in Bremen on 2 December. This was followed, two weeks later, by a special concert to mark the fiftieth anniversary of Rubinstein's first appearance at the Leipzig Gewandhaus, when Tableaux 3, 4, 6, and 7 of *Moses* were given in a concert performance.[26] After the concert the Gewandhaus administration made an address and presented the composer with "a gift (a very elegant thing),"[27] which Rubinstein promptly sent off to his son-in-law for collection in St. Petersburg. Finally, on Christmas Day, he conducted *Das Verlorene Paradies* in Stuttgart.

The New Year brought little change to the hectic pace of Rubinstein's concert routine. He was indefatigable in his endeavors to promote his work. As he told Sofiya on 28 January 1893: "Now I have to set out on my musical peregrinations once again, so my work has to be halted; this is something dreadfully abhorrent, but it has to be done, both for myself and for my publishers who are demanding that I do not let the public forget about me."[28] Before setting out for Cologne, Rubinstein found time to respond to Vladimir Stasov's request for his correspondence with Liszt to be deposited at the Imperial Library in St. Petersburg for safekeeping. "I have nothing against this," he told Anna. "They are at Mamma's place. If she did not mislay them, then I request Sergey Dmitriyevich [Rebezov] to take them to V. V. Stasov at the library on my behalf."[29] Stasov had already made copies of these letters in 1886 after Liszt's death, but, as noted earlier, Rubinstein's wife refused to give up the originals, and only in 1937 did Rubinstein's grandchildren surrender them to the State Public Library. Before setting out on his travels, Rubinstein also wrote to Yasha, who had requested money from him. In a firm, but benevolent, letter Rubinstein reminded his son that he had already settled his debts twice, once in Tashkent and once St. Petersburg. His first thought was to refuse, but then he declared: "My heart is not made of stone, and since this year I have received additional royalties from my book that I was not expecting, I am giving you eight hundred rubles; at the same time I have to tell you not to expect anything else in the future—'das schönste Mädchen kann nicht mehr geben, als was sie besitzt' [The prettiest girl cannot give more than she possesses (Germ.)]."[30]

Again taking on the old role of "comis voyageur" as in the mid-1850s, Rubinstein's first appearance was in Cologne on 7 February. After this, the route took him to Frankfurt-am-Main and Bonn, where he gave a charity concert to raise money for the fund to restore Beethoven's house, then Hamburg and back to Dresden. Sofiya Yakimovskaya and Anna Zherebtsova took part in most of these concerts. On 16 March Rubinstein conducted *Das Verlorene Paradies* at the Großer Musikvereinssaal in Vienna.[31] The cast included:

Bertha von Asztalos	soprano
Bertha Gutmann	soprano
Camilla Norwill	alto

Gabriele Gabriel	alto
Gustav Walter	tenor
Franz von Reichenberg	bass
Josef Ritter	bass

From Vienna he returned to Dresden for a few weeks and then proceeded to Berlin, where he conducted his First Symphony on 30 March 1893. A day or two later he was already back in Dresden, writing to his sister, Sofiya, about his plans for visiting Odessa in May. "You have many musical delights," he told her, "the Russian opera, Tchaikovsky, Sapelnikov, Auer, and heaven knows what else. You are lucky—I am starting to envy you. I am constantly on the move. I have to listen to, and conduct, the works 'of long past days,'" And paraphrasing part of a familiar line from Pushkin's *Ruslan and Lyudmila,* he added, on a wry note: "Si [la] jeunesse savait et si viellesse pouvait [If youth but knew, if age could do (French proverb)]." On 24 April he finally attended the long-awaited premiere of his ballet, *The Grapevine* [*Die Rebe*], which was given in a double bill with the opera *Unter Räubern* at the Berlin Königliche Theater. After the performance a delighted Rubinstein wrote to the director Graf von Hochberg to thank him for the fine production of *Unter Räubern,* which had been produced by Carl Tetzlaff and directed by Dr. Karl Muck, as well as "the magnificent mise-en-scène" of *The Grapevine.* All Rubinstein's future plans, however, were suddenly undermined by a serious deterioration in his son Sasha's state of health. He swiftly returned to St. Petersburg at the end of April, leaving the day after the Berlin performances. Sasha was diagnosed with galloping consumption, and there was an urgent need to take him to Italy where, it was hoped, the change in climate would aid in his recovery. Rubinstein's only consolation was that he would be able to continue with the composition of *Christus,* but he did so with a heavy heart. "What a terrible thing it is to live too long!" he declared to Sofiya in a tone of utter dejection.[32]

A few weeks later Rubinstein and his son left Russia for Cadenabbia on the shores of Lake Como. At the end of July Sasha and his mother made a trip to Rome for a consultation with the celebrated physician Guido Baccelli, who had evidently seen the boy as an infant during the earlier visit to Italy in 1874, and had even predicted the onset of the present illness at the age of twenty or twenty-one. During the summer months most of Rubinstein's immediate family took turns nursing Sasha, whose condition was becoming increasingly grave. Vera had not left her son's bedside for almost five months and was becoming ill with worry herself. Only the arrival of her elder son Yasha and her daughter Anna, who gave birth to a son, Konstantin, a few weeks later, afforded her a measure of consolation. For the sake of Sasha's health, Rubinstein had resigned himself to the prospect of having to go wherever the doctor instructed. In this depressed state of mind, he destroyed the autobiography he had been so eager to complete. As he told Sofiya: "I could not write it, I would have had to say too many malicious things about others and bring to the foreground many things that are repellent to me. Everyone knows a good deal about me, and what they do not know, forget about it. Let it remain unknown."[33]

By the end of July he had already completed two-thirds of *Christus,* and less than a month later the score was ready. It then transpired that Bulthaupt had insisted on an epilogue, and Rubinstein waited anxiously for news about the final edition of the text. "Oh, these writers of texts, what a headache they have caused me!" he complained bitterly to Senff.[34] The missing scene was composed during the second half of September 1893, when Rubinstein had already returned to Dresden. The opera proved to be his only distraction from the distressing news from Italy, and he confided to his sister, Sofiya: "Sasha is still not recovering. He is in bed all the time, and it is impossible to be certain about anything. He could die any day, or he could live for months or even years—but what sort of life is this? In my opinion death is preferable in such a situation."[35] He did not have long to wait for this presentiment to be fulfilled, for three weeks later Sasha died. "So, what everyone knew beforehand and expected has come to pass," he told Sofiya, "but it's also the case that however much people prepare themselves for a sad event, they are still terribly crushed by the loss of such a dear and close being."[36]

Never sentimental in such circumstances, Rubinstein threw himself into his work, but just a month later he learned about another death. Tchaikovsky had died from cholera in St. Petersburg on 25 October/6 November 1893. "This surely cannot be the will of God? What a loss for music in Russia! He was in the prime of life—he was only fifty [actually fifty-three—P.T.], and all this from a glass of water. What nonsense it all is—life, creativity, the whole lot!" he told Sofiya five days later.[37] He had never had much sympathy for his old pupil, but in these few lines, perhaps, there was a note of sincerity. Despite frequent outbursts of fury, Tchaikovsky had never ceased to respect Rubinstein, and just eighteen months earlier he had conducted a performance of *The Demon* given by Ippolit Pryanishnikov's private opera company in Moscow (22 April/4 May 1892). Yet Tchaikovsky's rise to fame had never in the slightest degree depended on Anton Rubinstein, and the composer of the celebrated *Simfonie Pathétique* was painfully aware of it. Perhaps the best assessment of their relations was given by Tchaikovsky himself when he told Eugen Zabel: "I adored in him not just a great pianist and a great composer but also a man of rare nobility, frank, loyal, generous, incapable of vulgar and petty feelings, with a clear and upright mind, and an infinite goodness—in a word, a man soaring very high above the common herd." After his graduation Tchaikovsky had felt a gulf separating him from his teacher, but he had hoped that by working steadfastly and conscientiously he might one day be able to bridge that gulf and have the honor of becoming Rubinstein's friend. "Not a bit of it," Tchaikovsky continued. "Almost thirty years have gone by since then, but the gulf has remained as wide as ever." He had never been and would never be the friend of Anton Rubinstein, even though he had always respected him as the greatest of artists and the noblest of men. As a young artist, he told Zabel, he had tried very hard to establish himself as a young, able composer (j'étais très impatient, de faire mon chemin). He had hoped that the great name of Rubinstein would have helped him along that road, "but it saddens me to confess that A. R. did nothing, absolutely nothing, to support my plans and projects. Never, to be sure, has he harmed me—he is too noble and too generous to poke sticks into the wheels of a colleague, but, with regard to me, he never departs from his tone of reserve and benevolent indifference. This has always grieved me deeply. The most likely assumption for this wounding tepidness is that R. does not like my music and that my musical individuality is antipathetic to him."[38]

* * *

With Sasha's death and the news from Russia, Rubinstein began to feel more and more homesick. The robust constitution that had supported him all through his many years on the concert platform was also beginning to falter. He had received many invitations to conduct his operas and symphonic works, but he had decided to return to St. Petersburg for the New Year. That autumn many Russian artists, including the great Lev Tolstoy, had celebrated the jubilee of the writer Dmitry Grigorovich, whose influential stories of peasant life had begun to appear in the mid-1840s. Rubinstein sent him a congratulatory telegram, signing it "a musical Anton Goremïka." Like the eponymous hero of Grigorovich's novella, whose very surname means "luckless," Rubinstein was publicly announcing his own sense of misfortune. That said, he had found an outlet for his thoughts in a collection of aphorisms, *Gedankenkorb* [A basket of thoughts], which, he told Sofiya, could be published after his death: "It is giving me a lot of amusement just now. What won't you find in there? It covers everything— serious subjects, humorous subjects—I think it isn't bad. I'm just afraid that one fine morning I shall read through it and tear it up."[39] Just a few more engagements prevented his returning to Russia before mid-December. On 12 December he conducted the first production of *Die Kinder der Haide* in Dresden, and on 15, 16, 17 December he gave three concerts in Berlin for the benefit of musicians and for students of the music schools. In these concerts he played a number of his own piano works as well as transcriptions of the dances from his operas *Feramors* and *The Demon.*

Before returning to Dresden in the New Year, Rubinstein appeared at a charity concert in St. Petersburg to raise money for the blind. This concert of 2/14 January 1894 proved to be his last appearance in Russia as a pianist and included his Variations in G, the *Léonore de Bürger* ballade, and the opera transcriptions from *Feramors* and *The Demon.*[40] Shortly afterward he returned to the Hôtel de l'Europe in Dresden. During February 1894 his pupil Anna Zherebtsova was due to appear in concerts given by the Odessa branch of the RMS. These concerts were conducted by Rimsky-Korsakov on 5/17 February (a Tchaikovsky program), 12/24 February (a Rimsky-Korsakov program), and an additional concert the following day for the benefit of the orchestra. Rubinstein wrote to Sofiya on 10 February, asking her to take note of the singer: "I am sending you our Anya Zherebtsova (Iretskaya's pupil) and one of my countless daughters.

You will love her, as we all love her, and you will hear her in Rimsky-Korsakov's concerts."[41] The next day Rubinstein set off for Rouen, where his *Néron* was staged at the Théâtre des Arts on 14 February. In Berlin he conducted his Fourth Symphony on 5 March and a week later gave the same work in Hamburg, where Josef Hofmann joined him for a performance of his Fourth Piano Concerto. As he lamented to Sofiya:

> Today I conduct an opera here, tomorrow it's a symphony there, and then I give a charity concert in some other place. So it goes on repeating itself without end—but always with enormous success!!! That is my life in total. I am bored to death. And what is most tedious of all is that I never know where I shall be tomorrow and that I can never tell you anything definite about myself. Suddenly, like a bolt from the blue, comes an invitation to conduct in such-and-such a place. Again I have to change my plans and postpone my intention of being somewhere on a particular date. And so it goes on, one after the other. I cannot wait for June and at least take a rest for the summer—I don't mean physically (I don't think about tiredness) but morally.[42]

The concerts continued throughout March and April in Vienna, Leipzig, and Berlin. On 14 April Anna Zherebtsova and Sofia Poznańska joined him at the Vienna Musikverein where he conducted his overture to *Dmitry Donskoy*, Zherebtsova sang an aria from *Die Kinder der Haide*, and Poznańska played the solo part in his Third Piano Concerto. The same concert also included Tableaux 3, 4, and 6 of *Moses*. Although these concerts were given largely for the benefit of Rubinstein's protégées, Barenboym implies that Vera was making sure that her husband did not give up his concert appearances and promotional work, as this might adversely affect the royalties from the performances. She had evidently been trying to goad her husband into getting his works performed in Milan, but in a letter to his son, Yasha, Rubinstein snapped back peevishly: "I do not desire any performances there except for *Die Maccabäer*, so nothing else can be of interest to me. If they really do want something, then let them consult the catalogue of my works."[43] At the end of April Josef Hofmann joined him for another performance of the Fourth Piano Concerto in Berlin, and some tableaux from *Christus* were performed for the first time. A complete concert performance of the sacred opera did not take place until 2 June at the Gewerbehalle [Trade Hall] in Stuttgart just a week after the composer had conducted *Die Maccabäer* at the Staatstheater in the same city. These two events marked Rubinstein's last appearances as the conductor of his own works, and the program of his piano pieces given for the students of the Stuttgart Conservatory on 4 June also signaled his last appearance on the concert platform.

Return to Russia and Last Days

The return to Peterhof in June was to be Rubinstein's last journey and perhaps he knew it. He found Vera still disconsolate after the loss of Sasha. With his death, she had channeled all her energy into ensuring the well-being of her one remaining son, and, against Rubinstein's wishes, Yasha had been sent to Italy for the sake of his education. With typically uncompromising brusqueness, Rubinstein had decided that his son should stand on his own feet and find a decent position for himself, quite unconvinced that the sojourn in Italy would bring any positive benefit: "I want to hear what he has learned there," he told Sofiya. "I do not think that he will amaze me. In general, I look upon this entire venture as lost time, effort, and money!!!—but si cela peut faire son bonheur, soit le [if that makes him happy, so be it]."[44] Rubinstein spent the last six months of his life in the relative calm of Peterhof: "I am living here quietly and pleasantly after a very tiring winter," he told Sofiya on 16 July, and he had even decided to embark on one more operatic work before giving up composition entirely. This was to be a setting of Byron's *Cain* to a libretto by Karl-August Heugel. The libretto had fascinated Rubinstein for more than twenty years, and he had asked Theodor Loewe, the director of the theater in Breslau, to revise it. In addition to his plans for the new opera during those last summer months, Rubinstein had also composed an orchestral Suite in E♭, Op. 119, dedicated to the Russian Music Society. The work was published by Senff for Austria and Germany in 1894, but Rubinstein also offered it to Jurgenson for Russia, France, England, and America, setting the royalty at six hundred rubles.

On 19 November Josef Hofmann gave a concert in London that included Rubinstein's recently composed Polonaise in E♭ minor. The reviewer for the *Times* was not overly impressed by the piece: "Mr. Hofmann played a polonaise by Rubinstein, dedicated to him by the composer; it is perhaps the least uninteresting of the six rather dull pieces that have lately appeared under the title 'Souvenir de Dresde.'" Two days later the *Times* and much of the Russian and foreign press widely reported Rubinstein's death at Peterhof on 8/20 November. It is a tribute to the esteem in which he was held throughout Europe that the *Times* devoted almost a full column to the obituary, and the final paragraph of the unsigned article reads:

> As a man he was of most lovable character, of superb generosity and unselfishness. Through his whole career he was eager to assist various charitable objects by the proceeds of his concerts, and in his farewell series not only were the concerts repeated for the instruction of musical students, but the whole profits were devoted to charity.

Rubinstein was eventually interred at the Alexander Nevsky Lavra in St. Petersburg near the graves of Dargomïzhsky and Tchaikovsky. During the funeral rites that continued for the entire week after his death, the music critic Nikolay Findeysen visited the Trinity Church on Izmaylovsky Prospekt where the composer's body lay in an open coffin. Two rows of soldiers lined the route from the railings surrounding the catafalque to the church pulpit, and the western entrance to the church was packed with police. The critic was horrified by the spectacle of orders being shouted to the men inside the church as if they were on a parade ground, and by the fact that the general public was not being admitted: "Outside there was swearing, shoving, arguing, police, and crowding!

And in the church—the deceased—a great man and . . . soldiers (i.e., not people but uniforms and troops ready for the attack)."[45] This extraordinary episode makes clear that even in death Rubinstein could never avoid bitter controversy.

Epilogue

On 12/24 December 1896 Nicholas II attended the inaugural address for the opening of the new St. Petersburg Conservatory building but, morose and annoyed at having to listen to a thirty-minute historical essay delivered by César Cui, he left without hearing the concert that followed. This concert included the *Triumphal Overture*, later published as Op. 120, that Rubinstein had completed shortly before his death to commemorate the reconstruction of the Conservatory. He had not lived to hear it, but it was entirely appropriate that the man who had devoted so much of his life to the Conservatory should be honored in this way. A few years later the overture was heard again in a concert of 7/19 April 1901 to celebrate the opening of the new Moscow Conservatory. The program was as follows:

The tsarist anthem
Glinka: Overture to *Ruslan and Lyudmila*
Tchaikovsky: Fantasy overture *Francesca da Rimini*
Borodin: In Central Asia
Rubinstein: Triumphal Overture, Op. 120
Beethoven: Symphony No. 9

Safonov, who conducted, gave an official speech in which he said:

Let us express the wish that our hall should serve for the glory of our native art, that the great people whose portraits adorn this hall should serve as an example to many generations, inspiring our young talents to serve humanity, and who knows? Perhaps it will be our dear homeland that gives the world a new Beethoven. . . . This evening the walls of our hall will ring to the sounds of the father of Russian music—Glinka, and three great Russian symphonists—Tchaikovsky, Borodin, and Rubinstein. After them, the greatest work of instrumental music, Beethoven's Ninth Symphony, will ring forth. Let the hymn of joy that concludes this symphony be the hymn of our joy.[46]

The symbolism of Safonov's address would, no doubt, have greatly pleased Rubinstein. His words could be seen as a fitting tribute to the achievements of a man whose energy and determination had led to the foundation of one of Russia's greatest institutions. In the final analysis, that was perhaps his greatest legacy. When the fiftieth anniversary of the St. Petersburg Conservatory was celebrated in September 1912, Glazunov composed a *Prelude-Cantata* for orchestra and mixed choir, set to words by the composer and teacher Nikolay Sokolov. The cantata was conceived as a tribute to Rubinstein and Tchaikovsky, who had both died within a year of each other, and appropriately it contains quotations from Rubinstein's Fourth Piano Concerto and from Tchaikovsky's fantasy overture *Romeo and Juliet*. During the grandiose ceremony, in which all the leading lights of the Conservatory took part, Rubinstein's daughter, Anna, presented the manuscript of her father's last orchestral composition. The score of the overture for the opening of the Conservatory is held to this day in the manuscripts department of the St. Petersburg Conservatory.[47]

The genius of Rubinstein the pianist had made him a legend, but the legend survived only as long as the people who had been fortunate enough to hear him play could remember. With one or two exceptions, his compositions were virtually forgotten as repertory pieces within twenty-five years of his death. With their faded charm and lack of a strong individual voice, they perished all too quickly, as Rimsky-Korsakov predicted they would:

> I'm coming to the sad conclusion that Anton Grigoryevich's symphonic music can be characterized as follows: if, while listening to something you don't know, you have the feeling that it's either bad Beethoven or poorly orchestrated Mendelssohn, and if, at the same time, it never strikes you as downright tasteless or ugly, but, on the other hand, there's nothing daring about it—on the contrary everything about it seems proper and decent, even if hopelessly monotonous—then you can be sure you're listening to one of Rubinstein's many works of this kind. I would exclude from this category, of course, a few excerpts from his vocal and Eastern music (the choruses from *The Tower of Babel*, the dances from *The Demon* and *Feramors*, some of *The Maccabees*, *Azra*, the *Persian Songs*, etc.). The only more or less pleasing exception among his symphonic pieces is, I think, *Don Quixote*, which Rubinstein once said he composed as a parody of Liszt. God must have punished him, for, as luck would have it, this "parody" turned out to be his greatest success.[48]

In Europe and America, too, audiences quickly forgot the artist whom they had once fêted so lavishly. Among Rubinstein's sixteen completed operas, nine had received their premieres in the German-speaking empires of Prussia and Austria, but they enjoyed only brief success. Ultimately they were powerless to resist the compelling force of Wagnerism, which so dramatically changed the course of European musical history. In his last years Rubinstein had even foreseen that his works would barely outlive him, but he still held out a hope that time would yet be his greatest justification. As he wrote in *Gedankenkorb*: "A composer who is now ignored must console himself with the hope that sometime, possibly even in the field of music, excavations will yield him up when the right time comes" (see Appendix E, no. 14). To some extent this rehabilitation has commenced with performances of *Das Verlorene Paradies* and *Moses* in Germany, recent productions of *The Demon* in Russia, Ireland, and France, and the issuing of most of his major works on compact discs. To what extent this will result in a major reevaluation of Rubinstein as a composer, time will yet tell.

Appendix A

Rubinstein's Works

Juvenile Works in the First Series of Opus Numbers (1842–48)

Op. 1   *Ondine* ("Souvenir de Ems"), a study in D♭ (Moderato e sempre legato). Dedicated to Madame la Princesse Wolkhonsky, née Comtesse Benckendorf (1842). Berlin, Schlesinger, 1842

Op. 2   Zuruf aus der Ferne von E. Weiden (1841–42). Schloss, Köln 1843

Op. 3   Romance "Comment disaient-ils" (Victor Hugo) (1843–44). Moscow, Gresser

Op. 4   Молитва [A prayer] (Lermontov) (1843–44). Moscow, Gresser

Op. 5   Die Nachtigall (1843–44). Moscow, Gresser

Op. 6   Die Lerche (1844). Moscow, Gresser

Op. 7   Homage à Jenny Lind. Airs suédois transcrits pour piano (1845–46). Berlin, Schlesinger

Op. 8   Voix antérieures (1847), Vienna, Wessely
      Volkslied, C major
      Rêverie, F minor
      Impromptu, A major

Op. 9   Trois mélodies caractéristiques pour piano à quatre mains, Vienna, Haslinger
      Chanson russe, G minor
      Nocturne sur l'eau, A major
      La Cataracte, E minor

Op. 10   Two nocturnes (1848). Dedicated to Amélie Kronenberg. Vienna, Haslinger.[1]
      Andante, F major
      Moderato, G major

Mature Compositions

Op. 1 Schnaderhürfel. Six Songs in the low German dialect of Rudolf Loevenstein (1848).
   1 "Unerklärlich"
   2 "Beim Fenstergehen"
   3 "Liebeshändel"
   4 "Das gebrochene Herz"
   5 "Abschied"
   6 "Beruhigung"

Op. 2 Two Fantasies on Russian folk melodies (1850)
Вниз по матушке по Волге [Down mother Volga]; Лучинушка? [Torch light]

Op. 3 Deux Mélodies (1852)

---

1. British Library copy marked in blue crayon, top right-hand corner "Aus Liszts Nachlass, Hofgärtnerei, Weimar 1886."

    (i) Moderato, F major

    (ii) Andante non troppo, B major

Op. 4 Mazurka-Fantasie in G (before 1854)

Op. 5 Trois Pièces (1852)

    (i) Polonaise in C minor;

    (ii) Krakowiak in E♭;

    (iii) Mazurka in E

Op. 6 Tarantella in B minor (1848)

Op. 7 Impromptu-Caprice in A minor (1848–1854)

Op. 8 Six Russian Songs (1850), published by Senff in German translation in 1856

    1 "Der Traum" (Zhukovsky; trans. W.Osterwald)

    2 "Frühlingsgefühl" (Zhukovsky; trans. W.Osterwald)

    3 "Das Blättchen" (Zhukovsky; trans. W.Osterwald)

    4 "Die Blume" (Zhukovsky; trans. W.Osterwald)

    5 "Sehnsucht" (Lermontov; trans. W.Osterwald)

    6 "Der Schiffer" (Davydov; trans. W.Osterwald)

Op. 9 Octet for Piano, Violin, Viola, Cello, Double-bass, Flute, Clarinet, Horn (reworked from the abandoned Piano Concerto in D minor) (1856). Leipzig, Peters

Op. 10 Kamennïy-Ostrov [Kamennoi Ostrow]. *Album de portraits.* 24 pieces (1853–54) Mayence, Schott

    (i) Allegro, E minor (H. F.)

    (ii) Moderato, F major (M. A.)

    (iii) Allegro, G minor (B. P.)

    (iv) Allegro capriccioso, A♭ major (M. N.)

    (v) Moderato assai, F major[2]

    (vi) Allegretto con moto, B♭ major (A. D.)

    (vii) Moderato, E♭ major (C. M.)

    (viii) Moderato, A minor (P.)

    (ix) Allegro capriccioso, G major (S.)

    (x) Moderato con moto, F minor (Madame Apraxina) Yekaterina Vladimirova (1770–1854)

    (xi) Allegretto, E♭ major (Mademoiselle Edith de Raden)

    (xii) Moderato con moto, C major (Elise de Euler)[3]

    (xiii) Moderato, F major (Lidiya Khrushchova)

    (xiv) Allegro non troppo, E♭ major (Hélène de Strandman)

    (xv) Allegretto, A minor (Hélène de Staal)

    (xvi) Allegro moderato, F major (Bertha de Preen)

    (xvii) Allegro appassionato, G minor (Madame Baratynskaya)

    (xviii) Allegro, C♯ minor (Madame de Helmersen)

    (xix) Agitato, D minor (Mademoiselle la Comtesse Antoinette de Bludova)

    (xx) Allegretto con moto, G♯ minor (Madame Marie de Weymarn)

    (xxi) Allegretto con moto in A♭ major (Madame Lucie de Naryshkina)

    (xxii) Moderato, F♯ major (Mademoiselle Anna de Friedebourg)[4]

    (xxiii) Moderato, F♯ major (Mademoiselle Alexandrine Sokolova)

---

2. Later published as "Romance."

3. Probably a publisher's misprint for Yelizaveta Eiler.

4. In later Russian editions this is sometimes called "La Gondolière."

(xxiv) Quasi presto, G major (Mesdemoiselles Julie and Isabella Grünberg)

Op. 11, No. 1 Three Pieces for violin and piano (1854). Dedicated to Joseph Joachim.

    (i) Allegro appassionato

    (ii) Andante

    (iii) Allegro

Op. 11, No. 2 Three Pieces for Cello and Piano (1853–54)

    (i) Andante quasi Adagio

    (ii) Allegro con moto

    (iii) Allegro risoluto

Op. 11, No.3 Three Pieces for Viola and Piano (1854)

    (i) Moderato con moto

    (ii) Allegro con moto

    (iii) Allegretto

Op. 12 Piano Sonata No. 1 in E (1848–54). Dedicated to Prince Vladimir Odoyevsky

    (i) Allegro appassionato

    (ii) Andante largamente

    (iii) Moderato

    (iv) Moderato con fuoco

Op. 13 Sonata No. 1 for Violin and Piano in G major (1851). Dedicated to Nikolay Yusupov

    (i) Moderato

    (ii) Moderato and two variations

    (iii) Scherzo (Prestissimo)

    (iv) Finale (Adagio non troppo—Moderato con moto—Adagio non troppo)

Op. 14 Le Bal. Fantaise pour le piano en dis numéros (1854). Dedicated to Princess Sophie of Nassau

    (i) Impatience (Allegro agitato in B♭ major)

    (ii) Polonaise in E♭ major

    (iii) Contredance

        (a) Tempo 1, C major

        (b) Allegretto non tanto, F major

        (c) Allegro, A major

        (d) Allegretto vivace, D major

        (e) Allegro non troppo, G major

        (f) Allegro molto, C major

    (iv) Valse A♭ (Allegro)

    (v) Intermezzo (Andante—Presto—Allegro), F major

    (vi) Polka (Allegretto con moto), E♭ major

    (vii) Polka-Mazurka (Allegretto), F major

    (viii) Mazurka, D major

    (ix) Galop (Allegro molto), B major

    (x) Le rêve (Andante—vivace—Andante con moto), B♭ major

Op. 15, No. 1 Piano Trio No. 1 in F (1851)

    (i) Con moto—moderato

    (ii) Moderato

    (iii) Moderato con moto

Op. 15 No. 2 Piano Trio No. 2 in G minor (1851)

    (i) Moderato

    (ii) Adagio

    (iii) Allegro assai

    (iv) Moderato. Adagio. Tempo I

Op. 16 Trois Pièces (1855). Dedicated to Madame Nadine de Lomakina

    (i) Impromtu, F major (Allegro non troppo)

    (ii) Berceuse, D major (Allegretto)

    (iii) Sérénade, G minor (Moderato)

Op. 17, No. 1 String Quartet No. 1 in G major (1852)

    (i) Moderato con moto

    (ii) Andante con moto

    (iii) Presto—Allegro moderato

    (iv) Allegro assai

Op. 17, No. 2 String Quartet No. 2 in C minor (1852)

    (i) Moderto

    (ii) Allegro molto vivace

    (iii) Molto lento

    (iv) Moderato

Op. 17, No. 3 String Quartet No. 3 in F major (1853)

Op. 18 Sonata for Cello and Piano No. 1 in D major (1852)

    (i) Allegro moderato

    (ii) Moderato assai

    (iii) Moderato

Op. 19 Sonata for Violin and Piano No. 2 in A minor (1853)

    (i) Allegro non troppo

    (ii) Scherzo (Allegro assai)

    (iii) Adagio non troppo

    (iv) Allegro

Op. 20 Piano Sonata No. 2 in C minor (1848–54)

    (i) Allegro con moto

    (ii) Andante: Tema con variazione

    (iii) Vivace

Op. 21 Trois Caprices (1855)

    (i) Allegretto scherzando, F♯ major

    (ii) Allegro, D minor/D major

    (iii) Allegro risoluto—Andante—Tempo I, E♭ major

Op. 22 Three Serenades (1855)

    (i) Andante con moto, F major. Dedicated to Comtesse Aleka de Pahlen

    (ii) Moderato, G minor. Dedicated to Mademoiselle Sophie de Norova

    (iii) Allegretto con moto, E♭. Dedicated to Mademoiselle Eugenie de Senyavina

Op. 23 Six Études (1849–50)

    (i) Allegro, F major

    (ii) Allegro vivace, C major

    (iii) Moderato assai, C♯ minor

    (iv) Moderato assai, E♭ major

    (v) Presto, F major

    (vi) Moderato con moto, G major

Op. 24 Six Preludes Dedicated to Clara Schumann (1854)

    (i) A♭, Moderato con moto

    (ii) F minor, Allegro molto

(iii) E major, Allegretto con moto

(iv) B minor, Moderato

(v) G major, Allegro non troppo

(vi) C minor, Grave

Op. 25 Piano Concerto No. 1 in E minor (1850)

  (i) Moderato

  (ii) Andante con moto

  (iii) Con moto

Op. 26 Deux Pièces (1854–58)

  (i) Romance: Andante, F major

  (ii) Impromptu: A minor

Op. 27 Nine Koltsov Settings (German trans. Von Viedert)

  1 "Fliehe hin, Nachtigall"

  2 "Lebewohl"

  3 "Gieb' o heil'ge Geisternacht"

  4 "Die Nachtigall und die Rose" (dedicated to Frau Betty Bury)

  5 "Das Ringelein"

  6 "Kleine Wolke ist es" (Aus dem XVI Jahrhundert)

  7 "Keine Frühlingsluft"

  8 "Wenn ich kommen dich seh"

  9 "Sturmeswinde"

Op. 28 Deux Pièces (1856)

  (i) Nocturne: Andante non troppo, G♭ major

  (ii) Caprice: E♭ major

Op. 29 Two Funeral Marches

  (i) Funeral March for an Artist in F minor (1851)

  (ii) Funeral March for a Hero in C minor (1856)

Op. 30 Deux Pièces

  (i) Barcarolle: Moderato, F minor (1852)

  (ii) Allegro appassionato, D minor (1856)

Op. 31 Six German Songs, 4 male vv (1854)

  1 "Die schlanke Wasserlilie" (Heine)

  2 "Trinklied" (Mirza Schaffy)

  3 "Meeresstille und glückliche Fahrt" (Goethe)

  4 "Jagdlust" (Tieck)

  5 "Die Rache" (Uhland)

  6 "Wiederhall"

Op. 32 Six Heine Settings (1856)

  1 Frühlingslied "Leise zieht durch mein Gemüth"

  2 Frühlingslied "Die blauen Frühlingsaugen"

  3 Frühlingslied "In dem Walde spriesst's und grünt es"

  4 Lied "Es war ein alter König"

  5 Lied "Du bist wie eine Blume"

  6 "Der Asra"

Op. 33 Six German Songs (1856)

  1 "Morgenlied" (Uhland)

  2 Lied "An der Rose Busen schmiegt sich" (Hoffmann von Fallersleben)

  3 "Die Lerche" (Theodor von Sacken)

4 "Räthsel"

5 Lied "Siehe, der Frühling währet nich lang" (Hoffmann von Fallersleben)

6 "Nachhall" (Mosenthal)

Op. 34 Twelve Persian Songs (1854) Mirza Schaffy with German translations by Friedrich Bodenstedt and Russian translations by Tchaikovsky. Dedicated to Grand Duchess Sophie of Weimar

1 "Nicht mit Engeln" ["Зулеиха"]

2 "Mein Herz schmückt sich mit dir" ["Как солнце небесам, ты свет"]

3 "Seh' ich deine zarten Füßchen an" ["Как увижу твои ножки"]

4 "Es hat die Rose sich beklagt" ["Мне розан жалобно сказал"]

5 "Die Weise guter Zecher ist" ["Тому, что хочет жить легко"]

6 "Ich fühle deinen Odem" ["Нас по одной дороге"]

7 "Schlag' die Tschadra zurück" ["Скинь чадру с головы"]

8 "Neig' schöne Knospe dich zu mir" ["Нераспустившийся цветочек"]

9 "Gelb rollt mir zu Füßen" ["Клубится волною"]

10 "Die helle Sonne leuchtet" ["Над морем солнце блещет"]

11 "Thu' nicht so spröde, schönes Kind" ["Не будь сурово, милый друг"]

12 "Gott hieß die Sonne glühen" ["Велел Создатель солнцу"]

Op. 35 Piano Concerto No. 2 in F (1851)

(i) Allegro vivace assai

(ii) Adagio non troppo

(iii) Moderato

Op. 36 Twelve Russian Songs in the German trans. by Bodenstedt (1849–51)

1 "Утес" ["Der Felsen"] (Lermontov)

2 "Слышу-ли голос твой" ["Wenn deine Stimme mir tönt"](Lermontov)

3 "Парус" ["Das Schiff"] (Lermontov)

4 "Тучи" ["Die Wolken"] (Lermontov)

5 "Кинжал" ["Der Dolch"] (Pushkin)

6 "Не спрашивай о чем тоскую" ["O frage nicht"] (Voskresensky)

7 "Певец" ["Vernahmet ihr"] (Pushkin)

8 "Пью за здоровье Мери" ["Auf dein Wohl trink'ich"] (Pushkin)

9 "Исступление" ["Die Erde ruht"] (Koltsov)

10 "Не весна тогда" ["Sie singt ein Lied"] (Countess Rostopchina)

11 "Падучая звезда" ["Der fallende Stern"] (Countess Rostopchina)

12 "Дуют ветры, ветры буйные" ["Weht es, heult es trüb"] (Countess Rostopchina)

Op. 37 An Acrostic (1856; published by Spina in 1857). Dedicated to Laura Sveykovskaya

No. 1 (L) F major

No. 2 (A) G minor

No. 3 (U) B♭ major

No. 4 (R) D minor,

No. 5 (A) F major

Op. 38 Suite in Ten Movements (1855)

(i) Prelude in D major

(ii) Minuet in E♭ major

(iii) Gigue in G major

(iv) Sarabande in B minor

(v) Gavotte: Allegretto, F♯ major

(vi) Passacaglia in A major

    (vii) Allemande in E major

    (viii) Courante in A minor

    (ix) Passepied in F major

    (x) Bourée in D major

Op. 39 Sonata for Cello and Piano No. 2 in G

    (i) Adagio

    (ii) Allegretto con moto

    (iii) Andante

    (iv) Allegro

Op. 40 Symphony No. 1 in F (1850). Dedicated to Julius Stern

    (i) Allegro con fuoco

    (ii) Allegro

    (iii) Moderato con moto

    (iv) Allegro

Op. 41 Piano Sonata No. 3 in F (1855). Dedicated to Countess Marie Kalergis

    (i) Allegro risoluto e con fuoco

    (ii) Allegretto con moto

    (iii) Andante

    (iv) Allegro vivace

Op. 42 Symphony No. 2 in C major—*The Ocean*. Dedicated to Franz Liszt

(four-movement version, 1851; published by Senff in 1857)

    (i) Allegro maestoso

    (ii) Adagio, ma non tanto

    (iii) Allegro

    (iv) Adagio—Allegro con fuoco

(six-movement version, 1863; published by Senff in 1871)

    (i) Allegro maestoso

    (ii) Adagio (D major)

    (iii) Allegro

    (iv) Adagio (E minor)

    (v) Presto (Scherzo)

    (vi) Adagio—Allegro con fuoco

(seven-movement version, 1880; published by Senff in 1882)

    (i) Allegro maestoso (C major)

    (ii) Lento assai (A minor)

    (iii) Adagio (D major)

    (iv) Allegro (G major)

    (v) Adagio (E minor)

    (vi) Presto (Scherzo) (F major)

    (vii) Adagio (C minor)—Allegro con fuoco (C major)

Op. 43a Triumphal Overture for the Coronation of Alexander II (1855)

Op. 43b Ballade of Leonora by G. A. Bürger (see: "Miscéllanées," Op. 93)

Op. 44 Soirées à Saint-Pétersbourg; six pieces (1860)

    (i) Romance: Moderato, E♭ major[5]

    (ii) Scherzo in A minor

    (iii) Preghiera: Andante con moto, B♭ major

    (iv) Impromptu in G major

---

5. Also arranged as the song "Night" to words by Pushkin.

   (v) Nocturne in F major

   (vi) Appassionato in B minor.

Op. 45 Piano Concerto No. 3 in G (1853–54). Dedicated to Moscheles

   (i) Moderato assai

   (ii) Moderato

   (iii) Allegro non troppo

Op. 45b Barcarolle No. 2 (1857)

   Moderato assai, A minor

Op. 46 Violin Concerto in G (1857)

   (i) Moderato assai

   (ii) Andante

   (iii) Moderato assai

Op. 47 No. 1 String Quartet No.4 in E minor (1856)

Op. 47 No. 2 String Quartet No.5 in B♭ (1856)

Op. 47 No. 3 String Quartet No.6 in D minor (1856)

Op. 48 Twelve Duets Set to Russian Texts (1852)

   1 "Ангел" ["Der Engel"] (Lermontov)

   2 "Пела, пела пташечка" ["Sang das Vögelein"] (Delvig)

   3 "Есть тихая роща" ["Im heimischen Land"] (Alekseyev)

   4 "Народная песня" ["Volkslied"]

   5 "Горные вершины спят во тьме ночной" ["Wanderers Nachtlied"] (Lermontov)

   6 "Прощаясь в аллее сидели" ["Beim Scheiden"] (Grekov)

   7 "Ночь" ["Die Nacht"] (Zhukovsky)

   8 "Туча" ["Die Wolke"] (Pushkin)

   9 "Беззаботность птички" ["Das Vöglein"] (Pushkin)

   10 "Горлица и прихожий" ["Der Turteltaube und der Wanderer"] (Dmitriyev)

   11 "Вечер в июне" ["Am Abend"] (Davïdov)

   12 "Светит солнышко" ["Volkslied"] (Koltsov)

Op. 49 Sonata for Viola and Piano in F minor (1855)

   (i) Moderato

   (ii) Andante

   (iii) Moderato con moto

   (iv) Allegro assai

Op. 50 Six Characteristic Pictures for Four Hands (1854–58)

   (i) Nocturne in E major

   (ii) Scherzo in F major

   (iii) Barcarolle in G minor

   (iv) Capriccio in A major

   (v) Berceuse in B minor

   (vi) March in C major

Op. 50b Barcarolle No. 3 (arr. by the composer of Op. 50, No. 3, for 2 hands): Moderato con moto, G minor

Op. 51 Six Pieces (1857)

   (i) Mélancholie in G minor

   (ii) Enjouement in B♭ major

   (iii) Rêverie in A minor

   (iv) Caprice in D♭ major

   (v) Passion in F major

   (vi) Coquetterie in B♭ major

Op. 52 Piano Trio No. 3 in B♭ (1857)
   (i) Moderato assai
   (ii) Andante
   (iii) Allegro moderato
   (iv) Allegro appassionato
Op. 53 Six Preludes and Fugues in a Free Style (1857)
   (i) A♭ major
   (ii) F minor
   (iii) E major
   (iv) B minor
   (v) G major
   (vi) C minor
Op. 54 Das Verlorene Paradies (sacred oratorio in 3 acts, A.Schloenbach, after Milton), 1856, perf. Düsseldorf, 1875
Op. 55 Wind Quintet in F for Piano, Flute, Horn, Clarinet, and Bassoon (1855, rev. 1860)
   (i) Allegro non troppo
   (ii) Scherzo: Allegro assai
   (iii) Andante con moto
   (iv) Allegro appassionato
Op. 56 Symphony No. 3 in A (1854–55). Dedicated to Leopold Zellner
   (i) Allegro risoluto
   (ii) Adagio
   (iii) Scherzo (Allegro vivace assai)
   (iv) Finale (Allegro maestoso)
Op. 57 Six German Songs (1864)
   1 "Frühmorgens" (Emanuel von Geibel)
   2 "Nun die Schatten dunkeln" (Geibel)
   3 "Neue Liebe" (Geibel)
   4 "Clärchens Lied" (Goethe)
   5 "Freisinn" (Goethe)
   6 "Tragödie" (Heine)
Op. 58 È dunque ver (M. Pinto) Scene and Aria for Soprano and Orchestra
Op. 59 String Quintet in F (1859)
Op.60 Concert Overture in B♭ (1853)—first movement of abortive symphony
Op. 61 Three Part-Songs on German Texts for Male Voices (1861)
   1 "Kriegslied" (Geibel)
   2 "Liebesfeier" (Lenau)
   3 "Vinum hungaricum" (Löwenstein)
Op. 62 Six Part-Songs on German Texts for Soprano, Contralto, Tenor, and Bass (1861)
   1 "Gondelfahrt" (Grün)
   2 "Durch Erd' und Himmel leise" (Geibel)
   3 "Ein Fichtenbaum" (Heine)
   4 "Um Mitternacht" (Mörike)
   5 "Die erwachte Rose" (Salis)
   6 "Die Heinzelmännchen" (Kopisch)
Op. 63 Rusalka (Lermontov) for Female Voice Choir and Orchestra (1861)
Op. 64 Six Krïlov Fables (1849–50). Bernard. Republished by Senff in 1863 as "Fünf Fabeln" in a German translation by R.Sprato. In this edition No. 6 was omitted.
   1 "Кукушка и орел" [The cuckoo and the eagle]

2 "Осел и соловей" [The donkey and the nightingale]

3 "Стрекоза и муравей" [The dragonfly and the ant]

4 "Квартет" [Quartet]

5 "Парнас" [Parnassum]

6 "Ворона и курица" [The crow and the hen]

Op. 65 Concerto for Cello and Orchestra No. 1 in A minor (1864)

   (i) Moderato con moto

   (ii) Adagio

   (iii) Allegro con fuoco

Op. 66 Piano Quartet in C

Op. 67 Six German Songs

1 "Lied der Vögelein" (Ernst Schultze)

2 "Waldlied" (Lenau)

3 "Frühlingsglaube" (Uhland)

4 "Vorüber" (Hermann Kletke)

5 "Meeresabend" (Moritz von Strachwitz)

6 Lied "Die Lotusblume ängstigt sich" (Heine)

Op. 68 Faust, a Musical Picture after Goethe (published 1864)—discarded movement from the *Faust Symphony*. Dedicated to Niels Gade.

Op. 69 Five Pieces (1867)

   (i) Caprice in A♭ major

   (ii) Nocture in G major

   (iii) Scherzo in A minor

   (iv) Romance in B minor

   (v) Toccata in D minor

Op. 70 Piano Concerto No. 4 in D minor (1864). Dedicated to Ferdinand David

   (i) Moderato assai

   (ii) Andante

   (iii) Allegro

Op. 71 Three Pieces (1867)

   (i) Nocturne in A♭ major

   (ii) Mazurka in F minor

   (iii) Scherzo in D♭ major

Op. 72 Six German Songs for Low Voice (1864). Dedicated to Julius Stockhausen. Russian translations by Tchaikovsky

1 "Es blinkt der Thau" ["Блестит роса"] (G. von Boddien)

2 "Wie eine Lerch' in blauer Luft" (G. von Boddien)

3 "Die Waldhexe" (G. von Boddien)

4 "Morgens" (Theodor Storm)

5 "Veilchen vom Berg" (Karl von Lemcke)

6 "Verlust" (Karl von Lemcke)

Op. 73 Fantasy in F minor for 2 Pianos (1864)

   (i) Lento. Allegro con fuoco

   (ii) Moderato vivace

   (iii) Andante con moto con variazioni

Op. 74 Cantata "Утро" [Morning] (Polonsky) for Male Voice Choir and Orchestra (1866)

Op. 75 Album de Péterhof. 12 pieces (1866)

   (i) Souvenir in C major

   (ii) Aubade in E♭ major

    (iii) Marche funèbre in G minor

    (iv) Impromptu in E♭ major

     (v) Rêverie in D minor

    (vi) Caprice russe in F major

    (vii) Pensées in F♯ minor

    (viii) Nocturne in G major

    (ix) Prélude in D major

    (x) Mazurka: Allegro non troppo, D minor

    (xi) Romance in B♭ major

    (xii) Scherzo in F major

Op. 76 Six German Songs (1867) Russian translations by Tchaikovsky

  1 "Waldeinsamkeit" ["Чаща лесная"] (Eichendorff)

  2 "Nacht" ["Ночь"](Eichendorff)

  3 "An den Frühling" ["К весне"](Lenau)

  4 "Frühlingsblick" (Lenau)

  5 "Bedeckt mich mit Blumen" (Geibel/P.Heyse)

  6 "Klinge, klinge, mein Pandero" ["Ах, играй же, мой пандеро"] (Geibel)

Op. 77 Fantasy in E minor (1866). Dedicated to Thalberg

    (i) Adagio—Allegro con fuoco

    (ii) Moderato assai

    (iii) Allegro moderato—Moderato—Allegro molto—Poco meno mosso—Presto

    (iv) Molto lento—Vivace assai—Tempo rubato—Quasi presto

Op. 78 Twelve Russian Songs (1868). German translations by W.Osterwald

  1 "Еврейская мелодия" [Hebrew melody] "Hebräische Melodie" (Lermontov)

  2 "Взором твоим я утешен" [I am consoled by your look] "Könnt'ich doch stets in deine blauen Augen" (Venediktov)

  3 "Ангел" [The angel] "Der Engel" (Pushkin)

  4 "Буря" [The storm] "Der Sturm" (Pushkin)

  5 "Ах, зачем меня силой выдали?" [Ah, why was I given away by force?] "O wie schwer die Pein?" (Koltsov)

  6 "Узник" [The captive] "Der Gefangene" (Pushkin)

  7 "Новогреческая песня" [New Greek song] "Neugriechisches Lied" (Lermontov)

  8 "Элегия" [Elegy] "Elegie" (Maykov)

  9 "Песня" [A song] "Wie der Quell ist mein Lied" (Polonsky)

 10 "Дума" [A thought] "Sinngedicht" (Polonsky)

 11 "Ворон к ворону летит" [The raven flies to the raven] "Rab' zum Raben fliegt daher" (Pushkin)

 12 "Сцена из цыган" [Gypsy scene] "Alter Mann, grimmer Mann" (Pushkin)

Op. 79 *Ivan the Terrible*, a musical characteristic picture (1869). Dedicated to Count Vladimir Sollogub

Op. 80 *Der Thurm zu Babel* (sacred oratorio, Rodenberg), 1869, perf. Köningsberg, 1870

Op. 81 Six Études (1870)

    (i) F minor

    (ii) A major

    (iii) G minor

    (iv) E major

    (v) D minor

    (vi) E♭ major

Op. 82 Album of Popular Dances of Different Nations (1868)

    (i) Russian dance and trepak, C major (Russie)

    (ii) Lezghinka, G major (Caucase)

    (iii) Mazurka, D major (Pologne)

    (iv) Csyrdás, E minor (Hongrie)

    (v) Tarantella, G minor (Italie)

    (vi) Lyndler, F major (Allemagne)

    (vii) Polka, Moderato, G major (Bohème)

Op. 83 Ten Songs to English, French, and Italian Texts

    1 "Rappelle-toi" (de Musset)

    2 "A Saint-Blaize" (de Musset)

    3 "Chanson de Barberine" (de Musset)

    4 "La prière de femme" (Lamartine)

    5 "Tanto gentile" (Dante)

    6 "La rondinella pelegrina" (Tom. Grossi)

    7 "La prima viola" (A.Maffei)

    8 "The Tear" (Thomas Moore)

    9 "Good Night" (Thomas Moore)

    10 "A Dream" (Thomas Moore)

Op. 84 Fantasia for Piano and Orchestra in C (1869)

    (i) Allegro moderato

    (ii) Moderato

    (iii) Moderato assai

    (iv) Allegro

Op. 85 Piano Trio No. 4 in A minor (1870)

Op. 86 Romance and Caprice for Violin (1870)

Op. 87 *Don Quixote,* musical characteristic picture after Cervantes, 1870. Dedicated to Maksimilian Fredro

Op. 88 Thème et Variations in G (1871). Dedicated to Yu. Berens

    Theme (Lento—Allegro moderato)

    Variation 1 (Allegro)

    Variation 2 (Andante con moto)

    Variation 3 (Moderato con moto)

    Variation 4 (Moderato)

    Variation 5 (Moderato)

    Variation 6 (Allegro non troppo)

    Variation 7 (Moderato assai)

    Variation 8 (Moderato assai)

    Variation 9 (Moderato)

    Variation 10 (Moderato)

    Variation 11 (Allegro)

    Variation 12 (Allegro moderato)

Op. 89 Sonata in D for Four Hands (1870). Dedicated to Baroness Emma de Wöhrmann

    (i) Moderato con moto—Allegro non troppo

    (ii) Allegro molto vivace—Moderato con fuoco

    (iii) Andante

    (iv) Coda—Allegro non troppo

Op. 90 No. 1 String Quartet No.7 in G minor (1871)

Op. 90 No. 2 String Quartet No.8 in E minor (1871, rev. 1892)

Op. 91 Songs and Requiem for Mignon (from Goethe's 'Wilhelm Meister') for Solo Voice and Piano (1872)

No. 1. Der Harfner: "Was hör'ich draussen vor dem Thor?"
No. 2. Der Harfner: "Wer nie sein Brot mit Tränen aß"
No. 3. Der Harfner: "Wer sich der Einsamkeit ergibt"
No. 4. Mignon: "Kennst du das Land?"
No. 5. Spottlied: "Ich armer Teufel, Herr Baron"
No. 6. Der Harfner: "Ihm färbt der Morgensonne Licht"
No. 7. Mignon under der Harfner: "Nur wer die Sehnsucht kennt"
No. 8. Philine: "Singet nicht in Trauertönen"
No. 9. Der Harfner: "An die Thüren will ich schleichen"
No. 10. Mignon: "Heiß mich nicht reden"
No. 11. Aurelie: "Ich hatt' ihn einzig mir erkoren"
No. 12. Mignon: "So laßt mich scheinen, bis ich werde"
No. 13. Requiem für Mignon: "Wen bringt ihr uns zur stillen Gesellschaft?"
No. 14. Friedrich: "O ihr werdet Wunder sehen"

Op. 92 No. 1 Hecuba (Ludwig Goldhann) Aria for Contralto and Orchestra (1872). Dedicated to the pianist and singer Karoline Gomperz-Bettelheim

Op. 92 No. 2 *Hagar in der Wüste* [Hagar in the Desert (Ferdinand von Saar), dramatic scene for soprano, contralto, tenor and orchestra, dedicated to Yelizaveta Lavrovskaya

Op. 93 Miscellaneous Pieces (Miscellanées) in Nine Books (1872–73)

Op. 93, No. 1 Ballad "Léonore de Bürger." Dedicated to Monsieur E. F.Wenzel

Op. 93, No. 2 Deux grandes études. Dedicated to Professor Kross of the St. Petersburg Conservatory

No. 1 Moderato con moto, D minor
No. 2 Allegro, A major

Op. 93, No. 3 Doumka in G minor (Lento). Dedicated to Monica Terminskaya
Polonaise in E major (Allegro moderato). Dedicated to Monica Terminskaya

Op. 93, No. 4 Cinquième barcarolle (A minor, Andante con moto)

Op. 93, No. 5 Scherzo in F major (Allegro moderato). Dedicated to Pyotr Tchaikovsky

Op. 93, No. 6 Deux sérénades russes. Dedicated to Sophie Smiryagina

No. 1 Andante con moto, D minor
No. 2 Lento—Moderato—Lento, A minor

Op. 93, No.7 Nouvelle mélodie in F♯ minor (Andante con moto). Dedicated to Cathinka Phrym
Impromptu in A♭ major (Allegro con moto). Dedicated to Cathinka Phrym

Op. 93, No. 8 Variations sur l'air "Yankee Doodle" (Adagio—Allegro non troppo), A major. Dedicated to William Mason.

Op, 93, No. 9 Miniatures. Dedicated to Madame Aglaë Massart

Près du ruisseau (Vivace), D major
Menuet (Moderato assai), E♭ major
Berceuse (Moderato assai), G major
Hallali (Allegro), A♭ major
Sérénade (Moderato), D minor
L'Hermite (Adagio), E♭ major
El Dachtarawan. Marche orientale (Allegretto con moto), G minor
Valse in F (Allegro non troppo)
Chevalier et Payse (Con moto), B♭ major

A la fenêtre (Andante con espressione), C major

Revoir (Moderato con moto), G major

Le cortège (Andante), A♭ major

Op. 94 Piano Concerto No. 5 in E♭ (1874). Dedicated to Alkan

   (i) Allegro moderato

   (ii) Andante

   (iii) Allegro

Op. 95 Symphony No. 4 in D minor *The Dramatic* (1874)

   (i) Lento—Allegro

   (ii) Presto

   (iii) Adagio

   (iv) Largo—Allegro con fuoco

Op. 96 Concerto for Cello and Orchestra No. 2 in D minor (1874)

   (i) Allegro moderato

   (ii) Andante

   (iii) Allegro

Op. 97 String Sextet in D (1876)

Op. 98 Sonata for Violin and Piano No. 3 in B minor (1876)

Op. 99 Piano Quintet in G minor (1876). Dedicated to Henri Jacques

   (i) Molto lento—Allegro moderato

   (ii) Moderato

   (iii) Variations

   (iv) Moderato

Op. 100 Piano Sonata No. 4 in A minor (1877)

   (i) Moderato con moto

   (ii) Allegro vivace

   (iii) Andante

   (iv) Allegro assai

Op. 101 Twelve Aleksey Tolstoy Settings (1877). German texts by Caroline von Pawloff

   1 "Коль любит, так без рассудку" ["Wie es sein muss"]

   2 "Грядой клубится белой над озером туман" ["Nebel und Gram"]

   3 "Дробится и плещет и брызжет волна" ["Am Meeresstrand"]

   4 "Дождя отшумевшего капли, тихонько по листям текли" ["In stiller Nacht"]

   5 "Звонче жаворонка пенья" ["Frühling"]

   6 "Волки" ["Die Wölfe"]

   7 "Не ветер, вея с высоты" ["Sanftes Walten"]

   8 "Вздымаются волны как горы" ["Vergängliches"]

   9 "Усни, печальный друг" ["Schlaf' ein"]

   10 "Кабы знала я, кабы ведала" ["Hätt' ich da gewusst, hätt' ich das geahnt"]

   11 "Князь Ростислав" ["Fürst Rostislav"]

   12 "Бор сосновый в стране одинокой" ["Des Baches Geplauder"]

Op. 102 Caprice Russe for Piano and Orchestra in C minor (1878). Dedicated to Anna Yesipova

Op. 103 Bal Costumé for 2 Pianos. Twenty numbers (1879)

   1 Introduction

   2 Astrologue et Bohémienne

   3 Berger et Bergère

   4 Marquis et Marquise

   5 Pêcheur napolitain et Napolitaine

6 Chevalier et Châtelaine
7 Toréador et Andalouse
8 Pèlerin et Fantaisie (Etoile du soir)
9 Polonais et Polonaise
10 Bojar et Bojarine
11 Cossaque et Petite-Russienne
12 Pasha et Almée
13 Seigneur et Dame
14 Sauvage et Indienne
15 Patricien allemand et Demoiselle
16 Chevalier et Soubrette
17 Corsaire et femme grecque
18 Royal Tambour et Vivandière
19 Troubadour et Dame souveraine
20 Danses

Op. 104 Six Pieces (1882–85)
  (i) Elegy in D minor
  (ii) Variations in A♭
  (iii) Study in C
  (iv) Barcarolle No. 6 in C minor
  (v) Impromtu in G
  (vi) Ballade in A minor

Op. 105 Ten Songs Based on Serbian Melodies (1877). German translation by Theodore Hauptner
  1 "Wie war't ihr fröhlich, gold'ne Mädchentage"
  2 "Warum musst du welken, schöne Rose"
  3 "Rosendüfte füllen rings die Lüfte"
  4 "Schüchtern brach der Mond durch Wolkenschatten"
  5 "Weithin rief die Mutter nach der Tochter"
  6 "Einen Bruder hatt'ich, einen Geliebten"
  7 "O Gott, wo ist mein Auserwählter"
  8 "Wie so launisch bist du, o Sonnenschein"
  9 "Willst du einen Ehemann erkennen"
  10 "Geh bei Tagesanbruch auf die Strasse"

Op. 106 No. 1 String Quartet No. 9 in A♭ (1880)
Op. 106 No. 2 String Quartet No. 10 in F minor (1880, rev. 1892)
Op. 107 Symphony No. 5 in G minor *The Russian* (1880)
  (i) Moderato assai
  (ii) Allegro non troppo—Moderato assai
  (iii) Andante
  (iv) Allegro vivace
Op. 108 Piano Trio No. 5 in C minor (1883)
Op. 109 Soirées Musicales. Nine pieces (1884)
  (i) Prélude in A minor
  (ii) Valse in E minor
  (iii) Nocturne in F major
  (iv) Scherzo in D major
  (v) Impromptu in G major
  (vi) Rêverie-caprice in G minor

(vii) Badinages
      I   Allegro con moto, D♭ major
     II   Presto, F major
    III Con moto, D minor
   IV Allegro moderato, C major
    V Allegro, B♭ major
   VI Andante, F major
  VII Con moto assai, B♭ minor
 VIII Allegro con moto, F♯ major
   IX Moderato con moto, D♭ major

(viii) Thème varié in D

(ix) Étude in E♭.

Op. 110 Fantasy *Eroica* (1884)

Op. 111 Symphony No. 6 in A minor (1886)
   (i) Moderato con moto
   (ii) Moderato assai
   (iii) Allegro vivace
   (iv) Moderato assai

Op. 112 *Moses* (sacred opera, eight scenes, Mosenthal), 1885–89, perf. Prague, 1892

Op. 113 Konzertstück in A♭ for Piano and Orchestra (1889)
   (i) Moderato assai
   (ii) Con moto moderato
   (iii) Allegro vivace

Op. 114 Acrostic No. 2 (1890). Dedicated to Sofia Poznańska
   (i) (S) Andante con moto, F minor
   (ii) (O) Allegretto in D♭ major
   (iii) (F) Tempo di mazurka, A♭ major
   (iv) (I) Adagio, C minor
   (v) (A) Allegro non troppo, F major

Op. 115 Ten German Songs
   1 "Das erste Sommergras und vor der Ernte" (Martin Greif)
   2 "Was thut's" (Siegfried Lipiner)
   3 "Am Strande" (Georg Scherer)
   4 "Seefahrt" (Rudolf Baumbach)
   5 "An die Vögel" (Robert Hammeling)
   6 "Liebeslied" (Otto von Leixner)
   7 "Der einsame See" (Max Kalbeck)
   8 "Lass mich deine Augen fragen" (Peter Cornelius)
   9 "Gebet" (Wilhelm Kunze)
  10 "Der Dichter" (Julius Sturm)

Op. 116 Overture *Antony and Cleopatra* (1890)

Op. 117 *Christus* (sacred opera, seven scenes with a prologue and an epilogue, H.Bulthaupt), 1887–93, perf. Bremen, 1895

Op. 118 Souvenir de Dresde. 6 pieces (1894)
   (i) Simplicitas in F major
   (ii) Appassionata in C minor
   (iii) Novellette in A major
   (iv) Caprice in C major

(v) Nocturne in A♭ major

(vi) Polonaise in E♭ major. Dedicated to Joseph Hofmann

Op. 119 Suite in E♭ (1894)

Op. 120 Overture for the Opening of the New Building of the St. Petersburg Conservatory (1894)

Op. 121 Polka, C major, pf.

Works without Opus Numbers

Operas

Dmitry Donskoy [Дмитрий Донской] (three acts, Count V. A. Sollogub and V. R. Zotov, after Ozerov), 1849–50, perf. St. Petersburg, 1852

Sibirskiye okhotniki [Сибирские охотники [Die Sibirischen Jäger] (one act, A. Zherebtsov), perf. 1852, Weimar, 1854

Hadji Abrek [Хаджи Абрек] (one act, A. I. Zhemchuznikov, after Lermontov), 1852–53, St. Petersburg, 1858 [?] as Месть [Vengeance]

Fomka the Fool [Фомка Дурачок] (one act, M. L. Mikhaylovich), 1853, perf. St. Petersburg, 1853

Die Kinder der Haide (four acts, S. H. Mosenthal, after Beck), 1860, perf. Vienna 1861

Feramors (three acts, J.Rodenberg, after "Lallah Rooke" by Thomas Moore), 1862, perf. Dresden, 1863

The Demon [Демон] (three acts, P. A. Viskovatov, after Lermontov), 1871, perf. St. Petersburg, 1875

Die Maccabäer (three acts, Mosenthal, after Otto Ludwig), 1874, perf. Berlin, 1875

Néron (four acts, Jules Barbier), 1875–76, perf. Hamburg, 1879

The Merchant Kalashnikov [Купец Калашников] (three acts, N. Kulikov, after Lermontov), 1877–79, perf. St. Petersburg, 1880

Sulamith (opera-oratorio, five scenes, Rodenberg, after the Song of Songs, 1882–83, perf. Hamburg, 1883

Unter Räubern (comic opera, one act, E.Wichert), 1883, perf. Hamburg 1883

Der Papagei (comic opera, one act, H. Wittmann, after a Persian tale), 1884, perf. Hamburg, 1884

Goryusha [Горюша] (four acts, D. Averkiyev), 1888, perf. St. Petersburg, 1889

Ballet

The Grapevine [Die Rebe] (three acts), 1882, perf. Berlin, 1893

Orchestra

Konzertstück for Piano and Orchestra (1877, destroyed)

Piano Concerto in F (first movement only) (1847) (lost?)

Piano Concerto in C major (1848) (lost?)

Piano Concerto in D minor (1849) (reworked into the Octet, Op. 9)

Symphony in B♭ (1853) (first movement published as the Concert Overture, Op. 60, and second and third movements added to the 1863 six-movement version of the Ocean Symphony)

Faust Symphony (1854) (the first movement was subsequently reused as the "Faust Overture," Op.68, published 1864
Russia, symphonic piece (1882)

Chamber

Grand Duo for Violin and Piano on Motifs from Meyerbeer's *Le Prophète* (with Vieuxtemps) (1849)

Piano

Quadrille (juvenile works of the mid-1830s, lost)
Four polkas (1843–44). Later reissued with titles:
    No. 1. Amalie-Polka, C major
    No. 2 Henriette-Polka, A♭ major
    No. 3 Flora-Polka, B♭ major
    No. 4 Natalie-Polka, E♭ major
Transcriptions for four hands:
    Paraphrase on Meyerbeer's *Les Huguenots* (1843)
    Liszt: Marche héroïque en style hongrois (1843)
Sailor's Song (1847) (lost?)
Turkish March from the Ruins of Athens (1848)
Variations on a Theme of Varlamov "Like a stray nightingale" (1849)[6]
Arrangement of the overture to Meyerbeer's *Ein Feldlager in Schlesien* (1849) (lost)
Euphémie-polka in E♭ major (1849), Bernard
Cavalry Trot (1850), Gresser
Marie-Polka in E♭ major (1853)
Mazurka in A♭ major[7] (1856)
Fantaisie sur les mélodies hongroises (1858)
Points d'orgue. Cadenzas for Beethoven's Piano Concertos 1–4 (1861)
Points d'orgue. Cadenzas for Mozart's Piano Concerto in D minor, K. 466 (1861). Published by Schott, 1863
Two concert studies:
    (i) Moderato, C major "On False Notes" (1867)
    (ii) C major (1868)
Arrangement of Beethoven's Egmont Overture (1868)
Valse-caprice: Vivace, E♭ major (1870). Dedicated to Countess Louisa de Mercy-Argenteau
Barcarolle No. 4: Allegretto con moto, G major (1870)
Sérénade russe, composée pour l'Album Bellini, in B minor (1879)
Transcription of the Dances from *The Demon* (1880)
Transcription of the Dances from *Feramors* (1893?)
Bluette in A♭ (1885)
Valse in A♭ (1891)
Finger Exercises [Fingerübungen], ed. Villoing

---

6. Varlanov died in October 1848 and Rubinstein, Henseit, and others contributed variations on the theme of Varlamov's song.
7. See Georg Kinsky, Manuskripte Briefe Dokumente: Katalog der Musikautographen—Sammlung Louis Koch (Stuttgart: Hoffmannsche Buchdruckerei Felix Arais, 1953), p. 283. The mazurka (beginning) was intended for the album of Princess Wittgenstein and is dated 10 August 1856, Weimar.

Vocal

"Чижик" [The siskin] (Grot), 1843–44

"Ласточка" [The swallow] (M. Sukhanov)[8] (1849)

Romance: "Не бейся тревожно в груди, ретивое" *[Do not beat so anxiously in my breast, dear heart] (A.Polovtsev) (1849)*

"Dors pendant que je veille" (Alfred de Musset), Bernard (1850?)[9]

Russian Church Chorus for the Choir of Prince Sheremetyev (1851) (lost)

"Возращение" [The Return] (Meri) (1854)

"Молитва перед битвой" *[A prayer before the battle] (A.Maykov) for voice and orchestra (1854)*

Solemn Overture on the Theme Heil dir im Siegerkranz for Chorus, Organ, and Orchestra (1854)

"Ночь" *[Night]* "Мой голос для тебя и ласковый и томный" *(Pushkin) (1860?). Arrangement of Op. 44 No.1: Romance in E♭*

Six German Songs (1872–75)

    1 "Wir drei" (Backody)

    2 "Bitte" (Lenau)

    3 "Mein Herzensschatz" (Herm. Oelschläger)

    4 "Verschiedene Wege" (Bodenstedt)

    5 "Die drei Zigeuner" (Lenau) (1873)

    6 "Die Heimath meiner Lieder" (Boddien) (1872)

"Узница" [The prisoner] (Polonsky) (1878?)

"Chanson d'Amour" (Hugo) (1879)

Bacchic Song (Pushkin) for Baritone, Male Choir, and Piano "Was schweigt unser fröhlicher Chor?" (1879)

Liebeswunder: "A quoi bon entendre les oiseaux des bois?" (Hugo) (1879)

Fatme "Schlanke Fatme, hohe Palme" (Felix Dahn) (1881)

Four German Songs (1881)

    1 "Mitternach" (Rückert)

    2 "Die Blume der Ergebenheit" (Rückert)

    3 "Hüte dich, Nachtigall" (Linge)

    4 "Wenn ich dieses Klage" (D.Strauss)

Mädchens Abendgedanken "Wer der Meine wohl wird werden" (F. T. Fischer) (1882)

"Весенний вечер" *[Spring evening]:* "Гуляют тучи золотые" *[The golden clouds go strolling] (Ivan Turgenev) (1885)*

"Das begrabene Lied" (Rudolph Baumbach), ballad for tenor and piano (1890)

"Glück," *duet for soprano and tenor with piano accompaniment "Was rauscht vor der Thüre?" (Faust Pachler), (1890)*

Six Russian Songs (1891). Dedicated to Natalya Iretskaya

    No. 1 "Весна" [Spring] (Semyon Nadson);

    No. 2 "Литовская песня" [Lithuanian song] (Władysław Syrokomla);

---

8. This was probably Mikhail Sukhanov (d. 1843), an amateur poet of peasant stock from the province of Arkhangel'sk. His poems first appeared in Russkiy invalid and other journals, and several volumes were published in St. Petersburg during the 1830s, including collections of folk songs.
9. See CBFA, p. 387; and Larry Sitsky, Anton Rubinstein: An Annotated Catalogue of Piano Works and Biography, Music Reference Collection, No. 72 (Westport, Conn., and London: Greenwood, 1998), p. 195.

No. 3 "Сияет весна золотая" [Golden spring shines] (Pavel Kozlov);

No. 4 "С тобой, моя печаль" [With you, my sorrow] (Dmitry Merezhkovsky);

No. 5 "Южная ночь" [Southern night] (Dmitry Merezhkovsky);

No. 6 "Не говорите мне: 'он умер'" [Do not say to me "he has died"] (Semyon Nadson).

"Осень" [Autumn] (Eristov)[10] (1891). Published in Germany as "Herbstgedanken." Dedicated to Mikhail Ivanovich Mikhaylov

"Зеркало" [The looking-glass] (Eristov) (1891). Dedicated to Ivan Korganov

"О дитя, живое сердце" [O child, dear heart] (Merezhkovsky), (1891). Dedicated to Nikolay Figner

Serenade: "Тянутся по небу тучи тяжелые" [The heavy clouds reach across the sky]. Published in Germany as "Durch die laue Nacht" (N. Minsky) (1891). Dedicated to I. V. Tartakov

Ballad (Ivan Turgenev) (1891): "Перед воеводой молча он стоит" [Silently before the Voyevoda he stands], for baritone and piano. Dedicated to Fyodor Stravinsky

"Я на тебя гляжу" [I look at you] (KR) (1893)

"Wo wird einst des Wandermüden" (Heine) (1893)

Projected and Unfinished Works

Psalm Settings for Prince Sheremetyev's Choir (1851)

Stepan Razin [Степан Разин] opera to a libretto by M. Voskresensky (1852)

Poltava [Полтава] after Pushin. Projected opera (1853)

Symphony in B♭ major (1853). Destroyed. Some material was used in the Concert Overture in B♭, Op. 60, and two movements were added to the six-movement version of the Ocean Symphony in 1863

Faust Symphony (1854–55). Destroyed. First movement published as the Faust Overture, Op. 68, in 1864

The Maid of Pskov [Псковитянка], opera to a libretto by Vsevolod Krestovsky (1864)

Figlia del Tintoretto, opera by an unknown librettist (1864)

Rudin [Рудин], opera to a libretto by Ivan Turgenev (1864)

Rosvita, opera to a libretto by Moritz Hartmann (1864)

The Oprichnik [Опричник], opera to a libretto by Pyotr Kalashnikov (1864)

Joab, projected opera in collaboration with Julius Rodenberg (1869)

Don Quixote, projected opera in collaboration with Julius Rodenberg (1869)

Konzertstück for Piano and Orchestra (1877)

The Gypsies [Цыгане], after Pushkin, to a libretto by Yevgeny Ganzeyer (1891 or 1892)

Cain, projected opera. Libretto commissioned from Karl-August Heugel in 1870. Reworked by Theodor Loewe in 1894

(e) Literary Works

"Report to the Minister of Education"
Original language: French

---

10. Barenboym, perhaps mistakenly, attributes this setting to Turgenev, presumably having in mind the lyric poem *Как грустный взгляд, люблю я осень*, but most other sources (Catherine Drinker Bowen, Larry Sitsky, and Grove) attribute it to D. Eristavi.

Russian translation by Dmitry Stasov: *RMG*, 1909
LN, 1:43–46

"Russische Komponisten" [Russian composers]
Original language: German
Blätter für Musik, Theater und Kunst, 1855
Russian translation: I. Glebov [B. V. Asaf'yev] Anton Grigor'yevich Rubinshteyn, Moscow, 1929

"О музыке в России" ["O muzïkye v Rossii" (On music in Russia)]
Original language: Russian
First published in the journal *Vek*, 1861
LN, 1:46–60

"Речь на открытии Петербургской консерватории" ["*Rech' na otkrïtii Peterburgskoy konservatorii*" (Speech on the opening of the St. Petersburg Conservatory)], 1862
Original language: Russian
LN, 1:53–55

"*Speech on the Ninth Anniversary of the Founding of the St. Petersburg Conservatory*"
Original language: French
Published in Journal de St.-Pétersbourg, 1871, 12/24 September
LN, 1:55

"*Über die Edition der Klassiker*" [On editing the classics]
Original language: German
Published in Signale für der musikalische Welt, 1883, no. 32
Russian translation F. M. Marmorshteyn
LN, 1:55–60

"*Die geistliche Oper*" [Spiritual opera]
Original language: German
First published in Vor den Coulissen, Berlin, 1882
German text (with English translation) in Alexander M'Arthur, Anton Rubinstein: A Biographical Sketch, Edinburgh, 1889, pp. 53–82

"По поводу сотого представления оперы *Демон* [*Po povodu sotogo predstavleniya operï Demon* (On the hundredth performance of the opera The Demon)], 1884
Original language: Russian
Originally published in RMG, 1910
LN, 1:60–62

"Докладная записка в Дирекцию С.-Петербургского отделения Русского музыкального общества" ["*Dokladnaya zapiska v Direktsiyu S.-Peterburgskogo otdeleniya Russkogo muzïkal'nogo obshchestva*" (Report to the Directorate of the St. Petersburg division of the Russian Music Society)], 1887
Original language: Russian
LN, 1:64–5

"Докладная записка Великой Княгине Александре Иосифовне" ["*Dokladnaya zapiska Velikoy Knyaginye Aleksandrye Iosifovnye*" (Report to the grand duchess Aleksandra Iosifovna)], 1887

Original language: Russian
LN, 1:62–63

"Докладная записка Александру III" *["Dokladnaya zapiska Aleksandru III" (Report to Alexander III)]*, 1889
Original language: Russian
First published in RMG, 1909
LN, 1:104–7

"Ещё о консерваториях" ["Eshchyo o konservatoriyakh" (More on the conservatories)]
Original language: Russian
First published in *Novoye vremya*, 1889, 11/23 July
LN, 1:107–110

Автобиографические воспоминания [Avtobiograficheskiya vospominaniya (Autobiographical reminiscences)]
Original language: Russian
First published in Russkaya starina, November 1889
LN, 1:65–104, as Avtobiograficheskiye rasskazï

Ein Gespräch über Musik. Die Musik und ihre Meister
Original language: German
Senff, Leipzig 1892
Russian translation by Rubinstein himself as Музыка и ея представители. Разговор о музыке [Muzïka i yeya predstaviteli. Razgovor o muzïkye (Music and its representatives. A conversation about music)]
LN, 1:110–62
English translation published as Music and Its Masters, translated by Mrs. John P. Morgan, London 1921

Die geistliche Oper
Original language: German
Published in *Die Zukunft* 3, Jahrgang (1894), no. 10: 456–461

Gedankenkorb
Original language: German
First published with a foreword by Hermann Wolff in Vom Fels zum Meer 16, Jahrgang, bk. 1 (October 1896–March 1897), vol. 2 (April–September 1897)
The Russian translation appeared as:
Мысли и афоризмы [Mïsli i aforizmï (Thoughts and aphorisms)], translated from the German by N. N. Shtraukh, St. Petersburg, 1904.
Partial Russian translation by S. L. Ginzburg and F. M. Marmorshteyn
LN, 1:163–204

Appendix B

Synopsis of *Die Kinder der Haide*

Act 1. A deserted place outside a village. The steppes and hills. An overcast evening. Isbrana is pining for her lover Wania, while her fellow Gypsy, Grigori, is mending a frying pan. They are joined by two more Gypsies, Pawel and Bogdan, who conspire with Grigori to rob an inn on the estate of Count Waldemar. The inn belongs to the foreigner Conrad who lives there with his daughter, Maria. The Count's herdsman, Wania, arrives, but he is cool toward Isbrana. As proof of her love, she reveals to him the plot she has overheard to rob the inn. Through Wania's foreknowledge, the robbery plan is foiled, and as a reward Conrad offers him the hand of his daughter. Maria, however, has a secret love, but she does not even know who he is.

Act 2. An open gallery in Conrad's house. The scene is set for the wedding of Wania and Maria. Alone, she reveals to her father her secret love and learns from him that the unknown man is none other than Count Waldemar. During the choruses of jubilation in honor of the couple, Isbrana appears and sings a dark song about treacherous love and vengeance. At this point Count Waldemar arrives and is shaken to see that the woman of his dreams is about to marry another. The crowd drags Wania away to play cards and drink, leaving the Count and Maria to acknowledge their love for each other. They are interrupted by Conrad, who reminds Maria of her duty to her husband, but Waldemar is resolute and Maria falls into a faint. In the mêlée that follows and the resumption of the wedding festivities, the Count and Isbrana each see their chance: the former to wrench Maria from Wania's clutches and the latter to take vengeance on her rival.

Act 3. Same as act 2. Isbrana finds Wania still asleep after the drunken revels. In an angry altercation Isbrana declares that Maria is unfaithful, but Wania does not believe her. As proof, she intercepts a letter from the Count to Maria asking for a secret rendezvous. Initially she attempts to use this to discredit Maria in the eyes of her husband, but the two women are reconciled as they come to understand the strength of their own passions. The truth of the situation is revealed, however, when Wania finds Maria and the Count together, and in a violent exchange between the two men the Count is killed. In an extended finale, Isbrana and the Gypsies defend Wania against Conrad and the Count's men, and make their escape.

Act 4. A rocky location in a forest. Isbrana is vainly trying to comfort Wania, who is now living as an exile. Conrad arrives with Maria who has lost her reason. Wania's attempts to console Maria only serve to infuriate Isbrana. Conrad and Maria leave, declaring that nothing but the grave is left for them, and Wania has to defend them against the other Gypsies who want to rob them as a parting gift. The argument is interrupted by a Gypsy who runs in to announce that soldiers are approaching. Isbrana implores Wania to flee with her, but he steadfastly refuses. As the soldiers approach to arrest him, she seizes a dagger from his belt and stabs herself.

Synopsis of *The Demon*

Prologue. A richly luxurious locality with trees, flowers, rocks, mountains, and caves, and in the distance the castle of Prince Gudal. A storm is raging and amid a chorus of evil spirits the commanding figure of the Demon appears. In the aria "Proklyatïy mir! Prezrennïy mir! Neschastnïy, nenavistnïy mne mir!" [Accursed world! Despicable world! Wretched, hateful world!] he expresses complete disillusionment. Humanity is so frail, weak, and insignificant that it is no challenge to his might and his power. Made miserable by intolerable ennui, he no longer even feels pleasure in committing acts of evil. An Angel appears and reminds the Demon that the power of love can reconcile him with heaven. This proposal is angrily rejected by the Demon: it is not slavery and blind obedience to a tyrannical god that he desires but freedom and wild passions. The Angel warns the Demon not to touch anything that is dear to heaven, but the latter relishes a fight and warns heaven to be on its guard.

Act 1, scene 1. Some girls are filling their pitchers with water on the banks of the river Aragva. Prince Gudal's daughter, Tamara, appears, accompanied by her nanny and hand-maidens. The sight of her has aroused long-forgotten feelings in the Demon's soul, but his presence confounds the girl, who believes that some danger is oppressing her. The nanny sings a song about the bridegroom who is hastening to join her: "Skachet k neveste zhenikh na kone" [A bridegroom is galloping on horseback to his bride]. This momen-tarily relieves her anxieties, but then the Demon appears, imploring her to love him. Tamara alone can see him and hear his voice, and her companions are perplexed by what she tells them about the stranger who has spoken to her. Worried by Tamara's agitated look, the nanny leads her back to the castle. As she leaves Tamara glances back and hears the Demon calling to her again: "I budesh' tï tsaritsey mira, podruga vechnaya moya" [And you shall be mistress of the world, my eternal companion].

Scene 2. A wild place in the mountains. Tamara's betrothed, Prince Sinodal, has stopped for the night with his caravan. An avalanche has blocked their path and de-layed their arrival at the castle of Prince Gudal. The prince orders a messenger to be sent on ahead to tell his future father-in-law that he will come at midday the following day. In his imagination Sinodal transforms himself into a falcon flying to his beloved: "Obernuvshis' sokolom, i k tebe, moya gorlitsa puglivaya, poletel bï ya" [Transformed into a falcon, my timid turtledove, I would fly to you]. The prince's old retainer consoles his master, and the camp makes preparation for the night. Servants pour wine, and everyone congratulates him on his forthcoming wedding: "Za zdorov'ye knyazya, ura!" [For the health of the Prince, hurrah!] The old retainer upbraids them for carousing in such an evil place and points to a distant chapel where a saint had once been slain. He begs the prince to say a prayer at the chapel before retiring, but the prince says they will do this as they set off on the morrow. The image of Tamara will protect him against evil. The camp falls silent, and in the darkness the Demon lulls the prince to sleep with visions of his beloved. Suddenly dark shadows creep toward the camp, and a band of Tartars falls on the sleeping men. In the skirmish that follows the prince is mortally wounded, and the old retainer tearfully confesses that his master will not live to see the dawn. The De-mon appears, and Sinodal dies with the name of Tamara on his lips.

Act 2, scene 1. A hall in Prince Gudal's castle. Guests are awaiting the arrival of the bridegroom. The messenger enters and delivers the news that Sinodal will arrive by mid-day. The guests drink a toast to the prince and princess: "Vino, vino, dayot ono vesel'ye i lyubov" [Wine brings joviality and love]. This is followed by two exotic dances, one for male dancers and one for female dancers. The high spirits are quickly dispelled, however, by off-stage noises, and a moment later the body of the prince is brought in. Tamara tries in vain to revive the corpse, but when she realizes that all is lost she tears off her wedding veil and sobs beside her beloved. The Demon, whom only Tamara can see, appears and tries to console her: "Nye plach', ditya" [Do not weep, child], but this only confuses her still more. Prince Gudal orders the corpse to be removed, believing that Tamara's strange apparition has been sent by God. The Demon appears to her again: "Na vozdushom okeanye, bez rulya i bez vetril" [On the ocean of the air, without rudder or sails], telling her that as soon as night shrouds the mountaintops he will come to her. Prince Gudal believes that his daughter has lost her reason, and she implores him to allow her to retire to a convent where the Lord will protect her. Eventually he agrees, and Tamara leaves with her handmaidens, the nanny, and the old retainer. Gudal, tormented by Tamara's affliction and outraged by the death of the prince, swears to avenge his death and leads his men from the castle with unsheathed sabers.

Act 3, scene 1. Part of a convent enclosure with the window of Tamara's cell visible. It is night and the old retainer sounds the vigil by striking a metal plate: "Spit khristianskiy mir" [The Christian world sleeps]. As he leaves, the Demon approaches and gazes at the illuminated window of the cell but fears entering the enclosure. He confesses that the moment he saw Tamara he began to envy the imperfect joys of earthly life; "Da ya yeyo lyublyu, da obnovleniye naydu! Chego zhe medlit'. Dlya dobra otkrit' moy dukh, i ya voydu!" [Yes, I love her, I shall find renewal! Why delay? My soul is open to goodness and I shall enter]. His way, however, is barred by the Angel, who warns him not to touch that which is dear to heaven. The Demon angrily disregards the Angel's words and enters the enclosure.

Scene 2. Tamara's cell with the narrow entrance to a little chapel that is illuminated by a lamp in front of an icon case. Tamara cannot sleep. She is constantly disturbed by a dream about a stranger and wonders who he might be: "Noch' tepla, noch' tikha, nye mogu ya usnut" [The night is warm, the night is calm, I cannot sleep]. Outside, the old retainer keeps up his vigil, but Tamara's thoughts about the stranger are answered by the sudden appearance of the Demon. The lamp in the chapel goes out and the two figures gaze intently at each other in the moonlight: "Ya tot, kotoromu vnimala ti v polunochnoy tishinye" [I am the one to whom you listened at the midnight hour], the Demon tells her. Tamara commands him to be silent, but he confesses that in her he has found all that he sought before he was cast out of heaven, and implores her to understand and acknowledge his suffering. The Demon rejects Tamara's fear of God and eternal damnation, because God is concerned with heaven and not earth. She feels compassion for his suffering but, acknowledging her own feminine frailty, entreats him to foreswear evil. "Otryoksya ya ot staroy mesti, otryoksya ya ot gordïkh dum; khochu ya s nebom primirit'sya, khochu lyubit', khochu molit'sya, khochu ya verovat' dobru" [I have renounced old vengeance, I have renounced proud thoughts, I want reconciliation with heaven, I want to love, I want to pray, I want to believe in goodness], the Demon swears. A chorus of distant nuns is heard singing matins, and Tamara, exhausted by her moral struggle, calls upon the Creator. The Demon, however, does not relent in his endeavors to win over Tamara and tells her that the fate of the earth is in her hands, for it is within her power to banish all evil. Unable to withstand the Demon's powerful arguments, she declares her love for him. The Demon kisses her and the angels are horrified. The little chapel to the side of Tamara's cell is suddenly brilliantly illuminated by the icon lamp and the Angel emerges, pointing to the ghost of the murdered Prince Sinodal. Tamara tears herself from the Demon's embrace and falls dead at the feet of the Angel.

Epilogue. The Angel conjures the Demon to be gone: "Skroysya, mrachnïy dukh" [Be gone, gloomy spirit!] Once more the Demon is abandoned and alone, and he curses heaven and earth. As the Angel prepares to lift up Tamara's body, smoke rises from below and fills the stage. To the sound of thunder and lightning the convent collapses. Apotheosis. The angels bear Tamara's body to heaven: "Mï dushu greshnuyu, dushu lyubivshuyu, dushu stradavshuyu k nebu" [We bear the sinful soul, the soul that loved and suffered, to heaven].

Synopsis of *Die Maccabäer*

Act. 1. The town of Modin. Children sitting on the steps of some houses weaving wreaths and garlands from flowers and ribbons. Leah greets her sons, Joarim, Benjamin, and Eleazar, but she has disowned her firstborn, Judah, for his shameful marriage to the Semite Naomi. Leah tells of the dream she has had in which, while pregnant with Eleazar, heaven had announced to her that God would grant a savior who would one day mount David's throne. A procession of shepherds and shepherdesses, led by Naomi, passes by Leah's house. Naomi offers Leah a wreath of lamb's fleece, but she refuses to accept it. Naomi bursts into tears, and at that moment Judah enters with a lion's hide. Leah chides him for his behavior and bemoans the fact that there is no hero who can free them from the Syrians. Naomi's father, Boas, together with Simei and the chorus of Semites accompanying Naomi, declare that the enemy is too strong and they are too weak to fight. This is enough to justify her opposition to her son's union with Naomi. The aged priest Jojakim appears, seeking out Leah and announces to her that God has chosen her sons to deliver the people of Israel. Leah realizes that her dream will be fulfilled. Jojakim tells her that she must choose one of her sons to follow him, and after a moment's hesitation she chooses Judah. He refuses, and Leah then turns to her second-born, Eleazar. Amri, one of the Semites, runs in to announce that the Syrian king Antiochus has taken Zion and that his troops are fast approaching Modin. With that, they appear at the gates, and Greek priests enter accompanied by a chorus of boys with incense burners. The Syrian commander Gorgias announces to the crowd that Zeus now reigns in the temple of Zion and that a temple to Pallas Athenae is to be built in Modin. The Syrians immediately erect an altar from the town walls and crown it with a golden effigy of the goddess. Horrified, Leah tries to spur Eleazar into action, but Amri and the Semites meekly accept the orders of Gorgias. Leah and Naomi refuse to worship the idol, and when Boas is forced to be a sacrifice to Pallas, Judah seizes Gorgias's sword, cuts Boas down, and destroys the altar. With this action Judah sparks the revolt against the Syrians. Naomi is left grief-stricken at the death of her father killed by the hand of her own husband, and Amri and the Semites declare a shameful end to Judah for his slaying of Boas.

Act 2, scene 1. A hill near Emaus; an open place. Judah and his army have defeated the Syrians. Judah wants to continue the fight, but Jojakim implores him to observe the Sabbath and rest before renewing the battle even if it means being overwhelmed by the enemy. The dilemma is resolved by the appearance of the Syrians who slaughter the praying Jojakim and the Israelites. Only Judah has taken up arms and disappears in the battle.

Scene 2. The apartments of Cleopatra, the daughter of King Antiochus. As Cleopatra reclines on a couch dreaming of Eros, she is joined by Eleazar who has fallen in love with her. He tells her about his lineage, and she announces that her father will grant him the crown of Zion. Hand in hand they depart for Jerusalem.

Scene 3. The streets of Modin. The people hail Leah and in the aria "Schlaget die

Pauke" she sings the praises of the Creator. Only Amri, Simei, and the Semites are not convinced by the rejoicing and foresee their destruction. Sarcastically they inform her that Eleazar has become Cleopatra's lover and demand vengeance for Boas's blood. With her remaining two sons, Benjamin and Joarim, Leah declares that victory is still possible, but the Semites mock her and try to wrest her sons from her. At this moment Naomi appears in mourning dress. Amri and Simei demand that Leah's sons be immediately led to Antiochus. Naomi's pleas are to no avail, and they are led away. The two women are left alone, and Leah finally realizes that she has been unjust to Naomi. Now united in their endeavors, the women rush off to Antiochus's camp.

Act 3, scene 1. Night at a place near Jerusalem. The crowd is praying before a temple, asking for deliverance. Judah appears full of shame at the death of his warriors, but the people rally to him. Naomi appears and tells him that his brothers have been seized and taken to the king. As the sun rises, they leave together.

Scene 2. The royal tent of Antiochus in the Syrian camp. The king enters gloomily, attended by Cleopatra and Eleazar, and their retinues. The cause of Antiochus's gloomy mood is a bad dream in which he has been denied David's crown. Encouraged by Cleopatra and Eleazar, however, his resolve is restored. Gorgias leads Leah into the tent, the latter having come to plead for her children's lives, but Antiochus is implacable. Only when Eleazar intervenes does the king relent, and he orders Benjamin and Joarim to be led in. Their lives will be spared, he tells them, if Leah will instruct them to accept Zeus as their god. The tyranny of Antiochus horrifies even Eleazar. Thunder peals out, and he orders Benjamin and Joarim to be burned alive. Eleazar rushes forward to join them, and Leah once again acknowledges him as her son. Gorgias leads the three brothers to their death in the flames. Their singing is heard off-stage accompanied by more peals of thunder. Suddenly Antiochus clutches at his breast in convulsions. The army led by Judah scatters the Syrian troops, and briefly Leah is reunited with her firstborn son before she, too, dies from grief. Naomi falls on her knees before Leah's corpse, and, as Judah proclaims, "The King of Zion is God alone," the opera ends.

Synopsis of *Néron*

Act 1. The home of Epicaris. As Epicaris welcomes her guests, Sacchus, Terpnos, Vindex, Rufus, and Pison, she rebukes them for their seditious talk about the feckless emperor and leads all except Vindex to drunken pleasures. Vindex ponders on the decline of Rome's glory: "Loin de ta grandeur vaine, loin d'un people déchu dont le César est le Dieu." He is approached by Chrysis, who begs for his protection from the drunken men who have accosted her. She tells him how she had grown up near the temple of Evander without knowing her mother. Masked Augustans (Chysis's persecutors) appear, and Vindex leads her to a side gallery. Among the revelers are the emperor Nero, Tigellinus, and Balbillus, who have seen the girl enter Epicharis's house. Epicaris herself confronts the intruders and demands that they remove their masks, but Nero orders his men to search the house at sword point, and Vindex and the girl are discovered. When Chrysis is brought forth she recognizes her mother, Epicharis, and falls into her arms. A mock marriage ceremony is acted out between Nero and Chrysis, and Epicaris slips a sleeping draught into her daughter's wine in the hope of saving her from disgrace. Dancers surround Nero and Chrysis, acting out an orgy and bacchanale. Vindex celebrates the event in an Epithalamium "Hymen! Hymen! fils d'Uranie." The act ends as Chrysis falls in a swoon and Epicharis claims to have killed her. Nero's anger turns on Vindex, and he is arrested.

Act 2. Poppaea's rooms in the imperial palace. Balbillus has informed her about the events in Epicharis's house, and he slips away as the emperor arrives. Poppaea's feelings of jealousy toward Nero's wife, Octavia, are allayed when she learns that Octavia, accused of adultery, has been killed. Nero declares Poppaea the new empress and presents her with a gift from Agrippina, a box of jewels, among which is a bracelet bearing a portrait of Chrysis. As her handmaidens deck her in the jewels, Nero sings his strophes "O lumière du jour." Vindex, who has been condemned for his actions, is brought before the emperor, but Poppaea demands to know his crime: "J'ai chanté l'Epithalame de Chrysis et de Néron," Videx replies. At this moment Epicharis arrives, pleading for the return of her daughter, abducted, so she believes, by Nero. With this revelation, everyone learns that the supposed death of Chrysis was only pretence. Nero is outraged, but through the intercession of Poppaea the lives of Vindex and Epicharis are spared.

Scene 2. A square in front of the temple of Evanders where various groups of people —Gauls, Germans, Ethiopians, and Christians—are assembled. One of the Christians makes a threatening gesture at the temple with his fist, and the Roman populace, demanding vengeance, drags him off. Epicharis and Vindex, now liberated, appear among the crowd singing praises to the glory of Caesar. A divertissement ensues with warriors and a group of bacchantes. Preceded by an elaborate procession, Nero finally appears in a chariot followed by Agrippina in whose honor the emperor promises grandiose games. Meanwhile Poppaea, guided by Balbillus, slips furtively into the nearby house belonging to Epicharis and informs her and Vindex that Chrysis is being held by Agrippina. On the steps of the temple Nero declares himself a god, and the crowd hails him.

Act 3, scene 1. Chrysis is alone in the little house where she grew up. Vindex enters and calms her; she declares that her Christian god will give her strength. They are joined by Epicharis, who informs them that Agrippina is dead but that their flight from Rome is prevented by a curfew on the streets. Vindex nevertheless leaves, and Chrysis falls into a sleep at her mother's feet. The two women are surprised by the sudden appearance of Nero who promises to exile Poppaea if Chrysis will follow him. Nero's vain attempts to seduce her finally turn to anger, but further action is halted by the appearance of Poppaea herself who now sees the proof of Caesar's infidelity. He calls his guard, but Vindex appears with a bared sword and, to Nero's annoyance, Chrysis and Epicharis are able to escape. Nero, dagger in hand, is contemplating Poppaea's punishment, but Saccus runs in to announce that Rome is in flames. It is Nero himself who gave the order for the burning of the city, and he plans to blame the Christians for it.

Scene 2. A square in Rome. Groups of frightened people rush in, fleeing the conflagration and cursing the Christians. As the people disperse, Epicharis, Vindex, and Chrysis enter. Nero now appears at the top of the Tower of Maecenas with Poppaea, Saccus, Tigellinus, and Balbillus. The emperor admires the scene of devastation and, asking for his lyre, sings strophes to Pergamum "O Pergame, o Pergame." The conflagration grows more intense, and, heeding the emperor's commands, the populace renews its demand for vengeance against the Christians. Chrysis confronts the populace in defense of her faith, but the people are in no mood for her protestations. Nero, who has seen the events taking place below, descends onto the square with his retinue. He tries to protect Chrysis from the mob but to no avail, and she is struck down and dies in her mother's arms. Vindex, sword in hand, rushes from the square, which is being slowly engulfed by flames. Nero, the court, and the populace leave hastily, but Epicharis remains with the corpse of her daughter to perish in the conflagration.

Act 4. A square in Rome. Nero has disappeared, and Tigellinus and Balbillus, sensing danger, prepare to flee from Rome, their pockets stuffed with gold and precious stones.

Lupus enters to issue a proclamation about the murder of Poppaea and the emperor's madness and flight. A force led by Vindex marches into the city.

Scene 2. The mausoleum of Augustus. A violent thunderstorm rages, and the doors fly open to admit the fugitive Nero. The ghosts of Claudius, Britannicus, Octavia, Agrippina, Poppaea, Chrysis, and other victims of Nero's tyranny appear to him.

Scene 3. The road to Rome. Vindex and his legions swear vengeance against Nero and march off toward the city. When they have gone Nero and Saccus emerge from the shrubbery, but they are spotted by a centurion. Unable to kill himself, Nero orders Saccus to do the deed for him. Vindex returns to discover the emperor dead. A meteor in the form of a cross appears in the heavens.

Synopsis of *The Merchant Kalashnikov*

Act 1. The royal chambers at Aleksandrovskaya Sloboda. The oprichniks are complaining that they have to play the part of monks and sing prayers, while their thoughts are really about girls, feasting, and getting drunk. The tsar's henchman, Skuratov, appears with the court jester Nikitka. The jester is accused of having brought Moscow's entire *zemstvo* to the court. The jester amuses the oprichniks with an allegorical song "V krayu dalyokom oryol zhil" [In a distant land lived an eagle]. The oprichniks threaten him for his audacity, but the jester is saved by Skuratov who announces the tsar's arrival. They all assume devout and submissive poses. The tsar receives Efim, Sergey, and Kolchin, who have come to beg him to return to Moscow. In his absence the tsar has appointed his wife's brother, Prince Mikhail, to rule the city, but he has been unable to control the violators of the people. "Which violators?" the tsar asks. "Your oprichniks," Efim and the petitioners reply. The tsar says that his oprichniks are devoted to a life of prayer, but he will come to Moscow. The petitioners leave, and Ivan, overhearing seditious talk from Kolïchev, has him arrested and taken away for execution. Wine is brought forth, and a golden goblet is filled. Ivan drinks and passes the goblet around to the other oprichniks as they acclaim the tsar. Only Kiribeyevich does not drink. When Ivan questions him, Kiribeyevich confesses that his melancholy is caused by an all-consuming passion for Alyona Dmitriyevna, a distant beauty: "Kak ya syadu, poyedu na likhom konye" [I shall mount and go on a mettlesome horse]. The tsar gives Kiribeyevich a precious ring and a pearl necklace to lure the object of his desires. Gusli and balalaika players and dancers appear to entertain the oprichniks, who toast Kiribeyevich and his future mistress.

Act 2. A square in the Zamoskvorechye region of Moscow. Evening. People are about to enter a church when a band of oprichniks passes by. Alyona Dmitriyevna appears from a large house wearing a richly adorned coat and a veil. She laments the fate of daughters and wives, and expresses her alarm at the attention of a young oprichnik who has been pursuing her. She is joined by Solomonida, and they are about to set off for vespers when they are waylaid by Kiribeyevich and Gryazny. Horrified by Kiribeyevich's advances, Alyona tells him she is a married woman and that her children are waiting for her. This has no effect whatsoever, but after a struggle she manages to break free, leaving Kiribeyevich holding her kerchief and veil. He swears that she shall be his and hurries off in pursuit of her. Solomonida calumniates against Alyona, telling the neighbors that she had been the one at fault. The mounting hullabaloo is interrupted by the appearance of Kalashnikov who learns about the incident that has just taken place. Deeply aggrieved, Kalashnikov hastens home. Rumors spread through the crowd that there is to be a boxing match the next day and that the tsar will attend.

Scene 2. A room in Kalashnikov's house. Kalashnikov pours out his grief and anger at his wife's seducer. He hears a knock at the gate and assumes it to be his brothers, but a moment later Alyona appears in a disheveled state. He accuses her of having been the cause of his disgrace. She denies it and pleads with her husband, saying that Nikitka had helped her make her escape as the oprichniks clashed with the populace on the way to Aleksandrovskaya Sloboda. Kalashnikov is finally convinced of Alyona's innocence and swears vengeance against the man who has violated her. She goes out to see the children, and Kalashnikov's brothers, Efim and Sergey, arrive. Kalashnikov tells them that he will attend the boxing match the next day and challenge the oprichnik who has disgraced the family name.

Act 3. An open space on the frozen Moscow River. A lively crowd has gathered to see the spectacle. Some boys are fighting in imitation of the contest that is about to take place. More fighting breaks out, and a police officer tries to restore order as the ringing of church bells announces the tsar's arrival. Ivan is drawn on a magnificently gilded sledge preceded by heralds, and the crowd hails him. Ivan takes his seat on an especially prepared stool. The Tartar strongman Chelubey addresses the crowd, inviting anyone who is prepared to fight him to step forward. Nikitka and Timofey both humiliate him by cunning. Tiring of this game, the tsar instructs his heralds to announce a real fight. Kiribeyevich steps forward and bows to Ivan, and when the heralds repeat the challenge Kalashnikov forces his way through the crowd and also bows to the tsar. The fighters take up their positions and Kiribeyevich learns who his opponent is. In the fight that follows Kiribeyevich is killed, against the wishes of the tsar who has commanded that this is not to be a fight to the death. Despite Alyona's entreaties, the tsar demands the execution of Kalashnikov: 'Where is his terror of God? Where is his fear of the tsar?' When questioned by Ivan as to why he killed Kiribeyevich, Kalashnikov says that this is a matter for him and God alone, and asks for the tsar's mercy toward his wife, children, and brothers. This last request is granted, but Kalashnikov is led away to the scaffold.

Appendix C

Programs of the Historical Concerts

Recital 1

William Byrd: Variations "The Carman's Whistle"

John Bull: *The King's Hunt*

Couperin: La ténébreuse, allemande; Le réveil-matin; La favorite, chaconne; La Fleurie; Le bavolet-flotant; La bandoline

Rameau: Le rappel des oiseaux; La poule; Gavotte avec 6 doubles

Domenico Scarlatti: Sonata in G minor "The Cat's Fugue," Kk30; Sonata in A[1]

J. S. Bach: Preludes and fugues in C minor and D major; Preludes in E♭ minor, E♭, and B minor[2] from *Das wohltemperierte Klavier*; Chromatic fantasy and fugue; Gigue in B♭; Saraband; Gavotte

Handel: Fugue from Suite in E minor; Air and variations "The Harmonious Blacksmith" from the Suite in E; Sarabande and Pasacaglia from Suite in G minor; Gigue from Suite in A; Aria con variazioni in D minor

C. P. E. Bach: Rondo in B minor (ed. Bülow); La Xénophone-La Sibille in C♯; Les langueurs tendres in C minor; La complaisante in B♭

Haydn: Theme and variations in F minor

Mozart: Fantasia in C minor, K.475; Gigue in G, K.574; Rondo in A minor; "Alla Turca" from the Sonata in A, K331

Recital 2

Beethoven

Eight piano sonatas:

No.14 in C♯ minor, Op. 27, No.2; No. 17 in D minor, Op.31, No. 2; No. 21 in C, Op.53; No. 23 in F minor, Op.57; No.27 in E minor, Op.90; No. 28 in A, Op. 101; No. 30 in E, Op.109; No.32 in C minor, Op.111

Recital 3

Schubert: Fantasy in C; Moments musicaux 1–6; Minuet in B minor; Impromptus in C minor and E♭

Weber: Sonata in A♭; Momento capriccioso; L'Invitation à la Valse; Polonaise in E

Mendelssohn: Variations sérieuses, Op. 54; Caprice in E minor, Op. 16, No. 2; Lieder ohne Worte No. 1 in E; No. 2 in A minor; No. 12 in F♯ minor; No. 30 in A; No. 13 in E♭;

---

1. The specific Sonata performed is not clear.
2. Other sources state B♭ minor. See Larry Sitsky, *Anton Rubinstein: An Annotated Catalog of Piano Works and Biography* (Westport, Conn.: Greenwood, 1998), p. 155. This is supported by the *Times* review of 19 May 1886.

No. 35 in B minor; No. 36 in E; No. 19 in A♭; No. 20 in E♭; No. 22 in F; No. 23 in A minor; Scherzo a capriccio in F♯ minor

Recital 4

Schumann: Fantasy in C, Op.17; Kreisleriana, Op. 16; Études symphoniques, Op.13; Sonata in F♯ minor, Op. 11; Phantasiestücke: "Des Abends"; "In der Nacht"; "Traumeswirren"; "Warum?"; "Vogel als Prophet"; Romance in D minor (Larry Sitsky gives Romance in B♭ minor, Op. 28, No. 1); Carnaval, Op. 9

Recital 5

Field: Nocturnes in E♭, A, D (B♭?)
Moscheles: Charakteristische Studien "Réconciliation," "Juno," "Conte d'Enfant"
Clementi: Sonata in B♭ (first and last movements)
Hummel: Rondo in B minor
Henselt: "Poème d'amour"; "Si oiseau j'étais" (Twelve Characteristic Concert Studies, Op. 2, No. 6); "Berceuse"; "La fontaine"; "Schmerz im Glück"
Thalberg: Étude in A minor, Op.45; "Don Giovanni" fantasy, Op. 14
Liszt: Étude de Concert in D♭; Valse-caprice; Consolations in E and D♭; Au bord d'une Source (Années de Pèlerinage, Book 1, No. 4); Hungarian Rhapsodies No. 6 in D♭ and No. 12 in C♯ minor
Rossini-Liszt: La gita in gondola; La regata veneziana; Serenade; La Danza (Soirées musicales)
Schubert-Liszt: Barcarolle; Serenade; Der Erlkönig; Valse in A♭ from Soirées de Vienne;
Meyerbeer-Liszt: Reminiscence de Robert le Diable

Recital 6

Chopin
Fantasy in F minor, Op. 49
Preludes, Op. 28: E minor, A, A♭, B minor, D♭, D minor
Mazurkas: B minor (Op. 30, No. 2, or Op. 33, No. 4)
Mazurka in F♯ minor (Op. 6, No. 1, or Op. 59, No. 3)
Mazurka in C major (Op. 7, No. 5; Op. 24, No. 2; Op. 33, No. 3; Op. 56, No. 2; Op. 67, No. 3; Op. 68, No. 1; and the Mazurka in C [1833] no opus; all are in this key)
Mazurka in B♭ minor (Op. 24, No. 4)
Ballades 1–4
Impromptu: F♯, Op, 36; G♭, Op. 51
Nocturnes: D♭, Op. 27, No. 2; G major, Op. 37, No. 2; C minor, Op. 48, No. 1
Barcarolle, Op. 60
Valses: A♭, Op. 34, No. 1; A minor, Op. 34, No. 2; A♭, Op.42
Scherzo in B minor, Op. 20
Sonata in B♭ minor, Op. 35
Berceuse, Op. 57
Polonaises: F♯ minor, Op. 44; C minor, Op. 40, No. 2; A♭ major, Op. 53

Recital 7

Chopin: Études in A♭, F minor, E major, C minor, E♭ minor, E♭ major, B minor, A♭ major,
A minor, C♯ minor, C minor (the studies in E major, Op. 10, No. 3; E♭ minor, Op. 10,
No. 6; and B minor, Op. 25, No. 10, do not share a key with the corresponding set. A♭
occurs twice and therefore corresponds to Op. 10, No. 10, and also Op. 25, No. 1. C
minor also occurs twice and therefore corresponds to Op. 10, No. 12, "The Revolutionary," and to Op. 25, No. 12)

Glinka: Tarantella in A minor; Barcarolle in G; Reminiscence of a Mazurka in B♭

Balakirev: Scherzo in B minor; Mazurka (of Balakirev's seven mazurkas only the first
two had been published before 1886, and therefore it was either the Mazurka in A♭ or
the second one in C♯ minor); Islamey

Cui: Scherzo in B♭; Polonaise in C

Rimsky-Korsakov: Étude in D♭, Op. 11, No. 4; Novelette in B minor, Op. 11, No. 2; Waltz
in C♯ major, Op. 15, No. 1

Lyadov: Étude in A♭, Op. 5; Intermezzo (one of the two Intermezzi in Op. 7—either the
one in D major or the one in F major)

Tchaikovsky: Chant sans paroles, Op. 2, No. 3; Valse-Scherzo, Op. 7; Romance in F minor,
Op. 5; Scherzo à la Russe, Op. 1, No. 1

Anton Rubinstein: Piano Sonata No. 3 in F, Op. 41; Theme and variations from Sonata
No. 2; Scherzo from Sonata No. 4

Nikolay Rubinstein: Feuillet d'Album, Valse in A♭

Appendix D

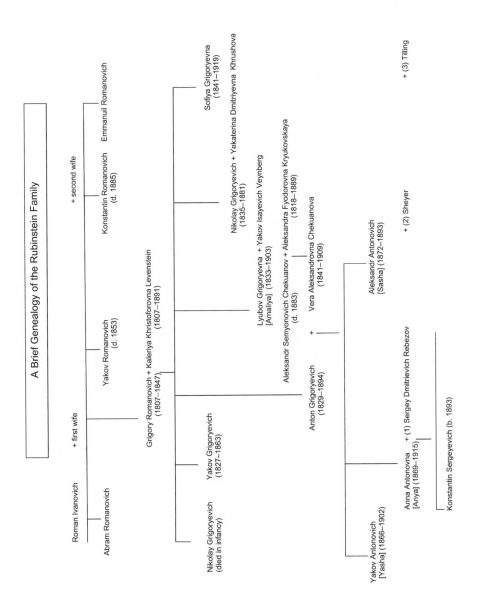

A Brief Genealogy of the Rubinstein Family

Roman Ivanovich

+ first wife

+ second wife

Abram Romanovich

Yakov Romanovich
(d. 1853)

Konstantin Romanovich
(d. 1885)

Emmanuil Romanovich

Grigory Romanovich + Kaleriya Khristoforovna Levenstein
(1807–1847)   (1807–1891)

Nikolay Grigoryevich
(died in infancy)

Yakov Grigoryevich
(1827–1863)

Lyubov Grigoryevna + Yakov Isayevich Veynberg
[Amaliya] (1833–1903)

Nikolay Grigoryevich + Yekaterina Dmitriyevna Khrushova
(1835–1881)

Sofiya Grigoryevna
(1841–1919)

Anton Grigoryevich
(1829–1894)

+

Aleksandr Semyonovich Chekuanov + Aleksandra Fyodorovna Kryukovskaya
(d. 1883)   (1818–1889)

Vera Aleksandrovna Chekuanova
(1841–1909)

Aleksandr Antonovich
[Sasha] (1872–1893)

Yakov Antonovich
[Yasha] (1866–1902)

Anna Antonovna + (1) Sergey Dmitrievich Rebezov
[Anya] (1869–1915)

+ (2) Sheyer

+ (3) Tilling

Konstantin Sergeyevich (b. 1893)

Appendix E

Rubinstein—Selected Topics from *Gedankenkorb* by Subject

Art and Musical Aesthetics

(1) A man feels within himself a calling for a certain profession, art, for instance; it fills his being and all his efforts are directed toward achieving something great, beautiful, and good in this field; he devotes his life to this profession. But in the end it turns out that he would have been better off choosing something else, because he was *not one of the elect*. How could God be so heartless as to lead a human child all his life along a false path without giving him any sign to desist? This is enough to make him an atheist. And the most tragic thing in this is that the artist will always find people who will say of his works: "I liked them!"

(2) There are artists who display startling achievements, who are even irreproachable in their art, but whose influence with the public is limited or even quite negligible. On the other hand, there are others whose work has many shortcomings, but the public is enthralled by it. It would appear that the public, in its perception of an artistic work, is subject to some magnetic force, that the artist's personality carried great weight in the evaluation of his work, that there still exists a certain moral magnetism.

(3) In its perception of works of art the public is very condescending and that is something to wonder at. Why is it? Is it indifference, goodness of nature, or stupidity? I think, most likely, it is contempt (it's not worth getting agitated over this!). Things will stay like that so long as art serves only to entertain, satisfy, and kill time, and, consequently, until it is seen as something that can have a serious impact on life.

(4) I distinguish three different trends in art up to the present time. The first lasted approximately until 1855. At this time absolute virtuosity predominated and was acknowledged in all branches [of art]. Only Italian opera and the operas of Meyerbeer were listened to with enjoyment (and even this, for the most part, was because of the virtuoso performances of male and female singers). It was a time when people only enjoyed the charms of fantasies or variations on celebrated opera themes, slight and vapid salon pieces, dance rhythms with the addition of concerto bravura. After this, approximately until 1880, the public and artists turned toward the works of the classic composers and demonstrably rejected anything new. The symphony concert, and even chamber music (the quartet), could count on the widespread support of the attending public, and the opera fantasy on a concert program was despised as anti-artistic. And, finally, the present time, when everything strives toward the modern, sees the past only from the point of view of historical interest, and desires the transcendental in all branches of the art. Will this latest trend in taste last, or will a reaction set in? Or will the question of something else arise? What could this "something else" be? Folk music? That means starting from the beginning all over again!

(5) In music it is not possible to prove anything—whether it is beautiful or ugly. If someone were to say Beethoven's Ninth Symphony is ugly music, you might turn away from him, but it would be impossible to prove to him that he was talking nonsense. Musical and aesthetic education helps to distinguish in music the beautiful and the ugly and then only conditionally, because subjective feelings play too great a role in this. Music is something akin to faith: proving that God exists is also impossible. Happy are they who have the true feeling in both instances.

(6) The correct declamation of words set to music is a straightjacket for melody. The poetry gains through this, the music often doesn't. And another big question—what would the listener prefer?

(7) Brahms I consider the heir of Schumann, myself the heir of Schubert and Chopin, and the both of us the last representatives of the third epoch of musical art.

(8) When examining present-day musical compositions it becomes apparent that, despite all the unusual and even very interesting methods of notation, the musical thought in them for the most part is actually commonplace and sometimes banal.

(9) When there is a lack of musical ideas, a leitmotif comes in very handy.

(10) The piano is my favorite instrument, because in the musical respect it represents something whole; every other instrument, the human voice included, in the musical sense is only a half.

(11) An opera composer must not fear the "too much," the "too long," the "too expansive" in his work; this is food for the conductor who would consider his dignity affronted if there were not anything to shorten, cross out, or axe in a composition. Otherwise the composer risks having the main thing or the best thing crossed out because shortening *there has to be*—that is the *conditio sine qua non* of having something accepted for production.

(12) Our present-day art, in all its fields, is guided by realism, tendentiousness, and programs, and for that reason it denies an absolute artistic character since it entails reflection. The arts no longer serve as an expression of that striving for the unknown but are the articulation of cognitive thinking. Many people consider this more correct, but for me it seems to demean the significance of art: it takes away its mystical and mythological character.

(13) It is a mistake to suppose that music is a universal language; it is indeed a language, but, like any language, it has to be studied in order to be intelligible and to give pleasure. There is artistic music, and there is folk music. The former may become accessible to the educated classes of all nations—and more likely in its vocal (opera) rather than in its instrumental manifestation. This is the same thing as making a thorough study of a foreign language, but its spirit will remain quite alien to another person; to the uneducated classes it will be unintelligible in both its manifestations. Folk music is perfectly intelligible and affords pleasure only to its people, and moreover as much to the educated as the uneducated classes. The language of music requires the same study as other languages, that is, he who studies it from childhood will master it—in more advanced years learning it will scarcely be possible. And just as the ancient Hebrew or Sanskrit languages are a pleasure for those who understand them and only gobbledegook for those who do not, so music for those who do not understand is at best only a pleasant sound, whereas for those who do understand, it is the language of the heavens.

(14) A composer who is now ignored must console himself with the hope that sometime, possibly even in the field of music, excavations will yield him up when the right time comes.

Artists and Performers

(1) An artist must not be born to wealth. Concerns about his daily bread have a good effect on his *Sturm und Drang* period; they give a dramatic element to his art. But they must not last too long. The artist must, in the end, achieve a life free of material concerns otherwise cares about his subsistence might restrict or even completely destroy his art.

(2) An artist, especially a creative artist, cannot exist without recognition; without it his art will dry up from the bitterness of doubts in his own abilities. This does not need to be widespread recognition—the recognition of a small circle, sometimes just a few adherents, is sufficient. It is therefore a good thing for those happy composers who manage to acquire fanatical adherents, that is to say, proselytes.

(3) Success affects a noble artistic nature in a stimulating and invigorating way, but on a less artistic nature it leads to self-adulation, and sometimes to a halt in development or even a decline. Failure, even if it pains the former, does not make them despair but rouses them to continue the struggle and to strive forward, whereas the latter are killed by it.

(4) The phonogram can immortalize a musical performance. Artists, beware!

(5) A young woman could ridicule a sixty-year-old man, who speaks to her of love. The public could do the same with regard to a sixty-year-old artist singing or playing about love. Performers should take note of this.

(6) Playing the piano means moving your fingers; performing on the piano means moving your soul. Nowadays you hear mostly the former.

Creative Work

(1) There are artists (painters, sculptors, etc.) who toil all their lives on one and the same work in order to bring it to perfection; there are others who during their lives produce an incalculable number of works, which are, however, far from perfection. The latter seem to me the more logical. There cannot be absolute perfection in any human work, but in imperfect works there may be as much beauty and things worthy to be appreciated as you like. In creative productivity there is something attractive because it is naïve, but at the same time faith in the possibility of creating something perfect bears on it the stamp of self-importance.

Religion

(1) Allegory and symbol—these are the weapons used by the Church when it wants seriously to tread on someone's toes. "This is an allegory" or "This is conceived symbolically"—such is its reply to scientific proof that threatens to become embarrassing.

(2) What is the highest aim of the believer? Pleasing his God. And of the nonbeliever? Pleasing humanity. The latter seems to me nearer the ideal, because the believer is certain of his reward, whereas the nonbeliever just does his duty without thinking about a reward.

(3) "Everyone must save his own soul"—this is a wise saying. After all, in each person there is the feeling that over him there is something or someone who is invisible and inexplicable, but powerful and definitive, to which he can turn in his grief, sorrow, joy, or

gratitude. Whether he holds this sacred in stone or in an animal, in a natural or a supernatural being, in Jehovah, Christ, Allah, Mahomet, Buddha, Ormuz, Ariman, Brahma, or Vishnu, etc., makes no difference, so long as he recognizes a morality that can improve him and set him on the path of goodness. Consequently he must not be governed by religion but by morality; therefore I can understand preachers and missionaries only as teachers of morality but not as teachers of religion. I really cannot understand at all why people have to be Christians, Jews, or Mohammedans—and least of all why Catholics, Orthodox Christians, and Protestants! People would be so much calmer and happier if they were taught to think and to act only in the spirit of goodness and [mutual] benefit, in the spirit of justice and love for one's neighbor, and leave them to believe in, and pray to, whatever they want, and thereby not have religion foisted on them. Until this principle is acknowledged, any real progress in humanity will be called into question.

(4) I was at a "Children's Charity" festival in London at St. Paul's Cathedral. Thousands of children were arranged in a circle, singing anthems and chorales to the accompaniment of the organ. This produced such a powerful impression on me that I could not restrain my tears. The most inveterate atheist would not have been able to resist thinking about the Creator. The priest concluded the ceremony with a sermon. This gave me the impression that the preacher did not want to let God speak for himself.

(5) If you think how much exaggeration, understatement, embellishment, and distortion is contained in the verbal retelling of an event, even one that only occurred the day before, how much of the personal, the malicious, the excessively condescending, the critical, the laudatory, the factional, the improbable, and the fictitious is written in newspaper reports (and afterward it is they that largely serve as the sources for biographies and history) about public figures, then the reading of biographies and the study of history (except for the historical facts) will seem superfluous or useless. And how much more, to an even greater degree, this concerns religious traditions, both oral and written. Nonetheless all religions are based on them, even our faith itself.

(6) It is a mistake to suppose that an artist (painter, poet, musician, or sculptor) must believe in God and be pious in order to fashion a religious subject correctly and well. This is the same thing as saying an artist working on a mythological subject needs to be a pagan. Art is pantheistic. In each blade of grass it sees divinity and thereby something even more—artistic material. The religion of art is aesthetics; it does not require from the artist any church religion, whereas he can make his forms sacred. Let that serve as a reply to those who are amazed that I, for all my non-religiousness, prefer to work with spiritual subjects.

History and Politics

(1) When, after 1871, I was traveling down the Rhine from Mainz to Rotterdam, this is what I felt: this river could flow calmly now, it has finished with the fighting, and now it has only to put up on its waves with English ladies and American misses, putting pencil marks in their beautiful Baedeckers against the Loreley Rock, Stolzenfels, Rolandseck, etc. While I was sailing down the Danube from Vienna to Galati, I was looking at the passengers on the steamboat (Germans, Hungarians, Serbs, Romanians, Turks, and Russians), and it became clear to me that here a terrible tragedy was yet to be played out, the subject of which would be the Eastern Question, and that the peace in Europe depended more than anything on the outcome of this tragedy.

(2) Of all five continents in the world, Europe deserves the greatest pity. So worthy

of amazement in terms of the growing progress of civilization, but in the political sense, even to the present time, it has clung steadfastly to the mediaeval theory of conquest and the rule of might. But now, when nations have started to think and express themselves, they can pose the question: "How did it happen that we belong to this and not some other country? Why are we a part of another country and not an independent entity," etc., etc.? For that reason, peace in Europe is only conceivable if Europe can be divided up on a *completely new basis* according to the religious, linguistic, and commercial (or industrial) interests of the peoples, because, as it stands today, there is not even a tiny stretch of it that could not be the cause of a general war. Therefore all the present-day peace congresses can only cause an ironic smile.

(3) In my opinion, in the very near future two great turning points will face us: one in the field of politics—a war which will change the face of Europe; the other in the field of social affairs—the development of socialism, which will question even private ownership. I am not so bound to life, but I would like to live long enough to see one or the other turning points, because I am sure that the result will be something completely new in human thinking in all fields (including art) and, I hope, more interesting than what seems to be new to us today.

(4) It is in vain that governments allow the socialist question to develop from below. This question is so important and so unforeseen in its consequences that governments ought in their own interests to study it and master it if they do not wish to be drawn into a universal social catastrophe or at least a full-scale social upheaval. Whether this is good or bad in itself—who can say beforehand with any certainty? In any case, this has the effect of an avalanche, and for its coming we shall not have long to wait.

(5) It is not the need for large numbers of troops that is impeding the start of the next war, but the terrible and daily increasing inventions for defense and destruction, and the endless financial resources needed for this.

(6) Europe is interesting for its past, America for its future. There is little to console one in the present on either side of the globe.

(7) Germany can, in part, thank the neutrality of Russia in 1870 for its unification and for its present-day staggering power. That Germany understands this and sees in Russia a deus ex machina of the political future is borne out by the brilliant chess movement of the triple alliance (Germany, Austria, and Italy); but the dual alliance (Russia and France) brought about by this can be considered checkmate for Germany.

(8) Monarchs never find their people sufficiently mature for freedom.

(9) A people strive for enlightenment, the despot gives it—only instead of electric or gas lighting (in the figurative sense) the people get tallow candles. Should we be surprised that the people are dissatisfied and inclined to revolution?

(10) Russia has a brilliant future, for the Russian has a gift [to strive] for the best. For now she is "La Belle au bois dormant" guarded by despotism. But if Prince "Freedom" awakens her with a kiss, then, after she has first gone through a certain transitional period, she will be able to surpass all the other countries of Europe, not only in political might but in genuine and high-principled strength.

(11) However much I love my country and my nation, I can express the wish for it to submit, that is, be beaten in the war that is going to come soon. That is because the consequence of this would probably be a complete change in the form of government, and thereby an awakening from the lethargy in which it has slumbered until now. Another result would be to fashion and alter its character and intellectual strength, even if this is attended for a time by disturbances and misfortunes; in other words, it could expect a brilliant future. If, on the other hand, it should be the victor in the next war, it will

be subject to the present status quo for an incalculable period of time—that is, it will remain a nation of superbly gifted and eternally speechless children.

Social Issues

(1) I feel no compassion for someone who gets into trouble out of laziness, but I feel the greatest pity for someone who looks for work and cannot find it—and nowadays there are more and more of such people. The state and society must answer for this, and they will pay dearly unless they can find a radical solution quickly.

Education

(1) Something outstanding rarely comes from the children of rich parents. In safeguarding their material future, they hide from them the understanding that work and self-reliance are needed. Is it not possible to think up some means whereby children could only find out about the material property of their parents when their education is complete, and let them be so certain that they were poor that they would have to achieve everything through their own efforts?

(2) At one time people had great belief in upbringing, now they are more for education. The combination of both these requirements is an ideal; but where you encounter them singly, I prefer the former to the latter.

(3) The upbringing of children is a great responsibility not only to society but toward the state. In our times parents do not recognize this sufficiently. It [should be] based less on the education of children than on developing the essential qualities of their character. The ancient Spartans had a sure sense of this, if not in the principles then in its fundamental ideas.

Domestic Matters

(1) Cooking smells in a house are offensive, but for me far more offensive in a house is the smell of gold.

(2) I would like to have as much money as my needs in life require. For surplus I have no taste, and to amass a fortune, even for the sake of leaving it to my children, I consider a bad thing. Even if this is harsh, I find it far more correct to force my sons, after the completion of their education, to earn money for themselves, and for my daughters, when they get married, to give as a dowry only as much as necessary so that any husband with a vile material position would not reprimand her for the fact he has to feed her.

Morality

(1) A twenty-year-old youth dies from consumption. At the same time a seventy-two year-old man is playing lawn tennis in the neighboring garden. "The ways of providence are inscrutable"; I know this well, but I would still like to ask for some kind of logic.

(2) As salt and pepper do to food, so a struggle gives life flavor.

(3) I live in a constant state of contradiction with myself, that is, I think differently from the way I feel. In the ecclesiastical and religious sense I am an atheist, but I am convinced that it would be a misfortune if people had no religion, no church, no God. I am a republican, but I am convinced that the only true form of government for people

that is suitable for their own existence is strictly monarchical. I love my neighbor as I do myself, but I am convinced that people scarcely deserve anything better than disrespect, etc. And all this relates not to uncultured but to cultured and even outstanding people. This contradiction in my nature poisons my life, because, logically speaking, it ought to be that a person thinks the way he feels and feels the way he thinks. Can it really be that I am a monster?

(4) Die—willingly, just don't get decrepit.

(5) Death often comes so suddenly and so unexpectedly that I am always obsessed by the thought: just another minute and you might not be here. That is the cause of my possibly excessive industry. After all, I, too, would like to say something to humanity.

Aesthetics

(1) Nature has forms, but it does not have any limiting conventions—art, on the other hand, cannot do without them. The stage for drama, and on it—the action; the frame for a picture; movements for a symphony, etc. Therefore realism without limitations in art becomes unnatural.

(2) It seems to me that when you sit at a writing table illuminated by an electric lamp your thoughts acquire a different character than when the table is illuminated by stearin or tallow candles. In the case of the former your thoughts become more optimistic, and in the case of the latter more pessimistic. Should this not be a description of pessimism as a whole? That it arises by a lack of lighting?

Paradoxes and Irony

(1) I planned to write a work—"Love: Theme and Variations"—but abandoned it because there was once a time when I could find the theme but didn't have sufficient knowledge for the variations, whereas now I could easily write the variations but lack the necessary ability for the theme.

(2) The best way to pass time under a monarchy, where all expression is forbidden, is to play cards. I am also for such card playing (except with regard to games of chance, of course) in republics, where people seek open expression, because I agree with the saying *La parole est d'argent, le silence est d'or,* and not only in politics.

(3) When a performer is asked to play something else at the end of a set program during a court concert, he must never imagine that this is out of a sense of rapture on the part of the audience but simply because the clock has not yet chimed the hour for them to depart.

(4) Usually, thanks to the stories and descriptions of travelers, people get to know countries and nations better, and acquire for themselves a more accurate idea of them than that which was formed through ignorance or prejudice. Only with regard to Russia and its people can one not say this. This surprises me most of all in artists (Germans, Frenchmen, and Italians), who have been coming here constantly and in multitudes. They are greeted in the most brilliant, the most cordial, and the most generous way by the court, the public, and by private persons, but when they return to their homelands— with very rare exceptions—they have not found it worthy to make the effort, or have had no desire in general, to correct the false notions about this country. Ingratitude—that is putting it mildly!

(5) I seem illogical even to myself—a republican and a radical in life but a conservative and a despot in art.

(6) For the most part, people think about God when they act. If they always thought only about humanity when they act, they would act less frivolously because God is merciful whereas people are not.

(7) There are people who appeared too early in the world with their caste of thoughts, and there are also those who appeared too late; the former are called martyrs, and the latter are called failures. To appear in the world at the right time—now that's the thing. Only the few can manage it!

Axioms

(1) Writing is a pleasure, being published—a responsibility.

(2) Cosmopolitanism can be acquired, patriotism is inborn.

(3) I judge a town by the number of bookshops in it.

(4) Life is the enigma—death is the solution.

(5) If you want to get a good reception somewhere, you have to appear there but rarely.

(6) You can tell a nation's level of culture by the way it amuses itself.

(7) That mankind has created art makes him equal to God.

Cynicism

(1) How did it happen that mankind must pay for his food, and if he cannot do this, then die from starvation, whereas all the other living souls have their food for nothing? He must also pay for his birth, and also for his death. This means that money is the chief condition for having the right to be a person. But how does this relate to the creation of the world? Was it not that Satan's serpent showed to our great primogenitress not just the apple but the sparkle of gold?

(2) Let each person do everything of which he is capable, but let the rest not concern him.

(3) If you want some action to be unnoticed by people around you, you have to announce your intention loudly. If you make a secret of it, then this will arouse curiosity, suspicion, and misinterpretation—and will become the topic of the day.

(4) For Jews I am a Christian, for Christians I am a Jew; for Russians I am a German, for Germans I am a Russian; for the classicists I am an innovator, for the innovators I am a reactionary, etc. Conclusion: not fish, nor flesh, a pitiful character.

Journalism and Critics

(1) I willingly acknowledge the freedom of the press but not its impudence. In our times newspapers have such a detrimental character that I would have no qualms about calling these journalists anarchists, and their newspapers—bombs. Their methods, in political and artistic matters, as well as social and private (!) affairs, are so indecent, so unrestricted, and so offensive that it becomes necessary to hide from them because it has become almost impossible to get away from them. This can be said most of all about France, but all the time it is becoming more noticeable in other countries as well.

Notes

Introduction

1. Cuthbert Cronk, *Anton Rubinstein: A Study* (London: Novello, 1900), p. 10.

2. The *kuchkists* were members of the group of nationalist composers headed by Balakirev from the late 1850s. The terms *kuchka* (handful) and *moguchaya kuchka* (mighty handful) were coined by Stasov in the late 1860s or early 1870s as a sobriquet for the group that consisted of five main composers: Balakirev, Rimsky-Korsakov, Musorgsky, Borodin, and Cui. The term *kuchkism* could be defined as a style of compositional technique established by Glinka and subsequently developed by the nationalist composers.

3. Richard Taruskin, *Defining Russia Musically* (Princeton, N.J.: Princeton University Press, 1997), p. xiii.

4. Egon Gartenberg, *Vienna: Its Musical Heritage* (University Park: Pennsylvania State University Press, 1968), p.175.

5. L. A. Barenboym, ed., *A. G. Rubinshteyn: Literaturnoye naslediye* [A. G. Rubinstein: Literary heritage], 3 vols. (Moscow: Muzïka, 1983–86), 3:89.

6. Ibid., 3:109.

7. This reluctance was partly owing to the second autobiography that Rubinstein began to write early in 1890 but later destroyed. See his letter to Senff of 22 August–3 September 1892: "I do not wish to tell E. I. Zabel anything, since the biography written by me at the moment can be of interest only if it contains something new; if everything was already known beforehand, that terrible 'why' looms up. Therefore I will categorically not take part personally in any reports or corrections concerning my biography" (Barenboym, *Literaturnoye naslediye*, 3:130–31).

8. Marina Frolova-Walker, "The Disowning of Anton Rubinstein," in *"Samuel" Goldenberg und "Schmuyle": Jüdisches und Antisemitisches in der russischen Musikkultur,* Studia Slavica Musicologica 27 (Berlin: Verlag Ernst Kuhn, 2003).

9. Grade 2 of the Russian civil hierarchy equal to a general in the land forces.

1. Prologue: The Historical Context

1. See F. A. Brockhaus and I. A. Efron, eds., *Entsiklopedicheskiy slovar': Rossiya* [Encylopaedic dictionary: Russia] (St. Petersburg, 1898; reprint. Leningrad: Lenizdat, 1991), p. 473.

2. A further estate, the *meshchanstvo* (ordinary townsfolk), was later introduced to define a class of petty artisans that could not be counted among the more wealthy merchants.

3. J. Klier: "Jewish Emancipation," in *Civil Rights in Imperial Russia,* ed. Olga Crisp and Linda Edmondson (Oxford: Clarendon, 1989), p. 126.

4. Ibid., p. 124.

5. Michael Florinsky, *Russia: A History and an Interpretation,* 2 vols. (New York: Macmillian, 1953/1960), 2:806 n. 6.

6. These details are given in *AGR*, vol 1. In the version by Findeyzen the issue of this first marriage was two sons (Grigory and Emmanuil) and a daughter, who "is unknown."

7. CBFA, p. 3.

8. *AGR*, 1:14.

9. FOZD, p. 3.

10. *NGR*, p. 16.

11. Ibid., p. 6.

12. *AR*, 1:65. The inconsistency in dates was picked up by the *Times*. The author of Rubinstein's obituary remarked: "The precise date of his birth is usually given as November 30, but in his so-called autobiography, a series of desultory reminiscences published at the time of his artistic jubilee in 1889, he states that, though born on November 16, he had been so long in the habit of regarding November 18 as his birthday that he had no intention of changing it. The point, by a curious chance, has acquired some importance, as, on the assumption that his own date was the right one, he had completed his 65th year, but not if the ordinary date be correct" (*Times*, 21 November 1894, p. 10).

13. *AR*, 1:66.

14. The population was 352,000 in 1863, growing to 1,036,000, almost a threefold increase, by the end of the century. See Brockhaus and Efron, *Entsiklopedicheskiy slovar' Rossii*, p. 79.

15. An area of the Zamoskvorechye; the name is still preserved in Moscow street names (the four Golutvinskiye pereulki).

16. Quoted in *NGR*, p. 18.

17. *CPSS*, 8:72.

18. *AR*, 1:66.

19. Letter to Kaleriya Khristoforovna, 28 December/9 January 1890, in *LN*, 3:111.

20. *Po Moskve. Progulki po Moskvye i eya khudozhestvennïm i prosvetitel'nïm uchrezhdeniyam* [Around Moscow. Walks around Moscow and its artistic and educational establishments), ed. N. A. Genyike et al. (Moscow: Sabashnikov, 1917; reprint, Moscow: Izobrazitel'noye iskusstvo, 1991, p. 307).

21. These details, first provided by Neustroyev in *Russkaya starina*, served as the basis for the accounts of Villoing's early career given by Findeyzen and Catherine Drinker Bowen.

22. *AR*, 1:67.

23. NEUS, p. 253.

24. "A. G. Rubinshteyn, vstrecha s nim v 1839 g." [A. G. Rubinstein, a meeting with him in 1839], *Russkaya starina* (May 1886), pp. 440–41.

25. NEUS, p. 253.

26. Ibid.

27. *AR*, 1:68.

28. In *AR* Rubinstein mistakenly reported: "I stayed in Paris the whole year" (LN, 1:68). In fact, he only returned to Paris in the late spring of 1842, after a long tour of Germany, Austria, Britain, and Scandinavia.

29. NEUS, p. 253.

30. The Allegro was not performed with an orchestra but with a second piano. Neustroyev gives the name of the second pianist as "Shiman" [Schiemann?] and Barenboym as "Shimon."

31. Alan Walker, *Franz Liszt: The Virtuoso Years, 1811–1847* (London and Boston: Faber and Faber, 1988), p. 130.

32. Robert Wangermée, "Conscience et inconscience du virtuose romantique. A propos des années parisiennes de Franz Liszt," in *Musical Life in 19th-Century France,* ed. Peter Bloom, Vol. 4, *Music in Paris in the Eighteen-Thirties* (New York: Stuyvesant, 1987), pp. 553–56.

33. Impromptu No. 2 in F♯ major, Op. 36; completed in 1839.

34. *LN,* 3:195.

35. *AR,* 1:69.

36. The original program of 9 January is reproduced in CBFA, p. 37.

37. NEUS, p. 259.

38. NSCJT, p. 194.

39. NEUS, p. 254.

40. Rubinstein's first piano composition, the little study *Ondine,* was published by Schlesinger in Berlin in 1843. It was dedicated to Countess Mariya Aleksandrovna Benkendorf (1820–1880), who had married Prince Grigory Petrovich Volkonky (1808–1882) in 1838. Schumann wrote a brief and encouraging review of the piece for the *Neue Zeitschrift für Musik.*

41. Gebel died a few months later, on 3 May 1843 (n.s.).

42. *AR,* 1:70.

43. *NGR,* p. 26.

44. *AR,* 1:70.

45. Siegfried Dehn, *Theoretisch-praktische Harmonielehre mit angefügten Generalbassbeispielen* (Berlin, 1840).

46. Rudolph Levenstein (or Lewenstein) may have been a relative of Kaleriya Khristoforovna

47. Quoted in *AGR,* 1:72. *Oskolki proshlogo* [Fragments of the past], the unfinished reminiscences of Vera Rubinstein, remained for many years in the hands of Anton's granddaughter, A. S. Rubinstein. They were later handed over to the Leningrad [St. Petersburg] Public Library.

48. *AR,* 1:69.

49. Lev Ginzburg, *Henri Vieuxtemps,* ed. Herbert R. Axelrod, trans. I. Levin (Neptune, N.J.: Paganiniana, 1984), p. 154.

50. *AR,* 1:72.

51. Ibid.

52. Ibid., 1:73.

53. Christoph Wilhelm Hufeland, editor, among others, of the *Enzyklopädisches Wörterbuch der medizinischen Wissenschaften,* Berlin, 1828–49. His book on the art of prolonging life was translated into several languages.

54. Emanuel Geibel was made a member of the Society on 25 January 1846. See *LN,* 1:209.

55. *AR,* 1:74.

2. Return to Russia and First Opera, 1848–53

1. *AR,* 1:69.

2. Henselt remained in Russia. For a time he taught music at the St. Petersburg

School of Jurisprudence, and then in 1863 he was appointed inspector of the Imperial Women's Institutes.

3. *AGR*, 1:146.

4. S. Vengerov, "Recent Literature," in F. A. Brockhaus and I. A. Efron, eds., *Entsiklopedicheskiy slovar': Rossiya* [Encylopaedic dictionary: Russia] (St. Petersburg, 1898; reprint, Leningrad: Lenizdat, 1991), p. 634.

5. Joseph Frank, *Dostoevsky: The Seeds of Revolt, 1821–1849* (London: Robson Books, 1977), p. 275.

6. In the period from 1841 to 1852 Count Lev Alekseyevich Perovsky headed the ministry.

7. *NGR*, p. 33.

8. FOZD, p. 35.

9. The early Concerto in F major probably disappeared with Rubinstein's confiscated trunk, the one in C was performed but is lost, and the Concerto in D minor was reworked as the Octet, Op. 9.

10. Jeremy Norris, *The Russian Piano Concerto,* Vol. 1, *The Nineteenth Century* (Bloomington: Indiana University Press, 1994), p. 25.

11. Carl Schuberth arrived in Russia from Germany in 1835 and two years later was appointed director of music at St. Petersburg University. In 1842 he was appointed director of the St. Petersburg Philharmonic Society, a position he held until his death in 1863.

12. Letter to Zotov, 4/16 February 1850, *LN*, 2:22.

13. The full program of the concert is given in James Stuart Campbell, ed. and trans., *Russians on Russian Music: An Anthology,* Vol. 1, 1830–80 (Cambridge: Cambridge University Press, 1994), p. 48.

14. Letter to Bernhard, 12/24 June 1850, *LN*, 2:22. Bernhard was a pupil of Field and founded his music shop in St. Petersburg in 1829.

15. Bernhard actually published them in 1851, although they were later republished as Rubinstein's Op. 64.

16. On 17/29 December Rubinstein took part in a concert given by Nissen-Saloman, where he played the solo part in Mendelssohn's Piano Concerto in G minor.

17. *AR*, 1:81.

18. Ibid.

19. Letter to Kaleriya Khristoforovna, 28 December 1859/9 January 1851, *LN*, 2:25.

20. In 1851 Yelena Pavlovna's daughter, Yekaterina Mikhaylovna, married Georg August of Mecklenburg-Strelitz.

21. Letter to Kaleriya Khristoforovna, 12/24 January 1851, in *LN*, 2:27.

22. *LN*, 2:29.

23. Ibid., 2:25

24. Rossini's *Guillaume Tell* was staged in Moscow in the fall of 1849 under the title *Charles the Bold.*

25. Letter to Kaleriya Khristoforovna, 12/24 January 1851, *LN*, 2:27.

26. Ibid., 26 March/7 April 1851, 2:31–32.

27. *LN*, 2:30.

28. Ibid., 2:31–32.

29. FOZD, pp. 31–32.

30. Letter to Kaleriya Khristoforovna 16/28 April 1851, *LN*, 2:32.

31. Ibid., 8/20 August 1851, *LN*, 2:32.

32. Ibid.

33. Ibid., 27 September/9 October 1851, *LN*, 2:33.

34. Lev Aronovich Barenboym, ed., *A. G. Rubinshteyn: Izbrannïye pis'ma* [A. G. Rubinshteyn: Selected letters] (Moscow, 1954).

35. Ibid., n.d. (presumably 1852), *LN*, 2:34.

36. Ibid., 21 April/3 May 1852, *LN*, 2:36.

37. "Russkaya opera v Peterburgye," in A. N. Serov, *Stat'i o muzïkye v 7-i vïpuskakh* [Articles on music in 7 volumes] (Moscow: Muzïka, 1984–87), 1:180–94.

38. Ibid., 1:190.

39. *LN*, 2:190.

40. Quite possibly Potocka may have meant Princess Mariya Vasilyevna Trubetskaya (1819–1895), a close friend of the grand duchess Mariya Nikolayevna, and the woman to whom Sollogub refers as "a lioness" of St. Petersburg high society in the 1840s. In 1839 she married Aleksey Grigoryevich Stolïpin, a colonel of a life guards hussars' regiment, but he died of cholera in 1847. Five years later, the princess married Semyon Mikhaylovich Vorontsov (1823–1882).

41. Letter to Kaleriya Khristoforovna 4/16 June 1852, *LN*, 2:37–38.

42. Her name is sometimes given with the German spelling "Rahden." The family originated from the bishopric of Osnabrück and settled in Courland in the sixteenth century.

43. *AR*, 1:79.

44. Letter to Kaleriya Khristoforovna 15/27 October 1852, *LN*, 2:39.

45. *LN*, 1:43–46.

46. Details of this concert are given in *AGR*, 1:147; and in *Istoriya russkoy muzïki* [The history of Russian music], ed. Yury Vsevolodovich Keldïsh et al., 10 vols. (Moscow: Muzïka, 1983–1997), 6:344.

47. Letter to Kaleriya Khristoforovna 12/24 January 1853, *LN*, 2:42.

48. *AR*, 1:43.

49. *LN*, 2:43.

50. Countess Aniela Potocka, *Theodore Leschetizky: An Intimate Study of the Man and the Musician,* translated from the French by Geneviève Seymour Lincoln (New York: Century, 1903), p. 203.

51. *LN*, 2:43.

52. Letter to Kaleriya Khristoforovna, 9/21 March 1853, *LN*, 2:44.

53. *LN*, 2:45.

54. Ibid.

55. Ibid., 6/18 May 1853, *LN*, 2:45–46.

56. Ibid.

57. Ibid.

58. *AR*, 1:82.

59. Trinklied der Sulima "Edlen Wein" was published in Berlin in 1871.

60. Letter to the writer and playwright Fyodor Alekseyevich Koni [between 6/18 April and 18/30 June 1853], *LN*, 2:46–47.

61. Neil Cornwell, *V. F. Odoyevsky: His Life, Times, and Milieu* (Athens: Ohio University Press, 1986), p. 121.

62. Olga Lanskaya was the sister of the future Minister of the Interior Sergey Lanskoy.

63. *LN*, 2:44. The original in French is kept at the Institute of Russian Literature of

the Academy of Sciences. The letter has only been published in F. M. Marmorshteyn's Russian translation.

64. Cornwell, *V. F.Odoyevsky,* p. 336.

65. In 1858 Rachel died of consumption, and in January, February, and March of that year Serov wrote three articles for the journal *Teatral'nïy i muzïkal'nïy vestnik* (see Serov, *Stat'i o muzïkye,* 3:333–43). The articles are indicative of the high esteem in which Rachel was held in Russia.

66. *LN,* 2:49.

67. Ibid., 2:48.

68. Ibid., 1:192. Quote also in Norris, *Russian Piano Concerto,* 1:31.

69. *LN,* 2:48.

70. Letter to Kaleriya Khristoforovna, 22 November/4 December 1853, *LN,* 2:49.

3. Foreign Tour, 1854–59

1. Rubinstein performed his Maykov setting, *Molitva pered Bitvoy* [A prayer before the battle].

2. Letter to Kaleriya Khristoforovna, 21 April/3 May 1854, *LN,* 2:49.

3. Letter to Yakov from Berlin, 17/29 May 1854, *LN,* 2:50.

4. Letter to Fredro 15/27 July 1854, *LN,* 2:53.

5. La Mara: *Briefwechsel zwischen Franz Liszt und Hans von Bülow* (Leipzig, 1898), p. 89.

6. *LN,* 2:55.

7. Letter to Fredro 15/27 July 1854, *LN,* 2:54.

8. Ibid.

9. Letter to Kaleriya Khristoforovna from Hamburg, 21 June/3 July 1854, *LN,* 2:51.

10. Adrian Williams, ed. and trans., *Franz Liszt: Selected Letters* (Oxford: Clarendon, 1998), p. 362.

11. *LN,* 2:51.

12. Fétis became director of the Brussels Conservatory in 1833, having relinquished control over his Parisian music journal, *Revue Musicale.*

13. *LN,* 2:54.

14. *AR,* 1:82.

15. The complete correspondence in the original French is in *Briefe hervorragender Zeitgenossen an Franz Liszt,* ed. La Mara, vols. 1–3 (Leipzig, 1895). Ossovsky also translated the letters into Russian for publication in *RMG* in 1896.

16. *LN,* 2:52.

17. Letter to Liszt, 5 August 1854, *LN,* 2:55.

18. *AR,* 1:83.

19. *LN,* 2:53–54.

20. Letter to Liszt, 5 August 1854, *LN,* 2:55–56.

21. Alan Walker, *Franz Liszt: The Weimar Years, 1848–1861* (Ithaca, N.Y.: Cornell University Press, 1989), p. 228.

22. Letter from Liszt to Karl Klindworth, 2 July 1854.

23. *LN,* 2:52.

24. Letter to Liszt, 5 August 1854, LMBHZ, 1:347.

25. Letter to Liszt, 9 August 1854, *LN,* 2:56.

26. *Kamennïy Ostrov,* Op. 10, published by Schott in 1855.

27. Letter to Liszt, 5 August 1854, LMBHZ, 1:347.

28. *LN*, 2:58.

29. Letter to Brendel, 19 November 1854. *The Letters of Franz Liszt*, Vol. 1, *From Paris to Rome: Years of Travel as a Virtuoso*, trans. Constance Bache (London, 1893). See: http://www.ibiblio.org/gutenberg/cgi-bin/sdb/t9.cgi

30. Letter to Kaleriya Khristoforovna, 11/23 July 1854, *LN*, 2:53.

31. LMBHZ, 1:348.

32. Andrey Krayevsky at that time was editor of the leading Russian newspaper *Sankt-Peterburgskiye vedomosti.*

33. Letter to Yakov, 21 August/2 September 1854, *LN*, 2:58.

34. LN, 2:59.

35. Heinrich Konrad Schleinitz, one of the directors of the Gewandhaus and Leipzig Conservatory.

36. LMBHZ, 1:351.

37. "Senff m'a laissé une odeur de souffre après que je l'ai vu, c'est un diable, et je désespère de l'amadouer s'il n'est pas bon diable. Härtel et consort se tiennent sur leur défensive avec moi, je me contente de manœuvrer afin de les tenir toujour en haleine, je ne compte leur livrer bataille que quand le vent me sera favorable qui doit souffler de l'Océan" (LMBHZ, 1:351).

38. Agnès was briefly married to Captain Ernest Denis-Street (an Englishman brought up in Vienna).

39. Alan Walker: *Franz Liszt: The Weimar Years, 1848–1861* (Ithaca, N.Y.: Cornell University Press, 1989), p. 213.

40. See Fritz Hennenberg, *Das Leipziger Gewandhausorchester* (Leipzig, 1984), pp. 29–30.

41. LMBHZ, 1:364.

42. Letter to Kaleriya Khristoforovna, 5/17 November, *LN*, 2:62.

43. LMBHZ, 1:365.

44. Emile Smidak, *Isaak-Ignaz Moscheles* (Aldershot: Scholar, 1989), p. 182.

45. Daughter of Wilhelm II of the Netherlands; she married Grand Duke Carl Alexander of Weimar in 1842.

46. Otto E Albrecht, *A Census of Autograph Music Manuscripts of European Composers in American Libraries* (Philadelphia: University of Pennsylvania Press, 1953).

47. *LN*, 2:65.

48. Ibid., 2:63,

49. See Nancy B. Reich, *Clara Schumann: The Artist and the Woman* (London: Gollancz, 1985), p. 149.

50. Letter to Liszt, 15 December 1854, LMBHZ, 1:365.

51. *LN*, 2:64.

52. LMBHZ, 2:7.

53. *LN*, 2:66.

54. Ibid.

55. LMBHZ, 2:8.

56. See http://www.gutenberg.org/dirs/etext03/1/of/10.txt; Letter 132..

57. Letter to Liszt, 24 March 1855, LMBHZ, 2:14–15.

58. The Symphony No. 3 in A major was published in 1861.

59. *LN*, 2:67.

60. The Suite for piano, Op. 38.

61. The 10 pieces, Op. 14, published by Bote und Bock in 1854.

62. LMBHZ, 2:14–15.

63. *LN*, 2:69.

64. *NGR*, p. 48.

65. CBFA, p. 192.

66. *LN*, 2:70.

67. Letter to Kaleriya Khristoforovna 6/18 August 1855, *LN*, 2:72.

68. Ibid., 10/22 May 1855, *LN*, 2:69.

69. *LN*, 2:70.

70. Letter to Liszt, 7 July 1855, LMBHZ, 2:35.

71. *The Letters of Franz Liszt*, Vol. 1, *From Paris to Rome: Years of Travel as a Virtuoso*, trans. Constance Bache (London, 1893). See http://www.ibiblio.org/gutenberg/cgi-bin/sdb/t9.cgi.

72. *LN*, 2:69.

73. Marina Frolova-Walker, "The Disowning of Anton Rubinstein," in *"Samuel" Goldenberg und "Schmuyle": Jüdisches und Antisemitisches in der russischen Musikkultur,* Studia Slavica Musicologica 27 (Berlin: Verlag Ernst Kuhn, 2003), pp. 34–35.

74. *AR*, 1:83.

75. T. N. Livanova et al., eds, *M. I. Glinka: Polnoye sobraniye sochineniy: Literaturnïye proizvedeniya i perepiska* [Literary works and correspondence], vols. 2(A) and 2(B) (Moscow: Muzïka, 1975/1977), 2(B):102. The text was censored in the Soviet "academic" edition, but Catherine Drinker Bowen restores the cut: "covering the impudent Jew with confusion. Barthold wrote it. He put sufficient chill into it, and the Jew suffered a thorough trouncing" (CBFA, p. 130).

76. Letter to Kaleriya Khristoforovna, 27 June/9 July 1855, *LN*, 2:72.

77. Ibid., 6/18 August 1855, p. 73.

78. Ibid., 22 October/3 November 1855, p. 74.

79. *LN*, 2:75.

80. LMBHZ, 2:55.

81. Letter to Raden, 5 /17 January 1856.

82. LMBHZ, 2:68. "Pour le salon il n'est pas assez gracieux, pour la salle de concert il n'est pas assez fougueux, pour le champs, il n'est pas assez primitif, pour la ville, pas assez général—j'ai peu de foi en ces natures-là."

83. Ibid., 2:67–68.

84. *LN*, 2:81.

85. Ibid.

86. Robert Ignatius Letellier, ed. and trans, *The Diaries of Giacomo Meyerbeer,* 4 vols., Vol. 3, *The Years of Celebrity, 1850–1856* (Cranbury, N.J.: Associated University Press, 2002), 3:396.

87. Mikhail Ivanovich Glinka, *Literaturnoye naslediye. Pis'ma i dokumentï* [Literary heritage. Letters and documents], ed. V. Bogdanov-Berezovskiy, vol. 2 (Leningrad: Gosudarstvennoye muzïkal'noye izdatel'stvo, 1953), p. 615.

88. *AR*, 1:83.

89. Ibid., 1:84

90. Michael Florinsky, *Russia: A History and an Interpretation,* 2 vols. (New York: Macmillan, 1953–1960), 2:953.

91. Sardinia had supported France and Great Britain in the conflict, and therefore Victor Emanuel sought to reestablish diplomatic relations with Russia.

92. *AR*, 1:84.

93. Letter to Kaleriya Khristoforovna, 23 January/4 February 1857, *LN*, 2:83.

94. *LN*, 2:84.

95. String Quartet, Op. 17, No. 2. Jacquard and Lalo were members of the quartet founded by Jules Armingaud in 1855.

96. This is paraphrased slightly; the original reads, "The success of yesterday's concert was brilliant, but it was not the sparkle of gold, but the sparkle of honours" (*LN*, 2:84).

97. The program included some of the pieces from *Kamennïy Ostrov*, the "Polonaise" and "Waltz" from *Le Bal*, the *Romance*, Op. 26, No. 1, *Barcarolle No. 2*; Field: *Nocturne in E♭*; Mozart: *Gigue* in G; Mendelssohn: two of the *Lieder ohne Worte*; Chopin: *Berceuse*.

98. MABS, p. 36.

99. Ibid.

100. NSCJT, p. 196.

101. Patrick Waddington, *Turgenev and England* (London: Macmillan, 1980), p. 26.

102. This quote is reproduced in John Ella, ed., *Record of the Musical Union* (London, 1845–80).

103. *LN*, 2:87.

104. It is not clear what this libretto was. Annakatrin Täuschel has suggested that it may have been a libretto by Max Ring whose collaboration Rubinstein had sought the previous summer or, more likely, one commissioned from Friedrich Hebbel and later rejected as unusable.

105. Letter to Kaleriya Khristoforovna from Pest, 29 December/10 January 1858, *LN*, 2:87.

106. *LN*, 2:87.

107. Ibid., 2:88.

108. The vocal score of the oratorio was published by Cramer in the late 1870s with an English translation by Henry Hersee.

109. Camille Saint-Saëns: *Portraits et Souvenirs* (Paris, 1900), p. 103.

110. Ibid., p. 104.

111. Bennett's overture *The Naiaids*, Op. 15, was later performed in Moscow at a concert sponsored by the Russian Music Society and conducted by Nikolay Rubinstein in November 1869.

112. Rubinstein was in Weimar on 22 July 1858. See Serov's article, *Pis'ma iz-za granitsï* [Letters from abroad]: "I shall note in passing: yesterday for a few hours ahead of me Rubinstein visited Liszt (he stopped by to say farewell before his departure for Russia]. See A. N. Serov, *Stat'i o muzïkye v 7-i vïpuskakh* [Articles on music in 7 volumes] (Moscow: Muzïka, 1984–87), 3:282.

113. Quoted in *NGR*, p. 52, on the basis of N. D. Kashkin, *Dve muzïkal'nïye pamyatki: N. G. Rubinshteyn i M. P.Musorgskiy*, published in *Russkaya mïsl'*, 1906.

114. *NGR*, p. 58.

115. A. F. Tyutcheva, *Pri dvorye dvukh imperatorov. Vospominaniya. Dnevnik 1853–82.* (Moscow: Zakharov, 2002), p. 302.

116. Letter to Kaleriya Khristoforovna, 13/25 October1858, *LN*, 2:91.

117. Ibid., 12/24 November 1858, *LN*, 2:92.

118. *LN*, 2:92–93.

119. Letter to Hellmesberger, 24 January/5 February 1859, *LN*, 2:93–94.

120. See *AGR*, 1:327.

121. Richard Taruskin, *Musorgsky—Eight Essays and an Epilogue* (Princeton, N.J.: Princeton University Press, 1993), p. 99.

122. Ibid.

123. Marina Cherkashina, *Aleksandr Nikolayevich Serov* (Moscow: Muzïka, 1985), p. 101.

124. Quoted in Yury Kremlyov, *Russkaya mïsl' o muzykye* [Russian thought on music], 2 vols. (Leningrad: Gosudarstvennoye muzïkal'noye izdatel'stvo, 1954/1958), 1:208.

125. Ibid., 1:209.

126. Serov *Stat'i o muzyke*, 1:56.

127. *AR*, 1:89.

128. RMM, p. 43.

129. Letter to the Danish musician Siegfried Saloman in Frankfurt-am-Main of 13/25 May 1859, *LN*, 2:98. The original (in German) is housed at the Musikhistoriska Museet in Stockholm.

130. Meyerbeer attended a concert given by Rubinstein and Joachim on 5 July 1859. See Letellier, *The Diaries of Giacomo Meyerbeer*, 4:126.

131. Wilhelm Ganz, *Memories of a Musician: Reminiscences of Seventy Years of Musical Life* (London: John Murray, 1913), p. 115.

132. Letter of Vladimir Stasov to Balakirev, 27 August 1859, in *Perepiska M. A. Balakireva s V. V. Stasovïm* [Correspondence between M. A. Balakirev and V. V. Stasov], ed. Vladimir Karenin (V. D. Komarova), vol. 1 (1858–69) (Moscow: Ozgiz-Muzgiz, 1935), p. 54.

133. *LN*, 2:105.

134. Letter to Kaleriya Khristoforovna, 16/28 September 1859, *LN*, 2:99.

135. Ibid., 2:100.

136. Ibid., 2:101.

137. Ibid., 12/24 October 1859, *LN*, 2:100–101.

138. Ibid., 2:202.

4. The Founding of the Russian Music Society and Russia's First Conservatory, 1859–67

1. Michael Florinsky, *Russia: A History and an Interpretation* 2 vols. (New York: Macmillian, 1953/1960), 2:883.

2. *AR*, 1:86.

3. The Symphonic Society of Musical Amateurs [Simfonicheskoye obshchestvo lyubiteley muzïki], organized in 1841 by the Wielhorski brothers and Anton Gerke.

4. Quoted in *Istoriya russkoy muzïki* [The history of Russian music], ed. Yury Vsevolodovich Keldïsh et al., 10 vols. (Moscow: Muzïka, 1983–2004), 6:203.

5. Letter to Matvey Wielhorski of 17/29 September (original in French). See *AGR*, 1:246–50.

6. These were managed by the Administration of the Empress Marie (Mariinskoye vedomstvo, which had operated since 1828 as Section IV of His Majesty's Chancery). See Florinsky *Russia: A History and an Interpretation*, 2:1040.

7. Gunke became a teacher at the Imperial Cappella in 1864. He published one of the early theoretical works on harmony in Russia, titled *A Brief Handbook for the Study of Harmony*, published in St. Petersburg in 1852.

8. Ivan Femistoklovich Nelisov was a pupil of Henselt, Dehn, and Liszt.

9. Letter to Liszt, 12/24 November 1859, *LN*, 2:103.

10. *LN*, 2:98.

11. Ibid.

12. Letter to Kaleriya Khristoforovna, 1/13 December 1859, *LN*, 2:105.

13. A chorus from Cui's opera, *A Prisoner in the Caucasus*, was also performed on 18/30 January 1860.

14. M. P. Musorgsky, *Pis'ma* [Letters] (Moscow: Muzïka, 1981), p. 22.

15. Grubinstein: a pun on Rubinstein's name formed from the Russian word *grubïy*, meaning "coarse."

16. Vladimir Karenin (V. D. Komarova), ed., *Perepiska M. A. Balakireva s V. V. Stasovïm* [Correspondence between M. A. Balakirev and V. V. Stasov], vol. 1 (1858–69) (Moscow: Ozgiz-Muzgiz, 1935), p. 124. The work in question was Balakirev's Piano Concerto in E♭, completed posthumously by Lyapunov in 1909.

17. Rubinstein gave three concerts at the city theater in Riga on 4/16 March, 6/18 April, and 7/19 April.

18. *LN*, 1:205.

19. *LN*, 1:43.

20. *LN*, 1:45.

21. Zaremba was Polish by origin. He had been educated in the law faculty of St. Petersburg University and afterward worked for a time in the Ministry of State Property.

22. Fyodor Ivanovich Begrov (1835–1885) studied under Anton Gerke and then at the Leipzig Conservatory under Moscheles, Hauptmann, Richter, and Rietz. He taught at the St. Petersburg Conservatory until 1879.

23. Dmitry Stasov, *Muzïkal'nïye vospominaniya* [Musical reminiscences], *RMG*, 1909.

24. Afansyev's string quartet "The Volga" and the cantata *The Feast of Peter the Great* were included in RMS programs, as were excerpts from Fitinghof-Shel's opera, *The Demon* (later renamed *Tamara* to avoid confusion with Rubinstein's own opera).

25. Quoted in V. Napravnik *Eduard Frantsovich Napravnik i yego sovremenniki* (Leningrad: Muzïka, 1991), p. 68.

26. *Literaturnoye nasledstvo*, vols. 22–24, "Dnevnik V. F. Odoyevskogo" (Moscow, 1935), p. 120.

27. Ibid.

28. *LN*, 2:109.

29. Ibid., 2:110.

30. Ibid.

31. Ibid., 2:111.

32. The full text of *O muzïkye v Rossii* is in *LN*, 1:46–53.

33. *LN*, 1:46.

34. Ibid., 1:47–48.

35. Letter to Balakirev, 13/25 January 1861, in Musorgsky, *Pis'ma*, p. 24.

36. *Conservatories in Russia* is reprinted in V. V. Stasov, *Stat'i o muzïkye v 5-I vïpuskakh* [Articles on music in 5 volumes] (Moscow: Muzïka, 1974–80), 2:5–10.

37. Ibid., 2:9; the word *creativity* is emphasized in the original.

38. Ibid.

39. Letter from Stasov to Balakirev, 1/13 March 1861, in *Perepiska M. A. Balakireva s V. V. Stasovïm*, ed. Vladimir Karenin (V. D. Komarova), vol. 1 (Moscow: Ozgiz-Muzgiz, 1935), pp. 96–97.

40. Ibid., p. 102.

41. Quoted by Yury Kremlyov, *Russkaya mïsl' o muzïke* 2 vols. (Leningrad: Gosudarstvennoye muzïkal'noye izdatel'stvo, 1954/1958), 2:62 et seq. The entire article is also given in an English translation in *Russians on Russian Music, 1830–1880: An Anthology*, ed. and trans. Stuart Campbell (Cambridge: Cambridge University Press, 1994), pp. 80–85.

42. Letter to Kaleriya Khristoforovna, 10/22 June 1861, *LN*, 2:112.

43. *LN*, 2:113.

44. Under the revised charter, which was finally approved in June 1863, the University of St. Petersburg gained considerable autonomy.

45. More recently published in *Iz istorii Leningradskoy konservatorii. Materialï i dokumentï 1862–1917* [From the history of the Leningrad Conservatory. Materials and documents 1862–1917] (Leningrad, 1964), pp. 11–15.

46. *LN*, 2:116. Barenboym's dating of this letter as 12/24 November is doubtful. The charter was published in *Senatskiye vedomosti* on 17/29 October, and Rubinstein tells Kologrivov "our charter concerning the Conservatory, declared without any change, is to be printed in *Senatskiye vedomosti* in a few days." This implies that the letter was written before that date. Rubinstein left Berlin on 11/23 October, and therefore he would have been in St. Petersburg by about 15/27 October. This date seems more probable.

47. *AR*, 1:88.

48. Letters to Davïdov (4/16 January) and Nissen-Saloman (15/27 February 1862), *LN*, 2:117–18.

49. The notion of detaching the personality from the artist probably derived from Rubinstein's experiences in Tunnel über der Spree, the literary group in Berlin, of which he had been a member in 1847.

50. *LN*, 2:118–19, and accompanying note. Barenboym quotes the original French here for the sake of the pun on the word César: Bendez [*sic*!] à ces arts ce qui est dû à ces arts, *LN*, 2:207. The entire original has not been published. The present English translation is based on F. Marmorshteyn's Russian translation in *LN*, 2:118–19.

51. Jean Becker (1833–1884), the so-called German Paganini, and Karl Davïdov arrived in St. Petersburg that spring. Rubinstein recommended both for Yelena Pavlovna's quartet evenings. At this period Becker was leader of the orchestra of the Nationalstheater in Mannheim and a few years later founded the Quartetto Fiorentino with Enrico Massi, Luigi Chiostri, and Friedrich Hilpert. For many years this was regarded as one of the finest quartets of the period. Rubinstein appeared in a public concert with Becker and Karl Davïdov on 14/26 March 1862.

52. *LN*, 2:120–21.

53. The concert took place on 12/24 March and included Field: Nocturne in A flat; Mendelssohn: Lied ohne Worte in E; and Rubinstein: Barcarolle, Op.30, No.1; Polonaise (C minor?).

54. Letter from Musorgsky to Balakirev, 31 March/12 April 1862, in Musorgsky, *Pis'ma*, p. 32. Dubinstein and Tupinstein (in the quote below) are puns on Rubinstein's name derived from the Russian words *dubovïy* [wooden-headed] and *tupoy* [stupid, dense].

55. Letter from Musorgsky to Balakirev, 28 April/10 May 1862, in ibid., pp. 32–33.

56. *LN*, 2:122.

57. The opera *Feramors* was dedicated to Friedrich Wilhelm of Hessen-Kassel and Princess Anna von Preussen.

58. Letter to Kologrivov, 22 June/4 July 1862, *LN*, 2:123.

59. Rubinstein's inaugural speech is published in full in *Iz istorii Leningradskoy konservatorii,* pp. 264–265; and *LN,* 1:53–55.

60. German Avgustovich Larosh [Herman Laroche] was born on 25 May 1845 in St. Petersburg. His father was a Hanoverian and his mother's maiden name was Frederizzi. He was highly educated and spoke Russian, German, French, and English. Later, during the last third of the nineteenth century, he became one of the most prominent music critics in Russia.

61. A *stolonachal'nik* was a "head of a desk" in the Civil Service, that is, the person in charge of an assigned duty at the Ministry of Justice. In actuality, Tchaikovsky was not the *stolonachal'nik* but only his senior assistant.

62. Laroche indicates that Joseph Ludger was of half-German, half-English stock. His father was a translator at the Admiralty. Joseph studied with Dreyschock but failed to graduate until 1871. He died in Paris in 1889, accidentally crushed by the wheel of the open carriage from which he had leapt onto the roadway.

63. Keldïsh et al., *Istoriya russkoy muzïki,* 6:171–72.

64. Letter to Leopold Zeller of 15/27 October 1862, *LN,* 2:125.

65. *Nurmahal* or *Das Rosenfest von Caschmir* was first staged at the Berlin opera in May 1822.

66. The *Grove* article on Wieniawski gives the date of the first performance as "St. Petersburg, 27 November 1862." This corresponds to the last of the November concerts listed in Keldïsh et al., *Istoriya russkoy muzïki,* 6:357–58, where the dates of Rubinstein's concerts are given as 30 October, 6, 13, 20, 27 November, and 4, 18 December (o.s.).

67. Keldïsh et al., *Istoriya russkoy muzïki,* 6:224.

68. RMM, pp. 73–75.

69. Aniela Potocka, *Theodor Leschetizky: An Intimate Study of the Man and the Musician,* translated from the French by Geneviève Seymour Lincoln (New York: Century, 1903), p. 238.

70. Villoing took Russian citizenship in October 1862 in order to be eligible to receive the "Free Artist" award. The same year his book, *Shkola dlya fortepyano* [Piano school], was published with a dedication to the grand duchess Yelena Pavlovna.

71. Quoted in *LN,* 2:208.

72. *Feramors* was not staged in Berlin until 1879.

73. Letter to Julius Rodenberg, 15/23 February 1863, *LN,* 2:127.

74. Ibid., 2:129.

75. Letter to Rodenberg from Dresden, 11/23 July 1863, *LN,* 2:129.

76. LIS, 2:287.

77. Letter to Konstantin Lyadov, 9/21 March 1864, *LN,* 2:131.

78. Letter to Raden, 15/27 March 1864, *LN,* 2:132.

79. In his article "On Music in Russia" Rubinstein had pointed out that the Theater School and the Court Cappella were the only government institutions for music, remarking also that their purpose was to train officials and not "free artists."

80. Letter to Kologrivov, 9/21 May 1864, *LN,* 2:132.

81. Ibid., 2:133.

82. Quoted in Ts. A. Kyui, *Izbrannïye pis'ma* [Selected letters] (Leningrad: Gosudarstvennoye muzïkal'noye izdatel'stvo, 1955), p. 498.

83. Barenboym supports this assertion by referring to the unpublished diary of Rubinstein's pupils Ye. and K. Loginova (*LN,* 2:209; note 3 to letter 149).

84. Letter to Raden—this and other letters to her are published in *Sovetskaya Muzïka*, no. 11 (1980).

85. Jeremy Norris, *The Russian Piano Concerto*, vol. 1, *The Nineteenth Century* (Bloomington: Indiana University Press, 1994), p. 31.

86. Letter to Kologrivov from Baden-Baden, 15/27 June 1864, *LN*, 2:136.

87. Gade's Sixth Symphony was performed in an RMS concert in Moscow that season.

88. Modest Chaykovskiy, *Zhizn' Petra Il'icha Chaykovskago*, 3 vols. (Moscow and Leipzig: Jurgenson, 1903), 3:331–32.

89. Heinrich Bellermann's *Der Kontrapunkt* was published in Berlin in 1862.

90. LIS, 2:284.

91. Ibid., 2:285.

92. Laroche was not quite correct in this. Tchaikovsky's use of the orchestra in the "Storm" overture was not really so "heretical." In the *Ocean Symphony* Rubinstein himself had introduced a harp in the Adagio (D major), and the Adagio (E minor) of the same work contains lengthy passages of triplet thirty-second notes with divided strings. It was perhaps more a case of students being forbidden to use these effects.

93. LIS, 2:p.286.

94. François-August Gevaert, *Traité général d'instrumentation* (Ghent, 1863).

95. See Rubinstein's reply to Abert of 24 December/5 January 1865. *LN*, 2:139.

96. *AGR*, 1:342.

97. *LN*, 2:140.

98. In the 1860s Count V. F. Adlerberg headed the Ministry of the Court.

99. Letter to Rodenberg, 4/16 June 1865, *LN*, 2:141.

100. Ibid., 2:141.

101. Letter to Kaleriya Khristoforvna from Stuttgart, 1/13 July 1865, *LN*, 2:141–42.

102. Ibid.

103. AGR, 1:233.

104. April Fitzlyon, *The Price of Genius: A Life of Pauline Viardot* (London: John Calder, 1964), p. 382.

105. Unidentified person. It may have been Vera Vasilyevna Ivasheva, who married Aleksandr Aleksandrovich Cherkesov (1839–1908), a member of the Land and Freedom group founded by Nikolay Aleksandrovich Serno-Solovevich in 1862. Cherkesov owned a public library and bookshops in St. Petersburg and Moscow and, as an attorney at law, was a councilor for the defense in the so-called trial of the 139, when four thousand persons were arrested for their involvement in the Going to the People campaign of the 1870s.

106. Letter to Kaleriya Khristoforvna from Stuttgart, 1/13 July, *LN*, 2:141–42.

107. Ibid., 2:144.

108. Tchaikovsky composed his *Oprichnik* on the same subject in 1870 but to his own libretto.

109. *Dni i godï P. I. Chaykovskogo* [Days and years of P. I. Tchaikovsky (Leningrad and Moscow, 1940), p. 41.

110. Gustav Gustavovich Kross was one of Henselt's best pupils. He had already appeared in public concerts and was considered a fine pianist. Despite this, he studied in Rubinstein's piano class for the full three-year course. He later became a teacher in the piano faculty of the Conservatory.

111. Letter to Kaleriya Khristoforovna, 7/19 January 1866, *LN*, 2:145–46.

112. AR, 1:87.

113. *LN*, 2:145.

114. Tchaikovsky's diploma was not formally signed until 1870.

115. This letter was published by Rubinstein's son, Yakov, in the newspaper *Rossiya* (1899, no. 46, p. 2) where it was mistakenly attributed to Turgenev. It seems that the handwriting is not Turgenev's (the signature is also illegible), and it is now assumed that the letter was actually written by Vladimir Sollogub. The original letter is in French and is housed at the St. Petersburg Public Library. See *LN*, 2:212; note 5 to letter 164.

116. Yury Engel', *V operye* (Moscow: Jurgenson, 1911), p. 233.

117. Laroche wrote an enthusiastic description of this work when Bessel published the vocal score in the early 1870s. See Laroche, *Muzïkal'no-kriticheskiya stat'i* [Critical articles on music] (St. Petersburg: Bessel', 1894), pp. 112–14.

118. See *CPSS*, 5:107 n. 3.

119. Ibid., 5:129.

120. Barenboym's 1954 edition of the letters, no.25.

121. See Keldïsh et al., *Istoriya russkoy muzïki*, 6:366. Possibly an error for Gade's overture *I højlandene* [In the highlands], Op. 7.

122. Letter to the Council of Professors of the Conservatory, 21 October /2 November 1866, *LN*, 2:146–47.

123. Ibid., 23 December/4 January 1867, *LN*, 2:147–48.

124. *LN*, 2:212–13, n. 3 to letter 169.

125. Letter from Yelena Pavlovna to the RMS Directorate dated 7/19 April 1867, partially quoted, *LN*, 2:213.

126. See Edward Garden, *Balakirev: A Critical Study of His Life and Music* (London: Faber and Faber, 1967), pp. 70–76.

127. See note 39, above.

128. Musorgsky, *Pis'ma*, 48–49.

129. See Keldïsh et al., *Istoriya russkoy muzïki*, 6:174.

130. Letter to Kaleriya Khristoforovna from Paris, 3/15 July 1867, *LN*, 2:150.

131. Ibid., *LN*, 2:151.

5. Europe and America Concert Tour, 1867–73

1. *AGR*, 1:340, letter to Kaleriya Khristoforovna, 17/29 October 1867, from Graz.

2. Stasov's article *Po povodu pis'ma g-ina Famintsïna* [*A propos the letter of Mr.Famintsïn*] in V. V.Stasov *Stat'i o muzïkye* (Moscow, 1976), 2:197–98.

3. Letter to Kaleriya Khristoforvna from Ghent, 18 February/1 March 1868, *LN*, 2:159.

4. Letter to Rodenberg, 21 September/3 October 1867, *LN*, 2:152.

5. Letter to Kaleriya Khristoforovna, 10/22 October 1867, *LN*, 2:152.

6. Ibid., 2:153.

7. Ibid.

8. Ibid.

9. Letter to Kaleriya Khristoforovna, 17/29 December 1867, from Baden-Baden, *LN*, 2:154.

10. Ibid.

11. Barenboym assumes that Rubinstein was referring to the Moscow Conservatory, observing: "Here Anton Grigoryevich's position was contradictory; on the one hand, he assisted N. G. Rubinstein in every way to found a conservatory in Moscow; on the other hand, he also considered the foundation of a second conservatory in Russia premature" (*LN*, 2:214).

12. Gromov and Vargunin were wealthy Russian merchant-industrialists, whose contributions had helped to support the Conservatory.

13. Letter to Edith Raden of 31 January/12 February 1868, *LN*, 2:155–56.

14. "Liszt tenait de l'aigle et Rubinstein du lion" (Saint-Saëns, *Portraits et souvenirs* [Paris, 1900], p. 106).

15. "Et quand il s'adjoignait à l'orchestre lui-même, quel rôle surprenant de l'instrument ne jouait-il pas sous ses doigts à travers cette mer de sonorités ! la foudre, traversant une nuée orageuse, peut seule en donner l'idée . . . et quelle façon de faire chanter le piano ! par quel sortilège ces sons de velours avaient-ils une durée indéfinie qu'ils n'ont pas, qu'ils ne peuvent pas avoir sous les doigts des autres" (ibid.).

16. "Je n'ai pas encore dirigé d'orchestre à Paris; donnez donc un concert pour que j'aie l'occasion de tenir le bâton" (ibid., p. 105).

17. Letter to Kaleriya Khristoforovna, 2/14 April 1868, *LN*, 2:162.

18. Aleksandr Gertsen, *Sobraniye sochineniy v 30-ti tomakh*, vol. 29, book 1 (Moscow, 1963), p. 306.

19. Letter to Edith Raden, 10 April–14 April 1868, *LN*, 2:160–61.

20. Letter to Siegfried Saloman from London, 23 May/4 June, *LN*, 2:164.

21. Letter to Kaleriya Khristoforovna, 2/14 April 1868, *LN*, 2:161–62.

22. Letter to Edith Raden, 23 May/4 June 1868, *LN*, 2:162.

23. Ibid., 2:163.

24. Letter to Siegfried Saloman of 23 May/4th June 1868, *LN*, 2:163.

25. *CPSS*, 5:145.

26. *LN*, 2:165.

27. Ibid.

28. Letter to Kaleriya Khristoforovna, 16/28 December 1868, *LN*, 2:166.

29. Letter to Edith Raden, 31 January/12 February 1869 from Brussels, *LN*, 2:167.

30. Adrian Williams, ed. and trans., *Franz Liszt: Selected Letters* (Oxford: Clarendon, 1998), pp. 699–700.

31. *LN*, 2:167.

32. Letter to Rodenberg, 23 July/4 August from Berlin, *LN*, 2:168.

33. Letter to Kaleriya Khristoforovna, 15/27 August 1869 from Vienna, *LN*, 2:169.

34. Here Rubinstein refers to Mariya Kalergis-Mukhanova to whom he had dedicated his Piano Sonata No. 3, Op. 41, in 1855.

35. *Sovetskaya muzïka*, 11 (1980): 110. The same letter to Raden is given in *LN*, 2:167, but the above passage is omitted.

36. *LN*, 2:163.

37. LIS, 4:49–50.

38. Styra Avins, ed., *Johannes Brahms: Life and Letters* (Oxford: Oxford University Press, 1997), p. 406.

39. Letter to Nikolay Rubinstein wrongly dated 14/26 May (the probable date is 27 May/8 June), *LN*, 2:173.

40. Letter to Edith Raden 6/18 May 1870, *LN*, 2:172.

41. See Tchaikovsky's letter to Klimenko, 26 October 1870: "Anton Rubinstein is

staying here. He has opened the season and played in the first concert the Schumann Concerto (unsuccessfully), Mendelssohn's variations and Schumann's studies (superbly!). At a quartet evening he played his new trio, which I did not like. An orchestral rehearsal for his new orchestral fantasy *Don Quixote* was arranged for him. Very interesting and superb in places. Besides that, he has composed a Violin Concerto and many small pieces." (*CPSS*, 5:238.

42. LIS, 4:68–69.

43. Quoted in Yu. Kremlyov, *Russkaya mïsl' o muzïkye*, 2:187.

44. Quoted in Viskovatov's reminiscences, but the actual letter from which he was quoting is not extant. It is not clear why Rubinstein mentions the Zoroastrian Pharisees in his scenario. In Lermontov's poem, as in the final libretto of the opera, Prince Sinodal's convoy is attacked by Tartars.

45. *AR*, 1:92.

46. Ibid., 1:93.

47. Letter to Jurgenson, 3/15 March 1871, *LN*, 2:178.

48. Ibid., 25 March/6 April 1871, *LN*, 2:180.

49. Letter to Kaleriya Khristoforovna, 16/28 March 1871, *LN*, 2:179.

50. *LN*, 2:180–81.

51. Letter to Dmitry Stasov, 17/29 April 1871, *LN*, 2:180–81.

52. Letter to Kaleriya Khristoforovna, 18/30 April 1871, *LN*, 2:181.

53. Letter to Liszt, 6/18 July 1871, *LN*, 2:182–3.

54. Williams, *Franz Liszt: Selected Letters*, p. 730.

55. *LN*, 2:183.

56. Williams, *Franz Liszt: Selected Letters*, p. 730.

57. A. V. Knowles, ed. and trans., *Turgenev's Letters* (London: Athlone, 1983), p. 182.

58. *LN*, 1:12.

59. Letter of 11/23 September 1871, in M. P. Musorgsky, *Pis'ma* [Letters] (Moscow: Muzïka, 1981), pp. 93–94.

60. See Jay Leyda and Sergei Bertensson, eds., *The Musorgsky Reader* (New York: Norton, 1947), pp. 170–71, where the date of this gathering is wrongly given as 17 September.

61. *LN*, 2:184–85.

62. Letter to Rodenberg of 4 November (n.s.) 1871, *LN*, 2:185.

63. Ivor Keys, *Johannes Brahms*, (London: Christopher Helm, 1989), p. 68.

64. Letter to Edith von Raden, 5/17 November 1871, *LN*, 2:185–86.

65. Ibid.

66. Maurice Grau had arrived in New York as a five year old in 1854. He came from a Jewish family whose origins were the Austrian city of Brünn in Moravia (see Henry Edward Krehbiel, *Chapters of Opera*, Project Gutenberg, May 29, 2005, chaps. 17 and 19. Available at http://www.gutenberg.org/files/5995/5995-8.txt

67. *AR*, 1:94.

68. Wladyslaw Duleba, *Wieniawski*, trans. Grazyna Czerny (Neptune, N.J.: Paganiniana, 1984), p. 135.

69. V. Yakovlev, ed., *P. I. Chaykovskiy: Muzïkal'no-kriticheskiye stat'i* [Critical articles on music] (Moscow, 1953), p. 39.

70. German Laroche, *Muzïkal'no-kriticheskiya stat'i* [Critical articles on music] (St. Petersburg: Bessel', 1894), pp. 114–23.

71. Williams, *Franz Liszt: Selected Letters*, p. 736.

72. Ibid., p. 739.

73. Letter to Hermann Levi, 15 January 1872, in *Johannes Brahms: Life and Letters,* ed. Styra Avins (Oxford: Oxford University Press, 1997), p. 434.

74. Letter to Liszt, 27 (n.s.) February 1872, *LN,* 3:9.

75. Beethoven's concerto in C of 1790–92 was published in Vienna in 1879. It received the opus No. Wo05.

76. Yakovlev, *P. I. Chaykovskiy. Muzïkal'no-kriticheskiye stat'i,* pp. 109–10.

77. The Russian Quartet consisted of the following players: Panov (vn); Leonov (vn); Yegorov (vla); A.V.Kuznetsov (vc).

78. Yakovlev, *P. I. Chaykovskiy,* 114.

79. Letter to Rodenberg of late April or early May 1872, *LN,* 3:9–10.

80. *LN,* 3:9.

81. Liszt's letter to Carolyne von Sayn-Wittgenstein, 29 May 1872, in Williams, *Franz Liszt: Selected Letters,* pp. 745–46.

82. Letter to Edith von Raden, 31 January/12 February 1868, *LN,* 2:158.

83. *AR,* 1:95.

84. Letter to Senff from Salzburg, 9 August (n.s.) 1872, *LN,* 3:11.

85. *LN,* 3:11–12.

86. The Music Academy opened in 1854 with a performance of *Norma.* It continued to function as an opera house and concert hall for many years but was demolished in 1926. It was located on the corner of East 14th Street and Irving Place near the site of the Steinway Hall (on the opposite side of Irving Place). The Steinway Hall was demolished ten years earlier in 1916.

87. Translated from *AGR,* 2:137–38.

88. *AR,* 1:94–95.

89. Ibid., 1:94.

90. LN, 3:12.

91. Letter to Kaleriya Khristoforovna from Detroit, 12 March 1873, *LN,* 3:13–14.

92. Ibid., p. 14.

93. Ibid.

94. The full programs of these concerts are given in Larry Sitsky, *Anton Rubinstein: An Annotated Catalog of Piano Works and Biography* (Westport, Conn.: Greenwood, 1998), pp. 162–63.

6. A Villa at Peterhof and Operatic Successes, 1873–85

1. Letter to Kaleriya Khristoforovna from Leipzig, 7 June 1873 (n.s.), *LN,* 3:15.

2. V. Yakovlev, ed., *Dni i godï P. I. Chaykovskogo* [Days and years of P. I. Tchaikovsky] (Moscow and Leningrad, 1940), pp. 100–101.

3. V. Yakovlev, ed., *P. I. Chaykovskiy: Muzïkal'no-kriticheskiye stat'i* [Critical articles on music] (Moscow, 1953), p. 182.

4. Ibid., p. 183.

5. Letter to Kaleriya Khristoforovna, 13/25 May 1874, *LN,* 3:21.

6. Letter to Mosenthal, 26 May/7 June 1874, *LN,* 3:23.

7. Letter to Senff, 5/17 July 1874, p. 24.

8. The arrangement for cello and piano appeared in 1875, the full score in 1896.

9. There is further discussion later in this chapter regarding the Moscow premiere of the opera at the Bolshoy Theater and some contemporary critical reaction to it.

10. Letter to Kaleriya Khristoforovna from Vienna, 19 February/3 March 1875, *LN*, 3:28.

11. Letter to Senff, 26 February/10 March 1875, *LN*, 3:29.

12. Letter to Kaleriya Khristoforovna from Paris, 10/22 April 1875, *LN*, 3:29.

13. Yakovlev, *P. I. Chaykovskiy: Muzïkal'no-kriticheskiye stat'i*, p. 251.

14. LIS, 4:231.

15. Yakovlev, *P. I. Chaykovskiy: Muzïkal'no-kriticheskiye stat'i*, p. 276.

16. Percy A. Scholes, ed., *The Mirror of Music, 1844–1944*, 2 vols. (London: Novello and Oxford University Press, 1947), 1:313.

17. See NSCJT, pp. 206–7.

18. *LN*, 3:33.

19. *AR*, 1:98.

20. P. E. Vaydman and G. I. Belonovich, *P. I. Chaykovskiy: Al'manakh* [P. I. Tchaikovsky: Almanac], Vol. 1, *Zabïtoye i novoye* [The forgotten and the new] (Moscow: IIF "Mir i kul'tura," 1995), p. 126. Even in this edition, which attempts to restore many cuts in Tchaikovsky's correspondence and eliminate the editorial tampering so characteristic of earlier Soviet publications, the expression *[rastudït?] vashu mat'* is rather stronger than "go to hell."

21. Rubinstein did play four of them several years later in a concert of 3/15 April 1883.

22. On 16/28 November 1874 Nápravník had conducted part 2 of *Das Verlorene Paradies*, but this was the first complete performance.

23. Quoted in Yu. Kremlyov, *Russkaya mïsl' o muzïkye*, 2:188.

24. G. A. Laroche, *Muzïkal'no-kriticheskiya stat'i* [Critical articles on music] (St. Petersburg: Bessel', 1894), pp. 55–73.

25. John Ella, *Musical Sketches Abroad and at Home*, ed. John Belcher, 3rd rev. ed. (London: William Reeves, 1878), p. 262.

26. The previous summer the Russian newspapers had reported that Rubinstein was going blind. His failing eyesight was caused by a cataract forming on the right eye, and Rubinstein had been at pains to reassure his mother in March 1876 that his eyesight would be completely restored once the cataract had been surgically removed.

27. Between 7 and 29 May Wagner and Hans Richter conducted eight concerts at London's Albert Hall.

28. Judging by Rubinstein's letter to Senff of 10/22 September, the composer destroyed this work.

29. These songs were published by Bessel in St. Petersburg in 1877 as Rubinstein's Op. 101.

30. Nikolay Solovyov gleefully pointed out in the Russian press that, although Tchaikovsky's *Romance [Chanson] sans Paroles* was announced in the program, Nikolay Rubinstein had actually substituted for it Chopin's *Nocturne* in D♭.

31. N. Simakova, ed., *V. V. Stasov: Stat'i o muzïkye* [V. V. Stasov: Articles on music], 5 vols. (Moscow: Muzïka, 1974–80), 2:353.

32. *CPSS*, 8:146.

33. E. E. Bortnikova, *Vospominaniya o P. I. Chaykovskom* [Reminiscences of P. I. Tchaikovsky], 3rd rev. ed. (Moscow: Muzïka, 1979), pp. 144–45.

34. *CPSS*, 8:156.

35. Possibly Rubinstein had in mind the Russian ethnographer and folklorist Ivan Petrovich Sakharov.

36. *LN*, 3:46–7.

37. Vladimir Napravnik, *Eduard Frantsovich Napravnik i yego sovremenniki* [Eduard Napravnik and his contemporaries] (Leningrad: Muzïka, 1991), p. 160.

38. LIS, 3:263.

39. Ethel Smyth, *Impressions That Remained. Memoirs.* 2 vols. (London: Longmans, Green, 1919), 1:283.

40. Letter to Pavel Petersen from Cologne, 3/15 December 1879, *LN*, 3:50.

41. Letter to Faltin from Peterhof, 17/29 July, *LN*, 3:53.

42. *LN*, 3:54.

43. LIS, 4:228.

44. *LN*, 3:55.

45. Barenboym gives 14 November; Täuschel revises it to 19 November.

46. Täuschel suggests that Barenboym's dating of the performance of *Die Maccabäer* in Köningsberg on 19 January is a misprint and that the actual date was 19 February 1882. See Annakatrim Täuschel, *Anton Rubinstein als Opernkomponist* (Berlin: Verlag Ernst Kuhn, 2001), p. 274.

47. Letter to Davïdov from Köningsberg, 4/16 January 1881, *LN*, 3:56.

48. According to Barenboym, at this period Sofiya was under police surveillance for revolutionary activities and was forbidden to visit either Moscow or St. Petersburg. For more than a year she had been associated with the revolutionary "chaykovtsï" movement and was once threatened with arrest. In 1875 the police authorities had arrested many of the members of the Pan-Russian Social Revolutionary Organization (sometimes called the "Moscow Circle") for spreading seditious propaganda among factory workers. The organization had members in Kiev and Odessa, but it is not known whether Sofiya had any affiliation with this group.

49. Letter to Sofiya Rubinstein, 11/23 March 1881, *LN*, 3:56.

50. *NGR*, p. 247.

51. David Brown, *Tchaikovsky: A Biographical and Critical Study,* 4 vols. (London: Victor Gollanz, 1978–1991), 3:136.

52. Scholes, *The Mirror of Music,* 1:113.

53. "Rubinstein's 'Il Demonio,'" *The Times,* 22 June 1881.

54. Letter to Senff, 15/27 October, *LN*, 3:58. Senff published the full seven-movement symphony in 1882, and the title page reads: "Nouvelle édition en sept morceaux."

55. LIS, 4:225.

56. Allan James Foley [Signor Foli] was an Irish bass, who had enjoyed great success in Russia with his performances of Rossini's *Moïse.*

57. Bilse was also a serious musician, and in the same year his Bilsesche Kapelle laid the foundations of the Berlin Philharmonic Orchestra.

58. Yakovlev, *Dni i godï P. I. Chaykovskogo,* p. 271.

59. M. A. Balakirev and V. V. Stasov, *Perepiska* [Correspondence], 2 vols. (Moscow: Muzïka, 1970–71), 2:37.

60. *LN*, 3:63.

61. In about 1890 Rubinstein wrote a second version of the above article, which he sent to the German writer Rudolf Lewenstein. The substance of the second article repeated the basic ideas of the earlier work but included a plan for the staging of *Das Verlorene Paradies.* Lewenstein died in 1891, and the second article (*Die geistliche Oper*) was only published in a fall edition of the journal *Die Zunkunft*, after Rubinstein's death. The earlier article was translated into Russian and appeared in the journal *Muzïkal'nïy*

mir in 1882, and in N. M. Lisovsky, *Anton Grigor'yevich Rubinshteyn. Pyat'desyat let ego muzykal'noy deyatel'nosti* (St. Petersburg, 1889), appendixes, pp. 27–34. The second version was never translated into Russian. The original article also appears in German and English in MABS, pp. 53–75.

62. *LN*, 3:66.

63. Letter to Jurgenson, 4/16 January 1883, *LN*, 3:66.

64. *LN*, 3:68.

65. Modest Chaykovskiy, *Pis'ma. P. I. Chaykovskiy i S. I. Taneyev* [Correspondence of P. I. Tchaikovsky and S. I. Taneyev] (Moscow: Jurgenson, 1916), p. 96.

66. Letter to Kaleriya Khristoforovna, 26 February/10 March 1883, *LN*, 3:68.

67. V. A. Zhdanov and N. T. Zhegin, eds., *P. I. Chaykovskiy: Perepiska s N. F. fon Mekk* [P. I. Tchaikovsky: Correspondence with N. F. von Meck], 3 vols. (Moscow-Leningrad: Academia, 1934–36), 3:185.

68. *LN*, 3:69.

69. Ibid., 1:55–60.

70. Ibid., 3:69.

71. Adapted from the synopsis given in Annakatrin Täuschel's *Anton Rubinstein als Opernkomponist* (Berlin: Verlag Ernst Kuhn, 2001), p. 257.

72. *LN*, 3:70.

73. Täuschel, *Anton Rubinstein als Opernkomponist*, p. 256.

74. Letter to Kaleriya Khristoforovna, 26 September/8 October 1883, *LN*, 3:71.

75. Letter to Pyotr Jurgenson, 17/29 June 1880, *LN*, 3:53.

76. Ippolit Chaykovskiy, ed., *Dnevniki P. I. Chaykovskogo* [Diaries of P. I. Tchaikovsky] (Moscow and Petrograd: Gosudatstvennoye izdatel'stvo, Muzïkal'nïy sector, 1923), p. 41.

77. Letter to Kaleriya Khristoforovna, 13/25 December 1883, *LN*, 3:73.

78. Ibid.

79. Ibid., 3:74.

80. Ibid., 3:75.

81. Letter to Senff, 4/16 February 1884, *LN*, 3:75.

82. Letter to Kaleriya Khristoforovna, 9/21 April 1884, *LN*, 3:76. Contemporary estimates suggest that from the 1880s to the early 1890s Rubinstein gave away approximately three hundred thousand rubles to charitable causes.

83. Adapted from the synopsis given in Täuschel's *Anton Rubinstein als Opernkomponist*, p. 257.

84. *LN*, 3:78.

85. Ibid., 3:79.

86. This "interview" was first published in *RMG* in 1910.

87. This monument was not unveiled until 1912 and was demolished by the Bolsheviks six years later.

88. From Lafontaine's fable *Le Corbeau et le Renard:* "Sans mentir, si votre ramage se rapporte à votre plumage. Vous êtes le Phénix des hôtes de ces bois [Without lying, if your warbling is as good as your plumage, then you are the Phoenix of the denizens of these woods]."

89. Letter to Senff from Hamburg, 31 October/12 November 1994, *LN*, 3:80.

90. Ibid.

91. *LN*, 3:82.

92. Ibid.

93. Letter to Kaleriya Khristoforovna, 7/19 April 1885, *LN*, 3:84.
94. *AR*, 1:99.

7. The Historical Concerts and Second Term as Director of the St. Petersburg Conservatory, 1885–91

1. *CPSS*, 13:269, letter to Nadezhda von Meck.
2. A small demonstration hall belonging to the Witzmann "piano depot" on Lanzheronovskaya Street.
3. *LN*, 3:86.
4. Ibid.
5. Ibid., 3:88.
6. Ibid., 3:89.
7. *CPSS*, 13:262.
8. Ibid., 13:269.
9. Ibid., 13:278.
10. Ibid., 13:272.
11. *LN*, 3:223–24; letter 396, note 1.
12. Letter to Kaleriya Khristoforovna, 18/30 April 1886, *LN*, 3:91.
13. Ibid., 3:90.
14. Ganz, *Memories of a Musician*.
15. *LN*, 3:92.
16. Ibid.
17. *AR*, 1:83.
18. *LN*, 3:93.
19. Oskar von Riesemann, *Rachmaninoff's Recollections Told to Oskar von Riesemann* (London: Allen and Unwin, 1934), p. 50.
20. *CPSS*, 13:449.
21. Erdmannsdörfer conducted the Moscow premiere of the symphony on 20 December/1 January 1887.
22. Letter to Kaleriya Khristoforovna, 18/30 October 1886, *LN*, 3:93–4.
23. The full programs are given in Larry Sitsky, *Anton Rubinstein: An Annotated Catalog of Piano Works and Biography* (Westport, Conn.: Greenwood, 1998), pp.171–72.
24. *LN*, 3:95.
25. The report was published in *LN*, 1:62–63.
26. See *Iz istorii Leningradskoy konservatorii: Materialï i dokumentï, 1862–1917* [From the History of the Leningrad Conservatory: Materials and documents, 1862–1917] (Leningrad, 1964), pp. 64–76.
27. *LN*, 1:64–65.
28. *LN*, 1:207.
29. Letter to Tchaikovsky, 28 March/9 April 1887, *LN*, 3:95–96.
30. Alexander Poznansky and Brett Langston, eds., *The Tchaikovsky Handbook*, 2 vols. (Bloomington: Indiana University Press, 2002), 1:404.
31. Adapted from the synopsis in Annakatrin Täuschel's *Anton Rubinstein als Opernkomponist* (Berlin: Verlag Ernst Kuhn, 2001), p. 259.
32. *LN*, 3:95.
33. M. A. Balakirev and V. V. Stasov, *Perepiska* [Correspondence], 2 vols. (Moscow: Muzïka, 1970–71), 2:113.

34. Bettina Walker, *My Musical Experiences* (London: R. Bentley, 1892), p. 251.

35. Balakirev and Stasov, *Perepiska,* 2:105.

36. A. A. Orlova and V. N. Rimsky-Korsakov, *Stranitsï zhizni N.A.Rimskogo-Korsakova: Letopis' zhizni i tvorchestva* [Pages from the life of N. A. Rimsky-Korsakov: A chronicle of his life and work], Vol. 2, 1867–93 (Leningrad: Muzïka, 1971), p. 255.

37. Ibid., p. 256.

38. *LN,* 3:97.

39. Letter to Karl Reinecke, 14/26 April 1887, *LN,* 3:96.

40. The detailed contents of these lectures are in Larry Sitsky, *Anton Rubinstein: An Annotated Catalog of Piano Works and Biography* (Westport, Conn.: Greenwood, 1998), pp. 157–61.

41. Letter to Kaleriya Khristoforovna, 2/14 May 1889, *LN,* 3:107.

42. Rubinstein's wife refused to give up the originals. Only in 1937 did Rubinstein's grandchildren surrender them to the State Public Library.

43. Balakirev and Stasov, *Perepiska,* 2:115.

44. Letter to Kaleriya Khristoforovna, 29 January/10 February 1888, *LN,* 3:102.

45. Vladamir Napravnik, *Eduard Frantsovich Napravnik i ego sovremenniki* [Eduard Frantsovich Napravnik and his contemporaries] (Leningrad: Muzïka, 1991), p. 257.

46. Letter to Averkiyev, 2/14 July 1888, *LN,* 3:103.

47. Balakirev and Stasov, *Perepiska,* 2:133.

48. Napravnik, *Eduard Frantsovich Napravnik i ego sovremenniki,* p. 256.

49. Ibid., p. 257.

50. *LN,* 3:105.

51. L. I. Kuz'mina, *Avgusteyshiy poet,* (St. Petersburg: Izdatel'stvo "Liki Rossii," 1995), pp. 101–2.

52. Quoted in *LN,* 2:228 on the basis of V. Lamsdorf, *Dnevniki, 1886–1890,* (Moscow, 1926), p. 96.

53. Aleksandr Polovtsov, *Dnevnik gosudarstvennogo sekretarya* [Diary of the state secretary], 2 vols. (Moscow: Tsentrpoligraf, 2005), 2:160.

54. *LN,* 3:106.

55. Kuz'mina, *Avgusteyshiy poet,* p. 110.

56. *LN,* 3:106-7.

57. Letter to Kaleriya Khristoforovna, 2/14 May, *LN,* 3:107.

58. A sardonic reference to the unperformed ballet *The Grapevine.*

59. Napravnik, *Eduard Frantsovich Napravnik i ego sovremenniki,* p. 261.

60. The full text in Russian is given in *LN,* 1:107–10.

61. *CPSS,* 15(a):201. Aleksey Suvorin was one of the principal editors of *Novoye vremya.*

62. *LN,* 1:21.

63. *LN,* 3:109-10. The original of this letter is lost. It was published posthumously in *Vossiche Zeitung* (Morgen Ausgabe), 2 February 1912. A Russian translation appeared at almost the same time in *Birzhevïye vedomosti* and later that year in *RMG.*

64. *LN,* 1:23.

65. Ibid.

66. The second edition was published by *Russkaya starina* in 1889. Quoted by Barenboym in *LN,* 1:23.

67. Yury Engel', *V operye,* (Moscow: Jurgenson, 1911), p. 240.

68. Marina Frolova-Walker, "The Disowning of Anton Rubinstein," in *"Samuel"*

Goldenberg und "Schmuyle": Jüdisches und Antisemitisches in der russischen Musikkultur, Studia Slavica Musicologica 27 (Berlin: Verlag Ernst Kuhn, 2003), p. 53.

69. E. E. Bortnikova et al., *Vospominaniya o P. I. Chaykovskom* [Reminiscences of P. I. Tchaikovsky], 3rd rev. ed. (Moscow, 1979), pp. 156–58.

70. Ibid.

71. Ibid.

72. M. L. Presman, "Ugolok muzïkal'noy Moskvï vosmidesyatïkh godov," in *Vospominaniya o Rakhmaninovye* [Reminiscences about Rachmaninov], ed. Z. Apetyan, 2 vols. (Moscow: Muzïka, 1974), 1:198.

73. See Nikolay Fyodorovich Findeyzen, *Iz moikh vospominaniy* [From my recollections], vol. 8 (St. Petersburg, Rossiyskaya natsional'naya biblioteka, 2004), p. 210

74. Letter to Kaleriya Khristoforovna, 16/28 April 1890, *LN*, 3:112.

75. Stanislav Gabel (1849–1924) taught at the St. Petersburg/Petrograd Conservatory from 1879 to 1923.

76. *LN*, 3:113.

77. Letter to Kaleriya Khristoforovna, 16/28 July 1890, *LN*, 3:116. Barenboym gives 16/28 August but this may be a mistake. Rubinstein's wedding anniversary fell on 12 July (o.s.), and it is far more likely that he was talking about an event that was four days old and not over a month.

78. Letter to Anna Rubinstein, 23 June/5 July 1890, *LN*, 3:113.

79. Ibid.

80. Ibid., *LN*, 3:114.

81. Ibid.

82. Barenboym suggests that the mysterious lady might have been Edith von Raden, but she had died five years earlier. More likely, the lady was entirely fictitious. The use of dialogue was simply a literary device intended to give the book a more satisfactory structure.

83. RMM, p. 65.

84. Ibid., p. 67.

85. *LN*, 3:232. These remarks were published in *Peterburgskaya gazeta* on 5/27 November 1890 as *Besedï s A. G. Rubinshteynom* [Conversations with A. G. Rubinstein].

8. Dresden, 1891–94

1. Yury Vsevolodovich Keldïsh, ed., *E. F. Napravnik: Avtobiograficheskiye, tvorcheskiye materialï, dokumentï, pis'ma* [Autobiographical and creative material, documents, and letters], comp. and introduction and notes by L. M. Kutateladze (Leningrad: Gosudarstvennoye muzïkal'noye izdatel'stvo, 1959), pp. 172–73.

2. *LN*, 3:117.

3. Ibid., 3:120.

4. Synopsis adapted from Annakatrin Täuschel's *Rubinstein als Opernkomponist*, (Berlin: Verlag Ernst Kuhn, 2001), p. 258.

5. M. P. Pryashnikova and O. M. Tompakova, eds., *Letopis' zhizni i tvorchestva A. N. Skryabina* [A chronicle of the life and work of A. N. Scriabin] (Moscow: Muzïka, 1985), p. 32.

6. Letter to Anna Rubinstein from the Hôtel de l'Europe, Dresden, 7 March 1892, *LN*, 3:124.

7. Ibid.

8. Letter to Sergey Rebezov, 4/16 April 1892, *LN,* 3:126.

9. Barenboym gives the dates as 27 and 28 June, but Annakatrin Täuschel has revised this to 25 and 27 June.

10. *LN,* 3:125.

11. Ibid., 3:127.

12. Ibid., 3:128.

13. Ibid., 3:129.

14. Abram Chasins, *Speaking of Pianists,* 4th ed. (New York: Da Capo, 1988), p. 17.

15. *LN,* 3:130.

16. N. A. Alekseyev, *Chaykovskiy i zarubezhnïye muzykantï* [Tchaikovsky and foreign musicians] (Leningrad: Muzïka, 1970), pp. 72–73.

17. *LN,* 3:130.

18. Ibid. A slightly misquoted dictum attributed to Talleyrand: "Je m'humilie quand je me juge, je m'enorgueillis quand je me compare" [I humble myself when I judge myself, I become proud when I compare myself].

19. H. E. Krehbiel, "A Second Book of Operas." Available at http://www.ibiblio.org/gutenberg/cgi-bin/sdb/t9.cgi?author=Krehbiel

20. Adapted from the synopsis in Täuschel's *Rubinstein als Opernkomponist,* p. 260.

21. *LN,* 3:131.

22. Ibid.

23. Ibid., 3:132.

24. Ibid.

25. Barenboym concludes his selection of letters for 1892 with this one addressed to the publisher Philippe Maquet. It has no date and, according to Barenboym, was originally published in Imbert Hugues, *Profiles d'artistes contemporaines* (Paris, 1897), p. 272. See *LN,* 3:236.

26. Barenboym gives the date as 15 December; Annakatrin Täuschel as 11–12 December.

27. *LN,* 3:133.

28. Ibid., 3:134.

29. Ibid., 3:133.

30. Ibid., 3:134.

31. See http://www.wienersingakademie.at/archive/1893.html

32. *LN,* 3:137.

33. Ibid., 3:138.

34. Ibid., 3:139.

35. Ibid.

36. Letter to Sofiya from Dresden, 23 September/5 October 1893, *LN,* 3:140.

37. Ibid.

38. Letter to Eugen Zabel, 24 May/5 June 1892, *CPSS,* 16(b):100–106.

39. *LN,* 3:141.

40. See *AGR,* 2:400. Findeyzen asserts, however, that the date of Rubinstein's final concert in St. Petersburg was 6/18 January (see Nikolay Fyodorovich Findeyzen, *Iz moikh vospominaniy* [From my recollections], vol. 8 (St. Petersburg: Rossiyskaya natsional'naya biblioteka, 2004), p. 211.

41. *LN,* 3:142.

42. Ibid.

43. Letter to Yasha Rubinstein, 25 March/6 April 1894, *LN,* 3:143.

44. *LN*, 3:144.

45. Nikolay Fyodorovich Findeyzen, *Dnevniki, 1892–1901* [Diaries, 1892–1901] (St. Petersburg: Izdatel'stvo Dmitriya Bulanina, 2004), p. 153–54.

46. Quoted in N. N. Sokolov, ed., *M. M. Ippolitov-Ivanov: Pis'ma, stat'I, vospominaniya* [M. M. Ippolitov-Ivanov: Letters, articles, reminiscences] (Moscow, 1986), pp. 118–19, with reference to *Otchyot po postroyke i torzhestvennomu otkritiyu zdaniya konservatorii* (Moscow, 1905), p. 16.

47. See L. G. Dan'ko and T. Z. Skvirskaya, eds., *Peterburgskiy muzikal'niy arkhiv* [The St. Petersburg musical archive], Vol. 1 (St. Petersburg: Izdatel'stvo "Kanon," 1997), pp. 148–53.

48. V. V. Yastrebtsev, *Reminiscences of Rimsky-Korsakov,* ed. and trans. Florence Jonas (New York: Columbia University Press, 1985), p. 100.

Bibliography

Abraham, Gerald. *On Russian Music*. New York: Books for Libraries Press, 1970.

——. *Studies in Russian Music*. London: William Reeves, 1969.

——. *The Tradition of Western Music*. Oxford: Oxford University Press, 1974.

Alekseyev, N. A., ed. *Chaykovskiy i zarubezhnïye muzïkantï* [Tchaikovsky and foreign musicians]. Leningrad: Muzïka, 1970.

"Anton Rubinstein." *Monthly Musical Record* 16, no. 186 (June 1886).

Apetyan, Z., ed. *Vospominaniya o Rakhmaninovye* [Reminiscences about Rachmaninov]. 2 vols. Moscow: Muzïka, 1974.

Avins, Styra, ed. *Johannes Brahms: Life and Letters*. Oxford: Oxford University Press, 1997.

Bache, Constance, trans. *The Letters of Franz Liszt*, Vol. 1, *From Paris to Rome: Years of Travel as a Virtuoso*, London, 1893. Available at http://www.ibiblio.org/gutenberg/cgi-bin/sdb/t9.cgi

Balakirev, M. A., and V. V. Stasov. *Perepiska* [Correspondence]. 2 vols. Moscow: Muzïka, 1970–71.

Barenboym, L. A., ed. *A. G. Rubinsteyn: Literaturnoye naslediye* [A. G. Rubinstein: Literary heritage]. 3 vols. Moscow: Muzïka, 1983–86.

——. *Anton Grigor'yevich Rubinshteyn: Zhizn', artisticheskiy put', tvorchestvo, muzïkal'no-obshchestvennaya deyatel'nost'* [Life, artistic career, creative work, public work in the field of music]. 2 vols. Leningrad, 1959/1962.

——. "Iz pisem A. G. Rubinshteyna k E. F. Raden." *Sovetskaya muzïka* [Soviet music], no. 11 (1980): 101–13.

——. *Nikolay Grigor'yevich Rubinshteyn: Istoriya zhizni i deyatel'nosti* [Nikolay Grigor'yevich Rubinshteyn: History of his life and work]. Moscow: Muzïka, 1982.

Barenboym, Lev Aronovich, ed. *A. G. Rubinshteyn: Izbrannïye pis'ma* [A. G. Rubinshteyn: Selected letters]. Moscow, 1954.

Bekman-Shcherbina, E. A. *Moi vospominaniya*. Moscow, 1982.

Berger, Francesco. *Reminiscences, Impressions, Anecdotes*. London: Sampson, Low, Marston, 1913.

Blaukopf, Kurt. *Mahler*. English translation of *Gustav Mahler oder der Zeitgenosse der Zukunft* by Inge Goodwin. London: Futura, 1973.

Bloom, Peter, ed. *Musical Life in 19th-Century France*. Vol. 4, *Music in Paris in the Eighteen-thirties*. New York: Stuyvesant, 1987.

Borodin, A. P. *Pis'ma* [Letters]. Foreword and notes by S. A. Dianin. 2 vols. Moscow, 1928/1936.

Bortnikova, E. E., et al. *Vospominaniya o P. I. Chaykovskom* [Reminiscences of P. I. Tchaikovsky]. 3rd rev. ed. Moscow, 1979.

Brockhaus, F. A., and I. A. Efron, eds. *Entsiklopedicheskiy slovar': Rossiya* [Encyclopaedic dictionary: Russia]. St. Petersburg, 1898; reprint, Leningrad: Lenizdat, 1991.

Brody, Elaine. *Paris: The Musical Kaleidoscope, 1870–1925*. London: Robson, 1988.

Brook, Donald. *Masters of the Keyboard*. London: Rockliff, 1946.

Brown, David. *Mikhail Glinka: A Biographical and Critical Study*. Oxford: Oxford University Press, 1974.

——. *Tchaikovsky: A Biographical and Critical Study*. 4 vols. London: Victor Gollancz, 1978–91.

Buckler, Julie A. *The Literary Lorgnette: Attending Opera in Imperial Russia*. Stanford: Stanford University Press, 2000.

Calvocoressi, M. D., and Gerald Abraham. *Masters of Russian Music*. London: Duckworth, 1936.

Campbell, James Stuart, ed. and trans. *Russians on Russian Music: An Anthology*, Vol. 1, 1830–80, Vol. 2, 1880–1917. Cambridge: Cambridge University Press, 1994/2003.

Chasins, Abram. *Speaking of Pianists*. 4th ed. New York: Da Capo, 1988.

Chaykovskiy, Ippolit, ed. *Dnevniki P. I. Chaykovskogo* [Diaries of P. I. Tchaikovsky]. Moscow and Petrograd: Gosudarstvennoye izdatel'stvo, Muzïkal'nïy sector, 1923.

Chaykovskiy, Modest. *Zhizn' Petra Il'icha Chaykovskago* [Life of Pyotr Il'ich Tchaikovsky]. 3 vols. Moscow, Leipzig: Jurgenson, 1903.

——, ed. *Pis'ma P. I. Chaykovskago i S. I. Taneyeva* [Correspondence of P. I. Tchaikovsky and S. I. Taneyev]. Moscow: Jurgenson, 1916

Cherkashina, M. R. *Aleksandr Nikolayevich Serov*. Moscow: Muzïka, 1985.

Clowes, Edith W., Samuel D. Kassow, and James West, eds. *Between Tsar and People: Educated Society and the Quest for Public Identity in Late Imperial Russia*. Princeton, N.J.: Princeton University Press, 1991.

Cornwell, Neil. *V. F. Odoyevsky: His Life, Times, and Milieu*. Athens: Ohio University Press, 1986.

Crisp, Olga, and Linda Edmondson, eds. *Civil Rights in Imperial Russia*. Oxford: Clarendon, 1989.

Cronk, Cuthbert. *The Works of Anton Rubinstein: A Study*. London: Novello, 1900.

Cui, César. *Izbrannïye pis'ma* [Selected letters]. Leningrad: Gosudarstvennoye muzïkal'noye izdatel'stvo, 1955.

——. *La Musique en Russie*. Paris, 1880, reprinted by Zentralantiquariat, Leipzig, 1974.

Dan'ko, L. G., and T. Z. Skvirskaya, eds. *Peterburgskiy muzïkal'nïy arkhiv* [The St. Petersburg musical archive]. Vol. 1. St. Petersburg, Izdatel'stvo "Kanon," 1997.

Drinker-Bowen, Catherine. *Free Artist: The Story of Anton and Nicholas Rubinstein*. New York: Random House, 1939.

Duleba, Wladyslaw. *Wieniawski*. Neptune, N.J.: Paganiniana, 1984.

Ella, John. *Musical Sketches Abroad and at Home*. Edited by John Belcher. 3rd rev. ed. London: William Reeves, 1878.

Ella, John, ed. *Record of the Musical Union*. London, 1845–80.

Ellis, Katherine. "Music Criticism in Nineteenth-century France." In *La Revue et Gazette musical de Paris, 1834–1880*. Cambridge: Cambridge University Press, 1995.

Engel', Yury. *V operye*. Moscow: Jurgenson, 1911.

Evans, Edward. *Tchaikovsky: "The Master Musicians."* London: J. M. Dent, 1935 [1906].

Fabbri, Rossella. *Cesare Ciardi: un flautista toscano alla corte dello zar*. Lucca: Akademos, 1999.

Fedorchenko, Valery. *Dvor rossiyskikh imperatorov* [The court of the Russian emperors]. Krasnoyarsk: "Izdatel'skiye proyektï"; Moscow: "AST," 2004.

Findeyzen, Nikolay Fyodorovich. *A. G. Rubinshteyn: Ocherk yego zhizni i muzïkal'noy deyatel'nosti* [A. G. Rubinshteyn: An outline of his life and musical activities]. Moscow, 1907.

———. *Dnevniki, 1892–1901* [Diaries, 1892–1901]. Edited by M. L. Kosmovskaya. St. Petersburg: Izdatel'stvo Dmitriya Bulanina, 2004.

———. *Iz moikh vospominaniy* [From my recollections]. Vol. 8. St. Petersburg: Rossiyskaya natsional'naya biblioteka, 2004.

Fitzlyon, April. *The Price of Genius: A Life of Pauline Viardot.* London: John Calder, 1964.

Florinsky, Michael. *Russia: A History and an Interpretation.* 2 vols. New York: Macmillan, 1953/1960.

Foster, Myles Birket. *History of the Philharmonic Society of London, 1813–1912.* London: John Lane, 1912.

Frank, Joseph. *Dostoevsky: The Seeds of Revolt, 1821–1849.* London: Robson Books, 1977.

Frolova-Walker, Marina. "The Disowning of Anton Rubinstein." In *"Samuel" Goldenberg und "Schmuyle."* Studia Slavica Musicologica 27. Berlin: Verlag Ernst Kuhn, 2003.

Ganz, Wilhelm. *Memories of a Musician: Reminiscences of Seventy Years of Musical Life.* London: John Murray, 1913.

Garden, Edward. *Balakirev: A Critical Study of His Life and Music.* London: Faber and Faber, 1967.

———. *Tchaikovsky.* London: J. M. Dent, 1973.

Gartenberg, Egon. *Vienna: Its Musical Heritage.* University Park: Pennsylvania State University Press, 1968.

Gevaert, François-August. *Traité general d'instrumentation.* Ghent, 1863.

Geynike, N. A., et al., eds. *Po Moskvye: Progulki po Moskvye i yeya khudozhestvennïm i prosvetitiel'nïm uchrezhdeniyam* [Around Moscow: Walks around Moscow and its artistic and educational establishments]. Reprint of the Sabashnikov edition of 1917. Moscow: Izobrazitel'noye iskusstvo, 1971.

Ginzburg, Lev. *Henri Vieuxtemps.* Edited by Herbert R. Axelrod. Translated by I. Levin. Neptune, N.J.: Paganiniana, 1984.

Glinka, Mikhail Ivanovich. *Literaturnoye naslediye. Pis'ma i dokumentï* [Literary heritage. Letters and documents]. Edited by V. Bogdanov-Berezovskiy. Vol. 2. Leningrad: Gosudarstvennoye muzïkal'noye izdatel'stvo, 1953.

Gozenpud, Abram Akimovich. *Russkiy opernïy teatr na rubezhe XIX–XX vekov i Shalyapin, 1890–1904* [The Russian opera theater at the turn of the 19th and 20th centuries and Shalyapin, 1890–1904]. Leningrad: Muzïka, 1974.

Hanslick, Eduard. *Vienna's Golden Years of Music, 1850–1900.* Edited and translated by Henry Pleasants III. New York: Simon and Schuster, 1950.

Harding, James. *Saint-Saëns and His Circle.* London: Chapman and Hall, 1965.

Headley, Arthur. *Chopin.* London: J. M. Dent, 1972.

Hennenberg, Fritz. *Das Leipziger Gewandhausorcheste.* Leipzig: VEB Bibliographisches Institut, 1984.

Herlihy, Patricia. *Odessa: A History, 1794–1914.* Cambridge, Mass.: Harvard University Press, 1991.

Hervey, Arthur. *Rubinstein.* Mayfair Biographies series. London: Chappell 1948.

Hingley, Ronald. *Russian Writers and Society in the Nineteenth Century.* 2nd rev. ed. London: Weidenfeld and Nicolson, 1977.

Hughes, Gervase. *Sidelights on a Century of Music, 1825–1924.* London: Macdonald, 1969.

Hullah, Annette. *Theodor Leschetizky.* Living Masters of Music series. London: John Lane, The Bodley Head, 1923.

Huneker, James. *Mezzotints in Modern Music.* London: William Reeves, 1913.

Irvine, Demar. *Massenet: A Chronicle of His Life and Times.* Portland, Ore.: Amadeus, 1994.

Iz istorii Leningradskoy konservatorii: Materialï i documentï, 1862–1917 [From the history of the Leningrad Conservatory: Materials and documents, 1862–1917]. Leningrad, 1964.

Jonas, Florence, ed. and trans. *Vladimir Vasilevich Stasov: Selected Essays on Music*. London: Barrie and Rockliff, 1968.

Karenin, Vladimir [V. D. Komarova], ed. *Perepiska M. A. Balakireva s V. V. Stasovïm* [Correspondence between M. A. Balakirev and V. V. Stasov]. Vol. 1 (1858–69). Moscow: Ozgiz-Muzgiz, 1935.

Kearney, Leslie, ed. *Tchaikovsky and His World*. Princeton, N.J.: Princeton University Press, 1998.

Keldïsh, Yury Vsevolodovich, ed. *E. F. Napravnik: Avtobiograficheskiye, tvorcheskiye materialï, dokumentï, pis'ma* [Autobiographical and creative material, documents, and letters]. Compiled and introduction and notes by L. M. Kutateladze. Leningrad: Gosudarstvennoye muzïkal'noye izdatel'stvo, 1959.

Keldïsh, Yury Vsevolodovich et al., eds. *Istoriya russkoy muzïki* [The history of Russian music]. 10 vols. Moscow: Muzïka, 1983–1997.

———. *Muzïkal'nïy entsiklopedicheskiy slovar'* [Encyclopaedic dictionary of music]. Moscow: Sovetskaya entsiklopediya, 1990.

Keys, Ivor. *Johannes Brahms*. London: Christopher Helm, 1989.

Kinsky, Georg. *Manuskripte Briefe Dokumente: Katalog der Musikautographen: Sammlung Louis Koch*. Stuttgart: Hoffmannsche Buchdruckerei Felix Arais, 1953.

Knowles, A. V., ed and trans. *Turgenev's Letters*. London: Athlone, 1983.

Kozhevnikov, V. M., and P. A. Nikolayev, eds. *Literaturnïy entsiklopedicheskiy slovar'* [Encyclopaedic dictionary of literature]. Moscow: Sovetskaya entsiklopediya, 1997.

Krehbiel, Henry Edward. *Chapters of Opera*. Project Gutenberg, May 29, 2005. Available at www.gutenberg.org/files/5995/5995-8.txt

———. *A Second Book of Operas*. Project Gutenberg, May 29, 2005. Available at http://www.gutenberg.org/dirs/etext03/2opra10.txt

Kremlyov, Yu. *Russkaya mïsl' o muzïkye* [Russian thought about music]. 2 vols. Leningrad: Gosudarstvennoye muzïkal'noye izdatel'stvo, 1954/1958.

Kryukov, Andrey N. *Moguchaya Kuchka: Stranitsï istorii peterburgskogo kruzhka muzïkantov* [The Mighty Handful: Pages from the history of the St. Petersburg circle of musicians]. Leningrad: Lenizdat, 1977.

Kuz'mina, Lyudmila Ivanovna. *Avgusteyshiy poet: KR. Stikhi raznïkh let: Lichnost'. Tvorchestvo* [The most august poet. KR. Verses from different years. Personality. Work]. St. Petersburg: Izdatel'stvo "Liki Rossii," 1995.

La Mara [Ida Lipsius]. *Briefe hervorragender Zeitgenossen an Franz Liszt*. Nach den Handschriften der Weimarer Liszt-Museums mit Unterstützung von dessen Custos Geheimrath Gille herausgegeben von La Mara. Vols. 1–2. Leipzig, 1895.

———. *Briefwechsel zwischen Franz Liszt und Hans von Bülow*. Herausgegeben von La Mara. Leipzig, 1898.

Laroche, German. *Izbrannïye stat'i v 5-i vïpuskakh* [Selected articles in 5 volumes]. Leningrad: Muzïka, 1975 (vol. 2); 1976 (vol. 3); 1977 (vol. 4).

———. *Muzïkal'no-kriticheskiya stat'i* [Critical articles on music]. St. Petersburg: Bessel', 1894.

Lebedev, A. K., and A. V. Solodovnikov. *V. V. Stasov*. Moscow: Iskusstvo, 1982.

Leonard, Richard Anthony. *A History of Russian Music*. London: Jarrolds, 1956.

Lermontov, M. Yu. *Sobraniye sochineniy v 4-kh tomakh* [Collected works in 4 volumes]. Moscow: Khudozhestvennaya literatura, 1975–76.

Letellier, Robert Ignatius, ed. and trans. *The Diaries of Giacomo Meyerbeer.* 4 vols. Vol. 2, *The Prussian Years and Le Prophète, 1840–1849.* Vol. 3, *The Years of Celebrity, 1850–1856.* Vol. 4, *The Last Years, 1857–1864.* Cranbury, N.J.: Associated University Presses, 2001–2004.

Leyda, Jay, and Sergei Bertensson, eds. *The Musorgsky Reader.* New York: Norton, 1947.

———. *Sergei Rachmaninov.* London: Allen and Unwin, 1965.

Lieberman, Richard, K. *Steinway & Sons.* New Haven, Conn.: Yale University Press, 1995.

Lieven, Dominic. *The Aristocracy in Europe, 1815–1914.* London, 1992.

Literaturnoye nasledstvo. Vols. 22–24, "Dnevnik V. F. Odoyevskogo." Moscow, 1935.

Livanova, T. N., et al., eds. *M. Glinka: Polnoye sobraniye sochineniy. Literaturnïye proizvedeniya i perepiska* [Literary works and correspondence]. Vols. 2(a) and 2(b). Moscow: Muzïka, 1975/1977.

———. *Muzïkal'naya bibliografiya russkoy periodicheskoy pechati XIX veka* [Musical bibliography of the Russian periodic press of the 19th century]. Vol. 6: 1871–1880. Moscow: Sovetskiy kompozitor, 1976.

Lokhvitsky, I. V. "A. G. Rubinshteyn, vstrecha s nim v 1839 g." *Russkaya starina* (May 1886): 440–41.

Longley, David. *The Longman Guide to Imperial Russia.* Harlow: Longmans, 2000.

Lott, R. Allen. American Itinerary of Anton Rubinstein (1872–73). 2003. http://rallenlott.info/itin4ar.htm.

Magocsi, Paul Robert. *Historical Atlas of East Central Europe.* Seattle: University of Washington Press, 1993.

M'Arthur, Alexander [Lillian McArthur]. *Anton Rubinstein: A Biographical Sketch.* Edinburgh: Adam and Charles Black, 1889.

McClelland, James C. *Autocrats and Academics: Education, Culture, and Society in Tsarist Russia.* Chicago: University of Chicago Press, 1979.

Mikhaylov, M. L. *Adam Adamïch i drugiye: Izbrannïye proizvedeniya.* Moscow, 1991.

Mikheyeva, Lyudmila Vikent'yevna. *Eduard Frantsevich Napravnik.* Moscow: Muzïka, 1985.

Mirsky, D. S. *A History of Russian Literature from Its Beginnings to 1900.* New York: Vintage Books, 1958.

Moldon, David. *A Bibliography of Russian Composers.* London: White Lion, 1976.

Montagu-Nathan, M. *An Introduction to Russian Music.* London: William Reeves, 1916.

———. *History of Russian Music.* 2nd ed. London: William Reeves, 1918.

Moser, Charles A., ed. *The Cambridge History of Russian Literature.* Rev. ed. Cambridge: Cambridge University Press, 1992.

Musorgsky, M. P. *Pis'ma* [Letters]. Moscow, Muzïka, 1981.

Napravnik, Vladimir. *Eduard Frantsovich Napravnik i ego sovremenniki* [Eduard Frantsovich Napravnik and his contemporaries]. Leningrad: Muzïka, 1991.

Neustroyev, A. A. "Aleksandr Villoing i pervoye kontsertnoye puteshestviye po Evropye A. G. Rubinshteyna, 1840–1842" [Alexander Villoing and A. G. Rubinstein's first European concert tour, 1840–1842]. *Russkaya starina* 65, no. 1 (January 1890).

Newmarch, Rosa. *The Russian Opera.* London: Herbert Jenkins, 1912.

———. *Tchaikovsky: His Life and Works, with Extracts from His Writings, and the Diary of His Tour Abroad in 1888.* London: Grant Richards, 1900.

Newmarch, Rosa, ed. *The Life and Letters of Peter Ilich Tchaikovsky.* London: John Lane, The Bodley Head, 1906.

Newmarch, Rosa, and Edwin Evans. *Tchaikovsky: His Life and Works, with Extracts from His Writings, and the Diary of His Tour Abroad in 1888.* London: William Reeves, 1908.

Newmarch, Rosa, and Alfred Habets. *Borodin and Liszt*. 2nd ed. London: Digby, Long, 1895.

Norris, Gerald. *A Musical Gazetteer of Great Britain and Ireland*. Newton Abbot, England: David and Charles, 1981.

———. *Stanford, the Cambridge Jubilee, and Tchaikovsky*. Newton Abbot, England: David and Charles, 1980.

Norris, Jeremy. *The Russian Piano Concerto*. Vol. 1, *The Nineteenth Century*. Bloomington: Indiana University Press, 1994.

Odoyevsky, V. F. *Dnevnik* [Diary]. Vols. 22–24. Moscow: Literaturnoye nasledstvo, 1935.

———. *Sochineniya v 2-kh tomakh* [Works in two volumes]. Moscow, 1981.

Orlova, Alexandra, ed. *Musorgsky Remembered*. Bloomington: Indiana University Press, 1991.

Orlova, A. A., and V. N. Rimsky-Korsakov. *Stranitsï zhizni N. A. Rimskogo-Korsakova: Letopis' zhizni i tvorchestva* [Pages from the life of N. A. Rimsky-Korsakov: A chronicle of his life and work]. Vol. 2, 1867–93. Leningrad: Muzïka, 1971.

Orlovsky, Daniel T. *The Limits of Reform: The Ministry of Internal Affairs in Imperial Russia, 1802–1881*. Cambridge, Mass.: Harvard University Press, 1981.

Osborne, Charles. *Letters of Giuseppe Verdi*. London: Victor Gollancz, 1971.

Pekelis, M. S. *Aleksandr Sergeyvich Dargomïzhsky i yego okruzheniye* [Aleksandr Segeyevich Dargomïzhsky and his circle]. Vol. 2, Moscow, 1973. Vol. 3, Moscow: Muzïka, 1983.

Pïlyayev, M. I. *Starïy Peterburg* [Old St. Petersburg]. Leningrad: Titul, 1990; reprinted from the 1889 edition.

Polovtsov, Aleksandr. *Dnevnik gosudarstvennogo sekretarya* [Diary of the state secretary]. 2 vols. Moscow: Tsentrpoligraf, 2005.

Potocka, Aniela. *Theodore Leschetizky: An Intimate Study of the Man and the Musician*. New York: Century, 1903.

Poznansky, Alexander. *Tchaikovsky through Others' Eyes*. Bloomington: Indiana University Press, 1999.

———. *Tchaikovsky: The Quest for the Inner Man*. London: Limetree, 1993.

Poznansky, Alexander, and Brett Langston, eds. *The Tchaikovsky Handbook*. 2 vols. Bloomington: Indiana University Press, 2002.

Prokhorov, A. M., ed. *Bol'shoy entsiklopedicheskiy slovar'* [Large encyclopaedic dictionary]. 2nd rev. and enl. ed. St. Petersburg: Norint, 1998.

Pryashnikova, M. P., and O. M. Tompakova, eds. *Letopis' zhizni i tvorchestva A. N. Skryabina* [A chronicle of the life and work of A. N. Scriabin]. Moscow: Muzïka, 1985.

Raeff, Marc. *Understanding Imperial Russia; State and Society in the Old Regime*. New York: Columbia University Press, 1984.

Rees, Brian. *Camille Saint-Saëns: A Life*. London: Chatto and Windus, 1999.

Reich, Nancy. *Clara Schumann: The Artist and the Woman*. London: Victor Gollancz, 1985.

Ridenour, Robert C. *Nationalism, Modernism, and Personal Rivalry in Nineteenth-Century Russian Music*. Ann Arbor, Mich.: UMI Research, 1981.

Riesemann, Oskar von. *Moussorgsky*, Translated from the German by Paul England. New York: Tudor, 1935.

———. *Rachmaninoff's Recollections as Told to Oskar von Riesemann*. London: Allen and Unwin, 1934.

Rimsky-Korsakov, N. A. *Letopis' moyey muzïkal'noy zhizni* [A chronicle of my musical life]. 8th ed. Moscow, 1980.

———. *Polnoye sobraniye sochineniye: Literaturnïye proizvedeniya i perepiska* [Complete collected works: Literary works and correspondence]. Vols. 1–8. Moscow, 1955–81.

Ringer, Alexander, ed. *The Early Romantic Era: Between Revolutions, 1789 and 1848.* Vol. 6, *Man and Music.* Basingstoke: Macmillan, 1990.

Rubinstein, Anton. *Music and Its Masters: A Conversation.* Translated by Mrs. J. P. Morgan. 2nd ed. London: Augener, [1921?].

Sabaneyev, L. L. "Iz moikh lichnïkh vospominaniy ob Antonye Grigor'yevichye Rubinsteynye" [From my personal reminiscences of Anton Grigoryevich Rubinstein]. In *Vospominaniya o Rossii.* Moscow: Klassika-XXI, 2005.

Sadie, Stanley, and George Grove. *New Grove Dictionary of Music and Musicians.* 20 vols. London: Macmillan, 1980.

Saint-Saëns, Camille. *Portraits et Souvenirs.* Paris, 1900.

Scholes, Percy A., ed. *The Mirror of Music, 1844–1944.* 2 vols. London: Novello and Oxford University Press, 1947.

Seaman, Gerald R. *History of Russian Music.* Vol. 1, *From Its Origins to Dargomyzhsky.* Oxford: Basil Blackwell, 1967.

Serov, A. N. *Stat'i o muzïkye v 7-i vïpuskakh* [Articles on music in 7 volumes]. Moscow: Muzïka, 1984–87.

Simakova, N., ed. *V. V. Stasov: Stat'i o muzïkye* [Articles on music]. 5 vols. Moscow: Muzïka, 1974–80.

Simeone, Nigel. *Paris: A Musical Gazetteer.* New Haven, Conn.: Yale University Press, 2000.

Sitsky, Larry. *Anton Rubinstein: An Annotated Catalog of Piano Works and Biography.* Music Reference Collection, No. 72. Westport, Conn., and London: Greenwood, 1998.

Skonechnaya, Ada Davïdovna. *Moskovskiy parnas* [The Moscow Parnassus]. Moscow: Moskovsky rabochiy, 1983.

Slonimsky, Nicholas. *A Lexicon of Musical Invective.* Seattle: University of Washington Press, 1965.

Smidak, Emil F. *Isaak-Ignaz Moscheles: The Life of the Composer and His Encounters with Beethoven, Liszt, Chopin, and Mendelssohn.* Aldershot: Scholar, 1989.

Smyth, Ethel. *Impressions That Remained. Memoirs.* 2 vols. London: Longmans, Green, 1919.

Sollogub, V. A. *Graf V. A. Sollogub: Vospominaniya.* [Count V. A. Sollogub: Memoirs]. Moscow: Slovo, 1998.

Sokolov, N. N., ed. *Grove Dictionary of Opera.* 4 vols. London: Macmillan, 1992.

———. *M. M. Ippolitov-Ivanov: Pism'a, stat'i, vospominaniya* [M. M. Ippolitov-Ivanov: Letters, articles, reminiscences]. Moscow: Sovetskiy kompozitor, 1986.

Stanislawski, Michael. *Tsar Nicholas I and the Jews: The Transformation of Jewish Society in Russia, 1825–1855.* Philadelphia: Jewish Publication Society of America, 1983.

Stasov, V. V. *Stat'i o muzïke v 5-i vïpuskakh* [Articles on music in 5 volumes]. Moscow: Muzïka, 1974–80.

Stegemann, Michael. Translated by Ann C. Sherwin. *Camille Saint-Saëns and the French Solo Concerto from 1850 to 1920.* Aldershot: Scholar, 1991.

Szabolcsi, Bence. *The Twilight of F. Liszt.* Budapest: Publishing House of the Hungarian Academy of Sciences, 1959.

Täuschel, Annakatrim. *Anton Rubinstein als Opernkomponist.* Berlin: Verlag Ernst Kuhn, 2001.

Taruskin, Richard. *Defining Russia Musically.* Princeton, N.J.: Princeton University Press, 1997.

——. *Musorgsky: Eight Essays and an Epilogue.* Princeton, N.J.: Princeton University Press, 1993.

——. *Opera and Drama in Russia as Preached and Practiced in the 1860s.* Rochester, N.Y.: University of Rochester Press, 1993.

Tchaikovsky, P. I. *P. I. Chaykovskiy: Polnoye sobraniye sochineniy. Literaturnïye proizvedeniya* [Complete collected works. Literary works]. 18 vols. Moscow: Gosudarstvennoye muzïkal'noye izdatel'stvo / Muzïka, 1953–81.

Turundayevskaya, I. G., ed. *Rossiya: Entsiklopedicheskiy slovar'.* Off-set reprint of vols. 54 and 55 of the Brockhaus and Efron encyclopaedia, St. Petersburg, 1898. Leningrad: Lenizdat, 1991.

Tyutcheva, Anna. *Pri dvorye dvukh imperatorov: Vospominaniya. Dnevnik* [At the court of two emperors: Memoirs and diary]. Moscow: Zakharov, 2002.

Vaydman, P. E., and G. I. Belonovich. *P. I. Chaykovsky: Al'manakh* [P. I. Tchaikovsky: Almanac]. Vol. 1, *Zabïtoye i novoye* [The forgotten and the new]. Moscow: IIF "Mir i kul'tura," 1995.

Volkov, Solomon. *St. Petersburg: A Cultural History.* London: Sinclair-Stevenson, 1996.

Waddington, Patrick. *Turgenev and England.* London: Macmillan, 1980.

Walker, Alan. *Franz Liszt: The Final Years, 1861–1886.* Ithaca, N.Y.: Cornell University Press, 1997.

——. *Franz Liszt: The Virtuoso Years, 1811–1847.* London and Boston: Faber and Faber, 1988.

——. *Franz Liszt: The Weimar Years, 1848–1861.* Ithaca, N.Y.: Cornell University Press, 1989.

Walker, Bettina. *My Musical Experiences.* London: R. Bentley, 1892.

Walsh, T. J. *Second Empire Opera: The Théâtre Lyrique, Paris 1851–1870.* London: John Calder, 1981.

Warrack, John. *Tchaikovsky.* London: Hamish Hamilton, 1973.

West, James L., and Iurii A. Petrov, eds. *Merchant Moscow: Images of Russia's Vanished Bourgeoisie.* Princeton, N.J.: Princeton University Press, 1998.

Williams, Adrian, ed. and trans. *Franz Liszt: Selected Letters.* Oxford: Clarendon, 1998.

Wirtschafter, Elise Kimerling. *Social Identity in Imperial Russia.* Dekalb: Northern Illinois University Press, 1997.

Yakovlev, V., ed. *Dni i godï P. I. Chaykovskogo* [Days and years of P. I. Tchaikovsky]. Moscow and Leningrad: Muzgiz, 1940.

——. *P. I. Chaykovskiy: Muzïkal'no-kriticheskiye stat'i* [Critical articles on music]. Moscow, 1953.

Yastrebtsev, V. V. *Reminiscences of Rimsky-Korsakov.* Edited and translated by Florence Jonas. New York: Columbia University Press, 1985.

Ysaÿe, Antoine. *Eugène Ysaÿe: Étude biographique et documentaire illustrée sur sa vie, son œuvre, son influence, par son fils Antoine.* Brussels: Éditions Ysaÿe, 1972.

Zhdanov, V. A., and N. T. Zhegin, eds. *P. I. Chaykovskiy: Perepiska s N. F. fon Mekk* [P. I. Tchaikovsky: Correspondence with N. F. von Meck]. 3 vols. Moscow-Leningrad: Academia, 1934–36.

Articles from the *Times*

"Herr Anton Rubinstein," May 6, 1876.

"Herr Rubinstein," June 8, 1877.

"Herr Rubinstein," 3 June 1881.

"A Rubinstein Concert," 14 June 1881.
"Rubinstein's 'Il Demonio,'" 22 June 1881.
"Herr Rubinstein's Recitals," 25 June 1881.
Untitled review, 18 May 1886.
"Rubinstein's First Recital," 19 May 1886.
"Rubinstein's recital," 14 June 1886.
"Anton Rubinstein. His Obituary," 21 November 1894.

Index

Dubossarï, 4
Dubuque, Aleksandr Ivanovich, 131
Duchambge, Pauline, 12
Duchy of Finland, 1
Duchy of Saxe-Weimar-Eisenach, 47
Durante, Francesco, 33
Durov, Sergey, Fyodorovich, 24
Düsseldorf, Germany, 127, 136, 146, 149

Eckert, Carl, 61, 170
Edinburgh, Scotland, 166
Eiler, Yelizaveta Pavlovna. *See* Wittgenstein, Yelizaveta Pavlovna
Eisenach, Germany, 135
Elberfeld, Germany, 127, 131
Elbing, 131, 169
Eliot, George (pseudomyn of Marian Evans), 48, 164; *Daniel Deronda,* 164
Elkamb, 32
Ella, John, 70, 71, 78, 132, 164, 166
Elmira, New York, 151
Ems, Germany, 13
Ende, Nikolay Grigoryevich, 169
Engel, Yury Dmitriyevich, 117, 214
Engelgardt, Vasily, 65
Erdmannsdörfer, Max, 185, 196, 304n21
Erie, Pennsylvania, 153
Eristov, Prince Rafail Davidovich, 222
Ernst, Heinrich Wilhelm, 115
Escudier, 157
Esztergom, Hungary, 68
Evansville, Indiana, 152
Ewing, Alexander, 163
Examiner, 14

Faltin, Friedrich, 175
Famintsïn, Aleksandr Sergeyevich, 166
Fan Ark, Karl Karlovich, 101
Farmington, Connecticut, 153
Farnol, Eleonor, 181
Fedotova, Glikeriya Nikolayevna, 196
Fenna, Marian, 181
Ferrero, Ivan Isipovich, 101, 115
Fétis, François-Joseph, 49, 288n12
Field, John, 9, 16, 25, 74, 84, 131, 155, 286n14; nocturnes, 77, 79, 291n97, 294n53
Figner, Vera Nikolayevna, xxi, xxii, 184
Findeyzen, Nikolay Fyodorovich, 5, 6, 8, 25, 31, 35, 214, 236, 284n6, 284n21
Fitingof-Shel, Baron Boris Aleksandrovich, xix, 89, 138; *The Demon* (*Tamara*), 200, 293n24
Fitstum von Eckstedt, Aleksandr Ivanovich, 26
Fitzenhagen, Wilhelm, 137, 158

Florence, Italy, 157
Fontane, Theodor, 20
Fort Wayne, Indiana, 152
Fourier, Charles, François-Marie, 21, 24
Franck, César, 11
Franco-Prussian War, 136
Frankfurt-am-Main, Germany, 13, 127, 131, 189, 193, 231, 292n129
Franz, Robert, 66
Fredro, Count Alexander, 46
Fredro, Maksimilian Maksimilianovich, 46, 47–49, 52, 56
Frankfort, Kentucky, 152
Freiberg, Germany, 217
Frenz, Herr, 103
Fride, Antonina Aleksandrovna, 215
Friedebourg, Anna Karlovna, 37, 39, 63, 66, 99
Friedrich Wilhelm, Landgraf of Hessen-Kassel, 294n57
Fühl, Baron, 20
Fyodorov, Pavel Stepanovich, 105
Fyurer, Otto Robertovich, 200

Gabel, Stanislav Ivanovich, 217, 306n75
Gabriel, Gabriele, 232
Gade, Niels, 54, 100, 109, 112, 117; Hamlet Overture, Op. 37, 146; *I højlandene* (*In the Highlands*), Op. 7, 297n121; *In Scotland,* 118; Symphony No. 6 in G minor, Op. 32, 296n87
Galakhov, Aleksandr Pavlovich, 23
Galatea, 9
Galvani, Giacomo, 196
Gamieri, 101
Ganeyzer, Yevgeny Adolfovich, 222
Ganz, Leopold, 59, 60
Ganz, Moritz, 14
Ganz, Wilhelm (1833–1914), 79, 198
Garcia, Mañuel, 100
Gaulois, 186
Gautier, Théophile, 43; *Voyage en Espagne,* 187
Gebel, Franz Xavier, 9, 15, 16, 285n41
Gedeonov, Aleksander Mikhaylovich, 28, 29, 32, 41
Geibel, Emanuel, 21, 285n54
Genast, Emilie, 49, 58
Geneva, Switzerland, 128, 131
Genoa, Italy, 157
Gerber, Yuly Gustavovich, 30, 72, 158
Gerke, Anton Avgustovich, 101, 115, 292n3, 293n22
Gerke, Avgust Antonovich, 215
Gesellschaft für Musikfreunde. *See* Vienna
Gevaert, François-Auguste, 112, 296n94

Geyten, Lidiya Nikolayevna, 197
Gippius, Adelaida Eduardovna, 205
Glasgow, Scotland, 166
Glazunov, Aleksandr Konstantinovich, 184, 187, 237; *Prelude-Cantata,* 237; *Uvertyura na grecheskiye temï* (Overture on Greek Themes), Op. 3, 184
Glinka, Mikhail Ivanovich, xviii, xix, 18, 26, 27, 28, 35, 36, 42, 43, 46, 47, 64, 65, 68–69, 77, 84, 89, 92, 104, 106, 117, 138, 176, 180, 187, 211, 219, 237, 283n2; *Kamarinskaya,* 27; *A Life for the Tsar,* xix, 26, 27, 42, 64, 65, 120, 127, 157, 206; *Prince Kholmsky,* 147; *Ruslan and Lyudmila,* xix, 64, 77, 85, 120, 173, 206, 211; Spanish overtures, 27
Globe, 71
Glubokoye, 114, 132, 154
Gluck, Christoph Willibald, 184; *Orphée,* 121, 122
Godebski, Cyprien, 134
Goethe, Johann Wolfgang von, 21, 47, 91, 130, 133, 147; *Faust,* 42
Goetze, A., 132
Goffrie, Herr, 71, 74
Golden Horde, 28
Goldenweiser, Aleksandr Borisovich, 224
Goldhann, Ludwig, 147
Goldschmidt, Otto, 15; *Study,* 15
Goldshteyn, Eduard Yulyevich, 203
Golitsïn Hospita, 9
Goldmark, Karl, 146; *Regenlied,* Op. 10, 146
Golos, 160
Golovnin, Aleksandr Vasilyevich, 96
Gomperz-Bettelheim, Karoline, 150
Gorchakov, Prince Aleksandr Mikhaylovich, 69
Goss, John, 71; *Glee: "Ossian's Hymn to the Sun",* 71
Gorshkov, 105
Gothenburg, Sweden, 132
Gounod, Charles, 180; *Mireille,* 180
Grandmougin, Charles-Jean, 179
Grand Rapids, Michigan, 152
Grau, Maurice, 144, 299n66
Graz, Austria, 19
Grazhdanin, 207, 210, 211, 212
Great War of 1914–18, xv, 167
Grell, Eduard, 67
Gresser, Julius, 17
Grigorovich, Dmitry Vasilyevich, 234
Grigoryev, Pyotr, 200
Grillparzer, Franz, 147
Grimm, Julius Otto, 67
Grisi, Giulia, 11, 26, 33, 73

Grodno, 2, 194
Gromov, Vasily Fedulovich, 97, 126, 298n12
Grunberg (née Rozenberg), Vavara Bogdanovna, 9
Grunberg, Yuliya Lvovna, 9
Gryaznov, P. I., 6
Gržimali, Ivan Voytsekhovich, 158
Gulak-Artemovsky, Semyon Stepanovich, 32, 41
Guerrazzi, Francesco, 108
Gulf of Finland, xxii, 1, 37
Gumbin, Mr., 32
Gumbinnen, Russia, 131
Gunke, Josef, 84, 292n7
Gurilyov, Aleksandr Lvovich, 104, 105
Gurkhaus, K., 56, 58, 62
Gutmann, Bertha, 231

The Hague, Netherlands, 13, 127
Hainl, François, 129
Halévy, Jacques François Fromenthal, 129
Halle, Germany, 66, 131, 133
Hallé, Sir Charles, 166
Hamburg, Germany, 20, 31, 48, 66, 131, 164, 165, 174, 177, 190, 191, 192, 231, 235; Dammtor Theatre, 189; Staattheater, 163
Hamilton, Canada, 153
Hamilton, Lord George Gordon, Earl of Aberdeen, 37
Hammer, Richard, 73
Hampton, Isabel, 79, 80
Handel, Georg Frederick, 14, 16, 78, 104, 106, 155, 187, 219; Adagio and fugue, 14–15; Coronation Anthems, 143; *Israel in Egypt,* 49, 67, 187; *Jephtha,* 85; *Messiah,* 127; Suite in A major, Gigue, 15, 132; Suite in D minor, *Air and Variations,* 129; Variations in E, 145
Hanover, Germany, 66, 67, 131, 177
Hansen, Josef, 179
Hanslick, Eduard, xx, 71, 190
Harder, Mariya, 112
Harrisburg, Pennsylvania, 152
Hartford, Connecticut, 151, 152, 153
Härtel. *See* Breitkopf und Härtel
Hartmann, Moritz, 108
Haslinger, Karl, 61, 63
Hasidism, 4
Haskala, 17
Hassel-Barth, Anna, 29
Hauptmann, Moritz, 55, 293n22
Haydn, Josef, 26, 104, 155, 184, 219, 221;

Mamay, Khan, 28
Mamontov, Savva Ivanovich, 117, 215
Manchester, England, 166, 194
Mannheim, Germany, 135, 177, 294n51
Manns, August, 167, 178
Maquet, Philippe, 230, 307n25
Marcello, Benedetto, 106
Marchesi, Mathilde (de Castrone), 90, 180, 198
Marienbad, 190
Marini, 179
Mario, Giovanni, 11, 26, 30, 33, 73, 100
Markovich, Andrey Nikolayevich, 117, 121, 197, 201, 217, 219
Markovskaya, Yevgeniya Konstantinovna, 197
Marmorshteyn, Fanya Mikhaylovna, 294n50
Marseilles, France, 135, 209
Martucci, Giuseppe, 157
Marx, Adolf Berhard, 59, 110
Mason, William, 155
Massenet, Jules, 231; *Werther,* 231
Massi, Enrico, 294n51
Matchinsky, Ivan Vasilyevich, 200
Mattathias, 157
Maurer, Ludwig Wilhelm, 27, 39, 46, 84
Mayer, Charles, 84
Mayerhofe, Herr, 90
Maykov, Apollon Nikolayevich, 139, 288n1
Meadville, Pennsylvania, 152
Meck, Nadezhda Filaretovna von, 7, 170, 171, 186, 196, 197
Mecklenberg-Strelitz, Georg Alexander, 210, 214, 218
Mecklenberg Strelitz, Yekaterina Mikhaylovna. *See* Romanova, Grand Duchess Yekaterina Mikhaylovna
Melnikov, Ivan Aleksandrovich, 160
Memphis, Tennessee, 152, 154
Mendelssohn, Abram, 20
Mendelssohn, Felix, x, 4, 16, 17, 18, 20, 25, 26, 27, 34, 35, 54, 68, 71, 74, 78, 83, 100, 106, 108, 112, 115, 116, 124, 155, 206, 208, 219, 238; Cello Sonata No.2 in D major, Op.58, 83; *Die Erste Walpurgisnacht,* 89; *Lieder ohne Worte* [*Songs without Words*], x, 14, 79, 132, 291n97, 294n53; *Loreley,* 85; *Paulus,* 67, 136; Piano Concerto in G minor, Op. 25, 286n16; Psalm 114, 143; Octet, 99; Scherzo a capriccio in F sharp minor, 15, 127; *Lobegesang,* 227; variations, 299n41; Violin Concerto in E minor, 151
Mendelssohn, Moses, x, 17
Menshikova, Aleksandra Grigoryevna, 166
Menter, Sophie, 167, 189, 203, 204

Merezhkovsky, Dmitry Sergeyevich, 222
Meshchersky, Prince Vladimir Petrovich, 211, 212
Metzdorf, Hermann, 101
Mey, Lev Aleksandrovich, 107
Meyendorff, Baron Pyotr Kazimirovich, 19
Meyer, Léopold de, 14
Meyerbeer, Giacomo, xv, 17, 18, 20, 68, 79, 96, 128, 292n130; *L'Africaine,* 150; *Il Crociato in Egitto,* 133; *L'Étoile du Nord,* 17; *Ein Feldlager in Schlesien,* 17; *Les Huguenots,* 17, 68; *Le Pardon de Ploërmel,* 79, 86; *Le Prophète,* 32; *Robert le Diable,* 26; *Stuensee,* 146
Mikhaylov, Mikhail Larionovich, 42; *Adam Adamïch,* 42
Mikhaylova, Mariya Anempodistovna, 197
Mikhaylovskaya, 105
Milan, Italy, 100, 157, 224, 235; La Scala, 156; Teatro Del Verme, 157
Millais, Sir John Everett, 166
Miller, Augusta, 31
Milton, John, 59, 68
Milwaukee, Wisconsin, 152
Milyukova, Antonina, 170
Minsk, 2
Minsky, Nikolay Maksimovich, 222
Miretsky, 101
Mlodetsky, Ippolit Osipovich, 175
Mobile, Alabama, 152
Moldavia and Walachia, 2–3
Mogilev-Podolsky, 6
mogochaya kuchka [mighty handful], 283n2
Moniuszko, Stanisław, 112; *Nijola,* 112
Mons, Belgium, 129
Monthly Musical Record, 167, 198
Montreal, Canada, 153
Moore, Thomas, 21, 94
Moscow, Russia, 6–9, 112, 130, 134, 136, 147, 158, 162, 170, 174, 175, 178, 180, 184, 185, 188, 189, 192, 194, 200, 224, 226, 233; Artistic Circle, 140; Bolshoy Theatre, 32, 95, 117, 140, 173, 179, 180, 195, 196, 200, 202; Conservatory, 74, 121, 123, 128, 140, 142, 165, 170, 185, 189, 196, 201, 217, 224, 237, 298n11; Exhibition of Industry and Art, 179, 181, 183; Hall of the Nobility, 25, 112 131; Hermitage Restaurant, 171; Malïy Theatre, 170, 196; Petrovsky Park, 9; Philharmonic Society, 201
Moscow University, 4, 25, 41
Moscheles, Ignaz, xi, 9, 14, 16, 55, 57, 293n22
Mosenthal, Salomon Hermann, 85, 157, 159, 203
Moskovskiye vedomosti, 18, 173, 180, 212

Moszkowski, Moritz, 227

Mozart, Wolfgang Amadeus, 26, 27, 74, 105, 106, 112, 155, 219; *Don Giovanni,* 26; *Die Entführung aus dem Serail,* 94; *Gigue* in G, 15, 291n97; "Mi tradi" from *Don Giovanni,* 71; *Le Nozze di Figaro,* 33; Piano Concerto in D minor, K.466, 209; Quartet in D, 74; *Requiem,* 147; Rondo in A minor, 127, 151; Symphony No. 41, 147; *Die Zauberflöte,* 26

Mozhaysk, Russia, 10

Muck, Karl, 232

Mühler, 183

Mukhanov, Count Sergey Sergeyevich, 43

Munich, Germany, 13, 125, 129, 133, 135, 165, 174

Musical Times, 163, 178

Musorgsky, Modest Petrovich, xxix, xx, 36, 86, 92, 99, 120, 143, 187, 283n2; *Boris Godunov,* 176; Intermezzo in modo classico, 184; *King Oedipus,* 86; Scherzo in B flat, 86

Musset, Alfred de, 43

Muzïkal'nïy listok, 166

Myuller, Mr., 114

Nadson, Semyon Yakovlyevich, 222

Nanini, Giovanni Maria, 33

Naples, Italy, 157

Napoleon Buonaparte, 13

Napoleonic Wars, 3, 22

Napravnik, Eduard Frantsevich, 134, 160, 162, 169, 172, 175, 177, 201, 207, 210, 218, 220, 301n22

Napravnik, Vladimir Eduardovich, 172, 206, 207, 208

Narbut, Zhosefina Tsezarevna, 226

Nashville, Tennessee, 152

National Liberation movement, 22

Nazism, xv

Neisse, 131

Nelidova, Lidiya Mikhaylovna, 196

Nelisov, Ivan Femistoklovich, 85, 292n8

Nero, 161

Neruda, Franz, 31, 209

Neruda, Josef, 31

Nerudová-Wickenhauserová, Amalie, 31

Nerudová, Wilma, 31, 132

Nesselrode, Count Karl Vasilyevich, 36, 43

Neu-Weimar-Verein, xviii, 51, 60

Neue Berliner Musikzeitung, 177

Neue Freie Presse, 108

Neue Hannovershche Landreitung, 174

Neue Zeitschrift für Musik, 48, 88, 129, 285n40

Neumann, Angelo, 226

Neustroyev, A., 11, 284n21

Ney, Kazimir, 70

Newark, New Jersey 151, 152, 153

Newcastle, England 101

New Haven, Connecticut, 151, 153

New Orleans, Louisiana, 151, 152, 154

New Russia (Novorossiya), 1–2

New [Free] Russian School, xviii, 93, 99, 106, 112, 138, 169, 182, 204, 206

New York, 151–154, 200; Clarendon Hotel, 150; Metropolitan opera, 144, 227; Music Academy, 150, 300n86; Steinway Hall, 150, 151, 155, 300n86

Nice, France, 69, 70, 178

Nicholas I. *See* Romanov, Nikolay Pavlovich

Nicholas II. *See* Romanov, Nikolay Aleksandrovich

Nieman, 3

Nikitina, Mariya Dmitriyevna, 196

Nikisch, Arthur, 183

Nikolayev, Ukraine, 137

Nikolayevsky Institute for Orphans, 63, 80

Nikolsky, Fyodor Kalinovich, 105

Nissen-Saloman Henrietta, 29, 84, 88, 97, 101, 121, 123, 159, 286n16

Nizhïny Novgorod, Russia, 42, 86

Norwich Festival, 67

Norwill, Camilla, 231

Novoye vremya, 142, 168, 175, 186, 202, 210, 211

Nashi konservatorii [Our conservatories], 210

Nuvellist, 186

Oberammergau, Germany, 136, 217, 228

Obolensky, Count Dmitry Alekseyevich, 113, 118, 119, 120

October Revolution, xv

Odessa, 1–6, 28, 40, 46, 65, 80, 91, 130, 137, 141, 157, 166, 187, 189, 191, 194, 217, 221, 222, 232, 234; Witzmann Hall, 194, 304n2

Odoyevsky, Count Vladimir Fyodorovich, 17, 27, 28, 34, 42, 43, 53, 84, 89, 90, 93; *Russkiye nochi,* xv, 42

Offenbach, Jacques, 12, 144; *Les Contes d'Hoffmann,* 12

Offermann, Alfred, 164

Oldenburg, Prince Pyotr Georgiyevich, 35

Onslow, George, 71; Quartet in B flat, Op. 21, 71

Opochinin, rear-Admiral Vladimir Petrovich, 138

Oranienbaum, Russia, 37, 38

Ordïnka, 6, 8, 154

Orenburg, Russia, 127

Orlov, Prince Nikolay Alekseyevich, 134

Prokhorova (Prokhorova-Maurelli), Kseniya
Alekseyevna, 105
Providence, Rhode Island, 151, 152
Prut, 3
Pryanishnikov, Ippolit Petrovich, 233
Pugni, Cesare, 105
Pukireva, Yevdokiya Petrovna, 196
Pushilov, Konstantin Nikolayevich, 115
Pushkin, Aleksandr Sergeyevich, 42

Quartetto Fiorentino, 294n51
The Queen of Spades, 37
Quincy, Illinois, 152

Raab, Wilhelmina Ivanovna, 159, 165, 166
Rachel, Élisa, 36, 44, 288n65
Rachmaninov, Sergey Vasilyevich, 195, 200;
Prelude in C♯ minor, x
Raden, Baroness Edith Fyodorovna, 36, 37, 66,
90–91, 95, 96, 98, 99, 105–106, 108, 125,
127, 128–129, 132–136, 144, 149, 195,
287n42, 306n82
Radziwiłłs, 4, 5, 81
Raff, Joseph Joachim, Symphony No. 1, 117
Rameau, Jean Philippe, 106, 206
Razin, Stepan, 36
Rebezov, Konstantin Sergeyevich, 232
Rebezov, Sergey Dmitriyevich, 217, 225,
230, 231
Reichenberg, Franz von, 232
Reinecke, Karl, xxiii, 49, 56, 169, 186, 208;
Piano Concerto No.1 in F♯ minor, 186;
Zenobia Overture, 205
Reinthaler, Karl, 67, 135
Rellstab, Heinrich Friedrich Ludwig, 60
Rembielinski, 144
Repin, Ilya Yefimovich, 205
Reszke, Édouard de, 179
Revel, 18, 137
Revolutions of 1848, 21–22
Revue Musicale, 288n12
Revue et Gazette Musicale, 144, 150
Reyer, Ernest, 163
Reykhardt, 115, 116
Rïbasov, Ivan Iosifovich, 101, 115, 116
Ribeaupierre, Comtesse de (née Potyom-
kina), 36
Ribeaupierre, Aleksandr Ivanovich, 36
Rïbniţa, 5
Ricci, F., 115
Richter, Ernest Friedrich, 293n22
Richter, Hans, 301n27
Ricordi, 156, 224
Ries, Louis, 74

Rietz, Julius, 54–56, 66, 103, 124, 293n22
Riga, Latvia, 86, 134, 137, 293n17
Rimskaya-Korsakova, Nadezhda Nikolayevna,
204
Rimsky-Korsakov, Nikolay Andreyevich, xix,
xxi, 92, 105, 137, 138, 141, 143, 168, 187,
204, 205, 206, 234–235, 238, 283n2; *The
Maid of Pskov* (*Pskovityanka*), 108, 187,
206; *Sadko,* 146, 180
Rïndina, A. M., 180
Ring, Max, 68, 291n104
Risorgimento, 22
Ritter, Josef, 232
Rïzhov, Ivan Andreyevich, 197
Rochester, New York, 151
Rodenberg, Julius, 74, 88, 94, 95, 96, 100, 103,
104, 113, 121, 123, 133, 136, 143, 148, 149,
183, 188
Roller, Andrey Ivanovich, 32
Romanov, Aleksandr Aleksandrovich (Tsar
Alexander III), xxii, xxv, 185, 206, 207–
210, 221
Romanov, Aleksandr Nikolayevich (Tsar
Alexander II), xxii, 42, 69, 82, 96, 120, 207
Romanov, Aleksandr Pavlovich (Tsar
Alexander I), 13
Romanov, Grand Duke Konstantin Konstan-
tinovich, 208, 209
Romanov, Grand Duke Konstantin Niko-
layevich, 13, 15, 29, 82, 201
Romanov, Grand Duke Mikhail Pavlovich, 36
Romanov, Nikolay Aleksandrovich (Tsar
Nicholas II), 209, 327
Romanov, Nikolay Pavlovich (Tsar Nicholas I),
xvi, 2–3, 10, 15, 23, 29, 32, 36, 37, 43, 47,
62, 75, 82
Romanova, Empress Aleksandra Feodorovna,
15, 18, 37, 69
Romanova, Empress Mariya Aleksandrovna, 75
Romanova, Grand Duchess Aleksandra
Iosifovna, 201, 209, 217
Romanova, Anna Pavlovna, 13
Romanova, Catherine II, 1, 38
Romanova, Elizabeth, 1
Romanova, Mariya Pavlovna, 47, 50, 52, 60
Romanova, Grand Duchess Yelena Pavlovna,
xvii, 30, 35, 36, 37, 39, 42, 44, 47, 56, 64, 66,
67, 69, 70, 71, 74, 75, 80, 82–85, 90, 91, 93,
96–100, 102, 107, 109, 113, 116–119, 122,
142, 154, 214, 286n20, 294n51
Romanova, Grand Duchess Yekaterina
Mikhaylovna, 63, 286n20
Romanova, Grand Duchess Mariya Niko-
layevna, 287n40

Romanovka, 4

Rome, 96, 157, 232

Rossi, 73

Rossini, Gioacchino, 26; *Il Barbiere di Seviglia*, 26, 39, 79, 94; *Guillaume Tell*, 286n24

Rossiya, 297n115

Rostopchina, Countess Yevdokiya Petrovna, 44

Rostovtsev, General Yakov Ivanovich, 82

Rotterdam, Netherlands, 49, 127

Rouen, France, 235; Théâtre des Arts, 235

Rozenberg, Morits Bogdanovich, 8

Rozenblyum, Nikolay Germanovich, 213

Rubets, Aleksandr Ivanovich, 101

Rubini, Giovanni Battista, 11, 15, 26, 33

Rubinstein, A. S., 285n47

Rubinstein, Abram Romanovich, 4

Rubinstein, Aleksandr Grigoryevich (Sasha), xxii, 150, 174, 182, 190, 192, 194, 222, 225, 232, 233, 234, 235

Rubinstein, Anna Antonovna (Anya), xxii, xiii, xxiv, 132, 193, 217, 218, 221, 224–226, 230, 231, 232, 238

Rubinstein, Anton Grigoryevich (subentries in chronological order): early childhood in Bessarabia and Moscow xxiv, 5–10; confusion over date of birth 6, 284n12; studies with Aleksandr Villoing and first European tour 9–15; studies with Siegried Dehn, 18; confiscation of manuscripts, 23, 286, n9; Petrashevsky incident, 23–24; adopts a new sequence of opus numbers, 25; debut as conductor, 27; plan for a Music Academy, xvi, 38–39, 50, 87; Singing Academy, 75–76, 89, 90; marriage to Vera Chekuanova, xxii, 113–114; stipend, 138; raised to the hereditary nobility, 167; failing eyesight, 168, 179, 195, 301n26; death of Nikolay Rubinstein, 177–178; fiftieth jubilee celebrations, 209–210, 214; Historical Concerts, ix, 155, 175, 187, 193–198, 206; Rubinstein Competition and Prize, 197, 218; second term as director of the St. Petersburg Conservatory, 201–226; rift with his wife Vera, xxii, 217, 224–225; tutelage of Josef Hofmann: 227; funeral service, 236–237; legacy; 237–238. Literary works: *Autobiography* (*Avtobiograficheskiye vospominaniya*), xxiv, 6, 149, 163, 192, 213; *Die Geistliche Oper*, 136, 182–183, 228, 302–303n61; *Gedankenkorb* (A Basket of Thoughts), xxv, 44, 88, 111, 234, 238; *On Editing the Classics*, 186; *Lectures on the History of Piano Music*, 13, 205; *Music and its Masters* [*Die Musik und ihre Meister*], 102, 218–219, 221; *The*

Necessity of Opening a Music School in St. Petersburg, 94; *O muzïkye v Rossii* (*On Music in Russia*), 91–94, 295n79; *The Obligations and Rights of the Director of the Conservatory*, 113; "Po povodu sotogo predstavleniya operï *Demon*" (Concerning the Hundredth Performance of the opera *The Demon*), 192; *Provisions for the St. Petersburg Conservatory*, 202; Report to the Minister of Education, 87–88; "Russische Komponisten" ("Composers in Russia"), xviii, 51, 64–65; speech on the opening of the St. Petersburg Conservatory, 101, 295n59; speech on the ninth anniversary of the founding of the St. Petersburg Conservatory, 138; *Report to the Directorate of the St. Petersburg Division of the Russian Music Society*, 202; report to the Grand Duchess Aleksandra Iosifovna, 201; Second autobiography (destroyed), 213, 217, 218, 227, 230, 232; *Yeshcho o konservatoriyakh* (More on conservatories), 210

Musical compositions: Acrostic, Op.37, 47; Acrostic, Op. 114, 218; Album of popular dances of different nations, Op. 82, 130; *Anthony and Cleopatra*, Op. 116, 218, 221; *Le Bal*, Op. 14: 52, 290n61; No. 2 Polonaise in E♭, 291n97; No. 4 Waltz in A♭, 66, 291n97; *Bal costumé* for two pianos, Op. 103, 177, 196; Barcarolle No. 1 in F minor, Op. 30 No. 1, 34, 294n53; Barcarolle No.2, Op.45b, 77, 291n97; Barcarolle No. 5: See *Miscellanées*, Op. 93; *Das Begrabene Lied*, 218; *Cain*, 136, 236; Caprice russe for piano and orchestra, Op. 102, 168, 169, 177; Cello Concerto No. 1 in A minor, Op. 65, 108, 159; Cello Concerto No, 2 in D minor, Op. 96, 159, 177, 300n8; Cello Sonata No. 1 in D, op.18, 39, 71, 176; *Chanson d'Amour*, 196; *Christus*, Op. 117, 228–230, 232, 233, 235; Concert Overture in B♭, Op. 60, 44; *The Demon*, x, xi, 99, 137, 141–44, 150, 159, 164, 168, 173, 174, 177, 179, 180, 189, 191, 192, 200, 210, 233, 238, 300n9, 302n53; *Dmitry Donskoy*, 27–36, 167, 168, 172, 214, 235; *Don Quixote*, 133, 136, 238, 299n41; *Don Quixote*, Op. 87, 130, 136, 137, 180, 196; *Eroica Fantasy*, Op. 110, 192; Etude in C "On false notes", 127; *Fantasie sur les mélodies hongroises*, 72; Fantasy on two Russian folk songs, 27; Fantasy in C for piano and orchestra, Op. 84, 132, 134, 135, 169, 192; Fantasy in E minor for piano solo, Op. 77, 115, 124; Fantasy in F minor for two pianos, Op. 73, 107, 137, 162; Faust overture, Op. 68, 53, 109, 134; Faust Symphony, 53, 60, 109; *Feramors,* 94, 96, 100, 102–04, 135, 148–149, 156, 159, 167–170, 175, 177, 180, 186, 189, 210, 214, 215, 238, 295n72; *Fomka the Fool,* 39, 40, 41, 42, 49, 52–54; *Figlia del Tintoretto,* 108; Five pieces, Op.69: Caprice in A♭, 127; Nocturne in G, 127; Five Russian songs, 222; German part songs, Op. 61, 102; German part songs, Op.62, 102; *Glück,* 218; *Goryusha,* 172, 202, 205, 207, 210, 214; Grand duo violin and piano on motifs from Meyerbeer's *Le Prophète,* 22; *The Grapevine (Die Rebe),* 179, 181, 182, 184, 186, 210, 232, 305n58; *Gypsies,* 222; *Hagar in the Desert (Hagar in der Wüste),* Op. 92, No. 2, 147, 150; *Hecuba,* Op. 92, No. 1, 147, 150, 168; *Die Heimat meiner Lieder,* , 150; *Homage à Jenny Lind,* Op. 7, 18; *Ivan the Terrible,* Op. 79, 130, 131, 134, 137, 168, 208; *Joab,* 133; *Kamennïy Ostrov:* Op.10, 37, 39, 44, 52, 63, 288n26, 291n97; No. 22 Andante "Rêve angélique", 39; *Die Kinder der Haide,* [*Children of the Steppes*], 85, 86, 90, 96, 100, 105, 112, 117, 159, 200, 226, 231, 234, 235; *Konzertstück* for piano and orchestra (estroyed), 168; *Konzertstück* in A♭ for piano and orchestra, Op. 113, 210, 214, 216; Krakowiak in E♭, Op. 5 No. 2, 34; *Die Maccabäer* [*The Maccabees*], 159, 160, 163–165, 167, 168, 174, 177, 183, 185, 189, 196, 226, 230, 235, 238, 302n46; *The Maid of Pskov,* 107–108; Mazurka in E, Op. 5 No. 3, 34; Melodies: Op. 3 No. 1 B major, 34; Op. 3 No. 2 F major, x, 34; *The Merchant Kalashnikov* [*Kupets Kalashnikov*], 168, 171, 172, 174, 175, 177, 188, 189, 206–210; *Miscellanées:* Barcarolle No. 5 in A minor, 158, 159; Impromtu in A♭, 158; Léonore de Bürger, 234; Menuet in E flat, 158; Nouvelle mélodie in F sharp minor, 158; Op. 93, 158, 214; Près du ruisseau, 158; Sérénade, 158, 159; Valse in F, 158; Morning [Utro], cantata, 117; *Moses,* Op.112, 203, 205, 210, 212, 222, 226, 228, 230, 235, 238; *Néron,* 157, 161, 163, 164, 168, 174, 177, 186, 188–193, 197, 200, 208, 210, 230, 235; *Night,* Op. 44, No.1, 215; Nine

Koltsov settings, Op.27, 43; Ondine, 14, 16, 285n40; *The Oprichnik,* 115–117; Octet, Op.9, 58, 59 286n9; Ouverture triomphale in C, Op. 43, 62; Overture for the opening of the St. Petersburg Conservatory, Op.120, 237, 238; *Der Papagei* [*The Parrot*], 187, 190, 191, 192; Persian songs, Op. 34, 58, 62, 63, 70, 71, 134, 238; No. 9 Gelb rollt mir zu Füßen, x; No. 11 Thu' nicht so spröde schönes, 196; Piano Concerto in D minor, 22, 58, 286n9; Piano Concerto in C major, 22, 286 n9; Piano Concerto in F, 286, n9; Piano Concerto No.1 in E minor, Op. 25, 25, 27, 28, 31, 163; Piano Concerto No. 2 in F, Op. 35, 30, 34, 59, 61, 73, 77, 79, 86, 128, 167, 169, 217; Piano Concerto No. 3 in G, Op.45, 44, 46, 60, 65, 66, 70, 73, 85, 127, 221, 235; Piano Concerto No. 4 in D minor, Op.70, x, 108–109, 121, 124, 127, 134, 151, 163, 217, 235, 237; Piano Concerto No. 5 in E flat, Op. 94, 159, 160, 163, 168; Piano Quartet in C, Op. 66, x, 107, 124; Piano Quintet in G minor, Op. 99, 164, 166, 168; Piano Sonata No. 1 in E major, Op. 12, x, 52; Piano Sonata No. 2 in C minor, Op. 20, 52; Piano Sonata No. 3 in F, Op. 41, 43, 63, 298n34; Piano Sonata No. 4 in A minor, Op. 100, 115, 168; Piano Trio in F, Op. 15, No. 1, 31, 39, 46, 59; Piano Trio in G minor, Op. 15, No. 2, 63, 74, 125; Piano Trio in B♭, Op. 52, 71, 72, 80; Piano Trio in A minor, Op. 85, 136, 137, 147, 16; Piano Trio in C minor, Op.108, 187; Polkas, 17; Polonaise in C minor, Op.5 No 1, 294n53; *Poltava,* 43; Prayer before the battle, 288n1; *The Prisoner (Uznitsa),* 196; Psalm settings (projected or lost), 33; Romance and Caprice for violin and orchestra, Op. 86, 136, 137; Romance and Impromtu, Op. 26, 71, 77, 291n97; *Rosvita,* 108; *Rudin,* 108; Rusalka, Op. 63, 102, 180, 198, 214; Russia, 179, 181, 214; Russian liturgical concerto (projected or lost), 33; *Die Sibirischen Jäger (The Siberian Hunters),* 39, 48, 52–55; *Six Fables of Krïlov,* Op. 64, 28, 169, 286n15; Six fugues (en style libre) introduites de préludes, Op. 53, 63, 124; Six Heine settings: Op. 32, 134; No. 5 Lied: *Du bist wie eine Blume,* 71, 198; No. 6 Der Asra, x, 238; Six pieces: Op. 51: No. 1 Mélancholie in G minor; No. 4 Caprice in

18, 114, 125, 128, 129, 130, 132, 133, 135,
150, 154, 157, 160, 174, 190, 194, 224, 225,
232, 235, 285n47
Rubinstein, Yakov Antonovich, 125, 128, 129,
130, 133, 182, 183, 221, 224, 225, 231, 232,
235, 236, 297n115
Rubinstein, Yakov Grigoryevich, xxi, 5, 25, 46,
47, 54, 63, 72, 74, 81, 95, 96
Rubinstein, Yakov Romanovich, 4
Rubinstein Museum, 6
Runtsler, 99
Russian Music Society (RMS) xvi, xvii, xix,
26, 36, 43, 69, 76, 78, 82–90, 94–97, 99–106,
109, 112–113, 117–127, 130, 134, 137, 142,
145, 157, 158, 159, 161, 162, 164, 165, 168,
169, 179, 180, 181, 183, 184, 185, 187, 192,
196, 201, 202, 207, 211, 217, 220, 221, 224,
226, 234, 236, 291n111
Russian Ministry of the Court, xvii, 96, 97,
109, 113, 115
Russian National Opera Company, 179
Russian Quartet, 148, 300n77
Russkaya Muzïkal'naya Gazeta, 1894–1918),
38, 87, 305n63
Russkaya starina, 8, 213, 214, 217, 284n21,
284n24, 305n66
Russkiye vedomosti, 147, 157, 158, 161, 162
Russo-Turkish War, 167–169, 192
Ryazan (Russia), 134

Saar, Ferdinand von, 147
Sabinina, Martha von, 47
Safonov, Vasily Ilich, 217, 220, 224, 237
Saint-Georges, Jules Vernoy de, 129, 133
St. Louis, Missouri 151, 152
St. Petersburg: Aleksandrinsky Theatre, 26,
40; Bernardaki Hall, 31, 75, 104, 105, 112;
Chinizelli Circus, 217; City Duma, 106;
Demidov pereulok, 101, 117; Engelhardt
Hall, 15, 16; Hermitage Theatre, 117;
Kamennïy Ostrov (Rocky Island), 35, 36,
96; Lichtenthal Hall, 33, 35, 39, 46; Malaya
Morskaya, 33; Marble Palace, 209; Mariin-
sky Theatre, 86, 114, 141, 159, 164, 165,
174, 192, 200, 202, 214; Mikhaylovsky Pal-
ace, 30, 39, 42, 75, 83, 84, 89, 90, 91, 96, 97,
99, 115, 116, 121; Mikhaylovsky Manège,
106; Mikhaylovsky Square, 83; Mikhay-
lovsky Theatre, 22, 31, 46; Myatlev Hall, 46;
Theatre Square, 202; Troitskaya ulitsa, 205;
Troitsky pereulok, 139; Winter Palace, 15;
Zagorodnïy prospect, 101, 117
St. Petersburg Academy of Arts, 114, 126, 207

St. Petersburg Academy of Sciences, 37
St. Petersburg Bolshoy Theatre, 27, 28, 30, 31,
33, 77, 154, 202, 209, 210, 220, 221
St. Petersburg Conservatory, ix, xvi, xvii,
xviii, xix, xxi, 35, 92–97, 99–104, 106, 107,
109, 110, 112–113, 115–126, 128, 130, 138,
142, 156, 162, 189, 197, 201–207, 209, 210,
211, 214, 217–221, 224, 226, 227, 237, 238,
298n12
St. Petersburg Hall of the Nobility, 28, 31, 99,
104, 106, 109
St. Petersburg Passage, 31
St. Petersburg Philharmonic Society, 22, 46,
53, 59, 62, 83, 102, 165, 286n11
St. Petersburg Public Library, 231, 297n115
St. Petersburg Symphonic Society, 83, 292n3
St. Petersburg University, 26, 42, 96, 139, 214,
286n11, 294n44,
St. Petersburger Zeitung, 65, 166
Saint-Saëns, Camille, 73, 127, 133, 135, 162;
Danse Macabre, Op. 40, 162; Piano Con-
certo No. 2 in G minor, Op. 22, 128; Piano
Concerto No. 3 in E flat, Op. 29, 162; *Varia-
tions sur un thème de Beethoven,* Op. 35, 162
Saint-Simon, Henri de, 21
Sainton, Prosper, 71, 74
Salin, Vasily Zakharyevich, 115
Salzburg, 125, 150
Sakharov, Ivan Petrovich, 172, 301n35
Saloman, Siegfried, 84, 85, 130, 292n129
Samoylov, Vasily Vasilyevich, 142
Samoylova, Glafira Nikolayevna, 197
Santagano-Gorchakova, Aleksandra Aleksan-
drovna, 157
Sankt-Peterburgskiye vedomosti, 34, 77, 137,
161, 166, 179
Santis, Mikhail, 43, 75, 112
Sapelnikov, Vasily Lvovich, 218, 232
Saphir, Moritz Gottlieb, 20
Saratov, Russia, 222
Sauvage, Thomas, 133
Savanelli, 101
Sayn-Wittgenstein, Carolyne von, 49–50, 66,
68, 132, 145, 146, 149
Sbroevsky, 30
Scarlatti, Domenico, 155
Schefferdecker, Emiliya Avgustovna, 41. *See
also* Schefferdecker, Emiliya.
Scheffer, Ary, 53
Schiller, Johann, 47
Schleinitz, Countess Marie von, 146, 149
Schleinitz, Heinrich Konrad, 55, 289n35
Schlesinger, 16, 285n40

Teatral'nïy i muzïkal'nïy vestik, 288n65
Tenishev, Prince Vyacheslav Nikolayevich, 201
Terminskaya, Monika Vikentyevna, 118, 123, 177
Tetzlaff, Carl, 232
Terre Haute, Indiana 152
Thalberg, Sigismund, xi, 11–13, 16, 22, 79, 150, 155; Andante in D flat, Op. 32, 9, 15; *Fantasy on Don Giovanni,* Op. 14, 15; *Fantasy on Russian Themes,* Op. 17, 14, 15; Fantasy on themes from *Moïse,* 9, 15; Thème original et étude in A Minor, Op. 45, 14
Thomas, Ambroise, Hamlet, 128
Thomas, Theodore, 151, 200
Tiflis, Georgia, 184, 189
Tilsit, 169
Times, 74, 163, 167, 179, 236, 284n12, 302n53
Tiron, 101
Titusville, Pennsylvania, 152
Todleben, Count Eduard Ivanovich, 36
Toledo, Ohio, 152
Tolstoy, Count Aleksey Konstantinovich, 168
Tolstoy, Feofil Matveyevich, 138
Tolstoy, Count Lev Nikolayevich, 42, 234
Toronto, Canada, 152, 153
Toulouse, France, 135
Transdnistria, 5
Traunkirchen, Austria, 141, 142
Treaty of Bucharest, 3
Treatry of Paris, 69
Trebelli, Zélia, 179
Treffz, Henrietta, 14
Trepov, Fyodor Fyodorovich, 140
Tretyakova, Yelena Andreyevna, 189
Trieste, 125
Troy, New York, 151, 153
Trubetskaya, Princess Mariya Vasilyevna, 287n40
Tuczek, Leopoldine, 17
Tula, Russia, 97, 127
Tunnel über der Spree, 20–21, 294n49
Turgenev, Ivan Sergeyevich, 70, 73, 77, 107, 108, 142, 258n10, 297n115, Rudin, 108, 295n83
Turin, Italy, 157
Tyll Eulenspiegel, 20
Tyutcheva, Anna Fyodorovna, 75, 291n115

Upsala, Sweden, 132
Usatov, Dmitry Andreyevich, 196
Ustinova, Princess, 36
Utica, New York, 151
Utrecht, Netherlands, 194, 198
Uvarov, Count Sergey Semyonovich, 3

Valts, Karl Fyodorovich, 196, 200
Van II, 51
Varlamov, Aleksandr Yegorovich, 117, 173, 256n6
Vargunin, Aleksandr Ivanovich, 126, 298n12
Varnhagen von Ense, Karl August, 20
Varnhagen von Ense (née Levin), Rahel, 20
Venevitinov, Dmitry Vladimirovich, 42
Vek, 91
Venice, Italy, 157
Verdi, Giuseppe, 157, 224; *Ernani,* 26; *Giovanna d'Arco,* 26; *I Due Foscari,* 26; *Nabucco,* 33
Verhulst, Johannes, 49
Verigo, Sofya Yakovlyevna, 97
Verstovsky, Aleksey Nikolayevich, 26, 28, 84
Verzhbilovich, Aleksandr Valerianovich, 177, 180
Veykman, Ieronim Andreyevich, 75, 76, 84, 115, 137
Veynberg, Pyotr Isayevich, 7, 91, 219
Veynberg, Semyon Isayevich, 133
Veynberg, Yakov Isayevich, 30, 63
Viardot, Pauline, 11, 26, 33, 39, 41, 43, 70, 73, 107, 114, 126, 142
Victor Emmanuel, King of Sardinia, 69, 290n91
Victoria, Queen of England, 14, 164, 166
Vienna, Austria, 9, 13, 19, 20, 61, 64, 71, 73, 76, 85, 86, 91, 94, 96, 124, 125, 133, 135, 141, 145–149, 160, 164, 165, 186, 190, 193, 194, 195, 197, 226, 232, 235; Gesellschaft für Musikfreunde, 14, 19, 61, 76, 135, 138, 141, 143, 146; Großer Musikvereinssaal, 231; Kärntnetor Theatre, 90; Wiener Staatsoper, 148, 179
Vieuxtemps, Henri, 12, 19, 22, 33, 34, 70, 83, 107, 108, 121, 163, 181; Grand duo on motifs from Meyerbeer's 'Le Prophète', 22; Violin Concerto No. 1 in E, 12, 19; Vïkhvatinets, 5
Vilde, Nikolay Yevstafyevich, 196
Villa Abigore, Nice, 69
Villa Bermine, Nice, 69
Villa of Hofgärtnerei, 131
Villoing, Aleksandr Ivanovich, xxi, 9–16, 25, 63, 100, 103, 284n21, 285n44, 286n9, 295n70; Piano Concerto in C minor, 15; Shkola dlya fortepiano (Piano School), 295n70
Villoing, Jean, 9
Vilno, 2
Vindex, Gaius Iulius, 161
Vinnitsa, 6

PHILIP TAYLOR holds a Single Honors degree in Russian from the University of Wales, a Postgraduate diploma in technical translation from Polytechnic of Central London, and is a member of the Institute of Translating and Interpreting, U. K. Taylor has worked for many years in the international book trade and has been a freelance translator since 1994, contributing to the *New Grove Dictionary of Music and Musicians*, the Wexford Opera Festival, the Edinburgh Festival, the Aldeburgh Festival, and numerous recording labels.